Political Islam

As the topic of political Islam gains increased visibility in international politics and current affairs, it has become more difficult to navigate the vast literature that is devoted to explaining this phenomenon. This reader provides the student with an accessible and comprehensive introduction to the study of political Islam. Offering a clear route to the most influential literature in the field, the diverse range of viewpoints presented allows students to obtain a broad, enlightened, and cosmopolitan perspective on the most pressing questions of the post-9/11 era.

With detailed introductory chapters and clear presentation of existing literature, thematically-arranged sections cover:

- Modern understandings and explanations of Islamism
- The emergence and development of Islamist groups
- Political responses to the phenomenon
- Democracy and democratization
- Multiculturalism
- Political violence and terrorism
- Globalization
- The future of political Islam

This fascinating overview of political Islam will help students at all levels to appreciate its many manifestations and dimensions. A relevant text to introductory courses on history, international affairs, government and sociology, this reader is an essential tool for students of the Middle East, Muslim politics, religion in politics and Islamism.

Frédéric Volpi is Deputy Director of the Institute of Middle East and Central Asia Studies and Senior Lecturer in International Relations at the University of St Andrews. He is the author of a number of books on political Islam and democracy in the Muslim world, and is coordinator of the British Society for Middle Eastern Studies research network.

Political Islam

A critical reader

Edited by Frédéric Volpi

Routledge
Taylor & Francis Group

LONDON AND NEW YORK

First published 2011 by Routledge
2 Park Square, Milton Park, Abingdon, Oxo OX14 4RN

Simultaneously published in the USA and Canada
by Routledge
270 Madison Ave, New York, NY 10016

Routledge is an imprint of the Taylor & Francis Group, an informa business

Typeset in Perpetua and Bell Gothic by Glyph International
Printed and bound in Great Britain by the MPG Books Group

British Library Cataloguing in Publication Data
A catalogue record for this book is available from the British Library

Library of Congress Cataloging in Publication Data
Political Islam : a critical reader / edited by Frédéric Volpi.
p. cm.
Includes bibliographical references and index.
1. Islam and politics. I. Volpi, Frédéric.
BP173.7.P6525 2010
320.5'57–dc22   2010008362

ISBN 978-0-415-56027-6 (hbk)
ISBN 978-0-415-56028-3 (pbk)

Contents

Acknowledgements

The publishers would like to thank the following for permission to reprint their material:

American Academy of Arts and Sciences for permission to reprint James Piscatori, 'Religion and Realpolitik: Islamic Responses to the Gulf War', *Bulletin of the American Academy of Arts and Sciences* 45(1) 1991, pp. 17–39.

American Anthropological Association and the author for permission to reprint extract from Mahmood Mamdani, 'Good Muslim, bad Muslim: a political perspective on culture and terrorism', *American Anthropologist* 104(3) 2002. Reproduced by permission of the American Anthropological Association from *American Anthropologist* Volume 104(3), pp. 104 (3), pp. 766–775, 2002. Not for sale or further reproduction.

American Anthropological Assocation and the author for permission to reprint Charles Hirschkind, 'Civic virtue and religious reason: an Islamic counterpublic', *Cultural Anthropology* 16(1) 2001, pp. 3–7; pp. 15–22. Reproduced by permission of the American Anthropological Association from *Cultural Anthropology* Volume 16(1), pp. 3–34, 2001. Not for sale or further reproduction.

C. Hurst & Co. (Publishers) Ltd for permission to reprint Faisal Devji, 'Accounting for Al Qaeda', extract from *Landscape of the Jihad* (London: Hurst 2005), pp. 20–32.

Comparative Politics and the author for permission to reprint Carrie Rosefsky Wickham, 'The path to moderation: strategy and learning in the formation of Egypt's *Wasat* party', *Comparative Politics* 36(2) 2004, pp. 205–228.

Duke University Press for permission to reprint Nilüfer Göle, 'Islam in public: new visibilities and new imaginaries', *Public Culture* 14(1) 2002, pp. 177–190. Copyright, 2002 Duke University Press. All rights reserved. Used by permission of the publisher.

Fordham University Press for permission to reprint Talal Asad, 'Trying to Understand French Secularism', in H. de Vries and L. Sullivan (eds), *Political Theologies: Public Religions in a Post-Secular World* (Fordham University Press, 2006), pp. 500–504, pp. 522–526.

Koninklijke BRILL NV for permission to reprint extract from Gudrun Kramer, 'Visions of an Islamic republic: good governance according to the Islamists', in K. Hafez (ed), *The Islamic World and the West: An Introduction to Political Cultures and International Relations,* trans. M.A. Kenny (Leiden: Brill, 2000), pp. 33–45.

MERIP and *Middle East Report* for permission to reprint Charles Hirschkind, 'What is political Islam?', *Middle East Report*, No. 205, 1997, pp. 12–14.

Oxford University Press and *Sociology of Religion* for permission to reprint Robert W. Hefner, 'Public Islam and the Problem of Democratization', *Sociology of Religion* 62(4) 2001, pp. 491–500. By permission of Oxford University Press.

Palgrave Macmillan, a division of St Martins Press, LLC, for permission to reprint Graham E. Fuller, *The Future of Political Islam* (London: Palgrave Macmillan, 2004), pp. 173–203, and notes.

Princeton University Press for permission to reprint Jenny White, 'The End of Islamism? Turkey's Muslimhood Model', in R. Hefner (ed.), *Remaking Muslim Politics* (Princeton University Press, 2005), pp. 87–111. © 2005 by Princeton University Press. Reprinted by permission of Princeton University Press.

Sage for permission to reprint Pnina Werbner, 'The predicament of diaspora and millennial Islam: reflections on September 11, 2001', *Ethnicities* 4(4) 2004, pp. 459–476, copyright © 2001 by Sage. Reprinted by permission of SAGE.

Social Research for permission to reprint Saba Mahmood, 'Ethical formation and politics of individual autonomy in contemporary Egypt', *Social Research* 70(3) 2003, pp. 837–68. www.socres.org.

Stanford University Press for permission to reprint Asef Bayat, 'The politics of presence', extract from *Making Islam Democratic: Social Movements and the post-Islamist turn* (Stanford University Press 2007), pp. 194–205. Copyright © 2007 by the Board of Trustees of the Leland Stanford Jr. University.

Taylor & Francis Books (UK) for permission to reprint Peter Mandaville, 'Reimagining the Umma', in Ali Mohammadi (ed.), *Islam Encountering Globalisation*, pp. 61–90, © 2002 Routledge. Reproduced by permission of Taylor & Francis Books UK. www.taylorandfrancis.co.uk www.routledge.com

Taylor & Francis Journals and the Royal Society for Asian Affairs for permission to reprint Gilles Kepel, 'The origins and development of the Jihadist movement: from anti-communism to terrorism', *Asian Affairs* 34 (2) 2003, pp. 91–108, translated by Peter Clark. Copyright © Royal Society for Asian Affairs, reprinted by permission of Taylor & Francis Ltd. <http://www.tandf.co.uk/journals> on behalf of The Royal Society for Asian Affairs.

Taylor & Francis Ltd for permission to reprint John R. Bowen, 'Beyond migration: Islam as a transnational public space', *Journal of Ethnic and Migration Studies* 30(5) 2004, pp. 879–887. http://www.tandf.co.uk/journals

Taylor & Francis Ltd for permission to reprint Quintan Wiktorowicz, 'A genealogy of radical Islam', *Studies in Conflict and Terrorism* 28(2) 2005, pp. 75–97. http://www.tandf.co.uk/journals

The Academy of Political Science for permission to reprint Ahmet T. Kuru, 'Globalization and Diversification of Islamic Movements: Three Turkish Cases', *Political Science Quarterly*, Vol. 120, No. 2, 2005, pp. 253–274.

The Hedgehog Review for permission to reprint Olivier Roy, 'Islam in the West or Western Islam? The disconnect of religion and culture', *The Hedgehog Review* 8(1–2), 2006, pp. 127–133.

The Johns Hopkins University Press for permission to reprint Daniel Brumberg, 'Islamists and the politics of consensus', *Journal of Democracy*, 13:3 (2002), pp. 109–115. © National Endowment for Democracy and The Johns Hopkins University Press. Reprinted with permission of The Johns Hopkins University Press.

The Middle East Institute and *The Middle East Journal* for permission to reprint Thomas Hegghammer, 'Global Jihadism After the Iraq War', *The Middle East Journal* 60(1) 2006, pp. 11–32. Reprinted with permission of the author.

University of California Press for permission to reprint Barbara Metcalf, 'New Medinas: The Tablighi Jama'at in America and Europe', in B. Metcalf (ed.), *Making Muslim Space in North America and Europe* (University of California Press, 1996), pp. 110–127.

University of Indiana Press for permission to reprint Janine Clark, 'Social movement theory', extract from *Islam, Charity and Activism* (Indiana University Press, 2004), pp. 30–40. Reprinted with permission of Indiana University Press.

University of Texas Press for permission to reprint excerpt from 'Chapter 2, From national struggle to the disillusionments of "recolonization": the triple temporality of Islamism', pp. 31–48, and Notes to Chapter 2, pp. 159–163, from *Islamism in the Shadow of Al-Qaeda* by François Burgat, translated by Patrick Hutchinson, copyright © 2008. By permission of the University of Texas Press.

Wiley Blackwell for permission to reprint Salwa Ismail, 'Being Muslim: Islam, Islamism and identity politics', *Government and Opposition* 39(4) 2004, pp. 614–631. Copyright © 2004. Reproduced with permission of Blackwell Publishing Ltd.

Wiley Blackwell for permission to reprint Guilain Denoeux, 'The forgotten swamp: navigating political Islam', *Middle East Policy* 9(2) 2002, pp. 56–81. Copyright © 2002. Reproduced with permission of Blackwell Publishing Ltd.

Wiley Blackwell for permission to reprint Mohammed Ayoob, 'Deciphering Islam's multiple voices: intellectual luxury or strategic necessity?', *Middle East Policy* 12(3) 2005, pp. 79–90. Copyright © 2005. Reproduced with permission of Blackwell Publishing Ltd.

Zed Books Ltd. for permission to reprint Salman Sayyid, 'The Islamist impasse', extract from *A Fundamental Fear* (London and New York: Zed Books Ltd. 2003), page xiii to page xxii.

The publishers have made every effort to contact authors/copyright holders of works reprinted in *Political Islam: A critical reader*. This has not been possible in every case, however, and we would welcome correspondence from those individuals/companies whom we have been unable to trace.

Glossary

Alim (plural *ulama*): A scholar, someone who is knowledgeable. In the plural, the term describes a class of Islamic legal scholars. The *ulema*'s training in Islamic law makes them authoritative interpreters of the Islamic scriptures and a source of jurisprudence. In the modern period the traditional educational system of the *ulema* has been undermined and a new category of self-proclaimed *ulema* with non-traditional religious training has emerged.

Ayatollah: Literally meaning 'sign of God', the term refers to one of the highest ranks given to Shi'a clerics (the highest being Grand Ayatollah). It indicates that these scholars have become experts in Islamic Law and that they can be sources of emulation (marjaa) for the faithful.

Bidah: A type of innovation, creation or change in the religious, political or social field, which is deemed to deviate from the Islamic principles and is therefore regarded as sinful.

Caliph (Khalifa): The spiritual and political leader of the Muslim community (ummah) and Muslim 'nation' (Caliphate). For Sunni Muslims there has not been a widely recognized Caliph since the destitution of the Sultan of the Ottoman Empire in 1924.

Caliphate (Khilafa): An Islamic system of governance headed by the Caliph; it also refers to the area ruled by the Caliph. Contemporary Islamist movements commonly include the reconstruction of the Caliphate as one of their long-term objective, but they rarely specify the institutions that this political system would have in the modern context.

Dar al-salaam/Dar al-harb: Dar is the home or domain. Dar al-salaam means 'the house of peace'; it corresponds to domain that is under Islamic rule. In contrast, dar al-harb refers to 'the house of war', which comprises all the areas outside Muslim rule and therefore potentially in conflict with the Muslim lands.

Deobandi: A reform movement that began at the Dar al-Uloom madrasa in Deoband (India) in 1866. The Deobandi movement stresses the direct implementation of the Koranic recommendations. It also advocates a purification of Islam from the influence of the 'West' and from material pleasures more generally. In the

1920s it influenced the formation of the transnational pietist movement Tablighi Jamaat; and in the 1980s, it had an influence on the emergence of the Taliban movement in Pakistan.

Fatwa: An Islamic religious ruling or edict. It is an opinion on Islamic law tradition-ally given by a member of the ulema known as a mufti. The democratization of Islamic knowledge throughout the twentieth century has empowered new, non traditionally-trained Islamic 'authorities' who also increasingly issued fatwas.

Fiqh: Islamic jurisprudence. Fiqh is an extension of the Islamic law (Shari'a) con-cerned with the practical applicability and implications of the Koran and Sunnah. It is performed by a jurist (faqih). Unlike the Shari'a, fiqh is usually very codified and context specific.

Fitna: An upheaval, strife or any period of civil violence. The turbulent political his-tory of Islamic empires led religious authorities to stress doctrinal imperatives to avoid fitna. The threat of fitna is/has been repeatedly used by established religious and political authorities to avoid dissent and contestation of their rule.

Halal: Lawful and permissible according to Islamic Law.

Haram: That which is forbidden according to Islamic Law.

Hijab: It commonly refers to the type of head covering worn by Muslim women. In the Koran, the term hijab indicates firstly a spiritual veil that provides privacy. In the context of contemporary Islamism, it is perceived as a sign of political and religious militancy.

Hijra: Migration of the Prophet Muhammad and his followers from Mecca to Medina in AD 622, as Meccans refused to recognize his authority. In modern Islamist narratives, the term can also refer to the process of separation of a group of mili-tants from the rest of society in order to follow what they deem to be genuine Islamic practices.

Hizb: A part of. In the contemporary context, hizb also means a political party (e.g. Hizbollah – Party of God).

Ijmaa: Ijmaa refers in its broadest sense to the full consensus of the Muslim com-munity (ummah), and in its narrower sense to that of the Islamic scholars (ulema). Such agreement by consensus can constitute a source of Islamic Law (Shari'a).

Ijtihad: An Islamic legal term which refers to the process of independent interpreta-tion of the Koranic sources by an Islamic scholar recognized as a mujtahid. Traditionally, the recourse to ijtihad was deemed problematic and controversial; a view still held by contemporary ultra-orthodox Islamist movements. In the modern period, Islamist movements have increasingly validated the use of ijti-had in order to make Islamism relevant to new socio-political circumstances.

Imam: In the modern context, the spiritual leader of a Muslim community or of a mosque. In some parts of the Muslim world it is equivalent to the term mullah.

Islamization: A process through which a Muslim community increasingly uses Islamic laws and principles as the basis for organizing all relevant aspects of individual and communal life.

Jahiliyya: Historically, the age of pre-Islamic 'ignorance' associated with polytheism. It shows the lack of guidance of the community prior to the revelation of the Koran. For modern Islamist movements, the term can also refer to the situation of unbelief and corruption that characterizes contemporary societies worldwide.

Jamaat: A gathering or assembly. It is commonly used by Islamists as an alternative to the term party (hizb).

Jihad: The Arabic noun for 'struggle', which is also commonly used with the meaning of Holy war. Islamic doctrine refers to jihad not only as a physical struggle in defence of the Islamic faith and the ummah, but also as an individual or communal quest for self-betterment and the good Islamic life.

Kafir (plural kuffar): In the Islamic doctrine it designates the person who rejects Islam, the unbeliever. By extension, it implies a wilful covering up of the (Islamic) truth that leads to disbelief (kufr).

Khomeinism: The religious and political doctrine of Ayatollah Khomeini, including the notion of guardianship of the jurist (wilayat-al-faqih), on which the Islamic Republic of Iran was founded after the 1979 revolution.

Majlis al-shura: An advisory or consultative council. Historically, a majlis al-shura selected the incoming Caliph for the Islamic community.

Mujahid (plural mujahidin): An Islamic fighter, usually one involved in jihad. In the contemporary context, this title is commonly claimed by armed Islamist groups throughout the Muslim world.

Muslim Brotherhood: An Islamist movement founded by Hassan al-Banna in Egypt in 1928. The Muslim Brotherhood was the first modern mass-based movement seeking to bring Islam to the centre of a modernized political and social sphere.

Orientalism: An essentializing depiction by 'Western'(ized) observers of the socio-economic, political, religious and cultural characteristics of individuals and communities from the 'Orient' (as distinct from the 'Occident'). This perspective underpins most analyses of political Islam and the Muslim world phrased in terms of 'clash' or of 'exceptionalism'.

Qadi: A judge or magistrate of Islamic Law.

Salafi: Derived from the noun salaf, meaning a predecessor or ancestor, the term salafi applies to the dominant Sunni Islamist trend of the twentieth century. It is a movement that takes the 'uncorrupted' practices of the first generation(s) of Muslims as the example to follow for contemporary Muslims. Although the salafi movement generically stresses a return to the 'fundamentals' of Islam, different trends within it draw different conclusions regarding what this return actually means in practice.

Shahid: Literally a witness; it commonly designates the individual who performs the Islamic testimony of faith (shahada), the verbal and spiritual recognition that there is only one God and Muhammad is God's prophet. By derivation, shahid is often used as a synonym of martyr for Muslims who have died in defence of their faith.

Shari'a: The principles of law that are derived from the Koran and the Sunnah. It is meant to regulate the public and private lives of those who chose to live as an Islamic community. The Shari'a is more a set of general guidance than a corpus of specific legal codes or interpretations. While contemporary Islamist movements commonly want the Shari'a to be the source of the constitutional and legal system in Muslim-majority countries, there remain considerable disagreements regarding what its implementation would mean in practice.

Shi'a (also Shi'ites): A collective noun designating the partisans of Ali (shi'at Ali), the fourth Caliph. This branch of Islam only recognizes Ali and his descendents as the legitimate successors to the Prophet. Shi'a Muslims constitute less than 15% of the total Muslim population today. The largest community, the Twelver Shi'a, constitutes a majority in Iran and Iraq.

Sufi: A Muslim mystic following the inner dimension of Islam, sufism. Sufis are generally condemned by Islamist movements for promoting what Islamists consider to be heterodox Islamic practices.

Sunni: The largest Islamic denomination, with approximately 85% of all Muslims.

Takfir: The act of designating a Muslim or a group of Muslims as kafir (unbeliever). Disowning the teachings of Islam, the act of apostasy, is one of the most serious accusations in Islamic jurisprudence, commonly punishable by death.

Taqlid: Imitation by exactly adopting and implementing the interpretations of Islamic scholars (often posited as the opposite of ijtihad). In the modern period, this process has been increasingly criticized and discarded in favour of a process of examination of the Islamic scriptures.

Ummah: Short for ummat-al-mu'minin, the Islamic community or the Muslim people. As a community of beliefs defined by adherence to the Islamic faith and Islamic practices, the ummah transcends modern state institutions and boundaries.

Wahhabi/Wahhabism: An ultra-orthodox Sunni movement started by the Islamic scholar al-Wahhab in the Arabian Peninsula in the mid-eighteenth century. This reform movement sought to restore Islam to its pristine form by emphasizing a literalist interpretation of the Koran and by rejecting historical innovations and adaptations. The global expansion of this trend, dominant in Saudi Arabia, has been facilitated by the Saudi elite in the late twentieth century.

Zakat: A type of almsgiving that constitutes one of the five pillars of Islam. It is regarded as a means of spiritual betterment, as it contributes to the improvement of the Islamic community by redistributing wealth. Zakat is an important source of funding for Islamic movements of all tendencies.

Introduction

Critically studying political Islam

WHAT IS POLITICAL ISLAM, and why is it important to understand its role and significance in international affairs at the beginning of the twenty-first century? In the aftermath of the al-Qaeda attacks on the United States on September 11, 2001 (9/11), there has been a heightened interest in a phenomenon that suddenly became a byword for transnational political violence. The decade of the 'War on Terror', as the response of the US government became known, ensured that political Islam became one of the key elements of international politics in the early twenty-first century. But how far is this evocation of the al-Qaeda brand of violent transnational Islamism useful in understanding the dynamics of political Islam today? What are the main characteristics of contemporary Islamism? The perspectives developed in this Reader indicate that a security-minded approach is rather limiting for explaining the complex nature of the modern Islamist phenomenon. The basic argument that underpins this critical Reader on political Islam is that different scholarly and policy approaches offer specific insights into Islamism without ever fully encapsulating it.[1] Indeed, these insights need to be brought together and assembled in a meaningful way to obtain a useful picture – albeit an ever-changing one – of the role and significance of Islamism in contemporary world affairs.

The purpose of this Reader is to construct such an assemblage of insights in order to shed some light on the key dynamics and mechanisms of political Islam. In the following, the terms 'political Islam' and 'Islamism' will be used interchangeably. For the purpose of this Reader, political Islam is defined primarily as a construct that refers to what individuals in a particular socio-historical context think about the political and the religious. More specifically, Islamism refers to the political dynamics generated by the activities of those people who believe that Islam as a body of faith has something crucial to say about how society should be organized, and who seek to implement this idea as a matter of priority.

The international responses to the events of 9/11 illustrated well how analysts, policy-makers and the media prioritized different insights into Islamism according to their interests and roles. When presenting the views of the Islamists, the specialists of Muslim politics themselves carefully select those political actors, religious scholars and ideologues that they deem representative of the movement (Khomeini, Qutb, Bin Laden, Al Qaradawi, and so on). Yet, to date, such efforts to represent the Islamist phenomenon have been only moderately successful. This Reader will therefore not seek to present snapshots of the positions and views of Islamist leaders in their own words, as this does not readily provide a meaningful introduction to the complex issue of political Islam. Instead, the Reader introduces the analyses of specialists of Islamist movements and Muslim politics that contextualize these actors' views and behaviours in a meaningful conceptual framework. Ultimately, what is being proposed is a multi-disciplinary approach to Islamism that stresses the longer-term development of political Islam rather than a sensationalist approach that focuses on current affairs.

For many non-specialists, Islamism is seen as a modern phenomenon, something that really took off in the late 1970s and early 1980s with the Islamic revolution in Iran and the Mujahidin struggle against the Soviet Union in Afghanistan. It is a process that culminated at the turn of the century with the events of 9/11 and the decade of the 'War on Terror'. But is Islamism really that new? The first section of the Reader introduces the socio-historical context of political Islam. The perception of political Islam as a very recent phenomenon can be quite misleading, especially if we consider the social and ideological aspects of the movement. In historical terms, political Islam is indeed a new phenomenon with an intellectual impulse given at the end of the nineteenth century and a social base formed at the beginning of the twentieth century. It is thus a modern movement in the sense of belonging to the modern era of politics: the epoch of mass politics. It is nonetheless a much older trend in Muslim politics and in Islamic theological thinking that challenges established ('traditional') religious and political authorities in the name of a 'return' to the mode of religious and political governance inspired by the time of the Prophet and the so-called Golden Age of Islam. From a political perspective, this challenge is at once conservative and revolutionary. It is conservative in the sense that it harks back to a very old social and political tradition and ethos. Yet it is also revolutionary in the sense that it requires a dramatic change of practices and institutions to be realized in the contemporary context. Against this background, one can make sense of the slow but predictable transformation of Islamist movements that were confined to intellectual and political elites at the end of the nineteenth century, into more populist and mass-based organizations from the 1930s onward. At the dawn of the era of mass media, mass politics and mass ideology, organizations like the Muslim Brotherhood in Egypt or the Jamaat-i-Islami in British India (part of which would become Pakistan) laid down the modern foundations of Islamism and set new directions for the development of this phenomenon.

The range of challenges and problems that are posed by Islamism to scholars and policy makers attempting to deal with its practical political manifestations are introduced in Section Two of the Reader. In the background looms large the question of which theoretical perspectives are most useful to understand the modern evolution of Islamism. When considering the concepts that can most usefully be deployed to frame political Islam, it is important to bear in mind that modern social sciences and politics are heavily secularized disciplines in which the notion of religious rule is not commonly deemed to be a very realistic proposition. Clearly, there has been a noticeable evolution of the scholarly views on Islamism. What was being asked about (and expected of) political Islam fifty years ago, during the heyday of the decolonialization struggle, is quite different from what animates the debates today. Old expectations regarding a standard model of secularization and modernization in the Muslim world have been dramatically transformed, if not altogether abandoned.[2] The logics of decolonization and of the Cold War have been superseded by new trends in socio-economic and cultural globalization. The post-colonial condition and transnationalism have made porous the boundaries between international and domestic politics, not least in security terms.[3] In considering the significance of political Islam today, one of the key challenges is to inscribe it in these grand narratives of world order. Indeed, contemporary debates about Islamism are not simply about the internal dynamics of this movement, but also about which explanations of the contemporary dynamics of world politics best capture the dilemmas of our time.

The implications of political Islam for state governance in the Muslim world and for the international relations of Muslim-majority countries are considered in Section Three of the Reader. These debates are articulated around two key issues: that of the construction of a concrete system of Islamic governance – the debate about the Islamic state – and that of the international and foreign policy orientations of would-be Islamic regimes. Until 9/11, the international implications of Islamic-minded regimes were thought to be a relatively well understood matter.[4] In foreign policy analysis and in geostrategic schemes, the choices of these regimes were deemed to be influenced at the margin by their Islamic culture. This culturalist argument was most readily used to introduce the view of a tactical positioning by the ruling elites of Muslim-majority countries that would display their commitments to vague Islamic ideals on the international scene in order to gain some legitimacy/popularity at home. This cultural particularism was nonetheless a relatively straightforward matter to analyse for 'rational choice'-based explanations of the behaviour of these polities. However, in the post-9/11 context, the global reach of transnational Islamist networks have led scholars and analysts to revise some of these traditional assumptions regarding how far national elites could actually control Islamic activism via the institutions of the state.

The relation between Islamic models of governance and the mechanisms and institutions of modern democratic politics grounded in the 'western' tradition is considered in Section Four of the Reader. From the early days of the revival of political Islam in the Middle East and South Asia, Islamism put forward social and political projects that stood in stark opposition to the views of the political elites of the day. Yet, neither weakening colonial powers nor emerging nationalist movements believed that a return to the 'fundamentals' of Islam was a viable answer to the political, military and socio-economic challenges that confronted Muslim-majority countries at that time. Whilst these political actors could see the benefits of using Islamic rhetoric for challenging (or legitimizing) a political system, they usually did not seriously consider the institutional implications of an Islamist model of governance either before or after independence. Only in a few exceptional circumstances was this Islamic rhetoric put into practice: for state-building purposes in the Arabian Peninsula before the discovery of oil, or during the hectic period that followed the creation of Pakistan. It would not be until the 1979 Islamic revolution in Iran that a very specific Shi'a interpretation of Islamic governance – a Khomeinist view of it – would set the tone for the debate about the nature of an Islamic state in the Muslim world. This created an awkward situation, as the rest of the Muslim community is predominantly made up of Sunni Muslims with a rather suspicious view of Shi'a interpretations of Islam. Subsequent attempts to create a modern Sunni Islamic state would be far less successful and durable (e.g. Afghanistan, Sudan), leading some scholars to suggest that we were witnessing a general 'failure of political Islam'.[5] Yet, at the same time, what became increasingly noticeable was the slow but progressive Islamization of many aspects of social and political life through a process of internal reform of nationalist regimes in quest of legitimacy and popularity (e.g. Egypt, Malaysia). Rather than an overall failure of political Islam what took place was a repositioning of the components of Islamism, especially via the endorsement of the mechanisms of electoral democracy and the emphasis on reforming existing authoritarian and secularized institutions. This progressive and piecemeal Islamization of society and of the system of governance matches the internal articulation of Islamism, which does not have a fixed blueprint for state governance but relies instead on a normative and moral set of guidance. The progression of an Islamist style of doing politics, by opposition to a direct takeover of the state, coincides with the process of democratization that has been gaining strength in Muslim majority countries since the end of the Cold War.

The above-mentioned connection between Islamization and democratization is further explored, in relation to the 'periphery' of the Muslim world, in Section Five of the Reader. The social and political discourse of Islamism has found a receptive audience from the 1980s onward in Muslim diasporas around the world and particularly in the 'West'. Until then, diasporas were expected to integrate into the dominant social and cultural system of the host countries through a process of modernization and secularization of their views and practices. In this context, pastoral care and religious provisions were mainly organized by Islamic scholars imported from the core regions of the Muslim world, and they were seen by the state as a stopgap measure whose significance would decrease over time. In this perspective, the Islamic guidance proposed was generally based on the principle of 'exceptionalism', as it concerned Muslims living in non-Muslim and secularized societies where 'proper' Islamic rules and practices could not be readily implemented. Increasingly, however, this situation was transformed by a combination of the rediscovery of Islam by younger generations born outside core regions of the Muslim world, and by an increased level of activism by transnational Islamist movements. This repositioning of Islamic constituencies and authorities took place in many different ways, from the more inward-looking activities of pietist organizations to the turn towards political violence of groups linked to Islamist insurgencies in the Muslim world. The articulation of political Islam in the context of western multiculturalism also gave a new impulse to Islamism by revitalizing the debates about Islamic governance and by introducing insights from western social and political theory. From the more pragmatic positions taken by the European Council for Fatwas and Research (led by Yusuf al-Qaradawi) to the more innovative propositions of Tariq Ramadan, the role played by the western Muslim constituency in political Islam has become more prominent at the beginning of the twenty-first century.[6] The trends in Islamist mobilization in the 'West' illustrate well the new dilemmas and opportunities created by a democratization of authority in Islam in the context of democratic politics.

The implications of the democratization of Islamic authority and the apparently coincidental increase in violence by Islamist networks are considered in Section Six of the Reader. From very early on, political Islam was identified as troublesome by colonial powers and then post-colonial regimes, due to its ability to mobilize unrest against to ruling elites. Initially this violence was perceived and presented as reactionary and bound to decline over time as people realized the legitimacy and progressive nature of the modern state. Colonial and post-colonial regimes in the Muslim world considered Islamism to be the expression of conservative forces trying to maintain their privileges by manipulating the views of 'unenlightened' masses. In this context, the violence generated by political Islam was often not analysed as a 'normal' type of political resistance (like that of nationalist movements), but as emotional outbursts of unrest generated by religious tensions. Only in the late 1970s and early 1980s, with the Iranian revolution and the resistance of the Mujahidin against the Soviet Union in Afghanistan, did it become more 'natural' to consider political Islam as a movement that could use violence tactically and strategically to achieve its objectives. Even then, the lack of any notable success of the Islamists against the secularized and nationalist regimes that rule much of the Muslim world helped maintain the perception that Islamism was not able to organize effectively the social and political activism it had initiated. The perception of a movement dominated by uncontrollable (if not altogether irrational) outbursts of violence against ill-defined 'enemies' of Islam at home and abroad gained strength in the 1990s as an increasingly violent transnational activism began to shape the debate about political Islam. This transnational violence sometimes overshadowed the crucial dynamics of cooperation and repression created through the interactions between mass-based national Islamist movements and their respective domestic regime. The focus on 'transnational terror networks', as they became known after 9/11, gave the impulse for an intensive but brief period of study of political Islam primarily through the lenses of security and terrorism studies. The media and policy enthusiasm for this type of explanation slowly died down at the end of the decade of the 'War on Terror', when once more the notion of instrumental and strategic uses of violence by political actors was put forward as an explanation of Islamism (e.g. Iraq, Afghanistan).

One crucial aspect of the Islamist phenomenon that became prominent in explanations of its violent character after 9/11, the process of globalization of political Islam, is examined in Section Seven of the Reader. Although Islamism was from its very beginning an aspiring global movement due to the universalistic character of Islam as a religion, it is the process of compression of space and time characteristic of the late twentieth century globalization that empowered contemporary Islamism. More pervasive global networks of communication (satellite, internet, etc.), combined with faster and larger global exchanges of goods and people, facilitated the transformation of the notion of the ummah, as a worldwide community of believers, into a more tangible community of shared Islamic practices.[7] At the beginning of the twenty-first century, the key characteristic of the globalization of political Islam has often been presented as a violent challenge to the established international order. Yet, at the heart of this process of globalization of Islamism is a much more low-key activation of Islamic identities in all those communities affected by economic globalization, as well as the (re)discovery of an Islamic heritage by new generations of Muslims living in secularized settings. In such situations of reconstruction of Islamic practices, political violence always remains a possibility. What is of more consequence, however, are the long-term processes of social, political and religious reform that articulate modern Islamic perspectives onto the dominant secular and liberal-democratic worldviews. In the contemporary context, what has been missing from these internal efforts at reform is a cohesive centre of authority for political Islam. In these global transformations, large transnational anti-establishment movements like the Muslim Brotherhood compete with state-controlled international organizations like the Muslim World League (under the aegis of the Saudi monarchy). Transnational social movements proposing grassroots social reform compete with each other (e.g. Tablighi Jamaat, Fetullah Gulen), as well as with political movements (e.g. Hizb-ut-Tahrir) and with violent militant organizations (e.g. al-Qaeda). These tensions not-withstanding, it is increasingly noticeable that there is a basic consensus across this global ummah about the ideas and practices that are central to political Islam, even as the issue of their implementation remains thoroughly contested.

The future of political Islam is considered in Section Eight of the Reader. This exercise is not primarily one of forecasting but rather an analysis of the longer-term dynamics of the phenomenon. The different aspects of the Islamist movement outlined in the preceding sections are evolving at a different pace, and have different poten-tials and implications in the long term for both Muslim and non-Muslim communities. What can be said with a reasonable amount of confidence is that the near obsessive concern with 'Islamist terrorism' that marked the first decade of the twenty-first century is not going to last. What can also be advanced with a fair amount of certainty is that many of the trends that have characterized political Islam from its beginning are going to continue in the coming decades. These long-term transforma-tions include the democratization of Islamic knowledge and authority, the growing importance of the Muslim 'periphery' (by contrast with the core regions of the Middle East), the convergence of the processes of democratization and Islamization. Overall, the challenge remains to identify which new important dynamics will emerge as a result of interactions between these different trends within political Islam, as well as between Islamism and other political actors and ideologies. The great mistake that one could make in this respect is simply to assume that political Islam is static or that a concern with reviving the 'fundamentals' of Islam prevent the transformation and adaptation of Islamism in a changing modern (and postmodern) world. Not only is Islamism always repositioning itself – tactically, strategically and substantively – vis-à-vis other ideas and practices in the social, political and religious field, but it is also continuously re-examining what it means to follow the 'fundamentals' of Islam. Political Islam is not a fixed and well-defined field of religious practices but instead an open and ongoing debate about the meaning of Islamic religiosity and of its impli-cations for individuals and communities.

External descriptions of political Islam always have difficulties to capture well the internal dynamics of the phenomenon, especially as analysts are often very con-cerned with explaining what Islamism ought to be doing in order to become more acceptable to non-Muslims. In such accounts, expectations of success or failure of specific trends in Islamism are informed by value judgements about what constitutes a viable social and political order. Unsurprisingly, therefore, social scientists, policy makers and Islamic activists can have very different views of the prospects of the Islamist phenomenon as a whole, or in relation to specific trends and movements. The actions and policies that flow from these views in their turn contribute to shape the successes and failures of Islamism – sometimes even creating self-fulfilling prophecies – as well as give the impulse for new interactions that will shape the political Islam of tomorrow. In the contemporary context, the consequences of the violent confrontation between national and transnational Islamist movements and the advocates of the 'War on Terror' will continue to have a lingering effect on the evolution of Islamism. It remains to be seen how far other key processes like democratization, multiculturalism and so on will be able to rapidly provide a more peaceful context for the development of political Islam in the coming decades of the twenty-first century. In this respect, the Reader proposes to signpost some of the main avenues that will need to be explored in order to understand the current and future transformations of Islamism.

Notes

1   For a development of this argument see Frédéric Volpi, *Political Islam Observed* (New York: Columbia University Press, 2010).
2   See Dale F. Eickelman and James P. Piscatori, *Muslim Politics* (Princeton: Princeton University Press, 2004).
3   See Olivier Roy, *Globalized Islam: The Search for a New Ummah* (New York: Columbia University Press, 2004); Peter Mandaville, *Global Political Islam* (New York: Routledge, 2007).
4   See Fawaz A. Gerges, *America and Political Islam: Clash of Cultures or Clash of Interests?* (Cambridge: Cambridge University Press, 1999).
5   See Olivier Roy, *The Failure of Political Islam*, trans. C. Volk (Cambridge: Harvard University Press, 1996).
6   See Tariq Ramadan, *Western Muslims and the Future of Islam* (New York: Oxford University Press, 2003); Bettina Gräf and Jakob Skovgaard-Petersen (eds), The *Global Mufti: The Phenomenon of Yusuf al-Qaradawi* (New York: Columbia University Press, 2008).
7   See Peter Mandaville, *Transnational Muslim Politics: Reimagining the Umma* (London: Routledge, 2003); Olivier Roy, *Globalized Islam: The Search for a New Ummah* (New York: Columbia University Press, 2004).

Modern understandings and explanations of Islamism

Introduction

THIS SECTION PROVIDES an historical and conceptual context for the current thinking on the nature and identification of political Islam. The following articles illustrate how important it is to understand the historical breaks and continuities in Islamism in order to make sense of today's (and tomorrow's) developments. An appreciation of the historical and ideational context of political Islam enables the reader to address better one of the most challenging issues in studies of Islamism: how can political Islam be identified and represented. In generic terms, political Islam or Islamism refers to a set of worldviews and practices that places the Islamic doctrine at the centre of any organization of social order. Islamism describes the position of those individuals and institutions believing that the message of Islam is of the utmost importance and that it ought to be implemented as fully as possible, as soon as possible. In itself, however, this general description does say much about the practical implications of these views, since both what constitutes a proper understanding of Islam and what constitutes an adequately Islamic social and political order are heavily disputed among Muslims and non-Muslims alike.

What constitutes political Islam cannot be neatly encapsulated in a definition that is accepted by all and that refers to exactly the same set of ideas and practices. This is so because the views and processes that are at the heart of Islamism are themselves repeatedly re-constructed by individuals, communities and institutions. What the 'fundamentals' of Islam are, just like what the fundamentals of politics are, constitutes the contested terrain on which all debates about political Islam take place. While there is recognition that Islamic practice, like political practice, is organized around key norms and rules, their actual prioritization and implementation are always changing. These dynamics shape the views and preferences of individuals, communities and institutions for Muslims and non-Muslims alike.

Policy-oriented perspectives on political Islam focus on specific interpretations of the Islamic doctrine and on how politics are to be organized according to the proponents of such views. Today, the dominant perspectives about politics reflect a secular and liberal understanding of societal interactions organized by a system of sovereign nation-states. These views frame the boundaries of the legitimate and illegitimate, of the appropriate and the inappropriate, of the normal and the abnormal in both domestic and international affairs. From this perspective, what needs to be explained and defined in relation to political Islam is what makes it fall outside 'normal' political categories and practices. More specifically, a liberal-secular view seeks to understand how the religious dimension of Islamism transforms what would otherwise be standard political processes. Hence, it is now commonplace for policy-minded analysts to rank different forms of Islam from 'moderate' to 'radical'. Although such approaches to political Islam are common in policy circles and the mass media, they are only informative about Islamism in so far as the secular and liberal assumptions about politics on which they rely are fully appreciated. In circumstances where the social boundaries between the public and the private are questioned, where the recognition of the nation-state as having the monopoly of legitimate violence is in doubt, and so on, the particularities of political Islam cannot be immediately attributed to its religious character. A process of contextualization is required to understand the relevance of common western assumptions about politics and how far they are (in)appropriate in a different socio-historical context. The contributions included in this section provide such a situational introduction to the notion of political Islam.

Charles Hirschkind's short text encapsulates well the failures of many mainstream analyses of political Islam that depict a religious movement encroaching upon a 'naturally' nationalist and secularized political sphere. Hirschkind notes that the local population in Muslim-majority countries has often perceived the intrusion of the institutions of the state in their daily life to be far more disruptive than that of Islamic-phrased attempts at social and political governance. In order to make sense of what Islamism represents for the average Muslim in the core regions of the Muslim world, it is crucial to first identify the challenges created by the institutions of the state in those polities.

The second contribution, by Salwa Ismail, explores in more detail what it means to have an Islamist perspective on social and political relations for the population of such Muslim-majority countries. Ismail highlights the dynamics and mechanisms of Islamization of public life taking place at grassroots level, and their implications at the institutional level for the state. The formation of an Islamist identity is an inter-relational process that results in the production of many hybrids which reflect the complex social, political and cultural interactions existing in contemporary Muslim communities.

In the next extract, from *Islamism in the Shadow of al-Qaeda,* François Burgat looks past the (long) shadow cast in recent years by al-Qaeda on the study of political Islam in order to outline the long-term evolutions and re-articulations of the Islamist phenomenon since its nineteenth-century beginnings. From this perspective, Burgat indicates that there are three crucial articulations of Islamism that contributed to shape the contemporary practices and discourses of political Islam. These are the construction of a response to colonial powers, the re-articulation of these choices to interact with the postcolonial state, and the engagement with the multiple aspects of globalization, especially in the post-Cold War context.

The fourth contribution, by Mohammed Ayoob, takes the analysis of the positioning of Islamism in contemporary world politics one step further by outlining the international dynamics of the engagement with diverse manifestations of political Islam. He indicates how the historical process of internationalization of Islamist politics has to be viewed not merely as an indigenous development in Muslim-majority countries, but also as a consequence of the strategies and policies of political actors external to the Muslim world. Throughout the twentieth century, the successes and failures of specific Islamist movements and discourses have been directly influenced by international and regional power struggles.

Finally, the text by Guilain Denoeux takes a narrower political analysis angle in order to classify the different trends within contemporary political Islam. Focusing on the recent historical evolution of Islamism, Denoeux's policy perspective distinguishes how different strands of Islamism prioritize differently orthopraxy and political efficiency. In a political framework grounded in means-end calculations, the religious dimension of Islamism recedes into the background or becomes cumbersome in the face of realpolitik.

Charles Hirschkind

WHAT IS POLITICAL ISLAM?*

OVER THE LAST few decades, Islam has become a central point of reference for a wide range of political activities, arguments and opposition movements. The term "political Islam" has been adopted by many scholars in order to
identify this seemingly unprecedented irruption of Islamic religion into the secular
domain of politics and thus to distinguish these practices from the forms of personal
piety, belief, and ritual conventionally subsumed in Western scholarship under the
unmarked category "Islam". In the brief comments that follow, I suggest why we might
need to rethink this basic framework.

The claim that contemporary Muslim activists are putting Islam to use for political purposes seems, at least in some instances, to be warranted. Political parties such
as Hizb al-'Amal in Egypt or the Islamic Salvation Front (FIS) in Algeria that base their
appeal on their Islamic credentials appear to exemplify this instrumental relation to
religion. Yet a problem remains, even in such seemingly obvious examples: in what
way does the distinction between the political and nonpolitical domains of social life
hold today? Many scholars have argued that "political Islam" involves an illegitimate
extension of the Islamic tradition outside of the properly religious domain it has historically occupied. Few, however, have explored this trend in relation to the contemporaneous expansion of state power and concern into vast domains of social life
previously outside its purview – including that of religion.

As we know, through this ongoing process central to modern nation building,
such institutions as education, worship, social welfare and family have been incorporated to varying degrees within the regulatory apparatuses of the modernizing state.
Whether in entering into business contracts, selling wares on the street, disciplining
children, adding a room to a house, in all births, marriages, deaths – at each juncture
the state is present as overseer or guarantor, defining limits, procedures and necessary
preconditions.

As a consequence, modern politics and the forms of power it deploys have become a condition for the practice of many personal activities. As for religion, to the extent that the institutions enabling the cultivation of religious virtue become subsumed within (and transformed by) legal and administrative structures linked to the state, the (traditional) project of preserving those virtues will necessarily be "political" if it is to succeed. Within both public and private schools in Egypt, for example, the curriculum is mandated by the state: those wishing to promote or maintain Islamic pedagogical practices necessarily have to engage political power.

This does not mean that all forms of contemporary Islamic activism involve trying to "capture the state." The vast majority of these movements involve preaching and other *da'wa* (missionary) activities, alms-giving, providing medical care, mosque building, publishing and generally promoting what is considered in the society to be public virtue through community action. Nonetheless, these activities engage the domain we call the political both in the sense that they are subject to restrictions imposed by the state (licensing, etc.), and in so much as they must often compete with state or state-supported institutions (pedagogic, confessional, medical) promoting Western models of family, worship, leisure, social responsibility, etc. The success of even a conservative project to preserve a traditional form of personal piety will depend on its ability to engage with the legal, bureaucratic, disciplinary and technological resources of modern power that shape contemporary societies.

This argument diverges from the common one that Islam fuses religion and politics, *din wa dawla*, in a way incompatible with Western analytical categories. It is worth noting, however, that this frequently heard claim does not deny the fact that Muslim thinkers draw distinctions between *din* and *dawla*; only that the specific domains designated by these terms, and the structure of their interrelations do not mirror the situation in Europe in regard to European states and the Church. Moreover, this leaves aside the fact that the division between religious and political domains even in Western societies has always been far more porous than was previously assumed, as much recent work has made clear.[1] Indeed, as Tocqueville long ago observed, Protestant Christianity plays an extremely important role in US politics in setting the moral boundaries and concerns within which political discussion unfolds, and hence can be considered the premiere political institution in some sense. I do not refer here to the lobbying efforts of church groups and other religious advocacy associations, but rather to the way a pervasive Christianity has been to varying degrees a constitutive element of Western political institutions. What is clear, in any case, is that greater recognition must be given to the way Western concepts (religion, political, secular, temporal) reflect specific historical developments, and cannot be applied as a set of universal categories or natural domains.

Lastly, although discussions of political motivation or class interest should continue to be important parts of accounts of contemporary Islam, they are not necessarily germane to a description of every problem the analyst poses. Statements like the following have too long been *de rigeur* in accounts of the Islamic *sahwa* (awakening): "Marginalized male elites experience socioeconomic disparities as cultural loss, and they are drawn to participate in fundamentalist cadres in order to militate against nationalist structures that they deplore as un-Islamic because they are, above all, ineffective."[2] Such analyses reduce the movements to an expression of the socioeconomic conditions which gave rise to them. The "marginalized male elites" speak nothing new to us, as their arguments and projects, once properly translated into the language of political economy, seem entirely familiar. Lost, in other words, is any sense of the specificity of the claims and reasoning of the actors. This is brushed aside as we reiterate what we already know about the universal operation of socioeconomic disparities.

Grasping such complexity will require a much more subtle approach than one grounded in a simple distinction between (modern) political goals and (traditional) religious ones. Terms such as "political Islam" are inadequate here as they frame our inquiries around a posited distortion or corruption of properly religious practice. In this way, the disruptive intrusions or outright destruction enacted upon society by the modernizing state never even figure in the analysis. In contrast, the various attempts of religious people to respond to that disruption are rendered suspect, with almost no attempt to distinguish those instances where such a critical stance is warranted from those where it is not. It is not surprising, in this light, that militant violence and public intolerance have become the central issues of so many studies of *al-sahwa al-islamiyya* (Islamic awakening), while the extensive coercion and torture practiced by governments get relegated to a footnote.

Notes

* I wish to thank Talal Asad, Saba Mahmood, Hussein Agrama, Steve Niva and Lisa Hajjar for their comments and suggestions on this brief article. Its shortcomings are my responsibility alone.

1 See William Connolly, *The Ethos of Pluralization* (Minneapolis: University, of Minnesota Press, 1995).

2 Bruce Lawrence, *The Defenders of God: The Fundamentalist Revolt Against the Modern Age* (Columbia, South Carolina: University of South Carolina Press, 1995), p. 226.

Salwa Ismail

BEING MUSLIM: ISLAM, ISLAMISM AND IDENTITY POLITICS

THE BASES OF IDENTITY in the contemporary world vary, diverge and converge. It is commonplace to state that identities develop in reference to nation, religion, gender, language, socio-economic position and lifestyle. While identities are not fixed or unidimensional, they may be constructed in a manner which is exclusive of some other dimension of identity formation. For example, it is argued by some – such as secular French Republicans – that a secular national identity cannot be reconciled with a religious public identity. According to this view, the public space cannot accommodate religious symbols such as the *hijab* (headscarf). The problem here is that the *hijab* may be an expression of identity politics, used to deliver a message in the public sphere: a message that is not about religion per se, but about difference and a right for public recognition. Identity politics, in this respect, asserts difference in terms of distinctions in tastes, lifestyles and modes of representation in the public sphere. These distinctions are affirmed as politically viable, and not just culturally tolerable.

The intersection of religion and identity is complex and raises important questions both in public spheres presumed to be secular and in contexts where religion is thought to play a significant role in defining the public sphere. In secular polities, there is an assumption that religion is a private matter that is withdrawn from the public domain. In principle, it cannot and should not be used as a frame of reference to justify public policy on social issues (e.g. abortion, reproductive rights etc.), nor should any reference be made to religion in drawing up the framework of government or the principles of the polity. Yet, even in western secular polities, signs and symbols of religion can be found in the public domain (for example, Sunday shopping laws, Christian public holidays and commercialized Christmas celebrations). At times, the discourse of political leaders in these polities (e.g. Berlusconi, Blair, Bush) does not shy away from making reference to Judeo-Christian principles and heritage.

In the case of Islam, or countries where Islam is the dominant religion, the view propagated in western scholarly writings, as well as by many Muslims, is that religion is the defining element of Muslim identity. Other dimensions of identity-formation such as class, gender or national belonging are treated as secondary to religion. In this article, I seek to explore the various manifestations of identity politics in relation to the religion of Islam. This exploration is set against the background of the unfolding dynamics of Islamist politics over the last three decades. While the various contemporary constructions of 'being Muslim' cannot be equated to 'being Islamist', Muslim identities have, nonetheless, been articulated in recent years in relation to the claims of Islamist political movements. At the same time, the assertion of a Muslim identity does not necessarily represent an endorsement of these movements. There are processes at work in the construction of 'being Muslim' that reveal a complex web of interaction among the various expressions of identity politics involving Muslims and Islamists.

The interaction of religion and politics in the contemporary period has been associated with the rise of Islamist movements in the Middle East from the 1970s on. During that period, Islamist politics came to be characterized by a diversity of actors, modes of action and, to some extent, objectives. Islamist actors can be classified, largely, into militants, conservatives and moderates. Each of these groupings tends to be characterized by particular social origins and modes of action. On the whole, militants originate from lower-middle-class backgrounds. They have social and economic concerns at the heart of their agenda and have used violence as a means of action. Conservatives and moderates belong to the middle classes with professionals as their main supporters. Conservatives focus on morality issues and seek the Islamization of society and state institutions but not a take-over of political power.[1] Moderates attempt to work within the institutional channels of participation. For example, the Muslim Brotherhood Organization in Egypt ran candidates in alliance with state-sanctioned political parties. Members of the Organization have also been active within the professional syndicates. Conceptions of culture and identity are articulated by all these various actors.

In this article, 'Islamism' is used to encompass both Islamist politics and the process of re-Islamization. 'Islamist politics', meanwhile, refers to the activities of organizations and movements that agitate in the public sphere while deploying signs and symbols from Islamic traditions. It entails a political ideology articulating the idea of the necessity of establishing an Islamic government, understood as government which implements the shari'a (Islamic law). 'Islamization' or re-Islamization signifies a drive to Islamize the social sphere. It involves a process whereby various domains of social life are invested with signs and symbols associated with Islamic cultural traditions. Efforts aimed at Islamization are pursued by actors who are not necessarily adherents of the Islamist project. For instance, there are entrepreneurs who promote the principles of Islamic economics and veiled women who articulate some Islamic ideal of modesty and gender relations yet are not active in Islamist movements. However, their engagement in Islamization is political; it is a central strategy of identity politics which, like other forms of politics, is about claims and contestation. Islamist politics both diverge and converge with the process of Islamization, presenting us with some interesting questions on the interaction between religion and politics. I will go over the grounds of convergence and divergence in the course of reflecting on the dynamics of interaction between religion and the politics of identity. In doing so, I will elaborate on the different expressions of being Muslim discerned in the intersection of religion and other dimensions of identity formation: gender, class, age and lifestyle, for instance.

In exploring the issue of religion and identity formation, I begin by looking at differing conceptions of religion and Islam in order to see how they have presented us with particular frameworks for understanding identity politics. The discussion then turns to an examination of existing debates on modernity and post-modernity. I conclude by examining the workings of processes of identity-formation that emerge out of global experiences. Throughout, I stress the importance of conceiving religion and those aspects of our identity that it shapes as deriving from a whole range of social practices rather than a given set of theological doctrines.

Religion and the social

Some explanations of Islamism posit Islam as the determining factor, and view it as embodying some unchanged, essential beliefs and ideas that motivate the believers to act. From this perspective, Islamists are moved by the ideal of the early Muslim society and a belief in the unity of religion and politics.[2] Such an account is problematic, however. It gives rise to a central question about the terms in which inquiry into the subject is conceptualized and framed: what is the basis for privileging religion over class, nation or gender in the constitution of an individual's identity? In the case of Muslims, this account rests on an ontological principle that constructs Muslims as different to most other social beings. They are primarily determined by their religion that itself is understood in narrow terms as embodying fixed principles, key among which is the idea of the shari'a. Further, it is argued that Muslims are comparatively more devout than the adherents of other religions, and that their religiosity is intimately tied up with their politics. This sort of account is often countered by a related, but equally misleading, historicist view. Islamist politics are worked into a meta-narrative according to which religion declines in salience/importance with economic development and industrialization. Muslims are thus seen as existing at a lower stage of development and will experience secularism once they have advanced to a higher stage. Challenging this view are many historical studies which demonstrate that realms of secular governance and profane spaces existed in Muslim societies. Beyond this, religion continues to play a role in decidedly modern societies, from the political influence exercised by the Moral Majority in the USA to Christian socialist movements in Europe and other subtle invocations of religious symbols. The starting point of both these accounts is often textual and to some extent theological – reference is made to sacred texts and a body of religious interpretation and then invested with explanatory powers. It is the text and the tradition that explain the religious practices or, to some extent, dictate them. There is a need to assess this premise in terms of how religion interacts with the social and, more fundamentally, what is meant by religion. For what is left out is the sociality of religion.

Religion as a set of rules involving reference to the divine/transcendental cannot be understood outside the social context of practices. In this sense, conformity with or transgression against the rules cannot be solely referred back to the rules for explanation and interpretation. Looking at instances of practices where religious injunctions exist, we find that the everyday life provides us with the terms of understanding. To illustrate this point, I shall examine a number of cases of conformity with and transgression against socially and religiously sanctioned norms in Egypt and Morocco.[3] These cases concern adultery, abortion and divorce. They are intended to demonstrate that competing frames of reference and situational logic shape the everyday experience of the interaction between religion and the social. The argument here is that the situational and context-bound effects of all systems of meaning apply to norms articulated in reference to Islamic traditions.

The first case concerns an Egyptian woman involved in an extramarital affair. She consults the Lajnat al-Fatwa (committee of religious rulings in al-Azhar) on how to deal with a neighbour's threat to publicly expose the affair.[4] The threat is accompanied by an offer to keep silent in exchange for the woman's sexual favours. The woman refuses to succumb to the neighbour's blackmail, but fears public exposure. The fatwa of the Lajnat advises that she end the illicit affair and not succumb to threats of publicity. In another case of adultery, a married couple in Egypt consults a Shaykh in Sayyida Zaynab.[5] The wife has confessed to an adulterous affair with the landlord of the house in which the couple lives. The Shaykh advises that the husband forgive his wife and accept her repentance and that the marriage continue. The Lajnat's response in the first case and the Shaykh's response in the second both depart from the established norm of condemning adultery and seeking punishment following the transgressor's confession. Should the Lajnat and the Shaykh's opinion/advice be placed outside the realm of orthodoxy? In a case from Morocco, a Muslim woman helps an unmarried friend get an abortion.[6] In undertaking this action, she viewed her support as private and not subject to societal rulings of morality. Instead, she considered herself answerable to God alone and the matter to be strictly a private affair.[7]

In the adultery cases we may note that the Lajnat and the Shaykh drew on alternative traditions that discourage publicizing transgressions and recommend clemency rather than punishment. In the case from Morocco, the exercise of individual morality superseded any notion of transcendental morality. Cases such as these abound and demonstrate the limited benefit of relying on scripture for apprehending social norms even when they make explicit reference to religion, whether involving practising Muslims or individuals in positions of religious authority. The examples also confirm that norms are situated within alternative frames developed in reference to social situations and existing in public and semi-public spaces. Moreover, they compete with dominant representations in the public sphere that are sustained by power relations. In the adultery case, people sought to resolve the moral dilemma through the mediation of religion, by referral to the Lajnat and the Shaykh. The resolution was framed in the language of religion, but it did not amount simply to following the rule.[8] Nor was the resolution conditioned purely by religion. In the abortion case, the woman's mode of reasoning did not exclude the divine, but nor did it conform to religion as a set of rules. What is pertinent in these examples is that competing frames and situational logic shape the everyday experience of the interaction between religion and the social.

Looking at the inscription of religion in social life, we find that social *enjeux* structure the choices of the actors whose judgements and conduct are guided by religion.[9] To illustrate the social *enjeux*, let us look at a divorce case involving a lower-class woman employed as a domestic helper in an upper-middle-class Cairo household. The woman's divorce took the form of repudiation (the enunciation of *talaq*) by her husband following a dispute. According to religious convention, she was no longer his wife. The woman informed her employers about the situation, and they judged that it would be illicit (*haram*) for her to return to her husband's home or to resume marital relations with him. To be certain of the appropriateness of their position, they decided to call on the office of the mufti, which is responsible for issuing religious edicts and judgments. While awaiting the mufti's response, the woman decided to return to her home and took her neighbours' advice that the husband's repudiation did not qualify as a true declaration of divorce because he was angry when he enunciated *talaq*. What were the social *enjeux* underlying this case? There is no doubt that the social class background of the various actors influenced their positioning in relation to religious knowledge and their modes of arriving at ethical decisions. It can be argued that the upper-middle-class family placed more stock in the religious knowledge of formal religious authorities, while the lower-middle-class neighbours used common sense to arrive at a resolution that conforms to their sense of justice and that, ultimately, could not contradict Divine intentions.

The main points to be made here are not only that there are differing and divergent interpretations of the text and law, but also that, as frames of reference for individual and social relations, these interpretations are conditioned by other social practices and situational ethics. As Jean-Noël Ferrié insightfully puts it, the closed world of religion, totalizing the practices of the believers, does not exist.[10] In other words, in its interaction with the social, religion ceases to be religion (understood as fixed beliefs, dogma, immutable rites and so on). This observation does not simply apply to the modern and post-modern periods but has meta-theoretical implications.[11] This rests on a distinction between religion as faith involving direct and immediate relations with the divine – relations which are personal and intimate – and religion as a set of rules interpreted and negotiated in social settings where all situational and contextual considerations come to bear on the interpretations and negotiations.[12] Going beyond this distinction, Talal Asad suggests that the experience of the spiritual world is shaped by conditions in the social world. Asad also rejects all transhistorical conceptions of religion. He argues that 'there cannot be a universal definition of religion, not only because its constituent elements and relationships are historically specific, but because that definition is itself the historical product of discursive processes'.[13] Integral to Asad's view is the idea that religion cannot be separated conceptually from the domain of power. From this perspective, religious meanings cannot be established outside the disciplines and authorities that determine correct reading and apt practice.[14] This constitutes the domain of 'orthodoxy' which always remains open to contestation and redefinition.

Islamism, Islamization and identity politics, or locating Muslims on the modernity–post-modernity track

The discussion of the position of Islamism from both modernity and post-modernity ties in with debates on the nature of identity-construction in the contemporary period. Post-modernity signals the destabilization of the idea of absolute truth and the abandonment of certainties and essential modes and ways of being associated with the fixed, singular subject, the always- and already-there subject, in favour of a bracketing of ideas of truth and falsehood. Instead of singular subjects, post-modernity speaks of hybridity and multiplicity. Locating Islamism in relation to modernity and post-modernity has not simply represented an inquiry into the nature of Islamist movements, but an elaboration on the efforts to capture the particularities of Islam. In one view, Islamism/Fundamentalism is constructed as an anti-modern movement, which is explained in terms of the essentially traditional character of the religion. This perspective has been subject to much discussion and criticism and I will not go over this ground here. By contrast, others have affirmed Islamism as a modern phenomenon that captures the affinity between Islam and modernity. I will briefly discuss the second view as a point of entry into an exploration of how 'Islam' is worked into processes of identity construction.

The view of Islam's modern character or at least its compatibility with modernity is intriguingly argued by Ernest Gellner.[15] In his schema of Muslim society, Gellner posited a scriptural Islam or High Islam (assuming a position of orthodoxy) in opposition to an ecstatic Islam or Low Islam. The former is urban, egalitarian and puritanical, while the latter is practised by unlettered Bedouin. Gellner's scriptural Islam bears similarities to the Protestant ethic and reasserts itself with modernization. The expansion of literacy and communication technology contributes to this reaffirmation of orthodoxy, assuring its ultimate victory over Low Islam. Islamists are the rational fundamentalists whose zeal is unattenuated by the forced moderation experienced by the Christian zealots.[16]

The assumptions underlying these propositions are not questioned but modified in Bryan S. Turner's thesis that Islamism is a reaction against post-modernity – a thesis which is also advanced by Akbar Ahmed.[17] Indeed, Turner agrees with Ahmed that Muslims are threatened by icons of post-modernity such as Madonna. Along the same lines, Benjamin Barber contends that Jihad is unleashed by the forces of 'McWorld'.[18] Turner's analysis crystallizes much of the complexity of arguments about Islamism, modernity and post-modernity. In line with Gellner, he does not see a contradiction between Islam and modernity (Islam is rational, universalist etc.). Fundamentalism, then, is a reaction against the failure of modernization and a defence against post-modernity. It is a reassertion of a universalist quest and an insistence on established certainties and absolute truth in the context of a globalized system of exchange commodities that alter, in fundamental ways, the everyday life experience of ordinary persons. Post-modernity challenges faith and reorganizes belief through social transformation in everyday life brought about by the consumption of commodities in which there is a sense of inauthenticity of culture.[19] In this sense, fundamentalism is an attempt at redeeming a fragmented identity and an escape from the post-modern condition of anxiety.

This view is premised on the idea of an orthodox Islam understood as the true/authentic doctrine, that is now engaged in a struggle for universal dominance against other systems of faith, as well as against the relativism of post-modern cultures. From this perspective, hybrid forms of religious identity are seen as inauthentic and a confirmation of the triumph of globalization and post-modern consumerism.[20] My argument against this reading by Turner, Roy, Barber, Ahmed and others, is that they continue to hold on to a notion of essential Islam and an essential Islamism or fundamentalism. For example, although Turner concedes that Islam is subject to the dynamics of post-modernity (self-reflexivity, for instance), this self-reflexive Islam continues to maintain global pretences to homogenize and totalize the cultural identity of Muslims against the diversity of consumer cultures. We need to ask where is this Islam located? In what way can it stand outside the same processes it seeks to overcome? Where does the space of externality exist? The answer, it would seem, is in the text, the norm and tradition; that is, in the trans-historical Islam that overrides temporality and spatiality of the world. As demonstrated in the discussion of the interaction between religion and the social, this notion is untenable if we shift our focus to the level of practices, the sociality of religion or the everyday-life politics of the believers. Similarly, we should focus on the different terms of insertion of Muslims into the political sphere. With these injunctions in mind, let us examine how Muslims are positioned in relation to globalization and post-modernity.

Globalization, post-modernity and the construction of muslim identities

In current accounts of Islamism, we are presented with either the alienated subject of modernity or with the confused subject of post-modernity. Working within the classical sociological framework of urban change, scholars of Islamism posit the alienated and uprooted subject who is disenchanted with modernity.[21] Under post-modern conditions, the subject is self-reflexive and unhappy about uncertainties. S/he desires a coherent moral view. Abhorring risk, s/he takes a fundamentalist turn. Given that one of post-modernism's postulates is that there is no unitary subject, we should ask what has become of the multiplicity of subject positions and the fragmented selves? The issues that we need to zero in on here have to do with the construction of Muslim identity in the present. Clearly, the processes that shape identity construction in general are at work in the particular case of Muslim identities. As such, some scholars have argued that processes associated with modernity and with post-modernity, such as objectification, rationalization, individualization and relativization, have contributed to the definition of contemporary Muslim selves.

Dale Eickelman and James Piscatori have identified 'objectification' as the process at work in the production of Muslim identity.[22] By objectification, they mean Muslims coming to consciousness of their identity as Muslims and their reflection on that identity. Although they link this process to changes in forms of cultural production and structural social transformations, objectification appears contingent on subjectivist developments and changes in Muslims' self-perceptions, rather than on structural or infrastructural change. This is somewhat similar to the idea of 'self-reflexivity' articulated by Beck and Giddens.[23] With the spread of literacy and the expansion of education, Muslims no longer rely solely on religious authorities to understand and make sense of their religion. In their modern condition, they ask themselves what it means to be Muslim. Their answers come to form an 'objectified consciousness' constituted through the processes of modernization, particularly the expansion of literacy and print. These developments are associated with the breakdown of the clerics' monopoly over religion/religious life and hence the introduction of new actors, namely the Islamists: Muslims whose consciousness has been objectified.

This formulation carries tensions between the view – found in Gellner – that processes of modernization buttress rational fundamentalism and the view that high modernity provides the ground for self-reflexivity, inquiry into self-identity and remaking that identity. The problematic that arises for us here is how to deal with this juxtaposition of a fixed tradition in perpetual reaffirmation and a lived tradition subject to reproduction, redefinition and constituting a space of contestation and reconfiguration of identity. Objectification, as conceived by Eickelman and Piscatori, allows for shifts in forms of authority. But the question that remains is: does objectification translate into changes in the nature of religion and religious knowledge?

In examining the religious field in contemporary Muslim societies, we are confronted with an ongoing redefinition and reconfiguration of religiosity and the place of religion in society and politics. In *Being Modern in Iran*, Fariba Adelkhah methodically shows how Muslims reconstruct practices and redefine beliefs in the context of globalization and consumerism. She argues that the processes of rationalization and individualization could be observed in the production of Muslim identities.[24] The rationalization of religious practices and the accompanying emphasis on the individuality of the believers indicate an increased differentiation of the religious field. Further, these processes are part and parcel of the imbrication of religion in the social. As Iranians partake of the modern world, they redefine their Muslim identity(ies). The new forms of religious sociability and the reconfiguration of practices surrounding religious festivals attest to the sociality of religion. For example, the *jalseh*, as a form of religious meeting, serves as an opportunity to attend to everyday life matters such as finding suitable partners or exchanging consumer goods procured in the free trade zones.[25]

Processes of identity formation in the post-modern period have been linked to commercialization and commodification. Through consumption, individuals construct their identities and social relations in different ways. Consumption, as a process of meaning production, can be discerned in the multiple configurations of Islamism and Islamization. Islamism, for some, expresses a particular lifestyle and patterns of consumption. This has been labelled post-modern Islamism, post-Islamism or New Age Islamism.[26] However, these formulations obscure the differentiated positions occupied by Muslims in relation to processes of globalization and post-modernity. New and changing forms of religious identification may constitute the means by which some middle-class Muslims assert a modern or a post-modern lifestyle. However, for many others, whose experience of globalization is not predominantly in the consumption sphere (i.e. access to goods and commodities purveying a globalized lifestyle), but through incorporation into the informal labour and housing markets, Islamism reworks popular practices and operates within the infrastructures of action at the local level.

Commercialization and consumerism have entered into the making of identities whether Islamist, secularist or just Muslim. Symbols associated with Islamism have been recast in the marketplace. The insertion of the veil into the world of fashion underlines the commodification process – a process that is enmeshed in the web of class, gender, lifestyle and taste-related identities and politics. The layered and multiple meanings that the veil evokes challenge the dichotomy of 'modern' and 'traditional', as demonstrated by the hybrid dress adopted by Muslim women: veiled yet fashionable. Working women in countries such as Egypt have adopted colourful headscarves combined with figure-hugging dresses or jeans and T-shirts.

Indeed, Cairo fashion boutiques and shopping malls offer new brands of trendy 'Islamic' dress, adapting the latest international styles. In Turkey, the new veiling styles are paraded on the catwalks of fashion shows by western and westernized models.[27] Are these women Islamists or post-Islamists? What does this classification yield? Studies of veiling in Turkey point to the multiple appropriations of the veil. For instance, *tessetur* (a distinct urban style of veiling), by upwardly mobile educated women, expresses a particular lifestyle and is a marker of an elite Islamist identity, while, by lower-class women, it could be read as response to populist Islamist mobilization.[28] In another context, the reverse could be true. Yet, things are not that simple. Reasons for adopting the veil vary. They include economic, social, political, religious and cultural motivations. The symbolism of the veil continues to reinforce the idea of the Islamization of the public sphere because of its association with the Islamist project and because of the terms of reception.

The multiplication of choices in the consumption sphere extends to the educational sector. Schools are sites of differentiation of identity where the interplay of class, lifestyle and taste come into full view. In Egypt, the relatively recent phenomenon of 'Islamic' foreign language schools provides a good example of the interplay of these forces and identity formation. The Islamic foreign language schools are private and enrolment fees are often very high.[29] They are preferred by a segment of the upper-middle class because they teach students IT skills and make use of computers and the internet. They also teach foreign languages, primarily English, which is often the language of instruction. Their curriculum covers the subjects set by the Ministry of Education with the addition of expanded periods of religious teaching. The mixture here captures many of the features of the lifestyle of the Egyptian upper-middle class as a whole. Members of this stratum are upwardly mobile and view progress in terms of technology and the use of English, the dominant international language. The added Islamic teaching satisfies what appears to be a need on the part of a segment of that class, a need that is linked to the preservation of a 'self-identity' in the globalized world to which they 'willingly' belong. For this particular segment, the choice of Islamic schools is most likely part of a lifestyle preference that includes listening to the new preachers promoting the accumulation of wealth as a sign of God's blessing, preaching conformity to modesty codes as an expression of love of God and so on.

These devout upper-middle-class families are positioned differently from the lower-middle-class families I interviewed in popular Cairo neighbourhoods.[30] There, some parents send their daughters to public schools where the veil is enforced by the school principal in contravention of state regulations. These parents are concerned about declining morality in their neighbourhood. Their engagement with the instruments of globalization is limited and uneven. They get glimpses of the new commodities on television. They are also exposed to the lifestyles of expatriates returning from the Gulf. These latter sometimes bring with them a conservative morality, particular styles of dress and capital, all of which are part of the global flows characterizing transnationalism. In this case, the opportunities made possible by globalization are more restricted and differ from those available to the well-off segments of society.

In these Cairo neighbourhoods, the production and consumption of cultural items enter into strategies of social and political resistance through the carving-up of spaces of difference. In these neighbourhoods youths in general, and Islamist youths in particular, generate forms of identity by asserting their own distinctions vis-à-vis other social groups. Islamist youth culture is hybrid and mediated through complex spheres of interaction. In my fieldwork with youths in Cairo, I found a richly textured construction of Muslim identity through Islamic music bands, proselytizing groups, male fraternities and mosque study groups. It is interesting that we can find parallels of this Islamic youth subculture in Turkey, where 'green pop' has emerged as a music genre, blending Islamic chants with a synthesis of Turkish and western music.[31] In certain respects, the youth experience bears similarities to that of other youths and cannot be simply abstracted as Islamic or Islamist. In Cairo, I found that Islamist and non-Islamist male youths shared common views with regard to women and their status and position in society. They articulated a critique of lax morality evidenced in women's attire and conduct. Some held that a subversion of the veil's ethical significance was taking place, as women used it to cover up or hide their moral transgressions. Islamist interventions in popular neighbourhoods reinscribed modes of action that recalled traditional practices of spatial control and moral governance (e.g. monitoring of women and gender interaction, reinforcing the familial ethos and investing in networks of solidarity and mutual aid). Even here, we may find co-option of globalized practices. Sports, in particular football and martial arts, became part of the networks of sociability of Islamist youths and sympathizers.[32] The male fraternities that formed around these activities acquired an Islamic association. The youths' self-fashioning is carried out in relation to religious traditions and cultural messages about gender relations as played out in popular films and television series and narratives of the past.

The manner and aesthetics of Islamic identities represent different inner dynamics and forms of resistance that are shaped by the local contexts. If we turn to British Muslim youths' assertion of an Islamic identity, we find that they are differently positioned in relation to religious traditions. As members of migrant and minority communities outside mainstream society, but conscious of its dominant cultural texts, they are engaged in the invention of syncretic cultural traditions out of the multiple registers available to them. In Zadie Smith's *White Teeth*, the British-born Milat Iqbal, a resident of Hackney, tries to fashion himself as a Muslim in a manner that would retain his desire for becoming a Hollywood style gangster. He joins KEVIN (Keepers of the Eternal and Victorious Islamic Nation) because 'it's got a wicked kung-fu kick-arse sound name to it'.[33] Milat Iqbal and his fellow KEVIN members are engaged in a settling of accounts where migration, minority status and the history of imperial subjugation are concerned.

The expansion of consumerism into local societies has undoubtedly affected the everyday life or the lifestyles of Muslims. But we should not assume that their responses are uniform. Nor should we label whatever comes out of the interaction between the global and the local as inauthentic and somehow equate change with heresy, newness with fakeness. In matters of belief, religious practice and views of the faith, contemporary Muslims challenge received ideas and established authorities in a way that cannot be explained solely by reference to modernity and post-modernity. Rather, conformity and transgression against religious norms can be more appropriately explained by reference to alternative lifestyles and local social and cultural practices and norms. To illustrate, I recall the example of the woman who decided to return to her husband after his declaration of *talaq*. According to official Islam, it was illicit for her to cohabit with him again. Her decision may have been based on affective, economic or social considerations. She received both support and condemnation that expressed the socio-economic and cultural positions of the various actors. The upper-middle-class employers upheld an official-Islam position, while the woman herself and her neighbours followed their own rulings. One may argue that self-reflexivity allowed her to adopt a critical, empowering resolution, but what role did it play in the decision of the others?

Concluding remarks

Taking account of the sociality and historicity of religion is central to understanding the production of religious identity in the public sphere. In other words, the identity constructed is relational: it shapes and is shaped by other social dimensions such as gender, class and lifestyles. Muslims, as actors, occupy different positions in their social settings and in relation to the processes of globalization. They do not engage, in a uniform manner, in the construction of Muslim selves. Nor do they reproduce a monolithic Muslim identity. Rather, their engagement in identity construction informs us of the power struggles that are embedded in material local conditions and global processes, and that make use of a multiplicity of registers and frames of reference.

Notes

1   For a discussion of conservative Islamism see Salwa Ismail, 'Confronting the Other: Identity, Culture, Politics and Conservative Islamism in Egypt', *International Journal of Middle East Studies*, 30 (1998), pp. 199–225. Reprinted in Salwa Ismail, *Rethinking Islamist Politics: Culture, the State and Islamism*. London, I. B. Tauris, 2003.

2   See, for example, Hrair Dekmejian, 'Islamic Revival, Catalysts, Categories and Consequences', in Shireen Hunter (ed.), *The Politics of Islamic Revivalism*, Bloomington, Indiana University Press, 1988, pp. 3–22; John Obert Voll, *Islam, Continuity and Change in the Modern World*, 2nd edn, Syracuse, Syracuse University Press, 1994.

3   The following discussion of the adultery and abortion cases draws on Ismail, *Rethinking Islamist Politics*, op. cit., pp. 18–19.

4   Nabil Abd al-Fatah and Diya Rashwan, *Taqrir al-Hala al-Dinniya fi Misr* (Report on the Condition of Religion in Egypt), Cairo, Markaz al-Ahram lil-Buhuth al-Istratijiya, 1996.

5   This case is discussed in Nadia Abu Zahra, *The Pure and the Powerful: Comparative Studies in Contemporary Muslim Societies*, Reading, Ithaca Press, 1997.

6   This case is discussed in Jean-Noël Ferrié, 'Prier pour disposer de soi: Le sens et la fonction de la prière de demande dans l'Islam marocain actuel', *Annuaire de l'Afrique du Nord*, 33 (1994), pp. 113–27.

7   Some Islamist women's groups in Morocco provide support to unmarried women seeking abortions. Their rationale for extending this kind of support may be different from the case discussed here. It is likely that their intervention is part of a vision of reform and provision for repentance and self-improvement. See Connie Carøe Christiansen, 'Women's Islamic Activism: Between Self-Practices and Social Reform Efforts', in John L. Esposito and François Burgat (eds), *Modernizing Islam: Religion in*

the Public Sphere in Europe and the Middle East, New Brunswick, NJ, Rutgers University Press, 2003, pp. 145–65.

8   Ferrié, 'Prier pour disposer du soi', op. cit., p. 125.

9   Jean Noël Ferrié, 'Vers une anthropologie deconstructiviste des sociétés musulmanes du Maghreb', *Peuples méditerranéens*, 54–5 (January–June 1991), pp. 229–45.

10 Ibid.

11 For an elaboration on the idea of the historicity of Islamic reason see Muhammad Arkoun, *Tarikhiyat al-Fikr al-Arabi al-Islami* (The Historicity of Arab-Islamic Thought), Beirut, Markaz al-Inma' al-Qawmi, 1987.

12 My reading of Ferrié, 'Vers une anthropologie deconstructiviste', op. cit., p. 238.

13 Talal Asad, 'The Construction of Religion as an Anthropological Category', in Michael Lambeck (ed.), *A Reader in the Anthropology of Religion*, Oxford, Blackwell, 2002, p. 116.

14 Ibid., p. 128.

15 Ernest Gellner, *Muslim Society*, Cambridge, Cambridge University Press, 1982.

16 See Ernest Gellner, 'Civil Society in Historical Context', *International Social Science Journal*, 43: 3 (August 1991), pp. 496–510.

17 See Bryan S. Turner, *Orientalism, Postmodernism and Globalism*, London, Routledge, 1994; and Akbar Ahmed, *Post-Modernism and Islam*, London, Routledge, 1992.

18 Benjamin Barber, *Jihad Versus McWorld*, New York, Balantine Books, 1995.

19 Turner, *Orientalism, Postmodernism and Globalism*, op. cit., pp. 17, 78, 90, 92.

20 Olivier Roy, 'Le Post-islamisme', in Olivier Roy and Patrick Haenni (eds), *Revue du Monde Musulman et de la Méditerranée*, 85–6 (1999), pp. 11–30.

21 For a critical discussion of the psycho-social approach to Islamist movements, see Salwa Ismail, 'The Popular Movement Dimensions of Contemporary Militant Islamism: Socio-Spatial Determinants in the Cairo Urban Setting', *Comparative Studies in Society and History*, 42: 2 (2000), pp. 363–93. Reprinted in Ismail, *Rethinking Islamist Politics*, op. cit.

22 Dale Eickelman and James Piscatori, *Muslim Politics*, Princeton, Princeton University Press, 1996.

23 Ulrich Beck, *Risk Society*, London, Sage, 1992; Anthony Giddens, *Modernity and Self-Identity: Self and Society in the Late Modern Age*, Stanford, CA, Stanford University Press, 1991.

24 Fariba Adelkhah, *Being Modern in Iran*, London, Hurst, 1999. The comparison with the unfolding of projects of modernity in Malaysia is instructive. There, the shari'a courts are engaged in the production of an individualized Malaysian Muslim identity while also contributing to the rationalization, if not the dissolution, of the bonds of kinship and tribe. These efforts are inscribed in the broader state objective of instituting disciplinary mechanisms that are at the service of its project of modernity. See Michael G. Peletz, *Islamic Modern: Religious Courts and Cultural Politics in Malaysia*, Princeton, Princeton University Press, 2002, in particular pp. 204–22.

25 Adelkhah, *Being Modern in Iran*, op. cit., p. 110.

26 Patrick Haenni and Olivier Roy, 'Au-delà du repli identitaire, dans les espaces de convergence entre islamisation et globalisation', mimeo, September 2002.

27 Yael Navaro-Yashin, 'The Market for Identities: Secularism, Islamism, Commodities', in Deniz Kandiyoti and Ayse Saktanber (eds), *Fragments of Culture: The Everyday of Modern Turkey*, New Brunswick, NJ, Rutgers University Press, 2002, pp. 221–53.

28   Jenny White, 'The Islamist Paradox', in Kandiyoti and Saktanber, *Fragments of Culture*, op. cit., p. 208. The inscription of veiling in spatial and symbolic representations shaped by gender, the Islamist–secularist divide and class in Istanbul is examined in Anna J. Secor, 'The Veil and Urban Space in Istanbul: Women's Dress, Mobility and Islamic Knowledge', *Gender, Place and Culture*, 9: 1 (2002), pp. 5–22.

29   See Linda Herrera, 'Islamization and Education in Egypt: Between Politics, Culture and the Market', in John L. Esposito and François Burgat (eds), *Modernizing Islam: Religion in the Public Sphere in Europe and the Middle East*, New Brunswick, NJ, Rutgers University Press, 2003, pp. 167–89.

30   These interviews were part of field research I conducted on everyday politics in Cairo's new urban quarters (conventionally referred to as the informal housing communities) in 2000 and 2001. This research was funded by the Economic and Social Research Council of Great Britain.

31   Ayse Saktanbar, '"We Pray Like You Have Fun": New Islamic Youth in Turkey between Intellectualism and Popular Culture', in Kandiyoti and Saktanber, *Fragments of Culture*, op. cit., p. 265.

32   A parallel experience among youths in Algeria is documented in Miriem Vergès, 'Les jeunes, le stade, le FIS: Vers une analyse de l'action portestaire', *Maghreb-Machrek*, 154 (October–December 1996), pp. 48–54.

33   Zadie Smith, *White Teeth*, London, Hamish Hamilton, 2000, p. 295.

François Burgat

FROM NATIONAL STRUGGLE TO THE DISILLUSIONMENTS OF "RECOLONIZATION"

The triple temporality of Islamism

THE FACT THAT THE identity problematic applies more or less to the sum total of actors does not necessarily immunize the latter from history. Even if we can discern a common matrix behind the diversity and elements of continuity within the changes, the modalities of the makeover of an individual between two affiliations ("secular," "French," "religious," "Islamic," etc.) are not strictly speaking equivalent, whether in space (social or national) or in time. Therefore, though it may be legitimate to consider that each member of the successive "generations" of the Islamist mobilization participates in the same assertion of his Muslim identity in the face of the Western alter ego and the regimes accused of pandering to it, it is important to continually reconfigure within each historical context this homogeneity of the identity problematic, in space and time.

The diversity of Islamist itineraries

In the nineteenth century the initial responses of the Muslim world to the thrust of Western hegemony were of an intellectual nature. It was on the pediment of such reformist thought, within the context of enduring British occupation, that the initial expression of the ideas of the Muslim Brothers subsequently crystallized in Egypt during the first third of the twentieth century. The United Kingdom at the time was protecting a fragile parliamentary monarchy, whose elites nonetheless enjoyed a certain pluralism of parliamentary expression. A generation later, the national ideological environment had changed: borders, nations, and mental patterns had been disrupted by the creation of Israel, the thrust of Arab nationalism, and the tripartite expedition organized in 1956 by London, Paris, and Tel Aviv to counter the nationalization of the Suez Canal. Replenished by the dividends of their nationalist victories, the authoritarianism of the successive regimes grew more pronounced. The entry "into Islamism" is obviously, on multiple levels, tailored to individual histories and national contexts. In their reversion to the fold of religious thought, Nasserists and Egyptian, Syrian, Iraqi, or Arab Baathists did not follow the same itineraries as those who, in Sudan, Egypt, or elsewhere, set aside their traditional membership in Sufi brotherhoods to rally to the reformism of a less passive and therefore more political Islam.

In Yemen, the Muslim Brothers (formed in Cairo by Hassan al-Banna) initially received, in their struggle against an isolationist and conservative religious Imamate, the support of Hassan al-Banna and then that of Gamal 'Abd al-Nasser, at the very moment when the latter was subjecting their counterparts in Cairo to a terrible campaign of repression. While in 1995 Mohammed Atta (1968–2001), an Egyptian architecture student in Hamburg, had so far internalized the categories of Sayyid Qutb's theology that he was ready to place his life on the line to make it triumph, it was in reaction to current events beyond anything Qutb might have known or imagined that he nevertheless forged the death-bent determination which eventually led to the organization of the September 11 attacks.

To render as well as possible both this plurality and the chronological ratcheting up of Islamist logic, I propose here to distinguish three broad contexts and hence three successive overarching sequences in the deployment of its mobilization.

The first sequence was that of the emergence of Islamist mobilization as a foil to direct colonial presence. In order to define its mechanism, it is nonetheless necessary to recall, however briefly, the reformist preambles of the nineteenth century. The second sequence, immediately subsequent to independence, was that of the assertion of cultural options and of the increasingly authoritarian political formulas of the first generation of nationalist elites. The third began in 1990 following the collapse of the USSR with the birth of a so-called world order which increasingly revealed itself to be conspicuously "ordered" around solely American interests. During this third timeline, in the former colonial peripheries, the Western counterpart, with its convergence of interests with the national elites in power becoming more blatant every day, insensibly again became the main foil for oppositional struggle: faced with the progress of a sort of rampant "recolonization," the loss of autonomy of the "independentist" elites stripped them of their ranking as primary adversary, to the advantage of the global superpower.

Iraq after Saddam Hussein provides a paradigmatic example of such a configuration: even more than the new elites elevated into office by the American military occupier, it is the latter that has become target number one for the resistance to a political order justifiably perceived as imposed by the United States.

The reformist preambles of the Muslim Brothers: from al-Afghani to 'Abd al-Wahhab

During the *first temporality of Islamism*, the resources of the endogenous religious culture were progressively mobilized to fuel the political resistance to the direct stranglehold of the Western colonizer. In 1928, ten years after the carving up of the Ottoman Empire and four years after the dissolution of the caliphate, the last institutional expression of global Muslim unity, eight years before the Treaty of London, which recognized the independence of Egypt in 1936 (while retaining the British military presence in the canal zone), the foundation of the Muslim Brothers by Hassan al-Banna can be considered to be the very first manifestation of the "Islamist reaction."

Nonetheless, the emergence of the Brothers owed much to the heritage of prior intellectual mobilization, which proceeded from a very similar logic. The existential question ("What is to be done to resist Western pressure?") had indeed already been raised by the founders of the trend identified with the thought of Jamal al-Din al-Afghani (1838–1897), Muhammad Abduh (1849–1905), and Rashid Ridha (1865–1935). Essentially, the Muslim Brothers prolonged the first intellectual efforts of their predecessors by transposing them into the political field. The testimony of a large majority of "founding fathers" thus contradicts the existence of any rupture between contemporary Islamists and the reformist thought of their elders.[1]

On this ground, the Algerian experience of Malek Bennabi – already mentioned above – is particularly illuminating. Bennabi paradoxically rediscovered the Arab and Turkish Orient, from which he had been insulated by the dominant north–south flows of colonial exchange, by reading French Orientalist literature. The latter provided him with an aesthetically enhanced image of the Orient. But there was a dearth of the key readings necessary to empower an explanation of its terrible state of decline. As he explained in his memoirs, it was the works of Muhammad Abduh and the Lebanese reformist Ahmed Ridha (1872–1953) which gave him the – political – key to this Oriental decline:

> Finally and above all, I discovered at the En-Nadjah Bookshop the two books that I consider to be the earliest and most decisive sources of my intellectual vocation. I am referring to *La Faillite morale de la politique occidentale en Orient* (The Moral Bankruptcy of Western Policy in the Orient) by Ahmed Ridha and the *Rissalat al-tawhid* by Sheikh Muhammad Abduh, translated by Mustapha Abderrazak, in collaboration with a French Orientalist. These two works, I believe, made an impression on my entire generation at the *madrasa*.[2] In any case, I owe them my turn of mind from then on. Indeed, with an abundant documentation on the splendors of Muslim society at the apex of its civilization, Ridha's work gave me a precise yardstick with which to measure its currently depressing social distress. Abduh's work – I am thinking of the important introduction by its translators, which dwells on the wealth of Islamic thought over the centuries – gave me a point of reference by which to judge its appalling present state of intellectual poverty. This reading chastened my spleen, that nostalgia for the Orient which Pierre Loti, Claude Farrère, and even Alphonse Lamartine and François de Chateaubriand had imparted to me. They revealed to me a historically real Orient whose currently miserable condition I could no longer ignore. They constituted a force, an intellectual call of quite another order which prevented me from lapsing into the romanticism which at the time was so fashionable among that generation of Algerian intellectuals.

There exist numerous other "object lesson" illustrations of this continuity of thought between the reformists and the Brothers. At the other end of the Arab planet, in the Yemen of Imam Yahya, the modernizing movement of the "Free Yemenis,"[3] which we will return to below, never politically distinguished the influence of al-Banna's Muslim Brothers from that of the reformist currents which preceded them.[4]

In this Arabian Peninsula, in Yemen but also in Saudi Arabia, reformist endeavors had certainly been the forerunners of the al-Afghani current. Can they also be associated with the inception of the Islamism of the twentieth century? The least known are the initiatives of the Yemenis Muhammad ibn Isma'il al-Amir (d. 1769) and Muhammad al-Shawkani (1760–1834).[5] The latter, for almost forty years a Zaydi (Shiite) judge at the service of the imams of the uplands of North Yemen, was one of the first to denounce the bad effects of ill-considered imitation (*taqlid*) of tradition to the detriment of the innovative adaptations rendered possible by *ijtihad*. His thought also contained an embryo of reference to constitutionalism and to a limitation of the powers of rulers, whom he prompts to accept the advice of the nation.[6] His thoughts deeply inspired Abduh.[7] Finally, and above all, he attempted to transcend the divisions between the different legal schools and the Zaydi (Shiite) and Shafii (Sunni) sectarian allegiances.

These reformist antecedents to the colonial shock and the continuity between Abduh and his Yemeni ancestor al-Shawkani relativize the theory of a Muslim world which only confrontation with the West had been able to extricate from its doctrinal stasis. On the contrary, they support the idea that the reformist dynamic already underway before the colonial confrontation was plausibly derailed only when its contributions had been assimilated with possible concessions to the culture of the invader. The wellsprings of this reactive logic, which marked the whole epoch then opening, have been brilliantly demonstrated in the formula of Tariq al-Bishri, an Egyptian jurist close to the Muslim Brothers: "While we resist, do you think it is possible for us to advance?" (quoted by Bennabi).

Whatever the posterity of al-Shawkani's efforts, at least one argument nevertheless suggests not directly associating him with this sequence of a reformist preamble to contemporary Islamism: contrary to members of the later school of al-Afghani, al-Shawkani did not mobilize under the pressure of a clearly identified Western menace. He perhaps only sought to help the Zaydi Imams, whom he served faithfully for forty years, to emerge from the ghetto of their sectarian allegiance to better legitimize their domination over their Sunni Shafii vassals. Above all he sought to transcend the divisions among different juridical schools and their sectarian allegiances.

Among the reformists of the eighteenth century, one whose notoriety has widely survived is "the Saudi" Muhammad 'Abd al-Wahhab.[8] Beginning in 1744, the Najdi preacher undertook a rigorous reinstatement of monotheism and divine unicity. He placed his preaching at the service of the nascent dynasty of Muhammad ibn al-Saud, with whom he threw in his lot, providing what might be called the ideological underpinnings which enabled the sovereign to unify a large part of the Peninsula and to give birth to a stable and autonomous political entity. From the perspective of contemporary Islamism, the status of 'Abd al-Wahhab's approach is therefore somewhat more ambivalent than that of the Yemeni al-Shawkani.

Even if it was not the product of a reaction to the Western threat, its message did indeed have a "nationalist" resonance with international implications. It contributed to help a new Arab nation emerge, to the detriment of the Ottoman Empire. It had a federal dimension, since it enabled a centralized political power to transcend the divisions of the different Sunni schools. It also had reformist implications: the federalism of "Wahhabism" indeed denounced illegitimate political-religious forms, considered to be a challenge to divine unicity. It therefore waged war against Shiism and the "cult" of Ali in the East and, almost everywhere, against the intermediation of the saints

advocated by the Sufis. The stamp of Wahhabism, although often caricatured in contemporary literature,[9] left an indelible imprint on later expressions of the dynamics
of re-Islamization, including (in its reserve toward certain expressions of Sufism) the
thought of the Muslim Brothers.

Essentially, in the context of the colonial confrontation, the first Islamist generation then contributed to reaffirming the place of the religious reference within the
lexicon of pro-independence struggles, as not only intellectual but now also political.
Even if it was used a lot, the Islamic lexicon did not monopolize the expression of
pro-independence anti-Western mobilization.[10] The first generation of nationalists
drew heavily on the conceptual arsenal of the colonial power and even more so from
its Soviet alter ego and competitor. "Anti-imperialist" socialism as well as "ethnic"
nationalism – that is, the so-called secular Arabism, whose original ideologues, first
and foremost led by the Syrian Michel Aflaq, included a significant number of
Christians – occupied a wide swath of the space traditionally allocated to the religious
reference. Many future members of the Islamist generation passed through this universe of "socialist" and "secular" Arabism before experiencing, at the end of highly
diversified itineraries, an identical need to restore the religious reference to its place
in the expression of the pro-independence project.[11]

The first Islamist generation, notably in Tunisia and Algeria, nonetheless failed to
capitalize on the political fruits of its efforts and to control the state apparatus vacated
by the departure of the colonizers. Its representatives, be they the Egyptian Muslim
Brothers, the trend of Malek Bennabi and the Association of Ulamas founded by Sheikh
Ben Badis in Algeria, or the Tunisian Youssefists,[12] were almost systematically excluded
from the exercise of power, to the benefit of the so-called secular pro-independence
elites. All the complexities of this process, and particularly the role played by the colonial powers in the co-option of their pro-independence "interlocutors," especially in
the case of the Algerian NLF, have not yet been completely documented.[13]

The disillusions of decolonization: from cultural divide to political authoritarianism

The *second Islamist temporality* stretches from the period of independence until early in
the 1990s. This was the period of assertion of the political formula of indigenous elites
who had succeeded in coming to power. It was also the period of an increasing calling
into question of these same elites. Today the main political opponent of the founders of
al-Qaeda appears to be this "Nasserian" or, elsewhere in the region, "Nasserist" generation of pro-independence elites. It was progressively on the receiving end of a double
indictment on the part of the rising Islamist generation. One was having betrayed the
promises of independence by not having pursued a clear symbolical rupture from the
colonizer. The other, which emerged more slowly, was having merely responded to
the first demands for political participation with a repressive authoritarianism.

Between the Islamist trends, which were mainly in the opposition, and the elites
in power, the dispute focused primarily on a sort of "cultural" deficit observable in the
realizations of independence. The Islamists wanted to pursue on the ideological and
symbolical levels the process of putting the colonizer "at arm's length," which had just
been achieved in the political arena before being extended on the economic level with

the "nationalizations" (of oil, arable land, the Suez Canal, etc). They called for a rupture with the mainly Marxist categories of "anti-imperialism" and "Third-Worldism" applied throughout the first temporality of the nationalist dynamic. The modernizing elites in power were therefore criticized for not having carried out the expected cultural and symbolic rupture with the colonial universe – in other words, their inability to perfect the "distancing" of the foreign master by restoring the primacy of the "Islamic," that is, "endogenous," symbolic system. In the Maghreb, the tensions linked to the persistent use of the French language and the state's marginalizing of the religious institutions (notably the universities) inherited from the precolonial "Islamic" system provided the visible part of this process. The elites in power were very soon identified as belonging to "the French party." Indeed, as the Tunisian Rashid al-Ghannoushi, in exile from "Bourguiba's army of the vanquished" to use his own expression, testified, independence, "much more than a victory over the French occupier, constituted instead a victory over the Arabo-Islamic civilization of Tunisia."[14]

The cultural nature of these first claims subsequently expanded to include the more banal denunciation of the growing authoritarianism of regimes and the premises of an "Arab political formula," behind which the pro-independence elites having come to power very soon felt the need to protect themselves. This lock-out of the political field progressively appeared all the less acceptable for benefiting from a watchful tolerance and, often enough, explicit support on the part of the former colonial powers. Beyond any reaction to colonial violence in itself, it was as a stand against the repression brought to bear by the pro-independence elites (Nasser's repression of the Muslim Brothers is paradigmatic here) that the first radical offshoots (above all in the case of Qutb) emerged in the course of this second temporality. In the immense majority of cases, the expressions of Islamist mobilization were very soon denied access to the legal political arena. Hence their members were long confined to clandestine action or, in the most favorable cases, to the associative or trade-unionist institutional outer fringe of political life. The more their capacity for mobilization was asserted, the more the policies of exclusion of the regimes and the ostracism of the Western media cracked down.

Despite the diversity of national configurations, the recipe for the radicalization of part of the Islamist population gelled thanks to the same ingredients: the regimes, having exhausted the capital of nationalist (Algeria, Tunisia, Morocco) or revolutionary resources (gained in the course of popular revolutions following independence, Egypt, Libya), progressively harmonized their governmental practices within the mold of a quasi "Arab institutional norm." Despite the patent discrepancies with all the humanist precepts lionized by the West, they thus benefited from the active support of the latter.

After a phase of nationalist exuberance, an inversion in the trend of oil prices and the mechanisms of global economic integration inexorably led the pro-independence elites to accept, from the 1980s onward, new forms of dependency, making even more concessions to their Western environment as their own popular underpinnings weakened. Progressively, the heroes of independence and the other Third-Worldist revolutionaries – or their inheritors – were accused not only of rehashing the terms of cultural domination but, increasingly, of endorsing, under the most dehumanized arsenal of political repression, a new "re-dependence," first economic and then political (and even military in the Middle East, as soon as the states of the region stopped resisting Israel's demands).

In the conservative oil monarchies which had purportedly remained closest to the religious reference, the passage through a certain "secularization," then through autocracy and (re)dependence, was in fact very real and fueled identical tensions.[15] In Saudi Arabia during the 1980s (to which we will return below) the *ulamas* were reduced to the role of accessories to power, purveyors of financial *fatwas* legitimizing modes of development, or to silent opposition. The expropriation of the religious norm progressively narrowed to the space of mere personal status, conquering only one new field of action, that of so-called Islamic finance. In Arabia, the political price of dependency on the West was revealed to be proportional to the European and American appetite for oil. Authoritarianism and concussion with Western powers inexorably set up the podium from which the first Islamist demands and the subsequent radicalization of some of their members were to be launched.

Facing "recolonization": al-Qaeda and the third temporality of Islamism

> *After years of being perceived as a problem solver, the United States itself has now become a problem for the rest of the world. After having been the guarantor of political freedom and economic order for half a century, the United States appears more and more to be contributing to international disorder by maintaining where it can uncertainty and conflict.*
> —EMMANUEL TODD, *AFTER THE EMPIRE: THE BREAKDOWN OF THE AMERICAN ORDER* (2004)

> *Did you ever wonder why it wasn't Sweden that we attacked?*
> —OSAMA BIN LADEN, MESSAGE TO THE AMERICAN PEOPLE (NOVEMBER 2004)

The *third Islamist temporality*, during which the gravitational pull of al-Qaeda's influence began to come into its own, emerged in the early 1990s. It underwrote a sort of transfer, or better a "return," of the oppositional struggles of the Arab world to the international scene. For a whole political generation, the Western powers, with the United States as self-imposed leader, gradually "reverted" to the status of main adversary, just as they had been during the colonial period.

The image of a new transition "from close enemy to distant enemy" – used by the Egyptian Ayman al-Zawahiri to describe the strategy of his extremist organization – thus amounts to a return to the binary confrontation of the colonial configuration, the overwhelming power of the foreign enemy reasserting itself against the intermediation of local governing elites, reduced to the rank of protected go-betweens for the new holders of the title "empire."

Three great "denials of representation" were fundamentally instrumental in the radicalization and transnationalization of the rebellion which spread through part of the Islamist constituency. The first was the denial endured by a rising generation of opposition to Arab state regimes, which year after year has come up against the great firewall of conservative political engineering which almost everywhere has replaced the fugitive promises of "democratic transition." The second "failure of the political" was regional: it resulted from the exacerbation of the Israeli–Arab conflict, more "asymmetrical" than ever,[16] and from the state of abandonment in which the hopes of the Palestinian camp, already weakened by the collapse of its traditional Soviet ally, ended up when the paralysis of the 1993 Oslo Accords finally locked in. The third political dysfunction has been global: by bringing the division of the "Western camp" to an end, the collapse of the USSR has abrogated an essential means of regulating the bouts of bulimia of Washington, whose foreign policy from then on increasingly lurched toward unilateral interventionism. As Rashid Khalidi emphasizes, the 2003 American war against Iraq was fought

> ... firstly to demonstrate that it was possible to free the United States from subordination to international law or the U.N. Charter, from the need to obtain the approval of the United Nations for American actions, and from the constraints of operating within alliances.... it was a war fought because its planners ... saw the tragedy of 9/11 as a golden opportunity to achieve this long-cherished goal."[17]

The correlation of these three levels of crisis – national, regional, and global – gradually widened the gap of misunderstanding between, on the one hand, the millions of citizens in an entire region of the world who deem themselves to be its victims and, on the other, the coalition of those who, at the global, regional, or national domestic levels, stand to reap benefit from it: the American administration and its neo-conservative ideological henchmen, then Israel, largely supported by its public opinion and its powerful communication capabilities, and finally the Arab governing elites, more often than not completely devoid of any public support. It was arguably this general failure in political regulation of world tensions which, early in the 1990s, took the lid off the Pandora's box of Islamist radicalization. The al-Qaeda insurgency, that monstrous progeny of the world's most perverse injustices, can be considered one of its most hyperbolical expressions.

In the globally democratic Western environments, the claims of the alter-globalization movement have highlighted, through radically different means, political and economic malfunctions which, *mutatis mutandis*, are not entirely foreign to those which have nurtured the emergence of al-Qaeda. In lands where – oil interests and Israeli security so demand – Western domination has intensified to a particularly high pitch and where, above all, conservative local political arrangements have prohibited all forms of legal protest, the radicalization has been spun into the emergence of revolutionary rhetoric and practices and the sectarian radicalization of Osama Bin Laden and his operatives.

The impunity of the "Arab Pinochets"

The grip of the Arab "institutional norm," endorsed by the international order, manifests itself above all through the outlawing and gradual criminalization of real political forces.[18] Parties deprived of their existence or of all access to the legal political arena represent in their immense majority the mainstream of the Islamist trend. The regimes have substituted oppositional "partners," tailored to the requirements of a "pluralist" narrative intended above all to lend credence abroad to a democratic façade. By refusing to pay the price for the existence of genuine mechanisms of representation, these regimes have reverted to repression to confront the tensions inescapably born of this deep dichotomy between reality and institution.

From Riyad to Rabat, the use of torture has become banal and systematic. It targets not only political prisoners but very often also their close family, male or female.[19] The presence of an extremist fringe – but also its regular, often massive, manipulation in the scenographies of the mass media – provides the pretext for an iron foreclosure of the legal political scene. Egypt, in which President Mubarak could be "elected" again for a fifth six-year term in September 2005, has been living under a state of emergency since 1981. Almost everywhere, the electoral system, dispossessed of any grasp on the balance of power in the upper reaches of the state, or "defused," to adopt the excellent expression coined by the Moroccan political scientist Mohamed Tozy, is in fact running idle.[20]

Last but not least,[21] this "Arab political formula" has been consubstantial with practically unreserved Western support. The first contradiction of the new American world order has therefore been adapting to the profound discredit of the authoritarian regimes that underpin it. This shows an obstinate blindness, born notably from an American propensity, inherited from the 1979–1980 Iran crisis, to indiscriminately criminalize a whole Islamist generation. Or, alternatively, great lucidity concerning the nationalist bearing of the Islamist thrust and the advantages that, albeit at the price of sacrificing a few sacred principles, the present formula bestows on those who are its chief architects.

The wellsprings of the mobilizing resources of Bin Laden's followers therefore are replenished by the frustration of a political generation which perceives itself to be caught between the increasingly heavy hammer of American interventionism and the anvil of the repressive authoritarianism of its own governing elites. During the 1990s the strategies of liberation gradually came to focus on the American hand perceived as wielding that heavy hammer.

The walling-up of Palestine

At the dark heart of the malignant dysfunctions of the political regulation of the world there lies, unsurprisingly, the ever-recurrent Israeli–Arab conflict over Palestine. Through the 1990s, as the real contours of the Oslo Accords came progressively to light, the Palestine Liberation Organization (PLO), which had taken the spectacular step of officially recognizing the state of Israel, received only illusory administrative compensation. The image of an archipelago of asphyxiated Bantustans, ceaselessly redefined by colonial excrescences, was inexorably substituted for any viable form of a Palestinian state, whose creation was continually postponed. Long before Likud came to office, the Labor Party, reputedly composed of "supporters of peace," initiated this systematic colonization of the West Bank, which rendered meaningless the proclaimed principle of an "exchange of land for peace."

From the end of 2000 on, the second Intifada gave the hawks of the Sharon camp the pretext purely and simply to reoccupy the Palestinian enclaves and ratchet up the violence to a new level. Refugee camps were assaulted with heavy armor and bulldozers. Even more than in its principle, it was in its mapping that the "security wall," which authorized the annexation of hundreds of hectares of Palestinian land, demonstrated the reality of the Israeli strategy. For all Palestinians, and for those elsewhere in the world who have preserved the privilege of accessing relatively objective sources of information, it quickly became self-evident not only that the Israelis did not want peace but that they also coveted the land occupied since 1967. It also became clear that the American administration, whether under Bush Junior or under Clinton, did not harbor the least real intention of opposing this unacknowledged policy of annexation of great swaths of the West Bank.[22]

"Against God" rather than "Against His Saints": al-Qaeda attacks the American world order

At the beginning of the 1990s the postcolonial formula gave way to a new "imperial" order, even more obviously dominated by the United States than before.[23] The methods that Washington has employed to perpetuate or to perfect its hegemony are certainly not new. In 1973, in Chile, a first "September 11" gave birth, on the ashes of a "rebel" democracy, to a "subserviently" terrible dictatorship.[24] To the objectives targeted by the subjection of the entire South American continent[25] were added, in the case of the Middle East, the strategic nature of oil interests and the security requirements of Israel. The principle of the eviction of a government duly elected but considered excessively nationalist in favor of a more conciliatory authoritarian regime had been inaugurated in the region by the overthrow of the Iranian prime minister Mohammad Mossadegh, with British connivance, in August 1953.

The Second Gulf War in 1991 marked the overture of an American decade of intervention in the Peninsula. Hitherto a major ally of the United States, the Iraqi dictatorship was to pay the price for its "unfortunate" attempt, in August 1990, to seize the oil wells of Kuwait, bearing the brunt of a U-turn in American diplomacy and the mobilization of the United Nations. After the sacrifice of whole divisions of Saddam Hussein's army, carpet-bombed by B-52s, it was the Iraqi civilian population, by the hundreds of thousands, who would foot the bill for the economic embargo subsequently enforced by the coalition. The disarmament of the only regional power capable of militarily resisting Israel also gave Washington the opportunity to perpetuate its armed presence in countries neighboring Iraq, such as Saudi Arabia. The founding episode of the armed annexation of the largest oil reserve in the world had just been played out.[26] It was at the core of the incipient rebellion to be staged by the al-Qaeda camp.

The theater of operations of the most disputed initiatives of American and Western diplomacy in the 1990s was not limited to the Arabian Peninsula. The decade opened in Algeria with a double electoral victory (June 1990 and December 1991) for an opposition rallied under the umbrella of the "Islamic Salvation Front." The ISF was probably not significantly more democratic than the military whose interests it threatened, but hardly less so either. The all-powerful presidential institution, which forecloses the constitution and controls the armed forces, considerably limited the maneuvering space for its possible parliamentary majority. Under the pretext of "preserving democracy," Europe and the United States allowed the military junta to suppress the results of these first free elections ever and to implement, from January 1992 onward, an unusually perverse repressive strategy.

The silent approbation of the United States was echoed by the open political, economic, and media-hyped support of France under François Mitterrand. In the view of the vast majority of opinion, which, in the Muslim world, gave no credence to the explanation that Paris and Algiers were attempting to legitimize, the conviction of a cynical Western dualism was further reinforced. The same dualism was palpable in 1995, when, in Bosnia, thousands of Muslim citizens were massacred despite the presence of Western troops under a United Nations mandate, supposedly there to protect them.

Finally, beyond the Middle East but still on Muslim lands, the new American world order granted its former Russian enemy *carte blanche* to wage in Chechnya, amid the rubble of its own empire, a colonial war every bit as barbarous as the one which it had just lost in Afghanistan.[27]

From the transnationalism of security policies to the internationalization of "Islamic" resistance

In the mind of an entire generation, and not only among Islamists, the political crises within the Arab world and part of the Muslim world are ever more systematically associated with an order that claims to be global but increasingly seems to be solely American. Washington's propensity to resort to "hard power" has grown, in line with that of its Arab puppet states to have recourse to repression. Both convey a common deficit of political legitimacy. Not only is this world order "Americanizing" (due to the collapse of the Soviet counterpower), but it is becoming increasingly confessional as the neo-conservatives make growing use of Christian references. It is also tending more and more to forgo the endorsement of the ever less credible international institutions dominated by Washington.

For millions of citizens of the Arab world (and not only for them), the mirage of a disinterested, pacifist, and universalist global "new order" has irresistibly evaporated before the hard reality of the support which an arrogant and ever more obviously autistic superpower has by all means at its command, including military, granted to one of the camps, whose actors are easy to identify. These are, first, the bearers of its own financial interests and narrowing ideological vision, that is, respectively, a small military-industrial caste closely linked to those in power and a highly coordinated Christian and Jewish electorate; second, the regional state actors who connive in their defense: Israel on the one hand, the Arab authoritarian regimes on the other.

During the 1990s the correlation between American interventionism and the repressive clout of the domestic Arab state orders was becoming increasingly self-evident. Even before September 11, 2001, the systematization and institutionalization of security cooperation endowed it with a heightened expression. The "War on Terrorism" would lead to the identification of certain Arab regimes with the American order and, conversely, of American interests with the durability of such regimes, notwithstanding their obvious unpopularity.

The formula which welds together this illegitimate transaction between the world order and sundry dictatorships rests on an exchange of resources: the authoritarian regimes "repay" Western silence and support with concessions which may range from massive arms orders to help in controlling oil prices, not to speak of more personal emoluments – which will leave lasting scars on not only the history of bilateral American–Saudi relations, of course, but also that of Franco–Algerian relations.

The first major world summit against (Islamic) terrorism at Sharm-al-Sheikh in March 1996 amounted to a particularly emblematic expression of this process. It was held some five months before Bin Laden's first call for "War against Americans," made on August 23, 1996. A significant double convergence in policy and rhetoric locked in, between the titleholders of the American order and their Arab and Israeli allies. The common enemy of the likes of Bill Clinton, Vladimir Putin, and Benjamin Netanyahu, and also of all Arab dictators, was thereafter characterized as "Islamic terrorism." An alliance involving the American and European (including Russian) security apparatuses, the Israeli services, and the repressive machinery of the most dictatorial Arab regimes was forthwith proclaimed. The enemy was indiscriminately dubbed "Islamic terrorism." It encompassed a wide medley of realities: that of Palestine for Netanyahu, of Chechnya for Boris Yeltsin and then for Putin, of the Algeria of the generals and the Tunisia of Zine al-Abidine Ben Ali.

The rhetoric of Sharm-al-Sheikh to some degree sanctioned the criminalization of all resistance, armed or not, to the dysfunctions of a very wide array of national, regional, or global authoritarianisms. All the actors in these oppositions and this resistance thus came, by an identical stigmatization, to be "invited" to identify with one another. Where this symbolic and political coordination had not already taken place, this was indeed what was to happen. In the eyes of many of those who were designated as being "on the receiving end," the transnational extension of the repression of all forms of protest or oppositional expression employing an Islamic lexicon reinforced the legitimacy of and the necessity for a correspondingly transnational extension of resistance.

For the militants of al-Qaeda, the "distant" American "enemy" thus sealed its own fate, henceforth to be shared with the "close" and long top-priority "enemy" represented by the Arab regimes. In the Islamic sphere, the internationalization and the reterritorialization of the armed struggle took shape concomitantly, echoing the American globalization of an increasingly disputed order.

"Mujahidin without borders" or the role of Afghanistan

The integration of several thousand young Muslims (between 10,000 and 15,000) into the ranks of the Afghan resistance to the Soviet occupation (from 1979 to 1989) constituted an episode that the analysis of the al-Qaeda generation must obviously take into consideration. This "Afghan factor" – and the opportunity given to several, thousand militants to participate in a victorious armed struggle against the second global superpower of the period – clearly played a significant role in the crystallization and self-affirmation of the al-Qaeda generation, just as the conflicts in the former Yugoslavia and, later, in Chechnya also did to a certain degree. It cannot, however, be inflated into the sole or even the central explanatory factor.

More than being just an opportunity for military training, it no doubt facilitated the "path to action" by accelerating the circulation and transnationalization of revolutionary strategy. It also boosted, at the expense of other political strategies, the credibility of the efficacy or simply the feasibility of armed struggle against one of the pillars of the world order. The thrust of the "rejectionist camp," composed of a minority of proponents of armed action, was indeed favored as much by the failure of the struggles waged within the "national" arenas (notably in Egypt and Algeria) as by the blatant absence of any alternative route offered by the world order and its local intermediaries to the legalism of the central nexus of Islamist movements, notably and above all the Muslim Brothers.

The Afghan episode was constructed around successive and relatively different phases and processes. The first, at the beginning of the 1980s, was that of the legal, even official (from both the Arab and the American point of view), mobilization of thousands of young volunteers in the ranks of the resistance to the Soviet occupation. The legal presence of these "combatants without borders," for a long time known as "Arab Afghans" (even if they came from the entire Muslim world), coincided with the victory, which was also theirs, of the coalition of opponents to the Kabul regime and the subsequent withdrawal of Soviet forces.

In 1992 began a four-year civil war between the victors. At first the "Arabs" bore the brunt. The necessity for most of them to fall back on positions outside the Afghan sanctuary coincided with the beginning of a phase of increased repression by the regimes of their respective countries (notably Saudi Arabia and Algeria), which were wary of such operatives too rashly sent or allowed to go abroad for training in *jihad*. In the eyes of the Western media, these "combatants of the faith" abruptly morphed into "God's madmen."

The rise to power of the Taliban in 1996 once again inverted the regional situation. The deal struck with them by Osama Bin Laden received the support of Ayman al-Zawahiri and the members of his Egyptian organization Jihad – the second, with Jamaa Islamiyya, of the two branches of Egyptian radical Islamism in open revolt against the regime – which had survived the particularly effective repression of previous years. Al-Zawahiri then decided to relocate the front of his old (and inconclusive) struggle against the "close" enemy, the Egyptian state, to an admittedly "distant" (American) enemy, against which an exponentially increasing number of malcontents could be recruited. This last phase gave the signal for the "legal" (from the point of view of their Afghan hosts) deployment of the international networks of al-Qaeda.[28]

The accusations and claims that the Islamist generation had long directed at their respective regimes were thus turned in top priority against the former European colonial powers or, more precisely, against the – American – apex of the global power structure, which, following the defeat of the USSR, seamlessly took over their role.

It was in this context that, in April 1996, an Egyptian named Mohammed Atta sat down to write his will. It was also on that date that most of the perpetrators of the September 11 attacks set out with him on the long road which, via Afghanistan, Hamburg, and a handful of American civil aviation schools, culminated one morning in September 2001 in the firestorm of the World Trade Center.

Notes

1   See, above all, the thesis of Tariq Ramadan, *Aux sources du renouveau musulman, d'al-Afghani à Hassan al-Banna: un siècle de réforme islamique* (Paris: Bayard/Centurion, 1998).

2   An educational establishment for Algerian Muslim students. [The French edition gives no source for this quotation – Trans.]

3   Leigh Douglas, *The Free Yemeni Movement, 1935–1962* (Beirut: AUB, 1987).

4   François Burgat and Mohamed Sbitli, "Les Libres' yéménites, le courant réformiste et les Frères musulmans: premiers repères pour l'analyse," in Chérif al-Maher and Salam Kawakibi (eds.), *Le Courant réformiste musulman et sa réception dans les sociétés arabes*,

Aleppo Symposium marking the hundredth anniversary of the death of Sheikh 'Abd al-Rahman al-Kawakibi, May 31–June 1, 2002 (Damascus: IFPO, 2003).

5   See in particular Bernard Haykel, *Revival and Reform in Islam: The Legacy of Muhammad al-Shawkani* (Cambridge: Cambridge University Press, 2003).

6   See in particular Franck Mermier, Bernard Haykel, and Gabriele Vom Bruck, in Franck Mermier et al. (eds.), *Le Yémen contemporain* (Paris: Karthala, 2003). "On the one hand, he who governs in the name of Islam has a responsibility toward the nation. On the other hand, the nation itself has obligations toward him. One of the former is obedience. The other is to provide council."

7   He wrote: "I raised my voice to call for two very great undertakings … The first was to liberate thought from imitation [*taqlid*]. The second … was the necessity to differentiate the obedience that the people owe to the government and the right of the people to justice from the government" (quoted by Ahmed Amin, *Zu'ama al-Islah fi al-'Asr al-Hadith* [The Fathers of Reform in the Contemporary Era] [Beirut: Dar al-Kitab al-'Arabi, 1979], p. 84).

8   See Natana J. Delong-Bas, *Wahhabi Islam: From Revival and Reform to Global Jihad* (Oxford/New York: I. B. Tauris, 2004); Alexei Vassiliev, *The History of Saudi Arabia* (New York: New York University Press, 2000); Guido Steinberg, *Religion und Staat in Saudi-Arabien: Die wahhabitischen Gelehrten, 1902–1953* (Würzburg: Ergon, 2002); see also *La Pensée* 335 (July–September 2003).

9   Pascal Ménoret, "Wahhabisme, arme fatale du néo-orientalisme," *Mouvements* (November 2004).

10   Albert Hourani, *Arabic Thought in the Liberal Age, 1798–1939* (Cambridge: Cambridge University Press, 1983); French translation: *La Pensée arabe et l'Occident* (Brussels: Naufal, 1992). For Algeria, see, for example, Jean-Robert Henry and Claude Collot, *Le Mouvement national algérien: textes* (Paris: L'Harmattan-OPU, 1978).

11   See Henry Laurens, *L'Orient arabe: arabisme et islamisme de 1798 à 1945* (Paris: Armand Colin, 1993).

12   The modernity of this is perfectly illustrated by the thought of Malek Bennabi (see Malek Bennabi, *Vocation de l'islam* [Paris: Seuil, 1954]).

13   One of the most emblematic situations is no doubt that of certain future high-ranking Algerian military officers: young officers in the French Army, many of whom only deserted to join the freedom struggle a few months before Independence. They then succeeded in taking a very firm hold on power and, in the 1980s and 1990s, played a well-documented role in foreclosing the political system.

14   Quoted in François Burgat, *L'Islamisme en face*, 3rd ed. (Paris: La Découverte, 2002), pp. 48ff.; English translation: *Face to Face with Political Islam* (London/New York: I. B. Tauris Publishers, 1999).

15   See Pascal Ménoret, *L'Énigme saoudienne* (Paris: La Découverte, 2004).

16   Bertrand Badie, "Palestine, quelles perspectives?" conference held at the Paris Institut d'Études Politiques (IEP), January 19, 2004.

17   Rashid Khalidi, *Resurrecting Empire: Western Footprints and America's Perilous Path in the Middle East* (Boston: Beacon Press, 2004), p. x.

18   See in particular François Burgat, "De A comme Arafat à Z comme Zîn al-'Abidîn Ben Ali: la pérennité de la formule politique arabe," in *L'Islamisme en face*, pp. 244ff.

19   Other than the converging reports of Amnesty International, see in particular Comité pour le Respect des Libertés et des Droits de l'Homme en Tunisie, *La Torture en Tunisie 1987–2000: plaidoyer pour son abolition et contre l'impunité* (Paris: Le Temps des Cerises, 2004); Mahmoud Khelili, *La Torture en Algérie (1991–2001)*, Algeria-Watch,

October 2001; Youcef Bedjaoui, Abbas Aroua, and Meziane Aït-Larbi, *An Inquiry into the Algerian Massacres* (Geneva: Hoggar, 1999); Lahouari Addi, "La torture comme pratique d'État dans les pays du Maghreb," *Confluences* 51 (October 2004).

Egyptian human rights organizations named around twenty people killed under torture in 2003 and 2004 and 292 avowed cases of torture between January 1993 and April 1994. The Egyptian state refused to allow the visit of the UN special envoy on torture (which the Egyptian National Council for Human Rights, in its first report in April 2005, emphasized was "normal investigation practice").

20 Mohamed Tozy, "Représentation/Intercession: les enjeux de pouvoir dans les 'champs politiques désamorcés' au Maroc," in Michel Camau (ed.), *Changements politiques au Maghreb* (Paris: CNRS, 1991), pp. 153–168. In a manner less academic but quite as eloquent, Mohamed Qahtan, one of the leaders of the Yemeni opposition, close to the Muslim Brothers, described electoral competition in the Arab world as being like a football match in which, "unlike the opposition team, the team in power is allowed to use its hands." "But we like the sport," he adds, "so we play anyway" (interview with the author, Sanaa, March 2003).

21 In English in the original – Trans.

22 Jean-François Legrain, "La Palestine, de la terre perdue à la reconquête du territoire," *Cultures et conflits*, "L'international sans territoire," 2005; Laetitia Bucaille, *Génération Intifada* (Paris: Hachette Littératures, 2002).

23 The phrases "Against God" and "Against His Saints" in the subhead derive from the commonly used French idiom: "Il vaut mieux s'adresser à Dieu qu'à Ses Saints" (i.e., when in urgent need, it is preferable to circumvent the intermediate levels of a power structure or a hierarchical bureaucracy) – Trans.

24 It was on September 11, 1973, in Chile that General Augusto Pinochet overthrew, with the help of the CIA, the regime of the elected president, Salvador Allende. The junta, with renewed American support, subsequently tortured and liquidated many of the members of this "Marxist" opposition, who supposedly threatened Washington's economic interests.

25 "The United States has never officially owned colonies in Latin America, but it has owned *de facto* colonies. From the beginning of the nineteenth century until the 1930s, the 'big stick' policy – armed interventions and occupation of sovereign states – enabled Washington to prepare the ground for the dictators who would later, to the great woe of their peoples, behave as perfect auxiliaries" (Maurice Lemoine, "Du 'destin manifeste' des États-Unis," *Le Monde Diplomatique* [May 2003] 20).

26 "The Iraq War was fought secondly with the aim of establishing long-term American military bases in a key country in the heart of the Middle East ... America saw these as replacements for the increasingly contested bases established in Saudi Arabia in the wake of the 1991 Gulf War. It was a war fought thirdly to destroy one of the last of the third world dictatorships that had at times defied the United States and its allies (notably Israel). ... It was a war fought finally to reshape, along the radical free-market lines so dear to Bush administration ideologues, the economy of a country with the world's second-largest proven reserves of oil." (Khalidi, *Resurrecting Empire*, x–xi).

27 See Comité Tchétchénie, *Tchétchénie: dix clés pour comprendre* (Chechnya: Ten Keys for Understanding) (Paris: La Découverte, www.editionsladecouverte.fr).

28 Since December 2001 Ayman al-Zawahiri has argued his strategy in a tract whose essential tenets have been reported, in eight issues (nos. 8405 to 8411), by the London Arabic-language daily *Al-Sharq al-Awsat*, under the title "Knights under the Prophet's Banner."

Mohammed Ayoob*

DECIPHERING ISLAM'S MULTIPLE VOICES

Intellectual luxury or strategic necessity?

THE QUESTION "Who Speaks for Islam?" has become of fundamental importance to the West in light of the terrorist attacks of 9/11 as well as the subsequent violence in parts of the Muslim world, most notably in Iraq, ostensibly undertaken in the name of Islam. This sequence of events has left the distinct impression in many quarters that such attacks presage a clash of civilizations between "Islam" and the "West." The clash of civilizations thesis in its latest incarnation, inspired by Princeton historian Bernard Lewis[1] and most vividly presented by Harvard political scientist Samuel Huntington,[2] in fact predates the events of 9/11. However, the terrorist attacks on New York and Washington and subsequent events have given the thesis much greater credibility among the Western public than had been the case earlier. Predicated upon an essentialist interpretation of Islam, the thesis has created a monolithic impression of Islam and Muslims that conceals the enormous diversity not only among Muslim opinion, in general, but even among those groups characterized as fundamentalists or Islamists.[3] In fact, as Michael Doran has argued, the United States has in part become the target of ire on the part of certain Islamists because it has interposed itself in what is in substantial measure an intra-Islamic battle over political ideas and strategies for political action.[4]

The major impact of this essentialist and monolithic interpretation of Islam on Western perceptions is not merely to paint all Muslims with the same black brush but also to accord the most extremist and violent elements in the Muslim world the position of authentic spokespersons for Islam. The latter assessment is based on the mere fact that these elements are able to quote selectively from the Quran and the traditions of the Prophet, and stretch the meanings of such quotes through very creative interpretations, to justify killing civilians.[5] Nothing could be farther from the truth. Just as there is no Islamic monolith, currently there is no single individual, group or institution that can rightfully claim to speak for Muslims, let alone on behalf of Islam. As Robert Hefner has pointed out, today "most Muslim societies are marked by deep disagreements over just who is qualified to speak as a religious authority and over just how seriously ordinary Muslims should take the pronouncements of individual scholars."[6]

However, this is not a new quandary for most Muslims. The question "Who Speaks for Islam?" has historically been difficult to answer. Islam has neither a pope nor a clearly delineated religious hierarchy. While a loose hierarchical tradition does exist among the Shia clergy, even in Shia Islam, which is the minority branch, there is currently no single individual or organization that can authoritatively decide theological issues. An attempt was made in the middle of the nineteenth century in Iran to establish a single source of religious authority in Shia Islam with the title *marja-i-taqlid*, meaning the source of imitation.[7] However, this system broke previously down after the death of Ayatollah Burujerdi in 1961. Since then several leading religious figures have enjoyed the prerogative to issue edicts or rulings that become binding but only on their respective followers, that is on those who have chosen these particular figures as sources of emulation.[8]

These rulings are not considered binding on the followers of other religious figures of equal status. It was, therefore, no surprise that Ayatollah Khomeini's arrogation of the right to speak on behalf of all of Iranian Shia Islam was greatly resented by many leading ayatollahs, several of whom outranked him in the religious hierarchy before the Iranian Revolution. These divisions of opinion have been very important in the political realm dividing those endorsing politically quietist interpretations of Islamic injunctions from those advocating politically activist interpretations of religious doctrines and the various shades of opinion in between. While Ayatollah Burujerdi advocated a quietist line, Ayatollah Khomeini expounded an activist position. Ayatollah Sistani, currently the de facto *marja* of the Iraqi Shias, falls somewhere in between.[9]

The problem of locating religious authority becomes much more acute in the majority Sunni tradition where multiple religious voices have historically been the rule rather than the exception. Traditionally, numerous senior *ulama*, the learned in the law, have exercised the right to issue religious rulings based on meticulous research of the sources of Islamic law, including the context in which particular revelations occurred, and of accumulated precedents. It is not uncommon to find edicts issued by different *fuquha* (jurists, from the singular *faqih*) to be at variance with each other, depending upon the different weight they have accorded to sources from which they have sought guidance and on the different contexts within which they have issued rulings.

The tradition legitimizing multiple sources of religious authority was institutionalized in the ninth century CE with the consolidation of five major schools of Islamic jurisprudence, four among the predominant Sunnis and one among the Shia. Followers of the major schools were expected to accord equal status and respect to each one of them and consider the decisions of their representative ulama as binding upon the followers of each respective school. This policy of live and let live produced several benefits over the centuries. It helped preclude the establishment of a single orthodoxy that in alliance with the state could suppress all dissenting tendencies and oppress their followers as happened in Christian Europe during the medieval and early modern periods. Wars of religion and persecution of "heretical" sects were, therefore, infrequent in the classical age of Islam again in contrast with Christendom.

The dispersal of religious authority in Islam also prevented a direct clash between temporal and religious authority, as happened in medieval Christendom, while simultaneously preventing the total control of the religious establishment by temporal rulers. A combination of these factors promoted the creation of distinct religious and political spheres that respected each other's autonomy. As long as the rulers did not unduly interfere in matters of religious belief, the ulama adopted a largely politically quietist stand. Furthermore, they normally exhorted their followers to accept established authority lest dissension lead to *fitna* (anarchy) and the fragmentation of the *umma*, the community of believers. "Rather than a divine right of rule, Islam came to recognize a divinely sanctioned need for rule."[10]

However, despite this decentralization of religious authority, there was a general consensus during the pre-modern era on the answer to the question, "Who Speaks for Islam?" It was commonly recognized that those learned in the religious sciences and Islamic jurisprudence, and recognized as such by their peers, had the right to speak for and about Islamic doctrines regarding both moral and societal issues. This consensus was ruptured in the nineteenth century by the intrusion of modernity through its various agents – European colonialism, the print revolution, and mass literacy the chief among them. The cacophony we hear in the Muslim world today is the culmination of the process that started with the breakdown of this Islamic consensus in the nineteenth century regarding the role of the ulama as the sole legitimate interpreters of religion.

European colonial domination reopened the whole question of the nature of authority in Islam by decimating the then existing political structures and by undercutting the legitimacy of the religious authorities. Both parties to the original contract between the temporal and the religious – the Muslim potentates who presided over a minimalist state and the largely politically quietist ulama – were discredited. Many lay thinkers in the Muslim world held the religious establishment as responsible as the temporal rulers for Muslim political decline because of their perceived collaboration with, or at least tolerance of, decadent regimes. They also considered the ulama as practicing a fossilized form of Islam that had neither answers to contemporary problems nor a vision of the future. This last conclusion is not completely true since many ulama demonstrated considerable intellectual agility and doctrinal flexibility in an effort to respond to new issues and problems as they arose during the past two centuries. Some creatively reinterpreted earlier rulings made by jurists to fit modern circumstances, while others attempted to think through contemporary problems *de novo*.[11] Nonetheless, the image has persisted because the majority of the ulama, not trained in the modern sciences, have continued to speak a language that appears largely pre-modern especially to the more advanced sections of Muslim societies. It is no coincidence that it is these modern strata that have been responsible for producing many lay Islamist thinkers.

The undermining of the ulama's status as interpreters of true religion was accelerated by the print revolution and the increase in literacy in Muslim countries beginning in the mid-nineteenth century. Consequently, the Muslim world found itself in a situation analogous to that of Western Christendom in the fifteenth and sixteenth centuries when the printed word became accessible to lay individuals and paved the way for the Reformation in Europe. Two ingredients that were integral to the Reformation – scriptural literalism and the 'priesthood of the individual' – also appeared in the Muslim world and with pretty much the same consequences. Just as Christian fundamentalism, which rejected the accumulated wisdom of religious tradition, was a product of the Reformation, its Islamic counterpart was born out of the proto-Reformation that swept the Muslim world once lay Muslims gained direct access to the fundamental texts of Islam.[12] Religiously inclined individuals, often educated in non-religious schools and engaged in secular professions, began exercising their right of individual interpretation of the Muslim scriptures in near total disregard of precedents and interpretations accumulated over centuries by those trained in religion and jurisprudence.

Today's Islamists are direct descendants of the nineteenth and early twentieth century *salafi* thinkers (the term *salaf* is a shortened form of *salaf al-salih*, which means the "righteous ancestors," and salafis are those who make the first generation of Muslims their primary source of emulation). They advocated a return to the golden age of Islam that they imagined on the basis of their reading of the fundamental texts. To be fair to the original salafis, leading figures among them, such as Muhammad Abduh of Egypt, advocated the return to a pristine faith because they believed it to be in total accord with scientific positivism and rationality that underpinned modernity.[13]

However, this modernist interpretation was overshadowed by those among the salafis who interpreted the return to the golden age in literal terms and advocated the creation of an authentic Islamic polity based on their imagined model of the Islamic society at the time of the Prophet and his immediate successors in seventh-century Arabia. Contemporary Islamists are heirs to this revivalist tendency although many of them have made significant concessions to the contemporary contexts in which they find themselves. As Daniel Brown points out, "While they staunchly defend the theoretical authority of the sunna, the revivalists' commitment to the reintroduction of Islamic law in *relevant* forms makes them pragmatists in practice."[14] These salafi/ Islamist thinkers, many of whom were not trained in the traditional seminaries that impart religious and legal knowledge, became the primary challengers in the scholarly realm to the ulama's authority to speak for Islam. Consequently, they contributed significantly to the crisis of religious authority in the Muslim world that was set off by the twin processes of literacy and the print revolution.

The ulama's authority was further undermined by the emergence of nation-states in the Muslim world during the twentieth century. The establishment of sovereign states within boundaries defined by the European imperial powers effectively put paid to the notion of the universal umma, the worldwide community of believers, as a politically relevant category. While the Muslim world had been de facto divided among several empires, kingdoms, and principalities beginning with the breakaway of Umayyad Spain from the Abbasid Caliphate in the second half of the eighth century CE, the ideal of the political unity of the umma had been maintained at least amongst the Sunnis, among other things by the continuation of the institution of the Caliphate. This institution was brought to an end with the defeat of the Ottoman Empire in World War I and the subsequent proclamation of the Republic of Turkey in 1923.

Nation-states that became the rule in the Muslim world in the twentieth century were conceptually very different from the pre-modern kingdoms and principalities into which the Muslim world had been divided. The ideal of nationalism posed a fundamental doctrinal as well as practical challenge to the concept of the umma. It did so by demanding that the nation-state, created in the image of European states and recognizing no superior, become the exclusive repository of its citizens' allegiance. A return to the ideal of a united umma, even as a hypothetical scenario, was no longer a feasible proposition.

The victory of the nationalist doctrine is demonstrated by the fact that the restoration of the Caliphate, even as a symbolic institution, is supported only by a very tiny minority among Muslims and by fringe organizations, such as the London-based Hizb-ut-Tahrir. Most Muslims, including most Islamists, have internalized the values of the sovereign state system and are perfectly at ease working within the parameters of the nation-state. The division of the umma into multiple sovereignties is now taken as given.

The partition of the Muslim world into sovereign nation-states led to two major outcomes. First, despite the spread of communication in the twentieth century, the ulama's reach and authority became restricted within specific national boundaries. For example, edicts issued by the Egyptian ulama were considered binding only within Egypt just as the edicts issued by the Pakistani ulama could be applied only in Pakistan. For all practical purposes, the religious authority of the learned in the law was nationalized. Moreover, as the modern state began to penetrate society in a way that the pre-modern Muslim empires had never done, it expanded its control of the religious establishment. This was accomplished above all by nationalizing the control of the religious endowments, the *awqaf* (plural of *waqf*), on which religious seminaries, mosques, and large numbers of the ulama subsisted. This drastically reduced the financial, and therefore the intellectual and political, autonomy of the religious classes many of whom became salaried functionaries of the state often ruled by unrepresentative and authoritarian regimes. This was particularly true of the Sunni countries, although the shah attempted a similar strategy in Iran as a part of his "White Revolution." Unfortunately for him, the strategy boomeranged and was responsible in substantial part for the growing hostility of the Shia clergy towards the Pahlavi dynasty.

Second, since Islam continued to be part of the regimes' legitimacy formula in most Muslim countries, leaders of Muslim states often portrayed their national and regime goals as Islamic ones. They used the subservient ulama to bolster their image as Islam's spokespersons, thus adding to the cacophony of ostensibly religious voices in the Muslim world. This was and is particularly true of self-proclaimed Islamic states, such as Saudi Arabia, Iran and Pakistan, as well as Egypt, the seat of the most prestigious Islamic institution, Al-Azhar. However, it is clear to discerning observers that much of their "Islamic" rhetoric was little more than subterfuge that they utilized to enhance their regime or national interests. This has been as much the case with "revolutionary" Islamic regimes, such as Iran, as with "conservative" ones, such as Saudi Arabia. In the process, however, the rhetoric of these regimes further confused Western audiences as to who really speaks for Islam.

The derogation in the authority of the ulama consequent upon their subservience to unrepresentative regimes, as well as the division of the Muslim world into fifty-odd nation-states, provided the opportunity and the space for Islamist groups of various hues to become important players in the political game. These groups, such as the Jamaat-i-Islami in Pakistan and the Muslim Brotherhood in Egypt, while they emerged out of the earlier salafi movements, were much more modern in their organization and much more in tune with their political environments. Although committed in theory to transforming their polities into Islamic states through the Islamization of society and the eventual enforcement of sharia law, they were adept at making compromises and working within the national frameworks and the constitutional constraints imposed upon them.[15] While paying rhetorical obeisance to the concept of the universal umma, these political formations did not challenge the existence of the nation-states within which they operated. In essence, they became exponents of what Olivier Roy has called "Islamo-nationalism."[16] Their basic objectives were and are to improve the quality of governance in existing states by making it conform to Islamic law and to change the moral condition of their societies by making them correspond to Islamic norms. These are national, not universal, goals.

These Islamist political formations have succeeded in carving out substantial constituencies within important Muslim states, allowing them to stake a claim to speak for Islam and Muslims within their national boundaries. They have been able to do so primarily because of the nature of many Muslim regimes, especially in the Middle East. Authoritarian and repressive in character, these regimes have been successful in stifling political debate and ruthlessly suppressing political dissent. Their effective decimation of nearly all secular opposition has created a vast political vacuum in their countries that Islamist formations have moved in to fill. The Islamists have been successful in doing so because of the vocabulary they use and the institutions they employ to advance their political objectives. It is very difficult for even the most repressive regimes to outlaw or successfully counter the use of religious idiom for the expression of political dissent. Similarly, it is almost impossible for regimes fully to control religious institutions and charitable networks linked to such institutions. These institutions provide the Islamist groups with the organizational base through which they are able to mobilize support.

Consequently, Islamist formations have in many cases been able to present themselves as the primary, and in some cases the sole, avenue of opposition to unrepresentative regimes. By suffering for their defiance of dictatorial regimes, they are also able to portray themselves as champions of human rights within their societies. This strategy has bought them a great deal of goodwill from those whom one cannot consider to be Islamists either in religious or political terms. This is why, even while Islamist groups have in many cases become targets of state suppression, they have simultaneously emerged in several instances as the only credible alternative to repressive regimes. As a result, many analysts have concluded that, if and when authoritarian and semi-authoritarian regimes in Muslim countries, especially in the Middle East, collapse, they are likely to be replaced by Islamist groups and parties through democratic elections. The recent electoral endorsement of the religiously based Shia parties in Iraq testifies to the validity of this assertion. This has led some commentators, such as Reuel Gerecht, to deduce that Shiite clerics and Sunni Islamists are the most likely vehicles for the spread of democracy in the Arab world.[17]

The Sunni Islamist formations are largely distinct from, and often antagonistic toward, the traditional ulama. Several of their leading figures have in the past condemned the ulama for practicing and preaching an ossified form of Islam incapable of responding to contemporary challenges. For example, Sayyid Qutb, the chief ideologue of the Egyptian Muslim Brotherhood in the 1950s and 1960s, denounced "the very idea of 'men of religion, who take from religion a profession,' corrupting the Qur'anic message to suit their needs and attributing to God what He did not reveal."[18] There are, however, exceptions to this rule, such as the nexus between the radical ulama and the lay Islamists that has produced a form of neo-Wahhabism both in Saudi Arabia and in parts of Pakistan.[19]

The situation in Shia Iran is somewhat different. The fact that a group of ulama led by Ayatollah Khomeini became the primary vehicle for Islamism and the Islamic

Revolution in Iran is a function of the difference between the ways the Shia ulama are organized as compared to their Sunni counterparts. Their financial independence from the Iranian state in contrast to the Sunni ulama's dependence on state patronage provides a part of the explanation. This independence was achieved to a large extent through the payment of *khums*, one-fifth of a person's income, by the religious laity to their chosen *marja*, or source of emulation, among the senior clerics. Also, the robust Shia tradition of *ijtihad* (innovative interpretation to suit changing times and circumstances) allowed a politically activist faction of the Iranian clergy inspired by Khomeini to adapt its strategy to the circumstances in which it found itself in the 1960s and 1970s.

Iranian Shia Islam's doctrinal flexibility helped the ulama to project themselves as the leading force of opposition to the shah's oppressive regime. The same predilection for innovation provided Khomeini the space to advocate his theory of Islamic government as one to be guided by the supreme jurist, with the Shia ulama the ultimate repositories of both moral and political rectitude.[20] This did not mean that lay Islamist radicals were totally absent from the Iranian scene. The writings and speeches of lay activists, such as Ali Shariati, contributed substantially to the delegitimization of the shah's regime. Non-clerical forces, both secular and avowedly Muslim, contributed substantially to the success of the revolution. However, in the final analysis they could not compete with the ulama for the control of post-revolution Iran because of the latter's superior organization, much greater financial resources, and divisions among the non-clerical forces.[21]

The Shia ulama have demonstrated, above all, a much greater capacity to remain relevant to contemporary issues than have their Sunni counterparts. This does not mean that the Sunni ulama have remained completely fossilized in terms of their interpretation of Islamic doctrines. Indeed, as Muhammad Qasim Zaman has demonstrated, the Sunni ulama have played a significant role as agents of change in Muslim countries.[22] However, the pace of change among them has been considerably slower than among the Shia clerics. This has led to their political and social role being overshadowed by that of the college-educated "new religious intellectuals," the lay Islamists, drawn from the secular professions.[23]

It is worth reiterating that while in theory Islamist groups, both Sunni and Shia, advocate a return to pristine Islam, in practice they have become prisoners of their own context provided by the nation-state and the discrete problems facing diverse Muslim societies. They are as much products of modernity as they are reactions to it. In fact, it can be argued quite convincingly, "they represent a vision of renewed Islam which is not only authentic to the ideal Islamic past but also adapted to the modern situation of Muslims."[24] Their greatest strength lies in their ability to combine their image of the ideal past with a vision that is considered by a substantial number of Muslims as being relevant to the contemporary situation.

Their rhetoric, which promises to bring Islam back to life and thereby provide solutions to the ills of their societies, resonates with large segments of Muslim populations. This is because Islam as a solution has not been tried and because other models imported from the West, including secular nationalism, capitalism and socialism, have largely failed to deliver either wealth or power or dignity to Muslim peoples. Moreover, Islamist groups appear to be paragons of probity when compared to the corrupt regimes that they seek to displace. However, if they come to power, Islamist parties will have to demonstrate the validity of their slogan "Islam is the solution" by addressing the concrete economic and social problems of their societies. It is then that their prescription that Islam possesses the solution to all social, economic, and political problems will be tested.

What cannot be disputed is the fact that the overwhelming majority of Islamist formations are primarily engaged in promoting their domestic agendas through largely peaceful means. They have participated in many cases in political processes under severe constitutional restraints and with the political cards visibly stacked against them. There are, however, extremist offshoots of some of the Islamist movements, such as the Egyptian Islamic Jihad, that have taken to violence against their own regimes. Some have made the United States their primary target because, among other things, they have come to the conclusion that the road to Cairo or Riyadh lies through Washington. This change in strategy is partly a function of their failure to overthrow local regimes supported by the United States and partly of their belief that the United States is bent upon dominating the Muslim world, especially the Middle East, for reasons relating to oil and Israel.

However, despite their dramatic exploits of the past few years, 9/11 above all, these groups, lacking national bases and loosely connected in an international "network of networks," are fringe elements among the Islamists themselves. Their resort to indiscriminate violence, first domestically as in Egypt in the 1990s and then globally, signifies that they have given up on attaining political power within Muslim societies and shifted to dramatic acts of international terror in order to capture the imagination of the disgruntled Muslim youth. Since sensational acts speak louder than words, they have captured Western imaginations as well and thus have been able to portray themselves as Islam's spokespersons especially to the Western world. Consequently, political Islam and terror have become synonymous in much of the discourse in the Western media and even in parts of academia.

In fact, these radical networks that espouse terror constitute a very small fringe of the Islamist tendencies. Their actions have been repudiated not only by the vast majority of the ulama and the governments in the Muslim world, but by mainstream Islamist movements as well. They add to the cacophony in the Muslim world and make it appear threatening to Western eyes, but they are not its true representatives. Moreover, as Wiktorowicz has argued, their "increasingly expansive violence ... may erode popular support for Al Qaeda, as increased violence did to the GIA in Algeria, but in the meantime more groups of people will likely find themselves on the jihadi list of legitimate targets ... attacks may become increasingly deadly as well."[25] The deadliness of their attacks, however, does not make them Islam's foremost spokespersons. In fact, it discredits them within the Muslim world itself, as does the absence of a realistic political agenda that informs their activities.

This article has attempted to do several things. First, it has tried to give a historical account of why religious authority has traditionally been dispersed and decentralized in the Muslim world. Second, it has attempted to analyze why the traditional religious authority of the ulama, the religious scholars, even if decentralized, has been gravely challenged during the past 200 years by the onset of colonialism, the print revolution, and mass literacy. Third, it has argued that the adoption of the nation-state model has fundamentally altered the nature of the debate in the Muslim world about religious authority by nationalizing religious establishments and putting them directly under the control of the state. Fourth, it has tried to analyze movements and groups, especially those which we call Islamist that emerged in the twentieth century as a result of what can be termed the proto-Reformation in Islam. These groups have projected themselves as spokespersons for Islam and Muslims often in opposition to the ulama, but sometimes in concert with sections of the ulama themselves. The article has argued that their current popularity is largely a function of the nature of regimes in the Muslim world and the failure of imported models of governance and development because of their gross distortion by unrepresentative ruling elites.

Fifth, the article has contended that the transnational networks of violence and terrorism, such as al-Qaeda, although ideologically offshoots of Islamist groups, are extreme fringe elements without societal base. Their popularity has been exaggerated because of the electronic revolution that has given them high visibility through audio- and video-cassettes and websites on the Internet. They may have the capacity to undertake dramatic acts of violence but are for the most part irrelevant to the political struggles, including those for democracy and social justice that are taking place on the ground in Muslim countries.

What is worth noting in this context is that the precursors of groups like al-Qaeda that were recruited from across the Muslim world and operated in Afghanistan in the 1980s were financed and armed in large measure by the United States to fight the Soviet presence in that country. Without the American-supported proxy war in Afghanistan, the various components of the al-Qaeda leadership and rank and file would not have come into contact with each other and been able to construct the global network that sustains them today. Nor would they have learned the tools of their trade, which they have turned against the United States with such lethal effect. Above all, without the experience of the American-supported Afghan war, the idea of a global *jihad* undertaken by a motley group of transnational fighters would have never captured the imagination of even the miniscule minority now engaged in this venture.[26]

Finally, and fundamentally, this article has tried to argue that there is no individual or group or tendency that can speak authoritatively for Islam and Muslims. The Muslim world is too diverse and too divided, along national, jurisprudential, and ideological lines, for a single set of spokes-persons to be acceptable to all major components of the worldwide umma, the community of believers. Despite the attempt by the most extreme elements to usurp the right to speak for Islam, what we have today is a cacophony of different, often competing, views and opinions in the Muslim world rather than the deliberate orchestration of a single dominant voice. The Islamist voices among these are divided primarily along national lines with Islamist political formations principally preoccupied with issues that matter within the territorial confines of the states in which they operate.

It is important for Western strategic analysts and policy makers to be aware of the fact that there are multiple and competing groups aspiring to speak for Islam, and that the vast majority of them are confined within discrete national boundaries. Responding to them successfully will require three major adjustments in Western thinking. One, Western policy makers and analysts must discard the notion of political Islam as a monolith and must begin to appreciate the multiple manifestations of political Islam. Two, at the same time, they must shed their obsession with the most extreme and violent transnational groups. These may be a nuisance and may even pose serious physical threats in the short term, but they do not have a serious constituency in the Muslim world and do not play a major part in formulating Muslim political perceptions, including those of the West. Crafting policy toward the Muslim world primarily in light of the terrorist challenge posed by these groups would be playing into their hands and alienating the vast majority of Muslims who would normally prefer to have no truck with terrorist groups. It could very well end up by turning the "clash of civilizations" thesis into a self-fulfilling prophecy.

Three, Western policy makers and analysts must develop empathy for the concrete grievances of Muslim populations. Graham Fuller has put this very succinctly: "The real issue is not what Islam is, but what Muslims want."[27] Festering, unaddressed grievances generate support for Islamist groupings that are increasingly perceived in the Muslim world as the foremost articulators of their people's political aspirations. These grievances range from issues of national self-determination, as in the case of Palestine, to freedom from oppressive regimes, as in the case of Egypt. Addressing such grievances sympathetically and spending political capital to redress them will significantly reduce hostility in the Muslim world toward the West, in general, and the United States, in particular. It will also help remove much of the anti-Western edge from Islamist political rhetoric itself. Deciphering Islam's multiple voices and discriminating among them is no longer an intellectual luxury for policy makers and analysts in the West. It has become a strategic necessity.

Notes

*   This article was inspired by my participation in a workshop in Amman in December 2004 on "Who speaks for Islam? Who Speaks for the West?" It was jointly organized by Dialogues: Islamic World-US-the West, a program earlier based at New School University and currently housed at New York University, and Majlis El Hassan, the non-governmental organization run by HRH Prince El Hassan bin Talal. I would like to thank Mustapha Tlili, Director of Dialogues, for stimulating my interest in this very important subject.

1   See, for example, his "Roots of Muslim Rage," *Atlantic Monthly*, September 1990, pp. 47–60.

2   Most famously, his book *The Clash of Civilizations and the Remaking of World Order* (Simon and Schuster, New York, 1996).

3   For a succinct analysis of different types of Islamists, see International Crisis Group, *Understanding Islamism*, Middle East/North Africa Report No. 37, March 2, 2005, available on the Internet at http://www.crisisgroup.org/library/documents/middle_east_north_africa/egypt_north_africa/37_understanding_islamism.pdf.

4   Michael Scott Doran, "Somebody Else's Civil War," *Foreign Affairs*, Vol. 81, No. 1, January/February 2002, pp. 22–42.

5   For an insightful discussion of their arguments justifying the killing of civilians, see Quintan Wiktorowicz, "A Genealogy of Radical Islam," *Studies in Conflict and Terrorism*, Vol. 28, No. 2, March–April 2005, especially pp. 86–92.

6   Robert W. Hefner, "Introduction: Modernity and the Remaking of Muslim Politics," in Robert W. Hefner, ed., *Remaking Muslim Politics: Pluralism, Contestation, Democratization* (Princeton University Press, Princeton, NJ, 2005), p. 6.

7   Hamid Enayat, *Modern Islamic Political Thought* (University of Texas Press, Austin, TX, 1982) p. 162.

8   Nikki Keddie, *Modern Iran: Roots and Results of Revolution* (Yale University Press, New Haven, 2003) p. 146.

9   According to one report, "While Sistani's thought is far from the radical Shiite lead-ers who led the Iranian revolution, it isn't accurate to say it's apolitical. While he himself leaves politics to politicians, Sistani's understanding of religious law leaves very little of the world beyond the scrutiny of religious leaders." Philip Kennicott, "The Religious Face of Iraq," *The Washington Post*, February 18, 2005.

10   L. Carl Brown, *Religion and State: The Muslim Approach to Politics* (Columbia University Press, New York, 2000), p. 54.

11   For a convincing argument that this has been the case, see Muhammad Qasim Zaman, "Pluralism, Democracy, and the 'Ulama,'" in Robert W. Hefner, ed., *Remaking Muslim Politics: Pluralism, Contestation, Democratization* (Princeton University Press, Princeton, NJ, 2000, 2005), pp. 60–86.

12   For details of this argument, see Carl W. Ernst, *Following Muhammad: Rethinking Islam in the Contemporary World* (Chapel Hill, NC, University of North Carolina Press, 2003), pp. 66–67, and Richard W. Bulliet, "The Crisis Within Islam," *Wilson Quarterly*, Winter 2002, pp. 11–19.

13   L. Carl Brown, *Religion and State: The Muslim Approach to Politics* (Columbia University Press, New York, 2000), pp. 93–98.

14   Daniel Brown, *Rethinking Tradition in Modern Islamic Thought* (Cambridge University Press, New York, 1999), p. 112. Italics in the original.

15   See, Carrie Rosefsky Wickham, *Mobilizing Islam: Religion, Activism, and Political Change in Egypt* (Columbia University Press, New York, 2002) on Egypt, and Seyyed Vali Reza Nasr, *The Vanguard of the Islamic Revolution: The Jama'at-I-Islami of Pakistan* (University of California Press, Berkeley, 1994), on Pakistan.

16   Olivier Roy, *The Failure of Political Islam* (Harvard University Press, Cambridge, MA, 1996), p. 26.

17   Reuel Marc Gerecht, *The Islamic Paradox: Shiite Clerics, Sunni Fundamentalists, and the Coming of Arab Democracy* (AEI Press, Washington, DC, 2004).

18   Charles Tripp, "Sayyid Qutb: The Political Vision," in Ali Rahnema, ed., *Pioneers of Islamic Revival* (Zed Books, London, 1994), p. 178.

19   For Saudi Arabia, see Gilles Kepel, *The War for Muslim Minds: Islam and the West* (Belknap, Cambridge, MA, 2004), ch. 5; for Pakistan, see Vali Nasr, "Military Rule, Islamism, and Democracy in Pakistan," *Middle East Journal*, Vol. 58, No. 2, Spring 2004, p. 205.

20   See Daniel Brumberg, *Reinventing Khomeini: The Struggle for Reform in Iran* (University of Chicago Press, Chicago, 2001), for Khomeini's innovative ideas about the structure of Islamic government.

21   Nikki Keddie, *Modern Iran: Roots and Results of Revolution* (Yale University Press, New Haven, CT, 2003), chs. 9 and 10.

22   See, Muhammad Qasim Zaman, *The Ulama in Contemporary Islam: Custodians of Change* (Princeton University Press, Princeton, NJ, 2002).

23   The term "new religious intellectuals" is borrowed from Dale F. Eickelman and James Piscatori, *Muslim Politics* (Princeton University Press, Princeton, NJ, 1996), p. 44.

24   Daniel Brown, *Rethinking Tradition in Modern Islamic Thought* (Cambridge University Press, New York, 1999), p. 141.

25   Quintan Wiktorowicz, "A Genealogy of Radical Islam," *Studies in Conflict and Terrorism*, Vol. 28, No. 2, March–April 2005, especially p. 94.

26   For further details, see Mahmood Mamdani, *Good Muslim, Bad Muslim* (Pantheon, New York, 2004).

27   Graham Fuller, "The Future of Political Islam," *Foreign Affairs*, Vol. 81, No. 2, March/April 2002, p. 50.

Guilain Denoeux

THE FORGOTTEN SWAMP
Navigating political Islam

W**E NEED TO** "drain the swamp." This expression has recurred like a leit-motif in the comments of pundits and policy officials asked to justify Washington's ever-expanding war on terrorism. But, alas, one critically important mud flat has received scant attention in the intense media coverage that has accompanied the war in Afghanistan and its extension to new settings: the swamp of analytical confusion surrounding the use of words such as "Islamic fundamentalists" or "Islamic radicals." Terms have been thrown around lightly, often without a real understanding of their connotations and limitations. There has been little appreciation for the fact that they are artificial constructs, usually elaborated by outsiders, and that they some-times may confuse more than they explain. For instance, do "Islamic fundamentalists" differ from "Islamic radicals," or can the two terms be employed interchangeably? Are "Muslim fundamentalists" merely the expression, within the Islamic world, of a broader "fundamentalist" trend visible in other great religious traditions? Why do so many scholars prefer the term "Islamism" to "fundamentalism"? In what context did the transnational radical Islam of Osama bin Laden develop, and how does it relate to earlier variants of radical Islam? Has the nature of Islamism itself changed significantly over the past 30 years? And where does the Taliban movement fit in the broader spec-trum of Islamist phenomena?

Answering such basic questions would seem to be a prerequisite to any substan-tive discussion of Islam's changing role and manifestations in Middle East politics. The task should be relatively easy considering that, since the 1970s, a substantial body of both academic and policy-oriented literature has developed on political Islam. By and large, however, the public debate thus far has tapped into only a fraction of that exper-tise. Yet, at this critical juncture – when more than ever we need to pause, reflect on and debate what our long-term strategy toward political Islam should be – it is imperative that the concepts used in that discussion be fully understood in their complexity and ramifications.

The central objective of this paper is to contribute to such a goal. Drawing on the existing literature, it aims to provide, in one place, a succinct presentation of key concepts and issues required to analyze political Islam, particularly in its more radical manifestations. It is hoped that such an endeavor will benefit as broad an audience as possible, answering the question still on the lips of many, "Who are those people and what do they want?"

"Muslim" or "Islamic"?

The two terms are often used interchangeably. For instance, one may refer to "Islamic civilization" or to "Muslim civilization." Yet of course a "Muslim scholar" (a scholar who is also a Muslim) is not the same as an "Islamic scholar" (a scholar, Muslim or not, who specializes in the study of Islam). But there are also more subtle differences in the usage of these two words as adjectives. For instance, one of the leading students of political Islam observes that he uses "Muslim" to refer to a fact, a cultural reality, while by "Islamic" he means to convey political intent.[1] According to that distinction, for instance, a "Muslim country" is merely "a country in which the majority of the population is Muslim." By contrast, an "Islamic state" designates "a state that bases its legitimacy on Islam" – a state in which Islam presumably plays a central role in public life and in legitimizing the existing sociopolitical order, and in which the government is committed to upholding values and modes of behavior that it deems to be in conformity with Islam. Similarly, a "Muslim intellectual" is "an intellectual of Muslim origin and culture," while the expression "Islamic intellectual" may be used to describe "an intellectual who consciously organizes his thought within the conceptual framework of Islam."[2]

According to those standards, Iran and Saudi Arabia are both "Islamic states" (though very different ones at that!), while Egypt is a Muslim country, but not an Islamic state. For the same reasons, a journalist in Beirut may think of herself as a Muslim professional (for reasons of birth and because she thinks Islam is an important component of her identity) but she may refute the label of "Islamic writer" (because her writing is not driven by Islamic referents).

Islamic fundamentalism

As a way of referring to the variety of movements and ideas that have become increasingly central to the public life and political scene of many countries in the Muslim world over the past 30 years, the expression "Islamic fundamentalism" is both useful and problematic. It is useful in that it draws attention to the fact that, like other forms of fundamentalism, what these movements and ideas have in common is a call for restoring the original purity and integrity of the faith through a literal reading of the founding religious texts. (In the case of Islam, these texts consist of the Quran, Islam's holy book, and the Sunna or *hadith*, which is the reported collection of the words and deeds of Prophet Muhammad.) The expression "Islamic fundamentalism" also implies that many Muslims' advocacy of a return to the foundations of their faith is merely the Islamic variant of a broader "fundamentalist" trend found in all the major religious traditions. Seen in this light, the demands of Islamic fundamentalists echo similar ones emanating from many Christians, Hindus, Sikhs and Jews. Thus the expression has the merit of inviting a comparative approach to that phenomenon, the understanding of which presumably has much to gain from what has been learned about fundamentalist movements and ideologies in other cultures. Certainly, like other manifestations of fundamentalism around the globe, Islamic fundamentalism can be seen as a reactive movement, driven by individuals who have come to feel that their faith faces a deadly threat to its survival, and that it can only be saved through a return to its original principles and values. Two prominent students of religious fundamentalism have noted that the concept applies to "beleaguered believers" who, when confronted with "the encroachment of outsiders who threaten to draw [them] into a syncretistic, are-ligious, or irreligious cultural milieu," go back to their faith's basic doctrines and practices in an effort to "preserve their distinctive identity as a people or group."[3]

Still, some analysts believe that the expression "Islamic fundamentalism" is inad-equate, since the word "fundamentalism" originated in a cultural context – American protestantism at the beginning of the twentieth century – very removed from Islam. Thus, the reasoning goes, the term comes with certain connotations that may be deeply misleading when applied to Islam. For instance, what was supposed to set Protestant fundamentalists apart from other Protestants was their conviction that the Bible was the true word of God and that it should be understood literally.[4] All believing Muslims, however, are expected to regard the Quran as the literal, infallible Word of God; such a tenet lies at the very core of Islam. In that respect, therefore, all Muslims are "fundamentalists": they hold their holy book to be a verbatim record of God's rev-elations to Prophet Muhammad. And yet most Muslims are hardly "fundamentalists" in the sense of believing that their behavior should be guided exclusively by religious scriptures. Nor do they assume that these scriptures should be understood literally or that they are open to only one interpretation. In these and other respects, the concept of "fundamentalism," when applied to Islam, confuses more than it explains.

To argue that Islamic fundamentalists are Muslims who want to go back to "the fundamentals" of their faith is also deceptive in two respects. First, the vast majority of Muslims agree on the fundamental tenets of their faith (such as the belief in the unity and oneness of God, the sacred nature of the Quran, Muhammad's role as God's messenger and as a source of emulation, etc.). Second, many of those usually referred to as "Islamic fundamentalists" do not, in fact, go back to the "fundamentals" of Islam. Instead, they selectively emphasize some of those presumed fundamentals while downplaying or ignoring others. Furthermore, within their alleged "fundamentalist thought," those elements that are selected from the sacred tradition are very often merged with ideas and practices that have no clear link with the Islamic past.

Problematic as well is the fact that fundamentalism suggests a monolithic move-ment, whereas one should really speak of "fundamentalisms" since fundamentalist thought is diverse and its modes of expression extremely varied – perhaps nowhere more so than in the Middle East and North Africa. Most important, to the extent that Islamic fundamentalists do not necessarily claim to have a political project and do not necessarily enter the political arena, the word "fundamentalism" is not well-suited to analyzing those movements that use Islamic referents to wage political battles. To describe this phenomenon, and to refer to hybrid ideologies that mix concepts bor-rowed from the Islamic tradition and ideas that are more distinctly modern, scholars have come to use instead the expressions "Islamism" or "political Islam" (see below).

There is, finally, another ground on which to question the notion that Islamic activism shares structural similarities or "family resemblances" with, for instance, Christian and Jewish fundamentalisms, and, therefore, that it can best be explained through the framework of "comparative fundamentalisms."[5] Such an argument fails to take into account the critical differences in the political contexts within which these trends have emerged. For one, most Christian and Jewish fundamentalist ideologies and movements have developed within democratic political environments, whereas one shared feature of the political settings that have witnessed the rise of Islamist movements has been the lack of real prospects for a genuine, peaceful alternation of power. Furthermore, to establish parallels between Christian, Jewish and Muslim "fundamentalisms" conceals the imbalance in power and resources between those environments within which Jewish and Christian fundamentalisms have grown (the "Judeo-Christian" North) and those where Islamic activism has appeared. It also fails to reflect that a critical driving force of Islamic activism has been the questioning of this basic imbalance of power, whereas neither Christian nor Jewish fundamentalisms have challenged explicitly the foundations of the existing international political and economic order. For the same reason, those who have sought to account for the demise of the Oslo peace process by, among other things, highlighting the "joint" opposition to that process by Jewish and Muslim "fundamentalists," insisting that these movements have been "mirror images" of each other, may confuse more than eluci-date the situation on the ground. In particular, they fail to highlight that military occupation and the neocolonial exploitation of one side by the other have been key forces behind the rise of so-called "Muslim fundamentalism" in Palestine.[6]

Salafism (*al-Salafiyya*)

Within the Islamic context, the tradition that comes the closest to the western con-cept of "fundamentalism" is what is known as Salafism (*al-Salafiyya* in Arabic), a cur-rent of thought which emerged during the second half of the nineteenth century. The word comes from *al-Salaf*, which refers to the companions of the Prophet Muhammad, and is usually used as part of the expression *al-salaf al-salih*, i.e., the "virtuous forefa-thers." Salafism urged believers to return to the pristine, pure, unadulterated form of Islam practiced by Muhammad and his companions. It rejected any practice (such as Sufi rituals), belief (such as the belief in saints) or behavior (for example those anchored in customary law) not directly supported by the Quran or for which there was no precedent in Muhammad's acts and sayings. Salafi thinkers also refused the idea that Muslims should accept blindly the interpretations of religious texts devel-oped by theologians over the centuries. Instead, they insisted on the individual believ-er's right to interpret those texts for himself or herself through the practice of *ijtihad* (independent reasoning).[7]

Salafism did not develop as a monolithic movement but rather as a broad philoso-phy, a frame of mind. To this day, there is no single Salafi ideology or organization. Instead, since the late nineteenth century, Salafism has expressed itself in a multiplic-ity of movements and currents of thought that have reflected specific historical circumstances and local conditions. Most have been primarily intellectual-cultural undertakings that generally have eschewed the political arena. In the past two decades, however, one particular brand of Salafi ideology – the Saudi variant known as

Wahhabism – has known particular success, and it is to that specific expression of Salafi thought which we now turn.

Wahhabism

Wahhabism draws its name from an eighteenth-century religious reformer known as Muhammad Ibn Abd al-Wahhab (1703–91) who preached in central Arabia. Abd al-Wahhab was incensed by what he saw as the laxity and moral corruption of the society in which he lived. In his eyes, that society had turned its back on Islam, neglecting basic religious duties while tolerating practices and beliefs which he saw as unacceptable deviations from the basic tenets of the faith. Idolatry, superstitions, the cult of saints and even the veneration of trees and stones were indeed ascendant in Arabia at the time. Abd al-Wahhab was determined to fight such heresies, and castigated his contemporaries for having reverted to a state of unbelief and ignorance of God's commandments. Consequently, he stressed the need to return to the monotheism that Islam had once introduced in that desert society. But he also went further than that, and strove to eradicate from Islam anything that was not consistent with a strict, literal interpretation of the Quran and the Sunna. What eventually emerged was a particularly puritanical, bland, ultra-orthodox and forbidding interpretation of Islam, concerned, if not obsessed, with notions of moral corruption and the need for purity. To this day, Wahhabism remains characterized by its intolerance toward any perceived deviation from the dogmatic interpretation of Islam that it preaches.

Wahhabism would likely have remained a marginal doctrine within Islamic thought had it not been for the alliance that Abd al-Wahhab struck with the House of Saud in 1745. From then on, the political fortunes of the Saud family and the potential audience for Abd al-Wahhab's ideas were closely tied to each other. Ultimately, when Abd al-Aziz Ibn Saud succeeded in unifying the tribes of Arabia under his control and into what became the Kingdom of Saudi Arabia in 1932, Wahhabism became the country's state-sanctioned ideology and code of behavior.

For some 40 years after that, however, the audience and appeal of Wahhabism remained for the most part confined to Saudi Arabia. That situation began to change following the 1973 oil boom. Blessed with new riches, the Saudi regime engaged in a major effort to spread Wahhabi ideology overseas – partly out of conviction, and partly to counter the appeal of ideologies that it perceived as a threat to its national security. Saudi money was instrumental to the building and the operation of thousands of mosques, Islamic centers and madrasas (religious schools) from Lahore to London, and from Morocco to Malaysia. There, the Wahhabi message was presented to ever-expanding audiences. Following the Iranian revolution of 1979, the Saudi authorities also endeavored to promote Wahhabi ideas as a counterweight to the new Iranian regime's stated goal of exporting its Shiite revolution overseas. At the end of that same year, the Soviet invasion of Afghanistan provided new, unprecedented opportunities for Saudi Arabia to spread Wahhabi views, especially in Pakistan. The Taliban phenomenon, which owes so much to Saudi support, was born out of this process.

In the end, one is struck by the extent to which a unique configuration of geological circumstances and world events led to the unexpected, rapid expansion of a rather sectarian branch of Islam which historically had been on the fringes of Islamic civilization. The "accident" of oil wealth, the Soviet invasion of Afghanistan, and America's blessing for (or complacent attitude toward) the Saudi regime's militant promotion of Wahhabism all combined to give this minority quasi-sect within Islam a level of influence entirely out of proportion to what it could have achieved on its own.

"Islamism" or "political Islam"

Unlike "Salafism" and "fundamentalism," the label "Islamism" is relatively recent. It was coined during the 1970s to refer to the rise of movements and ideologies drawing on Islamic referents – terms, symbols and events taken from the Islamic tradition – in order to articulate a distinctly political agenda (hence the expression "political Islam," which is usually seen as synonymous with Islamism).

Typically, the Islamist project provides a comprehensive critique of the existing order, challenges it and aims to change it. It addresses the social, political, economic and cultural challenges faced by contemporary Muslim societies and claims to provide solutions to them. It makes a more or less sustained and persuasive effort to reflect on what an "Islamic economy" or "Islamic society" might look like. Islamism, in short, is a form of instrumentalization of Islam by individuals, groups and organizations that pursue political objectives. It provides political responses to today's societal challenges by imagining a future, the foundations for which rest on reappropriated, reinvented concepts borrowed from the Islamic tradition.

Islamism and modernity

A defining characteristic of Islamist movements, organizations and ideologies is their two-sided relation to modernity and the West. On the one hand, at the very heart of Islamist ideology lies a powerful, comprehensive critique of the West and of what Islamists see as the corrupting political and cultural influence of the West on Middle Eastern societies. The Islamists' reliance on concepts drawn from the Islamic tradition also indicates a desire to break away from Western terminology. On the other hand, Islamism is a decidedly modern phenomenon in at least two critical respects: the profile of its leaders and its reliance on Western technology.

As far as the first of these two features is concerned, the cadres and ideologues of Islamist movements have been, overwhelmingly, products of the modern, secular educational system. "Radical Islamists," for instance, are not usually clerics but young, university-educated intellectuals who claim for themselves the right to interpret the true meaning of religion (their actual knowledge of Islam is typically sketchy). Most of them are graduates in engineering and the modern sciences, not in the humanities or theology. Some have studied in Western Europe or North America. For instance, two leading Islamist thinkers, the Iranian Ali Shariati (whose writings had the greatest influence on the young generation that participated in the Islamic revolution) and the Sudanese Hassan al-Turabi, received their doctorates from the Sorbonne in Paris. In their twenties and thirties, the cadres of radical Islamist movements typically belong to a *"lumpen intelligentsia."* They are frustrated by the discrepancy between, on the one hand, their relatively high level of educational achievement, and, on the other, their low social status and dim prospects for upward mobility in countries characterized by poor economic performance and the disproportionate importance of social connections to professional success. And if the leadership of Islamist movements is a product of modernization, so are the foot soldiers, who often consist of recently urbanized masses, lower-class youth and the downwardly mobile middle classes. As for the cadres of more "moderate" or "mainstream" Islamist movements, they usually consist of professionals and businesspersons employed in the modern sector of the economy – indeed often in the most technologically advanced and outward-oriented segments of that sector. Overall, therefore, what is noteworthy is the extent to which Islamist movements have drawn their main activists from the "new middle class" that scholars in the 1960s had expected to be a major source of secularization and Westernization in Middle Eastern societies.

Striking as well is the Islamists' heavy reliance on Western technology (faxes, cassettes and, more recently, the internet and cellular phones) in order to achieve their goals. In many ways, Islamists have harnessed modern technology and Western inventions to fight, or hold at bay, Western influences and the cultural and social evils they see as associated with modernity. Thus, with their choice of tools to disseminate their ideas and organize, radical Islamists have shown themselves quite capable of keeping up with advances in information and communication technologies. Consequently, the sophistication of the devices on which they have drawn has been characterized by a staggering improvement over the past quarter-century. Back in 1978, much was made of the critical contribution that cassettes containing Khomeini's sermons made to the success of the Iranian revolution. Recorded in France, where the ayatollah had been granted political asylum, these tapes were subsequently distributed throughout Iran, copied and played and replayed in thousands of homes and mosques. Similarly, in the mid-1990s, the main group in the Islamist opposition to the Saudi regime, the Committee for the Defense of Legitimate Rights in Saudi Arabia (CDLR), used its headquarters in London to disseminate its virulent attacks on the Saudi royal family through faxes, tapes and the internet. From the mid-1990s onward, numerous Islamist groups began to develop their own websites. Most dramatically, in the wake of the September 11 attacks on the Twin Towers and the Pentagon, U.S. intelligence worried about the use of encryption technology by members of Al Qaeda. Through their mastery of encryption tools, the latter may have been able to hide messages within apparently innocuous e-mails, music files and pictures sent instantaneously from one continent to another. They also may have been able to embed such messages in the graphics or images found on certain websites. Such a development underscores the technological sophistication of the tools now used by some radical Islamists to communicate with each other undetected. What is clear is that they are not behind the times technologically.

Islamism versus fundamentalism or Salafism

Though Islamism and fundamentalism or Salafism share certain traits, they also differ in several important respects. What they have in common is an idealized view of early Islamic history, a desire to restore the original purity of the faith, and the call for a return to a strict interpretation of the Quran and the Sunna. However, they clearly part ways on the following issues:

- Politics lies at the heart of Islamism, which ultimately has far more to do with power than with religion. To Islamists, Islam is more a political blueprint than a faith, and the Islamist discourse is to a large extent a political discourse in religious garb. Thus, while fundamentalists are typically concerned primarily with ideas and religious exegesis, Islamists are action-oriented; they are preoccupied first and foremost with changing their world. They believe, in particular, that political action is essential to the transformation of society into a truly Islamic one. They aim to exercise political power, and they are extremely critical of governments which they accuse of having turned their back on Islam. By contrast, politics does not feature prominently in Salafi thought. Unlike Islamists, fundamentalists do not claim to have a global, comprehensive political program. More interested in theology than politics, Salafists usually refrain from challenging governments and are generally reluctant to become involved in the political fray. They shy away from raising the issue of the political and religious legitimacy (or illegitimacy) of the powers-that-be, whereas that issue is perhaps the most prominent one on the Islamists' minds.

- Even though they constantly invoke concepts drawn from the Islamic past, Islamists are social and political activists intent on building a new type of society. In that respect, they are forward-looking, whereas fundamentalists tend to be fixated on an earlier, idealized era. Islamists usually aspire to reshape people's daily lives according to a more or less clearly defined political and cultural vision that harks back to a mostly mythical, invented Islamic past. While that vision draws on Islamic terms, symbols and events, it infuses them with new meanings that are typically alien to the actual historical and current experiences of Muslims. Islamists are engaged in a process of intellectual, political and social engineering which, through the familiar language of Islam, aims to legitimize a thorough restructuring of society and polity along lines that have no precedent in history. Under the pretense of re-establishing an old order, what is intended is the making of a new one.

- Fundamentalists are primarily concerned with issues of morality and personal behavior, and/or with theological issues, while Islamists, through the capture of the state or the Islamization of society, aim to bring about a radical transformation of political, social and economic relations within modern society.

- Islamists and fundamentalists also differ in their attitudes toward the *sharia* (Islamic law) and women.[8] Fundamentalists would like to see a strict implementation of the sharia and argue that all laws should be based exclusively on it. To them, applying Islamic law should be a priority since it is the most reliable way of making society more truly Islamic. And whenever political and social conditions are not "ripe" for an immediate application of the sharia, fundamentalists believe that working toward a gradual, incremental Islamization of laws and mores should be the driving force of their action. Islamists, too, favor an Islamization of laws, but to them full implementation of the sharia makes sense only after a genuinely Islamic order has been created (through the capture of political power). In short, the line dividing fundamentalists and Islamists on this issue revolves around the most effective way of making individuals more (Islamically) "virtuous." Is it, as Islamists advocate, through an Islamic revolution that will create an environment in which implementation of the sharia becomes inevitable because society itself has become more genuinely Islamic? Or is it, as fundamentalists are prone to believe, by pressuring individuals into abiding by certain moral and behavioral codes based on the sharia, which in turn ultimately and naturally will lead to the establishment of an Islamic state? Unlike fundamentalists, Islamists fear that trying to impose Islamic law on a society that has not yet become truly Islamic may be doomed to fail, and may even create new problems. In their eyes, it is likely to lead to the spread of hypocrisy, fake individual and collective displays of piety, and glaring discrepancies between public and private behavior – between who individuals profess to be and who they really are.

Similarly, whereas fundamentalists typically oppose the idea of women playing an active role in public life (arguing that it goes against Islamic teachings and that it will encourage moral corruption and laxity), Islamists overall are far more open on the issue. They usually support the education of women. Unlike fundamentalists, who tend to believe that the proper role of a woman is at home raising children, many Islamists have no problem with the idea of women playing an active part in the public and professional sphere, as long as the latter is sex-segregated. Islamist organizations often include women's sections, and modern-educated women activists represent an important constituency for many Islamist groups.[9] In Iran and elsewhere, women since the 1990s have been at the forefront of efforts to develop a form of "Islamic feminism" that blends Islam and modernity, often in an effort to secure further gains for women in the public sphere. In those efforts, they usually have faced considerable resistance from organized Islamic fundamentalist interests and power groups.

- As a rule, fundamentalist ideas have a much greater chance of finding a receptive audience among men of religion (ulama) than is the case for Islamist views. After all, Islamists are far more likely to be engineers, physicians or agronomists than clerics. Unlike clerics, they did not go through formal religious training (and consequently know little about Islamic jurisprudence), and their roots lie in the modern society that produced them, not in the relatively insulated religious institution. Most important, the official citadels of fundamentalist thought and power are usually closely tied to the political authorities and consequently very ill-disposed toward the "subversive" ideas of Islamists. Thus, for instance, the religious establishment in both Saudi Arabia and Egypt has been used by these countries' respective governments to rebut the arguments of the Islamists on religious grounds.

- In several respects, the typical modern Islamist intellectual is even anti-clerical. Across the region, Islamists have criticized the subservience of the religious establishment to the political authorities. In a handful of cases, radical Islamist militants have targeted senior clerics they saw as puppets of the government. Even in Iran, where a small segment of the Shiite clergy played a leading role in the triumph of the Islamic revolution, radical clerics initially formed only one rather small component of a broad-based revolutionary coalition. The core activists within that coalition were university-educated lay Islamists, not products of the country's religious seminaries. Moreover, Iran's revolutionary clerics, often former students of Khomeini, were themselves only a minority within the religious establishment. By contrast, the most senior and respected clerics (such as Ayatollah Shariatmadari) were decidedly opposed to Khomeini and his militant, radical interpretation of Islam. Ultimately, the clerics who, after the triumph of the revolution, rose to the top of the political pyramid and were given leadership positions within the religious institution itself were not those best known for their religious scholarly expertise, but those who had the best revolutionary credentials. Significantly, in a famous statement issued in 1989, Khomeini noted that in case of conflict between "the logic of the revolution" and strict respect for the sharia, the former should take precedence over the latter. That was his way of saying that, in his view, Iran's revolution had been an Islamist phenomenon, not a fundamentalist one.

From Islamism to neofundamentalism

The line dividing Islamists from fundamentalists should not be overdrawn. Some scholars have argued that from the mid-1980s onward, Islamism began to drift into "neofundamentalism" – a trend which, in the view of these analysts, became even more pronounced through the 1990s.[10] Several critical features distinguish "neofundamentalists" from "Islamists": their greater emphasis on mores, "virtue" and "purity"; their less exclusive focus on politics and different approach to political action; and their more rigid views on women and the sharia.

Unlike Islamists, neofundamentalists are less concerned with the immediate seizure of political power than with grass-roots action aimed at the moral regeneration of the individual and the gradual transformation of society into a more "Islamic" one. It is not that neofundamentalists always eschew politics. On the contrary, they do enter the political arena, seeking representation and influence in institutions ranging from parliaments to professional syndicates. But they see the establishment of a truly Islamic society as a long-term goal that involves the slow, step-by-step return to strict Islamic practices by individuals, a goal which itself necessitates constant efforts at education, persuasion, preaching, proselytizing and lobbying the authorities. To the Islamists of the 1970s, the capture of the state would open the door automatically to the establishment of a truly Islamic order. By contrast, neofundamentalists have regarded political action primarily as one of several means toward moral and spiritual reform, both at the individual and the societal level.

Similarly, the imposition of the sharia occupies a central role in the program of neofundamentalists (and of Islamists-turned-neofundamentalists), whereas it was not that critical to the first generation of Islamists during the 1970s. Neofundamentalists are also more conservative on the issue of women's role in society. Overall, they are more preoccupied than the Islamists with issues of morality, and with the need for cleansing souls and societies which they see as having been thoroughly corrupted by Western influence. One may say that the primary target of the 1970s generation of Islamists was the "infidel ruler" who was denounced for having betrayed Islam, sold out to the West, and allowed society to retrogress to a pre-Islamic state of unbelief. In comparison, the main concerns of neofundamentalists are the decline in religious practice and the spread of un-Islamic mores and moral decay (drug addiction, alcohol consumption, popular forms of entertainment, sex outside marriage, etc.).

Although neofundamentalists are distinct from fundamentalists, they share with Islamists some important socio-economic characteristics. Like Islamists, they often are products of modern education and are far more likely to be involved in the professions than is the case of fundamentalists. Furthermore, unlike fundamentalists but like Islamists, neofundamentalists espouse political action. Unlike Islamists, however, their approach to politics places far more hope in grass-roots activism than in the prospect for an immediate capture of the state, and their program tends to revolve almost exclusively on the application of the sharia.

Saudi support for a broad range of neofundamentalist movements from Algeria to Pakistan sustained the trend toward a transformation of Islamism into neofundamentalism. In retrospect, the Saudi authorities were remarkably successful in redirecting some of the energies originally harnessed by Islamism in the direction of a neofundamentalism that was much more consistent with the rigid Wahhabi ethos and the narrow interests of the Saud family than had been the case with the initial, revolutionary Islamist impulse of the 1970s. What some analysts refer to as "the failure of political Islam" was critical as well.[11] By the mid-to-late 1980s, indeed, Islamists had been unable to seize power in any single Arab country. Their earlier ambition of riding an Islamist wave that would sweep across the region had failed to materialize. More generally, Islamists had been unsuccessful in their bid to alter significantly the political landscape of Middle Eastern and North African societies. The Iranian revolution had been contained. Elsewhere, Islamists had been repressed, cowed or co-opted. Though they sometimes had proven to be a force to be reckoned with, Islamists had neither brought down regimes nor changed the basic logic of Arab politics. As for Islamist thought, it had shown itself to be relatively scant and bland, often unpersuasive and flawed to even sympathetic observers.

Failing to differentiate between the desirable and the possible, Islamism, it seemed, had promised more than it had delivered. It had not measured up to the great hopes which its supporters had originally placed in it when it had first emerged, filling the ideological vacuum created by the death of pan-Arab dreams on the battlefields of the 1967 war. According to proponents of the "failure of political Islam" thesis, once it became clear that the original Islamist project based on the revolutionary seizure of power in order to "Islamize" society from the top down had failed, a new generation of Islamist militants turned to a strategy aimed instead at Islamizing society and politics from the bottom up. In the process, they became less "Islamist" and more "neofundamentalist." The dream of an Islamic revolution and of a quick, relatively easy seizure of the state having been shattered, neofundamentalists refocused efforts on the conquest of society through grass-roots activism and the infiltration or takeover of the institutions of civil society.

The Taliban phenomenon does not fit easily into any of the categories discussed in this paper; it is really a product of the unique environment that gave rise to it in the early 1990s in Kandahar. But, with its emphasis on a literal interpretation of the Quran and its forced imposition of a particularly rigid moral order, the Taliban movement may be seen as an extreme manifestation of neofundamentalism. Indeed, this particularly obscurantist and exclusionary form might even be described as "neofundamentalism gone mad." Such a label seems warranted by the movement's oppression of women, its hostility to any form of entertainment and, more generally, its repressive rules and commandments. The latter, one should note, often had less to do with the sharia than with the Pashtun tribal code of behavior and were also shaped by the austere, parochial, largely illiterate and for the most part totally male environment from which so many Taliban leaders hailed.[12]

"Radical Islam" or "radical Islams"?

The two separate meanings of the adjective "radical" – first, growing from a root and, second, being politically extreme – define the essence of "radical Islam."[13] Consequently, radical Islamic groups can be described as politico-religious movements which, through extreme methods, strive to bring about drastic sociopolitical changes based on a revolutionary reinterpretation of Islamic doctrine that claims to go back to the fundamental meaning and message of the faith. In this context, violence is legitimized as a way of bringing down a social and political order deemed un-Islamic, and of replacing it with one that will restore Islam's original purity.

Understood in this fashion, the expression "radical Islam" sheds light on what motivates adherents of movements said to fall under that label. Yet one also must remain aware of the limitations of such an expression. Just as we have come to appreciate the enormous diversity of phenomena grouped under the label of "Islamic resurgence," it is perhaps more accurate to speak of "radical Islams" than of "radical Islam." For instance, one might fruitfully distinguish between radical Sunni and radical Shiite movements. They have their own separate political and intellectual histories, distinct trajectories over the past two decades, and different "founding fathers" (the Egyptian Sayyid Qutb and the Pakistani Mawdudi in the case of Sunnis, Ayatollah Khomeini and to some extent Shaikh Fadlallah in Lebanon in the case of Shiite Islam). Similarly, the forces that fuel radical Islamic groups and the reasons that prompt individuals (usually young men) to join them vary greatly from one country to the other. Those who have drifted into these movements primarily because of their aversion to Western forms of modernity may have little in common with Palestinians driven into Hamas cells because of their hatred of Israel, the occupation of Palestinian land, and the accumulated feelings of anger and humiliation created by Israeli policies in the West Bank and Gaza. And in their outlook and motives, both types of militants differ in turn from those involved in the most violent groups of Algeria's Islamic insurgency, which emerged out of the specific context created by a bankrupt post-colonial state and a botched democratization experiment.

It is also critical to distinguish between the vast majority of radical Islamic groups, which have had a primarily nationalist and country-specific agenda (as has been the case of Hizballah in Lebanon, Hamas in Palestine and the Gamaa Islamiyya in Egypt), and the more recent transnational type of radical Islamic network embodied in Al Qaeda. The former type's struggles have been for the most part contained within a particular territory, and their goals have been limited to it. By contrast, the latter type has been transnational in its goals, recruitment patterns and modes of operation. It has aimed to wage *jihad* on a global scale, not merely within a given country (though Bin Laden himself appears to have been driven primarily by objectives having to do with Saudi Arabia: ridding the kingdom of American military forces, and more generally of American influence, as well as overthrowing the ruling family). It has recruited most of its cadres among a transnational, uprooted intelligentsia of young Arabs studying in the West, while its foot soldiers also have been drawn from a multiplicity of Arab countries. Its intended audience is not primarily the population of a single country, but the entire *umma* (community of believers). And, ultimately, its target is not just one government, not even that of the United States. While it has identified America as its main enemy, it tends to portray its actions not merely as a war against a well-defined, narrowly circumscribed opponent, but rather as a cosmic struggle against evil forces bent on Islam's destruction. The United States is singled out to a large extent because it is the source of so many of these forces, and because American power has been the main instrument through which they are exercised (as is the case, for instance, of globalization).

Jihadist Salafism

"Jihadist Salafi" is a label that is sometimes applied to a nebula of "second generation" radical Islamist movements that emerged during the 1980s and rose in influence during the 1990s. The war in Afghanistan (1980–89) served as the incubator for this explosive mixture of Salafi outlook and call to violence. "Jihadist Salafis" embrace a strict, literal interpretation of Islam, but combine it with an emphasis on jihad, understood here as holy war. To them, jihad becomes the prime instrument through which the "Salafi" desire to "return" to the original message of Islam will be turned into reality.[14]

The prime targets of jihadist-Salafi organizations vary according to the country and the organization involved. Some concentrate their attacks on the "infidel regimes" at the helm of the country in which they operate. Such regimes are denounced as Muslim in name only and for having become completely subservient to the West. Jihadist Salafis also may engage in random violence against an entire society seen as having reverted to a state of pre-Islamic ignorance (of God's commandments), and rejected for failing to side with "true Muslims" in their struggle against the regime (a rationale invoked by some radical Islamic groups in Algeria to justify their massacres of civilians). But for most jihadist-Salafi organizations (most prominently the transnational Al Qaeda), the main enemy is the United States. It is singled out because of its support for Israel (and therefore Israeli control over the al-Aqsa mosque in Jerusalem), because of its alleged "crimes" against Muslims (including the sanctions on Iraq), because of its support for Middle Eastern regimes and leaders that have betrayed Islam and oppress Muslims, and (the decisive factor insofar as Bin Laden is concerned) because of its military presence in Saudi Arabia near the holy mosques.

The increasing success of jihadist-Salafi ideology during the 1980s and, especially, the 1990s stemmed from the merging of two trends. One was the spread throughout the region of Salafi-neofundamentalist worldviews, which themselves owed much of their growing audience to the financial support of Gulf regimes, especially Saudi Arabia, and Gulf-based Salafi organizations. The second critical factor was the war in Afghanistan, which radicalized many Arab Salafis and indeed had the effect of converting to the cause of jihad an entire segment of the transnational Salafi movement. To be sure, many groups involved in the loose "Salafi international" continued to refrain from direct involvement in politics. Others, while politically active, relied on legal and peaceful means to achieve their goals. They avoided direct criticism of existing regimes and rejected the resort to violence and terrorism. However, galvanized by the success of the Afghan *mujahideen*, more Arab Salafis came to believe in the need for jihad. Al Qaeda, created in 1988, emerged and developed within that context.

By the time the last Soviet soldier left Afghanistan in February 1989, Arab militants who had made the trip to Afghanistan to join the jihad against the Soviet Union had convinced themselves that they had been the primary reason behind the Soviet defeat.

Emboldened, they felt that the experience of the Afghan jihad could now be duplicated successfully elsewhere. Besides, in the wake of the Soviet withdrawal, these "Arab Afghans" were in search of a new cause – or, rather, of new horizons to which the cause of the jihad could be brought. Thousands of these battle-hardened fighters began to return home, where, as in Algeria and Egypt, they were to play a key role in the radical Islamist insurgencies that broke out in 1992. And when those insurgencies reached a dead end in 1997–98, Al Qaeda was there to redirect the energies of many radical Islamists toward the global struggle against the United States.

As the preceding account makes clear, several features separate "jihadist Salafis" from traditional Salafis, from the radical Islamists who preceded them, and from the Taliban. Unlike traditional Salafis, jihadist Salafis embrace violence and the cause of jihad. Jihadist Salafis are also distinct from the earlier generation of Islamist radicals in two respects. First, their Salafi worldview implies adherence to an orthodox, literalist interpretation of Islam, as well as an implicit or explicit belief in the need for a degree of societal coercion in order to ensure that individuals abide by strict "Islamic rules." Such a fundamentalist outlook, as noted earlier, was not found among the original Islamist militants of the 1970s, who were more modernist and future-oriented. Second, the violence of the earlier generation of radical Islamists was targeted almost exclusively at the "unbelieving" ruler, government and senior officials (including, occasionally, senior members of the religious establishment) of the countries in which these groups operated. That is no longer the case with jihadist Salafis, who have sought to export jihad to new settings, identified new enemies, and tend to see jihad as a global struggle that knows no borders.

The emphasis on a literal interpretation of the Quran, combined with the embrace of jihad, are features shared by the Taliban movement and the jihadist-Salafi international. Both phenomena coalesced around the same time, in the same Pakistano-Afghan region. Both, though in different ways, were a legacy of the Soviet-Afghan war. They stemmed from the unresolved tensions, internal disorder, devastation and continued regional competition left by that conflict. These common characteristics, however, should not obscure critical differences. For instance, unlike jihadist Salafis, the Taliban were exclusively a product of the madrasa system, and they were heavily influenced by the *deobandi* tradition (an Islamic revivalist movement born among the Muslims of India in the latter third of the nineteenth century). In addition, when their movement emerged in 1994, the Taliban had very circumscribed goals: restoring peace, order and security within Afghanistan and creating a new order consistent with the sharia. They had no inclination to engage in a sustained effort to spread their version of Islam beyond that country.[15] In short, unlike so many jihadist Salafis, they had no global agenda and no real interest in international politics and the world beyond Afghanistan.

Furthermore, the "typical" Taliban – a poor, largely uneducated Pahstun of peasant origin, born in a Pakistani refugee camp and with extremely limited horizons – was strikingly different from the "typical" jihadist-Salafi Arab: rather cosmopolitan, well-traveled and often well-educated. For that matter, Mullah Omar and Osama bin Laden were strange bedfellows. The marriage of convenience that they struck in 1996–97, which would prove to be the undoing of the Taliban regime, was certainly not a natural pairing. It was a coalition of interests and circumstances that could not have been anticipated. Omar, born into a family of poor, landless peasants, was a village mullah who did not know anything about the world and was not interested in it, even as he founded his Taliban movement. Bin Laden, the privileged child of one of the richest Saudi self-made men, grew up in a Westernized environment and even had spent time during his childhood in such countries as Sweden and Great Britain. By the mid-1990s, he was at the head of a multinational terrorist network with a global reach, one that aimed at striking at the very centers of America's international power. By comparison, at that time, Mullah Omar's goal was still limited to overthrowing the corrupt government in Kabul. It would take at least two more years before the village cleric would be converted to the internationalist agenda of his benefactor. Even then, the two men could not have remained more different. The reclusive Omar was ill at ease in public and avoided all contact with foreign journalists. By contrast, his Saudi "guest," a master at manipulating symbols and poses, was relentless in his use of modern means of communication to disseminate his message.

"Radical Islamists" versus "moderate Islamists"

The category "radical Islam" usually presupposes the existence of another type of Islamist movements, variously referred to as "moderate," "mainstream" or "pragmatic." Indeed, students of Islamism have stressed the importance of differentiating between the "radical fringe," which represents only a minority of Islamists and operates underground, and the broader Islamist mainstream, which has a much larger constituency and is often allowed or tolerated by the authorities. The differences between "radical Islamists" and "moderate Islamists" are said to boil down to the following.

- Radicals advocate and legitimize the use of violence for political ends, while moderates condemn it.
- The radicals' project is a revolutionary one aiming at the seizure of power in order to establish a new Islamic order. By contrast, the moderates are said to favor a legalist, incremental approach that relies on personal conversion, compromise and the force of example. Moderates seek not to overthrow the system, but to transform it from within through a pragmatic, step-by-step process that focuses on persuasion of the population and lobbying the authorities.
- Because moderates aim to change the system progressively from below, they rely heavily on social and charitable activities. Grass-roots activism, therefore, is critical to their strategy. It is designed to bring about a gradual Islamization of society from below, and to convince the population that "Islam is the way," that there can be concrete "Islamic" solutions to the social and economic ills faced by Middle Eastern societies. This is not to say that moderates eschew the political arena. On the contrary, whenever they are given the chance, they actively participate in electoral contests. But their approach is less exclusively concerned with political power than that of the radicals. To moderates, winning hearts and souls is at least as important as gaining representation in state institutions. By contrast, the radicals typically place far more emphasis on politics, specifically on the capture of the state. They do not agree to play by the rules of regimes and societies that they denounce for having turned their backs on Islam. Unlike moderates, who believe that society and the individual can be reformed gradually, radicals argue that society can be purified only if power is seized. In several

respects, their strategy follows a Leninist approach. It envisions the creation of a small, well-organized "vanguard" party led by committed, professional Islamist revolutionaries who will overthrow existing governments and then use state power to restructure society from above, along "Islamic" lines.

- Radicals reject democracy. They do not believe in sovereignty of the people, but in the sovereignty of God (*hakimiyya*), and cannot accept that the latter would take a back seat to the former. In their view, the sharia – which they see as God's will regarding how human society ought to be organized and how it should manage its affairs – must take precedence over the will of the majority. It also should determine what is the "rightful" place of women and minorities in an Islamic society (which, to democrats, means the legitimation of state-sanctioned discrimination against minorities and women). By contrast, moderates are said to believe in the compatibility of Islam and democracy. They often claim to find precedents for democratic principles in such Islamic concepts as *shura* (consultation) and *ijma* (consensus). Most important, they assert (with varying degrees of emphasis and credibility) that if they were to come to power they would respect democratic rules, abide by the will of the majority as reflected in elections, and protect human rights and civil liberties as well as the pluralistic nature of society.

How valid is the distinction between "moderates" and "radicals"?

Differentiating between "extremist" and "mainstream" Islamists has the merit of drawing attention to the enormous diversity of organizations that seek to change their society by using vocabulary and ideals drawn from the Islamic tradition. It underscores that Islamism is not a monolithic movement, but a complex, multifaceted phenomenon that expresses itself through groups that differ considerably in their strategies and objectives.[16] Those who stress the importance of distinguishing between "moderates" and "radicals" are usually intimately familiar with the societies they study and with the "Islamic resurgence" in particular.

Some analysts, however, have questioned the validity of differentiating between moderates and radicals. They note that (1) actual Islamist groups do not necessarily fall neatly into either of these ideal-type categories; (2) the line between both categories is actually less clearly drawn than is sometimes suggested; and (3) movements frequently change their identity over time, becoming radicalized or more "mainstream" as a result of the evolving sets of incentives, rewards and deterrents with which their environments present them. More specifically, one may summarize as follows the arguments of those who caution against placing too much faith in the radicals-versus-moderates mode of analysis.[17]

- In the end, no matter how divided they are over strategies, tactics and methods, both extremists and moderates share the goal of establishing a state governed by the sharia, one in which religious law will be the law of the land. When one focuses on their fundamental convictions, their most cherished values, and the kind of society and political order they aspire to create, moderates have far more in common with radicals than they do with Western-style democrats.
- One should not take the moderates' rhetoric at face value. On issues such as the use of violence, the legitimacy of a democratic order, human rights and

pluralism, the moderates' real positions may be at significant variance with their public statements. Moderates may be merely more patient than the radicals, more willing to bide their time. They may share the radicals' basic agenda, while being more pragmatic and realistic regarding their ability to advance such an agenda given the powerful forces they confront.

- What if the moderates succeed in their strategy of Islamizing society from below? Will they then not have paved the way for the establishment of an Islamic state, which is the radicals' goal? And if such a state is established, will there be space for dissenters, secularists, women's-rights activists and pluralism? Some analysts even go so far as to claim that the moderates pose a more insidious threat, and therefore a greater one, than the radicals. Through their community-oriented activities and because of the freedom of maneuver that they sometimes are granted by the authorities, they are progressively subverting, from within, the nominally secular systems in which they operate. Ultimately, the argument goes, they will be able to take over that system without a fight.

- A related argument is that the gradual Islamization of public discourse and society produced by the moderates, or by the courting of "Islamist moderates" by the authorities, may over time create an environment in which extremism can flourish. Pakistan illustrates this scenario. Beginning with the administration of General Zia ul-Haq (1977–88), the state strove to appease and co-opt religious parties, Muslim clerics and Islamist intellectuals. It Islamized law and infused its discourse with Islamic vocabulary and symbols. It turned a blind eye, indeed even encouraged, connections between Islamist groups and the military-intelligence apparatus. It granted "mainstream Islamist parties" and "religious intellectuals" unprecedented freedom of operation, while encouraging the proliferation of religious schools and organizations. It brought Islamists into the inner circles of power, at the higher echelons of the civil service and the military and intelligence agencies. And it used extremist Islamist groups as instruments of its foreign policy, both in Afghanistan and in Indian-controlled Kashmir.

That policy now has come back to haunt President Musharraf, who himself has longstanding connections to some Islamists and seized power in October 1999 with the blessing of many of them. After all, the 1999 coup that brought down the elected civilian government of Nawaz Sharif was orchestrated and carried out by the military high command, in which pro-Islamist elements were dominant, and it received the enthusiastic support of the country's Islamist parties. Musharraf's recent policy U-turn has been an implicit admission of the bankruptcy and unsustainability of previous policies. Certainly, his recent crackdown on violent Islamist groups was prompted by the war in Afghanistan, direct U.S. pressure and mounting tensions with India (especially in the wake of the attack on the Indian Parliament in mid-December 2001). But these events may merely have precipitated the day of reckoning for Pakistan's ruler. It already had become clear that complacency toward Islamism had bred religious extremism at all levels of society, that it had resulted in rising and increasingly bloody sectarian clashes between the country's Shiite and Sunni populations, and, more generally, that it had contributed to the spread of a culture of violence throughout the country and indeed in the entire region. The state's handling of political Islam had seriously damaged Pakistan's international image while dangerously building up tensions with India. It also raised the prospect of a religious take-over of the state by militant religious elements – one that presumably would be facilitated by the well-known and increasingly visible connections between the military-security apparatus and extremist religious groups, and between the latter and the criminal underworld.

Pakistan's case is certainly not unique. Many analysts have argued that the rise of radical Islam under President Sadat (1970–81) was fueled in part by the Egyptian president's efforts to use religion as a counterweight to Nasserist and leftist influence, and by his release from jail of members of the "mainstream Muslim Brotherhood" in the early 1970s. More recently, the Egyptian government's efforts to co-opt Islamic rhetoric, and the tolerance the Mubarak regime has shown toward the spread of fundamentalist views throughout society, are widely seen as having contributed to rising anti-Coptic violence and religious intolerance. Likewise, in Indonesia, the Islamization of political discourse during the rule of President Suharto (1966–98) has been blamed for having contributed to growing communal tensions and the development of radical Islamist movements over the past several years.

- Specific Islamist movements labeled as either "moderate" or "radical" may in fact exhibit characteristics that do not lend themselves to such easy classifications. Often that is because within a single Islamist movement, "moderate" and "radical" wings coexist (more or less easily). Consider the Islamic Salvation Front (FIS), which won the December 1991 parliamentary elections in Algeria, before the military cancelled the results of the elections on January 11, 1992, and put an end to the democratic process. The FIS was frequently described at the time as a "moderate Islamist party." Its leader, Abbasi Madani, spoke the language of pluralism, democracy, and respect for the constitution and legality. His core support was among Algeria's religiously oriented middle classes. But the FIS also featured an influential radical wing headed by Madani's second-in-command, Ali Belhaj. Belhaj, who enjoyed a significant following among Algeria's poor and disenfranchised, spoke a far more radical language. He was explicitly hostile to democracy, which he had denounced repeatedly as an alien concept, a western evil and a heresy. Similar tensions can be found among many other Islamist groups. Hamas's leadership, for instance, has long been torn between "insiders" (based in the West Bank and Gaza) and "outsiders" (exiled leaders). On the two key issues of confrontation with Israel and attitude toward the Palestinian Authority, insiders were always far more moderate than outsiders, more aware of the constraints on Hamas and the limits of its power, and more prone to engage in conciliation and compromise (at least until the recent radicalization produced by the general deterioration of the situation in Palestine).

- Describing a specific Islamist movement as either "radical" or "moderate" may also be misleading because, in practice, the frontier between "radical" and "moderate" Islamism is often elusive or porous.

    1. Most Islamist movements are divided into competing tendencies that are themselves located at different points along a radical-to-moderate axis. Therefore, where the movement as a whole stands on the continuum depends largely on the changing balance of power between "moderate"

and "radical" tendencies within it, as well as by the shifting political environment that often determines the evolution of that balance.

2. Islamist movements generally described as radical may also be capable of engaging in the give-and-take of democratic politics, as Hizballah deputies have done in Lebanon's parliament since 1992. Armed resistance to occupation does not preclude pragmatic, legalistic action in other arenas. Similarly, since its founding in 1988, Hamas has behaved in a manner that contrasts sharply with the widespread but misleading image of it as a dogmatic, ideologically-driven movement that is not amenable to the kind of cost-benefit calculations associated with pluralistic politics. In reality, Hamas has shown far more flexibility than it is usually given credit for. It has responded in a very pragmatic manner to changing political circumstances and adjusted its rhetoric and behavior accordingly. It has not let itself become a prisoner of its past rhetoric. In its attitude toward Israel, the peace process and the Palestinian Authority, it has shown itself capable of taking into account new opportunities and constraints as they have arisen.[18]

3. Islamist movements are not frozen in time as either radical or moderate. Radical Islamist movements can moderate their attitude over time, while mainstream Islamists can be radicalized. Such evolutions largely reflect changing political conditions and the shifting sets of opportunities and constraints that they create for Islamist movements, as well as the evolving balance of power between "radicals" and "moderates" within these movements. For instance, Algeria's FIS experienced a sharp radicalization following the military coup of January 1992, which discredited moderates within it while appearing to vindicate those radicals who had denounced the democratic process as a sham and warned that the military would never allow Islamists to win a free and fair election. Conversely, during the 1990s, Lebanon's Hizballah was able to change its image from terrorist, revolutionary organization to mainstream political party. It publicly dropped its goal of creating an Islamic republic and instead accepted Lebanon's multiconfessional system. In the Chamber of Deputies, its representatives showed themselves to be pragmatic, savvy politicians. By behaving responsibly and following the rules of legislative politics, they contributed to a marked improvement in the general perception of Hizballah, both within and outside of Lebanon. Israel's withdrawal from south Lebanon in May 2000 created new incentives for Hizballah to complete its transformation from guerrilla organization to political machine. Having lost a major trump card (its role as a vanguard of the Lebanese resistance to Israeli occupation) but also basking in the glow of its victory over Israel, Hizballah was expected to redirect its energies inward, focusing on broadening its political base by addressing the practical concerns of an electorate weary of war and politics-as-usual. The reality has been more nuanced: while Hizballah has redoubled its effort to gain political ground through savvy media campaigns and skillful positioning, it has not abandoned armed activities against Israel. In so doing, the organization has shown that pragmatic, mainstream behavior on domestic issues can go hand in hand with more aggressive, militant stances on foreign-policy

questions, especially those seen as threats to national security and sovereignty, or as matters of pan-Arab solidarity.

Though less clearly drawn than Hizballah's, the cases of Egypt's and Algeria's radical Islamist groups are also revealing. In Egypt, following a failed Islamist insurgency that lasted from 1992 until 1997, key members of the Gamaa Islamiyya called, from jail, for a unilateral cessation of violence against the state and subsequently asked permission to establish a political party (a request that was turned down by the authorities). Though exiled political leaders condemned this new policy, and while many observers saw it as more a tactical decision than a genuine and sincere change of strategy and approach, other analysts concluded that the new attitude of former Gamaa activists represented a fundamental shift in their ideology. In Algeria, too, leaders of the Islamic rebellion concluded in 1997 that the policies followed by radical Islamists had been self-defeating and had alienated society. Consequently, they called for a unilateral ceasefire. Unlike in Egypt, however, a large segment of the Islamist tendency was allowed to take part in the political process, and several of its key leaders even endorsed the candidacy of Abdelaziz Bouteflika, elected president in April 1999.

4. The fluid nature of the frontier between extremist and moderate Islamist groups is also evident when supposedly "mainstream" Islamists refuse to disavow unambiguously the violence of radical groups, or disavow it publicly while privately adopting a more ambivalent stance. Similarly, there may be close personal relationships and ideological affinities between radical Islamists and those affiliated with more moderate tendencies. While moderates may disagree with the methods of the extremists, they may share some of the same ultimate objectives, including the establishment of a state based on the sharia. After all, the social and political order that "jihadist Salafis" seek to establish is not significantly different from that espoused by more quietist Salafis. Such shared outlooks can generate solidarities that transcend disagreements over particular tactics and strategies. Significantly, throughout the 1980s and 1990s, jihadist Salafis received generous financial support from wealthy, reform-oriented Salafi contributors in the Gulf.

5. Radical Islamist ideologies often trace their roots to mainstream Islamist worldviews, and extremist Islamist movements often have developed out of moderate ones. Consider for instance the forebear of all Islamist groups in the Middle East, the Muslim Brotherhood (MB), created in Egypt in 1928 by a schoolteacher named Hassan al-Banna. The MB is usually described as a "mainstream organization." Originally, it was intended merely as a movement for spiritual and moral reform, and its emphasis was less on politics than on charitable activities and religious education. Yet, as it expanded during the 1930s, and as it became active on the Egyptian political scene, the MB also became host to a variety of more militant tendencies. Some broke off from the MB and created their own organizations. But within the MB itself, a secret paramilitary wing was formed in the late 1930s called the "secret apparatus" (al-jihaz al-sirri). That group carried out attacks against the British, the monarchy and senior officials. In 1948–49, shortly after the MB played a key role in mobilizing and sending volunteers to

fight in the war in Palestine, its conflict with the monarchy reached its climax. Concerned with the increasing assertiveness and popularity of the MB, as well as with rumors that it was plotting a coup d'état, Prime Minister Nuqrashi Pasha disbanded it on December 8, 1948. Less than three weeks later, the MB retaliated by assassinating the prime minister. That in turn prompted the murder of al-Banna, presumably by a government agent, on February 12, 1949. In 1954, the MB was blamed for allegedly having tried to assassinate Gamal Abdel Nasser. That event resulted in a crackdown on the movement, the execution of its top leadership, and the jailing of thousands of its active members.

This brief history illustrates how easily "mainstream" Islamist movements can be radicalized, and how quickly the ensuing conflict with the authorities can spin out of control. A focus on the MB also reveals that radical groups often emerge from more "moderate" ones. The core members of radical Islamist groups in Egypt during the 1970s were often former MB activists who had languished (and been radicalized) in Nasser's jails. Similarly, the Palestinian Hamas emerged in 1988 out of an internal coup within the Muslim Brotherhood, when a younger, more activist generation of modest social origins broke off from the MB, which at the time was dominated by an "old guard" of well-to-do merchants reluctant to confront Israel and openly resist the occupation.[19]

- Finally, the notion that radical Islamist groups give priority to violent political action, while moderate ones are more apt to rely on grass-roots charitable and educational activities also distorts a more complex reality. In fact, social work has been critical to the appeal and success of groups such as Hizballah and Hamas, which are usually labeled "radical." Hamas's deep roots in Palestinian society have much to do with the services it provides to the community through the hospitals, clinics, welfare organizations, schools, libraries, kindergartens and clubs attached to it. Similarly, in Lebanon, Hizballah has benefited considerably from the many years it has spent delivering relief, health and educational services. This activism has fed its appeal among the more impoverished segments of the population. Back in 1988, after intra-Christian clashes in East Beirut had left the residents of Beirut's southern suburbs without potable water and electricity, Hizballah provided generators and ensured a daily replenishment of local reservoirs by using trucks to bring water to affected areas. Three years later, during the harsh 1991–92 winter that hit the Bekaa Valley particularly hard, Hizballah stepped into the vacuum left by the government and organized teams of relief workers who cleared roads blocked by snow and distributed blankets and food to the poor. More recently, in the wake of Israel's devastating April 1996 Operation Grapes of Wrath, Hizballah helped repair or rebuild an estimated 5,000 homes as well as many bridges and roads destroyed or damaged by Israeli shelling.

On a day-to-day basis, Hizballah runs community centers and provides subsidized services and goods. It manages supermarkets and cooperatives that sell food at discounted prices. It cares for orphans, elderly persons and the families of those killed or wounded in attacks against Israel. Its schools provide a low-cost education which is often of higher quality than that of state-run schools. It awards scholarships and offers interest-free loans to the needy. It manages dispensaries, clinics and four hospitals. Even those services and goods for which Hizballah usually charges a fee are provided free to impoverished families, including medicine and hospitalization in Hizballah's hospitals and clinics, education in the schools run by Hizballah staff, and food packages in Hizballah-run supermarkets.[20]

Policy implications

Distinguishing between moderate and radical Islamists has clear policy implications, both for host governments and for the United States. While fleshing out those implications and looking at the empirical bases for them goes beyond the scope of this paper, I will summarize the essence of the debate.[21]

Those who stress the need to differentiate between "mainstream" and "extremist" forms of political Islam usually suggest that the main drift of government policy should be to isolate, delegitimize and marginalize the extremists, while providing the moderates with the incentives and rewards to play a constructive political and social role. Implicit or explicit in this reasoning are several interrelated assumptions or claims:

(a)   When "mainstream" Islamist movements are given an opportunity to express themselves relatively freely and are allowed to pursue their objectives within the confines of the legal political system, they typically refrain from violence and can play the role of a loyal opposition. Consequently, the argument goes, the more open the political system, the stronger moderate Islamists are likely to be relative to their more radical counterparts, the more likely it becomes that moderate Islamists will show a propensity to engage in the give-and-take of democratic politics, and the more religious radicalism will be held in check. Even when the participation of moderate Islamists in the system appears to be driven by opportunism and tactical considerations, that situation may change over time. With the proper incentives and rewards, moderate Islamists may develop a stake in the existing sociopolitical order and therefore a more genuine attachment to it.

(b)   By contrast, regimes whose response to Islamism revolves primarily or exclusively around an undifferentiated repression of Islamist movements will play into the hands of the violent fringe. Across-the-board repression will discredit the moderates, give credence to the positions embraced by the radicals, and drive many of the former into the arms of the latter. Instead, government policy should seek to multiply opportunities for moderate Islamists to play a constructive political role and use them as safety valves against radical tendencies. It should involve a carefully considered mix of carrots and sticks, cracking down on violent organizations while seeking to bring moderate groups into the political process. Such a two-track policy will serve to demonstrate that violence will not be tolerated, whereas moderation pays off and results in tangible benefits.

The reasoning that has just been articulated is not devoid of merits, but it also leaves some important questions unanswered. For one, what happens if and when "moderate" Islamists, benefiting from a relatively open political process, come to power and then change their position regarding their earlier-stated desire to preserve a pluralistic, democratic order? What if their previous embrace of the "one person, one vote" principle turns into a position that can be summarized as "one person, one vote, one time"? What if moderate Islamists use the democratic process to come to power and then abolish that process?[22] An academic observer may have the luxury of saying that the only way to determine whether moderate Islamists are truly committed to democracy, and/or whether they are capable of controlling more radical factions, is to "test" them. Allow them to take part in a relatively open political process and see how democratically they behave if and when they rise to power. That, however, is a position with which policy makers – or those likely to suffer under a repressive government that discriminates against minorities, women and secular-oriented individuals – are likely to feel uncomfortable. For the United States, the problem is compounded by the possibility that "moderate Islamists" may be "moderate" insofar as their domestic-policy orientations are concerned, but that their positions on regional issues, such as relations between Israel and the Arab world, may be in sharp contrast to Washington's.

Finally, to the extent that a given Islamist movement is often composed of several wings that hold different if not contradictory views regarding democracy, human rights and relations with the outside world, how can a coherent policy toward such a movement be developed? Even if "moderates" appear to constitute the dominant trend within that movement, how can government policy toward it reflect the possibility that the extremists might use the moderates as a front or that under some circumstances the former might displace the latter? How can policy reduce the likelihood that moderates will be outflanked by more radical factions? After all, between 1989 and 1991 in Algeria, the FIS was widely viewed by experts as a "mainstream" Islamist movement, but moderates in its ranks were very quickly bypassed and neutralized by extremists after January 1992. Besides, historically, when movements split between moderates and radicals have come to power, more often than not it is (at least in the early stages) the radicals who have been able to displace the moderates, not the other way around (in the region, the Iranian revolution may be seen as the latest manifestation of that phenomenon).

These and other considerations lead some analysts to question the appropriateness, for policy purposes, of drawing a distinction between moderate and radical Islamists. Such analysts believe that Islamists cannot truly be accommodated within a democratic system. In their view, Islamists may profess a commitment to democracy but only for tactical reasons, when they stand to benefit from greater political space. At heart, they never espouse wholeheartedly democracy and its values. The kind of society and political order that they envision is irreconcilable with a liberal, competitive political system that does not discriminate against certain groups and constituencies. Moreover, they contend, there is no strong evidence that policies of accommodation prompt Islamist parties and leaders to moderate their views and become more genuinely tolerant of, and open to, alternative viewpoints and ideas. In fact, quite the opposite may take place, as Islamists become emboldened by their increasing influence.

In fact, according to those same analysts, efforts to appease, co-opt or integrate Islamist movements into the political process are likely to backfire, creating a context within which political radicalism and/or social intolerance ultimately may prevail. Islamists may make inroads into centers of power, and their norms and outlook may spread to ever-wider segments of society. According to this view, accommodation of political Islam is therefore a dangerous and self-defeating behavior. A desire to placate or appeal to moderate Islamists may prompt regimes to adopt policies that slowly change, for the worse, the face and social fabric of their countries, undermining a tradition of tolerance, threatening peaceful coexistence with religious minorities, making societies more rigid, and progressively creating an environment in which extremist views may flourish.

Ultimately, the validity of such claims must be tested against the weight of the empirical evidence. A close examination of this record, followed by a broad-based debate on its significance, is more than ever necessary if the United States is to make informed policy choices regarding one of the most difficult challenges it has ever confronted.

Notes

1   Olivier Roy, *The Failure of Political Islam* (Cambridge: Harvard University Press, 1994), p. viii.
2   Ibid.
3   Martin E. Marty and R. Scott Appleby, "Foreword," *Islamic Fundamentalisms and the Gulf Crisis*, James Piscatori, ed. (Chicago: The American Academy of Arts and Sciences, 1991), p. xii.
4   See for instance Joel Beinin and Joe Stork, "On Modernity, Historical Specificity, and International Context of Political Islam," *Political Islam* (Berkeley and Los Angeles: University of California Press, 1997), pp. 3–4.
5   That argument is developed in Marty and Appleby, op. cit., pp. x–xi.
6   François Burgat, *L'islamisme en face* (Paris: La Découverte, 2002), pp. 275–276.
7   Roy, op. cit., p. 33.
8   See ibid., pp. 38–39 and p. 197.
9   See Chapter 11, "L'islamisme et les femmes," Burgat, op. cit.
10   That argument was first advanced in Roy, op. cit., especially Chapter 5 and Conclusion.
11   Roy, op. cit., was the first to develop that thesis, which at the time went against the conventional wisdom. More recently, see Gilles Kepel, *Jihad: expansion et déclin de l'islamisme* (Paris: Gallimard, 2000).
12   See Ahmed Rashid, *Taliban: Militant Islam, Oil & Fundamentalism in Central Asia* (New Haven: Yale University Press, 2000).
13   See for instance Bruno Etienne, *L'Islamisme radical* (Paris: Hachette, 1987).
14   On jihadist Salafism, see Kepel, op. cit., especially pp. 223–238, and Quintan Wiktorowicz, "The New Global Threat: Transnational Salafis and Jihad," *Middle East Policy*, Vol. VIII, No. 4, December 2001, pp. 18–38.
15   Kepel, op. cit., p. 228.
16   One of the most effective and comprehensive presentations of this feature can still be found in John L. Esposito, *The Islamic Threat: Myth or Reality?* (New York: Oxford University Press, 1999).

17 Many of these arguments can be found in Scott W. Hibbard and David Little, *Islamic Activism and U.S. Foreign Policy* (Washington, DC: United States Institute of Peace Press, 1997). See also Fawaz A. Gerges, *America and Political Islam: Clash of Cultures or Clash of Interests?* (Cambridge University Press, 1999), as well as the debate between Mumtaz Ahmad and I. William Zartman, "Political Islam: Can it Become a Loyal Opposition?" *Middle East Policy*, Vol. V, No. 1, January 1997, pp. 68–84.

18 See the excellent analysis conducted by two Israeli scholars in Shaul Mishal and Avraham Sela, *The Palestinian Hamas: Vision, Violence, and Coexistence* (New York: Columbia University Press, 2000).

19 Glenn E. Robinson, *Building a Palestinian State: The Incomplete Revolution* (Bloomington: Indiana University Press, 1997), Chapter 6.

20 A brief analysis of Hizballah from the perspective of this paper can be found in Augustus Richard Norton, "Hizballah: From Radicalism to Pragmatism?" *Middle East Policy*, Vol. V, No. 4, January 1998, pp. 147–158.

21 See Hibbard and Little, op. cit., and Esposito, op. cit., pp. 273–275.

22 Robert Pelletreau, assistant secretary of state for Near Eastern Affairs during the Clinton administration, as well as his predecessor, Edward Djerejian, repeatedly voiced such concerns publicly.

Further reading

Aziz al-Azmeh, *Islams and Modernities*, 3rd edition (London: Verso, 2009)
> An insightful analysis of the modern ideological and political reconfigurations of Islam and Islamism.

Roxanne L. Euben, *Enemy in the Mirror: Islamic Fundamentalism and the Limits of Modern Rationalism: A Work of Comparative Political Theory* (Princeton: Princeton University Press, 1999)
> An insightful account of the convergence and divergence between contemporary Islamist and western political thinking.

Roxanne L. Euben and Muhammad Qasim Zaman (eds.) *Princeton Readings in Islamist Thought: Texts and Contexts from al-Banna to Bin Laden* (Princeton: Princeton University Press, 2009)
> A carefully selected and presented collection of key texts from leading Islamist ideologues.

Saba Mahmood, *Politics of Piety: The Islamic Revival and the Feminist Subject* (Princeton: Princeton University Press, 2005)
> A sophisticated account of the grassroots modes of formation of Islamist identity among women activists.

Peter Mandaville, *Global Political Islam* (New York: Routledge, 2007)
> A comprehensive and well-balanced introduction to the key trends in Islamism in a global context.

Salman Sayyid, *A Fundamental Fear Eurocentrism and the Emergence of Islamism*, 2nd edition (London: Zed Books, 2003)
> An insightful account of the historical and conceptual framing of Islamism in Eurocentric representations of the non-western world.

Frédéric Volpi, *Political Islam Observed* (New York: Columbia University Press, 2010)
> A comprehensive overview of the approaches to, and representations of, Islamism in contemporary social sciences.

Political Islam, the state and political power

Introduction

THE PREVIOUS SECTION helped to provide a better understanding of the processes that shape the dynamics and identity of political Islam in relation to other forms of political activity. The task in this section is to move into the domain of explanation to assess the many theories about Islamism and how successful (or not) they have been in deciphering the key aspects of the Islamist phenomenon for domestic and international politics. Contemporary debates about political Islam reflect a set of dilemmas that have emerged in the twentieth century regarding the position of a politically active global religion in a world of sovereign and secular nation-states. As indicated earlier, part of this dilemma has been generated by the expansion of a western model of nation-state throughout the Muslim world. As traditional forms of social organization and legal frameworks supported by Islamic models of legitimization were transformed first by the colonial empires then by the post-colonial state, resistance to these new types of sovereignty invoked the Islamic repertoire to construct alternative modes of domestic and international allegiance.

These reconstructed Islamist models of political organization tried hard to show that they could be the solution to the local, national and international predicaments of Muslim polities, with varying success. The most noticeable difference between the dilemmas of the twentieth century and those of the twenty-first century have to do with the increased globalization of political Islam. Up to the decolonization period, political Islam was perceived by the main international powers to be primarily a domestic problem for Muslim-majority countries. Although it was deemed to hinder modernization and secularization, this problematic Islamist phenomenon was perceived to have limited implications for foreign policy. In the late twentieth century and more clearly in the early twenty-first century, by contrast, it is the global reach of transnational Islamist networks that are deemed to constitute a challenge, both for Muslim-majority countries and for the international system.

In the twentieth century, dilemmas involving political Islam commonly rested on assumptions about secularization that posited that religious opposition to the state would eventually die out as polities modernized. In the main, political Islam was viewed as a hindrance to the development of Muslim-majority countries that could be overcome through socio-economic advances and political education. Many analyses were thus concerned with explaining away the apparent vitality of Islamist movements in various parts of the Muslim world through a combination of socio-economic determinism – i.e. it will change when people get richer and better educated – and political accounts of the institutionalization and legitimization of the postcolonial state. The emphasis was on showing that the language of Islam expressed in a 'primitive' religious idiom some basic political concerns that local populations could not yet express using a modern political vocabulary and tools. It was often recognized that the postcolonial state was far from adequate to address the needs of its subjects. Yet, it was not until the Islamic revolution in Iran that political Islam was deemed to be a truly viable state actor – and analyses of the Islamic republic stressed how 'normally' the Islamic republic behaved in a world of nation-states.

The first text, by Gudrun Krämer, highlights what are, from an Islamist perspective, the key issues and dilemmas regarding the political practices promoted by the current (western) models of governance. Kramer indicates how the political programme of Islamism does not involve a precise blueprint for organizing political institutions. Ideologues and activists are more concerned with the morality required to sustain an Islamic public life, than with the technical procedures that would actually constitute an Islamic state. This situation gives them greater flexibility to address different sets of political circumstances, but it does not equip them well to handle state governance in a systematic way when they have a say in government.

The next contribution, by James Piscatori, considers the case of the first Gulf War to shed some light on the processes that intervene in the articulation of pro- or anti-'Islamist' positions in domestic and foreign policy. Piscatori outlines the way in which public opinion, international financial initiatives, military options and the use of political repression all contributed to the complex strategic calculations that regimes in the region had to make at the time. In their turn, these tactical choices reinforced – or on rare occasions changed – pre-existing patterns of interaction between Islamists and the state, in the region and beyond. These concrete expressions of foreign policy in a time of crisis brought to light the long-term political mechanisms that structure the interactions between government and opposition in the Middle East.

The third text, by Mahmood Mamdani, analyses in more detail how western policy makers approach the Islamist phenomenon from a culturalist perspective that instrumentalizes indigenous attempts at reform to their own advantage. Mamdani notes how the instrumentalization by foreign states of the Afghan mujahidin in the 1980s and of the Talibans in the 1990s contributed to articulate an Islamist message that was violent but tactically useful for the external actors involved in the conflict. Only when these Islamist organizations ceased to be useful for external sponsors, or became hindrances, did explanations of their dangerousness begin to be phrased in terms of their religious agenda. This instrumentalist approach to Islamism still dominates the contemporary international context and is clearly evidenced in many of the policies of the 'War on Terror'.

The final extract, from Salman Sayyid's *A Fundamental Fear*, delimits the realm of possibilities of action for political Islam. These options should not be viewed solely in terms of political calculations within a westernized geopolitical framework, but should also consider the potential for new positioning and expression of politics on the international scene. In particular, political Islam evokes the possibility of an international order less grounded on the notion of sovereign nation-states, which chimes with some of the transformations induced by the contemporary processes of globalization. Sayyid indicates that a key challenge for Islamist attempts at constructing a social and political order not based on western models of governance is an historical and international conjuncture now shaped by the confrontation between a US-led militaro-political order and globalized forms of Islamist resistance to it.

Gudrun Krämer

VISIONS OF AN ISLAMIC REPUBLIC GOOD GOVERNANCE ACCORDING TO THE ISLAMISTS

R ELATIONS BETWEEN THE Muslim world and the West are difficult and marked by mutual suspicion. This does not necessarily imply hostility; nor does it mean that each side has a clearly defined notion of the other as enemy. But each holds an image of the other that tends to be deeply critical; each fosters its own prejudices and misconceptions; and each believes that the other poses a threat. From a European perspective, perceived threats include migration caused by rapid population growth and political instability at the other side of the Mediterranean, and political Islam, if not Islam per se. Anxieties and apprehensions are not just a result of the close proximity between Europe and the Middle East. They are also due to the growing presence of Muslims inside Western Europe itself, which has led to the increasing blurring of the former distinction between domestic and foreign politics. Europeans today are more directly confronted with Islam, or rather with Muslim lifestyles, norms and aspirations, than they have been for centuries.

The debate on values

Mutual perceptions are greatly influenced by the debate on values, which even in Western Europe is no longer the domain of conservative circles: the unsettling effects of modernisation have provoked harsh criticism of modernity, and the search for a moral and social renewal has brought about a renaissance of virtues and values. While within Western society itself the "crisis of modernity" has generated a sense of insecurity, the West has largely maintained its posture of self-confidence towards the outside world. This is especially clear in the debate on human rights, civil society and the market economy ("good governance" and "best practices" in the neutral language of international organisations such as the United Nations, the *World Bank* and the *International Monetary Fund*). Particularly since the collapse of the Soviet empire, such values are held up as a panacea to the non-Western world. "Democracy-cum-market economy" presupposes the existence not only of a framework of rules and institutions, but also of specific values, first and foremost among them respect for the intrinsic value of the individual and the diversity of beliefs and opinions.

It is precisely this "ethics of tolerance" that is said to be lacking in Islam, both on a doctrinal and on a practical level. Not only do critics tend to identify religion with political culture, they also fail to make a distinction between theory and practice. They attribute to Islam a general disregard for the concept of freedom, for rational thought and the principle of responsibility. Also criticised is the absence of voluntary associations and of a self-confident middle class upholding modern, democratic ideas. And what Islam has not known in the past, it cannot produce in the future. Islam is said to promote collective thought and action, barbaric forms of corporal punishment, the repression of women and non-Muslims, and intolerance towards artists, intellectuals and independent minds of all kinds. On the Muslim side, criticism is equally strong, displaying a similar level of ignorance and an equally arbitrary confusion of theory and practice, past and present. The Occident is considered to be devoid of spirituality and ethical orientation. It is said to indulge in hedonistic materialism which finds expression in the degradation of women, the break-down of the family, the destruction of the cities and a general deterioration of "values." The West, it is claimed, propagates democracy and human rights on a global level, only to utterly disregard them when it so chooses.

The debate serves an obvious function: to prove one's own superiority in the domain of morals, ethics and humanity, and to deny those values to the other. Yet there are basic values shared by both sides: they range from the concept of human dignity and individual responsibility for society, politics and the environment, to the right to political participation and the ideal of the rule of law. Many Muslims today – especially the Islamists among them – consider religion, and more particularly Islam, as providing the only solid foundation for those values. In the West, on the other hand, it is often argued that modernity with the humanitarian values attached to it can only be attained by Muslims if they emulate developments in Europe and the West in general. The Reformation, the Enlightenment and secularisation are cited as processes which liberated Western society from the shackles of religion and freed it from the "iron cage of bondage" (Max Weber). The same path should be followed by the Muslim world. Some Europeans hope that the Muslims living among them will develop a liberal "Euro-Islam" reflecting their experiences in modern, democratic societies, and that this will eventually spread to the Islamic world. "Euro-Communism" was instrumental in overcoming the more rigid variants of communism in the East, and why should not "Euro-Islam" have a similar effect on the Orient? *Ex occidente lux*. It must be said that there are, as yet, few indications of the emergence of this liberal Euro-Islam. By and large, Muslim migrants living in Europe continue to look to the Islamic world for religious and spiritual guidance, and the Near and Middle East is still their main source of inspiration. It is to the Islamic world then, and more specifically to the Near and Middle East, that we must turn in order to find modern expressions of Islamic thought, including models of an "Islamic order" of morality, government and society.

Since the late 1970s, Islam has come to renewed prominence in the Muslim world as the guiding principle of individual behaviour and public life. This has gone hand-in-hand with the search for an "Islamic order" which might serve as an alternative to all known models of social, economic and political organisation. Such a system must fulfil two conditions: it must be "modern," i.e. respond to present-day demands and expectations, and it must be "authentic," demonstrating the cultural autonomy of the Muslim world from Morocco to Indonesia. Needless to say, the notion of "authenticity" is problematic. Even Muslims agree that it cannot simply be taken to stand for Islam writ large, since Islam (with a capital I) is commonly identified with the "grand tradition" or "orthodox Islam" as defined by the normative texts of the Koran and *Sunna*, at the expense of the numerous "little traditions" of Muslim life and spirituality based on oral traditions. Muslims, like the followers of other religions, are influenced by their social and cultural environments. Consequently, "Islamic" life-styles and "Islamic" norms display a large degree of diversity.

Even the most rigid scripturalists, who regard the Koran as their constitution and the Prophet Mohammed as their leader, will find that the authoritative sources do not contain precise guidelines for an Islamic order. While the Koran and the *Sunna*, i.e. the reports of the doings and sayings of the Prophet Mohammed, set down certain general rules regarding social and political life, they do not prescribe any particular model, not even the caliphate. There is no Islamic state independent of time and circumstance. Rather, there are various projects, some based on utopian thinking, others on existing models, such as the Islamic Republic of Iran and the Kingdom of Saudi Arabia, which differ from each other in important respects and are not even recognised as "truly Islamic" by many contemporary Muslims.

Most models for an "Islamic order" as an alternative to those existing both in the West and in Iran or Saudi Arabia have been outlined by adherents to the broad and heterogeneous Islamic, or Islamist, movement. This includes groups and organisations who vary as to their support of, or opposition to, the regimes in power. They range from the *Muslim Brotherhood* organisations in Egypt, Jordan and Palestine, the Algerian Salvation Front (*Front Islamique du Salut*, FIS), the Tunisian *Movement of the Islamic Tendency/Nahda* party and the Yemeni *Reform Movement* (*Islah*), to the Islamist opposition in Saudi Arabia, the Turkish *Refah Party* and Pakistan's *Jamaat-i Islami*. The Islamist movement also includes scholars and academics working at the institutions of classical Muslim learning and the non-religious state universities, as well as numerous "independent Islamic thinkers," intellectuals and activists who are not affiliated to any particular group or organisation. In terms of their social background, they tend to belong to the educated urban middle class, and the majority are men.

They all refer to the Koran, the *Sunna* and selected authors of the classical age, and nearly all claim to have outlined *the* ideal Islamic system. As suggested above, such assertions should be approached with caution. Islamists, like other Muslims, do no more than interpret the normative sources, and they cannot claim universal validity for their interpretations. The Muslim community does not recognise one single, central authority which can provide a binding definition of belief or unbelief, let alone of the Islamic state. The scholars at the *Sunni Azhar* University are not in a position to do so, nor are the Shiite Grand Ayatollahs like Imam Khomeini. Their interpretations are clearly rooted in the modern experience and reflect the needs, demands and ideals of the modern age – even when the authors believe they are resurrecting the golden age of Islam, a time when, due to the presence of the Prophet and ongoing revelation, belief and action were one.

Techniques and values

One of the most interesting, and at the same time most problematic aspects of the debate on an "Islamic order" is the distinction frequently made between techniques and values. Muslim scholars (*ulama*) and Islamist activists refer to this distinction, as do some of their staunchest critics – albeit for different reasons. Islamists hold that techniques are entirely neutral from a religious and moral perspective, and provided that Islamic values are preserved intact, they can be adopted from other civilisations without jeopardising Islamic authenticity. This applies not only to scientific discoveries and modern technology, but also to methods, instruments and institutions of economic, political and social organisation. This line of argument is of particular significance in the debate on human rights and democracy, since liberal and pluralist democracy, which is what most Muslims think of when discussing democracy in general, clearly encompasses both techniques and values.

Bassam Tibi, one of the best-known critics of fundamentalism, draws a similar distinction. He maintains that the fundamentalists (referred to here as Islamists) advocate the acquisition of modern technology, while rejecting modern values. What they want, he suggests, is merely "one half of modernity." Others, like the French political scientist François Burgat, have argued that it is precisely the reference to Islam which allows Muslims in general and Islamists in particular to assimilate the "essential references" of the "discourse of modernity," as it first evolved in the West. This includes democracy and human rights. According to Burgat, Islamists aim at an "Islamisation of modernity," and in his opinion they may very well achieve their objective. While Burgat has not substantiated his thesis, a closer look at contemporary models of "Islamic constitutions" may help to support his view, while at the same time revealing some of the contradictions inherent in the project of an "Islamic state."

Another, equally problematic, distinction should be mentioned here: that between a fixed and stable "core" of Islam and its time and place dependent "variables." Contemporary Islamists and Muslim jurists trained in the classical tradition contend that the core or essence of Islam was laid down by God and the Prophet, and cannot be affected by the changing circumstances of time and place. From this immutable core or essence, human minds derive positive norms and regulations in response to their specific needs and aspirations, which are of necessity flexible, reflecting human reasoning based on divine will, rather than divine will itself. Technically speaking, they practice *ijtihad*, which by force of legal reasoning based on the normative texts and regulated by certain procedural rules, derives the norms of social and political order, adapted to specific needs. Reason is given a prominent role in this context, but it is neither autonomous nor dissociated from divine will and guidance. The distinction between a stable core and its variable derivations may seem plausible, or even necessary, if the relevance and vitality of the Islamic message are to be preserved under the most diverse circumstances. But it is essentially arbitrary and subject to variation. For it is not God who made this distinction, but human beings, whose frail and fallible nature Islamists never cease to emphasise.

The distinction between the "core" and dependent "variables," the "stable" and the "flexible" constituents of Islam, is largely based on concepts of Islamic jurisprudence (*fiqh*), which are transferred to the sociopolitical sphere. Islamic jurisprudence distinguishes between "duties towards God" (Arabic: *ibadat*), which include the ritual obligations of prayer, fasting, alms-giving and pilgrimage, and "duties towards other human beings" (*muamalat*), covering all other fields of life from the family and politics to the economy and international relations. "Duties towards God" are classified as part of the immutable core of Islam, while "duties towards men" – with the exception of a limited number of issues definitively laid down in the Koran and *Sunna* – are subject to change and re-definition through *ijtihad*. There are obvious parallels with the occidental distinction between the "sacred" and the "profane" which did not, of course, spring directly from the Bible, but from a long and violent history culminating in the medieval dispute on the investiture of the high clergy, during which the respective rights of royalty and the church were defined. Muslim writers tend to avoid the terms "sacred" and "profane," and emphasise that all spheres of human life are subject to divine law. Nevertheless, the differentiation between an unchangeable and a flexible domain could allow for greater autonomy of the political sphere, and prepare the way for a process of secularisation – even though secularisation is certainly not among the aims of those who make the distinction.

That Islam is both "religion and state" (*al-islam din wa-daula*) is a basic assumption shared by contemporary Islamists, who have succeeded in dominating the Islamic discourse at least on this particular issue. Politics should therefore be determined by the "values of Islam." These values are contained in the *Sharia*, which regulates and shapes all aspects of life, and which for this reason is not confined to the legal sphere. Indeed, it can be argued that the "myth of the *Sharia*" (E. Sivan) has largely replaced the caliph as the symbol of Islamic identity and unity. Hopes of justice, clarity, order, and stability, which play such a crucial role in the thought of present-day Muslims, are vested in the *Sharia*. In this respect, one cannot but note an obvious contradiction: if the *Sharia* is to guarantee unity, order and stability and if it is to provide an inviolable foundation for individual life and the social order, which cannot be challenged by men no matter how powerful, the limits of its adaptability must be narrowly defined. As all adaptation is based on human interpretation and interest, the flexibility of the *Sharia* must be limited, particularly as there is always the risk that certain groups or individuals will claim a monopoly on interpretation. This has happened in the past, not only in Iran under Khomeini, but also in Tunisia under Habib Bourguiba (no advocate of Islamic fundamentalism), and there is no reason to think that it will not be repeated in the future. The risk of political manipulation can only be countered by securing the right of the Muslim community (or the people) to political participation, and by limiting the power of the ruler within the framework of a state of law. What is required, in other words, is a democratic system of government.

The basic values which Islamists consider fundamental to an Islamic order deserve close scrutiny. Interesting, if contradictory, signals come to light which seem to support the thesis of the "Islamisation of modernity" (or is it rather the "modernisation of Islam"?). Present-day authors, including committed Islamists, identify justice and the *jihad*, i.e. any effort on the path of Islam, as basic values of an Islamic order. But they also list freedom, equality and responsibility, which were not part of classical doctrines of Islamic governance, at least not in the politicised sense meant here. This reveals the influence of modern political thought not only in the domain of "techniques," but also in the area of "values." It is true that many Muslims will argue that freedom, equality and responsibility are nothing but the expression of true and unadulterated Islam, which was falsified during the course of history through a combination of error, tyranny and usurpation. Nevertheless, from an outside perspective it is the integration of the concepts of freedom and equality into the project of an Islamic state that matters.

The question remains to what extent the general references to freedom, equality and responsibility are translated into concrete rulings concerning specific areas of law and the social order. The Islamic state is characterised by the "application of the *Sharia*." Yet what is widely perceived as divine law essentially refers to positive norms derived from the Koran and the *Sunna* by (male) Muslim jurists. Islamic jurisprudence (*fiqh*) distinguishes in detail between different categories of people, who in important areas of private and public life do not enjoy equality before the law: men and women, Muslims and non-Muslims and, in pre-modern times, freemen and slaves. Consequently, the principle of equality can only be realised if the regulations of traditional *fiqh* were revised and the relevant stipulations of the Koran and *Sunna* given a radical re-interpretation. One way of doing this would be to refer to the ultimate objectives of the *Sharia*, its finality (*maqasid al-sharia*), and to the public interest (*al-maslaha al-amma*) which in cases of conflict are strong enough to overrule discriminating prescriptions of the law.

Many Muslim men and women – even some who regard themselves as Islamists – believe that this objective is attainable. It clearly presupposes extensive *ijtihad*. But what kind of political framework would such a revision require? Who should be authorised to define Islamic norms? Would Islam not be forced to sacrifice some of its traditional openness and plurality so that limits may be set – at least on the level of individual states or regions? To what extent should Muslim scholars and religious experts be involved, and what would be the role of the elected representatives of the people? The crucial question of legislative authority and political power is mentioned in the relevant literature, but it has yet to be given more rigorous thought.

The Islamic republic

As has been emphasised, there is no longer a universal model for an Islamic state – not even the caliphate, which began to decline in the Middle Ages, was abolished in 1924 by the newly established Turkish Republic and despite various attempts has not been re-established since. Even *Sunni* Islamists differ in their visions of an Islamic order which reflects the spirit of "true Islam" while at the same time meeting the demands of the modern age. It is nonetheless possible to sketch its essential outlines on the basis of a large body of written sources which include several detailed model constitutions.

There is general agreement that sovereignty in the Islamic state lies with God alone. In this sense it is a theocracy. God is not the political head of the polity, however. In the *Sunni* view, His direct intervention in the form of revelation ended with the death of the Prophet Mohammed. Divine sovereignty is manifested in the *Sharia* which contains the norms and values ruling human existence and the entire universe. The authority to "implement" God's law, which in medieval treatises on Islamic governance was the preserve of the imam or caliph assisted by the *ulama*, extends to the community of the faithful in its entirety. The faithful are equal before God. According to classical *fiqh*, this does not imply that they are equal before the law. Some authors, including committed Islamists, go beyond this to assert the equality of all human beings as descendants of Adam, on whom God has bestowed dignity and whom He has set on this earth as His trustees and representatives. The Koranic notion of human dignity and basic equality of all human beings regardless of gender, race or religious affiliation, could make a significant contribution to Islamic concepts of human rights. It requires further elaboration, however, and an effort to bring the general guidelines of the Koran as understood by these authors into harmony with the prescriptions of *Sharia* and *fiqh*.

It is commonly accepted that the "ruler" (the *imam*, caliph, or President) is no more than the representative of the community of believers (*umma*) from whom he derives his authority. In accordance with modern usage, it is often said that "all power originates in the *umma*." This constitutes a radical departure from medieval doctrines which held that the ruler, though subject to the *Sharia*, was God's representative or "shadow on earth." Modern *Sunni* writings paint a different picture: like any other human being, the Islamic head of state is responsible before God, but he is also answerable to the community (the latter is often referred to as the "nation" or the "people," allowing the possibility that non-Muslims or unbelievers may be included). In many respects, his position is similar to that of the American, French or Russian President. On the basis of its institutions, therefore, the Islamic state could be compared to a presidential republic – although its purpose as defined by the constitution would mark it as quite distinct.

As the Islamic state is founded on the *Sharia* with the explicit mandate to implement Islamic law and values, it cannot be neutral with regard to ethical and religious issues. This does not imply that the ruler or the authorities enjoy religious status. They are not "sacred," at least not for the *Sunni* majority who differs on this point from the Shiite minority who believes in the superior status of the *imams*. For present-day *Sunnis*, there is no place in Islam for a prince who rules by the grace of God, nor does the clergy hold the reigns of power. (In the *Sunni* understanding, Islam does not have any clergy.) The head of state may have religiously defined duties – he must apply the *Sharia*, defend the faith and lead the faithful in prayer – but he has no religious authority and is only authorised to interpret the law if he is properly qualified as a legal scholar (*alim*). *Sunni* Muslims do not accept Khomeini's doctrine of the "guardianship of the jurisconsult" (*wilayat al-faqih*) which, incidentally, is also disputed by high-ranking Shiite authorities because it presupposes a well-defined hierarchy among the class of scholars and assigns political leadership to the "most able one" among them.

With regard to the institutions and procedures regulating political life in the Islamic republic to be, the influence of Western models is obvious. These include the principles of representation and majority rule, the separation of powers and the independence of the judiciary. The adoption and adaptation of such principles are justified, and by the same token "Islamised," in terms of the Koran and *Sunna*. Thus the establishment of a consultative assembly as the Islamic counterpart of a Western parliament is based on the Koranic verses calling upon the faithful to practice "*shura*," i.e. to consult with each other on all important matters. Insofar as it is appropriate to consider these institutions and procedures as "techniques," considerable modernisation has taken place, for the current repertory of ideas and institutions would have been as alien to the scholars of classical Islam as to the thinkers of the European Middle Ages.

What has been preserved from classical doctrines is the characteristic reluctance to recognise the legitimacy of private interests and political dissent. According to our authors, consultation and decision-making must be guided entirely by the common good and must be free from personal interest, which is condemned as selfish and divisive. *Shura* is not meant to be a platform for different – and potentially antagonistic – ideas and interests. Its purpose rather is to even out divergent opinions and to preserve unity and harmony on the basis of the much-cited "framework of Islam," the *Sharia*. Argument and debate are not viewed as positively as they are in certain Western circles. On the contrary, there is a strong yearning for unity and harmony. The fact that reality in the Muslim world falls short of these ideals (in this it does not differ from reality elsewhere), merely helps to explain their ongoing appeal.

What are the implications of the debate on values, moral as well as democratic, for relations between "the West" and the Muslim world? It would be a significant achievement if both sides could be persuaded to devote the same level of critical evaluation to the theory and practice of the other as it demands for its own position. People living in the West would be well advised to take note of contemporary Islamic models of society and the state, which are not simply the outgrowth of outdated patterns of Islamic thought and lifestyles, but which reflect present-day needs and aspirations. Islamists should not be condemned as medieval or crypto-fascist simply because they see Islam as the only alternative to existing political systems and ideologies. Whereas it is important to denounce and combat intolerance, violence and authoritarianism among Islamists, or for that matter among any other political group engaged in the present debates and conflicts, the values shared by Muslims and non-Muslims must not be ignored.

Bibliography

Abd al-Karim, Khalil. 1995. *Al-islam baina al-daula al-diniyya wa-l-daula al-madaniyya* (Islam between a Religious and a Civil State). Cairo: Sina li-l-Nashr.

Aldeeb Abu-Sahlieh, Sami A. 1994. *Les Musulmans face aux droits de l'homme. Religion & droit & politique. Étude et documents*. Bochum: Dr. Dieter Winkler.

Ali, Haidar Ibrahim. 1996. *Al-tayyarat al-islamiyya wa-qadiyyat al-dimuqratiyya* (The Islamist Tendencies and the Question of Democracy). Beyrouth: Markaz Dirasat al-Wahda al-Arabiyya.

Ammara, Muhammad. 1988. *Al-daula al-islamiyya baina al-almaniyya wa-l-sulta al-diniyya* (The Islamic State between Secularism and Religious Authority). Cairo/Beyrouth: Dar Al-Shuruq.

Asad, Muhammad. 1980. *The Principles of State and Government in Islam*, new ed. Gibraltar: Dar al-Andalus.

Al-Awwa, Muhammad Salim. 1989. *Al-nizam al-siyasi li-l-daula al-islamiyya* (*The Political Organisation of the Islamic State*), 6th ed. Cairo/Beyrouth: Dar al-Shuruq.

Badry, Roswitha. 1998. *Die zeitgenössische Diskussion um den islamischen Beratungsgedanken (Shura)*. Stuttgart: Franz Steiner.

Binder, Leonard. 1988. *Islamic Liberalism. A Critique of Development Ideologies*. Chicago/London: The University of Chicago Press.

Burgat, François. 1995. *L'islamisme en face*. Paris: Édition La Découverte.

Enayat, Hamid, 1982. *Modern Islamic Political Thought*. Austin: University of Texas Press.

Esposito, John and John Voll. 1996. *Islam and Democracy*. Oxford: Oxford University Press.

Framework of an Islamic State. 1982. *The Muslim World League Journal*, April: 29–34.

Al-Ghannushi, Rashid. 1993. *Al-hurriyyat al-amma fi l-daula al-islamiyya* (Public Rights in the Islamic State). Beyrouth: Markaz Dirasat al-Wahda al-Arabiyya.

Huwaidi, Fahmi. 1992. *Al-islam wa-l-dimuqratiyya* (Islam and Democracy). Cairo: Markaz al-Ahram li-l-Tarjama wa-l-Nashr, Muassasat al-Ahram.

Jarisha, Ali (ed.) 1985. *Ilan dusturi islami* (Proclamation of an Islamic Constitution). Al-Mansura: Dar al-Wafa li-l-Tibaa wa-l-Nashr wa-l-Tauzi.

Jedaane, Fahmi. 1987. "Notions of the State in Contemporary Arab–Islamic Writings." In *The Foundations of the Arab State*, edited by Ghassan Salamé, 112–148. London et al.: Croom Helm.

Jürgensen, Carsten. 1994. *Demokratie und Menschenrechte in der arabischen Welt*. Hamburg: Deutsches Orient-Institut.

Kedourie, Elie. 1992. *Democracy and Arab Political Culture*. Washington, D.C.: Frank Cass.

Khalid, Khalid Muhammed. 1985. *Difa an al-dimuqratiyya* (In Defense of Democracy). Cairo (no publisher listed).

Al-Khalidi, Mahmud. 1986. *Al-dimuqratiyya al-gharbiyya fi dau al-sharia al-islamiyya* (Western democracy in the light of Islamic sharia). Amman (no publisher listed).

Krämer, Gudrun. 1994. "The Integration of the Integrists: a Comparative Study of Egypt, Jordan and Tunisia." In *Democracy Without Democrats? The Renewal of Politics in the Muslim World*, edited by Ghassan Salamé, 200–226. London/New York: Tauris.

Krämer, Gudrun. 1995. "Cross-Links and Double Talk? Islamist Movements in the Political Process." In *The Islamist Dilemma. The Political Role of Islamist Movements in the Contemporary Arab World*, edited by Laura Guazzone, 39–67. Reading: Ithaca Press.

Krämer, Gudrun. 1999. *Gottes Staat als Republik*. Baden-Baden: Nomos.

Kramer, Martin. 1993. Islam vs. Democracy. *Commentary* 1: 35–42.

Lewis, Bernard. 1993. Islam and Liberal Democracy. *The Atlantic Monthly*, February: 89–98.

Maududi, S.A.A. 1969. *The Islamic Law and Constitution*. Dacca.

Mayer, Ann Elizabeth (ed.). 1991. *Islam and Human Rights. Tradition and Politics*. Boulder: Westview.

Moussalli, Ahmad S. 1995. "Modern Islamic Fundamentalist Discourses on Civil Society, Pluralism and Democracy." In *Civil Society in the Middle East*, Vol. 1, edited by Augustus Richard Norton, 79–119. Leiden: Brill.

Al-Qaradawi, Yusuf. 1994. *Fatawa muasira* (Contemporary Responsa), 3rd ed. Al-Mansura: Dar al-Wafa li-l-Tibaa wa-l-Nashr wa-l-Tauzi.

Ramadan, Tariq. 1995. *Islam, le face à face des civilisations. Quel projet pour quelle modernité?* Lyon: Edition Tawhid.

Al-Rayyis, Muhammad Diya' al-Din. 1979. *Al-nazariyyat al-siyasiyya al-islamiyya* (Islamic Political Theories), 7th ed. Cairo: Maktabat Dar al-Turath.

Al-Shawi, Taufiq. 1992. *Fiqh al-shura wa-l-istishara* (The Rules and Regulations of Consultation). Al-Mansura: Dar al-Wafa li-l-Tibaa wa-l-Nashr wa-l-Tauzi.

Schwartländer, Johannes (ed.). 1993. *Freiheit der Religion. Christentum und Islam unter dem Anspruch der Menschenrechte*. Mainz: Grünewald.

Sivan, Emmanuel. 1995. *Mythes politiques arabes*. Paris: Fayard.

Tamimi, Azzam (ed.). 1993. *Power-Sharing Islam?* London: Liberty for Muslim World.

Tibi, Bassam. 1993. *Islamischer Fundamentalismus, moderne Wissenschaft und Technologie*, 2nd ed. Frankfurt: Suhrkamp.

Turabi, Hassan. 1983. "The Islamic State." In *Voices of Resurgent Islam*, edited by John Esposito, 241–249. New York/Oxford: Oxford University Press.

Zartman, I. William. 1992. Democracy and Islam: The Cultural Dialectic. *Annals. Journal of the American Academy of Political and Social Science* 524: 181–191.

James Piscatori

RELIGION AND REALPOLITIK
Islamic responses to the Gulf War

*T*HE FOLLOWING IS THE *first chapter of* Islamic Fundamentalisms and the Gulf Crisis, *edited by James Piscatori of the University of Wales. The book draws upon the expertise of participants in* The Fundamentalism Project, *a five-year interdisciplinary cross-cultural study of modern religious fundamentalisms conducted by the Academy with support from the John D. and Catherine T. MacArthur Foundation. The Project Director is Martin E. Marty, and the Associate Project Director is R. Scott Appleby (both of the University of Chicago).*

Commissioned in response to the Gulf crisis, the essays in this volume describe the major Islamic fundamentalist movements active in the nations of the region, review the rhetorical and organizational reactions of these movements to the Gulf crisis, and assess how both the crisis and the Islamic response affected the status and salience of each movement.

In the Gulf crisis of 1990–91, Saddam Hussein confidently promised the decisive victory against the forces of Western imperialism, but he will be remembered for another uncommon, and unexpected, achievement. He brought his regime and country to the brink of complete ruin, and yet, in the process, millions of Muslims throughout the world, often to the discomfort of their own governments, acclaimed him a Muslim hero. Although his air force and army embarrassingly took flight or dissolved, he gained in stature for standing alone against the mighty, principally American, military force arrayed against him. Moreover, his Scud missile attacks on Israel, though they inflicted relatively little actual damage, earned him immense credit for widening the conflict to the Arabs' nemesis. In effect, Saddam's invasion of Kuwait on 2 August 1990 and the diplomatic and military crisis that ensued not only challenged the region's interstate stability, but also emphasized the central importance that religion has in the political crises of the Muslim world.

Saddam did not always appreciate the power that religion exercises on the minds of men. But apparently on the eve of battle, he rallied his senior commanders by emotionally invoking God as the architect of the imminent war. "It is the Lord who wanted what has happened to happen. Our role in this decision is almost zero." Warming to his theme, he declared that, as the symbol of the Republican party was the elephant, the Qur'anic story of the defeat of the forces equipped with elephants which had attacked Mecca was a portent of the Iraqi victory to come. He was moved to cite the appropriate verses: "See you not how the Lord dealt with the companions of the elephant? Did He not make their treacherous plan go astray?" A tape recording of the meeting reveals that cries could be heard from the audience, "Yes, Mr. President, how history repeats itself!"

Prior to the Gulf crisis and particularly the dispatch of Western forces to Saudi Arabia, there were few in the Arab or Muslim world, except perhaps his most sycophantic supporters, who would have put Saddam in the front rank of defenders of Islam and of the pan-Islamic community (umma). Rather, the Ba'thist ideology to which he ascribed made the Arab nation the focal point and invested it with both socialist and secular meanings. The "republic of fear" which he systematically constructed in the name of these principles brooked no dissent, and politicized Shi'ite groups, which could conceivably stoke the fires of open rebellion among the Shi'ite majority of Iraq, were seen as especially dangerous. It was a regime terrifyingly consistent and lacking in all subtlety: any opponent – Shi'ite or Kurd, religious leader or Ba'thist apparatchik, man or woman – who defied the whim of Saddam's regime was eliminated. Ayatollah Muhammad Baqir al-Sadr, one of the preeminent religious authorities of the Shi'ite world, and his sister were publicly hanged in April 1980. This event evoked the Shi'ite traditional sense of oppression and martyrdom and hence became an emblem of Saddam's anti-Islamic brutality.

The ill-advised war with revolutionary and non-Arab Iran from 1980 to 1988 may arguably have added luster to Saddam's self-promoted image as defender of the Arab nation. But it also confirmed the universal view that Islam was, at best, of secondary importance to him. Referring to the celebrated battle in 637 at which Arab Muslims decisively defeated the non-Muslim Sassanid Persians, he scored a limited legitimizing point when he boasted that the battle with Iran, joined in September 1980, would soon yield another "Qadisiyya." However, the war was to grind on for eight bloody years, and Iraqi Shi'ite opposition groups, such as those which Amatzia Baram discusses, found natural support in the Iranian regime. While Tehran's Islamic rhetoric was as patently contrived for maximum domestic effect as was Saddam's Arabism, its demonization of Saddam fell on receptive ears in the broader Muslim world. Ayatollah Khomeini repeatedly spoke of the war as pitting faith against unbelief (kufr), and Saddam was relegated to the disagreeable company of the Shah of Iran, Ronald Reagan, and Menachem Begin as archenemies of Islam.

Saddam's recent transformation into Muslim hero – in many, though certainly not all, Muslim circles – were thus all the more striking. A number of complex factors were at work, and, in this story, the emotional appeal of the Palestinian issue, latent anger at the arrogant, nouveau riche states of the Gulf which had invited foreign troops into the holy peninsula, and a lingering suspicion of Western motives all played their part. Yet there were also limitations on the ability of Muslim movements and groups to maximize their position as a result of the Gulf crisis, and it must be seen as having both provided opportunities for and imposed constraints on the political agenda of Muslim fundamentalists.

Saddam and the political symbolism of Islam

The prevalence of anti-Saudi and anti-Israeli allusions in the rhetoric of Saddam Hussein and his regime was not simply accidental. "Saudi Arabia" and "Palestine" are emotionally charged, interconnected symbols in the Muslim political imagination. Together they represent the holiest cities of Islam – Mecca and Medina in Saudi Arabia, and Jerusalem in Palestine – which formed the setting in which the Prophet Muhammad lived his life. Even secularized Ba'thists could not have avoided the pervasiveness of these symbols and the meanings that they convey.

Born in the Arabian trading town of Mecca around A.D. 570, Muhammad began to receive the Revelation there. Forced to leave because of the hostility of his polytheistic townsmen, he and his early followers migrated to a nearby town in 622. Renamed Medina ("the city"), it became the seat of the first, and generally archetypical, Islamic state. The year of the migration (*hijra*) is now considered the first year of the Muslim calendar. The continuing relevance of these founding events of Islam is also affirmed by the obligation that Muslims have, if at all possible, to undertake a pilgrimage (*hajj*) once in their lives to Mecca. One of the five pillars of the Islamic faith, the pilgrimage has entailed great physical and financial hardships for Muslims throughout history, and the title "Hajji" has thus carried enviable social prestige. Medina, the final resting place of the Prophet, has also become a special place of devotion, and, although doctrine does not require it, tradition encourages a visit to the Prophet's mosque.

Jerusalem is central to the Muslim world-view because it is believed to be connected to two extraordinary journeys of the Prophet. The first is the "nocturnal journey" (*isra*) when the Prophet was transported on a winged horse from Mecca to Jerusalem in one night. According to the traditions, Muhammad met there Abraham, Moses, and Jesus, and the general journey is memorialized in the Qur'an: "Glory to Him who caused His servant to journey by night from the sacred place of worship [Mecca] to the further place of worship, which We have encircled with blessings, in order that We might show him some of our signs" (xvii: i). Although the Qur'an does not specify the exact location, that "further place" is now enshrined in al-Aqsa mosque (literally, "the further mosque") in Jerusalem, on the site that Muslims call "al-Haram al-Sharif" or "the Noble Precinct" and that Jews call the "Temple Mount," where they believe Solomon's temple once stood.

The second journey, which in most (but not all) accounts follows immediately from this nocturnal journey, is the Prophet's ascension to heaven (*mi'raj*). With his foot on a rock in the area of al-Haram al-Sharif, he ascended accompanied by the archangel Gabriel. Muhammad passed through the seven heavens and encountered God's earlier prophets along the way. When he reached the throne of Allah in the highest heaven, he was taught how the obligatory prayers must be performed. The Dome of the Rock, near to al-Aqsa mosque in the Haram area, stands as a visible reminder of this second journey.

Both Arabian and Palestinian lands are thus special preserves, and, because of this, they take on a wider importance, particularly in the competition for legitimacy that characterizes politics in the Middle East. The Palestinian dimension of Muslim politics is illustrative of this point.

The linkage between Arab and Muslim concern over Zionism in Palestine had existed since at least 1931 when the Jerusalem Congress, ostensibly called to revive the caliphate, attempted to put developments in Palestine on the Muslim agenda. But, after 1967 when Israel occupied Jerusalem and the West Bank, the matter assumed a far greater urgency. The religious officials (*ulama*) of al-Azhar, the venerable Islamic university in Cairo, had talked in 1956 of Israel as one of the "imperialist countries" and focused on the dangers of the Western-inspired Baghdad Pact. But now with Israeli occupation of one of Islam's defining centers, the discourse reflected a decidedly Islamic concern. In 1968, an international gathering of ulama condemned Israeli activities as an attack on the very fabric of Islamic Jerusalem: "[The usurpers] tore down several Muslim sites, including mosques, schools, and homes, all of which were held by religious endowments (*awqaf*)." Even more worrisome, the Zionists had detestable "schemes" for al-Aqsa mosque, "the first holy place in Islam."

When Saddam Hussein launched his "initiative" of 12 August, explicitly linking his withdrawal from Kuwait with Israeli withdrawal from the occupied territories, he was exploiting the profound sentiment which had become the Arab – and Muslim – consensus. It was, on one level, an obvious political ploy, a cost-free way of attempting to divert attention. He appeared to strike a blow for Palestinian liberation without doing a great deal to accomplish it. But by explicitly shifting focus to the Arab–Israeli conflict and restoring the question of Palestine to pride of place, he was, on another level, tapping into deep springs of Muslim concern. In the words of Shaikh Abd al-Aziz Bin Baz, the paramount religious scholar of Saudi Arabia, "the Palestinian problem is an Islamic problem first and last," and Muslims "must fight an Islamic *jihad* against the Jews until the land returns to its owners." In the case of Jordan, when Saddam gave expression to this consensus in his own inimitable manner, he found favor, if he had not already, on the streets of the Muslim world.

But as the theology is all of a piece, so too the political symbolism of Palestine is inevitably linked to that of the Arabian peninsula. Saddam was able to argue that, like Palestine, the land containing the holy cities of Mecca and Medina had itself fallen prey to occupation. He spoke of the need to liberate Mecca, "hostage of the Americans," from troops of the Western-led coalition. "Until the voice of right rises up in the Arab world, hit their interests wherever they are and rescue holy Mecca and rescue the grave of the Prophet Muhammad in Medina."

The response in the Muslim world to this call for jihad was not hesitant. A preacher at al-Aqsa mosque in Jerusalem sharply condemned the Saudi leadership before a congregation of some 10,000 worshippers: "Arab leaders are giving Moslem lands to the Americans." In Jordan, the Muslim Brotherhood called on Muslims "to purge the holy land of Palestine and Najd and Hijaz [provinces of Saudi Arabia] from the Zionists and imperialists." About 400 protestors shouted "shame" and "death to Fahd" outside the Saudi embassy in Belgrave Square in London; they were disturbed by the Saudis' seeming willingness to have their country occupied by "the enemies of Islam." Even among Muslims as far away from the Arab world as China, some believed that the dispatch of Western troops to Saudi Arabia had violated the integrity of Muslim territory. As a result, they felt that Islam had been insulted and that Saddam's opposition to the foreign troops deserved support.

These criticisms of Saudi policy were the latest version of the special derision which has been reserved for a monarchy that has referred to itself as "custodian of the Holy Places." In the eyes of many Muslims, the self-designation has been sententious at best and hypocritical at worst. Indeed, from the time in 1924 that the Saudi regime conquered Mecca, its control of the holy places and pilgrimage exercised the concern of great numbers of Muslims throughout the world. Many feared that Wahhabi opposition to folk practices and especially to the veneration of the Prophet himself and Muslim saints would lead it to destroy such shrines as the Prophet's tomb and force Shi'ite pilgrims to adopt Wahhabi practices. In the early nineteenth century, Wahhabi ancestors had attacked the shrine of Imam Hussein, the Prophet's martyred grandson, in Karbala in Iraq and destroyed a cemetery of special Shi'ite significance outside of Mecca. Bad feelings persisted, and only gradually did the new Saudi regime of King Abd al-Aziz (ca. 1880–1953) manage to reassure pilgrims throughout the world that it would not interfere in their religious duty. Formerly dependent to a significant extent on hajj revenues, the newly oil-rich Saudi regime began to spend large amounts of money on preserving the shrines and improving housing and sanitation conditions. In the process, guardianship of the pilgrimage and of Mecca and Medina became the heart of its formula for legitimacy.

Claiming in effect to be the protector of Islam, the Saudi royal family thereby made itself vulnerable to constant scrutiny and invited the scorn of other would-be protectors. Muammar Qaddafi, the erratic leader of Libya, accused the Saudis of defiling the holy places by allowing their American-made military aircraft to fly in the air space above Mecca and Medina, and called for their internationalization. Since the revolution in 1979, the Iranians have seen the Saudis as their natural rival for leadership of the Muslim world, and historical antipathies have been revived. The Iranian assault has, as a consequence, been sustained and insistent. For example, Ayatollah Khomeini, in his last will and testament, mocked the efforts of the Saudis in distributing Qur'ans throughout the world and called Wahhabism an "aggressive sect" (al-madhhab al-mu'adi) that leads unsuspecting people to be controlled by the superpowers, whose aim is to destroy true Islam."

The Iranians' desire to use the great cosmopolitan occasion of the pilgrimage to advance their notions of Islamic revolution naturally inspired agitation in Riyadh, and the stage was set for the often violent confrontations of the past decade. Small Iranian demonstrations occurred in the pilgrimage of 1980, but in 1981 and 1982 there were serious clashes between Iranian pilgrims and the Saudi security forces. In 1986, Iranian pilgrims who were thought to be importing arms were arrested and prevented from undertaking the hajj. The 1987 pilgrimage, however, was to prove the most violent, with 402 pilgrims killed and Saudi Arabia and Iran blaming each other. Iran convened an international conference to discuss the future of the holy places, but it accomplished little except to concentrate the anti-Saudi rhetoric that was already flowing from pro-Iranian circles in the Muslim world. Although Iran formally boycotted the hajj from 1987 to 1990, there were explosions during the 1989 pilgrimage, and in 1990 the Saudi reputation for efficient management was not enhanced when over 1,400 pilgrims were crushed to death in a tunnel. Hizbullah, a radical Lebanese Shi'ite group, spoke of "a new massacre," and Iran referred darkly to a "criminal conspiracy" and called for the Saudis to be stripped of their custodianship of the holy places.

Against this background Saddam Hussein leveled his attack on the Saudi regime for allowing Western, non-Muslim troops into the kingdom. Having faced a withering barrage of criticism for a considerable period of time, the Saudis were careful to secure a *fatwa* (religious ruling) from Shaikh Bin Baz, which sanctioned the presence of "diverse nationalities among the Muslims and others for the resistance of aggression and the defense of the country." The council of senior religious officials also specifically endorsed the King's decision and said that the *Shari'a* (Islamic law) required both that the Muslim ruler be prepared to defend Muslim land and that he "seek the help of whoever has the power that enables them to perform the task." Another fatwa in January 1991 sanctioned the use of force against the Iraqis and declared the battle against Saddam a jihad. Non-Muslim soldiers had an important role to play in defeating "the enemy of God."

But even Bin Baz's casuistic relegation of Western troops to the obscure category of "others" (*ghayhum*) could not disguise the fact that the vast majority of the half million troops on Saudi soil were not Muslim. Nor, apparently, did Saudi restrictions on the practice of Christian and Jewish religious services among the foreign troops defuse internal disquiet. Some religious scholars appear to have felt that the presence of Western troops violated the moral integrity of the holy peninsula and that the foreigners harbored their own nefarious goals. For example, Safar al-Hawali, dean of Islamic studies at Umm al-Qura University in Mecca and a well-known popular preacher, has chastised his fellow Muslims for putting their trust in the United States rather than in God: "America has become your God." Citing sources as diverse as the traditions of the Prophet, the memoirs of Richard Nixon, and *Foreign Affairs*, he concluded that the Westerners had long been looking for a pretext to occupy the Muslim heartland. Another scholar, Sulaiman al-Uwda, dean at the Muhammad Bin Saud University in Qasim, directed his fire closer to home. In a scarcely veiled reference to the royal family, he warned that nations decline when rulers maintain themselves in power through corruption and resist the Islamic duty of consultation with the ulama and others. Robert Fisk of the British newspaper *The Independent* reported on an unnamed religious official who pointedly asked him, "When are the Americans leaving?" An *imam* (prayer leader) at a Riyadh mosque asked somewhat more obliquely but not impenetrably, "If a dog has come onto your land, would you invite a lion to get rid of it?"

The apprehension, in fact, seemed to grow with time. According to reports, a number of ulama gave a detailed memorandum to the King on 18 May 1991 which outlined a comprehensive program of reform. It ostensibly called for the creation of a *majlis al-shura*, or consultative assembly, whose members would be chosen according to competence, and not according to rank or sex; "Islamization" of the judiciary, military, economy, and media; and abstention from all "non-Islamic pacts and treaties." The last clearly referred to the concern that the continuing presence of Western troops on Saudi soil produced. The memorandum may have been intended to pressure King Fahd into abdicating in favor of the Crown Prince, Abdullah, who is generally more acceptable to the ulama. But the most senior ulama issued a statement on 3 June which condemned the public manner in which the memorandum was presented, and pointedly reminded Saudis of the "bounty of security, stability, [and] unanimity" which the Saudi regime has presumably provided. But in endorsing the Islamic principles of consultation and advice between ruler and ruled in certain circumstances, and, rather cagily, in not specifically rejecting the reforms demanded, the senior ulama failed to dispel the sense of disquiet in the kingdom which the Gulf crisis helped to create.

Saddam exploited this profound sense of unease, and when he spoke of the Saudis having sold out to the Americans, he struck a responsive chord. His natural Ba'thist predilection would have been to denounce them both in anti-imperialist terms, but to invoke now the resonant terms of "infidel" and "jihad" served the same purpose and, in the circumstances, may have been more effective. Certainly, a significant portion of the Muslim public across the world was instinctively dubious of Saddam's Islamic qualifications; his brutal anti-Shi'ite policies at home were well known after all. And there is no reason to believe that the use of words like "jihad" automatically entails a social and political response; an Islamic vocabulary takes on specific meaning only in the context in which it is applied. Yet the context in this case was that infidel troops on Arabian soil had exposed the Saudi monarchy to the delegitimizing charge that it was consorting with the infidels and, by extension, with their natural allies, the Zionists.

When Saddam asked why his troops should withdraw from Arab land when the Israelis remained unopposed in their occupation of Arab land, he found a sympathetic hearing. It was preeminently seen as a matter of justice and fair play, but the Muslim proprietary interest in Palestine was also at work. When he said that the Saudis, by allowing Western troops on their soil, were now effectively in league with the Israelis, he drew the two powerfully related symbols of Muslim politics together: the sanctity of both Arabia and Palestine was really at stake, and he, Saddam, was the new Saladin, the restorer of Islamic rule to the holy lands.

The Muslim "street" and the fundamentalist response

Despite the political symbolism, the leadership of the Islamic movement across the Muslim world faced a dilemma: on the one hand, sentiment from the rank and file of membership was clearly in favor of Saddam, yet on the other hand, their very organizations were often financially dependent on the Gulf states, particularly Saudi Arabia and Kuwait.

Feelings from below were pronounced, partly for the reasons of political symbolism already cited. But other factors were also involved. First, the entire range of discontents that emanate from developing, inefficient, over-bureaucratized, and undemocratic societies crystallized in the illogical but no less real hope for some release. For example, Jordanians, including East Bank bedouins, had rioted as recently as April 1989, and despite the holding of parliamentary elections in November 1989, widespread discontent continued in the face of manifold and intransigent economic difficulties. Palestinians, the majority of inhabitants of Jordan, bore both the added grievance of opposition to Israeli occupation and a sense of disappointment that the *intifada*, the uprising in the occupied territories, had achieved so little in three years of near-constant turmoil. Similarly in Algeria, as Hugh Roberts points out, the perception that the socialist regime had wrought economic failure and moral bankruptcy stimulated civil unrest. Local elections in June 1990 ended in the rout of the ruling party, but far from being appeased, popular dissatisfaction was encouraged. In such situations, Saddam's claim to be striking a blow for liberation had its distracting appeal.

Second, the popular pro-Saddam sentiment that was found in many, but not all, places was fueled by the distinct unpopularity of the Gulf monarchies. Ostentatiously wealthy and often arrogantly claiming that God had chosen them for special favor, the "Gulfis" have incurred the envy, and more often the enmity, of poorer Arabs and Muslims. Despite the vast amounts of petro-dollars that they have expended in the causes of Arab brotherhood and Muslim unity and the good works that have undeniably been accomplished as a result, the Gulf Arab regimes have become widely synonymous with corruption, insincerity, and licentious, un-Islamic conduct. Though at some remove, one observer typically commented, "We Muslims in China are twice as devout as the Saudi and Kuwaiti shaikhs who spend their money in the brothels of Southeast Asia and Bahrain."

Related to this unflattering representation of the Gulf monarchies has been the mirror image of "riyalpolitik" that has developed (the riyal is the Saudi unit of currency). Rather than making gains as the result of the judicious usage of their financial resources, these states have lost influence among the Arab masses. This has occurred because of the perception that Gulf wealth, effectively subsidizing the American economy, is indirectly in turn supporting Israel. The Palestinian writer Sahar Khalifeh makes the point in her novel *Wild Thorns* [London: Al Saqi Books, 1985]: "They were listening to the news on a transistor radio. The American Secretary of Defense had made a new statement about arms shipments to Israel. Phantom jets. More and more Phantoms. Billions of dollars flooding into Israel's treasury. The old men muttered grim prayers, praising God and invoking blessings on the people of the Prophet Muhammad. The young men cursed and blasphemed. ... Arab oil revenue turned into Phantoms! So much for Arab unity!"

Third, in addition to the hope of escape from pressing social and economic difficulties and the unpopularity of the Gulf monarchies, latent suspicions of Western intentions in the Muslim world played into Saddam's hand. Much has been written about the supposed antipathy of Islam and the West, and the received wisdom appeared to acquire a new vitality during the Gulf crisis. A. M. Rosenthal wrote in the *New York Times* that "somehow the passion of Muslims against the West is presented as inevitable, unstoppable, a terrifying phenomenon based on justified anger and the Koran."

Such analyses, however, which build on the simplistic notion of an engrained "Muslim rage," must be set against the complex history of interaction between Islam and the West. Civilizations rarely, if ever, act as monolithic entities with single-minded, doctrinally defined interests or passions. As Islamic history demonstrates, political pluralism has been the norm within the Muslim world, and between it and the West there has been a pattern of alternating cooperation and competition, alliance and violent confrontation. Moreover, Muslim identities have been influenced by a variety of social experiences – race, class, nation, ethnicity, and education, among them. Political circumstance can also be consequential, at least in the short run. As Amatzia Baram points out, the Iraqi Shi'ites, while linking the Zionist enemy with Western imperialism, obviously found themselves on the same side as the West during the Gulf crisis. The result was a notable absence of rhetorical assault on the West in general and the United States in particular.

Yet anti-Westernism is surely not absent from the Muslim world, and its presence contributed to Saddam's popularity. Indeed, recognition of the variableness of the relationship between Islam and the West should not obscure the fact that the common historical memory of Muslims – as gauged by their rhetoric – largely dates today not from the distant Crusades, as is often assumed, but from the beginning of this century. As Jean-François Legrain makes clear in his discussion of the Palestinian

Muslims' response to the Gulf crisis, if they used the word "Crusade," they meant to signify neither wholehearted support for Saddam nor that any general struggle against the West was to take precedence over that for the liberation of Palestine. The memory that weighs heavily on the minds of the great generality of Muslims is of imperialist rule, Western antagonism toward Arab nationalism, the creation and fortifying of the state of Israel, and American hostility toward the Islamic revolution in Iran. The West has had its moments of a relatively benign image, of course, such as the one enjoyed by the United States in the wake of its opposition to the tripartite aggression against Egypt in the Suez crisis of 1956. But these have proved to be short-lived.

Washington, as well as London and Paris, has tended to have precious little political capital of a sustained kind in the Muslim world, and it has become an often bewildering fact of life that regardless of the act, the hand of Western imperialism is seen to be behind it. In the Gulf crisis, many thought it villainous that the United States, long tolerant of Saddam, had now turned so decisively against him. Mumtaz Ahmad quotes the influential intellectual and one of the leaders of Jamaat-i-Islami of Pakistan, Khurshid Ahmad: "The trap was to entangle Iraq in war so that it could provide the United States with a chance to interfere and advance its sinister design – to give an edge to Israel in the region and to control the Muslim oil." Similarly, al-Jama'a al-Islamiyya (The Islamic Group) in Morocco said the aim of the West was not to liberate Kuwait, but "to destroy the economic and military structures of Iraq which constitute an Arab force, with the goal of establishing a strong Israel and mastery over Arab oil wealth." Gehad Auda notes that the leader of the Jihad Organization of Egypt believed that one of the American objectives was to recondition the Muslim mind to accept humiliation and the supremacy of the West. The Jordanian newspaper *al-Ra'i* spoke of the people of the United States, Britain, and France as the "real enemies" of the Arabs, and a Moroccan policeman told a British reporter, "The West not only wants to destroy Iraq, but also to destabilize the whole Arab world in its interests and in those of Israel."

All three factors help to explain why Saddam Hussein had a natural constituency on the Muslim streets. They also help to explain the pressure that percolated upward from "below," causing a dilemma for both governments and, ironically, their Islamic opposition. Regimes as diverse as those of Algeria, Morocco, Tunisia, Egypt, Jordan, Syria, Pakistan, Bangladesh, Indonesia, and even Britain and South Africa faced demonstrations that expressed either direct popular support for Saddam Hussein or opposition to the level of destruction that the Western-led coalition was inflicting on the Iraqi people.

Despite the fact that it had contributed troops to the anti-Iraqi coalition, the Moroccan government was aware of the depth of public sentiment against the war. In February 1991, therefore, it allowed Moroccan Islamist groups, for only the third time in their history, to take part in a huge public march to express their views. In Tunisia the government began to collect blood to send to the Iraqis, and in Algeria the government newspaper, having earlier called for a mediated settlement of the conflict, became more militant: "The battle that has begun in the Gulf is not Iraq's, but that of all the Arab and Muslim countries against the great Western powers – the United States, Britain, France, and the West's creature, Israel." The then Foreign Minister (and now Prime Minister), Sid Ahmad Ghozali, went so far as to say that Iraq and Saddam "incarnate … the spirit of resistance" to those who wish to humble the Arabs.

The effect on the Islamic fundamentalist groups and movements was more telling. Many groups throughout the Muslim world have been supported by Saudi Arabia and Kuwait, either directly through their governments or indirectly through such agencies as the Saudi-backed World Muslim League (Rabitat al-'Alam al-Islami). The Jordanian Muslim Brotherhood is a case in point, as is the Algerian Front Islamique du Salut (FIS), both of which received Saudi financial backing. Jean-Françoise Legrain points out that the Kuwaitis claimed to have given some $60 million in 1989 to HAMAS (Harakat al-Muqawama al-Islamiyya), the main Islamic group in the West Bank and Gaza Strip.

These groups would have been imprudent if they had endangered such financial links, and yet they would have been reckless if they had failed to respond to the pro-Saddam sentiments from the ranks of their membership. The result was an understandable hesitance. Hamas, for example, preferred not to dwell on the crisis and thus hoped not to divert attention from the central Palestinian problem or to alienate its Gulf supporters. Moreover, mindful that its chief rival, the Palestine Liberation Organization (PLO), had embraced Saddam, it wanted to be seen neither to be lagging in support for Iraq, nor simply to be parroting the PLO's position. Other groups, like the Muslim Brotherhood in Egypt and Jordan, similarly partially dependent on Gulf patrons but with an eye also on political competitors at home, gradually asserted their opposition to the war against Iraq. As Gehad Auda and Mumtaz Ahmad point out, these groups also felt the pressure of Muslim groups outside of their countries that had taken a more assertively antiwar position. In the particular case of Egypt, the Brotherhood hoped not to be outbid in its desire for leadership of the international Islamic movement by the Muslim Brotherhood in Sudan. In the process, although they may well have endangered medium-range relations with the Saudis and Kuwaitis, they gained in the short term by being responsive, as well as giving voice, to popular feelings at home and across the Muslim world.

It would, of course, be a mistake to accord too much significance to this sentiment from below, and Charles Krauthammer is doubtless correct to warn that opinion is rarely uniform and is inevitably controlled to some degree by the security apparatuses of the state. Yet he goes too far when he dismisses "the street" in the Arab or Muslim worlds as "an echo of the Palace." The crisis in the Gulf clearly demonstrated that Muslim opinions remain free, or at the least partially free, of government control, if not on the street, then certainly in the religious schools (*madrasas*) and the mosques. Mumtaz Ahmad points out that even though the Pakistani government sent troops to the front, the elders of Pakistani madrasas had urged their students to regard the war as one against *kufr* (unbelief). Some 80,000 students were excused from classes and joined in the national day of protest against the war.

In the case of the mosque, many regimes try to prescribe an officially sanctioned sermon (*khutba*) in the Friday service, but even when they do, imams score political points by indirection and the well-timed invocation of metaphor. The Saudi imam, for example, would be foolhardy to launch a frontal assault on the corruption of the Saudi regime, but a subtle allusion to the probity of the Caliph Umar would not fail to impress on his audience the qualities of a Muslim ruler. Frequently, the sermon is much more direct and unnuanced: "The great days of Islam, the nobility of the past are evoked; Koranic references support the arguments. The analysis is simplistic, the colours are black and white and the expression hyperbolic. The audience, largely rural and often illiterate, responds with passion." [Akbar Ahmed, "Mosque Bros.," *New Statesman & Society*, 24 May 1991].

In effect, whether in Muslim demonstrations on the street, in lessons in the school, or in sermons in the mosque, "Islam" provides the arena in which political, and largely oppositional, sentiments can be expressed. In this way, the latent power of Islam was mobilized in the crisis to the advantage of Saddam Hussein – yet to the discomfort of many governments of the Muslim world, and often many Muslim fundamentalist groups themselves, whose financial self-interest dictated the need for a lower profile.

Islamic fundamentalism between power and revolution

This discernibly popular Islamic dimension to the Gulf conflict has intensified the perception in the West that now that the Communist threat has collapsed and the cold war has been won, the real challenge is an Islam which is at once illiberal and expansionist. Although writing before the Gulf War, Patrick J. Buchanan described Islam in threatening terms: "As the Salman Rushdie episode demonstrates, the followers of the Prophet, even in the West, have little use for the liberalism of J. S. Mill." Somewhat more sympathetic to Islam, the British columnist R. W. Johnson speaks nonetheless of Islamic fundamentalism as a "creed that refuses the whole objective of 'modernization'."

While the long run must remain an open question, the evidence to date, including that of the Gulf crisis of 1990–91, supports a rather less alarming conclusion. In mediating among three forces – the state, which they hope to capture; popular Muslim sentiment, which they do not always control; and Muslim patrons, on whom they are often dependent – Islamic fundamentalists must make compromises with each. Neither simply revolutionary nor merely accommodationist, these groups are preoccupied with reform within their societies and, in the process, continually adapt their thinking and strategies in ways which belie the simplicity of an "illiberal" or "angry" Islam.

One way in which they do this is the articulation of a social mission for Islam. Taking the traditional concept of *da'wa* ("call" to Islam), which formerly carried the connotation of missionary or proselytizing work among the unbelievers, Muslims have, in the present era, gradually transformed it, making its central purpose the return of nominal Muslims to the true Islamic path. In addition to the obvious emphasis on education, a social welfare network of impressive proportions has evolved as integral to this new sense of mission. Islamic hospitals and health clinics, housing cooperatives, and benevolent societies for widows and orphans operate in societies from Morocco to Indonesia, and as they do so they both attract followers to their cause and challenge the inefficient, competing institutions of the state.

The political implications of this kind of social mission are patent, and it is no surprise that President Mubarak of Egypt, to cite but one example, fears the delegitimizing impact of a rival Islamic social system. He cannot simply repress the fundamentalists, for fear of radicalizing the relative moderates; nor, because of the strength of their integrity or because of limitations on his resources, can he coopt all of them. His "carrot and stick" policy must thus be calibrated to the circumstances, and the responses of the Muslim groups, ranging from confrontation to "normalization," must be equally deft.

Another instance of the ambiguity of Muslim political attitudes is the difficulty in creating consensus on foreign policy or national security issues. As Gehad Auda points out, President Mubarak, while conceding latitude to Muslim groups in the domestic debate, has insisted that politics stops at the water's edge. When it is remembered that Anwar Sadat's rule was undermined in great part because of the peace treaty that he signed with Israel, the prudence of Mubarak's policy is obvious. In the Gulf crisis, however, this induced cautionary approach to international matters came under severe strain as all the main Islamic groups, with varying degrees of enthusiasm, expressed opposition to the deployment of Egyptian troops in the anti-Saddam coalition.

Yet, in spite of this, there was little agreement among the groups as to what the proper Islamic policy should be. Should jihad be directed only against the Western states in the coalition, as the Muslim Brotherhood came to argue, or against Saudi Arabia as well, as the Labor party insisted? Does "unbelief" apply to Saddam as well as the Americans, and can it be extended to include those Muslims fighting on the side of the Americans? The crucial factor in the difference of approach was the relationship with the Saudis, but the common result was uncertainty as to what such important concepts as jihad and kufr meant in international politics. This vagueness on foreign policy matters and the Muslim groups' lack of success in opposing the Egyptian government's war policy have, in turn, stimulated a rethinking of the strategy to adopt in domestic politics.

In addition to these factors, the experience of participation in government has provided its own kind of equivocation. On the one hand, Muslim groups have sustained themselves by the often unmitigatingly harsh criticism of the regimes that they feel are un-Islamic. Employing the powerfully negative term for the pre-Islamic period of ignorance, fundamentalists characteristically accuse today's authorities, both religious and political, of perpetuating *jahiliyya*. Complacency would be immoral in the face of a regime "that does not apply God's rules," and there is no doubt that one's religious duty is to wage jihad against such forces of repression and injustice within the Islamic community.

On the other hand, however, Muslim groups are, in several instances, becoming integrated into the political process. In Algeria, they have successfully contested local elections and intend to field a full slate of candidates in the national elections, which were promised for late June of 1991 but then postponed in the wake of serious riots early in June. In Egypt, Muslim Brothers have participated in parliamentary elections and won seats, though under the banner of other legally recognized parties. In Jordan, members of the Brotherhood and others who formed the umbrella Islamic Movement won stunning successes in the parliamentary election of November 1989, the first general election in twenty-two years in Jordan and the first in which women were allowed to vote. Although King Hussein at first declined to admit Muslim Brothers to the government, five Brothers and two other Islamists were given Cabinet portfolios in January 1991 in the midst of the general agitation over the Gulf crisis. They remained in office until the government re-shuffle of June 1991. In Pakistan, the governing coalition consists of three Islamic parties – Jamaat-i-Islami, Jamiyat Ulama-i-Islam, and Jamiyat Ulama-i-Pakistan.

Muslim groups have not been hesitant to use the political instruments at their disposal. Control of various ministerial portfolios, particularly those dealing with education and religious affairs, confers the advantage of direct influence over the young and over the religious authorities. This influence is important in stimulating mass support for their program. The activists have also found in Parliament a particularly useful instrument by which to magnify their voice and to intensify their pressure on the government. It was such pressure in Pakistan that led to the resignation of Yaqub Khan, the Foreign Minister, whose relatively pro-American sympathies had incurred the displeasure of a key partner in the Islamic ruling coalition.

If the Muslim street and the palace are now not so far removed from each other, the experience of proximity has proved as unsettling to the street as to the palace. Regimes such as those of Algeria, Pakistan, and Jordan may have felt impelled to distance themselves, in diverse ways, from criticism of Iraq. And in several countries, Daniel Brumberg points out, governments may have even gained the temporary advantage by initiating some form of liberalization of the political system, thereby putting the Islamic opposition on the defensive. But, at the same time, the Muslim participants in power have themselves felt impelled to act responsibly. For these Islamists, wishing still to reform the system and instill values in society that are consonant with the scriptural ordinances of Islam, participation in daily political life has demonstrated the efficacy of give-and-take, the value of compromise and consensus.

This is most obviously seen in the case of revolutionary Iran. As Said Arjomand indicates, there has been, generally since 1985 and certainly since the death of Ayatollah Khomeini in June 1989, a transformation in revolutionary commitment among the elite. Although pragmatism in one sphere, such as foreign policy, has not been automatically replicated in another sphere, such as economic policy, the formalization of the revolution over the past decade has produced a relatively greater preoccupation with domestic matters and the desire to normalize Iran's diplomatic relations, and lesser concern with exporting the revolution and confronting the satanic West.

In the Gulf crisis, Iran might have been expected to fulfill its self-proclaimed Islamic mission either by confronting the West or by actively supporting the Shi'ites in southern Iraq. In fact, it did neither. President Hashemi Rafsanjani and his allies were able to outmaneuver the radicals by leading the public outrage at Israeli actions in the occupied territories – particularly the Temple Mount killings in October 1990. And, nearly simultaneously, they were able to reassure Syria and the Gulf states that Iran would not endanger its new international relationships by decisive support for Islamic revolution in Iraq. Preemption of radicals at home and reassurance of potential allies abroad were the marks of a confident, institutionalized revolution and of an "Islam" comfortable with power.

The case of the Iraqi Shi'ites is, on one level, obviously different from that of the Iranians. The Iraqis have not only been supressed under Saddam's regime, but, when they revolted in the wake of the war in March 1991, they failed to receive any concrete outside help that would have given them the chance of seizing power. Yet, although they have thus not wielded power themselves, Iraqi Shi'ites have had, by the very fact of their weakness, to learn to deal with disparate groups, including the Communist party, whose ideological goals differ from their own. It is entirely possible that the concessions that they have made are merely tactical, an allowance to adverse circumstance. But, as Baram suggests, the Islamic Da'wa party's and

Amal's specific endorsement of parliamentary democracy for post-Ba'thist Iraq is a notable evolution in their rhetoric. It may also represent an ideological shift of some importance, as well as signal a serious disagreement with the Supreme Assembly for the Islamic Revolution in Iraq, a group dominated by ulama committed to the establishment of an Islamic state.

As this suggests, the Islamic dimensions of the Gulf crisis were often manipulated by various groups and governments for their own political advantage, and these Islamic concerns may have even been of secondary importance in the competition for power. Roberts points out, for example, that the FIS hoped to capture the high ground of Algerian politics and thereby improve its standing relative to other political groups, particularly the ruling Front de Liberation National. The riots of June 1991, which gave the group its first "martyrs," dramatically enhanced its standing relative to other groups and parties competing for influence in Algeria. In the West Bank and Gaza, Hamas hoped to circumscribe the influence of the PLO. Moreover, in Pakistan, the various Islamic parties were as outraged by the American decision to cut off all aid to Pakistan and by what was seen as an American–Soviet sellout of the Afghan *mujahidin*, as they were by Western military action in the Gulf. Yet this kind of political thinking is, in its own way, a sign of political flexibility. Rather than being unbending dogmatists, as is often assumed, many Islamic fundamentalists are at ease with the complex political calculus of means and ends, constraints and values which we in the West assume to be the normal stuff of politics.

Future Muslim generations will not remember Saddam Hussein as one of the great heroes of Islamic history, and the Gulf crisis of 1990–91 will not rank as the beginning of a new Crusade pitting East against West. But this crisis will have highlighted the important mobilizing role that Islamic symbolism and sentiment play in the politics of Muslims. It will also have shown the degree to which rulers and opponents must weigh principle with self-interest, ideology with political advantage.

Mahmood Mamdani

GOOD MUSLIM, BAD MUSLIM

A political perspective on culture and terrorism

MEDIA INTEREST IN ISLAM exploded in the months after September 11. What, many asked, is the link between Islam and terrorism? This question has fueled a fresh round of "culture talk": the predilection to define cultures according to their presumed "essential" characteristics, especially as regards politics. An earlier round of such discussion, associated with Samuel Huntington's widely cited but increasingly discredited *Clash of Civilizations* (1996), demonized Islam in its entirety. Its place has been taken by a modified line of argument: that the terrorist link is not with all of Islam, but with a very literal interpretation of it, one found in Wahhabi Islam.[1] First advanced by Stephen Schwartz in a lead article in the British weekly, *The Spectator* (2001), this point of view went to the ludicrous extent of claiming that all suicide couriers (bombers or hijackers), are Wahhabi and warned that this version of Islam, historically dominant in Saudi Arabia, had been exported to both Afghanistan and the United States in recent decades. The argument was echoed widely in many circles, including the *New York Times*.[2]

Culture talk has turned religious experience into a political category. "What Went Wrong with Muslim Civilization?" asks Bernard Lewis in a lead article in *The Atlantic Monthly* (2002). Democracy lags in the Muslim World, concludes a Freedom House study of political systems in the non-Western world.[3] The problem is larger than Islam, concludes Aryeh Neier (2001), former president of Human Rights Watch and now head of the Soros-funded Open Society Foundation: It lies with tribalists and fundamentalists, contemporary counterparts of Nazis, who have identified modernism as their enemy. Even the political leadership of the antiterrorism alliance, notably Tony Blair and George Bush, speak of the need to distinguish "good Muslims" from "bad Muslims." The implication is undisguised: Whether in Afghanistan, Palestine, or Pakistan, Islam must be quarantined and the devil must be exorcized from it by a civil war between good Muslims and bad Muslims.

I want to suggest that we lift the quarantine for analytical purposes, and turn the cultural theory of politics on its head. This, I suggest, will help our query in at least two ways. First, it will have the advantage of deconstructing not just one protagonist in the contemporary contest – Islam – but also the other, the West. My point goes beyond the simple but radical suggestion that if there are good Muslims and bad Muslims, there must also be good Westerners and bad Westerners. I intend to question the very tendency to read Islamist politics as an effect of Islamic civilization – whether good or bad – and Western power as an effect of Western civilization. Further, I shall suggest that both those politics and that power are born of an encounter, and neither can be understood in isolation, outside of the history of that encounter.

Second, I hope to question the very premise of culture talk. This is the tendency to think of culture in political – and therefore territorial – terms. Political units (states) are territorial; culture is not. Contemporary Islam is a global civilization: fewer Muslims live in the Middle East than in Africa or in South and Southeast Asia. If we can think of Christianity and Judaism as global religions – with Middle Eastern origins but a historical flow and a contemporary constellation that cannot be made sense of in terms of state boundaries – then why not try to understand Islam, too, in historical and extraterritorial terms?[4] Does it really make sense to write political histories of Islam that read like political histories of geographies like the Middle East, and political histories of Middle Eastern states as if these were no more than the political history of Islam in the Middle East?

My own work (1996) leads me to trace the modern roots of culture talk to the colonial project known as indirect rule, and to question the claim that anti-colonial political resistance really expresses a cultural lag and should be understood as a traditional cultural resistance to modernity. This claim downplays the crucial encounter with colonial power, which I think is central to the post September 11 analytical predicament I described above. I find culture talk troubling for two reasons. On the one hand, cultural explanations of political outcomes tend to avoid *history* and issues. By equating political tendencies with entire communities defined in nonhistorical cultural terms, such explanations encourage collective discipline and punishment – a practice characteristic of colonial encounters. This line of reasoning equates terrorists with Muslims, justifies a punishing war against an entire country (Afghanistan) and ignores the recent history that shaped both the current Afghan context and the emergence of political Islam. On the other hand, culture talk tends to think of individuals (from "traditional" cultures) in authentic and original terms, as if their identities are shaped entirely by the supposedly unchanging culture into which they are born. In so doing, it dehistoricizes the construction of political identities.

Rather than see contemporary Islamic politics as the outcome of an archaic culture, I suggest we see neither culture nor politics as archaic, but both as very contemporary outcomes of equally contemporary conditions, relations, and conflicts. Instead of dismissing history and politics, as culture talk does, I suggest we place cultural debates in historical and political contexts. Terrorism is not born of the residue of a premodern culture in modern politics. Rather, terrorism is a modern construction. Even when it harnesses one or another aspect of tradition and culture, the result is a modern ensemble at the service of a modern project.

Culture talk

Is our world really divided into the modern and premodern, such that the former makes culture in which the latter is a prisoner? This dichotomy is increasingly prevalent in Western discussions of relations with Muslim-majority countries. It presumes that culture stands for creativity, for what being human is all about, in one part of the world, that called "modern," but that in the other part, labeled "premodern," culture stands for habit, for some kind of instinctive activity whose rules are inscribed in early founding texts, usually religious, and mummified in early artifacts. When I read of Islam in the papers these days, I often feel I am reading of museumized peoples, of peoples who are said not to *make* culture, except at the beginning of creation, as some extraordinary, prophetic act. After that, it seems they – we Muslims – just *conform* to culture. Our culture seems to have no history, no politics, and no debates. It seems to have petrified into a lifeless custom. Even more, these people seem incapable of transforming their culture, the way they seem incapable of growing their own food. The implication is that their salvation lies, as always, in philanthropy, in being saved from the outside.

If the premodern peoples are said to lack a creative capacity, they are conversely said to have an abundant capacity for destruction. This is surely why culture talk has become the stuff of front-page news stories. It is, after all, the reason we are told to give serious attention to culture. It is said that culture is now a matter of life and death. To one whose recent academic preoccupation has been the institutional legacy of colonialism, this kind of writing is deeply reminiscent of tracts from the history of modern colonization. This history assumes that people's public behavior, specifically their political behavior, can be read from their religion. Could it be that a person who takes his or her religion literally is a potential terrorist? That only someone who thinks of a religious text as not literal, but as metaphorical or figurative, is better suited to civic life and the tolerance it calls for? How, one may ask, does the literal reading of sacred texts translate into hijacking, murder, and terrorism?

Some may object that I am presenting a caricature of what we read in the press. After all, is there not less talk about the clash of civilizations, and more about the clash inside Islamic civilization? Is that not the point of the articles I referred to earlier? Certainly, we are now told to distinguish between good Muslims and bad Muslims. Mind you, not between good and bad persons, nor between criminals and civic citizens, who both happen to be Muslims, but between good Muslims and bad Muslims. We are told that there is a fault line running through Islam, a line that separates moderate Islam, called "genuine Islam," from extremist political Islam. The terrorists of September 11, we are told, did not just hijack planes; they also hijacked Islam, meaning "genuine" Islam.

I would like to offer another version of the argument that the clash is inside – and not between – civilizations. The synthesis is my own, but no strand in the argument is fabricated. I rather think of this synthesis as an enlightened version, because it does not just speak of the "other," but also of self. It has little trace of ethnocentrism. This is how it goes: Islam and Christianity have in common a deeply messianic orientation, a sense of mission to civilize the world. Each is convinced that it possesses the sole truth, that the world beyond is a sea of ignorance that needs to be redeemed.[5] In the modern age, this kind of conviction goes beyond the religious to the secular, beyond the domain of doctrine to that of politics. Yet even seemingly secular colonial notions such as that of "a civilizing mission"—or its more racialized version, "the white man's burden" – or the 19th-century U.S. conviction of a "manifest destiny" have deep religious roots.

Like any living tradition, neither Islam nor Christianity is monolithic. Both harbor and indeed are propelled by diverse and contradictory tendencies. In both, righteous notions have been the focus of prolonged debates: Even if you should claim to know what is good for humanity, how do you proceed? By persuasion or force? Do you convince others of the validity of your truth or do you proceed by imposing it on them? Is religion a matter of conviction or legislation? The first alternative gives you reason and evangelism; the second gives you the Crusades and jihad. Take the example of Islam, and the notion of jihad, which roughly translated means "struggle." Scholars distinguish between two broad traditions of jihad: *jihad Akbar* (the greater jihad) and *jihad Asgar* (the lesser jihad). The greater jihad, it is said, is a struggle against weaknesses of self; it is about how to live and attain piety in a contaminated world. The lesser jihad, in contrast, is about self-preservation and self-defense; more externally directed, it is the source of Islamic notions of what Christians call "just war" (Noor 2001).

Scholars of Islam have been at pains since September 11 to explain to a non-Muslim reading public that Islam has rules even for the conduct of war: for example, Talal Asad (n.d.) points out that the Hanbali School of law practiced by followers of Wahhabi Islam in Saudi Arabia outlaws the killing of innocents in war. Historians of Islam have warned against a simple reading of Islamic practice from Islamic doctrine: After all, coexistence and toleration have been the norm, rather than the exception, in the political history of Islam. More to the point, not only religious creeds like Islam and Christianity, but also secular doctrines like liberalism and Marxism have had to face an ongoing contradiction between the impulse to universalism and respective traditions of tolerance and peaceful coexistence. The universalizing impulse gives the United States a fundamentalist orientation in doctrine, just as the tradition of tolerance makes for pluralism in practice and in doctrine.

Doctrinal tendencies aside, I remain deeply skeptical of the claim that we can read people's political behavior from their religion, or from their culture. Could it be true that an orthodox Muslim is a potential terrorist? Or, the same thing, that an Orthodox Jew or Christian is a potential terrorist and only a Reform Jew or a Christian convert to Darwinian evolutionary theory is capable of being tolerant of those who do not share his or her convictions?

I am aware that this does not exhaust the question of culture and politics. How do you make sense of a politics that consciously wears the mantle of religion? Take, for example, the politics of Osama bin Laden and al-Qaeda; both claim to be waging a jihad, a just war against the enemies of Islam. To try to understand this uneasy relationship between politics and religion, I find it necessary not only to shift focus from doctrinal to historical Islam, from doctrine and culture to history and politics, but also to broaden the focus beyond Islam to include larger historical encounters, of which bin Laden and al-Qaeda have been one outcome.

The Cold War after Indochina

Eqbal Ahmad draws our attention to the television image from 1985 of Ronald Reagan inviting a group of turbaned men, all Afghan, all leaders of the mujahideen, to the

White House lawn for an introduction to the media. "These gentlemen are the moral equivalents of America's founding fathers," said Reagan (Ahmad 2001). This was the moment when the United States tried to harness one version of Islam in a struggle against the Soviet Union. Before exploring its politics, let me provide some historical background to the moment.

I was a young lecturer at the University of Dar-es-Salaam in Tanzania in 1975. It was a momentous year in the decolonization of the world as we knew it: 1975 was the year of the U.S. defeat in Indochina, as it was of the collapse of the last European empire in Africa. In retrospect, it is clear that it was also the year that the center of gravity of the Cold War shifted from Southeast Asia to southern Africa. The strategic question was this: Who would pick up the pieces of the Portuguese empire in Africa, the United States or the Soviet Union? As the focal point of the Cold War shifted, there was a corresponding shift in U.S. strategy based on two key influences. First, the closing years of the Vietnam War saw the forging of a Nixon Doctrine, which held that "Asian boys must fight Asian wars." The Nixon doctrine was one lesson that the United States brought from the Vietnam debacle. Even if the hour was late to implement it in Indochina, the Nixon Doctrine guided U.S. initiatives in southern Africa. In the post-Vietnam world, the United States looked for more than local proxies; it needed regional powers as junior partners. In southern Africa, that role was fulfilled by apartheid South Africa. Faced with the possibility of a decisive MPLA victory in Angola,[6] the United States encouraged South Africa to intervene militarily. The result was a political debacle that was second only to the Bay of Pigs invasion of a decade before: No matter its military strength and geopolitical importance, apartheid South Africa was clearly a political liability for the United States. Second, the Angolan fiasco reinforced public resistance within the United States to further overseas Vietnam-type involvement. The clearest indication that popular pressures were finding expression among legislators was the 1975 Clark amendment, which outlawed covert aid to combatants in the ongoing Angolan civil war.

The Clark amendment was repealed at the start of Reagan's second term in 1985. Its decade-long duration failed to forestall the Cold Warriors, who looked for ways to bypass legislative restrictions on the freedom of executive action. CIA chief William Casey took the lead in orchestrating support for terrorist and prototerrorist movements around the world – from Contras in Nicaragua to the Mujahideen in Afghanistan, to Mozambican National Resistance (RENAMO) in Mozambique[7] and National Union for the Total Independence of Angola (UNITA) in Angola[8] – through third and fourth parties. Simply put, after the defeat in Vietnam and the Watergate scandal, the United States decided to harness, and even to cultivate, terrorism in the struggle against regimes it considered pro-Soviet. The high point of the U.S. embrace of terrorism came with the Contras. More than just tolerated and shielded, they were actively nurtured and directly assisted by Washington. But because the Contra story is so well known, I will focus on the nearly forgotten story of U.S. support for terrorism in Southern Africa to make my point.

South Africa became the Reagan Administration's preferred partner for a *constructive engagement*, a term coined by Reagan's Assistant Secretary of State for Africa, Chester Crocker. The point of "constructive engagement" was to bring South Africa out of its political isolation and tap its military potential in the war against militant – pro-Soviet – nationalism.[9] The effect of "constructive engagement" was to bring to

South African regional policy the sophistication of a blend of covert and overt opera-tions: In Mozambique, for example, South Africa combined an official peace accord (the 1984 Nkomati agreement) with continued clandestine material support for RENAMO terrorism.[10] Tragically, the United States entered the era of "constructive engagement" just as the South African military tightened its hold over government and shifted its regional policy from détente to "total onslaught."

I do not intend to explain the tragedy of Angola and Mozambique as the result of machinations by a single superpower. The Cold War was fought by two superpowers, and both subordinated local interests and consequences to global strategic consider-ations. Whether in Angola or in Mozambique, the *Cold War* interfaced with an internal *civil war*. An entire generation of African scholars has been preoccupied with under-standing the relation between external and internal factors in the making of contem-porary Africa and, in that context, the dynamic between the Cold War and the civil war in each case. My purpose is not to enter this broader debate. Here, my purpose is more modest. I am concerned not with the civil war, but only the Cold War and, furthermore, not with both adversaries in the Cold War, but only the United States. My limited purpose is to illuminate the context in which the United States embraced terrorism as it prepared to wage the Cold War to a finish.

The partnership between the United States and apartheid South Africa bolstered two key movements that used terror with abandon: RENAMO in Mozambique, and UNITA in Angola.[11] RENAMO was a *terrorist* outfit created by the Rhodesian army in the early 1970s – and patronized by the South African Defense Forces. UNITA was more of a *prototerrorist* movement with a local base, though one not strong enough to have survived the short bout of civil war in 1975 without sustained external assistance. UNITA was a contender for power, even if a weak one, while RENAMO was not – which is why the United States could never openly support this creation of Rhodesian and South African intelligence and military establishments. Because the 1975 debacle in Angola showed that South Africa could not be used as a direct link in U.S. assistance, and the Clark amendment barred U.S. covert aid in Angola, the CIA took the initiative to find fourth parties – such as Morocco – through which to train and support UNITA. Congressional testimony documented at least one instance of a $15-million-dollar payment to UNITA through Morocco in 1983. Savimbi, the UNITA chief, acknowl-edged the ineffectiveness of the Clark amendment when he told journalists, "A great country like the United States has other channels – the Clark amendment means nothing" (in Minter 1994:152).

By any reckoning, the cost of terrorism in Southern Africa was high. A State Department consultant who interviewed refugees and displaced persons concluded that RENAMO was responsible for 95 percent of instances of abuse of civilians in the war in Mozambique, including the murder of as many as 100,000 persons. A 1989 United Nations study estimated that Mozambique suffered an economic loss of approximately $15 billion between 1980 and 1988, a figure five and a half times its 1988 GDP (Minter 1994). Africa Watch researchers documented UNITA strategies aimed at starving civilians in government-held areas, through a combination of direct attacks, kidnappings, and the planting of land mines on paths used by peasants. The extensive use of land mines put Angola in the ranks of the most mined countries in the world (alongside Afghanistan and Cambodia), with amputees conservatively estimated at over 15,000. UNICEF calculated that 331,000 died of causes directly or indirectly related to the war. The UN estimated the total loss to the Angolan economy from 1980 to 1988 at $30 billion, six times the 1988 GDP (Minter 1994:4–5).

The CIA and the Pentagon called terrorism by another name: "low intensity conflict." Whatever the name, political terror brought a kind of war that Africa had never seen before. The hallmark of terror was that it targeted civilian life: blowing up infrastructure such as bridges and power stations, destroying health and educational centers, mining paths and fields. Terrorism distinguished itself from guerrilla war by making civilians its preferred target. If left-wing guerrillas claimed that they were like fish in water, rightwing terrorists were determined to drain the water – no matter what the cost to civilian life – so as to isolate the fish. What is now called collateral damage was not an unfortunate byproduct of the war; it was the very point of terrorism.

Following the repeal of the Clark amendment at the start of Reagan's second term, the United States provided $13 million worth of "humanitarian aid" to UNITA, then $15 million for "military assistance." Even when South African assistance to UNITA dried up following the internal Angolan settlement in May 1991, the United States stepped up its assistance to UNITA in spite of the fact that the Cold War was over. The hope was that terrorism would deliver a political victory in Angola, as it had in Nicaragua. The logic was simple: The people would surely vote the terrorists into power if the level of collateral damage could be made unacceptably high.

Even after the Cold War, U.S. tolerance for terror remained high, both in Africa and beyond. The callousness of Western response to the 1994 genocide in Rwanda was no exception. Or consider the aftermath of January 6, 1999, when Revolutionary United Front (RUF) gunmen maimed and raped their way across Freetown, the capital of Sierra Leone, killing over 5,000 civilians in a day. The British and U.S. response was to pressure the government to share power with RUF rebels.

Afghanistan: The high point in the Cold War

The shifting center of gravity of the Cold War was the major context in which Afghanistan policy was framed, but the Iranian Revolution of 1979 was also a crucial factor. Ayatollah Khomeini anointed the United States as the "Great Satan," and pro-U.S. Islamic countries as "American Islam." Rather than address specific sources of Iranian resentment against the United States, the Reagan administration resolved to expand the pro-U.S. Islamic lobby in order to isolate Iran. The strategy was two-pronged. First, with respect to Afghanistan, it hoped to unite a billion Muslims world-wide around a holy war, a crusade, against the Soviet Union. I use the word *crusade*, not *jihad*, because only the notion of crusade can accurately convey the frame of mind in which this initiative was taken. Second, the Reagan administration hoped to turn a doctrinal difference inside Islam between minority Shia and majority Sunni into a political divide. It hoped thereby to contain the influence of the Iranian Revolution as a minority Shia affair.

The plan went into high gear in 1986 when CIA chief William Casey took three significant measures (Rashid 2000: 129–130). The first was to convince Congress to step up the anti-Soviet war in Afghanistan by providing the mujahideen with U.S. advisors and U.S.-made Stinger antiaircraft missiles to shoot down Soviet planes.

The second was to expand the Islamic guerrilla war from Afghanistan into the Soviet Republics of Tajikistan and Uzbekistan, a decision reversed when the Soviet Union threatened to attack Pakistan in retaliation. The third was to recruit radical Muslims from around the world to come and train in Pakistan and fight with the Afghan mujahideen. The Islamic world had not seen an armed jihad for centuries. Now the CIA was determined to create one, to put a version of tradition at the service of politics. Thus was the tradition of jihad — of a just war with a religious sanction, non-existent in the last 400 years — revived with U.S. help in the 1980s. In a 1990 radio interview, Eqbal Ahmad explained how "CIA agents started going all over the Muslim world recruiting people to fight."[12] Pervez Hoodbhoy recalled,

> With Pakistan's Zia-ul-Haq as America's foremost ally, the CIA advertised for, and openly recruited, Islamic holy warriors from Egypt, Saudi Arabia, Sudan, and Algeria. Radical Islam went into overdrive as its superpower ally and mentor funneled support to the Mujahidin, and Ronald Reagan feted them on the lawn of the White House, lavishing praise on "brave freedom fighters challenging the Evil Empire." [2001]

This is the context in which a U.S./Saudi/Pakistani alliance was forged, and in which religious madrasahs were turned into political schools for training cadres. The CIA did not just fund the jihad; it also played "a key role in training the mujahideen" (Chossudovsky 2001). The point was to integrate guerrilla training with the teachings of Islam and, thus, create "Islamic guerrillas." The Indian journalist Dilip Hiro (1995) explained:

> Predominant themes were that Islam was a complete sociopolitical ideol-ogy, that holy Islam was being violated by (the) atheistic Soviet troops, and that the Islamic people of Afghanistan should reassert their indepen-dence by overthrowing the leftist Afghan regime propped up by Moscow. [in Chossudovsky 2001]

The CIA looked for, but was unable to find, a Saudi Prince to lead this crusade. It settled for the next best thing, the son of an illustrious family closely connected to the Saudi royal house. We need to remember that Osama bin Laden did not come from a backwater family steeped in premodernity, but from a cosmopolitan family. The bin Laden family is a patron of scholarship: it endows programs at universities like Harvard and Yale. Bin Laden was recruited with U.S. approval, and at the highest level, by Prince Turki al-Faisal, then head of Saudi intelligence (Blackburn 2001:3). This is the context in which Osama bin Laden helped build, in 1986, the Khost tunnel complex deep under the mountains close to the Pakistani border, a complex the CIA funded as a major arms depot, as a training facility, and as a medical center for the mujahideen. It is also the context in which bin Laden set up, in 1989, al-Qaeda, or military base, as a service center for Arab Afghans and their families (Rashid 2000:132).

The idea of an Islamic global war was not a brainchild of bin Laden; the CIA and Pakistan's Inter Services Intelligence (ISI) hoped to transform the Afghan jihad into a global war waged by Muslim states against the Soviet Union. Al-Qaeda networks spread out beyond Afghanistan: to Chechnya and Kosovo (Blackburn 2001:7), to Algeria and Egypt, even as far as Indonesia. The numbers involved were impressive by any reckoning. Writing in *Foreign Affairs*, Ahmad Rashid estimated that 35,000 Muslim radicals from 40 Islamic countries joined Afghanistan's fight in the decade between 1982 and 1992. Eventually Rashid notes, the Afghan jihad came to influence more than 100,000 foreign Muslim radicals (Rashid 1999). The non-Afghan recruits were known as the Afghan-Arabs or, more specifically, as the Afghan-Algerians or the Afghan-Indonesians. The Afghan-Arabs constituted an elite force and received the most sophisticated training (Chossudovsky 2001). Fighters in the Peshawar-based Muslim "international brigade" received the relatively high salary of around $1,500 per month (Stone 1997:183). Except at the top leadership level, fighters had no direct contact with Washington; most communication was mediated through Pakistani intelligence services (Chossudovsky 2001).

The Afghan jihad was the largest covert operation in the history of the CIA. In fiscal year 1987 alone, according to one estimate, clandestine U.S. military aid to the mujahideen amounted to 660 million dollars – "more than the total of American aid to the contras in Nicaragua" (Ahmad and Barnet 1988:44). Apart from direct U.S. funding, the CIA financed the war through the drug trade, just as in Nicaragua. The impact on Afghanistan and Pakistan was devastating. Prior to the Afghan jihad, there was no local production of heroin in Pakistan and Afghanistan; the production of opium (a very different drug than heroin) was directed to small regional markets. Michel Chossudovsky, Professor of Economics at University of Ottawa, estimates that within only two years of the CIA's entry into the Afghan jihad, "the Pakistan–Afghanistan borderlands became the world's top heroin producer, supplying 60 percent of U.S. demand" (2001:4). The lever for expanding the drug trade was simple: As the jihad spread inside Afghanistan, the mujahideen required peasants to pay an opium tax. Instead of waging a war on drugs, the CIA turned the drug trade into a way of financing the Cold War. By the end of the anti-Soviet jihad, the Central Asian region produced 75 percent of the world's opium, worth billions of dollars in revenue (McCoy 1997).[13]

The effect on Pakistan, the United States's key ally in waging the Cold War in Central Asia, was devastating. To begin with, the increase in opium production corresponded to an increase in local consumption, hardly an incidental relation: The UN Drug Control Program estimated that the heroin-addicted population in Pakistan went up from nearly zero in 1979 to 1.2 million by 1985, "a much steeper rise than in any nation" (McCoy 1997, in Chossudovsky 2001). There were two other ways in which the Afghan jihad affected Pakistan. The first was its impact on Pakistan's military and intelligence services, which were key to giving the CIA an effective reach in Afghanistan and, more generally, in Soviet Central Asia. The more the anti-Soviet jihad grew, the more the intelligence services, particularly the ISI, moved to the center of governmental power in Pakistan. The Islamization of the anti-Soviet struggle both drew inspiration from and reinforced the Islamization of the Pakistani state under Zia (Hoodbhoy 2001:7). Second, the more the Afghan jihad gathered momentum, the more it fed a regional offshoot, the Kashmiri jihad (Hoodbhoy 2001:7). The jihadi organizations were so pivotal in the functioning of the Pakistani state by the time Zia left office that the trend to Islamization of the state continued with post-Zia governments. Hudud Ordinances[14] and blasphemy laws remained in place.

The Jameet-e-Ulema-Islam, a key party in the alliance that was the Afghan jihad, became a part of Benazir Bhutto's governing coalition in 1993 (Chossudovsky 2001).

By now it should be clear that the CIA was key to forging the link between Islam and terror in Central Asia. The groups it trained and sponsored shared three characteristics: terror tactics, embrace of holy war, and the use of fighters from across national borders (the Afghan-Arabs). The consequences were evident in countries as diverse and far apart as Indonesia and Algeria. Today, the Laskar jihad in Indonesia is reportedly led by a dozen commanders who fought in the Afghan jihad (Solomon 2001:9). In Algeria, when the Islamic Salvation Front (FIS) was prevented from taking power by the Algerian military when it became evident that it would win the 1991 election, those in the political leadership of FIS who had pioneered the parliamentary road were eclipsed by those championing an armed jihad. The Algerian-Afghans "played an important role in the formation of the Islamic extremist groups of the post-Chadli crisis." Though their precise numbers are not known, Martin Stone reports that "the Pakistani embassy in Algiers alone issued 2,800 visas to Algerian volunteers during the mid-1980s." One of the most important leaders of the Algerian-Afghans, Kamerredin Kherbane, went on to serve on the FIS's executive council in exile (Stone 1997:183).

The Cold War created a political schism in Islam. In contrast to radical Islamist social movements like the pre-election FIS in Algeria, or the earlier revolutionaries in Iran, the Cold War has given the United States a state-driven conservative version of political Islam in countries like Pakistan and Afghanistan. In an essay on September 11, Olivier Roy has usefully contrasted these tendencies – radical political Islam as against conservative "neo-fundamentalism. Islamist social movements originated in the 20th century in the face of imperial occupation; they aimed to rejuvenate Islam, not just as "a mere religion," but as "a political ideology which should be integrated into all aspects of society (politics, law, economy, social justice, foreign policy, etc.)" (Roy 2001). Though it began by calling for the building of an *umma* (supranational Muslim community), radical Islamism adapted to the nation state and sprouted different national versions of Islamism. This shift has been the most dramatic in movements such as the Lebanese Hezbullah, which has given up the idea of an Islamic state and entered the electoral process, and Hamas, whose critique of the PLO is that it has betrayed not Islam, but the Palestinian nation. Where they are allowed, these movements operate within legal frameworks. Though not necessarily democratic, they strengthen the conditions for democracy by expanding participation in the political process. In contrast, state-driven neofundamentalist movements share a conservative agenda. Politically, their objective is limited to implementing Sharia (Islamic law). Socially, they share a conservatism evidenced by opposition to female presence in public life and a violent sectarianism (anti-Shia). Though originating in efforts by unpopular regimes to legitimize power, the history of neofundamentalist movements shows that these efforts have indeed backfired. Instead of developing national roots, neofundamentalism has turned supranational; uprooted, its members have broken with ties of family and country of origin. According to Roy, "while Islamists do adapt to the nation-state, neofundamentalists embody the crisis of the nation-state.

This new brand of supra-national fundamentalism is more a product of contemporary globalization than the Islamic past" (Roy 2001).

If the mujahideen and al-Qaeda were neofundamentalist products of the Cold War – trained, equipped, and financed by the CIA and its regional allies – the Taliban came out of the agony and the ashes of the war against the Soviet Union. The Taliban was a movement born across the border in Pakistan at a time when the entire population had been displaced not once but many times over, and when no educated class to speak of was left in the country. The *Talib* was a student and the student movement, Taliban, was born of warfare stretching into decades, of children born in cross-border refugee camps, of orphans with no camaraderie but that of fellow male students in madressas, of madressas that initially provided student recruits to defend the population – ironically, women and young boys – from the lust and the loot of mujahideen guerrillas. Born of a brutalized society, the Taliban was, tragically, to brutalize it further. An old man in a mosque in Kandahar, an architectural ruin, which was once an ancient city of gardens and fountains and palaces, told Eqbal Ahmad, "They have grown in darkness amidst death. They are angry and ignorant, and hate all things that bring joy to life" (1995).

Both those who see the Taliban as an Islamic movement and those who see it as a tribal (Pushtun) movement view it as a premodern residue in a modern world. But they miss the crucial point about the Taliban: Even if it evokes premodernity in its particular language and specific practices, the Taliban is the result of an encounter of a premodern people with modern imperial power. Given to a highly decentralized and localized mode of life, the Afghan people have been subjected to two highly centralized state projects in the past few decades: first, Soviet-supported Marxism, then, CIA-supported Islamization.[15] When I asked two colleagues, one an Afghan and the other a U.S. student of Afghanistan, how a movement that began in defense of women and youth could turn against both,[16] they asked me to put this development in a triple context: the shift from the forced gender equity of the communists to the forced misogyny of the Taliban, the combination of traditional male seclusion of the madressas with the militarism of the jihadi training, and, finally, the fear of Taliban leaders that their members would succumb to rape, a practice for which the mujahideen were notorious.[17] True, the CIA did not create the Taliban. But the CIA did create the mujahideen and embraced both bin Laden and the Taliban as alternatives to secular nationalism. Just as, in another context, the Israeli intelligence allowed *Hamas* to operate unhindered during the first *intifadah* – allowing it to open a university and bank accounts, and even possibly helping it with funding, hoping to play it off against the secular PLO – and reaped the whirlwind in the second intifadah.[18]

My point is simple: Contemporary "fundamentalism" is a modern political project, not a traditional cultural leftover. To be sure, one can trace many of the elements in the present "fundamentalist" project – such as opium production, madressas, and the very notion of jihad Akbar – to the era before modern colonization, just as one can identify forms of slavery prior to the era of merchant capitalism. Just as transatlantic slavery took a premodern institution and utilized it for purposes of capitalist accumulation – stretching its scale and brutality far beyond precapitalist practice or imagination – so Cold Warriors turned traditional institutions such as jihad Akbar and madressas, and traditional stimulants such as opium, to modern political purposes on a scale previously unimagined, with devastating consequences. Opium, madressas, jihad Akbar – all were reshaped as they were put into the service of a global U.S. campaign against "the evil empire."

When the Soviet Union was defeated in Afghanistan, this new terror was unleashed on Afghan people in the name of liberation. Eqbal Ahmad observed that the Soviet withdrawal turned out to be a moment of truth, rather than victory, for the mujahideen (Ahmad 1992a). As different factions of the mujahideen divided along regional (north versus south), linguistic (Farsi versus Pushto), doctrinal (Shia versus Sunni) and even external (pro-Iran versus pro-Saudi) lines, and fought each other, they shelled and destroyed their *own* cities with artillery. Precisely when they were ready to take power, the mujahideen lost the struggle for the hearts and minds of the people (Ahmad 1989, 1992a, 1992b).

The question of responsibility

Who bears responsibility for the present situation? To understand this question, it will help to contrast two situations, that after World War II and that after the Cold War, and compare how the question of responsibility was understood and addressed in two different contexts.

In spite of Pearl Harbor, World War II was fought in Europe and Asia, not in the United States. Europe, and not the United States, faced physical and civic destruction at the end of the war. The question of responsibility for postwar reconstruction arose as a political rather than a moral question. Its urgency was underscored by the changing political situation in Yugoslavia, Albania, and, particularly, Greece. This is the context in which the United States accepted responsibility for restoring conditions for decent civic life in noncommunist Europe. The resulting initiative was the Marshal Plan.

The Cold War was not fought in Europe, but in Southeast Asia, Southern Africa, and Central and South America. Should we, ordinary humanity, hold the United States responsible for its actions during the Cold War? Should the United States be held responsible for napalm bombing and spraying Agent Orange in Vietnam? Should it be held responsible for cultivating terrorist movements in Southern Africa, Central Africa, and Central Asia? The United States's embrace of terrorism did not end with the Cold War. Right up to September 10, 2001, the United States and Britain compelled African countries to reconcile with terrorist movements. The demand was that governments must share power with terrorist organizations in the name of *reconciliation* – in Mozambique, Sierra Leone, and Angola. Reconciliation turned into a codeword for impunity, disguising a strategy for undermining hard-won state independence. If terrorism was a Cold War brew, it turned into a local Angolan or Mozambican or Sierra Leonean brew after the Cold War. Whose responsibility is it? Like Afghanistan, are these countries hosting terrorism, or are they also hostage to terrorism? I think both.

Perhaps no other society paid a higher price for the defeat of the Soviet Union than did Afghanistan. Out of a population of roughly 20 million, a million died, another million and a half were maimed, and another five million became refugees. UN agencies estimate that nearly a million and a half have gone clinically insane as a consequence of decades of continuous war. Those who survived lived in the most mined country in the world.[19] Afghanistan was a brutalized society even before the present war began.

The United States has a habit of not taking responsibility for its own actions. Instead, it habitually looks for a high moral pretext for inaction. I was in Durban at the 2001 World Congress against Racism when the United States walked out of it. The Durban conference was about major crimes of the past, such as racism and xenophobia. I returned from Durban to New York to hear Condeleeza Rice talk about the need to forget slavery because, she said, the pursuit of civilized life requires that we forget the past. It is true that unless we learn to forget, life will turn into revenge seeking. Each of us will have nothing to nurse but a catalogue of wrongs done to a long line of ancestors. But civilization cannot be built on just forgetting. We must not only learn to forget, we must also not forget to learn. We must also memorialize, particularly monumental crimes. The United States was built on two monumental crimes: the genocide of Native Americans and the enslavement of African Americans. The tendency of the United States is to memorialize other peoples' crimes but to forget its own – to seek a high moral ground as a pretext to ignore real issues.

What is to be done

Several critics of the U.S. bombing of Afghanistan have argued that terrorism should be dealt with like any criminal act. If terrorism were simply an individual crime, it would not be a political problem. The distinction between political terror and crime is that the former makes an open claim for support. Unlike the criminal, the political terrorist is not easily deterred by punishment. Whatever we may think of their methods, terrorists have a cause, and a need to be heard. Notwithstanding Salman Rushdie's (2001) claim that terrorists are nihilists who wrap themselves up in objectives, but have none, and so we must remorselessly attack them, one needs to recognize that terrorism has no military solution. This is why the U.S. military establishment's bombing campaign in Afghanistan is more likely to be remembered as a combination of blood revenge and medieval-type exorcism than as a search for a solution to terrorism.

Bin Laden's strength does not lay in his religious but, rather, in his political message. Even a political child knows the answer to Bush's incredulous question, "Why do they hate us?" When it comes to the Middle East, we all know that the United States stands for cheap oil and not free speech. The only way of isolating individual terrorists is to do so politically, by addressing the issues in which terrorists "wrap themselves up." Without addressing the issues, there is no way of shifting the terrain of conflict from the military to the political, and drying up support for political terror. If we focus on issues, it should be clear that September 11 would not have happened had the United States ended the Cold War with demilitarization and a peace bonus. The United States did not dismantle the global apparatus of empire at the end of the Cold War; instead, it concentrated on ensuring that hostile states – branded rogue states – not acquire weapons of mass destruction. Similarly, the United States did not accept responsibility for the militarization of civilian and state life in regions where the Cold War was waged with devastating consequences, such as Southeast Asia, southern Africa, Central America and Central Asia; instead, it just walked away.

In the first weeks after September 11, the leaders of the United States and Britain were at pains to confirm aloud that theirs was a war not against Islam, nor even just Islamic terror, but against terrorism. To be convincing, though, they will have to face up to the relationship between their own policies and contemporary terrorism. A useful starting point would be to recognize the failure of the United States's Iraqi policy, give up a vendetta that refuses to distinguish between the Iraqi government and Iraqi people, and to pressure Israel to reverse its post-1967 occupation of Palestinian lands. It is the refusal to address issues that must count as the *first* major hurdle in our search for peace. For their part, Muslims need to break out of the straightjacket of a victim's point of view. This, too, requires a historical consciousness, for at least two good reasons. One, only a historical consciousness can bring home to Muslims the fact that Islam is today the banner for diverse and contradictory political projects. It is not only anti-imperialist Islamist movements but also imperialist projects, not only demands to extend participation in public life but also dictatorial agendas, which carry the banner of Islam. The minimum prerequisite for political action today must be the capacity to tell one from the other. The second prerequisite for action is to recognize that just as Islam has changed and become more complex, so too has the configuration of modern society. More and more Muslims live in societies with non-Muslim majorities. Just as non-Muslim majority societies are called on to realize an equal citizenship for all – regardless of cultural and religious differences – so Muslim-majority societies face the challenge of creating a single citizenship in the context of religious diversity. In matters of religion, says the Koran, there must be no compulsion. Islam can be more than a mere religion – indeed, a way of life – but the way of life does not have to be a compulsion. Islamist organizations will have to consider seriously the separation of the state from religion, notably as Hezbollah has in Lebanon. Instead of creating a national political Islam for each Muslim-majority state, the real challenge faced by Muslims is to shed the very notion of a nation-state. Whatever the terms of the nation-state – territorial or cultural, secular or religious – this political form exported by the modern West to the rest of the world is one part of Western modernity that needs to be rethought. The test of democracy in multireligious and multicultural societies is not simply to get the support of the majority, the nation, but to do so without losing the trust of the minority – so that both may belong to a single political community living by a single set of rules.

Notes

1   Wahhabi is a strictly orthodox Sunni sect; it is predominant in Saudi Arabia.
2   For an account of bad Muslims, see Harden 2001; for a portrayal of good Muslims, see Goodstein 2001: A20.
3   "While more than three-quarters of 145 non-Muslim nations around the world are now democracies, most countries with an Islamic majority continue to defy the trend, according to a survey by Freedom House, an independent monitor of political rights and civil liberties based in New York" (Crossette 2001:4).
4   Amartya Sen has highlighted the flip side of this argument in an interesting article on Indian civilization: To think of India as a Hindu civilization is to ignore the multiple sources from which historical India has drawn its cultural resources. Conversely, to try and box civilizations into discrete boxes – Hindu, Muslim, Christian, Buddhist – is to indulge in an ahistorical and one-dimensional understanding of complex contemporary civilizations. I would add to this a third claim: to see also

these discrete civilizational boxes as territorial entities is to harness cultural resources for a very specific political project (Sen 2001a, 2001b).

5   Think, for example, of the Arabic word *al-Jahaliya* that I have always known to mean the domain of ignorance. Think also of the legal distinction between *dar-ul-Islam* (the domain of Islam) and *dar-ul-harab* (the domain of war) that says that the rule of law applies only to the domain of Islam.

6   Popular Movement for the Liberation of Angola, then a rebel group backed by the Soviet Union and Cuba.

7   Mozambican National Resistance, a guerrilla organization formed in 1976 by white Rhodesian officers to overthrow the government of newly independent Mozambique.

8   UINTA, the MPLA's main rival for power after independence from Portugal in 1975.

9   The United States used its leverage with a variety of multilateral institutions to achieve this objective. It successfully urged the IMF to grant South Africa a $1.1 billion credit in November 1982, an amount that – coincidentally or not – equaled the increase in South African military expenditure from 1980 to 1982 (Minter 1994:149).

10   In less than a year after Nkomati, Mozambican forces captured a set of diaries belonging to a member of the RENAMO leadership. The 1985 Vaz diaries detailed continued South African Defense Force support for RENAMO (Vines 1991:24).

11   On Angola and Mozambique, see Minter 1994:2–5, 142–149, 152–168; Vines 1991:24, 39; Brittain 1988:63.

12   See Http://www.//pmagazine.org/articles/featahmad_134.shtml.

13   Chossudovsky has also synthesized available information on the growth of the drug trade.

14   The 1979 Hudud Ordinance declared all sex outside marriage unlawful. It also sanctioned the flogging of women accused of adultery.

15   "The ideologies at war – Marxism and Fundamentalism – are alien to Afghan culture. Afghanistan is a diverse and pluralistic society; centralizing, unitary agendas cannot appeal to it" (Ahmad 1991).

16   Rashid (1995) explains that the Taliban did not only ban women from public life, they also banned numerous activities for men, such as any game with a ball, music (except drums), lest any of these entice others socially (see also Ahmad 1995).

17   J. Rubin and Ashraf Ghani, conversation with author, November 16, 2001.

18   A former military commander of the Gaza Strip was quoted in 1986 to the effect that "we extend some financial aid to Islamic groups via mosques and religious schools in order to help create a force that would stand against the leftist forces which support the PLO" (in Usher 1993:19). The Israeli experts on defense policy, Ze'ev Schiff and Ehud Ya'ari give a short account of Israeli policies toward Hamas so far as bank transfers and other margins of maneuver are concerned (see Schiff and Ya'ari 1991:233–234). Finally, Khaled Hroub acknowledges that the Israelis used Hamas and the PLO against each other but discounts any deliberate Israeli role in aiding Hamas (see Hroub 2000:200–203).

19   United Nations Mine Action Program for Afghanistan (in Flanders 2001).

References

Ahmad, Eqbal. 1989. Stalemate at Jalabad. The Nation, October 9. Electronic document, http://www.bitsonline.net/eqbal/articles_by_eqbal_view. asp?id=28&cid=6.

——. 1991. In Afghanistan: Cease Fire Please. Dawn, Karachi, April 7.

——. 1992a. Endgame in Afghanistan. Dawn, Karachi, April 26.

——. 1992b. The War Without End. Dawn, Karachi, August 30.

——. 1995. In a Land without Music. Dawn, Karachi. Electronic document, http://www.bitsonline.net/eqbal/articles_by_eqbal_view. asp?id=29&cid6. Accessed July 23.

——. 2001. Genesis of International Terrorism. Speech originally given in October 1998. Dawn, Karachi, October 5.

Ahmad, Eqbal, and Richard J. Barnet. 1988. A Reporter at Large: Bloody Games. The New Yorker, April.

Asad, Talal N.d. Some Thoughts on the World Trade Center. Unpublished MS, October 2001.

Blackburn, Robin. 2001. Terror and Empire. Chapter 3: The U.S. Alliance with Militant Islam. Electronic document, http://www.counter-punch.org/robin3.html. Accessed December 20.

Brittain, Victoria. 1988. Hidden Lives, Hidden Deaths: South Africa's Crippling of a Continent. London: Faber and Faber.

Chossudovsky, Michel. 2001. Who Is Osama bin Laden? Montréal: Centre for Research for Globalisation. Electronic document, http://globalresearch.ca/articles/CHO109C.html. Accessed September 12.

Crossette, Barbara. 2001. Democracy Lags in Muslim World. International Herald Tribune, December 4: 24–25.

Flanders, Laura. 2001. Killer Food Drops. Working for Change. Electronic document, http://www.workingforchange.com/article.cfm?itemid=12097. Accessed October 8.

Goodstein, Laurie. 2001. Stereotyping Rankles Silent, Secular Majority of American Muslims. The New York Times, December 23: A20.

Harden, Blaine. 2001. Saudis Seek to Add U.S. Muslims to Their Sect. New York Times, October 20. Electronic document, http://query.nytimes.com/search/abstract?res=F40613FF3A5A0C738EDAA90994D9404482.

Hiro, Dilip. 1995. Fallout from Afghan Jihad. Interpress Services, November 21.

Hoodbhoy, Pervez. 2001. Muslims and the West after September 11. South Asia Citizens Wire, Dispatch #2. Electronic document, http://www.mnet.fr/aiiindex. Accessed December 10.

Hroub, Khaled. 2000. Hamas: Political Thought and Practice. Washington, DC: Institute for Palestinian Studies.

Huntington, Samuel. 1996. Clash of Civilizations and the Remaking of World Order. New York: Simon and Schuster.

Lewis, Bernard. 2002. What Went Wrong? Atlantic Monthly, January. Electronic document, http://www.theatlantic.com/issues/2002/01/lewis.htm.

Mamdani, Mahmood. 1996. Citizen and Subject: Contemporary Africa and the Legacy of Late Colonialism. Princeton: Princeton University Press.

McCoy, Alfred. 1997. Drug Fallout: the CIA's Forty-Year Complicity in the Narcotics Trade. The Progressive, August 1.

Minter, William. 1994. Apartheid's Contras: An Inquiry into the Roots of War in Angola and Mozambique. London: Zed Press.

Neier, Aryeh. 2001. Warring against Modernity. The Washington Post, October 9.

Noor, Farish A. 2001. The Evolution of Jihad in Islamist Political Discourse: How a Plastic Concept Became Harder. Social Science Research Council. Electronic document, http://www.ssrc.org/sept11/essays/noor.htm.

Rashid, Ahmad. 1999. The Taliban: Exporting Extremism. Foreign Affairs, November–December.

——. 2000. Taliban; Militant Islam, Oil and Fundamentalism in Central Asia. New Haven, CT: Yale University Press.

Roy, Olivier. 2001. Neo-Fundamentalism. Social Science Research Council, http://www.ssrc.org/sept11/essays/roy.htm.

Rushdie, Salman. 2001. Fighting the Forces of Invisibility. New York Times, October 2. Electronic document, http://www.Spectator.co.uk/article. php3?table=old&section=current&issue=2002-06-29&ID=1004&search text=.

Schiff, Ze'ev, and Ya'ari Ehud. 1991. Intifada. New York: Simon and Schuster.

Schwartz, Stephen. 2001. Ground Zero and the Saudi Connection. The Spectator, September 22.

Sen, Amartya. 2001a. A World Not Neatly Divided. The New York Times, November 23.

——. 2001b. Exclusion and Inclusion. South Asia Citizens Wire, Dispatch no. 2. Electronic document, http://www.mnet.fr/aiindex. Accessed November 28.

Solomon, Jay. 2001. Foreign Terrorists Are Tied to Indonesia. The Wall Street Journal, December 13.

Stone, Martin. 1997. The Agony of Algeria. New York: Columbia University Press.

Usher, Graham. 1993. The Rise of Political Islam in the Occupied Territories. Middle East International, London 453, June 25.

Vines, Alex. 1991. RENAMO: Terrorism in Mozambique. Bloomington: Indiana University Press.

Salman Sayyid

THE ISLAMIST IMPASSE?

MANY OF THE difficulties encountered by Islamists have been common to other historical attempts at transnational social transformations. Specifically, the Islamists face four main challenges to their ambitions to institutionalize a new order. First, in most Muslim societies a large section of the population remains committed to Westernization, and for various reasons Islamists have not been as successful in winning over this group. This section of the population believes itself to be secularist, modern and liberal; it certainly presents itself in these terms to Western audiences. Despite their love of liberalism and democracy, however, many of these people have been willing to support illiberal and anti-democratic measures taken by the state machinery against Islamists. The Islamists need to win over this group without diluting their appeal to their core constituencies. To win this group over, Islamists have to deconstruct the rather benign interpretation by which this group tends to 'understand' the West. This has to be done through a radical decolonization and not a demonization of the West (although it is unlikely that the defenders of Western hegemony will necessarily be able, or even willing, to differentiate between the two).

Second, the current divisions of the Muslim world are sanctioned by an international order enforced by the new concert of mainly Western powers. As such, most Islamist groups are forced into making accommodations to the nation-state, with the consequence that nationalism begins to penetrate their discourse (for example, the parties in Kuwait, who claim to be Islamist, are unwilling to allow non-Kuwaiti Muslims to become members). This nationalization of Islamism means that Islamist groups are prone to being isolated, and often forced into political positions which undermine their Islamist objectives – this can be seen in the way that Islamist groups have to pander to policies of ethnic and cultural homogenization even when dealing with Muslim minority ethnic groups. If the Islamists are to remain a distinct political force, they must continue to focus on transcending the nation-state and contribute towards the formation of a global Islamicate culture. This requires Islamists to engage in intellectual-moral reforms, which are geared towards a critique of xenophobic nationalism, and a celebration of an Islamicate identity. To this end, Islamists need to take a more active part in contributing towards a global all-inclusive *Ummatic* culture which is not reducible to any authoritative national (whether Iranian, Saudi, or Turkish), or sectarian (Shia or Sunni) model.

Third, the current global order is dominated by a discourse that privileges the subjectivity of a sovereign consumer. In this way, all values and convictions become matters for individual choice and consumption. Islamists, despite the energy spent on devising 'Islamic' economics, have largely failed to counter this discourse. Their attacks have been based on questions of moral regulation and rectitude rather than overcoming the fundamental logic of this discourse. In this important sense, they have not yet been able to articulate a counter-hegemonic project for the reorganization of the world political economy.[1] The Islamists have an urgent need to develop a response to the contemporary division of global spoils. A number of alternatives suggest themselves, including joining in with the anti-globalization critique of radical and leftist groups. The recent popular boycott in the Islamicate world of American brand names suggests another possibility. More fundamentally, however, Islamists need to articulate a vision in which conspicuous consumption is not the motor of individual gratification and self-realization. The articulation of desire beyond the logic of consumerism is necessary, and the Islamists have tended to deal with the question of desire in a punitive rather than a productive manner. To construct desire requires enculturation and not simply prohibitions or tighter law enforcement.

Fourth, the major difficulty faced by Islamists, despite all their rhetoric of Islam as a total system, a complete 'way of life', is that when it comes down to it, far too many of them have a very limited idea of what 'a way of life' is. It is not something that can be reduced to mere biological functions and religious rituals – there is more to life than this, for example, questions of aesthetics, joy, solidarity and so on ... Given the limited understanding of a 'total way of life', it is not surprising that so many Islamists are considered to be unequal to the task of managing the complexities of contemporary governance. Their capacity to make the 'trains run on time' or 'make sure the garbage is collected' is often put into question. The Islamist groups which seem to enjoy the largest base of support are those who have exercised a social welfare function among their communities, for example, Hizbollah in Lebanon, Hamas in Palestine, and to some extent the AK party (in its various incarnations with its management of municipalities) in Turkey. There is a need for Islamists to demonstrate great skill in dealing with the banality of governing. Islamist parties that seem to offer little more than injunctions to greater piety, without putting those systems and procedures that would encourage such behaviour into place, display a lack of governmental imagination, which restricts their capacity for effective governance. Islamists often give the impression that they have a rather limited conception of the nature and possibilities of the state. This difficulty is partly due to a larger problem in which Muslims and Islamists have tended to privilege a theological reading of their history. As a consequence, their capacity to conduct a conversation with their past is too often a rather terse affair. Thus the Islamists often share a difficulty with rest of the Islamicate world in accessing their own (non-canonical) history as a resource for the future.

Despite these four difficulties, the Islamist project is not necessarily over. The condition of possibility for Islamism was the product of a number of distinct developments and processes: the decentring of the West, a quest for a post-Caliphate order and globalization. It is worth considering whether those conditions that made Islamism possible in the first place continue to prevail.

De-centred West

In the wake of the US-sponsored war on terror and its seizure of Afghanistan and Iraq (to date), is it still possible to maintain that the West is de-centred? To the extent that the de-centring of the West was one of the main conditions of possibility for the emergence of Islamism, is it possible to see in the US-sponsored crusade on Islam(ism) the so-called war on terror, as a negation of a de-centred West? Does not the apparent retreat of Islamists in the face of American power point to the restoration of the West as centre? Are we not witnessing a re-centring of the Western cultural formation? Could the gap that appeared between the West and the universal be seen as a temporary blip, the result of decolonization and superpower bi-polarity? There are two factors, however, which suggest that the 'de-centring of the West' is not over, but rather, since the first publication of *A Fundamental Fear*, it has become even more intense.

First, the identity and coherence of the West continues to be contested. The controversial election of George Bush has helped to highlight the differences between the European and American fractions of what Martin Shaw describes as the Western conglomerate state.[2] The West was constituted principally by the globalization of the European formation and its appropriation of the Americas. The articulation of a substantive difference between Europe and America presents the possibility of the fragmentation of the unified Western centre. (While there has been an anti-European strand in both Anglo and Latin America, particularly during the nineteenth century, this anti-Europeanism has been subsumed by the idea that America, particularly the United States, exemplifies the best of a European heritage.) It could be argued that, given the highly contingent manner in which the neo-Reaganites have 'hijacked' the American establishment, the subsequent so-called 'Talibanization' of American public life is ephemeral and does not reflect any long-term strategic or structural change. Even if this is the case and the social changes in the US are producing a society less and less like the America envisioned by the neo-conservatives, it does not follow that the hegemony of the right is over. Hegemony does not require a consensus or a majority; it can suffice by preventing dissent from being organized into what is considered a viable alternative. In other words, hegemony means that those dissenters who do not or cannot speak through its language are considered mute and, as such, outside the framework of public discourse. While, in the long term, a disjunction between the neo-conservative rule and the more variegated experiences of the ruled may produce a crisis of legitimacy, it is possible for regimes and hegemonies to remain entrenched even as the gap between rulers and ruled expands. There is, however, reason to believe that the conservative transformation of American political culture is not an effect of Bush's victory, but rather the consequence of a process that has been under way for the last thirty or so years. A neo-conservative hegemony has been established so that public debate is dominated by neo-conservative tropes, and those who cannot speak through these tropes are considered to be outside the arena of politics.

As a consequence of these developments, the possibility of two powerful divergent interpretations and projections of the West comes closer to actualization. While it is still too early to be able to make a sharp distinction between American and European values and practices, it is, however, possible to imagine the Western conglomerate state becoming bifurcated in the future. This implies the further undermining of the identity and coherence of the West. This weakening of Western identity makes it difficult to maintain the distinction between the West and the Rest as the grammar of world order. The postcolonial dis-articulation between the universal and the West continues apace.

Second, power is at its most effective when it is able to present itself as a natural way of life; in other words, when power has become invisible it is no longer considered to be power, but seen as just the way the world has been and will be. Power finds its legitimacy in the fashioning of a culture in its image. Enculturation and socialization minimize the need for the use of force. Imperial enterprises that rely solely on the exercise of violence are unsustainable. In this light, the war on terror can be read as an admission of the failure of American hegemony over the Muslim *Ummah*.[3] It has failed to legitimize its occupation of parts of the Islamicate lands. It is these failures that necessitate the use of violence on a global scale in order to discipline a world that does not listen to America unless threatened with Cruise missiles and special forces. The crusade on Islam(ism) demonstrates the failure of legitimacy, and the difficulties Western cultural practices and values have in trying to pass themselves off as universal and natural.

Therefore, the de-centring of the West has not been halted. The postcolonial condition has not been, as yet, rolled back. While increasingly public policy and academic commentary suggest re-colonization as a way of restoring the world to order, it is not clear that the publics of the Western conglomerate state would support and sustain such imperial ventures. The postcolonial condition has penetrated Western culture to the extent that such imperial dreaming fails to fire the popular imagination. The project of Eurocentrism, that is, the attempt to suture the gap between the universal and the West, has become militarized in the years after the publication of *A Fundamental Fear*. The militarization of Eurocentrism is a sign not of its imminent success but rather of its current failure to close the gap.

Waiting for the Caliph

The second condition of enabling Islamism was the abolition of the Caliphate and the quest to establish an Islamically legitimate political order in its wake. It seems curious to argue that the institution of the Caliphate should have such political significance; after all, the Caliphate was contested since at least from the time of the Abbassid–Fatmid confrontation (if not from the very beginning of its institution with the Shia critique).[4] There is also a dispute as to what extent the early Ottomans actually emphasized their Caliphal status. Even if we were to accept the relative unimportance of the Caliphate in the past (and it is still far from clear that we should), it does not mean that the Caliphate did not become important in the post-Caliphate period.

After all, contrary to the tenets of Orientalism, Islam does not end with the siege of Vienna. The centrality of the Caliphate is not a purely historical matter for which detached historians act as judges and gatekeepers of what is permissible for today's Muslims.[5] I would argue that the significance the Caliphate has had over the period of Islamicate history has not been constant, but that does not invalidate its growing significance in a post-Ottoman universe. The place of the Caliphate can be (and has been) re-articulated at different moments according to different (re-)constructions of the present and projects for the future.

The attempt to restore the Caliphate is not only the direct aim of political parties such as Hizb-ut-Tahrir; more diffusely, one can also see in Khomeini's concept of *veliyat-I-faqih* an attempt to articulate a Caliphate that is acceptable to Shia opinion and thus able to transcend divisions between Shia and Sunni political thought. Khomeini's assumption of the office of *veliyat-I-faqih* and his personal stature provided the Islamicate world with a *de facto* Caliph. His interventions were instrumental in helping to shore up an Islamicate global presence.

The symbolic importance of the Caliphate that is presented in *A Fundamental Fear* tended to focus on its canonical response to the problem of a legitimate Islamic government. Perhaps what was not emphasized then, and needs to be emphasized now, is that the Caliphate also represents the idea of an Islamicate great power. A power that can lead, as well as guarantee, an independent and sovereign Islamicate presence in the world. The absence of an Islamicate great power points to the way in which Muslims remain unrepresented at the global level. Such a condition did not have much political significance during a period when Muslim identity was considered to be of minor relevance. The assertion of a Muslim identity in a context in which there is no Islamicate Great Power creates a situation in which large numbers of people are marginalized from the international system. The absence of the Caliphate is not only a metaphor for a normative vacuum in which the gap between the rulers and ruled within the Muslim world cannot be closed, it is also a metaphor for the missing Islamicate great power that could represent the Muslim *Ummah* at a global level. The Islamicate world can still be usefully described as being post-Caliphate. The significance of the Caliphate for the Muslim *Ummah* has not diminished, rather it still continues to act as a horizon. It is in this context that Al-Qaeda can be understood as an attempt to create a virtual Caliphate – a diasporic, Islamicate great power, able and willing to impose its will on a recalcitrant international system on behalf of those who it considers to be dispossessed and excluded from it. The politics of the Islamicate world continue to be conditioned by the absence of the Caliphate. The Caliphate represents not only political legitimacy for the *Ummah*, but also the possibility of its global political presence.

Islamism and globalization

Globalization, or the hollowing out of the Westphalian order, is often represented by two different trends. One trend sees in globalization the process by which an increasingly integrated world is becoming homogenous. The other trend sees globalization as producing greater heterogeneity. In this duel between integration and fragmentation, Islamist projects are seen as exemplars of the forces of fragmentation.

Islamism seems to be a retreat from global homogenization and a last-ditch effort to assert particularism in the face of the McDonaldization of the World. The idea that Islamism is a reaction to globalization, however, tends to ignore the way in which Islamism is enabled by globalization. Islam is a universal religion in that it is not specific to any location or any ethnicity. The interpretation of Islam as universal is well established among Muslims, even though, on occasion, parochialism and particularism creep in. For most Islamists, however, Islam is not reducible to cultural or national practices. Islamists in general see Islam as being for all of humankind.

The reorganization of the world along Westphalian lines contributed to the development of Islam that tended to deny its global and political character. The undermining of the Westphalian state system has created a space where an Islam unencumbered by national cultural accretions can operate.[6] Such a space allows for the articulation of Islam unconstrained by national or particularistic concerns, an Islam that is able to embrace the entire Muslim *Ummah*. The creation of a large Muslim diaspora is one of the key developments that has enabled the spread of a pan-Islamicate sense of Muslimness.[7] In the Muslim diaspora in Western plutocracies, Muslims, unified by experiences of racism and Islamopobia, are brought into contact with each other increasingly as Muslims rather than as members of ethnic or national communities. The growth of Muslim advocacy organizations and media outlets all demonstrate the construction of a nascent Islamicate civil society in the Muslim diaspora, which is multi-national and multi-ethnic in character. This can be seen in the way in which many *ordinary* Muslims responded to the Bosnian genocide, and in the way in which *support for the Palestinian cause has become part of the common sense of Muslim public opinion from Indonesia to Canada*. It can be increasingly seen in the way in which conflicts in Kashmir and Chechnya go beyond their specific locations to a find support in a wider range of Muslim public opinion. So the hollowing out of the Westphalian order continues at a pace.

The capacity of national governments to regulate their populations in their nominal jurisdictions, to tie 'their' people in knots of dependency and loyalty, are increasingly limited. This opening of national spaces enables the development of a trans-national Muslim identity. It is this trans-national Muslim subjectivity that Islamism benefits from, since it helps to form an interpretation of Islam, not simply as a social relationship historically associated with particular national societies, but rather as a matter of political choice that seeks to go beyond the conventional boundaries in which Islamicate identity was always considered to be secondary to national identity.

Islamism is a political discourse that benefits greatly from many of the processes associated with globalization. It is able to disarticulate globalization from Westernization, and offer itself as another paradigm of what lies beyond the nation-state. A trawl through the inmates of the American 'concentration camps' in Guantanamo Bay and elsewhere would readily reveal the trans-national nature of Al-Qaeda. This trans-nationality is not unique among some Islamist organizations. There is no reason to believe that Islamism will not continue to benefit from globalization. What remains to be seen is to what extent the regulatory and disciplinary strategies of the war on terrorism will bring about the end of globalization by enhancing the policing powers of national authorities, and strengthening, at least at the level of peripheral states, the Westphalian template.

Islamism and empire

The symbols of the American Imperium were not attacked because of the virtues of American society. They were not attacked because of resentment at American prosperity. The attacks on the United States were not psychotic or cosmological, but political.[8] To think that attacks on Western targets are simply a reaction to the wonders of Western civilization is to engage in a narcissistic fantasy. The significance of the attacks on the Pentagon and the World Trade Center resides in the way in which it transcended the barrier that separated centre and periphery. During the colonial struggles of the nineteenth century, the 'natives' could rarely, if ever, cross this barrier. Anti-colonial wars were waged, for the most part, on the soil of the colonized and the 'collateral damage' was confined to those residents in the colonies. Post-coloniality makes it increasingly difficult to maintain the separation between centre and periphery. It makes it difficult to enjoy democracy at home and support repressive regimes abroad.

There are voices among the new crusaders who dream of the transformation of the Islamicate world through an occupation modelled on post-war Germany or Japan, and who see Islamism as third in the line of ideologies after Nazism and communism, crushed by American power. Islamism, however, is not analogous to communism or Nazism. It could be argued that communism and Nazism are variants of an immanentist Christian heresy, in which salvation could be immediately found in new social order.[9] Islamism's relationship to Islam is not similar to the relationship of Nazism (or communism) to Christianity. It is not a secularized re-occupation of theological discourse. Islamism is an interpretation of Islam, which emphasizes its social and political import. It is not a replacement for Islam. Furthermore, the occupation and reconstruction of Germany and Japan was facilitated by the Soviet threat. The people of Japan and Germany were being offered not American occupation or liberation, but American occupation or the possibility of Soviet occupation. There is no credible geopolitical rival to the United States, the threat from which can be used by the United States to sell its occupation. Despite the nostalgia for empire being exhibited among some circles in Western plutocracies, it is a nostalgia that does not seem to resonate with those who were subjected to Western empires. It remains the case that despite all the disappointments and devastation visited upon ex-colonial societies in the wake of decolonization, there is hardly any popular movement in any major ex-colony demanding the restoration of imperial rule.

The success or failure of the war on terrorism will depend on the extent to which the project of Eurocentrism is able to close the gap between Western cultural formations and universal values. It is not the occupation of countries such as Afghanistan or Iraq (or whichever regime becomes the latest addition to the American government's list of rogue regimes) that is significant; the real challenge for Western supremacists is whether they can occupy the universal.

The challenge presented by contemporary Islamist movements goes beyond 'panics' about terrorism or weapons of mass destruction, for what Islamism points to is the end of 'the Age of the West' and thus the limits of Westernization as the future of the world. In other words, the study of the Islamicate world has to move beyond the paradigm of the 'West and Rest', in which the 'Rest' of the world is reduced to little more than the West's residue. This is the context which allows

A Fundamental Fear to be situated in a broader set of interventions in various fields (e.g. the so-called 'California school' of world history, some forms of cultural studies and post-colonial discourse theory), which have (in many different ways) begun to interrupt the West and Rest dyad as a way of apprehending the world.

The political turn of Islam cannot be understood outside the very complex ways in which it relates to the project of Western hegemony. Islamism is a project that draws much of its strength from a conviction that there is no need for a detour through the labyrinths of Western history, before one can arrive at a vision of the good life and a just order: universal values can be generated from Islam.

Notes

1 See also Anouar Majid (2000) *Unveiling Traditions: Postcolonial Islam in a Polycentric World*, Chapel Hill, NC: Duke University Press.

2 Martin Shaw (2000) *Theory of the Global State*, Cambridge: Cambridge University Press.

3 One indicator of this failure can be seen in the growth of 'anti-Americanism', not just in Islamicate communities but also in many other parts of the world. See, for example, a 44-country survey with 38,000 respondents on attitudes to the USA in light of the 'war on terror', Pew Global Attitudes Project, 2002.

4 For a discussion of the undermining of Caliphal legitimacy which allowed 'anti-Caliphs' to be established by the Fatimids and Umayyads, see Janina Safran (2001) *The Second Umayyad Caliphate: The Articulation of Caliphal Legitimacy in Al-Andalus*, Cambridge, MA: Harvard University Press.

5 Talal Asad (2003) makes a similar point in his discussion of the role of Muslim reformers in the reconfiguration of the law in colonial Egypt; see *Formations of the Secular: Christianity, Islam, Modernity*, Stanford, CA: Stanford University Press.

6 For further details of this argument see S. Sayyid (2000) 'Beyond Westphalia: Nations and Diasporas' in Barnor Hesse (ed.) *Un/settled Multiculturalism: Diasporas, Entanglements, Transruptions*, London: Zed Books.

7 For details of transnational Islamicate civil society see Peter Mandaville (2001) *Transnational Muslim Politics: Reimagining the Umma*, London: Routledge.

8 For an analysis of the way in which the war on terror is based on an attempted disavowal of its political nature see Barnor Hesse and S. Sayyid (2002) 'The "War" against Terrorism/The "War"' for Cynical Reason', *Ethnicities*, June 2 (2).

9 Michael Burleigh (2000) *The Third Reich: A New History*, London: Pan Books, p. 10.

Further reading

François Burgat, *Face to Face with Political Islam* (London: I. B. Tauris, 2003)
  A sophisticated presentation of important trends and ideologues in contemporary political Islam.
Dale F. Eickelman and James P. Piscatori, *Muslim Politics*, 2nd edition (Princeton: Princeton University Press, 2004)
  A detailed and sophisticated account of the multifaceted dynamics of Muslim politics and of the role played by Islamism.
Fred Halliday, *Islam and the Myth of Confrontation*, 2nd edition (London: I.B. Tauris, 2003)
  A well-informed analysis of politics and violence in the Middle East, and of the role played by Islamism.
Salwa Ismail, *Rethinking Islamist Politics: Culture, the State and Islamism* (London: I. B. Tauris, 2003)
  An insightful analysis of the trends in the social formation and political expression of Islamism in key Muslim polities.
Gilles Kepel, *Jihad: The Trail of Political Islam*, trans. A. Roberts (London: I B Tauris, 2002)
  A sound and comprehensive overview of the evolution of political Islam worldwide in the modern context.
Quintan Wiktorowicz (ed.), *Islamic Activism: A Social Movement Theory Approach* (Bloomington: Indiana University Press, 2004)
  An insightful collection of essays analysing the dynamics of Islamist mobilization from a social movement perspective.
Sami Zubaida, *Law and Power in the Islamic World* (London: I. B. Tauris, 2005)
  An insightful analysis of the relationship between religious and political power in the contemporary Muslim world.

Political Islam and democracy

Introduction

THIS SECTION PROVIDES the reader with detailed accounts of how
Islamist movements are involved in democratization processes. The cases that
have been selected involve prominent Islamist organizations and they highlight the
complexity of political Islam in relation to democratic developments in the Muslim
world. The question of democratization and political Islam came to the fore in the late
twentieth century, particularly after the collapse of the communist bloc, when the
issue of democratic change began to take a prominent place on the international
scene. Regarding Muslim-majority countries there was a slow recognition that Islamist
social forces were able to mobilize the kind of popular support that had underpinned
a liberal civil society in earlier waves of democratic transitions (Latin America,
Southern and Eastern Europe). This situation created new dilemmas for the study of
political Islam. The main theoretical dilemma involved framing how the modern democratic concept of 'sovereignty of the people' could be accommodated within the
Islamic notion of 'sovereignty of God'. Orientalist-inspired analyses of this issue took
one horn of the dilemma and answered that no Islamic order could be truly democratic since the sovereignty of God (and of all those who claimed authority to speak
in God's name) ultimately trumped the popular legitimacy on which any democratic
system was based. Post-orientalist views, by contrast, stressed that since God did not
intervene directly in political affairs and since the Holy Scriptures usually were not
very specific on such issues either, these grand dilemmas could be reduced to very
down-to-earth questions about the relationship between the views of the religious
leadership and those of the general public.

From a practical political perspective, the difficulties created by political Islam
for democratization initially had to do with ensuring that in the early stages of political competition, those Islamists who did not subscribe to the notion of electoral

democracy could not take undue advantage of the new institutional system. This fear of having Islamists 'hijacking' the democratization process – the so-called Islamist free election trap – was eventually met by two types of starkly different observations. On the one hand, secularized regimes in Muslim-majority countries refrained from making significant democratic reforms to the political system in order to 'save' their country from this Islamist 'threat', and in so doing entrenched their own brand of authoritarian governance. On the other hand, Islamist movements revised their discourse and practices to show that they had no particular problem with abiding by the rules of electoral democracy, even in a secularist framework (as in Turkey). The remaining practical dilemmas of democratization in Muslim-majority polities involve an Islamization of society that is seemingly facilitated by the liberalization of politics and the opening of the public sphere. Because democratization does not coincide with the secularization of public life according to a western model of development, it has been a moot point how far political Islam could durably produce a viable modern (or post-modern) type of social and political mobilization in the domestic and international context of the early twenty-first century. Thus, even when Islamist movements are willing and able to adopt the instruments of electoral democracy to organize political competition, there remain notable differences between the dominant model of liberal-democracy and those that are underpinned by an Islamist worldview.

The first extract, from Asef Bayat's *Making Islam Democratic*, stresses the local production of democratic practices that are set in motion by everyday 'Islamic' interactions between citizens at grassroots level. Bayat indicates that besides the political militancy of Islamist organizations, what effectively transforms societal practices is the diffusion of Islamist worldviews via social networking at the sub-political level. This slow and quiet social transformation underpins both the continuing political appeal of Islamist movements and the partial Islamization of the institutions of the state by secularized authoritarian institutions in quest of legitimacy. It counteracts what was previously seen as the dominant societal process in the region, namely the increasing reach of the nationalist and secularized state into traditional society.

The next extract, from Janine Clark's *Islam, Charity and Activism*, considers the mobilizing role played by Islamism from the perspective of social movement theory. Clark notes how the Islamization of the public sphere is not a uniform and straightforward process, but one that remains structured internally by competing constituencies and interest groups. In particular, the mere utilization of Islamist networks and social institutions by local people, and especially the poor, does not necessarily imply their endorsement of an Islamist political agenda. Individual users and Islamist activists use their resources tactically and strategically to make the most out of difficult social and political contexts.

The third text, by Robert Hefner, outlines some of the key trends in the debates regarding Islamism and democratization by examining the relationship between religiosity and political modernity. Warning against the tendency to over-generalize from particular doctrinal positions, Hefner stresses that different trends in Islam interact differently with those aspects of democratization that are deemed crucial in modern politics. In the case of Indonesia, he indicates how pro-democratic Islamist currents became an important element in the consolidation of democratic institutions in the country instead of playing the disruptive role that many analysts had hypothesized.

At the same time as their political input, however, they also produced an important social activism that facilitated the Islamization of society.

The final text, by Carrie Rosefsky Wickham, addresses directly the case of Islamist movements that were not previously sympathetic to (or interested in) the idea of democracy (as described in the western political tradition), but that have initiated an internal reform conducive to more democratic discourses and practices. In the case of Egypt, new movements have branched out of the Muslim Brotherhood (MB) networks to propose programmes that bypass the traditional dilemmas between Islamist and democratic politics. Whickham notes that this situation is not only the result of the more liberal trends within the MB expressing themselves, or of attempts by the movement to sidestep repressive actions taken by the regime. It corresponds also to a tentative strategic repositioning of the movement with regards to its societal project and what it requires in order to receive the support of the masses.

Asef Bayat

THE POLITICS OF PRESENCE

Social movements and political change

TO WHAT EXTENT THEN can social movements in the Middle East alter the political status quo without resorting to violent revolutions? The debate over social movements in general swirls intensely around the modalities of social mobilization, around how the movements are made. Few analyses of the relationship between social movements and sociopolitical change venture beyond what protest actions may entail in either repression or reform.[1] More significantly, little attention is paid to the interplay of social movement activism and state power.[2] The "Westocentric" orientation of social movement theory, rooted in the democratic structures of Western societies, treats social movements as merely the stuff of civil society, where collective protests, lobbying, and pressure are used to force legal change. For the most part, the state and its coercive power matter little. At the same time, the "decentered" understanding of power, notwithstanding its merits, has drastically undercut our attention to state power as a key medium of social and political transformation. For such thinkers as Alberto Melucci and Manuel Castells, for instance, the new social movements (feminist or environmentalist) are not against the dominant power but rather against "dominant codes," principally because no one knows where power lies, or because it is entirely diffused.[3] Foucault, among others, is right in insisting that altering the state's power might not necessarily lead to transformations in other areas of social life such as the family, the workplace, or gender relations,[4] but this should not downplay the debilitating role of the state against a social movement's forward march. At the same time, both the liberal and (orthodox) Marxian perspectives offer little help, since they regard the state either as a neutral and coherent institution that represents the public interest (a liberal view), or as the "executive organ of the ruling class" that cannot be won over without a violent revolution (an orthodox Marxian view). Joel Migdal's instructive point that the states' actual "practices" are different from, indeed more limited than, their apparent coherent and controlling "image" says, unfortunately, little about what this means to struggles that aim to change the polity.[5]

Perhaps Gramsci's perception of the state as the unity of consent and coercion, his rejection of the separation of civil society and the state, and his notions of "war of position" and "passive revolution" might signal a way out. "War of position" describes a strategy of the subaltern to establish societal hegemony – that is, to win over the hearts and minds of the majority by painstakingly working to capture trenches within civil society with the aim of encircling the state. "Passive revolution" is the political elites' strategy to avert social movements by appropriating their aims, so that the state, the original target of change, takes charge of the process. Although it unleashes some degree of reform, "passive revolution" ultimately aims to demobilize social actors. Gramsci's perspective can help us explore how societal processes, social movements as well as activism in everyday life, can contribute to refashioning state institutions and norms.

Drawing on the experience of Iran and Egypt, I suggest that multipurpose movements, such as Islamism and post-Islamism, generate change in four domains. The most common work of social movements is to pressure opponents or authorities to meet social demands.[6] This is carried out through mobilization, threatening disruption, or raising uncertainty.[7] For instance, the Islamist campaign in Egypt compelled the government to restrict many liberal publications, persecute authors, and prohibit films. Second, even if social movements are not engaged in a political campaign, they may still be involved in what Melucci calls "cultural production."[8] The very operation of a social movement is in itself a change, since it involves creating new social formations, groups, networks, and relationships. Its "animating effects," by enforcing and unfolding such alternative relations and institutions, enhance the cultural production of different value systems, norms, behavior, symbols, and discourse. This process of building "hegemony" is expressed in producing alternative ways of being and doing things. Islamism displays a most vivid example of such a moral and intellectual conquest of civil society, albeit in a conservative direction, through Islamic business, education, morality, fashions, weddings, welfare associations, and a "development model."

Third, social movements may also induce change by discretely operating on the faultline between the state and civil society – in educational, judicial, media, and other institutions. In the early 1990s, Egyptian Islamists succeeded in penetrating the state education system, influencing policy-makers, teachers, and above all a generation of students through their activities at teacher training colleges. Islamist judges, at times appearing in traditional garb, or *jalabiyas*, enforced Islamic law, punishing secular individuals while supporting Islamic-oriented legal suits. Even police and the military were not immune. Finally, social movements, if they are tolerated by the incumbent regimes, may be able to capture segments of governmental power through routine electoral means. The cases of Turkey's ruling Rifah Party and Iran's reform government are only two recent examples. Both movements managed to form legitimate governments.

However, the ability of social movements to effectively share political power depends on maintaining their popular support. Unlike the authoritarian states, which rest primarily on coercive force, social movements depend only on their capacity to mobilize their social basis; without this, movements cease to exist. The greatest challenge of a social movement is how to retain its movement character and at the same time exert governmental power. While sharing state power may enable social movements to turn some of their ideas into public policy, failure to do so, even though due to opponents' sabotage, would undermine their support base, thus rendering them powerless. First and foremost, it seems, social movements need to weave their institutional foundation into the fabric of society – something that Iran's reform movement failed to do, but Egypt's MB succeeded in doing. For not only can a solid social base compel opponents and states to undertake political reform, it can also protect movements from repression and ensure revival and continuity even after a period of downturn. Democracy movements must pay close attention to the economic dimension if they are to sustain popular support. People might prefer a populist dictator who brings them immediate prosperity over the promise of a democratic future. A UN survey of Latin America, which found that "a majority would choose a dictator over an elected leader if that provided economic benefits," indicates how real the possibility of "escape from freedom" can be.[9]

Still, crucial questions remain: To what extent can social movement mobilization enforce intended political and structural change? How far can states accommodate the radical projects of their social movement adversaries? And how far can a movement's conquest of civil society and encroachment into the political apparatus proceed? Political scientists have spoken of the possibility of a political pact in which a segment of ruling elites and the opposition come to an agreement to form a new regime. In Chile and Spain, the transition from military dictatorship to democracy took place through such a pact. On the other hand, political reform can occur when ruling groups, enveloped by popular and elite pressure (and possibly by international demand or economic crisis), see compromise as their only option. Such radical reform, or "refolution," as Kis put it, characterized Polish and Hungarian transitions to democracy.[10] In Mexico, the democracy movement (composed of students, peasants, and workers' organizations) managed a prolonged campaign that compelled the state to undertake a democratic transition in the 1990s.[11]

Middle Eastern saga

The Middle East experience has been quite different. Regimes have been too resistant to political change and democracy movements too feeble to force it. It is not that popular dissent has been absent or that the people are inherently indifferent to democracy. Looking back at recent history, one is struck by the extent to which popular movements arose in Syria, Iraq, Jordan, and Lebanon during the late 1950s, after Nasser nationalized the Suez Canal.[12]

The unsuccessful tripartite aggression by Britain, France, and Israel, in October 1956, to reclaim control of the canal caused an outpouring of popular protest from Arab countries in support of Egypt. Although 1956 was probably the last major pan-Arab solidarity movement until the 2002 wave of pro-Palestinian support, social protests by workers, artisans, women, and students for domestic social development, citizens' rights, and political participation have been quite significant. Labor movements in Lebanon, Syria, Egypt, Yemen, and Morocco have carried out strikes and street protests over both economic and political issues. Since the 1980s, during the era of IMF-recommended structural adjustment programs, Arab labor unions have tried to resist cancellations of consumer commodity subsidies, price rises, pay cuts, and layoffs. Despite no-strike deals and repression of activists, strike-induced work stoppages have occurred. Fear of popular resistance has often forced governments, such as those of Egypt, Jordan, and Morocco, to delay structural adjustment programs or retain certain social policies. Ordinary people have responded radically to the violation of traditional social contracts. Massive protests in Morocco, Tunis, the Sudan, Lebanon, Algeria, and Egypt during the 1980s sent strong messages to authoritarian regimes. Even though structural changes since the 1980s, such as de-peasantization, the growth of the informal sector, the fragmentation of labor, and the proliferation of NGOs have significantly diminished class-based mobilization, street protests have flourished when opportunity has allowed. Indeed, since early 2000, popular mobilization in support of Palestinian and Iraqi people has been remarkable. In 2002, hundreds of thousands of protestors marched in Yemen, Iraq, Khartoum, Rabat, Bahrain, and Damascus against the impending U.S. attack on Iraq. For a short while, it seemed, states lost their tight control over "the street," where new, publicly vocal opposition groups multiplied.

Yet these remarkable struggles, carried out largely by the political classes, were directed primarily against outside adversaries (Israel and the United States) with the tacit but cautious endorsement of the states where they occurred, rather than against the repressive rule of those states. If anything, campaigns against authoritarian regimes have been subsumed by powerful nationalist-nativist sentiment, the kind of mass politics that can easily lend itself to enigmatic demagogues or authoritarian populists.[13] Virtue lies not in opaque mass politics but in protracted social movements that have the potential to force systematic change, and whose members are motivated not by emotional impulses or ideological devotion but by their common interests and their leaders' actions.

In Iran and Egypt, social movements succeeded in winning the hearts and minds of the majority and even threatened their governments by forcing them to change some policies, but they ultimately failed to effectively reform their states. Iran's post-Islamist reform movement penetrated the state, only to face the classic dilemma of a parallel power structure in which Islamist opponents, through their control of coercive institutions and economic networks, managed to intercept its progress. And the ruling elite in Egypt continued to neutralize the forward march of Islamism through repression, violence, and a "passive revolution." Even though they left their mark, both movements were forced into retreat. Egypt's secular state tilted toward religion while Iran's religious state became more secular, but in both cases the structures of authoritarian rule remained intact. It was as if the authoritarian "secularreligious" state had become the destined manifestation of "passive revolution" in the Muslim-majority nations of the Middle East.

Precisely because of this exasperating impasse, some social actors have opted for foreign intervention as the only possible way to remove ossified autocratic regimes and "install democracy." The "removal" of the Taliban in Afghanistan and the rapid Anglo-U.S. overthrow of the Ba'athist regime in Iraq hoped those efforts would jump-start democratization in the Middle East. They often made reference to the democratizing experiences of Germany and Japan following their defeat in World War II, even though those countries' social structures, economies, and experience of war differed from those of the Middle East. Even more comparable "imposed democracies," such as the Philippines and Korea, had plunged into dictatorship by the 1970s. They had to wait until the 1980s and 1990s for their domestic social movements to push for homegrown democratic rules.[14]

If anything, foreign intervention in the Middle East has historically worked against, and not for, democratic governance. Most autocratic kingdoms, such as the Hashemite Kingdom of Jordan and those of the Persian Gulf, were created by Britain, which also supported Colonel Qaddafi and King Idris in Libya, both of whom went on to establish autocratic rule. The United States and Britain actively backed the Shah's dictatorship in Iran after helping to overthrow the democratic rule of Muhammad Musaddiq in the 1950s. Iraq's Ba'athist regime enjoyed U.S. and British support, as do most of the region's current authoritarian regimes: Saudi Arabia and the oil shaykhdoms, Jordan, the Turkish generals, Morocco's king, and Egypt's Mubarak. Even the Taliban once had U.S. backing, when UNOCAL wanted to build a gas pipeline through Afghanistan.

This is not to dismiss, a priori, any possible international intervention, solidarity, and support (whether from states or civil society organizations) for the project of political change.[15] The point rather is to explore how to manage foreign support. No doubt "democracy by conquest" is different from international multilateral pressure on repressive states, when it is initiated in association with endogenous pro-democracy movements in the region and draws on international consensus. It may take the form of international institutions or foreign states basing their diplomatic and economic relations on, for instance, respect for human rights. The case of apartheid in South Africa is an obvious example. Democratic Europe's political and economic pressure on its southern dictatorships (Greece, Portugal, and Spain) played a positive role. Even Turkey under Recep Tayyip Erdogan's "Islamic government" "has pulled Turkey further toward democracy than it had moved in the previous quarter century."[16] It has passed laws that have abolished the death penalty, put an end to army dominated security courts, removed curbs on free speech, brought the military budget under civilian control, authorized Kurdish-language broadcasting, and eased tension between Turkey and Greece.[17] These developments are at least partly a response to European Union demands in exchange for considering Turkey's membership.

In contrast, military occupation and war, even if launched in the name of "liberation," are not only immoral (because they presuppose domination, victimize innocent people, inflict destruction, and violate international consensus); they are also unlikely to succeed. The idea of "regime change" is rooted in the false assumption that installing "democracy" as the most noble value justifies drastic consequences and violations. The experience of Iraq confirms the point. Within the first year alone, the Anglo-U.S. occupation reportedly cost Iraq 100,000 dead, colossal material loss, and infrastructural destruction. Many people question whether "regime change" was worth the idea. Besides, at least in the Middle East, even though people long for democratic governance and participation,[18] they are unlikely to embrace it if it comes at the cost of their dignity. The march of American soldiers up and down Arab streets, even in the name of "freedom," violates Arab national dignity. It often turns people toward nativism or makes them susceptible to the demagogic manipulations of xenophobic populists who wail against democratic ideals and cosmopolitan association. Indeed, Israel's continuous occupation of Palestinian lands has already played a destructive, anti-democratic role in the Arab world. The U.S. invasion of Iraq is likely to reinforce this unfortunate legacy. Already signs are that the future of Iraq will be marred by either sectarian conflict or a centralized authoritarian state, unless a nationwide citizen movement for democracy emerges from below. Even a senior advisor to the occupation authority in Baghdad has conceded that the coalition occupation has greatly worsened the long-term prospects for democracy in Iraq.[19]

Politics of presence

The region's Muslim majority, it appears, is caught between, on the one hand, authoritarian regimes and Islamist opposition, both of which tend to impose severe social control in the name of nation and religion; and on the other, flagrant foreign intervention and occupation in the name of democratization. If "democracy by conquest" is not an option, and if authoritarian states resist the democratic quest of organized movements, then what strategy can ordinary citizens pursue? Does the answer, as some might propose, lie in a rapid and violent popular revolution to depose authoritarian states?

The proposition is not as simple as it appears. First, it is doubtful that revolutions can ever be planned. Even though revolutionaries do engage in plotting and preparing, revolutions do not necessarily result from prior schemes. Rather they often follow their own mysterious logic, subject to a highly complex mix of structural, international, coincidental, and psychological factors. We often analyze revolutions in retrospect, rarely engage in ones that are expected or desired. For revolutions are never predictable. Second, most people do not particularly wish to be involved in violent revolutionary strategies. Individuals often express cynicism about engaging in revolutions whose outcome they cannot foresee. At most, they wish to remain "free-riders," wanting *others* to carry them out on their behalf. Third, are revolutions necessarily desirable? Those who have experienced them usually identify violent revolution with massive disruption, destruction, and uncertainty. Besides, nothing guarantees that a democratic order will follow from a revolutionary change. Finally, supposing that revolutions are desirable and *can* be planned, what are people under authoritarian rule to do in the meantime? What options do they have in tackling their own repressive institutions and arrangements if they wish to avoid violent strategies?

Some might choose complicity or "loyalty" by joining mainstream currents. Others, while not approving of the status quo, might well disengage, surrendering their voice and exiting the political stage altogether in the hope that things will someday, somehow, change. Still others may choose to express their contention loudly and clearly, even if it means remaining at the margins of society – being vocal but marginal, or worse, irrelevant. It is, however, extremely challenging to be heavily *present* at the heart of society, and yet not to deviate from the objective, to be both effective and ethical. More precisely, I am referring to that delicate *art of presence* in harsh circumstances, the ability to create social space within which those individuals who refuse to exit can advance the cause of human rights, equality, and justice, and do so even under adverse political conditions. It is this difficult strategy, one that demands sharp vision, veracity, and above all endurance, that holds the most promise.

Meaningful change in the Muslim Middle East may eventually benefit from such a protracted strategy.

The public life and activism of Iranian Muslim women, such as Nobel Laureate Shirin Ebadi, may illustrate that art of persistent presence. Ebadi became the first female Muslim judge in Iran; she held the presidency of Tehran's city court until the Islamic revolution, when she was forced to resign on the grounds that Islam did not allow women to be judges. Yet she and a host of women activists (religious and non-religious) who had been demoted by the revolutionary regime refused to remain silent; they waged a relentless campaign by writing, reasoning, reinterpreting the Islamic texts, engaging in public debate, and lobbying to reverse the unjust ruling until women were once more able to serve as judges in the Islamic Republic. But such a struggle, this double strategy of no-silence and no-violence, could not have gone very far without broad societal support for change.

The idea that Muslim women should be allowed to serve as judges, only one example of the struggles taking place for gender equality in Islam, had already gained a great deal of public legitimacy through the grassroots campaigns of rights activists and ordinary men and women. Its appeal was further rooted in the yearning of Iranian women in general to assert their public presence in society, not necessarily by undertaking extraordinary activities, such as involvement in contentious politics, but through the practices of everyday life, such as working outside the home, pursuing higher education, engaging in sports, performing art and music, traveling, and executing banking transactions in place of their husbands. And these very ordinary practices, once normalized among the general public, were able to undermine gender hierarchy in society while imposing their logic on the state's political, legal, and economic institutions.

Understandably, reform of authoritarian states requires distinct and arduous struggles, the significance and difficulties of which I have already addressed. However, democratic societal change remains indispensable to meaningful and sustained democratic reform of the state. Change in society's sensibilities is the precondition for far-reaching democratic transformation. While social change might occur partly as the unintended outcome of structural processes, such as migration, urbanization, demographic shifts, or a rise in literacy, it is also partly the result of global factors and the exchange of ideas, information, and models. But the most crucial element for democratic reform is an active citizenry: a sustained presence of individuals, groups, and movements in every available social space, whether institutional or informal, collective or individual, where they assert their rights and fulfill their responsibilities. For it is precisely in such spaces that alternative ideas, practices, and politics are produced. The art of presence is ultimately about asserting collective will in spite of all odds, circumventing constraints, utilizing what is possible, and discovering new spaces within which to make oneself heard, seen, and felt. Authoritarian regimes may be able to suppress organized movements or silence collectives. But they are limited when it comes to stifling an entire society, the mass of ordinary citizens in their daily lives.

I envision a strategy whereby every social group generates change in society through active citizenship in their immediate domains: children at home and in schools, students in colleges, teachers in classrooms, workers on shop floors, athletes in stadiums, artists through their art, intellectuals through the media, women at home and in public. Not only are they to voice their claims, broadcast violations done unto them, and make themselves heard, but also to take responsibility for excelling at what they do. An authoritarian regime should not be a reason for not producing brilliant novels, intricate handicrafts, math champions, world-class athletes, dedicated teachers, or a global film industry. Excellence is power; it is identity. Through the art of presence, I imagine the way in which a society, through the practices of daily life, may regenerate itself by affirming the values that deject the authoritarian personality, gets ahead of its elites, and becomes capable of enforcing its collective sensibilities on the state and its henchmen. Citizens equipped with the art of presence would subvert authoritarian rule, since the state usually rules not as an externality to society, but by weaving its logic – through norms and institutions as well as coercion – into the fabric of society. Challenges to those norms, institutions, and the logic of power are likely to subvert a state's "governmentality," its ability to govern. In this regard, women's struggle to resist patriarchy in their day-to-day interactions becomes particularly critical, precisely because patriarchy is embedded in the perception and practice of religious authoritarian polity. Even though patriarchy may subordinate women's public presence (e.g., by bringing gender inequality into the public sphere), it cannot escape from the incrementally egalitarian effect of women's public role. When girls outnumber boys in colleges, women are more likely to become professionals whose authority men are compelled to accept, if not internalize. This alone would point to a significant shift in society's balance of power.

By the art of presence, or an active citizenry, I do not necessarily mean pervasive social movements or collective mobilization for political transformation; nor do I intend to privilege individual active citizenry over contentious movements; in fact, a citizenry of motivated individuals is likely to embrace and facilitate organized collective action. Yet I also recognize that authoritarian rule routinely impedes contentious collective actions and organized movements, and that it is unrealistic to expect a civil society to be in a constant state of vigor, vitality, and collective struggle. Society, after all, is made up of ordinary people who get tired, demoralized, and disheartened. Activism, the *extraordinary* practices that produce social change, is the stuff of *activists*, who may energize collective sentiment when the opportunity allows. The point is not to reiterate the political significance of contentious movements in causing political change, or to downplay the need to undercut the coercive power of the states. The point rather is to discover and recognize societal spaces in which lay citizens, through the ordinary practices of everyday life, through the art of presence, may recondition the established political elites and refashion state institutions into their sensibilities.

Such a refashioning of the state may result not only from an active citizenry, individual initiative, and education, but more pervasively from the long-term impact of social movement activism. Through their cultural production – establishing new social facts on the ground, new lifestyles, new modes of thinking, behaving, being, and doing – movements can acclimatize states to new societal trends. For instance, to gain legitimacy, the Egyptian government had to abide by the many, albeit conservative, codes, conducts, and institutions that Egyptian Islamism hegemonized in society. In a different setting, the Islamic Republic began to recognize the popular desire for secularization, democratic polity, and civil liberties, which Iran's social movements had helped to articulate. I call this laborious process of society influencing the state *socialization of the state*. It means conditioning the state and its henchmen to societal sensibilities, ideals, and expectations. Socialization of the state is in effect "governmentality" in reverse.[20]

It would be naive to romanticize "society" at the expense of demonizing the state. Just as states may be oppressive, societies can be divided, individualized, authoritarian, and exploitive. Feminists have long taken issue with "society" for its patriarchal disposition in the organization of the household and family life, in private relations, in science and technology, and in everyday language. We saw how Egyptian society in the 1990s pushed the state not in a democratic but in a conservative direction. In general, an effective state is indispensable in preventing not only societal abuses,[21] but also social collapse and disintegration. In short, socializing the polity (the state) to democratic values may not succeed without politicizing society in a democratic direction. Otherwise, an active citizenry can easily recede into co-optation, conservatism, orientation to market attractions, selfish individualism, or conventional globalized networks that transform it into a citizenry devoid of collective sensitivity and aspiration. It is thus crucial for an active citizenry to think and act politically, even within its own immediate sphere, even though its aim might not be revolution or regime change; but it must be concerned with solidarity, social justice, and an inclusive social order.[22]

An active citizenry of this sort cannot remain parochial, introverted, and nativist; it is compelled to join a cosmopolitan humanity, to link up with global civil activism, and to work for solidarity. Those actively present in the Muslim Middle East cannot expect global camaraderie if they remain ignorant or indifferent to the plight of people like themselves in other corners of the world – in Chiapas, in Darfur, or in the inner cities of the West. Nor can they afford any longer to treat the West as though it were a unitary category, without recognizing its internal divisions and struggles; they cannot afford to discount the sympathy of Western humanists for the struggles of Muslims within their own societies. In turn, global recognition and solidarity are crucial in encouraging and energizing those in the Muslim world who endure the plight of presence. I stress recognition and solidarity rather than acts of dismissing, stereotyping, or patronizing. But this requires a deep sensitivity to and understanding of the complex texture, multilayered dispositions, and seemingly contradictory directions of popular struggles in this part of the world.

Notes

1 See, for instance, Tarrow, *Power in Movement*. See also Giugni, "Was It Worth the Effort?"; Giugni, MacAdam, and Tilly, *From Contention to Democracy*.

2 Only as recently as 2003 did a book-length treatment of the subject appear. See Goldstone, *States, Parties and Social Movements*. Tarrow, *Power in Movements*, and Della Porta and Diani, *Social Movements*, do take up the issue, but the discussions do not go far beyond invoking notions of co-optation or repression.

3 See Melucci, "A Strange Kind of Newness," and his *Challenging Codes*. See also Castells, *The Power of Identity*, pp. 359–60.

4 Foucault, *Knowledge/Power*, pp. 55–62.

5 Migdal, *State in Society*.

6 This is what Polish sociologist Piotr Sztompka calls "manifest change"; *see* Sztompka, *Sociology of Social Change*, pp. 274–96.

7   Tarrow, *Power in Movement*.
8   Melucci, *Nomads of the Present*, p. 60. Melucci's "cultural production" is roughly what Sztompka calls "latent change"; see Sztompka, *Sociology of Social Change*.
9   Forero, "Latin America Graft and Poverty."
10   Kis, "Between Reform and Revolution."
11   Cadena-Roa, "State Pacts, Elites."
12   These passages heavily draw on Bayat, "The 'Street' and the Politics of Dissent."
13   This does not imply that "civil society" is missing in the Muslim Middle East, or that people have been passive in light of the new structural changes. I have described the alternative mode of mobilization in the Arab world in ibid.
14   Grugel, *Democratization*, pp. 42–43.
15   Mahmood Mamdani's otherwise fine book, *Good Muslims, Bad Muslims*, rejects any kind of foreign intervention.
16   Kinzer, "Will Turkey Make It?"
17   Ibid.
18   The World Value Survey (WVS) carried out between 1999 and 2002 in Algeria, Egypt, Jordan, and Morocco found that over 90 percent of respondents believed that, despite its problems, democracy is still the best form of government; cited in Tessler and Gao, "Gauging Arab Support for Democracy."
19   See Diamond, "What Went Wrong in Iraq."
20   Foucault describes "governmentality" in terms of the state devising mechanisms, methods, and ideas through which citizens govern themselves in accordance with the interests of those who govern. See Foucault, *Power*.
21   These range from Hobbes through the Marxists. See Held, *States and Societies*.
22   I am grateful to Kaveh Ehsani for bringing these important points to my attention. For a discussion, see Mamdani, *Citizens and Subjects*.

Bibliography

Bayet, Asef. "The 'Street' and the Politics of Dissent in the Arab World." *Middle East Report*, no. 226 (March 2003): 10–17.
Cadena-Roa, Jorge. "State Pacts, Elites, and Social Movement in Mexico's Transition to Democracy." In Jack Goldstone, ed. *States, Parties, and Social Movements*, pp. 107–43. Cambridge, UK: Cambridge University Press, 2003.
Castells, Manuel. *The Power of Identity*. Oxford, UK: Blackwell, 1997.
Della Porta, Donatella, and Mario Diani. *Social Movements: An Introduction*. Oxford, UK: Blackwell, 1999.
Diamond, Larry. "What Went Wrong in Iraq." *Foreign Affairs* (Sept.–Oct. 2004): 34–56.
Forero, Juan. "Latin America Graft and Poverty Trying Patience with Democracy." *New York Times*, June 24, 2004.
Foucault, M. *Knowledge/Power*. New York: Pantheon Books, 1972.
———. *Power*, New York: New Press, 1994.
Giugni, Marco. "Was It Worth the Effort? The Outcome and Consequences of Social Movements." *American Review of Sociology*, vol. 24: 341–93.
Giugni, Marco, Doug MacAdam, and Charles Tilly, eds. *From Contention to Democracy*. Lanham, Md.: Rowman and Littlefield, 1998.

Goldstone, Jack, ed. *States, Parties and Social Movements*. Cambridge, UK: Cambridge University Press, 2003.

Grugel, Jean. *Democratization: A Critical Introduction*. London: Palgrave, 2002.

Held, David. *States and Societies*. Oxford, UK: Martin Robertson, 1983.

Kinzer, Stephen. "Will Turkey Make It?" *New York Review of Books*, July 15, 2004.

Kis, Jonus. "Between Reform and Revolution: Three Hypotheses about the Nature of Regime Change," *Constellations*, vol. 1, no. 3: 399–421.

Mamdani, Mahmood. *Citizens and Subjects*. Princeton, N.J.: Princeton University Press, 1996.

———. *Good Muslims, Bad Muslims*. New York: Pantheon, 2004.

Melucci, Alberto. *Challenging Codes: Collective Action in the Information Age*. Cambridge, UK: Cambridge University Press, 1996.

———. *Nomads of the Present*. Cambridge, UK: Cambridge University Press, 1989.

———. "A Strange Kind of Newness: What's New about the 'New' Social Movements." In E. Larana et al., eds., *New Social Movements: From Ideology to Identity*. Philadelphia: Temple University Press, 1994.

Migdal, Joel. *State in Society*. Cambridge, UK: Cambridge University Press, 2001.

Sztompka, Piotr. *The Sociology of Social Change*. Oxford, UK: Blackwells 1999.

Tarrow, Sidney. *Power in Movement: Collective Action, Social Movements and Politics*. Cambridge, UK: Cambridge University Press, 1994.

Tessler, Mark, and Eleanor Gao. "Gauging Arab Support for Democracy." *Journal of Democracy*, vol. 16, no. 3 (July 2005): 86–87.

Janine Clark

SOCIAL MOVEMENT THEORY, SELECTIVE INCENTIVES, AND BENEFITS

ACCORDING TO THE social movement literature, participation in social movement organizations such as ISIs and the horizontal social networks in which they are embedded is to a large extent facilitated by the benefits that social movement organizations provide their participants. In the case of ISIs, these benefits include well-paying jobs, flexible work schedules, and private schools for their children. According to the literature, benefits, or "selective incentives," play a positive role. The study of ISIs, however, indicates that this is not always the case.

Debra Friedman and Doug McAdam confirm that networks draw individuals into collective action by providing incentives and rewards – both nonmaterial and material. Refusing to respond to the call of network partners means the potential loss of all benefits provided by that tie.[1] These benefits may be social, such as friendship or social honor, or material, such as jobs.[2] The encouragement of important others to participate is in itself a social incentive.[3] McAdam refers to the myriad of interpersonal rewards that ongoing participation in a group or informal association provides as the "structures of solidarity incentives."[4] Rodney Stark and William Bainbridge, citing the example of Protestant groups in predominantly Catholic Guatemala City, note that prior to joining, members had had especially weak social ties compared to their neighbors who remained Catholic. The act of joining Protestant groups thus provided gratifying relationships, and through them the members acquired and maintained Protestant beliefs. The two authors point out that the Ananda cult similarly provides its members with companionship unavailable in the larger society.[5] Regarding his study of the Moonies, Stark observes

> remarkable improvements in the ability of some members to manage interpersonal relations. They came to the group suffering greatly from low self-esteem and lack of confidence that disrupted their interactions with others.... Forging strong affective ties to other group members

quite noticeably raised the self-esteem of new recruits. ... Moreover, direct rewards available to cult and sect members are not limited to affection. Groups such as the Hare Krishnas and the Moonies offer specific material inducements – they clothe, feed, and shelter adherents. Indeed, they offer them a career that, at least within the group, enjoys considerable prestige. ... Furthermore, there is considerable scope for ambition. ... Some members can rise to positions of considerable status and power. Bainbridge found that the original core members of The Power lived in considerable luxury and exercised a great deal of authority over newer members (including sexual access).[6]

Indeed, ISIs are not the only groups to provide incentives to their participants. Many groups, aware of the seduction of incentives, consciously provide various forms of rewards. Stark and Bainbridge note that the Mormons' thirteen-step instructional program for recruiting new members reveals a strong priority on "showering tangible rewards upon potential new members."[7] And Snow, Zurcher, and Eckland-Olson observe that both the Moonies and the Nichiren Shoshu strategically go about "the business of 'luring' and 'securing' recruits." Both of their respective recruitment processes are organized to gradually "sell" potential members the benefits of participation and thereby provide them with reasons for joining and remaining members of the respective movements.[8]

So important are selective incentives that Mancur Olson argues that, other than coercion, there is really no other way to get collective action going.[9] Selective incentives may be positive or negative – they can punish a member for reneging or reward or induce one to participate. Only such an incentive, Olson argues, will stimulate a rational individual to act in a group-oriented way as opposed to pursuing individual interests. The incentives must be selective, in that they by and large are reserved for those in the group and not for outsiders. Olson concurs with other theorists that these incentives may be economic or they may be less tangible and include prestige, friendship, and social status. Olson does not discuss any negative side effects with regard to selective incentives – they play a necessary and positive role.

The case study of ISIs, however, challenges the prevailing view within resource mobilization theory that these rewards and benefits play a strictly positive role. In the case of ISIs we see that the provision of benefits by a social movement organization, such as well-paying jobs with flexible work schedules, can both help and hinder the organization and perhaps even the movement. While there is no doubt that various benefits have been pivotal to middle-class participation in ISIs, the very provision of benefits is creating a tension between the stated aims or goals of ISIs and the needs of the Islamist movement. While Islamists establish ISIs in order to address the needs of the poor, the requirements of ISIs (their need for a pool of educated doctors, for example) and the needs of the Islamist movement to expand its membership base by providing benefits for the middle class mean that ISIs do not necessarily prioritize the needs of the poor over those of the middle class. While the ICCS in Jordan loudly boasts of its efforts to alleviate poverty in Jordan, its most prominent "charity" activity is that of the Islamic Hospital – a relatively expensive hospital that is inaccessible to Jordan's poor.[10] In Egypt, the best Islamic clinics are located in the more affluent areas of Cairo – where the holders and donors of money are located. In Yemen, the

Islah Charitable Society in Hodeidah offers day camp for children during the summer at exorbitant rates. This tendency has not gone unnoticed by the general public, including the middle class. The mere fact that in Jordan the Islamic Hospital is commonly referred to as the "Criminal Hospital" – a reference to its high fees – is telling evidence of the negative side effects offering benefits can have.

However, few social movement theorists view any possible negative repercussion from the benefits social movement organizations have to offer. Hanspeter Kriesi briefly states that to the extent that the provision of selective incentives becomes an end in itself, the social movement organization has turned into a business enterprise.[11] He does not provide any empirical evidence, however. Frances Fox Piven and Richard Cloward have written in an in-depth manner on the deleterious effect of benefits and rewards. In their study of poor people's movements, they argue that "organization can hurt organizing." They argue that formal organization is detrimental to poor people's movements, such as the civil rights movement, because as they formalize, they become vulnerable to internal oligarchy and stasis and to external integration with and co-optation by the elites they are lobbying for changes. Organizational demands (and temptations) soon supersede the needs of the membership. Within this larger argument, the authors discuss the specific concerns of this book, the provision of benefits to members. One example they cite is that of the welfare rights movement in the United States. Established by middle-class activists, the movement offered poor, relatively powerless people various leadership positions. However, these positions soon became a source of intense preoccupation and competition. As they state:

> Considering the hard and dreary lives which most welfare recipients had previously led, the rewards of prestige and organizational influence which accrued to those who could win and hold office were enormous. An equally enormous investment in the politics of leadership naturally followed. These circumstances constrained the expansion of membership, for the leaders came to have an investment in membership stasis.[12]

Once a leader got into power, he/she tended to focus on cultivating and strengthening their ties with the group that brought them to power and not on increasing the movement's membership.[13] However, Piven and Cloward deal predominantly with the issue of organizational form and only tangentially with the issue of benefits and rewards.

The case study of ISIs strongly indicates that the strategy of luring and securing movement participants through the provision of various benefits can have a negative effect upon a movement. The case studies do not dispute the fact that benefits can and do aid the expansion of a social movement organization's participants; however, when the provision of benefits themselves comes at the expense of the stated goals of the organization, the long-term impact upon the movement can be detrimental. Particularly in the case of social movement organizations in which the goal of the organization is to serve a different audience than that of the membership of the movement, the provision of benefits to the movement's membership runs the risk of overriding or sacrificing the goals of the social movement organization. The very success of an organization at providing benefits to lure and secure movement members (or, ironically, to operationalize the goal of the social movement organization) can undermine a movement when they override the goals of the social movement organization or become the goals themselves.

Pulling it all together: Islamist networks and the new middle class in Egypt, Jordan, and Yemen

Based on the three case studies of Egypt, Jordan, and Yemen, I argue that Islamic social institutions are run by and for the middle class – specifically members of the educated middle class whose career ambitions rest on their secular, largely professional educations. Because of the operational and instrumental needs of Islamic social institutions and of the Islamist movement of which they are part, we consistently find that the needs of the poor are sacrificed. This is the result of the operating demands of the Islamic social institutions as well as of strategic decisions to cater to and thereby strengthen the largely middle-class membership of the movement. In the course of attending both to the operating imperatives of Islamic social institutions and to the interests of the middle class, strong middle-class social ties and networks are forged and reinforced. Islamic social institutions thus are embedded in middle-class social networks. As participants engage in ISI activities, a strong sense of teamwork, trust, and solidarity develops and new social networks are created. By bringing social networks, Islamist and non-Islamist, together in the provision of charity, ISIs facilitate the introduction of an activist or Islamist worldview to new social circles. However, I argue that while this gradual accumulation of social capital is the basis of a social movement, it is not a social revolution.[14] The case study of Islamic social institutions indicates that moderate Islamism seeks more to coexist and compete with the dominant institutions and social arrangements than to dramatically alter them. Most important, I argue that the strategy of catering to middle-class needs undermines the movement in the long term.

Each of the three ISIs under examination owes its existence and viability to its ability to attract educated middle-class donors, volunteers, and employees. The means by which the respective ISIs do so is their utilization of and dependence upon middle-class social networks – those who have time, money, and skills to offer. The heart and soul of ISI funding is through individual appeals – largely verbal, sometimes written – to neighbors, fellow workers, and friends. Quite simply, for an ISI to succeed, it needs an active and well-connected director or board of directors. Directors of ICCS branch centers energetically write, telephone, and visit their friends both within Jordan and abroad for regular donations. In Yemen, volunteers for the Islah Charitable Society approach friends for donations at the end of Qur'anic study group sessions. In Cairo, founders of an Islamic medical clinic encourage neighboring community members to donate cement, iron pillars, and windows, and electrical wiring in the building of the clinic. In this sense, the overlapping networks between the home, mosque, workplace, other ISIs, clubs, and even friends living abroad make the establishment and continuation of an ISI possible. These same middle-class networks provide necessary contacts in the bureaucracy to facilitate the legal registration of the ISI. Without connections within the government – friends, former army mates, or schoolmates – ISIs would not be able to expedite the frustrating bureaucratic quagmire necessary to register an NGO and ensure a successful outcome. Middle-class networks are also the most important source of volunteers and "skilled" labor. The case study of Islamic medical clinics in Cairo reveals that the vast majority of clinics hire their doctors and nurses by word of mouth – without advertising, targeted recruiting, or interviewing. Through conversations among friends, clinic directors learn of the brother of a friend of a friend who is a doctor and is looking for extra income or experience in the evenings.

Beyond appeals to friends, ISIs must be able to attract doctors and nurses to their organizations on a professional level. ISIs must be able to meet middle-class needs that are not being met (or are being insufficiently addressed) elsewhere. When possible, ISIs thus engage in strategic decisions concerning hiring and adopt strategies of providing incentives for a middle-class doctor to work in an Islamic clinic as opposed to elsewhere (or in addition to elsewhere). They must lure and secure employees and volunteers by offering various benefits or selective incentives.[15] In Egypt, where the underemployment rate among doctors is extremely high, this is less problematic. The high underemployment rate means that positions in Islamic clinics can be highly sought after, particularly by interns and junior doctors. Islamic clinics can sometimes offer these doctors experience, income, and a potential client base should they open their own private practices. Where underemployment among doctors is not such a problem, ISIs are often more strategic. In the case of Jordan, doctors are lured to Islamic clinics and hospitals by flexible work schedules and the prospect of working on some of the finest equipment in the country. ISIs associated with the ICCS regularly adopt a strategy of purchasing limited pieces of sophisticated, specialized, and, as a result, expensive medical equipment as opposed to more numerous pieces of lower-quality equipment. While this strategy has a certain symbolic appeal in terms of demonstrating (or boasting of) the viability and/or superiority of the Islamic alternative, it is also strategically chosen with the desires of Jordanian doctors in mind. Professionally it makes sense to work in an ISI. In this way ISIs are assured a secure supply of an educated labor force. By addressing the economic, professional, and other needs of middle-class professionals, ISIs assure their own viability and sustainability.

Thus, the founding and running of ISIs involves middle-class contacts and ties on a one-time and ongoing basis. It involves loosely and tightly knit networks of people who donate time, energy, skills, and money on a regular or irregular basis and branch out to include hundreds of people who may in fact have never visited the ISI in question. These networks include both Islamists and non-Islamists.

In this regard, the operational needs of an ISI largely dictate that ISIs cater to the middle class, specifically the educated middle class (e.g., doctors and interns) and, as a result, become embedded in middle-class networks. ISIs need doctors, nurses, and teachers in order to provide their services to the poor. They furthermore need those with resources – or material – to donate. However, the expansion or embeddedness of middle-class networks is also due to the demands of the Islamist movement itself. Doctors, lawyers, engineers, and university students make up the bulk of the support of the Islamist movement. In the context of states that cannot provide adequate economic and other opportunities for their citizenries, the movement seeks to provide for the needs and demands of its membership. There is thus a push from within the movement itself to establish private schools and hospitals that cater strictly to middle-class needs. The ICCS in Jordan runs both private (and expensive) institutions, such as the Islamic Hospital, and welfare institutions, such as those that provide free lessons to orphans on the Qur'an, all in the name of charity. This push is further fueled by the ideological endeavor of creating alternative institutions – the belief in activist *da'wa*. The expansion of ISIs to include private enterprises further enlarges the middle-class web in which ISIs are situated.

The result is that ISIs can be divided into two types: Islamic commercial institutions (ICIs) and Islamic welfare institutions. Islamic welfare institutions (IWIs) are those ISIs catering to the welfare of the poor. They provide financial aid to orphans and reduced-price medical services to the poor, for example. ICIs are those ISIs that are mostly private commercial (albeit nonprofit) institutions that cater, as evidenced by their relatively high fees, to the middle class – the movement's membership. One ISI, such as Jordan's ICCS, can have both IWIs and ICIs.

ISIs are thus embedded in ever-overlapping social networks largely comprising educated middle-class professionals. As are social movements elsewhere, these networks are not exclusively composed of the educated middle class, but they are overwhelmingly homogenous in nature. The head of an Islamic women's charity and a member of an Islamic political party may attend the same Qur'anic study group. The former may also attend classes at a commercial Islamic university where she encourages friends to also participate in the study group. She may ask her tailor to sew school uniforms at cost for orphan children at Ramadan or she may organize a book sale at the state university in order to raise money for her charity. Similarly, she may ask for donations at the closing of the Qur'anic study group. Alternatively, the director of an Islamic school may also be the founder of an Islamic marriage society that aids the poor by providing inexpensive wedding services and may also be active in an Islamic political party. His/her daughter may be on the student council at state university representing the Islamic List and write in the student newspaper. At each one of these institutions, she/he will overlap with other social networks, including Islamist networks, of the same socioeconomic level. In this manner, the middle-class nature of ISIs and their associated networks reproduces and reinforces itself as the social networks expand. Like-minded people generally associate with one another and prefer to share opinions with each other.

Those who work in ISIs are not all Islamists. Neither does one automatically become an Islamist by working in or contributing to an ISI. Volunteers, employees, and directors of ISIs have numerous and varied reasons for working in an ISI. Indeed, part of the success of ISIs lies in their flexibility. The networks that sustain ISIs include those who may only donate once per year on the occasion of Ramadan, those who are simply looking for an extra income, supporters of a variety of different (including non-Islamic) political parties, those wanting to fulfill a largely personal Muslim obligation, and more committed Islamists. Many volunteers and employees do not view their activities in ISIs in any political light. Working or volunteering in an ISI does not mean one becomes a committed Islamist.

In stating this, I am making a distinction between different levels of movement support within an ISI. A participant in an ISI – a volunteer or an employee – may or may not identify with the ideology or goals of the ISI or the Islamist movement. This becomes more evident when we examine the numerous employees (as opposed to volunteers) in ISIs. Particularly given the economic situations in Egypt, Jordan, and Yemen in which jobs, even for professionals, are not available or secure, we cannot assume that employees work in ISIs because they identify with their ideology and/or goals. They may simply be seeking a job.

I therefore am making a distinction within this book between members and non-member participants. A nonmember participant is a person who works within an ISI, a doctor, for example, and in this sense is a participant but one who does not necessarily identify with the Islamist movement. A donor or volunteer who sees his/her act as one of simple charity is also a nonmember participant. A member, on the other hand, is one who actively regards his/her activities within the ISIs as part of his/her identity as an Islamist, as an act of *da'wa*, and as an important component in the Islamist movement. In this case, a director, for example, would be far more integrated into the middle-class social networks that link his ISI with other Islamist institutions. It would be relatively rare to find a director of an ISI who is a nonmember participant; the same cannot be said of the employees. In some instances, depending on the tightness of fit between the goals of the social movement organization and the goals of the social movement, this distinction may not apply. However, in the case of ISIs – where the goal is to provide for the poor – and the Islamist movement – where the goal is to expand its middle-class membership base – the "fit" is not always tight.[16] Participants in ISIs may identify with one or the other goal, with both, or with neither. There is a difference between a doctor who comes in the evenings to work in an Islamic clinic for extra income, does not pray on a regular basis, does not socialize with fellow workers, and simply returns home at the end of the evening, and the doctor who socializes with the members of the board of directors, may have another family member working in the clinic, prays at the community mosque, and is friends with numerous community members who drop by the clinic for social chats. Time constraints, religious conviction, political persuasion, and personality all influence the degree of identification with movement goals and integration in activist social networks.

However, donating to, volunteering for, or working in ISIs gradually creates a sense of teamwork and middle-class networks of trust and solidarity. Indeed, it is this sense of teamwork, family-like relations, and solidarity that marks ISIs and largely sets them apart from other NGOs. What makes ISIs "Islamic" is less the implementation of Islamic rules and procedures than this invisible process of building social capital. The Islamic nature of ISIs is thus not necessarily apparent to outsiders – those outside the associated middle-class networks. This sense of solidarity and commitment is reinforced by the benefits the middle class receives – jobs or better working conditions, higher incomes, educational and health services, a sense of purpose and self-confidence, leadership roles, and friendships. Furthermore, by bringing different social networks together in the provision of charity, ISIs facilitate the creation of new social networks and the introduction of Islamist networks and worldviews to non-Islamists. In doing so, ISIs indirectly contribute to the potential diffusion of Islamist worldviews and the breakdown and rebuilding of social networks with an activist understanding of Islam.

The poor

ISIs can be conceptualized as being situated within two networks of horizontal linkages – those of the directors and middle-class professionals who run the ISIs and benefit from their welfare and commercial institutions and their related networks – and those of the poor – the clients of Islamic welfare institutions. This book argues that

ISIs do not forge strong vertical ties between the two. Indeed, this is entirely in keeping with the experiences of social movements elsewhere. This is not to state that the
poor do not benefit or that those who work in the Islamic welfare institutions do not
care about the poor but that to a large extent, due to operational and strategic reasons, there are more benefits for the middle class and the poor are not integrated into
the middle-class social networks that are the backbone of ISIs and ultimately of the
Islamist movement. The poor are neglected or, more accurately, alienated from the
Islamist social and political vision. Furthermore, while the poor receive numerous
benefits from ISIs, it is doubtful that their experiences within ISIs provide the same
sense of shared meaning. As members of different social networks, the poor are not
participants in (and are largely not privy to) the trust and solidarity building among
the middle class that works in and benefits from ISIs.

In all three countries, there is a large diversity of the types of ISIs and a disparity
in the quantity and quality of services they offer. While the middle class benefits from
the better Islamic welfare institutions and the five-star services offered in private
commercial institutions, those services targeted explicitly for the poor are often of
inferior quality and are inconsistent on a year-to-year basis. In Cairo the quantity and
quality of ISIs differ dramatically in accordance with the socioeconomic milieu of the
surrounding neighborhood. The most successful Islamic medical clinics in terms of
available services and sustainability are simply not in the poorer areas of Cairo. Rather,
these areas are dominated by clinics that have one doctor, have few or no supplies
or equipment, are often inconsistent in their operational hours, and teeter on the
verge of closure. In Jordan, the jewel in the ICCS's crown is the Islamic Hospital in
Amman — a nonprofit hospital that charges rates the poor cannot afford even with
the subsidies offered by the hospital's Fund for the Sick and Poor. None of the profits
from the hospital are directed toward other branches of the ICCS, such as those dealing explicitly with the poor. Indeed, the commercialization of many of the ICCS's
"charity" services led one prominent Jordanian Islamist to complain to me that the
Muslim Brotherhood had abandoned the poor.

The analysis of the three case studies of Egypt, Jordan, and Yemen furthermore
highlights that there is nothing uniquely Islamic about ISIs. The experiences of the
poor in ISIs are similar to their experiences in other social institutions or NGOs.
Indeed, the poor reach out for any help they can receive, including services offered by
nonreligious NGOs and by the government. ISIs are important and necessary provid-
ers of a technical and charitable service. However, in terms of a "demonstration effect"
(whether or not ISIs demonstrate that Islamic medical facilities are superior to government medical facilities), the poor are not necessarily exposed to "superior" Islamic
medical services that demonstrate the illegitimacy of public services and confirm the
viability, efficacy, or preferability of an Islamic state. ISIs are "Islamic" solely in the
sense that they perform charity work for the poor, not in terms of their organizational
structure, regulations, or functions. Stated differently, they are Islamic in the hearts
and minds of those who provide the services or in the sentiment or attitude with
which they are run.[17] Very few, if any, ISIs differ in their operational procedures from
private, philanthropic, or other social welfare associations. In this regard, they do not
provide a model for or alternative to the state.

ISIs are often one of several options the poor regularly frequent for services.
Indeed, ISIs complement the services of the government and other secular NGOs;

they do not replace them. In Jordan, for example, many of the ICCS centers dealing specifically with the poor have "social workers" on staff. One of their duties is to ensure that the recipients of monthly subsidies are not receiving monthly allowances from other charity sources and thereby raising their combined (undeclared) "income" to a level that technically excludes them from charity programs.[18] The poor take advantage of whatever means is available – regardless of political ideology.

Finally, while the poor are not nameless clients in ISIs, they are also not members of the executive decision-making bodies of ISIs or of their general assemblies.[19] It goes without saying that they cannot afford the schools and other commercial services of which the middle class can take advantage. Furthermore, more informal social gatherings among the middle class, such as Qur'anic study groups, also generally exclude the poor as they are not part of middle-class social circles and generally do not have the time to engage in such leisure activities. They thus have little access to middle-class social networks.

What emerges is a picture that is very different for the poor and the middle class. More to the point, the economic benefits and the meaning, solidarity, and satisfaction that may be experienced by the middle class in ISIs is not being expanded to the lower classes. The Islamization or recruitment of the poor appears to be neither the intent nor the result of ISIs. Indeed, Asef Bayat's examination of the Islamist movement in Egypt confirms that Islamic social welfare organizations are not places for Islamist political activism among the poor.[20] ISIs appear to be run by middle-class Islamists for their middle-class supporters and voting constituency.

Middle-class benefits

ISIs offer both services the middle class demands and jobs the middle class needs. The middle class is employed in ISIs, often in good-paying positions as doctors, and benefits from private schools and hospitals for themselves and their families – all in the name of charity. This is both due to the operational requirements of ISIs and due to the movement's desire to cater to its membership and increase that membership. I argue, however, that contrary to the prevailing literature on social movement theory, the catering of ISIs to middle-class needs, often at the expense of the poor, may in fact be detrimental to the movement. It may be backfiring among potential middle-class members – the potential recipients of those very benefits.

The three case studies thus indicate that when the provisions of benefits to pro-spective members and members supersedes the goals of the organization, this can have a deleterious effect upon the movement. This tendency is most pronounced in Jordan, where there are strong indications that the tension between the needs of the movement – to address the demands of the middle-class membership by offering benefits – and the stated goals of the ISI – to help the poor – has resulted in a per-ceived sense of hypocrisy among Jordanians that undermines the movement and its recruitment potential. Quite simply, ISIs are seen as betraying their values, and this reflects negatively upon the movement.

My argument – that benefits under these conditions can hurt a movement – provides a contribution to the literature on social movements in which the prevailing view is that benefits can only help secure membership expansion. In the context of states that cannot adequately provide for the various needs of the educated middle class, including jobs, the provision of these needs takes an extremely important role in the movement. In addition, ISIs need middle-class participants in order to fulfill their goal of providing for the poor. The result is that the provision of middle-class benefits can come to dominate ISIs – at the expense of the poor. When this occurs, the fit between the goals of the movement and that of the social movement organization begins to break down or loosen – to the detriment of both.

Notes

1   Alternatively, those who know numerous other people who are participating in a social movement, such as the peace movement, stand a much higher chance of being asked if they are participating and of getting negative reactions if they are not. The costs of nonparticipation, which may include losing one's friends, are thus very high. Klandermans and Oegema, "Potentials, Networks, Motivations, and Barriers," 527.

2   Debra Friedman and Doug McAdam, "Collective Identity and Activism: Networks, Choices, and the Life of a Social Movement," in *Frontiers in Social Movement Theory*, ed. Aldon D. Morris and Carol McClurg Mueller (New Haven, Conn.: Yale University Press, 1992), 161.

3   Karl-Dieter Opp and Christiane Gern, "Dissident Groups, Personal Networks, and Spontaneous Cooperation: The East German Revolution of 1989," *American Sociological Review* 58 (October 1993), 661.

4   McAdam, "Micromobilization Contexts and Resource Mobilization," 135.

5   Stark and Bainbridge, "Networks of Faith," 1381, 1384.

6   Ibid., 1393.

7   Ibid., 1393–1394.

8   Snow, Zurcher, and Eckland-Olson, "Social Networks," 795.

9   Mancur Olson, *The Logic of Collective Action* (Cambridge, Mass.: Harvard University Press, 1965), 133; Hanspeter Kriesi, "The Organizational Structure of New Social Movements in a Political Context," in *Comparative Perspectives on Social Movements: Political Opportunities, Mobilizing Structures, and Cultural Framings*, ed. Doug McAdam John D. McCarthy, and Mayer N. Zald (New York: Cambridge University Press, 1996), 156.

10   The poor do receive some limited financial aid from the hospital.

11   Kriesi, "Organizational Structure," 156.

12   Frances Fox Piven and Richard A. Cloward, *Poor People's Movements* (New York: Vintage Press, 1979), 310.

13   In her examination of Kuwaiti women's organizations, both secular and religious, Haya al-Mughni notes a similar phenomenon. She states that in almost all women's organizations in Kuwait, the *rab'a* (a tight network of friends and kin) is an important source of control and a strategy for perpetuating power. In order to retain their influence and avoid a redistribution of power, the leaders bring their own friends and relatives into the organization. Leadership positions have therefore remained in the hands of a relative few and it is these few who have gained popularity and prestige. Leaders meet with government officials, give interviews to the press, and travel all over the world to attend conferences on women's issues.

As al-Mughni states: "Given all these privileges, it is perhaps not surprising that they are so reluctant to give up their positions and return to anonymity." Haya al-Mughni, *Women in Kuwait: The Politics of Gender* (London: Saqi Books, 2001), 119.

14   I use these terms as originally employed by Asef Bayat. See Bayat, "Revolution without Movement, Movement without Revolution: Comparing Islamic Activism in Iran and Egypt," *Society for Comparative Study of Society and History* 40, no. 1 (January 1998), 136–169.

15   Olson defines a selective incentive as a form of benefit that a nonmember cannot obtain. This meaning of the term selective incentives applies to some, but not all, of the benefits that participants in ISIs receive.

16   Maren Lockwood Carden, "The Institutionalization of Social Movements in Voluntary Organizations," in *Research in Social Movements, Conflicts and Change*, 11 (1989), 143–161. In her research on the women's movement in the United States, Carden argues that voluntary organizations may or may not share the same ideology and goals as the social movement to which they ostensibly belong. Carden found that many voluntary groups have very specific or narrow goals, such as helping an identified needy group such as homeless families, but do not always realign their organizational activities in keeping with the larger social movement that is pursuing social problems or the welfare of deprived people in general. The goals of the social movement organization and the social movement may not always fit, and tensions may arise between the social movement organization and the social movement. Carden found that members in voluntary organizations join an organization to pursue *its* goals and not the goals of the social movement.

17   Wiktorowicz agrees. See *Management of Islamic Activism*, 85.

18   The case studies of ISIs in Egypt, Jordan, and Yemen appear to confirm a growing body of research that argues that the poor avoid becoming trapped in any system of authority that may limit their options elsewhere. See, for example, Asef Bayat, *Street Politics: Poor People's Movements in Iran* (New York: Columbia University Press, 1997).

19   Poor patients and members of the community will drop by the director's office and discuss concerns. See Janine A. Clark, "Islamic Social Welfare Organizations in Cairo: Islamization from Below?" *Arab Studies Quarterly* 17, no. 4 (Fall 1995), 11–28.

20   Bayat, "Revolution without Movement," 157. See also Bayat, *Street Politics*.

Robert W. Hefner

PUBLIC ISLAM AND THE PROBLEM OF DEMOCRATIZATION

A KEY FEATURE of world politics in recent years has been the resurgence of religious issues and organizations into public affairs. Whether with the Christian Coalition in the U.S., Hindu nationalism in India, militant Buddhism in Sri Lanka, or Islamist movements in the Muslim world, the end of the twentieth century demonstrated convincingly that high modernist reports of religion's demise were, to say the least, premature. As José Casanova (1994) has shown, in many places the upsurge of public religion appears compatible with democracy and political civility. Indeed, Casanova argues, public religion can act as a significant counterweight to the otherwise hegemonic institutions of the market and the modern state. But whether all public religions are equally good at playing such a civility-enhancing role is another question.

Nowhere has this last question generated greater controversy than with regard to the second largest of the world's religions, Islam. As is well known, the Harvard political scientist and U.S. State Department advisor, Samuel Huntington, has argued that not all societies or civilizations are likely to develop democratic institutions, because the principles of democracy contradict the cultures of many. Professor Huntington reserves some of his most pessimistic observations on democracy's incompatibilities for the Muslim world. "Conflict along the fault line between Western and Islamic civilizations has been going on for 1,300 years," he has written, and in the future this "*military interaction* between the West and Islam is unlikely to decline" (emphasis added; Huntington 1993:29; cf. Huntington 1996). In the face of the slaughter in Algeria or Taliban brutalization of schoolgirls in Afghanistan, other commentators sound equally dire warnings, hinting of a new Cold War in which a resurgent Islam might play the role earlier assumed by Soviet communism (cf. al-Azmeh 1993; Lawrence 1998).

In this article I want to present a preliminary overview as to how we might think about the relationship of this revitalized *public* Islam to civil society and democratization.

My discussion is intended to be general and comparative. However, a significant portion of the case material I present toward the end of the paper will be drawn from recent events in the majority Muslim nation of Indonesia. For many Westerners, of course, Indonesia is not what first comes to mind when one thinks of the Muslim world. But Indonesia is the fourth most populous nation in the world and also the world's largest majority-Muslim country. Some 88 percent of this nation's 210 million people officially profess Islam. An investigation of Muslim politics that includes this often overlooked portion of the Islamic world has the additional benefit of allowing us to distinguish features of Muslim politics that owe more to Middle Eastern circumstances than Muslim civilization as a whole. Marginalized in treatments of classical Islam, Indonesia is an important point of entry to an understanding of the diversity of modern Muslim politics.

The pluralism of Muslim politics

It is a truism of comparative historical sociology that religion in the post-Enlightenment West was marked by widespread privatization, which is to say, the growing tendency for religion to be seen as a matter of private personal ethics rather than public political order (Wilson 1966; cf. Martin 1978). In light of recent developments around the world, however, we now realize this privatization may have had as much to do with circumstances peculiar to modern Europe and Western Christianity than it did any universal developmental tendency. We also now understand that this privatization was never as extensive as portrayed by some modernist enthusiasts of Enlightenment secularism. After all, the Post-Enlightenment West witnessed not merely attacks on public religion but new religious movements, such as Methodism in England, Pietism in Germany, and the United States' Great Awakening (Outram 1995; Thompson 1963:350–400). It was no accident, after all, that the great French sociologist Alexis de Tocqueville concluded that congregational Christianity was a vital element in the democratic culture of early nineteenth century America (Tocqueville 1969). De Tocqueville understood that the American separation of church and state took government out of the business of coercing conformity, but it did not take religion out of public life. Religion remained one of the most important of institutions in American civil society. It was characterized, not by the smooth consensualism of "civil religion," but by vigorous denominational competition and ethical debate (Casanova 1994:211–34; Wuthnow 1988).

In light of our revised understanding of Western religion and modernity, we should not be surprised to see that privatized understandings of religion and modernity run into problems when applied to contemporary Muslim societies. Although the Muslim world has its share of secular modernists, many practicing Muslims continue to look to their religion for principles of public order as well as personal spirituality. The political ideals they derive from their tradition, however, are not immutable, but vary in a manner that reflect competing views as to how Muslims should respond to the challenges of the late modern world. The more significant "clash of civilizations" taking place in today's Muslim world has less to do with an alleged struggle between "Islam" and the "West," than it does with rival visions of Muslim politics.

To begin to understand the pluralism of Muslim politics, then, we need to dispense with theoretical models that assume that Muslim politics and religion are all of a single stripe. Viewed historically, in fact, it is clear that Muslim politics was never monolithic but, like politics and culture in all great civilizations, plural and changing (Eickelman and Piscatori 1996; Esposito and Voll 1996). Even in the early classical period of the Umayyad and Abbasid empires during Islam's first centuries, there was a lively pattern of extra-state religious organizations, centered around the twin institutions of learned Muslim scholars (the *ulama*) and religious law; neither was totally controlled by the state. From a sociological perspective, this differentiation of religious leaders from state authorities was inevitable as the Muslim community developed from a small, relatively homogeneous movement into a vast, multiethnic empire. From a religious perspective, too, many Muslim scholars (*ulama*) concluded that some measure of separation was necessary if the transcendent truth of Islam was not to be subordinated to the whims of all-too-human rulers (Lambton 1981; Munson 1993).

More than Western Europe during the same period, medieval Muslim societies retained a considerable measure of religious pluralism, with Muslims living alongside Christians, Jews, Hindus, and others (Esposito and Voll 1996:4–10; Goldberg 1993). At several times in Muslim history, there were notable attempts to develop an ideology and practice of toleration, although, as in every other premodern tradition, no systematic theology on the matter was ever devised. On issues such as conversion from Islam, the major schools of Muslim law were anything but tolerant, stipulating death, for example, for apostates (*murtad*; see Mottahedeh 1993).

All this being said, premodern Muslim societies were varied in their social and political organization. Contrary to the claims of today's conservative Islamists and Occidentalist critics alike, most societies displayed a significant separation of religious and state authority. Religious scholars learned to hold themselves at a distance from government – despite the fact that official legal commentaries often spoke as if the ideal state was one in which the ruler is such an ardent defender of Islam that his interests are identical to those of the *ulama* (Lapidus 1975).

It was not just scholars, however, who developed the notable habit of distancing themselves from state authorities. So too did many of the great mystical brotherhoods that served as vehicles for popular religious participation (Eaton 1993; Villalón 1995). During the long Muslim middle ages, social precedents like these insured that concepts of sacred kingship coexisted in uneasy tension with contractual notions of governance, with the result that religious leaders sometimes challenged rulers' authority (Munson 1993:35–55). For reasons that will become clearer in the Indonesian case, however, Muslim scholars during this same period were unwilling or unable to "scale up" (Evans 1996) these local precedents for pluralism and civic autonomy into an explicit theory of public freedom and political checks and balances. The full reformation of Muslim politics awaited the great upheavals of the modern era.

In the early modern era, reform-minded rulers in the Muslim world initiated modernizations intended to respond to the political challenge of the West. The enormity of Western colonization also prompted Muslim reformists outside of the state to demand that the door of religious interpretation (*ijtihad*) be reopened. Over the course of its long history, the Muslim world had seen a series of religious reformations, most of which called for a return to scripture and the recorded example of the

Prophet Muhammad. But the reformers of the late nineteenth and early twentieth century gave this scripturalist imperative a new twist. For them, the message of Islam required that Muslims avail themselves of science, education, and modern forms of association. *This* reformation was intended to give Muslims, not just the purity of the Word, but the resources and aptitudes of political modernism (Keddie 1968; Rahnema 1994).

By the middle of the twentieth century, however, the great experiment of Islamic modernism seemed to have settled into a stale orthodoxy. In several Middle Eastern countries, Muslim brotherhoods continued to call for the establishment of an Islamic state (Mitchell 1969; Zasr 1994). But these movements did not play a dominant role in the politics of their homelands. Equally important, they appeared reluctant to take the spirit of rational religious interpretation seriously and engage the terms of Muslim politics in a new and critical manner. In the postwar period, the dominant political discourse in most Muslim countries was socialist and secular nationalist, not Islamist. Politics was visualized through the shapes and colors of the nation-state (Piscatori 1986), and the nation to which the state was supposed to conform had, if any, an only vaguely Islamic hue.

However secure the idea of the nation might have appeared at mid-century, the social world of ordinary Muslims was anything but stable. At the beginning of the twentieth century, the vast majority of Muslims lived in agrarian communities. By mid-century, however, the circumstances of ordinary Muslims had changed forever. Nationalist regimes launched ambitious programs of mass-education (Eickelman 1992). They also developed roads, markets, mass media, and intrusive state administrations. Local communities were opened wider than ever to outside ideas and powers. Mass migrations to cities and distant nations furthered this detraditionalization, forcing whole populations to develop new habits of livelihood and association. In the 1980s and 1990s, this restructuring of lifeworlds went further with the expansion of high-speed travel and electronic communications, both of which made Muslim societies even more permeable to new information and lifestyles. As in other parts of the world, the resulting "global ecumene" (Hannerz 1992:217) heightened popular awareness of the world's pluralism and posed serious challenges to settled authorities and solidarities.

In this manner, social change in the late modern age drew great masses of Muslims onto a teeming public stage. Having done so, it gave special urgency to the question of the political and ethical scripts by which they were to act once there. This "participatory" revolution in society did not yet amount to a democratic revolution, however, because a consensus on the terms for the refiguring of Muslim politics remained unformulated. What *was* clearly occurring in Muslim societies, however, was a pluralization of religious authority and, with it, an intensification of debates over Islam's social meaning and the authorities by whom it was to be defined.

In a pattern that resembles the competition between Protestant fundamentalists and liberal modernists in the United States a century ago (Marsden 1980; Wuthnow 1988), this destabilization of religious hierarchies unleashed "competition and contest over both the interpretation of [religious] symbols and control of the institutions, formal and informal, that produce and sustain them" (Eickelman and Piscatori 1996:5). Mass education and mass marketing only intensified the competition, creating vast but segmented audiences for Islamic books, newspapers, and arts (Atiyeh 1995).

In line with this trend, the newly pluralized social landscape also saw the appearance of a host of religious activists with backgrounds and interests different from those of classically-educated Muslim scholars (*ulama*). Today populist preachers (Gaffney 1994), neotraditionalist Sufi masters (Mardin 1989), and secularly educated "new Muslim intellectuals" (Meeker 1991; Roy 1994) challenge the monopoly of religious power earlier enjoyed by classically trained religious scholars (*ulama*).

Having originated in circles apart from the *ulama*, these new activists tend to orient themselves to a broad public rather than a few scholarly virtuosos. In place of esoteric legal debates, the proponents of the new public Islam present their faith in quasi-ideological terms, as a source of practical knowledge "that can be differentiated from others and consciously reworked" (Roy 1994:3). For many traditionally trained Muslim scholars, of course, the language and interests of these new Muslim activists appear bizarrely eclectic or even un-Islamic. Activist commentaries mix passages from the Qur'an with discussions of current affairs and, sometimes, Western political theory. However unfamiliar it may be to traditional scholars, this eclectic mix makes the new public Islam all the more attractive to mass audiences.

In this manner, Islam in recent years has drifted away from its classical moorings among educated elites into an unsteady societal sea. In a fashion that resembles the expansion of evangelical Protestantism in contemporary Latin America (Martin 1990; Smith 1995), one segment of the new Islamic leadership has moved down-market in its appeals, crafting its message for an audience of ordinary and, sometimes, destitute Muslims. More than is the case for Latin American evangelicals (although not unlike their North American counterparts), however, others have moved up market into the political and philosophical debates of public intellectuals. A few others, finally, have been drawn into the netherworld of off-stage intrigue and parapolitical violence. The long-term fate of Muslim politics everywhere depends on the balance struck between these divergent tendencies.

A Muslim public sphere?

In certain respects, what is happening in the Muslim world resembles what the German social philosopher Jurgen Habermas described some years ago as the emergence of the "public sphere" in the West (Habermas 1989). Habermas's study of eighteenth-century European society emphasized that public arenas like coffee houses, literary clubs, journals, and "moral weeklies" helped to create an open and egalitarian culture of participation. Habermas suggests that this development provided vital precedents for the next century's struggles for democratic representation.

Habermas has been criticized for overlooking the degree to which there were competing notions of public interaction in eighteenth-century Europe, and other public spheres, not least of all religious. Habermas has also been rightly faulted for exaggerating the egalitarianism of the eighteenth-century public by overlooking exclusions based on wealth, gender, and religion (Calhoun 1992; Landes 1988). Like Alexis de Tocqueville's observations on democracy in America, however, Habermas's analysis has the virtue of emphasizing that democratic life depends, not just on the formal structures of government, but on informal resources and dispositions operative in society at large. Formal democracy requires a civil culture and organization greater than itself.

The question this comparison raises, of course, is whether the heightened participation and pluralization so visible in the Muslim world heralds an impending strengthening of civil society and democratization. For some observers, the answer to this question is a resounding "no." These skeptics insist that the Muslim resurgence contradicts one of the central premises of democratic and Habermasian theory, namely, that for a society to democratize, religion must retreat from the public stage to the privacy of personal belief (Tibi 1990). Privatization, critics insist, is a condition of democratic peace.

As noted above, our revised understanding of religion in the West now casts doubt on the view that there is such a necessary linkage between democracy and religious privatization. Nonetheless, some specialists of Islam have lent their voices to this pessimistic view by arguing that Muslims have a unique cultural tendency toward religious authoritarianism. Bernard Lewis, a distinguished historian of Turkey and the Middle East, has invoked the oft-cited phrase that Islam is *din wa dawla*, "religion and state," to observe that Muslims have an entirely different understanding of religion from that of liberal Christianity or the post-Enlightenment West:

> When we in the Western world, nurtured in the Western tradition, use the words "Islam" and "Islamic," we tend to make a natural error and assume that religion means the same for Muslims as it has meant in the Western world, even in medieval times; that is to say, a section or compartment of life reserved for certain matters. ... That was not so in the Islamic world. It was never so in the past, and the attempt in modern times to make it so may perhaps be seen, in the longer perspective of history, as an unnatural aberration which in Iran has ended and in some other Islamic countries may also be nearing its end (Lewis 1988:2).

Lewis is right to emphasize that many Muslims regard their religion as a model for public order as well as personal ethics. His generalization is too sweeping, however, if it implies that no good Western democrat has ever viewed religion in an equally comprehensive manner. Conversely, his generalization is also mistaken if it implies that Muslims have just one way of interpreting *din wa dawla*, and one way, therefore, of organizing Muslim politics.

Recent events in the Muslim world demonstrate that there is an enormous range of opinion among Muslims on all of these matters. As with the Taliban in Afghanistan or the hardline conservatives battling the forces of reform in contemporary Islam, some activists *do* invoke the idea of Islam as "religion and state" to justify repressively coercive policies. They promote a fusion of state and society into an unchecked monolith on the grounds that this is a more truly "Islamic" state. According to this political formula, the only way to enforce the high standards of Muslim morality is to dissolve the boundary between public and private and use the disciplinary powers of the state to police both spheres. Other Muslims point out, however, that the Qur'an knows no such concept of an "Islamic" state, least of all one with the coercive appetites of modern totalitarianism. In fact, in their uncritical appropriation of the idea of a centralized state with a monopoly of social and ideological power, conservative Islamists show their debt to, not traditional Muslim conceptions, but the corporatist ambitions of high modernist political ideology (see Scott 1998).

The Qur'an speaks in favor of no such modernist leviathan; it also abhors compulsion in religion. For Muslim political thinkers like Nurcholish Madjid of Indonesia (Madjid 1987, 1992, 1999) or Abdolkarim Soroush of Iran (Soroush 2000), however, the greatest problem with this arrangement is that it ends by degrading Islam itself. By concentrating power in rulers' hands, such recipes only increase the likelihood that Islam's high ideals will be subordinated to vulgar intrigues. Time and time again, we see unscrupulous despots wrap themselves in the mantle of Muslim piety. Not coincidentally, the Islam they promote is typically a neofundamentalism hostile to pluralism, justice, and civil decency (Roy 1994).

But the "Islamic reformation" (Eickelman 1998) of the late-modern era is richer and more complex than the authoritarian claims of modernist tyrants and religious bullies. In part this is so because the Qur'an and its commentaries are rich with other, pluralistic possibilities. From a sociological perspective, however, this is also the case because the politics of the modern Muslim reformation depends not only on the recovery of hallowed textual truths but on a reading of the realities of the larger modern world. To quote the great Syrian Muslim theorist, Mohammad Shahrour, Muslims "have been used to reading this book [the Qur'an] with borrowed eyes for hundreds of years" (Shahrour 1997:8). More are reading it today with their own eyes. Like all thoughtful readers, however, they draw on what they see in the world around them to enrich their apprehension of the text. In so doing, they discover meanings previously overlooked. For many Muslims, the charge of this new reading is to recover and amplify Islam's democratic endowments, so as to provide the ethical resources for Muslims in a plural, mobile, and participatory world.

Civil Islam

In a larger study, I have referred to this pro-democracy and pro-pluralism wing of the modern Muslim reformation as "civic pluralist" or "civil" Islam (Hefner 2000). Civil Islam is an emergent and highly unfinished tradition associated with a broad assortment of social movements (see Dalacoura 1998; Kurzman 1998). One of its most consistent themes, however, is the claim that the modern ideals of equality, freedom, and democracy are not uniquely Western values, but modern necessities compatible with, and even required by, Muslim ideals.

Some skeptics have dismissed this diffusion of democratic ideas as "Westernization" pure and simple. Conservative Islamists typically agree, viewing the borrowed discourse of democracy as spiritual pollution. What is really at play in this process, however, is not Westernization, but a more subtle interaction between the local and the (relatively) global. Viewed from the ground of everyday practice rather than the dizzying heights of official canons, the normative diversity of preindustrial societies, Muslim and non-Muslim, was always greater than implied in classical Western sociology. Culture is nowhere a monolith, and people engage its varied streams in a manner that is responsive to their commitments and concerns (Barth 1993; Hefner 1985). Equally important, in all societies there are values and practices that hover closer to the ground than official discourse and carry latent possibilities, some of which may have egalitarian or democratic dimensions. These low-lying precedents may not be heard in high-flying cultural canons. Nonetheless, because culture is hetero-vocalic and unfinished, these messages are in some sense "available" to those seeking guidance on what to become when the world takes a new turn.

As Robert Weller (1998) has shown in his study of China's prodemocracy movement, local actors there seized on what at first looked like the exogenous idioms of democracy and civil society to legitimate principles of equality and participation in public life. Weller demonstrates that these principles were already "present" in indigenous Chinese kinship and folk Confucianism, although in an undeveloped and politically bracketed way. The concept of democracy proved useful for Chinese activists, then, not just because it was in the global air (although this certainly helped), but because it "scaled up" (Evans 1996) social resources and cultural meanings long latent in Chinese society.

It is for Muslim democrats as it is for Chinese (Hefner 1998). The tumult of recent decades, and the emergence of a vastly more differentiated social order, has led many to aspire to a freer and more egalitarian public order. Although democratic, the political discourse these Muslims are forging is not merely derivative of Western liberalism. One reason this is so is that democratic Muslims look to their religion to provide some of the terms for this new public ethic. Another reason this is so, however, is more specifically sociological: namely, that the discourse of democracy in modern Muslim societies can take hold only if it responds to the criticisms of conservative Islamists. Inasmuch as this is so, some of the emphases of contemporary civil Islam show a different mix of ideas and themes than those of, say, contemporary liberals in the secular West.

In its emphasis on public virtue and justice, for example, civil Islam, if anything, recalls earlier Western traditions of civic republicanism (elements of which run through some variants of Western "communitarianism" today) rather than secular liberalism. To put the matter a bit differently, Muslim democrats tend be more *civil* democratic or Tocquevillian than they are (Atlantic) liberal in spirit. They deny the need for an Islamic state. But they also insist that society involves more than autonomous individuals, and democracy more than markets and the state. Democracy, Nurcholish Madjid (1999) points out, requires a noncoercive culture of civility that encourages citizens to respect the rights of others as well as to cherish their own. This public culture depends on mediating institutions in which citizens develop habits of free speech, participation, and toleration. In all this, Madjid and other civil Muslims say, there is nothing undemocratic about Muslim voluntary associations (as well as those of other religions) playing a role in the *public* life of civil society as well as in personal ethics.

The success of this civil or democratic Islam will ultimately depend on more than the ideas of a few great thinkers. In sociological terms, the reformation depends on the achievement of a delicate balance between structural changes in state and society, on one hand, and public culture and ethics, on the other.

References

Al-Azmeh, A. 1993. Modern 'culture' and the European tribe. In *Islams and Modernities*, edited by A. Al-Azmeh, 1–17. London: Verso.

Atiyeh, G. N. 1995. The book in the modern Arab world: The cases of Lebanon and Egypt. In *The book in the Islamic world: The written word and communication in the Middle East*, edited by G. N. Atiyeh, 232–53. Albany, NY: SUNY Press.

Barth, F. 1993. Coherence, hegemony, and productivity in knowledge. In *Balinese worlds*, edited by F. Barth, 305–323. Chicago: University of Chicago Press.

Calhoun, C., ed. 1992. *Habermas and the public sphere*. Cambridge, MA: MIT Press.

Casanova, J. 1994. *Public religions in the modern world*. Chicago: University of Chicago Press.

Dalacoura, K. 1998. *Islam, liberalism, and human rights: Implications for international relations*. London: I.B. Tauris.

Eaton, R. M. 1993. *The rise of Islam and the Bengal frontier, 1204–1760*. Berkeley: University of California Press.

Eickelman, D. F. 1992. Mass Higher education and the religious imagination in contemporary Arab societies. *American Ethnologist* 19:4:643–55.

———. 1998. Inside the Islamic reformation. *Wilson Quarterly* 22:1 (Winter):80–89

Eickelman, D. F., and J. Piscatori. 1996. *Muslim politics*. Princeton: Princeton University Press.

Esposito, J., L. Esposito, and J. O. Voll. 1996. *Islam and democracy*. New York and Oxford: Oxford University Press.

Evans, P. 1996. Government action, social capital and development: Reviewing the evidence on synergy. *World Development* 24:6:1119–1132.

Gaffney, P. D. 1994. *The prophet's pulpit: Islamic preaching in contemporary Egypt*. Berkeley: University of California Press.

Goldberg, E. 1993. Private goods, public wrongs, and civil society in some medieval Arab theory and practice. In *Rule and rights in the Middle East: Democracy, law, and society*, edited by E. Goldberg, R. Kasaba, and J. S. Migdal, 248–71. Seattle: University of Washington Press.

Habermas, J. [1962] 1989. *The structural transformation of the public sphere: An inquiry into a category of bourgeois society*. Translated by T. Berger with F. Lawrence. Cambridge, MA: MIT Press.

Hall, J. A. 1985. *Powers and liberties: The causes and consequences of the rise of the West*. Berkeley: University of California Press, 1985.

Hannerz, U. 1992. *Cultural complexity: Studies in the social organization of meaning*. New York: Columbia University Press.

Hefner, R. W. 1985. *Hindu Javanese: Tengger tradition and Islam*. Princeton: Princeton University Press.

———. 1998. A Muslim civil society? Indonesian reflections on the conditions of its possibility. In *Democratic civility: The history and cross-cultural possibility of a modern political idea*, edited by R. W. Hefner, 285–321. New Brunswick, NJ: Transaction Press.

———. 2000. *Civil Islam: Muslims and democratization in Indonesia*. Princeton: Princeton University Press.

Huntington, S. 1993. The Clash of civilizations? *Foreign Affairs* 72:3 (Summer): 14–33.

———. 1996. *The clash of civilizations and the remaking of world order*. New York: Simon & Schuster.

Keddie, N. R. 1968. *An Islamic response to imperialism: Political and religious writings of Sayyid Jamal ad-Din "Al-Afghani."* Berkeley: University of California Press.

Kurzman, C., ed. 1998. *Liberal Islam: A sourcebook*. New York: Oxford University Press.

Lambton, A. K. S. 1981. *State and government in medieval Islam: An introduction to the study of Islamic political theory*. Oxford: Oxford University Press.

Landes, J. B. 1988. *Women and the public sphere in the age of the Fench revolution*. Ithaca: Cornell University Press.

Lapidus, I. M. 1975. The separation of state and religion in the development of early Islamic society. In *International Journal of Middle East Studies* 6:4 (October):363–85.

Lawrence, B. B. 1998. *Shattering the myth: Islam beyond violence*. Princeton: Princeton University Press.

Lewis, Bd. 1988. *The political language of Islam*. Chicago: University of Chicago Press.

Madjid, N. 1987. *Islam, kemodernan, dan Keindonesiaan*. Bandung: Mizan.

———. 1992. *Islam, doktrin, dan Peradaban: Sebuah Telaah Kritis tentang Masalah Keimanan, Kemanusiaan, dan Kedmoderenan*. Jakarta: Paramadina.

———. 1999. *Cita-Cita politik Islam era reformasi*. Jakarta: Paramadina.

Mardin, S. 1989. *Religion and social change in Modern Turkey: The case of Bediuzzaman Said Nursi*. Albany, NY: State University of New York Press.

Marsden, G. M. 1980. *Fundamentalism and American culture: The shaping of twentieth century evangelicalism, 1870–1925*. Oxford: Oxford University Press.

Martin, D. 1978. *A general theory of secularization*. New York: Harper & Row.

———. 1990. *Tongues of fire: The explosion of Protestantism in Latin America*. Oxford: Blackwell.

Meeker, M. E. 1991. The new Muslim intellectuals in the Republic of Turkey. In *Islam in Modern Turkey: Religion, politics, and literature in a secular state*, edited by R. Tapper, 189–219. London: Tauris.

Mitchell, R. P. 1969. *The society of the Muslim brothers*. New York: Oxford University Press.

Mottahedeh, R. P. 1993. Toward an Islamic theology of toleration. In *Islamic law reform and human rights: Challenges and rejoinders*, edited by T. Lindholm and K. Vogt, 25–36. Copenhagen: Nordic Human Rights Publications.

Munson, H., Jr., 1993. *Religion and power in Morocco*. New Haven: Yale University Press.

Outram, D. *The enlightenment*. 1995. Cambridge: Cambridge University Press.

Piscatori, J. P. 1986. *Islam in a world of nation-states*. Cambridge: Cambridge University Press.

Rahnema, A., ed. 1994. *Pioneers of Islamic revival*. London: Zed Books.

Roy, O. R. 1994. *The failure of political Islam*. Cambridge, MA: Harvard University Press, 1994.

Scott, J. C. 1998. *Seeing like a state: How certain schemes to improve the human condition have failed*. New Haven, CT: Yale University Press.

Shahrour, M. 1997. The divine text and pluralism in Muslim societies. New York: *Muslim Politics Report No. 14*, Council of Foreign Relations, 8–10.

Smith, C. 1995. The spirit and democracy: base communities, Protestantism, and democratization in Latin America. In *Religion and democracy in Latin America*, edited by W. H. Swatos Jr., 27–44. New Brunswick: Transaction Books.

Soroush, A. 2000. *Reason, freedom, and democracy in Islam: Essential writings of Abdolkarim Soroush*. Edited by M. Sadri and A. Sadri. New York: Oxford University Press.

Thompson, E. P. 1963. *The making of the English working class*. New York: Vintage, 1963.

Tibi, B. 1990. *Islam and the cultural accommodation of social change*. Boulder: Westview Press.

Tocqueville, A. de. 1969. *Democracy in America*. Two Volumes, translated by G. Lawrence; edited by J. P. Mayer. Garden City, New York: Doubleday.

Villalón, L. A. 1995. *Islamic society and state power in Senegal: Disciples and citizens in Fatick*. Cambridge: Cambridge University Press.

Weller, R. P. 1998. Horizontal ties and civil institutions in Chinese societies. In *Democratic civility: The history and cross-cultural possibility of a modern political idea*, edited by Robert W. Hefner, 229–47. New Brunswick, NJ: Transaction Press.

Wilson, B. R. 1966. *Religion in secular society*. London: C.A. Watts.

Wuthnow, R. 1988. The *restructuring of American religion: Society and faith since the Second World War*. Princeton: Princeton University Press.

Zasr, S. V. R. 1994. *The vanguard of the Islamic revolution: The Jama'at-i Islami of Pakistan*. Berkeley: University of California Press.

Carrie Rosefsky Wickham

THE PATH TO MODERATION

Strategy and learning in the formation of Egypt's *Wasat* party

WHAT PROMPTS RADICAL opposition leaders to revise or abandon their ultimate goals and accommodate themselves to the give and take of democratic politics? This question has been explored largely by scholars seeking to explain the historic deradicalization of the left in western Europe and Latin America. According to a number of influential studies, radical socialist leaders and parties moderated their agendas in order to exploit the new opportunities for electoral participation created by democratization. Yet recent change in the ideological positions staked out by some leaders in Egypt's Islamic movement reveals that moderation can also occur in the absence of democratization. More limited institutional openings can be sufficient to generate strategic incentives for moderation and create opportunities for political learning, or experience-driven change in individual leaders' core values and beliefs.

A moderate political Islam?

The largest, best organized, and most popular opposition groups in the Arab world are those that seek the Islamic reform of society and state. Like earlier movements of the radical left in western Europe and Latin America, Arab Islamist movements are committed to a *telos*, or end-state, beyond the realm of competitive electoral politics. If the ultimate goal of the socialists was a classless society freed from all forms of bourgeois domination, for Islamists it is a moral community governed by *Shari'a*, or Islamic law. While a radically reconstructed *Shari'a* fully consistent with democratic norms is theoretically possible, the "historical *Shari'a*," the actual corpus of Islamic legal rulings, clearly violates some of the main principles of democratic citizenship, for example, by restricting the civil and political rights of women and religious minorities.[1] The position of Islamists committed to some form of *Shari'a* rule as the strongest opposition to many Arab regimes raises a question of vital importance for potential Arab democratization: can Islamist opposition leaders and groups be "tamed" by inclusion within the political process? Can the integration of Islamists within formal representative institutions induce them to moderate their goals?

Recent studies of Islamist political activity in a number of Arab states have demonstrated conclusively that political openings can encourage Islamist opposition leaders to moderate their tactics. When authoritarian leaders have opened their political systems to Islamist groups, many have responded by renouncing violence, accepting the rules of electoral competition, and developing party (or quasi-party) organizations to mobilize the popular vote.[2] Less clear is whether or not participation can trigger ideological moderation. Ideological moderation refers to the abandonment, postponement, or revision of radical goals that enables an opposition movement to accommodate itself to the give and take of "normal" competitive politics. It entails a shift toward a substantive commitment to democratic principles, including the peaceful alternation of power, ideological and political pluralism, and citizenship rights. This usage of a single, cross-cultural definition of moderation makes it possible to determine whether and to what extent radical Islamist groups are evolving ideologically in a way comparable to socialists in the West and, if so, to investigate whether their evolution is driven by similar causes.

Three further aspects of the definition of ideological moderation should be highlighted. First, it refers to the stated positions of Islamist leaders and groups regarding the organization of domestic politics, rather than economics or foreign policy. Second, it refers to change in the stated views of an opposition leader or group relative to their positions in the past. Defining moderation in this way makes it possible to track important changes in an opposition group's platform irrespective of its ideological starting and end points. Third, moderation may be uneven across issue areas. A single group may espouse moderate positions on some issues and radical positions on others and may undergo uneven moderation (or radicalization) over time.

Some scholars of Islamic revivalism would challenge the analysis presented here by arguing that Islamist moderation does not exist. Daniel Pipes is perhaps the strongest academic proponent of this view. He categorizes all individuals and groups that seek the Islamic reform of society and state as "fundamentalists" and defines fundamentalism as a radical utopian movement akin to Fascism and Communism that is by definition "antidemocratic," "antimoderate," "antisemitic," and "antiwestern." "Fundamentalist Muslim groups, ideologies, and tactics differ from each other in many ways ... but every one of them is inherently extremist."[3] From this perspective, the very concept of a moderate Islamist is, like that of a moderate Nazi, a contradiction in terms.

Other Middle East scholars are less inclined to cast all Islamist groups in the same net. To John Esposito, Graham Fuller, and Charles Kurzman, among others, there is a world of difference between Islamists who publicly endorse democracy, pluralism, and human rights (such as the Tunisian Islamist Rashid al-Ghannoushi and the leaders of Turkey's Justice and Development Party) and those who do not (such as the Egyptian organization Islamic Jihad, the former Taliban regime in Afghanistan, and members of *al-Qa'ida*).[4] Even scholars who appreciate the Islamic movement's internal ideological diversity, however, are often quick to point out the nondemocratic implications of what remains the primary objective of most Islamist groups, the call for *Shari'a* rule.[5] However, the perfunctory dismissal of all Islamist agendas as non-democratic obscures significant variation in Islamists' understanding of the content and meaning of *Shari'a* rule and diverts attention away from recent Islamist efforts to incorporate such ideas as pluralism, tolerance, and human rights in a *Shari'a* framework. While this evolution falls short of a full conversion to democracy, it is significant in its own right and has yet to be fully explained.

In recent decades, a quiet revolution of ideas has begun within certain Islamist intellectual and activist circles in Iran, Turkey, Indonesia, and some Arab states, characterized primarily by the call for *ijtihad*, the use of human reasoning to adapt enduring Islamic principles to modern times. While continuing to seek divine guidance in the Quran and the Sunna, these Islamists have formulated new interpretations of Islam's revealed texts that privilege ideas of pluralism, representation, and human rights.[6] A small but growing body of western scholarship on this trend describes it as the rise of a "liberal" Islam, "modern" Islam, or, drawing on Arabic language sources, the new "Islamic centrism" (*Wasatiyyah*).[7] In the Arab world the clearest attempt to turn these ideas into a political program can be found in Egypt, where a new Islamist party based on them was formed in 1996. Founded by a group of activists who broke away from Egypt's largest Islamist political organization, the Muslim Brotherhood, the Egyptian *Wasat*, or Center party, seeks to establish a political system based on Islamic law. Yet, in keeping with its emphasis on the need for a critical reassessment of the historical *Shari'a*, it affirms the principle of popular sovereignty as the basis of legitimate state power, endorses pluralism in all spheres of social and political life, and supports equal rights for all citizens, including women and non-Muslim minorities. Thus, it represents a form of political Islam that is qualitatively different from the ideological extremism of militant Islamist groups, as well as a more subtle, but nonetheless significant, departure from the religious conservatism of the Muslim Brotherhood and other mainstream Islamist groups. Further, the platform of the *Wasat* party represents a sharp break from the conservative interpretation of Islam previously embraced by its founders.

Three arguments explain this shift in the *Wasat* founders' goals. First, Islamist ideological moderation was driven in part by strategic calculation but was also a result of political learning, that is, of change in its leaders' core values and beliefs. Second, value change was facilitated by the interaction of Islamists and secular opposition leaders in pursuit of common goals, including reform of Egypt's authoritarian state. Third, the institutional opportunities and incentives for such interaction were created by a mix of regime accommodation and repression of the country's Islamist opposition groups.

Re-viewing Islamic rule: The *Wasat* party platform

The *Wasat* party represents a break away from Egypt's oldest and most influential Islamic political organization, the Muslim Brotherhood. Since the Brotherhood's founding in 1928, it has called for the establishment of an "Islamic order" based on the Quran and the Sunna.[8] In recent years senior Brotherhood leaders have incorporated rhetorical support for democracy, pluralism, and human rights into their official statements. Yet the Brotherhood's old guard continues to call for strict enforcement of traditional legal rulings contained in or supported by Islam's revealed texts. For example, in 1997 then Deputy Supreme Guide Ma'moun Hudeibi agreed to write a lengthy statement detailing the Brotherhood's positions on a number of key issues for publication in the *Harvard International Review*. Even in a testimonial aimed at a western audience, Hudeibi affirmed the Brotherhood's commitment to the enforcement of textually based Islamic rulings. "The *Shari'a* includes texts relating to systems which nowadays are considered to be an integral part of politics. We, the Muslim Brotherhood, demand that these particular Islamic injunctions be adhered to and acted upon. They cannot be disregarded, neglected, or their application and enforcement ignored."[9]

This approach to the *Shari'a* as a fixed and unchanging set of rules contrasts sharply with the position of the *Wasat* party, founded in January 1996 by a group of high profile, young Islamist leaders in the Muslim Brotherhood.[10] Headed by Abu Ayla Madi Abu Ayla, a forty-five-year old Islamist engineer, the *Wasat* party claims to assume a middle (or center) position between those promoting a rigid defense of Islamic tradition and those ready to jettison that tradition in its entirety in favor of values and institutions imported from the West. While affirming the core values of Arab-Islamic culture, it also calls for a multidimensional process of civilizational reform (*al-islah al-hadari*) as a vital precondition of the Arab-Islamic community's modern spiritual, political, and economic advancement.

Revised and expanded in 1998, the current platform of the *Wasat* party was authored by Salah 'Abd al-Karim, a former Brotherhood leader and professor of aero-nautical engineering at Cairo University.[11] While the *Wasat* party advocates a political system based on Islamic law, it also emphasizes the need for a thoroughgoing revision of the historical *Shari'a* through the use of *ijtihad* (independent reasoning). Toward this end, the *Wasat* platform distinguishes between the "enduring Islamic principles" of the *Shari'a* and what it describes as the "outdated" and "backward" ideas that entered it in medieval times. This formulation provides a rationale for the integration of such "modern" ideas as popular sovereignty, ideological and political pluralism, and equal citizenship rights into the *Wasat* group's broader project of Islamic reform.

The Brotherhood's characterization of textually based *Shari'a* rulings as binding on Muslims in all times and places suggests a profound tension between the democratic and religious elements of its agenda. The *Wasat* party platform does not resolve this tension completely but reduces it by defining the *Shari'a* as a general set of principles and advocating flexibility in their interpretation and application. As Abu Ayla Madi explained: "*Shari'a* is very simply a collection of guiding principles, which should be put to *ijtihad*, to a free interpretation in order to adapt them to a world in the process of change."[12]

Another key ideological difference between the *Wasat* party and the Muslim Brotherhood can be found in their positions on the role of popular sovereignty. In the past, the leading ideologues of the Muslim Brotherhood emphasized that all sovereign power belongs to God. In a seeming departure from this tenet, Ma'moun Hudeibi asserted in 1997 that the Brotherhood believes that "the *ummah* (nation) is the source of authority." But he immediately undercut this statement by adding that the Brotherhood also believes:

> That the Muslim Nation is obliged to submit to Allah alone and to sanctify
> the laws of the Glorious Qur'an and the blessed Sunnah [Tradition of

the Prophet], and believes that man does not have the right to rule except with that which was revealed by Allah in the form of *Shari'a*. In that sense, it cannot nominate anyone to act on its behalf except if he is willing to rule in accordance with the Law of Allah, and ready to train it [the nation] on the requirements of the principles of religion.[13]

By contrast, the *Wasat* platform's discussion of popular sovereignty contains no such qualifying statements. It asserts simply that "the *umma* [nation or community] is the first and original and only possessor of authority" and hence that "the constitution and all of its primary laws must be constituted by an assembly which speaks for the *umma*, and which is responsible for the constitution."[14]

On the subject of pluralism there are also clear differences. Both the Muslim Brotherhood and the *Wasat* party define pluralism as a Quranic principle that acknowledges human diversity as a part of God's creation.[15] But the *Wasat* platform elevates this principle to a new height. "The most important civilizational principle of our *umma*, and accordingly of the public order of the *umma*, is pluralism. And we mean pluralism in its many dimensions, and not just political pluralism, because this *umma* was established through history on the basis of religious and cultural and social pluralism and other types as well."[16] Particularly revealing is the platform's use of the term *umma*, conventionally defined as the community of believers, that is, of Muslims only, to refer to a broader cultural community that includes Egypt's Coptic Christians. As the platform states: "In the Islamic civilizational project, Muslim and Christian stand on equal footing, in belonging and role and authenticity. They are the children of one *umma* and one civilization despite their religious differences."

Finally, the *Wasat* party goes further than the Muslim Brotherhood, and much further than other Islamist opposition groups in the Arab world, in its support for full citizenship rights for women and non-Muslims. In recent years, the platform of the Muslim Brotherhood has evolved in the direction of supporting greater rights for women and Coptic Christians. Hence, while in 1999 parliamentary representatives from Kuwait's two largest Sunni Islamist opposition factions voted against the emir's proposal to enfranchise Kuwaiti women, an official position paper of Egypt's Muslim Brotherhood in 1994 endorsed women's suffrage.[17] Nevertheless, the Brotherhood's document acknowledged internal disagreement about whether women should be allowed to serve in representative councils and concluded that women should not be allowed to serve as head of state. Further, the document stated that women's exercise of political rights "should not lead to the violation of ethical rules laid down by the *Shari'a* and made binding by it." In sum, the Muslim Brotherhood continues to distinguish between the political rights of men and women and makes the exercise of political rights by the latter contingent upon the *Shari'a*, whose rulings remain vague and ill-defined.[18] By contrast, the *Wasat* platform contends that women are equal to men in all their public rights and responsibilities and affirms the right of women to serve in the highest positions of authority, such as judge and head of state.

The *Wasat* party is not an isolated phenomenon but rather bears the imprint of a broader intellectual current that seeks to revive what scholars have referred to as the liberal interpretive tradition in Islam.[19] Muslim thinkers affiliated with this trend acknowledge the divine origins of religion but emphasize that its understanding is human and hence open to change. The liberal interpretive tradition blossomed during the first two decades of the twentieth century, for example, in the movement of Islamic modernism associated with the Egyptian reformer Muhammad Abduh. Yet in subsequent decades it was largely eclipsed by the revivalist (or fundamentalist) tradition that aims to restore Islam to a pristine original state unpolluted by western cultural influences. The latter tradition, in various guises, inspired Hassan al-Banna, the founder of Egypt's Muslim Brotherhood, animated the Shi'ite clergy who led the Islamic revolution in Iran, and informs the *Salafi* and *Wahhabi* strands of Islam propagated by conservative Saudi and Pakistani Muslim clerics today.

After decades of marginalization, the liberal or modernist strand of political Islam experienced something of a renaissance in the Muslim world in the 1990s. This renaissance was in part a reflection of the increased global prestige of democratic norms after successful transitions to democracy elsewhere.[20] Transposing such ideas into an Islamic idiom (and drawing upon the earlier movement of Islamic modernism), a new generation of "liberal" Islamist intellectuals attracted a growing circle of adherents. Though positioned outside the mainstream of conservative Muslim religious opinion, such intellectuals in the 1980s and early 1990s attracted many of the Muslim Brotherhood's most dynamic younger leaders, some of whom went on to form the *Wasat* party in 1996.[21]

The revival of the liberal interpretive tradition within Islam set the stage for the *Wasat* party initiative but cannot in and of itself explain it. In Egypt and elsewhere in the Arab world, liberal Islamist intellectuals constitute a minority whose views have been disputed – and at times condemned outright – by members of the official religious establishment as well as by other Islamist leaders. More generally, the existence of a set of ideas is not sufficient to explain how and why they are adopted as a basis for political action. What prompted Abu Ayla Madi and other young leaders in the Brotherhood to depart from the conservative ideological mainstream of the Islamic movement and embrace a minor, and deeply contested, strand of Islamist discourse as the foundation for a new political party?

Comparative studies offer two different analytic approaches to explain how radical political actors become habituated to and ultimately support the give and take of democratic politics. The strategic and political learning approaches build on different assumptions about the motors of ideological change. Both are relevant to an explanation of Islamist ideological moderation.

Ideological moderation as an outcome of strategic calculation

According to one strand of comparative analysis, radical opposition leaders and groups moderate their agendas as a strategic adaptation to changes in their political environment. In *Capitalism and Social Democracy*, Adam Przeworski notes that the establishment of democratic political systems in Europe based on universal adult male suffrage presented radicals on the left with a choice: to pursue socialist revolution through direct confrontation in the workplace and the street or to work through political institutions. European socialist parties opted to participate in the electoral process for several reasons. Some socialists supported elections as a "ready-made forum for [socialist] organization, agitation and propaganda" but were certain that the bourgeoisie would never permit an elected government to abolish their privileges.[22]

A majority of socialists, however, believed that, because they had significant popular support, the establishment of universal suffrage would enable them to achieve revolution through the ballot box. As Przeworski notes: "Socialists entered into bourgeois politics to win elections, to obtain an overwhelming mandate for revolutionary transformation, and to legislate the society into socialism. This was their aim and this was their expectation."[23]

While elections offered the socialists a new route to political power, they also subjected them to new constraints. It eventually became clear to socialist leaders that any attempt to legislate a transition to socialism would provoke a far-reaching economic crisis that would deprive them of electoral support. Electoral pressures thus forced the socialists to abandon their ultimate goal of nationalization and settle for the pursuit of incremental reforms within the existing capitalist framework.

Similar arguments have been proposed to explain the more recent deradicalization of leftist parties and movements in southern Europe and Latin America. Scholars have argued that this deradicalization was inseparable from a broader process of democratization (or "redemocratization") involving complex negotiations between regime and opposition elites.[24] Hence the process of democratic transition itself created powerful incentives for radical opposition leaders to moderate their goals. Pressure for ideological moderation came from two sources. First, moderation was an implicit or explicit condition for inclusion in the new democratic system, a phenomenon Samuel Huntington referred to as the "participation-moderation tradeoff."[25] Socialists realized that it was necessary to moderate their agenda to gain acceptance by conservative adversaries and secure the right to participate in post-transition elections. They thus renounced violence, abandoned the goal of revolution, and accepted the basic institutions of capitalism and democracy.[26] Second, socialists also understood that moderation was key to their electoral success. As Donald Share notes, the dramatic deradicalization of the Spanish Socialist Workers' Party (PSOE) in the 1970s during Spain's transition was driven in large part by electoral considerations. "PSOE elites were aware that maximalist rhetoric, as well as the Party's continued insistence on a *ruptura* (a sharp break with the authoritarian past) would only alienate the electorate."[27] The PSOE leaders' commitment to moderation was reinforced after the 1977 elections, when it emerged as the largest opposition party in parliament. From this point forward, moderation became an integral part of the PSOE's strategy to obtain a parliamentary majority.[28]

In Latin America, a major factor prompting Chilean socialists to moderate their agenda was their desire to establish an electoral alliance with the centrist Christian Democrats that could defeat Pinochet at the ballot box. The left was particularly dependent on such a coalition because Pinochet's advisors had manipulated the electoral rules to their disadvantage. As Kenneth Roberts observes, "the transition process in Chile, and in particular the institutional constraints established by the Pinochet regime, gave powerful advantages to the party of the Left that was most adept in establishing an alliance with the Center."[29]

In sharp contrast to the situation in Europe and Latin America, where the moderation of leftists occurred in a context of democratization, the *Wasat* party was established in a period of intensified authoritarian rule. In the few years preceding the *Wasat* party's formation, the Muslim Brotherhood, and citizens active in Islamic groups more generally, were targets of increased repression, a trend interpreted by some observers as a retreat from the policy of controlled political liberalization that the regime had pursued during the previous decade. Indeed, one year before the *Wasat* party was announced, Mubarak's regime detained eighty-one of the Brotherhood's leading activists, including former members of parliament, university professors, syndicate officials, and businessmen. They were tried in military courts, and fifty-four received sentences of up to five years with hard labor.[30]

On the face of it, the formation of the *Wasat* party under conditions of increased repression is surprising, not only because the incentives for moderation created by democratization elsewhere were absent but because repression might more logically trigger Islamist radicalization. Yet Egypt demonstrates that increased repression can sometimes induce ideological moderation as "rational" opposition actors moderate their agendas not only to seize new political opportunities but also to evade new political constraints. Interviews with Abu Ayla Madi Abu Ayla and Esam Sultan, two of the party's founders, suggest that the *Wasat* party initiative was indeed partly a strategic move by leaders in the Muslim Brotherhood to avoid repression.[31] As Madi explained, the arrest of some of the Brotherhood's leading activists in 1995 confirmed that its secretive, insular "antisystem" form of organization had failed and that it was time for the Islamic movement to shed the handicap of illegality and secure the formal party status needed to participate in public life "like any normal party." As Madi claimed, by remaining aloof from secular opposition forces, relying on vague and to outsiders threatening slogans such as "Islam Is the Solution," and maintaining a "culture of confrontation" with the regime, the Brotherhood's leadership had provoked the hostility of potential allies in both the regime and opposition. The achievement of legal status would offer the Islamists a number of strategic advantages, the first of which was a measure of immunity from state repression. Further, at a time when democracy had emerged as a powerful global norm adjudicating the legitimacy of Arab regimes and oppositions alike, the articulation of a "democratic" platform would enable the Islamists to seize the moral high ground vis-à-vis the country's authoritarian rulers, facilitate alliances with secular opposition groups, and potentially increase domestic and external pressures that would open a democratic electoral route to political power.[32]

However, the *Wasat* Islamists' strategic ideological moderation cannot explain everything. The immediate payoff associated with moderation was uncertain and likely to be modest at best. Unlike the socialists of democratizing Spain or Chile, or for that matter Islamist opposition groups in Algeria or Jordan, Egypt's Islamists were never offered a trade-off between participation and moderation. Mubarak's regime never hinted that moderation of Islamist goals would pave the way toward legalization of an Islamist party. Indeed, the *Wasat* party's applications for legal party status (in 1996 and 1998) were summarily denied by the government's political parties committee, decisions that were upheld on appeal in court.

The *Wasat* founders may also have moderated their agenda to enhance their credibility with the Egyptian electorate or secure the cooperation of secular opposition groups, but here too the incentives for strategic moderation were relatively weak. It is not clear how much of the Egyptian electorate was put off by the Brotherhood's antidemocratic positions, but these positions did not prevent the Brotherhood from winning a series of stunning electoral victories in the professional associations from 1984 to 1993 among precisely those educated, middle class groups one might expect to be most committed to democratic norms. The *Wasat* party founders arguably did seek to address concerns raised by secular critics. However, a history of mutual suspicion and the conviction of some secularists that the *Wasat* leaders were masking their true intentions behind a democratic façade limited the short-term prospects for a broader political alliance between the *Wasat* Islamists and secular opposition groups. Simultaneously, the price that the *Wasat* founders paid for their moderation within the Islamist camp was quite high, for their embrace of ideas and institutions historically associated with the West opened them to accusations that they had betrayed Islam. As Madi noted in an *Economist* interview in January 2000: "We often find ourselves between two fires, the lack of a democratic state where we can express ourselves, and the risk of treading on what other Islamists feel are sacred principles."[33] Hence whatever support the *Wasat* Islamists hoped to gain from erstwhile critics at home or abroad as a result of their ideological moderation had to be weighed against the opprobrium it would provoke from Islamists committed to a stricter version of Islamic rule. While socialists pursuing moderation in Latin America and Europe also confronted accusations of betrayal from more radical party leaders, such accusations may have posed a greater risk to Egypt's moderate Islamists due to their minority status within the Islamist camp. The willingness of the *Wasat* Islamists to alienate conservative Muslim clerics and expose their own Islamic credentials to doubt suggests that moderation was a result not solely of rational cost-benefit calculations but also of political learning.

Political learning: the roots of democratic value change in authoritarian settings

In *Issues in Democratic Consolidation*, Scott Mainwaring observes that many studies of Latin American democratic transitions draw implicitly or explicitly on a strategic model of elite political behavior and hence have "downplayed the importance of a normative commitment to democracy on the part of political elites."[34] But "in Latin America, democracy has worked only where political elites saw it as a best solution, not as an instrumental means of securing some of their interests."[35] How and why did the region's political leaders come to internalize democratic values? According to Nancy Bermeo, one of the most striking features of recent transitions to democracy in southern Europe and Latin America is the development by political leaders across the ideological spectrum of a commitment to democracy under conditions of dictatorship, before a transition to democracy occurred. Bermeo suggests that "the experience of dictatorship can produce important cognitive change," or "political learning." Political learning refers specifically to "the process through which people modify their political beliefs and tactics as a result of severe crises, frustrations, and dramatic changes in environment." First, political learning occurs at an individual level; hence "the timing and nature of the learning experience may vary between individuals and between political groups. Second, "learning need not occur across the political spectrum. Third, learning can "involve means or ends or both," that is, it "can affect basic, ideological beliefs about political structures, or it can affect simply the means one prefers for achieving constant ends."[36]

Bermeo suggests several possible sources of political learning. Democratic learning under conditions of dictatorship was provoked by "processes of comparison and interaction," as authoritarian elites and opposition leaders in southern Europe and Latin America were affected by events in "reference states." Further, radical opposition leaders interacted in prison and in exile in ways that caused them to "reappraise past errors," while interactions between business and labor groups impressed upon both the potential advantages of bargaining and compromise.[37] Finally, "even the most ambitious dictatorships contain arenas within the state and society where the learning and diffusion of democratic ideas and tactics is possible," particularly "sanctioned organizations" that enjoy a certain immunity from state repression, including church organizations, professional associations, political parties, and business groups.[38] Two main points help in analyzing the roots of Islamist ideological moderation in Egypt: democratic learning can arise from formative experiences under conditions of dictatorship, and it is likely to occur within institutional spaces that retain a degree of autonomy from state control.

Political participation under conditions of authoritarian constraint

In the mid 1970s Egyptian President Anwar Sadat launched a process of controlled political liberalization, moving the country away from the Nasserist model of a single party corporatist state toward a new form of authoritarian rule described by Egyptian scholars as restricted pluralism (*al-ta'addudiyya al-muqayidda*). This new system was consolidated in the 1980s and 1990s by Hosni Mubarak. For the first time since the Free Officers assumed power in 1952, the country's parliament, professional syndicates, and university student unions were opened to electoral participation by opposition groups, including nonviolent Islamists. Especially in parliament, regime leaders engaged in a wide range of administrative and legal maneuvers, and at times outright coercion, to restrict Islamist gains and preempt a meaningful electoral challenge.

Despite its limitations, political liberalization created new opportunities for Islamists to participate in Egyptian public life. In the mid 1970s the Brotherhood's renunciation of violence led Sadat to permit its leaders to reestablish an office in Cairo and publish their own journal, *al-Da'wa* (*The Call*). At the same time, Sadat actively encouraged the formation of independent Islamic student associations, or *jama'at*, on Egyptian university campuses as a counterweight to the Nasserist and Marxist left. The *jama'at* soon replaced the left as the leading political force on university campuses, winning landslide victories in student union elections, especially in such technical fields as medicine, science, and engineering. Beginning in the mid 1980s, Islamist candidates affiliated with the Muslim Brotherhood ran for elections in parliament and the professional syndicates under the banner "Islam Is the Solution." Their most stunning victories occurred in the professional syndicates, where, unlike in parliament, they were permitted to run on their own list and government intervention was minimal. By the early 1990s Islamists controlled a majority of seats on the executive boards of five of the country's most prestigious syndicates (engineering, medicine, science, pharmacy, and law) and made significant inroads in several others.

The Islamists initially seized new opportunities for electoral participation not out of a commitment to democracy, but as a means to further their goal of establishing an Islamic state. But over time, in a manner unanticipated by the Brotherhood's senior leaders, the experience of participation led some of the movement's middle generation activists to reject the Brotherhood's "antisystem" strategies and goals and reinvent themselves as the founders of a moderate Islamist party seeking to "assist in the building of a democratic civil society.[39] Many of them experienced a dramatic ideological shift in the decade before the *Wasat* party was announced.

The Islamic Student Associations of the 1970s and *Weltanschauung* politics

Egypt's middle generation Islamists typically entered the movement as high school or university students in the 1970s. Within a few years the most dynamic and committed of them surfaced as the *amirs* or leaders, of Islamic student associations (*jama'at*) and were later elected to leadership positions in the student unions. The political orientations of these students were very different from what they are now. Reflecting the influence of the revivalist strand of Islam promoted by Hassan al-Banna, Sayyid Qutb, and other Brotherhood ideologues, the student activists, then in their teens and early twenties, saw themselves as the vanguard of a broad Islamic awakening that would purify Egyptian society of corrupting western influences and establish a system based on the strict application of Islamic law. Further, they embraced a highly literalist and conservative interpretation of *Shari'a* rule which, among other things, favored mandatory veiling and the gender segregation of public space.[40] Their conception of the *telos* of the Islamic movement was influenced in particular by Sayyid Qutb.[41] Drawing directly on Qutb's work, the *jama'at* of the time portrayed contemporary Egyptian society as existing in a state of *jahiliyya*, or wilful ignorance of god's will, emphasized that in contrast to the western concept of democracy, sovereignty and the right to legislate belonged to god alone, and portrayed the Islamic movement as resistant to all infidel political institutions and modes of thought.[42]

In the terms of Seymour Martin Lipset, the Islamist student leaders of the 1970s conformed to a *Weltanschauung* model of politics in which a group seeks to "make the world conform to their basic philosophy or world-view (*Weltanschauung*)." The members of such groups "do not see themselves as contestants in a give-and-take game of pressure politics" but rather "view the political or religious struggle as a contest between divine or historic truth on one side and fundamental error on the other." As Lipset observed, the leaders of such groups attempt to "encapsulate the lives of members within ideologically linked activities" and minimize contact with outsiders that might dilute their faith.[43] The behavior of Islamist student leaders in the 1970s conformed to a *Weltanschauung* model of politics in several ways. Such leaders typically grew a *lahya* (untrimmed beard) as a sign of religious devotion setting them apart from ordinary Muslims and spent a considerable amount of time in small group sessions devoted to intensive religious study and prayer. Further, they shunned cooperation with Marxist and Nasserist groups, minimized their social interaction with Coptic Christians and unveiled women, and boycotted mixed sex social events on campus.[44]

Despite their rejection of democracy as a western construct, Islamist student leaders became quite adept at competitive electoral politics. Further, once elected to leadership positions in student government, they successfully cultivated the image of competent administrators who arranged tutoring, gender-segregated transportation, and other services to address student needs and attract more recruits. Nevertheless, it is clear that as recently as the late 1970s this modification of tactics was not matched by a moderation of ultimate goals. In this period the majority of Egypt's middle generation Islamist leaders adhered to a conservative interpretation of the *Shari'a* not only different from, but also openly hostile to, liberal democracy. In this respect their views were quite similar to those of the Brotherhood's oldguard.[45]

The micro-foundations of Islamist political learning

After graduating from the university, Islamist student leaders confronted the question of how to sustain their activism. Some chose not to affiliate with Islamist political groups but rather channeled their energies into the parallel sector of Islamic health clinics, hospitals, schools, community centers, charitable foundations, newspapers, and publishing houses that were being established at the time, funded partly by donations from Egyptian and Gulf patrons enriched by the oil boom. A number of other student leaders, many from the economically underdeveloped region of Upper Egypt, proclaimed a *jihad* (holy war) against the country's "infidel" rulers and set up underground armed cells dedicated to overthrowing Sadat. But some of the country's most prominent student leaders eventually decided to join the Muslim Brotherhood. One of them was Abu Ayla Madi Abu Ayla, who in 1979 was a student leader in the Faculty of Engineering of Minya University in Upper Egypt. As Madi explained, "the idea was that we [young leaders] would breathe new life into the organization." Over the next decade the former student leaders spearheaded the Brotherhood's penetration of parliament, professional syndicates, university faculty clubs, and other spheres of Egyptian public life. Beginning in 1984, they represented the Brotherhood in elections for the syndicates' executive boards and by the early 1990s obtained controlling majorities in the doctors, engineers, scientists, pharmacists, and lawyers' syndicates.

Once the former Islamist student activists became syndicate officials, their immediate goals changed. They were now the elected leaders of large, national public institutions, charged with representing the interests of their profession and its members, irrespective of the latter's religious background and political orientations. As syndicate officials, the former *amirs*, now in their late twenties or early thirties, launched into their new roles with considerable enthusiasm. They organized advanced training courses, offered health and emergency insurance, extended low interest loans to help young members get married and/or establish their own small businesses, and facilitated the purchase of consumer durables and furniture on long-term installment plans. Further, in negotiations with the ministry of education and the Supreme Council of Universities, they demanded a reduction in university enrollments to minimize the labor surplus and lobbied for the establishment of liaison offices to help Egyptian professionals obtain work in other Arab states.[46]

The Islamists were also responsible for administering syndicate elections. Even losing candidates acknowledged that the Islamist-supervised elections were generally free and fair. In part, the Islamists were confident of their superior mobilization skills, which enabled them to win large victories under conditions of free competition.

But they wanted to cultivate a reputation as honest administrators, willing to place institutional interests ahead of partisan goals.

The assumption of these new roles was accompanied by conspicuous changes in the Islamists' appearance and daily routines. Gone were the untrimmed beards of their defiant student days; instead, most were now clean-shaven or had neatly trimmed beards and wore standard western or civil service style suits. From the air-conditioned offices of their syndicates' national headquarters in Cairo, they supervised a large staff, received visitors from the provinces, were interviewed by journalists, and met with other syndicate and party leaders to coordinate strategy on issues of shared concern. In the process, their behavior shifted, to paraphrase Max Weber, from a politics of principle to a politics of responsibility.[47] In order to fulfill their duties as syndicate officials the Islamists were forced to negotiate with government authorities and elicit the help of professionals and business leaders who did not share their views. Likewise, their duties required them to cooperate with the leaders of secular opposition parties and nongovernmental organizations and to communicate with local and foreign media outlets. In sum, the Islamists' new roles as elected syndicate leaders elicited higher levels of competence, pragmatism, and professionalism than had been required of them in the past.

The Islamist leaders of Egypt's professional syndicates also exploited their new status to raise issues of broader national concern. In published statements, conferences, and syndicate assembly meetings Islamic Trend leaders demanded the repeal of the country's emergency laws, condemned the torture of political detainees (the vast majority of whom were Islamists), and called for broader democratic reforms. The Islamists' efforts to mobilize a moral campaign against the authoritarian excesses of Mubarak's regime encouraged them to reach out to secular opposition groups, despite fundamental disagreements on questions of morality and religion. Convergence on the issue of political reform thus facilitated new forms of cooperation across partisan lines. For example, Islamists and secularists issued joint petitions at the six national professional association conferences organized by Islamist syndicate leaders between 1990 and 1994. The Islamists allied with secular opposition leaders on pan-Arab issues as well, joining Nasserists and Marxists in opposition to Egypt's participation in the U.S.-led alliance during the Gulf War.

Finally, Islamist syndicate officials gained new opportunities to travel outside the Arab world to the Balkans, Central Asia, western Europe, and the United States. In participating in conferences and working on humanitarian issues such as the distribution of financial aid and supplies to Muslim refugees in Bosnia and Chechnya, they worked not only with other Muslims, but also with European and American Christians and Jews.

In sum, during their ten years as elected syndicate leaders the Islamists assumed a high profile role in the promotion of national and international causes related only indirectly to the goal of Islamic reform. Their collaboration on such issues with non-Islamist individuals and groups appears to have led to a series of adjustments in their broader world-view. In the campaign for democracy and human rights, issues that were initially of only instrumental importance metamorphosed into matters of principle. For example, what began as opposition to the torture of suspected Islamic militants became opposition to torture as a basic violation of human rights, regardless of the identity of the perpetrators or the victims. Similarly, the call for the legalization of the Islamist opposition broadened over time into a call for freedom of assembly for all political parties.

Equally important, the pursuit of shared goals forced the Islamists to break out of the insular, ideologically uniform networks of Islamist *Weltanschauung* politics and enter into sustained interaction with leaders of parties and nongovernmental organizations, human rights activists, academics, and journalists outside the Islamist camp, including Coptic Christians and unveiled, assertive women. The impact of such interactions on their political thinking was profound. As Madi notes, it led his own thinking and that of some of his peers to evolve toward the recognition that "we don't monopolize the Truth" and "we have a human understanding of Islam."[48] As Esam Sultan explained:

> It is a mistake for us to say that a certain system represents an Islamic system. The ruling system in Sudan represents its understanding of Islam. Like Iran. … We differ with these understandings of Islam, but it is not possible for any of us to claim that this is not Islam. This is a mistake and this is dangerous. No, I am not able to say – no one in the *Wasat* party is able to say that the program of the *Wasat* Party, this is Islam. But I can say that the program of the *Wasat* party is my understanding of Islam. … It is possible for you to agree or disagree with me about it.[49]

Finally, the Islamists' interaction with civic and political activists outside the Islamist movement led to a qualitative shift in their positions on a number of sensitive issues. As Madi explained, his extensive contact (*ihtitkak*) with "many different types of people" in Egypt and abroad influenced his views on the rights of women, the status of Copts and the question of national unity, the scope for artistic creativity and expression, and relations with the West. In regard to the latter, Madi noted that his forty-seven trips abroad, including several trips to Europe and the United States, challenged his prior view of the West as a monolithic entity and convinced him of the possibility of a relationship with westerners based on mutual respect and dialogue rather than confrontation.[50]

Abu Ayla Madi Abu Ayla, Esam Sultan, Salah ʿAbd al-Karim, and other former Brotherhood leaders now affiliated with the *Wasat* party initiative describe the shift in their thinking as a "maturation" or "development" of their ideas rather than as an abandonment of their prior goals.[51] While Egypt's middle generation leaders remain committed to the comprehensive Islamic reform of society and state, they have articulated a new vision of what that reform should entail and how it should be pursued.

Political learning by middle generation Islamists set the stage for an unprecedented schism in the Brotherhood's ranks in the mid 1990s. *Wasat* leaders announced the party's formation over the objections of veteran Brotherhood leaders. On one level, this schism represented a power struggle between the Brotherhood's oldguard elite, then in their seventies and early eighties, who dominated its executive board, and its middle generation leaders, who, as the Brotherhood's most active force, sought a greater role in its direction. Yet, on another level, the schism reflected the emergence of two competing world-views within the Brotherhood community. In the mid 1990s a number of prominent middle generation Islamists began to criticize openly the *Weltanschauung* model of politics that informed the decision making of the

Brotherhood's executive board. In particular, they criticized the oldguard's insistence on secrecy, discipline, and ideological conformity, their regular flouting of internal democracy, and the "persecution mentality" that shaped their relationship with the regime. In addition, they criticized the Brotherhood's reliance on such vague slogans as "Islam Is the Solution" that implied that the Brotherhood spoke for Islam itself (hence all competing viewpoints and interpretations were illegitimate). Finally, they criticized the oldguard for remaining aloof from and hostile to other political trends, isolating the Brotherhood from potential allies, and rendering it more vulnerable to repression. As Esam Sultan explained:

> The Muslim Brotherhood ... doesn't believe in the democratic process, whether it concerns the state if it took power or the internal movement of the Brotherhood itself. The opinion of the leader is the opinion that is followed. ... The truth is that the most important, the clearest difference between the *Wasat* party and the Muslim Brotherhood is faith in these matters – faith in pluralism, faith in democracy, faith in freedom, faith in freedom of opinion, freedom of thought, freedom of creativity, relations with other currents. The Muslim Brotherhood isolates itself from other political currents because they are outside the group's religious frame-work. In relation to us, the *Wasat* party, we consider the other political currents part of the national framework. ... It is not possible to bring about a renaissance for the future nation without joining forces with these other groups.[52]

The limits of the *Wasat* party's democratic shift

While the *Wasat* party may be the first step toward the emergence of a moderate Islamism compatible with democratic politics, there remains significant tension between its religious and democratic commitments. First, in proclaiming that "*Shari'a* is the principle source of legislation*,*" it opens a Pandora's box of questions about who has the right to interpret Islamic law and what happens if those interpretations conflict with the popular will. When confronted by such questions, Abu Ayla Madi and Esam Sultan emphasized the special authority of religious scholars yet noted that they should serve only in an advisory role since "there is no authority higher than the will of the people." Nevertheless, it remains unclear how a conflict of opinion between an elected legislature and an official panel of *Shari'a* experts would be resolved.

Another source of tension is the limits the party appears to have placed on how much of the historical *Shari'a*, and of the Islamic heritage more generally, is open to reinterpretation. While emphasizing that "the scope for *ijtihad* is broad," the *Wasat* platform notes that "the civilizational reference (*marj'aiyya*) of the people – [which is] Arab-Islamic – constitutes the framework which should not be transcended, and from which is derived all visions and programs and systems." This statement echoes an argument advanced by Muhammad Salim al-'Awa, the Egyptian lawyer and "new Islamist intellectual" who is cited by the *Wasat* Islamists as a major influence on their thought. Al-'Awa calls for *ijtihad* but argues that new interpretations must be consistent with *thawabet al-umma* (the fixed or enduring values of the nation), in effect establishing an outward boundary for ideological change. As Gasser Abd al-Raziq, a secular human rights activist and director of the Hisham Mubarak Law Center, noted, the concept of *thawabet al-umma* is central to the thinking of the new Islamists and is broader and more flexible than *Shari'a*. But "at the end of the day, it's the same thing – there is a ceiling to everything. Even the most progressive Islamists have a ceiling. It may be a little higher than the conservatives, but it's still a ceiling."[53]

The cultural elements that the *Wasat* founders deem essential and thus apparently incontestable include the religious character of Arab-Islamic society and the position of the family, rather than the individual, as its basic social unit. In regard to the latter, the party notes the special responsibility of a woman to assume care of the family, "since no one beside her can take her place." Hence, while the party affirms that "women are equal to men in their civil and political rights and responsibilities," it also calls for the use of the media and other socializing institutions to "prevent the spread of western models of social relations which might lead to the fragmentation of the Egyptian family."[54] Underlying this determination to guard "the fixed values of the nation" is a deep anxiety about the spread of western values and lifestyles, and this defensive posture limits the extent to which the cultural patrimony can be revised.[55] While in theory the *thawabet* are themselves open to reinterpretation, the new Islamists have not yet crossed this frontier.

Even when the *Wasat* Islamists clearly depart from mainstream conservative Muslim opinion, they are careful to avoid western terminology. Although *Wasat* party leaders have expressed support for democracy in their speeches and interviews, the *Wasat* platform does not use the term. Similarly, *Wasat* party leaders and the independent Islamist intellectuals they cite as religious authorities avoid describing themselves as liberal, preferring instead such terms as moderate (*mu'tadil*), centrist (*mutawasit*), and open-minded (*mutafattih*). In this way they ward off accusations of too close an association with the secular political systems of the West.

The *Wasat* party's conception of Islam is not elastic enough to permit a full reconciliation of religious and democratic values. Yet their recognition of a distinction between the "fixed" and "variable" aspects of the Islamist heritage opens the space for a more radical critique of traditional Islamic norms and practices in the future. As Sayyid Naggar, the founder of the liberal New Civic Forum, notes, the "*marja'iyya al-islamiyya*" (the Islamic frame of reference) has the potential to be quite flexible; "it could be reconceptualized as a general commitment to social justice, or responsiveness to the people, rather than a mandate to apply rules and regulations developed one thousand years ago." Naggar knows both the veteran leaders of the Muslim Brotherhood and the *Wasat* founders personally and stresses that "there is a world of difference between them." "Of course, Naggar observes, Abu Ayla and the others are not liberal democrats, but I don't expect them to be. It is just a beginning, but it is a process that should be encouraged."[56]

The marginalization of the moderates

So far Mubarak's regime has rebuffed the *Wasat* party's bid for legal recognition. Far from guaranteeing it a secure foothold in the Egyptian political system, the *Wasat* party's moderation may have increased its perceived threat to the regime by making it a more viable competitor for power. Huntington's participation-moderation tradeoff evidently does not hold when the objective of regime leaders is the preservation of authoritarian rule, not democracy. Senior Brotherhood leaders also resented the *Wasat* party project because it was outside their control. In spring 1996 Ma'moun Hudeibi, then deputy supreme guide, allegedly ordered all Brotherhood members who had joined the new party to withdraw immediately or face expulsion. By the end of the year Madi and fifteen other *Wasat* members announced their resignation from the Brotherhood.[57] Their departure not only deprived the Brotherhood of some of its most popular and skilled activists, but also deprived them of their ties to Egypt's largest Islamic political organization.

Rebuffed by the regime and the Brotherhood, the *Wasat* Islamists remain marginal political actors without a mass base. In April 2000 they scored a modest victory when *Wasat* received approval to form a new nongovernmental association. According to its charter, the Egyptian Society for Culture and Dialogue (*Misr lil-Thaqafa wa-l-Hiwar*) will hold seminars and conferences, conduct and publish research, and assist in other ways to "strengthen the values of intellectual pluralism and cultural opening and encourage the country's development in various fields." By channeling the group's energies into largely intellectual pursuits, the new association has only reinforced its elitist, "salon" character. The regime has thus allowed the *Wasat* group a voice while denying it the party organization and resources it would need to compete for political power. Islamist critics of the *Wasat* initiative claim that its leaders gained legal recognition at the expense of their former visibility and influence. But the *Wasat* Islamists take a longer-term view. As Esam Sultan, secretary general of the new association, commented, at this juncture securing a legal foothold is the group's highest priority. "Once we have legal status we can concern ourselves with mobilization," adding "anyway, mobilization is what comes easiest to us."[58]

The sources of Islamist ideological moderation: some preliminary conclusions

What broader conclusions can be derived from the *Wasat* party initiative in Egypt? Islamist ideological moderation was an outcome of both strategic calculation and political learning, much as comparative theory would predict. Hence, though the extent of ideological moderation by Islamists in Egypt does not equal that of socialists in the West, the causal logic behind it is quite similar.

Yet the *Wasat* party is interesting precisely because it is a hard case, in which the precipitants of moderation are weak and/or the deterrents to moderation are strong. While socialists in Europe and Latin America moderated their agendas to mobilize support – and presumably win power – through the mechanism of electoral competition, the *Wasat* Islamists revised their ultimate goals and took a public stand in favor of values associated with a democratic civic culture when the regime was not democratic. The *Wasat* case suggests that limited political openings short of democratization can also induce radical opposition leaders to moderate their public goals. Islamist political organizations in Egypt have long been positioned outside and against the state establishment. Given the unwillingness of Mubarak's regime to risk an electoral challenge from any opposition group, the *Wasat* founders' moderation was unlikely to enhance their immediate prospects for legal recognition. Yet the *Wasat* Islamists appear to have wagered that their reorganization as an open, transparent, and democratic party would enable them to evade state repression, expand their visibility and influence, and reduce their isolation from other groups in Egyptian civil society. Moderation, then, can be seen partly as a strategic move not to benefit from inclusion, as in the case of the socialists, but rather to increase the prospects for inclusion in the future.

According to some observers, the story ends here. To their critics in the government and the secular opposition, the *Wasat* Islamists have cultivated a moderate public image in order to gain a legal foothold and eventually to win power through the ballot box. They are "wolves in lambs' clothing," hiding their antidemocratic intentions behind a democratic façade.[59] This appraisal is hard to refute, since any moderate rhetoric or behavior can be dismissed as strategically motivated. But it is at least plausible that strategic adaptation is only part of the story. It is not at all clear that the strategic benefits of ideological moderation outweighed its costs. Furthermore, a close study of the *Wasat* Islamists' participation in Egypt's professional syndicates during the decade before the party's creation revealed a set of potential triggers of political learning, of change in their core values and beliefs.

Egypt suggests that democratic learning in nondemocratic, nonwestern settings can be propelled by a mix of regime accommodation and repression. The partial opening of Egypt's authoritarian political system created new opportunities for Islamists to participate in public life, fostering democratic learning by permitting the emergence of quasi-autonomous institutions in which Islamists could compete for power and, as elected officials, represent the interests of a group much larger than their own ideological constituency. Hence the practice of democracy within institutions contributed to democratic learning even within an authoritarian regime. Paradoxically, though, democratic learning by Islamists in Egypt was also a response to their continued repression. As the representatives of a large but technically illegal opposition movement, the Islamists protested the continuation of emergency laws, restrictions on political party formation, and human rights violations by security services and police. Over time, their opposition to restrictions on Islamist political organization and expression appears to have metamorphosed into a principled opposition to authoritarian restraints on political freedom more generally. For example, in a 1997 interview Abu Ayla Madi stressed that all political trends, including the Communists, should have the right to form legal parties.[60] And in a November 2000 interview he noted that it was his own detention in the al-Qala' prison (a notorious interrogation and torture center) in 1982, when, though not tortured personally, he could hear the screams of Islamists being tortured in adjoining cells, that led him to a visceral rejection of all forms of dictatorship. As he explained, "if we repudiate the state's mistreatment of us, how could we justify doing the same to others?"[61]

Finally, repression contributed to democratic learning by creating incentives for sustained interaction and cooperation between Islamist and secular opposition leaders. Over time, both Egyptian leftists (Marxists, Nasserists, and independents) and Islamists, neither of whom had previously accorded a high priority to democracy, gravitated toward a democratic agenda, in part to assume the moral high ground vis-à-vis the country's authoritarian leaders and in part because, as victims of repression, they had come to value democracy more than in the past. The emergence of a shared democratic agenda created new incentives for leaders on the Islamic right and the secular left to break out of the ideologically insular networks of *Weltanschauung* politics and become active in a cross-partisan campaign for political reform. One sign of this trend is the multiplication over the past decade of seminars, salons, and conferences on such themes as democracy, pluralism, and human rights, in which Islamist and secular opposition leaders have jointly taken part. One of the conferences led to the drafting in October 1995 of a national charter (*mithaq al-wifaq al-watani*) that affirmed the right of the Egyptian people to a democratic government.

Islamist opposition groups elsewhere in the Arab world demonstrate that participation does not inevitably induce ideological moderation. The largest Islamist opposition groups in Kuwait and Yemen have participated in electoral politics for years but remain committed to a profoundly illiberal agenda based on support for an unreformed *Shari'a*. Why does formal political participation trigger ideological moderation in some instances but not others? The *Wasat* party initiative suggests that democratic learning is most likely when institutional openings create incentives and opportunities for radical opposition leaders to break out of the insular networks of movement politics and engage in sustained dialogue and cooperation with other groups. Further, it suggests that ideological positions initially staked out as a kind of democratic posturing can eventually metamorphose into actual convictions, a process that Dankwart Rustow referred to in a different context as "democratic habituation."[62] Strategic moderation triggers changes in the public rhetoric and behavior of political actors that, when reiterated and defended over time, can produce change in their ultimate goals. To borrow Suzanne Hoeber Rudolph's felicitous phrase, "the mask becomes the face."[63]

In conclusion, this study has focused on how domestic institutional arrangements encourage (or inhibit) Islamist moderation. But while the *Wasat* Islamists' political orientations are strongly affected by their domestic political environment, they also respond to broader regional and international trends. The *Wasat* Islamists are part of a broader transnational Islamic movement and thus respond to calls for Muslim solidarity in the face of external threats. Events in recent years, including the descent of Israeli-Palestinian relations into unprecedented violence, the attacks of September 11 and the ensuing U.S.-led "war on terror," and the recent war in Iraq, have all deepened the prevailing sense of siege and diminished the resonance of calls for cross-cultural dialogue and cooperation. Hence it may not be an exaggeration to describe the present juncture as one singularly unpropitious for the growth of a moderate Islamist current in the Arab world. Indeed, present trends threaten not only to diminish the resonance of moderate Islamist voices, but to encourage a reradicalization of the moderate current itself.

Notes

1   Abdullahi Ahmed An-Na'im, *Toward an Islamic Reformation: Civil Liberties, Human Rights and International Law* (Syracuse: Syracuse University Press, 1990), pp. 1–2; John Waterbury, "Democracy without Democrats? The Potential for Political Liberalization in the Middle East," in Ghassan Salame, ed., *Democracy without Democrats? The Renewal of Politics in the Muslim World* (New York: I. B. Tauris, 1994), pp. 40–41.

2   See Vicki Langohr, "Of Islamists and Ballot Boxes: Rethinking the Relationship between Islamisms and Electoral Politics," *International Journal of Middle East Studies*, 33 (November 2001), 591–610; Gudrun Kramer, "Cross-Links and Double Talk? Islamist Movements in the Political Process," in Laura Guazzone, ed., *The Islamist Dilemma* (Reading: Ithaca Press, 1995), pp. 39–67; Glenn E. Robinson, "Can Islamists Be Democrats? The Case of Jordan," *Middle East Journal*, 51 (1997).

3   Daniel Pipes, "There Are No Moderates: Dealing with Fundamentalist Islam," *The National Interest*, 41 (Fall 1995), 48–52, 54.

4   See John L. Esposito, *Unholy War: Terror in the Name of Islam* (New York: Oxford University Press, 2002), pp. 133–51; Graham Fuller, "The Future of Political Islam," *Foreign Affairs*, 81 (March–April, 2002); Charles Kurzman, ed., *Liberal Islam: A Sourcebook* (New York: Oxford University Press, 1998), pp. 3–26.

5   In the Middle East one notable exception is the Justice and Development Party in Turkey, which has pledged its support to the country's secular constitutional framework.

6   The Sunna are the sayings and actions of the Prophet Muhammad, as recalled by his companions and recorded in the *hadith* literature.

7   For an anthology of and introduction to the "new Islamic thought" within the broader context of contemporary Islamic thought, see Kurzman.

8   For a discussion of the Brotherhood's original conception of *an-nizam al-islami*, see Richard Mitchell, *The Society of the Muslim Brothers* (London: Oxford University Press, 1969), pp. 234–59.

9   Muhammad Ma'moun Hudeibi, *Politics in Islam* (10th Ramadan City, Egypt: Islamic Home for Publishing and Distribution, 1997), p. 21.

10 Early Arabic language coverage of the *Wasat* Party initiative included reports in *al-Hayat*, Jan. 18, 1996; *al-Wasat*, Jan. 22, 1996; *al-Mujtam'a*, Jan. 23, 1996; *al-Wasat*, Nov. 18, 1996. In English, see Andre Hammond, "Reconstructing Islamism," *Middle East Times*, Sept. 29–Oct. 5, 1996; Nabil Abd al-Fattah, "Politics and the Generations' Battle," *Al-Ahram Weekly*, Oct. 17–23, 1996. See also Joshua Stacher, "Post-Islamist Rumblings in Egypt: The Emergence of the Wasat Party," *Middle East Journal*, 56 (Summer 2002); Anthony Shadid, *Legacy of the Prophet: Despots, Democrats and the New Politics of Islam* (Boulder: Westview Press, 2001).

11 The platform of the Egyptian *Wasat* party is a revised and expanded version of the original *Wasat* party platform published in 1996. The new platform was submitted to the government's Political Parties Committee on May 11, 1998 and published as the *Papers of the Egyptian Wasat Party* (*Awraq Hizb al-Wasat al-Misri*) (the publisher, city, and year of publication are not listed). All translations from the Arabic are my own.

12 Eric Rouleau, "Egypt's Islamists Caught in a Bind," *Le Monde Diplomatique*, English edition, January 1998, p. 2, quoted in Stacher, p. 426.

13 Hudeibi, p. 24. Hudeibi notes that the views expressed in his "Politics in Islam" echo the Brotherhood's official statements and booklets, including "A Plain Statement to Men," published in 1995, and a booklet on women's involvement in public and political life, *shura* (consultation), and the multiparty system, published in 1994. Ibid., p. 23.

14 *Awraq Hizb al-Wasat al-Misri*, pp. 24–25.

15 For the Brotherhood's position, see Hudeibi, pp. 29–30.

16 *Awraq Hizb al-Wasat al-Misri*, p. 24.

17 "Kuwaiti Legislature Says 'No' to Women's Vote," *www.cnn.com*, Nov. 30, 1999.

18   For a discussion of how references to *Shari'a* dilute the rights provided by Islamist human rights schemes, see Ann Elizabeth Mayer, *Islam and Human Rights: Tradition and Politics*, 2nd ed. (Boulder: Westview Press, 1995).

19   See Kurzman, ed., pp. 5–13.

20   See Charles Kurzman, "The Globalization of Rights in Islamic Discourse," unpublished ms. (2000), pp. 2–6.

21   See Raymond Baker, "Invidious Comparisons: Realism, Postmodern Globalism, and Centrist Islamist Movements in Egypt," in John L. Esposito, *Political Islam: Revolution, Radicalism, or Reform?* (Boulder: Lynne Rienner, 1997), pp. 115–33. Tal'at Rumeih, *al-Wasat wa al-Ikhwan* [The Wasat and the Muslim Brotherhood] (Cairo: Jaffa Center for Studies and Research, 1997), pp. 179–90.

22   Adam Przeworksi, *Capitalism and Social Democracy* (Cambridge: Cambridge University Press, 1991) pp. 7–13.

23   Ibid., pp. 16–17.

24   Samuel P. Huntington, *The Third Wave: Democratization in the Late Twentieth Century* (Norman: University of Oklahoma Press, 1991), p. 165.

25   Ibid., pp. 169–71.

26   Ibid., p. 170.

27   Donald Share, "Two Transitions: Democratization and the Evolution of the Spanish Socialist Left," *West European Politics*, 8 (January 1985), 89.

28   Ibid., p. 92.

29   Kenneth M. Roberts, "From the Barricades to the Ballot Box: Re-Democratization and Political Realignment in the Chilean Left," *Politics and Society*, 23 (December 1995), 509.

30   Middle East News Agency Bulletin, Nov. 23, 1995.

31   Interviews with Abu Ayla Madi, founder of the *Wasat* party "under formation" (*taht at-ta'siis*), Cairo, November 6, 8, and 11, 2000; 'Esam Sultan, an Islamist lawyer and *Wasat* party founding member, Cairo, November 14, 2000.

32   For parallel strategic explanation of *Wasat* Islamists' ideological moderation, see Stacher, pp. 430–32.

33   "A Gentler Middle Eastern Islam?," *The Economist*, Jan. 29, 2000, p. 46.

34   Scott Mainwaring, "Transitions to Democracy and Democratic Consolidation: Theoretical and Comparative Issues," in Scott Mainwaring, Guillermo O'Donnell, and J. Samuel Valenzuela, eds., *Issues in Democratic Consolidation: The New South American Democracies in Comparative Perspective* (Notre Dame: University of Notre Dame Press, 1992), p. 308.

35   Ibid., p. 309.

36   Nancy Bermeo, "Democracy and the Lessons of Dictatorship," *Comparative Politics*, 24 (April 1992), 273–75.

37   Ibid., pp. 284–85.

38   Ibid., pp. 285–87.

39   Interview with Abu Ayla Madi Abu Ayla, November 2000.

40   For example, see the article by the prominent *amir* Esam ad-Din al-'Aryan published in *al-Da'wa* in 1980 and discussed in Gilles Kepel, *Muslim Extremism in Egypt: The Prophet and the Pharaoh* (Berkeley: University of California Press, 1993), pp. 152–56.

41   Kepel, p. 155, highlights the impact of Qutb's writings on the thought of Islamic student leaders. "Qutb's name crops up repeatedly in the mimeographed leaflets

and newsletter produced by the *jama'at* rank and file, and the young militants claimed allegiance to his memory, whereas the work of Hasan al-Hudaybi, the former [Brotherhood] Supreme Guide who upheld a moderate line against Qutb's radicalism, was virtually ignored."

42 Ibid., pp. 152–56.

43 Seymour Martin Lipset, "Some Social Requisites of Democracy: Economic Development and Political Legitimacy," *American Political Science Review*, 1 (March 1959), 92–94. Lipset notes that historically the two major nontotalitarian groupings that conformed to this model in the West were the Catholics and the Socialists.

44 Interview with Abu Ayla Madi Abu Ayla, November 2000. See also Gaafar Al-Ahmar, "Abu Ayla Madi through an Extensive Profile," *al-Hayat*, Dec. 25, 1996.

45 See Mitchell, pp. 234–59.

46 See Carrie Rosefsky Wickham, *Mobilizing Islam: Religion, Activism and Political Change in Egypt* (New York: Columbia University Press, 2002), pp. 176–203.

47 In "Politics as a Vocation," Weber notes that political conduct is either oriented to an "ethic of ultimate ends" or an "ethic of responsibility." See H. H. Gerth and C. Wright Mills, eds., *From Max Weber: Essays in Sociology* (New York: Oxford University Press, 1958), pp. 120–21. I thank Alexander Hicks for noting the relevance of Weber's work.

48 Interview with Abu Ayla Madi Abu Ayla, Cairo, July 1997.

49 Interview with Esam Sultan, in Shadid, p. 267.

50 Interview with Abu Ayla Madi Abu Ayla, Cairo, July 1997.

51 Middle generation Islamists who stayed within the Brotherhood fold use similar language. For example, the prominent Islamist activist and physician 'Abd al-Mun'em Abu-l-Futuh referred to the emergence of more progressive positions on such issues as pluralism and women's rights as "a development (*tatawur*) in our thinking." Interview with Abu-l-Futuh, November 16, 2000.

52 Interview with Esam Sultan, in Shadid, p. 262.

53 Interview with Gasser Abd al-Raziq, Hisham Mubarak Law Center, Cairo, November 9, 2000.

54 *Awraq Hizb al-Wasat al-Misri*, p. 31.

55 Ibid., pp. 28–29, 36–37.

56 Interview with Sayyid Naggar, Cairo, November 21, 2000.

57 See *al-Wasat*, Nov. 18, 1996.

58 Interview with Esam Sultan, November 14, 2000.

59 See Mona Makram-Ebeid, "Democratization in Egypt: The 'Algeria Complex,'" *Middle East Policy*, 3 (1994), 121.

60 Interview with Abu Ayla Madi Abu Ayla, Cairo, July 1997.

61 Interview with Abu Ayla Madi Abu Ayla, Cairo, November 2000.

62 Dankwart A. Rustow, "Transitions to Democracy: Toward a Dynamic Model," *Comparative Politics*, 2 (April 1970), reprinted in Lisa Anderson, ed., *Transitions to Democracy* (New York: Columbia University Press, 1999). For a discussion of democratic habituation, see Anderson, ed., pp. 32–35.

63 I am grateful to Suzanne Hoeber Rudolph for proposing this phrase at the Halle Institute for Global Learning Conference on Religion and Global Civil Society: Religious Rebellion, Pluralism and New Spiritualities, Emory University, January 25, 2003.

Further reading

Michaelle Browers, *Political Ideology in the Arab World: Accommodation and Transformation* (Cambridge: Cambridge University Press, 2009)
An insightful analysis of the ideological and political evolution of Islamism in relation to other ideologies and political practices in the Middle East.

Janine Clark, *Islam, Charity and Activism: Middle-Class Networks and Social Welfare in Egypt, Jordan, and Yemen* (Bloomington: Indiana University Press, 2004)
A detailed analysis of the patterns and limits of Islamization promoted by social movements in different Middle East polities.

Robert W. Hefner, *Civil Islam: Muslims and Democratization in Indonesia* (Princeton: Princeton University Press, 2000)
An insightful study of the role played by Islamist movements in the processes leading to the Indonesia democratic transition.

Jillian Schwedler, *Faith in Moderation: Islamist Parties in Jordan and Yemen* (Cambridge: Cambridge University Press, 2007)
An insightful study of the mechanisms of integration of Islamist parties in two semi-authoritarian political systems of the Middle East.

Jenny White, *Islamist Mobilization in Turkey: A Study in Vernacular Politics* (Seattle: University of Washington Press, 2002)
A detailed study of the pragmatic articulation of grassroots Islamism in a democratizing Turkish polity.

Carrie Rosefsky Wickham, *Mobilizing Islam: Religion, Activism, and Political Change in Egypt* (New York: Columbia University Press, 2002)
A detailed study of the transformation of the Islamism of the Muslim Brotherhood in the face of an authoritarian Egyptian regime.

M. Hakan Yavuz, *Islamic Political Identity in Turkey* (New York: Oxford University Press, 2003)
An insightful analysis of the process of empowerment and institutionalization of Islamist actors in a secularized Turkish polity.

Islamist movements in multicultural settings

Introduction

MOVING BEYOND THE core regions of the Muslim world, this section details how political Islam contributes to reshaping the relationship between Muslim and non-Muslim communities in westernized liberal-democratic settings. It shows, from a perspective of multiculturalism, the diversity of views on the issue of how far the Islamists' social project can be constructed alongside that of non-practitioners and/or non-Muslim majorities. This section also highlights how far the reconstruction of more observant Islamic communities transforms their secularized surroundings. In the late twentieth century and early twenty-first century, the issue of the rise of Islamism among Muslim minorities and in secularized societies gained a new prominence in western policy and academic debates. There was a realization that immigrant Muslim communities in western polities were not becoming secularized as much as the host countries had expected. Furthermore, many second and third generation migrants who had become citizens of these countries were experiencing a revival of their faith and displaying an increased religiosity. This situation brought to the fore new political and religious dilemmas having to do with both the secularized liberal framework of these polities, and the organization of authoritative Islamic discourses outside the core regions of the Muslim world. For those western polities whose institutions had been shaped by the interaction between the Christian faith and a secular state, the emergence of different religious traditions and discourses also led to a tentative reconsideration of the boundaries of the public and private spheres.

The issues of integration and accommodation of Muslim populations with increased levels of religiosity have been treated primarily as a practical institutional problem for the host state. Yet, at times, they are also presented as a challenge to the core values of the existing institutional order. In parallel, inside Muslim communities, the question of the organization of religious authority has also proved difficult to answer in practice. Because the Islamic doctrine has strong egalitarian tendencies, the religious institutions that structure Islamic practices in the core regions of the

Muslim world have a traditional-legal authority more than a doctrinal-theological one. As religious authority began to be structured among communities outside these traditional Muslim regions, the articulation of Islamism in new settings revived pre-existing ideological and political disputes. Two main sets of issues structure these internal Islamic debates. Firstly, there is the question of the choice of interpretation regarding what can constitute the norm for Muslims in these secularized and minority situations. Secondly, there is the issue of the practical organization of these norms by newly created organizations and institutions that articulate the views of the diasporas instead of reflecting primarily the ambitions of foreign states and transnational movements. Unavoidably the debates taking place within Muslim communities have had implications for the political choices made by host societies trying to revise their own views of integration and multiculturalism. In their turn, the initiatives taken by governments to include the Muslim component of their societies have impacted the organization of political Islam.

The first text, by John Bowen, outlines the complexity of the transnational phenomenon produced by Islamism, which is made up of multiple interconnections between communities of practice. Bowen details the parameters of a new common public space that is tentatively created between Muslim communities newly established in secularized polities around the world. The organization of this transnational Muslim community is habitually met with suspicion by governments wanting to ensure that their national priorities and political authority are not undermined or superseded by transnational ones. Yet, rather than being a case of either/or, the main issue in this context remains to understand how mutual accommodation can be organized in practice.

The next contribution, by Talal Asad, analyses what the vitality of Islamism in western societies implies for governments which had until then devised their social policies according to the view that the secularization of society was a straightforward and irreversible process. Asad notes that in order to implement their views regarding a 'properly' secular public domain, western states are increasingly forced to engage the religious field (and Islam in particular) to set specific boundaries for religious discourse and practice. In particular state policies have to become more involved with the micro-management of an increasing number of behaviours that are perceived to be encroaching on the public sphere and impacting upon the national ethos.

The third text, by Nilüfer Göle, highlights how Islamism as an embodiment of an alternative view of social order challenges by its very visibility secular conceptions of normality in a modern society. In the case of Turkey, a Muslim-majority country whose institutional system has been tailored to match that of the secular European republican systems, Göle analyses how the renewed visibility of Islamic religiosity in previously secularized spaces creates new political challenges for official discourses on modernization. Paying particular attention to the wearing of the Islamic veil, she details the multiple layers of meaning that construct these new forms of Islamic identification and the way in which they can be compatible with the secularized narratives on religion and politics.

The next contribution, by Pnina Werbner, details the processes of internal reconstruction of an Islamic ideal and practices by Muslim minorities located in the 'West' but interconnected with Muslim majorities in the 'East'. In this process of articulation of Islamist views, Werbner highlights the risk of marginalization of Muslim communities as perceptions of racial differences are turned into notions of cultural superiority in imbalanced multicultural situations. Considering in particular the case of British Muslims in the post 9/11 context, she notes how the South Asian diasporas could be forced into a defensive identity discourse in the face of governmental and social pressures for renewed proofs of loyalty to the state and the nation.

The final text, by Olivier Roy, considers the interaction between new Islamist trends in western societies and the multicultural policies that traditionally have been used by governments in order to manage migration and facilitate integration. Roy indicates how policies dealing with religion as a cultural artefact are inadequate for Islamist movements that propose a formalized blueprint for social and political order increasingly devoid of cultural references and applying to all Muslims regardless of their local circumstances. These new forms of transnational Islamism benefit from a globalized public sphere that weakens local and national particularisms.

John R. Bowen

BEYOND MIGRATION: ISLAM AS A TRANSNATIONAL PUBLIC SPACE

RECENT STUDIES OF transnational religious phenomena have emphasised the importance of distinguishing between transnational processes of migration and movement on the one hand, and diasporic forms of consciousness, identity
and cultural creation on the other (Levitt 2001a; Vertovec 2000). While this distinction is useful (and subtly deployed by these authors), it risks directing the study of
transnational social phenomena in certain, limited directions. If 'transnationalism' is
mainly about migration and its variable aftermaths, it is a short step to suggesting that
it be subsumed under the category of cultural assimilation (as recently advocated by
Kivisto 2001), leaving 'diaspora' to designate populations living outside putative
'homelands' as well as the self-understandings held by those populations (Saint-
Blancat 2002; Vertovec 1997).

Migration and diaspora do, of course, define a wide range of social processes and
experiences, but they do not exhaust transnationality. In particular, they insufficiently
take into account the possibility of quite distinct self-understandings about boundaries and legitimacy on the part of both 'host' countries and 'immigrant' populations.
I take Islam in France as an illuminating case in point because each of its two terms
challenges the possibility of self-defining through migration and diaspora. First,
Islam complicates current lines of transnational analysis by emphasising its own universal norms and its practices of deliberating about religious issues across national
boundaries.[1] Secondly, *France* raises the stakes of diasporic self-definition by challenging
the cultural, political, and even religious legitimacy of any sort of extension of a
citizen's life beyond state borders. The one resists national assimilation; the other
requires it; both question the legitimacy of 'diaspora' as a descriptive term for
portions of their membership.

In what follows I argue that transnational Islam creates and implies the existence
and legitimacy of a global public space of normative reference and debate, and that
this public space cannot be reduced to a dimension of migration or of transnational

religious movements. I offer two brief ethnographic examples of this transnational public space, and maintain that even as it develops references to Europe it implies neither a 'Euro-Islam' nor a 'post-national' sense of European membership and citizenship.

Three transnational dimensions of Islam

The phrase 'transnational Islam' can be used to refer to a variety of phenomena, among which I would emphasise three: demographic movements, transnational religious institutions, and the field of Islamic reference and debate. I will argue that a focus on the first two, and in general on phenomena of migration and movement, has obscured the importance of the third.

Muslims may move across national borders for social or economic reasons, and in this first respect can be said to participate in transnational movement in precisely the same way as do Haitians who move to North America or middle-class Europeans who live and work in more than one country. There is nothing necessarily 'Islamic' about these attachments and returns, although they *may* define or create trajectories along which religious ideas or forms are carried and changed. Many of the North or West Africans, Turks, or South Asians who migrated to European countries in search of work have remained profoundly attached to their countries of origin. Many of them make frequent trips to these countries; those who retained their original citizenship may return to vote; some have chosen to have their bodies 'repatriated' for burial: and in this sense these individuals participate in the transnational movements proposed for anthropology by Glick Schiller (1997), Portes (1999) and others.

Of course, different populations develop distinct trajectories: in France and Italy, West Africans seem to travel more frequently to origin countries than do North Africans, for reasons having in part to do with the greater participation by the former in transnational Sufi movements (Grillo 2001; Riccio 2001). In this respect Senegalese in Italy or France (and Turkish workers in Germany) resemble the now-classic cases of transnational movement between Caribbean countries and the eastern United States (Levitt 2001b; McAlister 1998).[2] To that extent, these Muslim populations fit quite well into the analytical category of transnational demographic movement.

Certain transnational practices *are* tied to religious practice, however, and these transnational religious institutions have been a second focus of study for those interested in 'transnational Islam'. Some Muslims belong to religious organisations that either promote cross-national movement as part of their religious practice, or encompass and promote cross-national communication within their religious hierarchy. One of the most prominent in France and elsewhere in Europe (and North America) is the Tablighi Jama'at (Kepel 1991; Masud 1999; Metcalf 1996, 2001). The movement has its origins and centre in northern India, and sends missions out to urge Muslims residing elsewhere in the world to return to the correct practice of Islam. Diverse Sufi orders also maintain ties and communication between new places of residence and their centres, as they have been doing since the tenth century. Their devotions focus on a living or dead saint, and they carry that devotional orientation with them as they travel. Sufis in Manchester or Paris have local leaders, but they also maintain their ties of devotion to saintly leaders in Pakistan, Senegal, or elsewhere (Riccio 2001; Werbner 2003). These groups maintain particularly strong ties to a homeland and maintain these ties across generations. In that respect these transnational religious movements develop a diasporic character in the form of representations and imaginations of a homeland.

In studies about Islam and transnationalism in Europe, it is these transnational, diasporic religious movements that have received the most attention (Grillo *supra*). In Britain, for example, anthropological and sociological studies of Islam have focused on the perduring ties between local mosques or associations and home-country institutions, particularly those in Kashmir and Bangladesh (Lewis 2002; Werbner 2003). In Germany, a great deal of attention is paid to the ties between Islamic organisations in Germany and Turkish political parties (e.g. Schiffauer 1999). The reasons for this research concentration are probably multiple. These movements provide a sociologically clear entity to study, with members, leaders and group activities. They involve movement and communication across borders, and so are clearly 'transnational' in a way that links their study both to migration literature and to current writing about globalisation. Finally, the Sufi ties of some of these organisations may make them intrinsically more attractive to some anthropologists and sociologists, intellectually so because they have their own rituals and genealogies, and perhaps ethically so to the extent that many social scientists prefer Sufism to the more pared-down versions of Islam associated with modernist and (non-Sufi) reformist movements.

This emphasis within sociological and anthropological studies has led to the relative neglect of a third form of transnational Islam: namely, the development of debates and discussions among Muslims about the nature and role of Islam in Europe and North America. These debates and discussions have led to the creation of networks, conferences, and increasingly formalised institutions for systematic reflection among scholars. These activities and institutions focus on the dilemmas faced by Muslims attempting to develop forms of Islamic life compatible with the range of Western norms, values and laws – in other words, how to become wholly 'here' and yet preserve a tradition of orientation toward Islamic institutions located 'over there' (Grillo 2001).

This third sense of 'transnational Islam' as a public space of reference and debate draws, of course, on Islam's history of movement, communication and institutional innovation. Islam has an intrinsic universality (which it shares with Christian religions) and also more specific universalistic dimensions. The message of the Qur'ân was to turn away from localised deities and worship the transcendent God. The capitals of Islamic polities shifted from one city to another (Baghdad, Damascus, Cairo, Istanbul), meaning the caliphate was and is not limited to one particular region or centre – and indeed in some contemporary imaginings can be entirely deterritorialised (Kahani-Hopkins and Hopkins 2002). Mecca remains the religious focal point of Islam, but the Islamic era began with the flight or migration (*hijra*) from Mecca to Medina (Eickelman and Piscatori 1990).

Other features of Islamic religious practice promote the sense of a worldwide community, the *umma*, among ordinary Muslims. The perduring role of Arabic as the primary language of scholarship and the development of a global jurisprudence (albeit with several schools or traditions) made possible international communication among scholars.[3] The standardisation of the Qur'ân, the requirement to pray in Arabic, and the popular enjoyment of reciting and writing verses of the Qur'ân promote among ordinary Muslims the sense of participation in a universal message (Hirschkind 2001). The annual pilgrimage brings together a sampling of Muslims, and the Saudi government's quota system ensures that pilgrims will meet a geographically wide range of fellow pilgrims. Daily, theoretically five times daily, Muslims turn their bodies in the direction of Mecca in order to carry out the obligatory rituals of worship (salât). Even those Muslims who refer to their allegiance to a spiritual leader or to the Shiite legacy of 'Ali more than to their membership in the worldwide umma would deny that Islam is or should be defined or bounded by local or national borders. This sense of Islam's transnational character is diffuse but powerful, and it derives its power from the ways in which rituals reproduce, and histories remind Muslims of, the shared duties and practices of Muslims across political boundaries. In its impulse to refuse particularistic loyalties to ethnic groups or to a nation-state, this consciousness first and foremost creates an imagination of an Islamic community transcending specific boundaries and borders.[4]

This consciousness in turn supports the legitimacy and indeed the imperative of searching anywhere in the world for the highest authority on Islamic matters. This imperative creates specific networks of authority, learning and communication that are more historically and sociologically specific than the general sense of global umma-hood. Some sources of religious authority – Meccan jurists, Cairene muftis – owe their status to their institutional associations and affiliations; they have been at least recognised, if not always acknowledged, by Muslims throughout the world and over the centuries. Other sources of authority, such as the currently mediatique Yûsuf Qardâwî of al-Jazîra television fame, have followed more specific paths to positions of authority, but nonetheless find audiences in many countries. Still others, such as the Syrian father and son al-Bouti mentioned below, have a smaller, but nonetheless enthusiastic body of followers.

The scope of influence of these authorities varies greatly, but in each case, and this is the critical point, it reaches far beyond the borders of the home country. The communications between these sites and Muslims living elsewhere in the world take many forms: newspaper columns, Internet sites, cable television, or books (Eickelman and Anderson 1999). Moreover, links to authority sites often demand a competence in Arabic and a familiarity with the genre conventions of the advice column or the fatwa. These sites are not the only ones available to Muslims, of course, and those in, say, northern India, Iran or Java require additional or distinct linguistic competencies and take different institutional forms. But to claim the highest level of scholarly expertise and authority, one must be able to read texts written in classical Arabic and perhaps be able to recite these texts as well.[5]

This orientation is more specific and can be more particularistic than that toward the umma, in that different populations of Muslims pay attention to different sources of authority (and scholars do so more than ordinary people) but it, too, draws on a general feature of Islam, namely, the idea that it is to the most learned, wherever they may reside, that the Muslim ought to listen. It has to do much more with the worldwide communication of ideas than with the movement of populations, and does not depend on it. Muslims may communicate and debate across political boundaries without necessarily migrating or forming transnational religious movements.

For the rest of this paper I wish to consider the implications of this transnational public space for the question of Islam's place in Europe, and I do so for the hardest case, that of France. Because the transnational public space of Islam is based on a set of extra-national social norms – the many interpretations of *shari'a*, 'God's plans and commands' – one will expect a higher level of conflict between transnational and national public claims in those states that make the stronger demands on their members for normative conformity or homogeneity. As the first example suggests, the more successful states are in organising Islam internally, the more visible will be those conflicts.

Conflicts of justification at *Le Bourget*

The scene is the 'Exhibition Park' at the former airport of *Le Bourget*, in April 2003, during the four-day annual assembly of the UOIF, the Union of Islamic Organisations of France (*Union des Organisations Islamiques de France*), an umbrella organisation of mosques and local Islamic associations in France. The UOIF is only one of several such national organisations; its main rivals are a network of mosques under the control of the Paris Mosque, which itself is financed and controlled by the Algerian government, and the FNMF (*Fédération Nationale des Musulmans de France*), controlled by Morocco.[6]

The assembly is part book fair, part marriage market, and part Islamic school, with speakers from several countries talking on spirituality, law and politics (for details see Bowen 2004). This assembly was the twentieth sponsored by the UOIF, and also occurred just after nation-wide elections for a new representative council of Muslims, the *Conseil Français du Culte Musulman* (CFCM). The previous December, the Minister of the Interior (who is also 'Minister of Cults'), Nicolas Sarkozy, had succeeded in convincing the major Islamic organisations to participate in these elections. One of the means by which he did so was to get all parties to agree that the first President of the Council would be the head of the Paris Mosque, Dalil Boubakeur, and that the leaders of the UOIF and the FNMF would supply vice-presidents. At the elections the latter two organisations, in some places in alliance with each other or with other groups (notably the Turks), crushed the Paris Mosque candidates. The UOIF/FNMF victories could be attributed to a number of factors, among them the Moroccan dominance of mosques (the electoral unit) and of Moroccan prominence in both the UOIF and the FNMF. But at Le Bourget the UOIF leadership celebrated the results and the large turnout as a vote of confidence in their organisation's willingness to follow Sarkozy's game.

The high point of this celebration was to be the prime-time moment, Saturday evening, when Sarkozy was to address the gathering – the first such visit by a minister. He arrived punctually and was loudly, repeatedly applauded (27 times, said one source), particularly when he called for treating all citizens equally, whatever their religion. But then came the moment that would dominate public discussion throughout France for the next 10 days (until debates over a new pension reform plan took the stage). Sarkozy said that because all are equal before the law, all must comply with the law that all residents must have their picture taken for identity cards with their heads uncovered: 'nothing would justify women of the Muslim confession benefiting from a different law'.

The booing and whistles took minutes to die down. The statement ruptured the mood, but logically it was merely an application of the general principles applauded moments before. The reasoning was impeccable: Muslims must obey the law, the law says no headcovering on identity cards, Muslim women must untie their scarves at such moments. The Minister simply recited a syllogism, a basic cultural fact of French mental life.

The UOIF officials immediately denounced the law in question, and said it was their right to work to overturn it – one official making the unfortunate comparison with what he saw as a similarly unjust law, the Nazi requirement that Jews wear yellow stars. This remark also was covered in the press. Less remarked on was the equally clear-cut recitation of how Islamic law should be followed that occurred in the same place two days after the Minister's speech, delivered as part of the UOIF's report on Islamic law. The organisation's spokesman on Islamic law, Ahmad Jaballah, issued a fatwa on behalf of the UOIF and the broader European network of which it is part, to the effect that Muslim women must wear headscarves. His speech came in response to a question, in the form of question and answer that defines the work of a mufti. The question concerned the obligation to wear 'le *hijâb*', which always means, in these discursive contexts, a headcovering. Jaballah said:

> This question [out the *hijâb*] was invoked earlier and the media have spoken about it. Many families find themselves obliged to have their daughters take off the hijab at work or at school. And as you know, many officials would like to pass a law forbidding it. But I should make several points. First, Islam requires women to wear the hijab, and here all schol-ars, in the past and today, agree. Secondly, we consider wearing the hijab to be an act of choice by a woman and not something forced upon her. Families should not oblige a girl to wear it if she does not want to. Third, when a Muslim woman wears the headscarf, she does it as an act of faith, and not as a political act or to signal her separate social identity. Fourth, the Conseil d'Etat [France's highest administrative tribunal] has decided that wearing the headscarf is not incompatible with *laïcité* [here, applause from the crowd], and this decision is consistent with the European Charter of Human Rights, where it guarantees the expression of reli-gious beliefs both in private and in public. Many denounce ostentation and proselytism, but these occur only when someone wishes to impose religion on someone else, and such practices are not found in Islam. Fifth, what must be done? Try dialogue and avoid confrontation. Some school principals have interpreted the Conseil's decision in the direction of permitting the headscarf. Cover the maximum possible with the *fou-lard*, and not just with a bandanna. Don't focus on the issue of its colour; the point is to cover up [more applause]. We need to have Muslim women in every sector of public life. Some work not because they have to but because they received education and want to contribute, and they need to do so with their headscarf. If you have to take it off at work because you are forced to do so, this does not mean that you should leave it off the rest of the time, only when obliged to. Finally, there is a decree

regarding the identity cards, but we must emphasise that no statute forbids wearing the headscarf, and legal specialists agree that such a law would be in conflict with the European convention. In 1983 the UOIF asked Gaston Deferre, then the Minister of the Interior, to allow Muslim women to keep their headscarves on when photographed for their identity cards, 'because the foulard is a part of their identity', and he agreed. We have the letter on file and it could become part of the jurisprudence [more applause].

Both Sarkozy and Jaballah were categorical and explicit: each of the two systems of norms, one enforced by the 'chief cop of France', as he had been introduced to the UOIF crowd, the other enforced by God, is absolute. No exceptions or exemptions can be tolerated. Indeed, Jaballah had devoted his own speech, earlier in the meeting, to the precise topic of the conditions under which exemptions can be made to an Islamic rule (*ahkam*), and his exposé did not allow for exemptions in cases such as that of the *hijâb*. It is important to note that the fatwa was not limited to France; it was originally the product of a European assembly of scholars, all individuals of non-European origin, although most now living in European countries, and of which the leader is the Egyptian scholar, resident in Qatar, Yûsuf Qardâwî (on the European council see Caeiro 2003).

What I wish to emphasise here is that the two structures of justification are identical in form, and that they have entirely different starting points. Sarkozy and others in the French government start from the positive laws of France, but quickly proceed to deduce these laws, and perhaps others that need to be passed, from a conception of the Republic. In March 2004 the French National Assembly and Senate passed a law that will forbid public school students from wearing clothing that calls attention to their religious affiliation. The legislators argued that the presence of the scarves contravened norms of gender equality and of *laïcité*, interpreted in the parliamentary debates to mean the absence of religious signs in the public sphere (see Baubérot 2000; Favell 2001). As I argue elsewhere (Bowen 2003), the deductive form taken by French arguments about *laïcité* make for particularly sharp confrontations with alternative ideas of justice or public comportment.

The UOIF, and many other Muslims, start from authoritative interpretations of Islamic norms ('I scholars, in the past and today, agree'). These interpretations are the more authoritative the less bound they are by space or time: better if they reflect the opinions of learned Muslims over the centuries, and across political boundaries. Indeed the more 'liberal' views of Islamic norms urge Muslims to begin their interpretations from the general principles of Islam rather than from the specifics of time and place. The value of generality helps explain why, at the beginning of the Dâr al-Fatwa session at which Jaballah spoke, the moderator was careful to emphasise that the session reflected the opinions of the European Council as well as the French one.

Now, as we saw above, the UOIF spokesman also refers to European norms of human rights and to the French Conseil d'Etat. This sort of reference has led Yasemin Soysal (2002) to argue that Muslims in Europe are justifying their claims to specific rights (to dress, food, or language) on the basis of 'natural' rights of individuals and human rights 'rather than drawing on religious teachings and traditions' (2002: 144).

Although she points to occasional 'alternative' references to 'God's law', she states that these should not detract from the 'prevalent universalistic forms of making claims by Muslim groups that are commonly overlooked' (2002: 145). This argument is part of the broader one that groups and states in Europe are moving towards 'post-national' forms of membership in Europe.

Soysal's claim usefully reminds us that some Muslims make such references, as Jaballah's discourse exemplifies. But we must ask what rhetorical position these references occupy in justifications of social claims made by key public Muslim actors. In trying to persuade other Muslims of the truth of their position on various religious matters, do Muslim public intellectuals base their justifications on general human rights grounds or on notions of European citizenship? No, they base them on Islamic norms, as did the UOIF with respect to headscarves. The normative force of wearing the *foulard*, its obligatory quality, comes from scripture, not from human rights, as is true for 'ordinary' women discussing their decisions to wear headscarves or not to do so (Souilamas 2001; Venel 1999). (Similarly, Sarkozy's counter-argument comes from French law, not from European laws or universal rights.) The references to non-Islamic normative sources are purely instrumental in Jaballah's speech on behalf of the Dâr al-Fatwa: the Conseil d'Etat has ruled that schoolgirls must be allowed to keep their headscarves on, and any new law that said otherwise would contravene the European Convention on Human Rights. These are useful ways to persuade French law-makers and school principals, but the specific norms invoked are entirely a function of the strategic advantages such citations will produce. If focusing on the contingencies of French court decisions best supports the case for the headscarves, then it is to those sources that most Muslim spokespersons and others will point. If that recourse becomes impossible because the law has changed, then the reference will change as well.

In any case, references to non-Islamic normative sources are secondary to a justificatory discourse that is based in Islamic jurisprudence, manifestly transnational, and not European. How precisely one interprets Islamic norms and jurisprudence is, however, open to debate, and Muslim public intellectuals writing and speaking in France have proposed a range of alternative positions, from a traditional reliance on one legal tradition (*madhhab*) to an effort to rethink Islamic norms in terms of broad ethical principles (see Bowen forthcoming). Moreover, Europe may define a set of shared contingencies, as evidenced in the willingness of Qardâwî and his European Council to allow Muslims to take out first mortgages because of the 'necessity' created by high European house rental rates (Bowen forthcoming; Caeiro 2003). However, the space of reference and debate on normative questions is one that includes the sources of greater authority to be found in the Arabic-speaking world.

Notes

1   I should emphasise that the authors referred to here are well aware of these internal formulations within Islam; see Vertovec (2000).

2   On the ways in which the movements of Turkish workers, made mainly for economic reasons, nonetheless shape religious consciousness, see Amiraux (2001) and Schiffauer (1999).

3   I have been struck by this use of Arabic in what might otherwise be unlikely places. Two examples will illustrate the general point. The Fiqh Council of North America does use English at their meetings but participants are expected to be able to converse in Arabic as well, despite the group's inclusion of American converts and South Asians. In the Gayo highlands of Aceh, Indonesia, where I worked for many years, 'traditionalist' religious scholars, all speakers of the Gayo language, generally write down the conclusions of their meetings in Arabic, a language none of them converse in fluently.

4   I omit discussion of the debates among Muslims about the ways to conceive of the 'Islamic world' and the rest: should they be considered as two distinct realms (*dâr*) based on the Islamic character of the society or the government? Or should one focus instead on the degree to which Muslims are free to pursue their religious activities in different countries? For historical and comparative perspectives on this question, see Abou El Fadl (1994); Bowen (forthcoming); Kahani-Hopkins and Hopkins (2002); and Ramadan (2002).

5   Zaman (2002) shows how scholarly writing and debates in today's Pakistan take place in Arabic, not in Urdu. Zaman has remarked (personal communication, 2003) that this fact explains the small number of Western scholars of Islam in South Asia competent to master the scholarly communications, in that Arabic has not been a regular part of the training of South Asianists.

6   In response to the North African domination of public Islamic activities, immigrants from Turkey formed their own grouping, as did a collection of Muslims from a broad array of places, including the Comoros, the West Indies, and West Africa. Because the strongest rivalries are among the three North African groups, sometimes mosques at which Muslims from more than one of these groups worship will choose someone from a smaller grouping to be the imam or mosque leader. In one mosque south of Paris, men from Algeria and Morocco laughingly (but meaningfully) recounted to me that only a Comoro man could have brought peace to their mosque. Mosques in the Paris region usually are multi-ethnic, and preach in Arabic or French and Arabic; in cities with large populations of non-Arabic speakers such as Marseille one finds ethnic-specific mosques.

References

Baubérot, J. (2000) *Histoire de la laïcité française*. Paris: Presses Universitaires de France.

Bowen, J.R. (2003) 'Two approaches to rights and religion in contemporary France', in Mitchell, J. and Wilson, R. (eds) *Rights in Global Perspective*. London: Routledge, 33–53.

Bowen, J.R. (2004) 'Does French Islam have borders? Dilemmas of domestication in a global religious field', *American Anthropologist*, 106(1): 43–55.

Bowen, J.R. (forthcoming 2005) 'Pluralism and normativity in French Islamic reasoning', in Hefner, R. (ed.) *Islam, Pluralism, and Democratization*. Princeton: Princeton University Press (in press).

Caeiro, A. (2003) *La Normativité Islamique à l'Epreuve de l'Occident: le cas du Conseil européen de la fatwa et de la recherche*. Paris: l'Harmattan.

Eickelman, D.F. and Anderson, J. (eds) (1999) *New Media in the Muslim World: The Emerging Public Sphere*. Bloomington: Indiana University Press.

Eickelman, D.F. and Piscatori, J. (eds) (1990) *Muslim Travelers: Pilgrimage, Migration, and the Religious Imagination*. Berkeley: University of California Press.

Favell, A. (2001) *Philosophies of Integration: Immigration and the Idea of Citizenship in France and Britain*. Houndmills: Palgrave (2nd edition).

Glick Schiller, N. (1997) 'The situation of transnational studies', *Identities*, 4(2): 155–66.

Grillo, R.D. (2001) *Transnational Migration and Multiculturalism in Europe*. Oxford: Transnational Communities Working Paper WPTC-01-08.

Hirschkind, C. (2001) 'The ethics of listening: cassette-sermon audition in contemporary Egypt', *American Ethnologist*, 28(3): 623–49.

Kahani-Hopkins, V. and Hopkins, N. (2002) '"Representing" British Muslims: the strategic dimension to identity construction', *Ethnic and Racial Studies*, 25(2): 288–309.

Kepel, G. (1991) *Les Banlieues de l'Islam: naissance d'une religion en France*. Paris: Seuil.

Kivisto, P. (2001) 'Theorizing transnational immigration: a critical review of current efforts', *Ethnic and Racial Studies*, 24(4): 549–77.

Levitt, P. (2001a) *Between God, Ethnicity, and Country: An Approach to the Study of Transnational Religion*. Oxford: Transnational Communities Working Paper WPTC-01-13.

Levitt, P. (2001b) *The Transnational Villagers*. Berkeley: University of California Press.

Lewis, P. (2002) *Islamic Britain: Religion, Politics, and Identity among British Muslims*. London: I.B. Tauris (2nd edition).

Masud, M.K. (ed.) (1999) *Travelers in Faith: Studies of the Tablighi Jamaat as a Transnational Islamic Movement for Faith Renewal*. Leiden: Brill.

McAlister, E. (1998) 'The Madonna of 115th Street revisited: Vodou and Haitian Catholicism in the age of transnationalism', in Warner, R.S. and Wittner, J. (eds) *Gatherings In Diaspora: Religious Communities and the New Immigration*. Philadelphia: Temple University Press, 123–60.

Metcalf, B.D. (1996) 'New Medinas: the Tablighi Jama'at in America and Europe', in Metcalf, B.D. (ed.) *Making Muslim Space in North America and Europe*. Berkeley: University of California Press, 110–27.

Metcalf, B.D. (2001) '"Traditionalist" Islamic activism: Deoband, Tablighis, and Talibs', in Calhoun, C., Price, P. and Timmer, A. (eds) *Understanding September 11*. New York: The New Press, 53–66.

Portes, A. (1999) 'Conclusion: toward a new world – the origins and effects of transnational activities', *Ethnic and Racial Studies*, 22(2): 463–77.

Riccio, B. (2001) 'From "ethnic group" to "transnational community"? Senegalese migrants' ambivalent experiences and multiple trajectories', *Journal of Ethnic and Migration Studies*, 27(4): 583–99.

Saint-Blancat, C. (2002) 'Islam in diaspora: between reterritorialization and extraterritoriality', *International Journal of Urban and Regional Research*, 26(1): 138–51.

Schiffauer, W. (1999) *Islamism in the Diaspora: The Fascination of Political Islam Among Second Generation German Turks*. Oxford: Transnational Communities Working Paper WPTC-99-06.

Souilamas, N.C. (2001) *Des "beurettes" aux descendantes d'immigrants nord-africains*. Paris: Grasset.

Soysal, Y.N. (2002) 'Citizenship and identity: living in diasporas in postwar Europe?', in Hedetoft, U. and Hjort, M. (eds) *The Postnational Self*. Minneapolis: University of Minnesota Press, 137–51.

Venel, N. (1999) *Musulmanes Françaises: des pratiquantes voilées à l'université*. Paris: L'Harmattan.

Vertovec, S. (1997) 'Three meanings of "diaspora", exemplified among South Asian religions', *Diaspora*, 6(3): 277–300.

Vertovec, S. (2000) *Religion and Diaspora*. Oxford: Transnational Communities Working Paper WPTC-01-01.

Werbner, P.S. (2003) *Pilgrims of Love: Anthropology of a Global Sufi Cult*. London: Hurst & Company.

Talal Asad

TRYING TO UNDERSTAND FRENCH SECULARISM

Reading signs

BECAUSE RELIGION IS of such capital importance to the lay Republic, the latter reserves for itself the final authority to determine whether the meaning of given symbols (by which I mean conventional signs) is "religious." One might object that this applies only to the meaning of signs in public places, but since the legal distinction between public and private spaces is itself a construction of the state, the scope and content of "public space" is primarily a function of the Republic's power.

The arguments presented in the media about the Islamic headscarf affair were therefore embedded in this power. They seemed to me not so much about tolerance toward Muslims in a religiously diverse society, not even about the strict separation between religion and the state: they were first and foremost about the structure of political liberties – about the relations of subordination and immunity, the recognition of oneself as a particular kind of self – on which this state is built, and about the structure of emotions that underlies those liberties. The dominant position in the debate assumed that in the event of a conflict between constitutional principles the state's right to defend its personality would trump all other rights. The state's inviolable personality was expressed in and through particular images, including those signifying the abstract individuals whom it represented and to which they in turn owed unconditional obedience. The headscarf worn by Muslim women was held to be a religious sign conflicting with the secular personality of the French Republic.

The eventual outcome of such debates about the Islamic headscarf in the media and elsewhere was the president's appointment of a commission of inquiry charged with reporting on the question of secularity in schools. The commission was headed by ex-minister Bernard Stasi, and it heard testimony from a wide array of persons. In December 2003, a report was finally submitted to the president, recommending a law that would prohibit the display of any "conspicuous religious signs [*des signes ostensibles*]" in public schools – including veils, kippas, and large crosses worn around the neck. On the other hand, medallions, little crosses, stars of David, hands of Fatima, or miniature Qur'ans, which the report designates "discreet signs [*les signes discrets*]," are authorized. In making all these stipulations, the commission clearly felt the need to appear evenhanded. The proposed law was formally passed by the National Assembly in February 2004 by an almost unanimous vote. There were some demonstrations by young Muslims – as there had been earlier when the Stasi commission had formally made its recommendation – but the numbers who protested openly were small. Most French Muslims seemed prepared to follow the new law, some reluctantly.[1]

I begin with something the Stasi report does not address: according to the Muslims who are against the ban for reasons of faith, the wearing of the headscarf by women in public is a religious *duty* but carrying "discreet signs" is not. Of course there are many Muslims, men and women, who maintain that the wearing of a veil is *not* a duty in Islam, and it is undoubtedly true that even those who wear it may do so for a variety of motives. But I do not offer a normative judgment about Islamic doctrine here. My point is not that wearing the veil *is* in fact a legal requirement. I simply note that *if* the wearer assumes the veil as an obligation of her faith, *if her conscience impels her to wear it as an act of piety*, the veil becomes for that reason an integral part of herself. For her it is not a *sign* intended to communicate something but *part of an orientation, of a way of being*. For the Stasi commission, by contrast, all the wearables mentioned *are* signs, and are regarded, furthermore, as *displaceable* signs. But there is more to the report than the veil as material sign.

The Stasi commission takes certain signs to have a "religious" meaning by virtue of their synecdochic relation to systems of collective representation – in which, for example, the kippa stands for "Judaism," the cross for "Christianity," the veil for "Islam." What a given sign signifies is therefore a central question. I stress that, although the Stasi report nowhere defines "religion," it assumes the existence of such a definition because the qualifying form of the term ("religious signs") rests on a substantive form ("religion").

Two points may be noted in this connection. First, precisely because there is disagreement among contemporary pious Muslims as to whether the headscarf is a divinely required accoutrement for women, its "religious" significance must be indeterminate for non-Muslims. Only by rejecting one available interpretation ("the headscarf has nothing whatever to do with real religion") in favor of another ("the veil is an Islamic symbol") can the Stasi commission insist on its being obviously a "religious" sign. This choice of the sign's meaning enables the commission to claim that the principle of *laïcité* is breached by the "Islamic veil," and that since *laïcité* is not negotiable the veil must be removed. (To some extent this variability of interpretation was played out subsequently in relation to the meaning of the Sikh turban.[2])

The second point is that the "religious" signs forbidden in school premises are distinguished by their gender dimension – the veil is worn by women, the kippa by men, and the cross by both sexes. The object of the whole exercise is, of course, to ban the Islamic veil partly because it is "religious" but also because it signifies "the low legal status of women in Muslim society" (a secular signification). The girls who are the object of the school ban are French, however, living in France; they are therefore subject to French law and not to the *shari'a*. Since French law no longer discriminates between citizens on grounds of gender or religious affiliation, *since it no longer allows, as it did until 1975, that a man may chastise his wife for insubordination*, the sign designates not a real status but an imaginary one, and therefore an imaginary transgression.

Ideally, the process of signification is both rational and clear, and precisely these qualities make it capable of being rationally criticized. It is assumed that a given sign signifies something that is clearly "religious." What is set aside in this assumption, however, is the entire realm of ongoing discourses and practices that provide authoritative meanings. The precision and fixity accorded to the relationship of signification is always an arbitrary act and often a spurious one, insofar as embodied language is concerned. In other words, what is signified by the headscarf is not some historical *reality* (the evolving Islamic tradition) but *another sign* (the eternally fixed "Islamic religion"), which, despite its overflowing character, is used to give the "Islamic veil" as a stable meaning.

Assuming, for the sake of argument, that certain signs are essentially religious, where and how may they be used to make a statement? According to the Stasi report, secularism does not insist on religion's being confined within the privacy of conscience, on its being denied public expression. On the contrary, it says that the free expression of religious signs (things, words, sounds that partake of a "religious" essence) is an integral part of the liberty of the individual. As such, it is not only legitimate but essential to the conduct of public debate in a secular democracy – so long as the representatives of different religious opinions do not attempt to dominate.[3] But what "domination" means when one is dealing with a religiously defined minority, whose traditional religion is actively practiced by a small proportion of that minority, is not very clear.

It is interesting that the determination of meanings by the commission was not confined to what was *visible*. It included the deciphering of psychological processes such as desire and will. Thus the wearer's *act of displaying the sign* was said to incorporate the actor's *will* to display it – and therefore became part of what the headscarf meant. As one of the commission members later explained, its use of the term "displaying [*manifestant*]" was meant to underline the fact that certain acts embodied "the will to [make] appear [*volonté d'apparaitre*]."[4] The *Muslim identity* of the headscarf wearer was crucial to the headscarf's meaning because the will to display it had to be read from that identity. (Another aspect of its meaning came from equating the will to make the veil appear with "Islamic fundamentalism" or "Islamism," terms used interchangeably to denote a range of different endorsements of public Islam.) Paradoxically, Republican law thus realizes its *universal* character through a *particular* (i.e., female Muslim) identity, that is, a particular psychological internality. However, the mere existence of an internal dimension that is accessible from outside is felicitous for secularism. It opens up the universal prospect of cultivating Republican selves in public schools. At any rate, "the will" itself is not seen but the visible veil points to it as one of its effects.

"Desire" is treated in an even more interesting way. The commission's concern with the desires of pupils is expressed in a distinction between those who didn't really want to wear the headscarf and those who did. It is not very clear exactly how these "genuine desires" were deciphered, although reference is made to pressure by traditional parents and communities, and one assumes that some statements to that effect must have been made to the commission.[5]

It is worth remarking that solicitude for the "real" desires of the pupils applied only to girls *who wore the headscarf*. No thought appears to have been given to determining the "real" desires of girls *who did not wear the headscarf*. Was it possible that some of them secretly wanted to wear a headscarf but were ashamed to do so because of what their French peers and people in the street might think and say? Or could it be that they were hesitant for other reasons? However, in their case surface appearance alone was sufficient for the commission: no headscarf worn *means* no desire to wear it. In this way "desire" is not discovered but semiotically constructed.

This asymmetry in the possible meanings of the headscarf as a sign again makes sense if the commission's concern is seen to be not simply a matter of scrupulousness in interpreting evidence in the abstract but of guiding a certain kind of behavior – hence the commission's employment of the simple binary "coerced or freely chosen" in defining desire. The point is that in ordinary life the wish to do one thing rather than another is rooted in dominant conventions, in loyalties and habits one has acquired over time, as well as in the anxieties and pleasures experienced in interaction with lovers and friends, with relatives, teachers, and other authority figures. But when "desire" is the objective of *discipline*, there are only two options: it must either be encouraged (hence "naturalized") or discouraged (hence declared "specious"). And the commission was certainly engaged in a disciplining project.

So the commission saw itself as being presented with a difficult decision between two forms of individual liberty – that of girls whose desire was to wear the headscarf (a minority) and that of girls who would rather not. It decided to accord freedom to the latter on majoritarian grounds.[6] This democratic decision is not inconsistent with *laïcité*, although it does conflict with the idea that religious freedom is an *inalienable right* of each citizen – which is what the Rights of Man (and, today, human rights) articulate.[7] But more important, I think, is the detachment of desire from its object (the veil), so that it becomes neutral, something to be counted, aggregated, and compared numerically. Desires are essentially neither "religious" nor "irreligious," they are simply socio-psychological facts.

Now I have been suggesting not only that government officials decide what sartorial signs mean but that they do so by privileged access to the wearer's motive and wil – to her subjectivity – and that this is facilitated by resort to a certain kind of semiotics. To the extent that this is so, the commission was a device to *constitute* meanings by drawing on internal (psychological) or external (social) signs, and it allowed certain desires and sentiments to be encouraged at the expense of others. A government commission of inquiry sought to bring "private" concerns, commitments, and sentiments into "public" scrutiny in order to assess their validity for a secular Republic. The public sphere, guarantee of liberal democracy, does not afford citizens a critical distance from state power here. It is the very terrain on which that power is deployed to ensure the proper formation of subjects.

From its beginning the idea of the secular Republic seems to have been torn in two conflicting directions – insistence on the withdrawal of the state from *all* matters of religion (which must include abstention from even trying to define "religious signs") and the responsibility of the state for forming *secular citizens* (by which I do not mean persons who are necessarily "irreligious"). The Stasi report seizes this basic contradiction as an occasion for creative interpretation. The trouble with the earlier legal judgments relating to the veil, it says, is that "the judge did not think he had the power to pronounce on the interpretation of the meaning of religious signs. Here was an inherent limit to the intervention of the judge. It seemed to him impossible to enter into the interpretation given to one or another sign by a religion. Consequently, he was not able to understand that the wearing of the veil by some young women can mean discrimination between man and woman. And that of course is contradictory to a basic principle of the Republic."[8] The Stasi report regrets that judges in these cases had refused to enter the domain of religious signs. It wants the law to fix meanings, and so it recommends legislation that will do just that. But first it has to *constitute* religious signs whose meanings can be deciphered according to objective rules. For what the commission calls "a sign" is nothing in itself. "Religious signs" are part of the game that the secular Republic plays. More precisely, it is in playing that game that the abstract being called the "modern state" is realized.

One might suggest that for the Stasi commission the headscarf worn by Muslim schoolgirls is more than a sign. It is an icon in the sense that it does not simply desig-nate but evoke. What is evoked is not a "headscarf [*un foulard*]" but "the Islamic veil [*le voile islamique*]." More than an image, the veil is an imaginary – a shrouded differ-ence waiting to be unveiled, to be brought into the light of reason, and made indifferent. [...]

Conclusion

Defenders and critics of the Islamic veil law represent it in different ways, but secular-ists, whether pro or con, employ the same political language, in which they assert something about the proper place of religion.[9] I think that in doing so most of them miss just how certain discourses can become part of the powerful practices that culti-vate particular sensibilities essential to a particular kind of contradictory individual – one who is morally sovereign and yet obedient to the laws of the secular Republic, flexible and tolerant yet fiercely principled. The liberal idea is that it is only when this individual sovereignty is invaded by something other than the representative demo-cratic state, which represents his individual will collectively, and by something other than the market, which is the state's dominant civil partner (as well as its indispens-able electoral technique), that free choice gives way to coerced behavior. But the fact that the notions of moral and political sovereignty are not coherent as descriptions of contemporary individual and collective life is less important than the facts that they are part of the apparatus of techniques for forming secular subject-citizens and that the public school has such an extraordinary ideological place in the Republic's self-presentation. Central to that apparatus is the proper deployment of signs, a topic with which I began this essay. So I end with a few further remarks about it.

The internationally famous Egyptian activist Nawal al-Saadawi describes a protest march of young women against the new law in February 2004:

> The slogan raised by the girls and young women who demonstrated against the announcement made by the government of France was "the veil is a doctrine not a symbol." Another argument used as a part of the brain-washing process is to consider the veil an integral part of the iden-tity of Islamic women and a reflection of their struggle against Western

imperialism, against its values, and against the cultural invasion of the Arab and Islamic countries. Yet in these demonstrations the young women and girls who marched in them wearing the veil were often clothed in tight fitting jeans, their faces covered with layers of make-up, their lips painted bright red, the lashes around their eyes thickened black or blue with heavy mascara. They walked along the streets swaying in high-heeled shoes, drinking out of bottles of Coca Cola or Sprite. Their demonstration was a proof of the link between Western capitalist consumerism and Islamic fundamentalism, how in both money and trade ride supreme, and bend to the rule of corporate globalization. It was an illustration of how a "false consciousness" is shot through with contradiction.[10]

What upsets Saadawi, of course, is the apparent mystification of the young women demonstrating against the French ban, which led them to express their self-negation, as it were. The interesting assumption that she and many others make is that a concern with adornment is incompatible with religious expressions, which, to be really "religious," ought to be concerned only with the transcendental and the unworldly, and that what is asserted to be mandatory Islamic behavior cannot be authentic if it is at the same time combined with "capitalist signs." (As always, particular definitions underlie the discourse about "religion," but it is curious that the *normative* character of this definition should so often go unnoticed by the "nonreligious.")

I have cited Saadawi for another reason, however. Contrary to the slogan of the young demonstrators — "the veil is a doctrine not a symbol" — Saadawi insists, like the Stasi commission, that it is precisely as a symbol that it is important. The interesting thing about symbols (i.e., conventional signs) is that they invite one to do a reading of them independently of people's stated intentions and commitments. Indeed, the reading becomes a way of retrospectively constituting "real desires." It facilitates the attempt to synthesize the psychological and juridical concepts of the liberal subject. Are these immature girls aware of what they are *really* saying when they assert their wish to wear the headscarf? Is their "contradictory" appearance an index of their confused desire to be modern? Can *that* desire be deciphered as a modern passion repressed by — and therefore in conflict with — the "fanatical" religiosity expressed by the Islamic veil? Doesn't emancipation require the freeing of what is repressed and the dismantling of fanaticism? These are the kinds of question that suggest themselves and that seem to demand authoritative answers.

Vincent Geisser records some of the authoritative answers that appeared in the French media. At first, he notes, the young women with headscarves were represented as victims of their relatives. But then, in response to the latest sociological studies on the wearing of the veil, which showed a complicated picture of the young women's motives for wearing it, the media chose an even more alarmist interpretation. "Henceforth it is the idea of 'voluntary servitude' that prevails in media analyses: that young French women should themselves choose to wear the headscarf is precisely what makes them even more dangerous. This act is no longer to be seen as the consequence of family pressure but as the sign of a personal — and therefore *fanatical* — commitment."[11] This, as Geisser points out, makes the veil appear even more threatening to the state school and to Republican values in general. Once one is in the business of uncovering dangerous hidden meanings, as in the Spanish Inquisitor's search for hidden beliefs, one will find what one is looking for. Where the power to read symbols includes the construction of (religious/secular) intentions attributable to practitioners, even the distinction, made in the 1905 law of separation between church and state, between "freedom of conscience" (a moral immunity) and "freedom of religious practice" (a legal right) becomes difficult to maintain with clarity.

Secularism is invoked to prevent two very different kinds of transgression: the perversion of politics by religious forces, on the one hand, and the state's restriction of religious freedom, on the other. The idea that religion is a system of symbols becomes especially attractive in the former case, I think, because in order to protect politics from religion (and especially certain kinds of religiously motivated behavior), in order to determine its acceptable forms within the polity, the state must identify "religion." To the extent that this work of identification becomes a matter for the law, the Republic acquires the theological function of defining religious signs and the power of imposing that definition on its subjects, of "assimilating" them. This may not be usually thought of as *coercive* power, but it is undoubtedly an intrusive one. The Stasi report does not pretend otherwise. The secular state, it insists, "cannot be content with withdrawing from all religious and spiritual matters."[12]

Pierre Tevanian, a critic of the new law, has written that secularism as defined by the laws of 1881, 1882, and 1886 applies to the premises, the school curricula, and the teachers, but not to the pupils. The latter are simply required to obey school rules, to attend all lessons properly, and to behave respectfully toward others.[13] These founding texts appear to be echoed in the Council of State judgment of November 27, 1989 (issued on the occasion of an earlier crisis concerning the veil), which the Stasi report cites ("education should be provided with regard, on the one hand, to neutral curricula and teachers and, on the other hand, to the liberty of conscience of the pupils"[14]) and which it then glosses in its own fashion. Instead of withdrawing completely from anything that describes itself as "religion" (while insisting that no behavior be allowed that disrupts the proper functioning of education) the Stasi report chooses to interfere with "religion" by seeking to define its acceptable place.

Today it seems that "religion" continues to infect "politics" in France – partly as parody (the "sacred" foundation of the secular Republic) and partly as civilization ("Judeo-Christian" values in the education of secular citizens). Whatever else *laïcité* may be, it is certainly not the total separation between religion and politics said to be required for living together harmoniously in a diverse modern society. It is, by contrast, a continuous attempt by state apparatuses to encourage subjects to make and recognize themselves through appropriate signs as properly secularized citizens who "know that they belong to France." (Only to France? Ultimately to France? Mainly to France?) Like other modes of secularism, *laïcité* is a modern form of political rule that seeks to define a particular kind of secular subject (whether "religious" or not) who can take part in the game of symbols – the right kind of conventional signs – to demonstrate his or her loyalty to the state.

Where does all this leave the notion of "a community of shared values," which is said to be minimally secured in a modern democratic society by secularism? My simple thought is that differences in class, gender, region, and ethnic origin do not constitute a community of shared values in France. Besides, modern France has always had a sizable body of immigrants, all bringing in "foreign" ideas, habits, and experiences. The only significant difference is that since the Second World War they have been largely from North Africa. The famous slogan "la République une et indivisible" reflects a *natio-nalist* aspiration, not a social reality. Like people everywhere, the French are imbued with complex emotions about their fellow citizens,[15] including a simple feeling that "France" belongs to *them* but not to Others. In any case, the question of feelings of belonging to the country is distinct from that of the rights and duties of citizenship; the former relates to dreams of nationalism, the latter to practices of civic responsibility.

Public arguments about equitable redistribution of national resources exist in France as they do in every liberal democracy. Like other political matters they are negotiated – secretly as well as openly, to the satisfaction of all parties or of only a few. The state's integrity is, of course, fundamental to this. Its administrative institutions may be able to carry through decisions politically arrived at, or they may find them-selves confronted with obstacles. But logically this process does not seem to me to require a principled reference by the state to "the proper place of religion" in a secular society – any more than it needs to have a principled reference to "the proper place" of *anything*. Viewed in historical perspective, the political culture of the modern nation-state is never homogeneous or unchanging, never unchallengeable or unchal-lenged. The ways in which the concept of "religion" operates in that culture as *motive* and as *effect*, how it mutates, what it affords and obstructs, what memories it shelters or excludes, are not eternally fixed. That is what makes varieties of secularism – including French *laïcité* – always unique.

If one accepts this conclusion, one may resist the temptation to think that one must either "defend secularism" or "attack civic religion." One might instead learn to argue about the best ways of supporting particular liberties while limiting others, of minimizing social and individual harm. In brief, one might content oneself with assessing *particular* demands and threats without having to confront the *general* "danger of religion."

Notes

1   The Union of Islamic Organizations of France (UOIF) ordered its youth wing, one of the organizers of the February 13 demonstration against the law, to desist from open struggle, although it did not discourage people from participating as individuals. At the annual meeting of the UOIF at Le Bourget in April 2004, its president denounced what he saw as the move from a "tolerant, open, and generous secularism, that is to say, a secularism aiming at integration [*une laïcité d'intégration*], to a secu-larism of exclusion [*une laïcité d'exclusion*]" signaled by the new law. See the account by Catherine Coroller, "UOIF: 'La Loi sur la laïcité est là et nous l'appliquerons,'" *Libération*, April 12, 2004.

2   French Sikhs made a special case to the president for boys to be allowed to wear the turban in schools. Their argument was that, since it is long hair that is prescribed for males by the Sikh religion and not the wearing of a turban, the latter was a *cultural* and not a *religious* sign, and that therefore the law banning religious signs should not apply to it. In April 2004 the ministry accepted the Sikh argument: the new law did not apply to "traditional costumes which testify to the attachment of those who wear them to a culture or to a customary way of dressing" (Luc Bronner, "François Fillon propose son 'mode d'emploi' de la loi sur le voile," *Le Monde*, April 12, 2004). This apparent exception was eventually voted down in August 2004 by the National

Assembly, who considered the ban to apply equally to the turban (but not to long hair) for Sikh men as an obvious religious sign. There was never any question of examining the categorical opposition of *cultural* to *religious*; what mattered was where the turban was to be placed as a sign. This ambiguity was resolved by law.

3   "Dans le cadre laïque, les choix spirituels ou religieux relèvent de la liberté indivi-duelle: cela ne signifie pas pour autant que ces questions soient confinées à l'inti-mité de la conscience, 'privatisées,' et que leur soient déniées tout dimension sociale ou capacité d'expression publique. La laïcité distingue la libre expression spiri-tuelle ou religieuse dans l'espace public, légitime et essentielle au débat démocra-tique, de l'emprise sur celui-ci, qui est illégitime. Les représentants des différentes options spirituelles sont fondés à ce titre dans le débat public, comme toute com-posante de la société [In the secular framework, religious or spiritual choices are a matter of individual freedom, yet this does not mean that these questions should be confined to the privacy of conscience, 'privatized,' and that they are denied all social dimensions or the possibility of public expression. Secularism distinguishes free religious or spiritual expression in public space, which is legitimate and essential to democratic debate, from control over the latter, which is illegitimate. Representatives of the different spiritual options are thus entitled to take part in public debate, as are all who make up society]" (*Laïcité et République*, 31).

4   Ghislaine Hudson, in an interview with a group of young people published as "Laïcité: Une loi nécessaire ou dangereuse?" *Le Monde*, December 11, 2003.

5   See *Laïcité et République*, 102–3.

6   "After we heard the evidence, we concluded that we faced a difficult choice with respect to young Muslim girls wearing the headscarf in state schools. Either we left the situation as it was, and thus supported a situation that denied freedom of choice to those – the very large majority – who do not want to wear the headscarf; or we endorsed a law that removed freedom of choice from those who do want to wear it. We decided to give freedom of choice to the former during the time they were in school, while the latter retain all their freedom for their life outside school" (Patrick Weil, "A Nation in Diversity: France, Muslims and the Headscarf"; www.opendemocracy.com, March 25, 2004).

7   The Stasi report cites various international court judgments in support of its argu-ment that the right to religious expression is always subject to certain conditions (*Laïcité et République*, 47–50). My point here is not that this right – or any other – *should* be absolute and unlimited; it is simply that a right *cannot* be inalien-able if it is subject (for whatever reason) to the superior power of the state's legal institutions to define and limit. To take away a right in part or in whole on grounds of utility (including public order) or morality means that it is alienable.

8   "Le juge n'a pas cru pouvoir se prononcer sur l'interprétation du sens des signes religieux: il s'agit là d'une limite inhérente à l'intervention du juge: Il lui a semblé impossible d'entrer dans l'interprétation donnée par une religion à tel ou tel signe. Par conséquent, il n'a pu appréhender les discriminations entre l'homme et la femme, contraires à un principe fondamental de la République, que pouvait revêtir le port du voile par certaines jeunes filles [The judge did not believe he was able to pronounce on the interpretation of the meaning of the religious signs. It was a matter of an inherent limit to a judge's intervention: it seemed to him impossible to enter into the interpretation given by a religion to such or such a sign. Consequently, he was unable to understand the discriminations between man and woman that the wearing of a veil by some young girls could assume – contrary to a

TRYING TO UNDERSTAND FRENCH SECULARISM 219

basic principle of the Republic]" (*Laïcité et République*, 69–70). Insofar as school is concerned, however, the report believes that, in dealing with some religious signs (texts), pupils should *not* concern themselves with theological meanings (ibid., 34).

9   See, e.g., Pena-Ruiz, "Laïcité et égalité, leviers d'émancipation," and Pierre Tevanian, "Une loi antilaïque, antiféministe et antisocial," both in *Le Monde diplomatique*, February 2004.

10 Nawal al-Saadawi, "An Unholy Alliance," *Al-Ahram Weekly*, February 18, 2004.

11 Vincent Geisser, *La Nouvelle Islamophobie* (Paris: La Découverte, 2003), 31; emphasis in original. Geisser cites the *Nouvel Observateur* for the picture now favored by much of the media: "Are these young girls from the St. Etienne suburb – a sinister territory controlled by fundamentalists – manipulated? They are, at any rate, indoctrinated by an active Muslim environment. In the course of their conversation, one learns that they benefit from educational help from an association close to the UOIF, that one of the girls goes every year to Nièvre in order to follow courses of religious education given by Saudi Arabian imams, that another devotes every Sunday to religion: recitation in the morning, the study of texts in the afternoon. They often go to the Islamic bookshops and to the new Association of Emancipated French Muslim Women in Lyon, and they talk calmly of militants of the pietistic Tabligh movement" (ibid., 32).

12 "Il ne peut se contenter d'un retrait des affaires religeuses et spirituelles [It cannot limit itself to withdrawal from religious or spiritual matters]" (*Laïcité et République*, 32).

13 Tevanian, "Une loi antilaïque, antiféministe et antisocial," 8.

14 "L'avis énonce que le principe de laïcité impose que 'l'enseignement soit dispensé dans le respect, d'une part, de cette neutralité par les programmes et par les enseignants, d'autre part, de la liberté de conscience des élèves' [The decree states that the principle of secularism demands that education be provided respecting, on the one hand, by that neutrality on the part of the programs and the teachers, and on the other hand, the freedom of conscience of pupils]" (*Laïcité et République*, 66).

15 A well-known example of this is the ambivalence with which many people in rural France regard Parisians.

Nilüfer Göle

ISLAM IN PUBLIC
New visibilities and new imaginaries

THE WAYS IN which Islam emerges into the public sphere defy modernist aspirations for a civilized (read Westernized) and emancipated self yet follow a similar pattern in regard to gender, body, and space issues. The covered woman deputy walking into the Turkish Parliament and walking out the same day serves as an icon: an image that crystallizes the tensions emanating from two different cultural programs in the making of the self and the public. A visibility that by the same token reveals the ways in which Parliament as a secular public sphere is imagined, constructed, and instituted in the Turkish Republican context. Therefore a two-layered reading is required. One concerns the modern self-presentation and its migration into the Turkish context of modernity. The second concerns the counterattack of Islamic practices as a competing form of pious self-making and social imaginary. And with this second reading, through an examination of the ways in which Islam is problematized in the public sphere, we become aware of the unspoken, implicit borders and the stigmatizing, exclusionary power structure of the secular public sphere.

The headscarf in the parliament: a "blowup"

For the first time in its Republican history, Turkey witnessed the election of a "covered" Muslim woman, an Istanbul deputy from the pro-Islamic party (Fazilet Partisi) during the last general elections (18 April 1999). But it was Merve Kavakçı's physical presentation in the Parliament, not her election, that provoked a public dispute, a blowup. On the very day of its opening on 2 May 1999, when Kavakçı, a thirty-one-year-old woman wearing a white headscarf with fashionable frameless eyeglasses and a long-skirted, modern two-piece suit, walked (over-)confidently into the meeting hall of the National Assembly for the opening session of the new Parliament. The men and women deputies stood up and protested against Kavakçı's presence with such vehemence—especially twelve women from the Democratic Left Party (DSP) – shouting "Merve out, ayatollahs to Iran," "Turkey is secular, will remain secular," that she was obliged to leave the Parliament without taking the oath.[1] Kavakçı's Islamic covering challenged the unwritten laws of the Parliament and enraged the deputies as well as (secular) public opinion.[2] The best-known secular women's association organized meetings and condemned the headscarf in the Parliament as an "ideological uniform of Islamic fundamentalism," challenging republican state power and secular reforms.[3] She was treated as an "agent provocateur" in the Turkish press, which accused her of having close links with the Palestinian group Hamas and working for foreign powers such as Iran and Libya. It was discovered that Kavakçı had become a U.S. citizen shortly after becoming a parliamentary candidate. As she had not officially noted that she was holding another passport, authorities were able to use this legal pretext to strip Kavakçı of her Turkish citizenship.[4]

The above story cannot be narrated as merely a political incident. At a microlevel, instantaneous social reality and the significant tensions that generate history can be condensed and concealed. The trivial can be revealed as meaningful. In Georg Simmel's words, in these "momentary images," snapshots (*Moment-bilder*), fragments of social reality, we are able to glimpse the meaning of the whole.[5] We can unpack the nature of the social discord between the secular and religious practices compressed in this political incident if we first take it as it is, that is, frame it as a picture or snapshot. Visualizing the story and the players will bring into focus the corporeal, gendered, and spatial aspects of the social cleavages. Second, we need to defamiliarize our gaze. The picture is taken from the present day. It is widely and commonly shared. Its accessibility makes its understanding even more difficult because it appears as "ordinary" and "natural" to the common eye, duplicating the given terms of public controversy. This trompe l'oeil poses a challenge to sociology. A sign must be interpreted using "thick description" and placed in historical perspective if we want to reveal all of its possible meanings.[6] We need to go back and forth between micro- and macrolevels of analysis, between empirical practices and theoretical readings.[7] If we introduce anthropological unfamiliarity, historical distance, and the shift between micro- and macrolevels, the ordinary will appear less ordinary, and the still picture will turn into a movie. In his film *Blow Up* (1966), Michelangelo Antonioni tells the story of a photographer who by chance takes a picture that appears at first incoherent and incomprehensible. But he then enlarges a detail of the photograph, and that detail leads him to read the whole picture differently.[8] Let us enlarge – "blow up" – the picture of the veiled deputy taken in the secular Turkish Parliament.

Merve Kavakçı's portrait is both representative and distinctive in relation to other Muslim women in the Islamic movement. The trajectory of the Muslim woman deputy follows a social dynamic similar to that of Islamic female students who have sought the right to attend university classes wearing headscarves since the beginning of the 1980s.[9] Access to higher education, daily experience of urban city life, and use of political idiom and action expose new female Islamic actors to modernity; this exposure is problematic for both secular actors and religious ones. The case of Merve Kavakçı, although not an exception, serves as an example that carries the process of interaction with a program of modernity to its extreme limits; it thereby blurs the oppositional boundaries. Kavakçı had access to higher education, became a computer engineer, trained at the University of Texas (the headscarf was banned in Turkish universities),

lived in the United States, had two children, divorced her Jordanian-American husband, returned to Turkey, and became a member of the pro-Islamic party. She had
access therefore to powerful symbols of modernity and was simultaneously engaged
in Islamic politics. Living in the United States (not in Saudi Arabia), speaking English
fluently, using new technologies, fashioning a public image (light-colored headscarf
and frameless eyeglasses) – these are all cultural symbols of distinction in a non-
Western context of modernity. And Islamists are not insensitive to acquiring such
cultural capital. In fact, though they are in an oppositional political struggle with the
modern secularists, they often mirror them and search for public representatives who
speak foreign languages and belong to the professional and intellectual elite. Even
Kavakçı's choice of a two-piece suit rather than an overcoat is a duplication of the
Republican women's dress code. With all of her elite credentials, Kavakçı could have
been used to bolster Islamic pride – if only she was not so "foreign."[10]

Her trajectory is not only a sign of distinction, it also distinguishes her from other
Muslim women and brings her socially closer to the Western-oriented, secular elites
of Turkey. It's a closeness that creates more enmity than sympathy. The appropriation
of social signs of modernity, such as language, comportment, politics, public
exposure, and being in contact with secular groups without giving up the Islamic
difference (marked by the headscarf) – this is the source of trouble. It is the "small
difference" and the small distance between her and the secular women that ignites
political passion. Only when there is this feeling of a stranger's intrusion into one's
own domain, places, and privileges is there an issue of rejection or recognition of
difference. The figure of the stranger, in a Simmelian approach, represents the
ambivalent relation of proximity and distance, identity and difference, through
which a group reproduces social life and structures hierarchically social space.[11] This
is why the small difference is so crucial in understanding the rejection of those that
are closest.

In Turkey, one of the arguments widely used against the headscarf is that it has
been appropriated as a political symbol, so the desire to wear it is not a disinterested
one. Many will say they are not against their grandmother's headscarf, that on the
contrary they remember it with affection and respect. This is certainly true to
the extent that "grandmothers" either sat in their corners at home and didn't step into
the sites of modernity or took off their headscarves as they walked out from indoors.
Such behavior is in conformity with the scenario of national progress and emancipation of women, key elements of the modern social imaginary in a non-Western context.
But today the play has changed and so have the actors. The Islamic headscarf is
deliberately appropriated, not passively carried and handed down from generation to
generation. It is claimed by a new generation of women who have had access to higher
education, notwithstanding their modest social origins (many come from the periphery of the big cities or from small towns). Instead of assimilating to the secular regime
of women's emancipation, they press for their embodied difference (e.g., Islamic
dress) and their public visibility (e.g., in schools, in Parliament) and create distur-
bances in modern social imaginaries. Islamic women hurt the feelings of modern
women and upset the status quo; they are playing with ambivalence, being both
Muslim and modern without wanting to give up one for the other. They are outside a
regime of imitation, critical of both subservient traditions and assimilative modernity.
One can almost twist the argument and say that they are neither Muslim nor modern.

The ambiguity of signs disturbs both the traditional Muslim and the secular modernist social groups. And this goes further than a question of abstract identity. It takes place in the public sphere, it involves a face-to-face relation, which means that difference is marked on the body; it is an embodied difference, one that is visible to others. Islamic visibility (and not solely the identity) creates such a malaise because it has a corporeal, ocular, and spatial dimension. These dimensions are only intensified in the case of Merve Kavakçı.

Kavakçı is both a local and a "foreigner" (in a literal sense as well, given that she became a U.S. citizen); she is from here but also from elsewhere. Her popular background and her choice to wear a headscarf recall the indigenous yet pre-modern Turkey, while her education, individualistic posture, and political language belong to the modern world; she is a woman who follows an Islamic dress code yet does not adopt the traditional dress, behavior, and representations. Professional and political ambitions as well as divorce are all indicators of a nontraditional life and personality. Furthermore, that she did not collapse into tears under heavy pressure and criticism, and does not speak the collective language of those who were persecuted, interposes a psychological distance between her and the Muslim community. The latter uses widely the idiom of suffering and victimization and through common emotional practices, such as crying and lamenting, reproduces a repertoire of cultural signs, a sense of social belonging, and a collective social movement. Meanwhile, Kavakçı's individualist and composed self-presentation creates trouble in the Islamic social imaginary. Secular women, too, were no less suspicious of her "cold-blooded attitude"; it was taken as one more strike against her, revealing her militant discipline and premeditated behavior at the service of a political conspiracy. Kavakçı cannot be situated in terms of geographical location, communitarian belonging, or cultural coding; as she crosses the boundaries, circulates among different locations – thereby placing them in "disjunctive" relation to one another – new social imaginaries are being shaped.[12]

Kavakçı's fearlessness in the face of intimidation and her insensitivity to established relations of domination between Muslim and secularist women are perceived as arrogant, but at the same time her carriage and discourse change the codes of interaction. Her political language is that of constitutional rights, which resonates more in a U.S.-style democracy than in Turkey, where the constitution tends to provide more trouble than rights. Her language makes reference to an ultramodern space, whereas her covered body suggests Muslim privacy and modesty. Again, she is from here but also from elsewhere; she is neither a replica of a local Muslim nor a Western other. On the one hand, she is no less modern than the Turkish women defending the secular national public sphere. On the other hand, her persistent wearing of the Islamic headscarf displays her embodied difference and reproduces and deepens the cleavage. The ambiguous signs carried by her presence create confusion and disturbance among Muslims and also among secularists (including journalists from CNN to whom her U.S.-inflected language was more familiar). The fact that she comes from "elsewhere" and makes reference to another mental space disturbs – and also helps to transgress – the social rules of conduct and interaction. As Erving Goffman writes, the rupture of the framework is used by those from below, trying to discredit and disturb an adversary.[13] Such surprising crossovers bring into question the fixity of categories and boundaries.

The social dispute generated by the public visibility of Islam is carried by corporeal performances and self-presentations rather than by textualized forms of subjectivities and discursive practices. The public sphere is not simply a preestablished arena; it is constituted and negotiated through performance. In addition to constituting the public sphere, these micropractices enact a way of being public. We can speak of what Victor Turner calls "performative reflexivity," " a condition in which a sociocultural group, or its most perceptive members acting representatively, turn, bend, or reflect back upon themselves, upon the relations, actions, symbols, meanings, and codes, roles, statuses, social structures, ethical and legal rules, and other sociocultural components which make up their public 'selves.'"[14] Islamic performance has a reflexive character to the extent that the codes and symbols embedded in the religious culture are critically appropriated and distanced from the traditional culture. The Islamic dress code exemplifies this performative reflexivity. The practice of veiling restores a link with past traditions; it signifies the immutability of religion and nonsecular time. Through repetition, rehearsal, and performance, the practice of veiling is reproduced again and again, acquiring legitimacy and authority and contributing to the making of a modest pious self. But veiling is not derived directly from prevailing cultural habits and preestablished conventions. On the contrary, it bears a new form, the outcome of a selective and reflexive attitude that amplifies and dramatizes the performative signs of "difference." It is transgressive with respect to Muslim traditions as well as to modern self-presentations. Consequently, the new covering suggests a more rather than less potent Islam, which accounts for secular counterattacks against the headscarf for being not an "innocent" religious convention but a powerful "political symbol."

Let us look back to secularist counterattacks. A brief detour to the linkage between women and the making of the public sphere will introduce a historical perspective into the picture without which we cannot explain the destabilizing force of Islam in secular social imaginaries. One has to remember that secularist women have entered into modernity through emancipation from religion, which was symbolized by taking off the veil. They have experimented with modernity as a tangible entity inscribed on their bodies, clothes, and ways of life – not exclusively as an abstract and distant category of citizenship. They are products of a historical, emotional, corporeal fracture with the Muslim identity; a fracture with the past that made it possible for them to have access to modernity.

Public site as visual secularism

The grand narratives on modernity typically describe the elements of modernity in non-Western contexts as insufficient. However, when the concepts of Western modernity travel into different contexts, they often acquire not only different meanings but also an unexpected intensity. Secularism is an example of this phenomenon. Secularism, because of its origins in the Western historical development, is expected to be a marginal element in other contexts, especially in Muslim ones. Yet in the Turkish case, for instance, we observe not only its role in nation-state building and its penetration into civil and military elite ideology but also its emergence in civil society and in particular in women's associations. Secularism works as a social imaginary.

It is possible to speak of an excess of secularism, when secularism becomes a fetish of modernity. Modern social imaginaries cross boundaries and circulate but take a different twist and a slightly modified accent in non-Western contexts – they take on a sense of extra. We can read *extra* both as external to the West and as additional and unordinary. The evolutionary concept of historical change can hardly imagine that there can be a surplus or excess of modernity in some domains of social life in non-Western contexts. Modernity functions as a fetish. In non-Western contexts, modernity's manifestations are overemphasized, as are the performances of belonging to modernity.[15] The excess of secularism in Muslim contexts of modernity is such an example. The public sphere becomes a site for modern and secular performances. In contrast with the formation of the public sphere in the West, characterized initially as a bourgeois sphere that excluded the working classes and women, in Muslim contexts of modernity, women function as a pivotal sign/site in the making and representing of the public sphere.[16]

In a Muslim context, women's visibility and the social mixing of men and women attest to the existence of a public sphere. Women as public citizens and women's rights are more salient than citizenship and civil rights in the Turkish modern imaginary. The removal of the veil, the establishment of compulsory coeducation for girls and boys, civil rights for women that include eligibility to vote and to hold office, and the abolition of Islamic family law guarantee the public visibility and citizenship of women. Women's participation in public life as citizens and as civil servants, their visibility in urban spaces, and their socialization with men all define the modern secular way of life and indicate a radical shift from the social organization and gender roles framed by Islam. In other words, in a Muslim context, secularism denotes a modern way of life, calling for the "emancipation" of women from religion, the removal of the veil, and the end of the spatial separation of sexes. Women are symbols of the social whole: home and outside, interior and exterior, private and public. They stand in for the making of the modern individual, for the modern ways of being private and public. Women's corporeal and civic visibility as well as the formation of heterosocial spaces underpin the stakes of modernity in a Muslim society.

Secularism is enacted as a modern social imaginary through gendered, corporeal, and spatial performances. In that respect, some common spaces are transformed as they gain additional symbolic value and become public sites of visual modernity and gendered secular performances. In addition to Parliament, schools, and the workplace, spaces such as beaches, opera and concert halls, coffeehouses, fashion shows, public gardens, and public transportation all become sites for modern self-presentations. They are instituted and imagined as public spaces through these daily micropractices in which men and women rehearse and improvise in public their new self-presentations, dress codes, bodily postures, aesthetic and cultural tastes, and leisure activities.

The implicit dimensions of modern social imaginaries, namely, the aspects that are embodied in the habitus of a population, in the modes of address, living, habitation, and taste, all become explicit features of performative modernity in a non-Western context. The public sphere denotes a space for the making of the new modern self while it excludes others, namely, those who do not conform to this "new life" and new habitus – Muslims, for example. Acts of performance as well as space are not socially neutral concepts; indeed, they are situated in and produced by social relations of domination and exclusion.

As Henri Lefevbre puts it, the notion of space refers not to an empty space but to a space of production of social relations, defining boundaries of exclusion and inclusion, of the licit and illicit.[17] Social space, moreover, implies virtual or actual assembling at a point; urban space brings together the masses, products, markets, acts, and symbols. It concentrates them, accumulates them. Speaking about urban space invokes as well a center and a centrality, actual or possible.[18] Through its invocation of the possibility of assembly and commonality, public space establishes its link with democracy.

The issue of recognition arises when the Other, perceived as different, becomes closer in proximity – spatially, socially, and corporeally. Recognition of difference is possible only when one finds similitude and commonality with the other. One has to discern the "concrete other" – single individuals with life histories – in order to be able to tolerate difference as part of a social bond.[19] Overpoliticized definitions of identity and arguments of conspiracy exclude the possibility of finding semblance and familiarity; indeed they reinforce the demoniacal definitions of the adversary. In Merve Kavakçı's case, she is not recognized as a woman, an individual, a Muslim, a deputy, and a citizen but is rejected and stigmatized as a militant, an Islamist, and an outsider.

The question of a social bond with the stigmatized and excluded is the essential problem of democracy.[20] In the case of Islam in the public sphere, there is a double movement that causes uneasiness: Islamists seek to enter into spaces of modernity, yet they display their distinctiveness. There is a problem of recognition to the extent that Islamists start sharing the same spaces of modernity, such as the Parliament, university classes, television programs, beaches, opera halls, and coffeehouses, and yet they fashion a counter-Islamic self. In contrast with being a Muslim, being an Islamist entails a reflexive performance; it involves collectively constructing, assembling, and restaging the symbolic materials to signify difference. The symbols of Muslim habitus are reworked, selectively processed, and staged in public. Performative acts of religious difference in the secular public space defy the limits of recognition and of social bonds and unsettle modern social imaginaries.

Choreographies of ambivalence

The Islamic critique of modernity can be interpreted as a new stage in the process of the indigenization of modernity in non-Western contexts. The Islamic subject is formed both through liberation from traditional definitions and roles of Muslim identity and through resistance to a cultural program of modernity and liberalism. Alain Touraine claims that the subject owes her existence to a social conflict or collective action that criticizes the established order, expected roles, and logic of power.[21] Thus the Islamic subject is created by a collective action that is critical of the subjugation of Muslim identity by both community (religious and otherwise) and modernity. The search for difference and authenticity expresses a critical resistance to the assimilative strategies and homogenizing practices of modernity. Especially in non-Western contexts, the reflexive nature of modernity, the critical capacity to surpass its limits, is weak.[22] Criticism of modernity is engendered when modernity becomes an indigenous, everyday practice. Indigenously defined modernity not only is a discursive regime that shapes subjectivity but also is constituted and negotiated through performances.[23] The Habermasian model of bourgeois public sphere as worked out by "rational-critical debate" does not always provide a frame to understand the performative basis of the indigenously defined modernity. In distinction from the Enlightenment notion of the public sphere, which endorsed gender blindness, gender movements and other identity-based movements display and make public sexual differences.[24] Performance of difference through corporeal and spatial practices requires a new reading of nonverbal communication, embodied information, and sensorial interaction.

The nonverbal "embodied information" and its link to "naked senses" provides one of the crucial communication conditions, according to Erving Goffman.[25] And of the sensory organs, the eye has a uniquely sociological function: the union and interaction of individuals is based upon mutual glances.[26] Especially where issues of religion and gender are in question, the vocabulary of gaze and spatial conventions acquire a greater salience. When Muslim women cross the borders between inside and out, multiple senses – sight, smell, touch, and hearing – feature in concerns over redefining borders, preserving decency, and separating genders. A public Islam needs to redefine and recreate the borders of the interior, intimate, illicit gendered space (*mahrem*).[27] The notion of modesty (*edep*) underpins the Muslim self and her relation to private and public spaces. The veiling suggests the importance of the ocular (avoiding the gaze, casting down one's eyes), and the segregation of spaces regulates gender sociability. These acts, counteraesthetics, body postures, and modes of address are public performances; they seek to gain authority and legitimacy through their repetitions and rehearsals. They are not alien to Muslim memory and culture. They are rooted in past traditions and memory, in the religious habitus. But they are not simple conventions that have always been there and that are unconsciously handed down from generation to generation. The habitus provides, in Pierre Bourdieu's account, a source of improvisations; it allows for a process of continual correction and adjustment.[28] However, Islamic public visibilities are not implicitly embodied in Muslim habitus. They mark a break with traditions. Islamism is a political means for the exacerbation of Muslim difference. This process of exacerbation makes the habitus (both secular and religious) explicit and conscious. Grandmother's veiling is acceptable because it is "natural." Whereas the new veiling is seen as not so innocent because it is not a movement among religious or interior women. Secularists are not wrong to read it as a symbol. Although not rendered discursively, a nonverbal embodied communication in the veil conveys information; it disobeys both traditional and secular ways of imagining self-emancipation and becoming public.

Islamic public visibility presents a critique of a secular version of the public sphere. The work of Richard Sennett has shown that the initial development of the public sphere in the West was inseparable from the ways in which people were experiencing their bodies; the body was linked to urban space by religious rituals.[29] According to Sennett, the dematerialization of the public sphere and its separation from the body is the secular version of the public sphere. The divorce of urban experience from religious understanding inhibits the creation of intense civic bonds and "civic compassion" in a multicultural city.[30] Drawing upon this analysis, one can suggest that Islamic public display recuperates a phenomenon that has been repressed by secularism. This public display attempts to reconstruct the social link between subjectivity and public space through the reintroduction of religious self-fashionings, performances, and rituals. Women are the principal actors in this process as they display the boundaries between private and public, licit and illicit, body and imaginary. Islamism reinforces the boundaries in social relations through regulating bodily practices in public spaces; this regulation, in turn, serves as a public display of Islamic subjectivity. The Muslim body becomes, for actors of Islamism, a site for resistance to secular modernity. It is a site where both difference and prohibition are linked to the formation of a new subject (neither Muslim nor modern) and a new sociability. On the one hand, this new subject becomes modern; on the other hand, she incorporates the limits, the boundaries, the interdictions; hence it is a "forbidden modern." Self-limitation and self-disciplining go together with becoming modern. Ambivalence, a feeling that is normally alien to both the religious and the modern, undergirds the contemporary Muslim psyche. In *Another Modernity, a Different Rationality*, Scott Lash draws on Kant's "reflective judgment" to define ambivalence as a third space, the margin between the same and the other, where difference is more primordial than either presence or absence and instead exists as an aporetic space of ambivalence and undecidability.[31]

Castoriadis insists on the complementary nature of social representations – without this complementarity, he writes, society would not be possible. For example, the relation between serf and lord – and feudal society itself – is made possible through the institutions and representations that bind them.[32] However, Islamic social imaginaries and practices are worked out through ambivalence rather than complementarity. Surprising crossovers between Muslim and modernity and between secular and religious practices take place, unsettling the fixity of positions and oppositional categories. Turkish experience provides us with a privileged terrain for this choreography of ambivalence. Voluntary modernization means a processed and displaced form of Western modernity as well as the absence of a colonial Other against which to direct Islamic oppositional discourse. Mutually inclusive categories create not binary oppositions, counterdiscourses, or emulations but multifaceted, intertwining modern performances. This ambivalence operates basically through crossing over, losing one's positionality, and circulating in different spaces, categories, and mental mappings. Rather than resulting in peaceful juxtapositions, hybridities, and augmentations, it is worked out in double negations (neither Muslim nor modern), ambiguities (forbidden and modern), resulting in fragmented subjectivities and transcultural performances. New social imaginaries are shaped by these circulatory, transcultured, and crossover performances. They are imagined, abstract, and implicit categories; they are carried in images, produced by bodily practices and in physical spaces. Islam displays a new "stage" in the making of modern social imaginaries; a stage in which ocular, corporeal, and spatial aspects underlie social action, confrontation, and cohabitation. It is the intrusion of senses, prelinguistic aspects of communication embodied in habitus, that makes the conflict between secularists and Islam so charged with corporeal stigma, affectivity, and political passion.

Notes

1   "The Revolt of Women," *Hürriyet*, 4 May 1999, 1. According to a survey on political and social values conducted in October 1999 by the Foundation of Political Science in Istanbul (IMV-SAM), 61 percent of the Turkish population thought that Kavakçı

should have taken off her headscarf while in the Parliament. Another covered woman deputy, from the Nationalist Party (MHP), had taken off her headscarf to attend the National Assembly and while giving her oath was applauded.

2   Nicole Pope, "Parliament Opens amid Controversy," TurkeyUpdate (Web publication at www.TurkeyUpdate.com), 3 May 1999.

3   "The Revolt of Women," 1.

4   Nicole Pope, "Islamist Deputy Stripped of Her Turkish Citizenship," TurkeyUpdate (Web publication at www.TurkeyUpdate.com), 17 May 1999.

5   David Frisby, *Fragments of Modernity: Theories of Modernity in the Work of Simmel, Kracauer, and Benjamin* (Cambridge, England: Polity, 1985), 6.

6   Clifford Geertz, "Thick Description: Toward an Interpretative Theory of Culture," in *The Interpretation of Cultures: Selected Essays* (New York: Basic Books, 1973).

7   Jacques Revel, "Micro-analyse et construction du social," in *Jeux d'échelles: La micro-analyse à l'expérience*, ed. Revel (Paris: Gallimard: Seuil, 1996).

8   Revel, *Jeux d'échelles*, 36. Revel uses this example to establish a parallelism with micro-history. Rather than privileging one scale over the other, he argues that the methodological principle is the variations between them.

9   Nilüfer Göle, *The Forbidden Modern: Civilization and Veiling* (Ann Arbor: University of Michigan Press, 1996).

10 For an analysis of the foreigner in terms of distance from and proximity to the social group, see Simmel's notion of "l'étranger": Georg Simmel, "Digressions sur l'étranger," in *L'école de Chicago: Naissance de l'écologie urbaine*, ed. Yves Grafmeyer and Isaac Joseph (Paris: Editions du Champ Urbain, 1979); for an English translation, see *The Sociology of Georg Simmel*, trans. Kurt Wolff (New York: Free Press, 1950).

11 Simonetta Tabboni, "Le multiculturalisme et l'ambivalence de l'étranger," in *Une société fragmentée? Le multiculturalisme en débat*, ed. Michel Wieviorka et al. (Paris: Editions La Découverte, 1997), 239–40.

12 For global circulations and modern social imaginaries, cf. Arjun Appadurai, *Modernity at Large: Cultural Dimensions of Globalization* (Minneapolis: University of Minnesota Press, 1996).

13 Erving Goffman, *Les cadres de l'expérience* (Paris: Minuit, 1991), 417; originally published as *Frame Analysis: An Essay on the Organization of Experience* (New York: Harper and Row, 1974).

14 Victor Turner, *The Anthropology of Performance* (New York: PAJ Publications, 1986), 24.

15 The concept of "extra-modernity" is developed in Göle, "Global Expectations."

16 On the public sphere in the West, see Jürgen Habermas, *The Structural Transformation of the Public Sphere: An Inquiry into a Category of Bourgeois Society*, trans. Thomas Burger with Frederick Lawrence (Cambridge: MIT Press, 1989); on the public sphere in a Muslim context, see Nilüfer Göle, "The Gendered Nature of the Public Sphere," *Public Culture* 10 (1997): 61–81.

17 Henri Lefebvre, *La production de l'espace*, 3d ed. (Paris: Editions Anthropos, 1986), 35.

18 Lefebvre, *Production de l'espace*, 121.

19 Seyla Benhabib, *Situating the Self: Gender, Community, and Postmodernism in Contemporary Politics* (London: Routledge, 1992).

20 Danilo Martuccelli, *Sociologies de la modernité: L'itinéraire du XXe siècle* (Paris: Gallimard, 1999), 447.

21   Alain Touraine, *Critique de la modernité* (Paris: Fayard, 1992), 337.

22   On reflexivity and modernity, see Ulrich Beck, Anthony Giddens, and Scott Lasch, *Reflexive Modernization: Politics, Tradition, and Aesthetics in the Modern Social Order* (Cambridge, England: Polity, 1994).

23   For a discussion of such an approach to performing modernity in the case of the Miao population in China, see Louisa Schein, "Performing Modernity," *Cultural Anthropology* 14 (1999): 361–95.

24   Michael Warner, "Public and Private," in *Critical Terms for the Study of Gender and Sexuality*, ed. Catharine R. Stimpson and Gil Herdt (Chicago: University of Chicago Press, in press).

25   Erving Goffman, *Behavior in Public Places: Notes on the Social Organization of Gatherings* (New York: Free Press, 1966), 15.

26   Goffman, *Behavior in Public Places*, 93.

27   The title of the Turkish edition of my book on veiling, *The Forbidden Modern*, is *Modern mahrem*.

28   Craig Calhoun, "Habitus, Field, and Capital: The Question of Historical Specificity," in *Bourdieu: Critical Perspectives*, ed. Craig Calhoun, Edward LiPuma, and Moishe Postone (Chicago: University of Chicago Press, 1993), 61–89.

29   Richard Sennett, *Flesh and Stone: The Body and the City in Western Civilization* (New York: Norton, 1996).

30   Sennett, *Flesh and Stone*, 370.

31   Scott Lash, *Another Modernity, a Different Rationality* (Oxford: Blackwell, 1999), 4.

32   Castoriadis, *Imaginary Institution*, 367.

Pnina Werbner

THE PREDICAMENT OF DIASPORA AND MILLENNIAL ISLAM

Reflections on September 11, 2001

Muslims in the UK: a spiral of alienation?

DESPITE SUCH MILLENNIAL discourses, for a while it seemed that new diasporas in the West had achieved a golden age: of creativity, freedom, civil rights, equal citizenship, and – along with these – prosperity. They were the fortunate few who had escaped postcolonial underdevelopment, poverty and oppression to create flourishing communities in the West. The dark side of diaspora – persecution, racism, exclusion – so familiar from the histories of the Jewish, Black, Armenian, Indian and Chinese diasporas, had been banished, or so it seemed, forever. Thus Karen Leonard (2000), writing about South Asians in America, highlights the efflorescence of voluntary activities and popular culture in what has increasingly become a successful, prosperous diaspora community, only occasionally divided by religious or national conflicts and loyalties. In the UK, too, the South Asian community has prospered overall, although Pakistanis in some depressed northern British towns have not shared this general affluence. Despite this, like other South Asians, they have felt themselves to be more fortunate than those they left behind on the subcontinent.

But global crises such as September 11 or the confrontation between India and Pakistan over Kashmir bring out the dark side of diaspora. They may also divide complex diaspora communities such as the South Asian one in the UK and, as a consequence, raise serious questions about multiculturalism and the kinds of cultural commitments minorities might legitimately foster. In the UK, the South Asian diaspora is segmented, encompassing Indians and Pakistanis, Bangladeshis and Sri Lankans. It is multi-faith and linguistically plural. Despite the fact that Pakistanis in the UK, like Sikhs and many Hindus, are mostly Punjabis – a fact expressed in their tastes, lifestyles, clothing, food, music, and customary wedding popular culture – they prefer to highlight their Muslim identity, especially in public political contexts. They increasingly see Islam as their most valued, high-cultural identity, especially as the British-born younger generation begin to lose touch with their Punjabi popular cultural roots. Pakistani parents insist that their children learn to read the Qur'an in Arabic and respect prohibitions on alcohol and premarital sex.

After September 11, however, privileging a Muslim identity in the public sphere has become potentially problematic. Alleged acts of Islamic terror have tarred local Punjabi Muslims, despite being for the most part aspiring bourgeois pragmatists, with the brush of Muslim extremism. These allegations have cast into jeopardy past Muslim demands for public respect and multicultural rights within British society. While Hindus and Sikhs seem to be on a path of progressive integration, South Asian Muslims, in many respects identical culturally, seem to be bent on a path of self-destructive self-exclusion and progressive alienation from the western societies in which they have voluntarily chosen to settle.

There are two trajectories evident within the South Asian community. One is positive, leading to mutual respect and toleration. The other is negative, leading to spiralling estrangement. Both trajectories contain their own contradictions. The first hint that British Pakistani Muslims were beginning to draw a line within the *Muslim* diaspora community between themselves and an alien – *also* Muslim – 'other', came following the arrest of more than a dozen Algerians in Leicester, a city widely known for its racial tolerance and progressive multicultural policies. Appalled by the arrest. Muslim leaders in Leicester, mostly South Asians by origin, announced that they 'were more shocked than anyone. We didn't know who these people were *but we knew they were not involved in our community*.' The Algerians arrested, they said, had 'almost no contact at all with Leicester's *mainstream indigenous Muslim community*' (Wright, 2002: 12, emphasis added).

Evident here are the linguistic contortions increasingly required by local Pakistanis to distinguish Good Muslims from Bad Muslims in the UK, 'our' Muslims from Muslim 'others' (in the upshot, most of those arrested were released without charge).

An important theoretical distinction is at stake here. The attack on the World Trade Center and Pentagon on September 11, 2001 may seem to have been the work of Muslims living in the diaspora. The suicide bombers were mainly overseas students, while Al Qaeda evidently consists of a transnational network of Muslim activists based outside their natal countries, including Osama bin Laden himself. Sociologically speaking, however, the need is to distinguish between temporary or itinerant transnationals and political exiles, and settled diaspora communities of economic migrants or refugees. Diaspora communities develop local roots and a stake in the continuity of their relationship to the country of settlement. They are permanent sojourners, in the sense that while they recognize a continued affinity and loyalty to the home country, they increasingly come to participate as active citizens in the country of settlement. By contrast, transnational itinerants or political exiles, to the extent that they see their sojourning as temporary, have no commitments and loyalties to the country of settlement, at least unless they begin to sink roots locally. Many never do. In terms of globalization theory, then, although there is increased mobility across national boundaries from the developing world to the West, not every migrant outside his or her country of origin is a 'diasporic' in the full sense of this term. September 11 was not the work of Muslim diasporics but of itinerant transnationals, most of them Saudi nationals. Hence the implicit reference of a local Muslim community leader to the loyalty of the 'mainstream indigenous Muslim community', is intended to differentiate the diaspora community from itinerants, refugees and asylum seekers.

Soon after this declaration, however, news reports announced that three young Pakistanis from Tipton, a little-known town in the English West Midlands, had been arrested in Afghanistan and taken to Camp X-Ray at Guantanamo Bay. All these young men were relatively educated, soccer players for local teams, and apparently integrated into British society, although two had belonged to Asian youth gangs earlier in their lives. Why did they join the Taliban?[1]

The debate in Britain about loyalty to the post-national state

The response to September 11 in the UK, as in the USA, threatened to precipitate a moral panic about Islam, multiculturalism and the toleration of difference. Moral panics work, as Stanley Cohen argued, by demonizing tangible surface targets through a process of 'displacement' (1972: 9). In a moral panic, underlying social contradictions converge on apparently concrete causes. As moral panics overlap, as the 'demons proliferate', the sense of threat reaches a point of crisis in which ordinary people begin to fear 'the breakdown of social life itself, the coming of chaos, the onset of anarchy' (Hall et al., 1978: 322–3) – in short, apocalypse, that only an 'exceptional' response can forestall.

September 11 became an event that seemed to threaten the social order of the world. Muslims settled in the West were in danger of becoming scapegoats for the crisis. In the UK, the news that young British Pakistanis had joined the ranks of the Taliban and Al Qaeda in Afghanistan led to a debate about whether they should be tried for treason or some other criminal offence (Hopkins, 2001). The issue was raised by the Defence Secretary, Geoff Hoon (Dodd et al., 2001), and debated live on TV in the British House of Commons. The debate reflected a growing moral panic about the limits of liberal multiculturalism. As Hugo Young, a journalist for the *Guardian* newspaper put it, multiculturalism can 'now be seen as a useful bible for any Muslim who insists that his religio-cultural priorities, including the defence of jihad against America, overrides his civic duties of loyalty, tolerance, justice and respect for democracy' (Young, 2001: 18). Counter-statements by Muslim leaders that these young radicals were merely a tiny, unrepresentative minority failed to convince fully. Such statements were pitched against surveys that reported widespread support by British Muslims for the Taliban (four in ten thought it right to fight for them according to a *Sunday Times* poll, Bassey, 2001 reports) and almost universal condemnation of the Allied war in Afghanistan, widely perceived to be an attack on Islam. There was pervasive denial that the West had proved its case against bin Laden.

Following revelations of the antagonisms of young Muslims in the West to the western alliance, the 'loyalty debate' in the UK took on a momentum of its own, carried forward by surveys, television forums, Radio Live phone-ins, and newspaper letter columns. An Asian weekly, *Eastern Eye*, attempted to counter such claims of disloyalty, announcing as its front-page caption in giant letters that 'British Asians are Proud to be British'. The article reported a survey it had commissioned in which Asians and Muslims were asked if they felt 'loyal' to the UK (*sic!*). About 90 percent claimed that they did (Taher, 2001: 1–6). British Ministers such as the Home Office

Secretary, David Blunkett, unveiled schemes for new immigrant education to citizen-ship and warned of the need to disperse Muslim 'ghettos' (*Eastern Eye*, 2001: 2). Another government minister, Estelle Morris, the Education Secretary, cautioned that religious schools 'must integrate in the community' (Wintour, 2001).

Such authoritarian state responses gloss over the tragic predicament of a diaspora caught between deeply felt loyalties, at an historical moment not of its own making. Most British Muslims in the diaspora witnessed the collapse of the World Trade Center's twin towers on television, sitting in their living rooms, with the same help-less sense of horror as other television viewers. As it emerged that an obscure Islamist, Osama bin Laden, and his Al Qaeda clandestine global network, were probably responsible for the devastation, it seemed that the clash of civilizations predicted by Huntington (1993) between Islam and the West had finally materialized. At that moment, diaspora Muslims in the West became symbolic victims of a global mythol-ogy, caught in a spiral of alienation and ambivalent identifications that no local protes-tations of innocence could counter.

Since September 11, global images of terror have invaded every home in the UK, France, Germany and the USA. They reveal the terrible vulnerability of Muslim diaspora communities in the West, susceptible to being essentialized as fanatical and irrational, a potential fifth column in a clash of civilizations. In the past, British Pakistani Muslims had always been a vocal minority, demanding equal citizenship rights and never being afraid to speak their minds even if their opinions – support for the Iranian *fatwa* against Salman Rushdie or for Saddam Hussein during the Gulf War – were out of line with British popular sentiments. They felt sufficiently secure in the UK to express their political opinions, however contentious, without fear. Indeed, in their own public arenas, in the diasporic public sphere they had created for them-selves as we have seen (see also Werbner, 2002a), Manchester Muslims articulated familiar visions of apocalyptic battles between Islam and the West, especially the USA, the source of all evil. So too, they used Islamist rhetoric to attack Middle Eastern regimes, criticizing them for their corruption and weakness in the face of the West.

Michael Ignatieff argues that faced with autocratic regimes which suppress all dissent:

> Muslim political opposition takes the form of apocalyptic nihilism, a rejection of the world as it is – the existence of the state of Israel, the failure of Arab leadership and its elites, the miserable inequalities of mod-ernisation in the Arab world. Modern jihad seeks escape in fantasies of violent expulsion of the infidel, the driving of the Israelis into the sea and mortal strikes against the Great Satan. (Ignatieff, 2001)

In imagining the different diasporas to which they 'belong' as matter of course – Pakistani, South Asian, Muslim – each with its own public spheres and performative arenas, local British Pakistanis tended in the past to position themselves imaginatively as the heroes of global battles. Now came the moment of real apocalypse, beyond the imagination, and with it a self-silencing by a people who felt tangibly the potential rage and terror of the West.

Unlike the 1978–1979 Iranian revolution or the Rushdie affair in the UK ten years later, the ensuing moral panic against Muslim minorities in the UK following September 11 was initially relatively muted. A massive police presence was mounted in vulnerable neighbourhoods. Some mosques were daubed with graffiti, an Afghan taxi driver was seriously injured in London the day after the bombings, Asians (not just Muslims) were insulted in streets, buses and pubs, as they went about their daily business (Chrisafis, 2001). In the USA, there was more violence, and two Asians were murdered. Above all, Asians and Muslims felt stigmatized as never before, associated with terror and subject to constant surveillance and suspicion. Young Asians moved around in groups. Women stayed home. Men avoided going out in the evenings. Businessmen suspected that customers were avoiding their firms. There was resentment as well as fear, a feeling of being perceived as unwanted outsiders. As new, draconian laws for non-citizens have been introduced by the British Parliament, infringing on basic rights, and as security at airports, targeting mostly Muslims, has been stepped up; as the rounding up of suspected terrorists in the UK, France, Italy, Spain and Germany continues to make the news headlines, this sense of alienation has grown. We are witnessing a process of what might be called the 'spiralling progressive alienation' of Muslim South Asians in the West, which began with the Rushdie affair.

Global images of terror, violence and fanaticism are contagious. As the world watched bin Laden and the Taliban condemning the West and calling for its destruction, and witnessed Muslim crowds in Pakistan and the Middle East burning American flags and Bush effigies in a violent display of hatred, it was hard for ordinary British men and women not to associate these images with their Asian Muslim neighbours next door. Nevertheless, a *Guardian* ICM poll found that 82 percent of Britons had not changed their feelings towards British Muslims, and 88 percent thought it unfair to link them to the terror attacks, according to an NOP *Daily Telegraph* survey (Travis, 2001). Tony Blair, the UK Prime Minister, stepped in at the very start of the crisis to declare that Islam was a religion of peace and that the Qur'an did not condone suicide bombings. The battle was not, he assured Muslims and the public at large, between the West and Islam, but against a small number of evil individuals – terrorists. By now Huntingdon's clash of civilizations – or its denial – had become the jargon of politicians and the media.

Akbar Ahmed (2001) points out that: 'The terrible and tragic events of September 11 have opened a Pandora's box of questions about Islam.' Among these, the status of suicide bombings remains unresolved. Arguably, the line between martyrdom and suicide in Islam is highly ambiguous, and the morality of suicide bombings continues to be debated by Muslim religious authorities. Nevertheless, the Prime Minister and Muslim clergy in the UK invoked a moderate Qur'anic interpretation that was clearly intended to protect local Muslims from a local backlash (Blair, 2001; Wintour and Carter, 2001). Muslim leaders, in turn, condemned the World Trade Center bombings as they gathered in Downing Street for a media and press conference. Dressed smartly in western suits and ties rather than traditional garments, they spoke in rational tones and lucid English. Gone were the Muslim mullahs of *The Satanic Verses* affair, with their beards and foreign accents, declaring death to Salman Rushdie in broken English. The men and women representing the Muslims of the UK in 2001 through the Muslim

Council of Britain (MCB) conveyed moderation and an awareness of the concerns of the wider British community. Here were representatives of an 'exemplary' diaspora; a diaspora that recognized its minority status and identified with its newly adopted nation.

Yet, before long, the representative status of the MCB was challenged as endemic internecine schisms and divisions between Muslim organizations also surfaced (see Body, 2001). Nevertheless, the organization initially appeared to have achieved a change in British policy for which they had been struggling since the Rushdie affair: the extension of the Race Relations Act to include a clause against incitement to religious hatred. They used the opportunity presented by the global crisis to extend their bid for equal citizenship.

In the end, the law was dropped, although it is now once again on the legislative agenda of the Commission for Racial Equality. But the victory it represented would have been in any case a bitter and double-edged one. The new law was intended as much to curb extremist Islamist rhetoric in British mosques, as it was anti-Muslim racist discourses. London had reputedly become a centre of world Islamic terror.[2] Quite explicitly, the envisaged law was not intended to silence pretentious postmodern writers such as Salman Rushdie or sacrilegious comedians who spoofed Islam. Yet the existence of such a law would probably have made the publication of *The Satanic Verses* actionable in court, even if the novel might ultimately have escaped banning or censorship.

In the early days of diasporic Muslim silence after September 11, whether sympathetic, pragmatic, or merely enforced, there were some lone voices of dissent. The Shaykh of the Naqshbandi mosque in Manchester with Deobandi sympathies, cited above, invited his congregation to raise their hands in support of the Taliban. A young imam at the Manchester Central Mosque told his youthful congregation in English that it was not bin Laden but the Jews who had in fact bombed the World Trade Center. This was proved by the fact, he said, that all the Jews had stayed away from the towers that day.[3] But, on the whole, criticism was muted. Muslims in the UK – and worldwide – were genuinely deeply shocked by the devastation and loss of life in Manhattan.

As American bombing in Afghanistan, and subsequently Iraq, assumed its fearful, monotonous pounding, however, so familiar from Vietnam, Cambodia or the Gulf War, and as scenes of wounded Afghan refugees or Iraqis and on-the-ground devastation filled television screens, the usual British Muslim transnational identity politics, with its anti-American and anti-Arab regime rhetoric, reasserted itself, but with one important difference. This time the diaspora joined a growing British peace movement critical of the war or the way it was being fought (Gledhill et al., 2001). Muslims could share the same anti-American, anti-war rhetoric with others in the society. Rather than being seen as deviant and out on a limb, diasporic Muslims succeeded in creating alliances with local activists – CND (Campaign for Nuclear Disarmament), the English Left, anti-globalization lobbyists, pacifists. Muslim, mostly Pakistani, spokespersons were young and articulate.

The war in Afghanistan in 2002, and even more so the war with Iraq in 2003, proved that a common enemy can create peaceful alliances across an apparently unbridgeable chasm. The Stop the War alliance in the UK, led by the British left and CND, consciously and deliberately incorporated the Muslim Association of Britain

(MAB), an organization encompassing Pakistanis along with Palestinians and other Muslims, as equal partners.

Alternative political visions and the public good

Political commitments can be very long term and passionate, embedded in moral narratives of self and community. In this sense they are *meroscopic*, that is, perspectival and positioned. If, as I have argued elsewhere (Werbner, 2002a), diasporas are transnational communities of co-responsibility, recognizing their mutual indebtedness across national boundaries, we need to disclose where their identifications, the centres of their subjective universe, lie. Undoubtedly, the sufferings of New Yorkers touched people worldwide. But not everyone saw New York, as Ien Ang has so eloquently argued, as 'their' global city and New Yorkers as compatriots (see Ang, 2002). The Evil Attack on the Free World, in the rhetoric of western leaders, meant something different to those for whom the Manhattan skyline had a beauty and permanence of its own; who saw its towering skyscrapers not merely as the expression of unbridled capitalism, but as cathedrals of modernity, embodiments of the human imagination and its desire to transcend itself. By the same token, while westerners might share Muslim concern for Kashmiri, Palestinian or Iraqi victims of war, the pain felt by Muslims in the face of this suffering was one of shared selfhood. For liberals, the essential fragility of the capitalist economy compounded the horror of the mass murder. For most Muslims this economy was a side show, if not itself an evil global plot. Everyone recognized that the attack was symbolic, but only westerners fully comprehended its potentially devastating consequences.

While people might agree that an act is heinous, as an aesthetic, embodied experience its impact varies between moral communities. This was a critical aspect of the global conflict over *The Satanic Verses* affair. That conflict could be seen above all as a passionate argument about the aesthetics of the religious imagination. So, too, ideas about politics and leadership differ. For many postcolonial Pakistanis, politics, even democratic politics, evokes a world of self-serving corruption and nepotism. As a result, they are deeply sceptical of all political leadership and state power. Yet they are passionate political actors themselves and so they go on believing that some place, somewhere, the ideal, exemplary political leader will emerge. Inevitably such a leader is envisioned as a charismatic saviour, bearing a religious mantle. In a society in which most people are deeply pious, dissent is often couched in religious terms. The Prophet Muhammad was the exemplary leader for all times: legislator, holy man, warrior and statesman. In speeches made in the diasporic public sphere in Manchester, outstanding individuals, from Muhammad Ali Jinnah, the founder of Pakistan, to Imran Khan, the great cricketer turned philanthropist and politician, are repeatedly mythologized in local narratives as exemplary, unique, God-chosen persons.

This stress on exemplary personhood in Pakistani political culture also makes sense of the ambivalences surrounding Saddam Hussein during the 1991 Gulf war, or Osama bin Laden in the international crisis a decade later. A Pakistani survey in October 2001 found that – against the judgement of their own president – 88 percent of the people of Pakistan believed there was no evidence linking Osama bin Laden to the World Trade Center bombings (Gallup Pakistan, 2001, reported on *Panorama*,

BBC, 2001). In his posture and appearance, bin Laden projects the classic image of a pious, saintly Muslim world renouncer, a man who has abandoned his great wealth to live an austere existence in the desert for the sake of Islam, dedicating his life to the battle against western domination. He speaks calmly and looks peaceful, almost ethereal. Such a man could not by definition be capable of mass murder. Nor, for many British Pakistanis, was it conceivable that *any* Muslim would be capable of such an atrocity. Hence the bizarre but nevertheless widely believed Jewish conspiracy theory, with the Jews accused, simultaneously, of being the evil arm of American imperialism and its hidden destroyers. Where westerners might see in bin Laden an evil megalomaniac, ordinary Muslims see a courageous *mujahid* contending with the evil forces that oppress Palestinians, Iraqis and Kashmiris, and which desecrate the holy lands of Islam.

This Manichean discourse of good and evil hides other diasporic vulnerabilities. Pakistanis in the UK are sensitive to the opinions of friends and relatives on the subcontinent. They watch Pakistani satellite TV (there are several stations) and read Pakistani daily newspapers. They fear for the fate of their families back home if violence and civil war erupt there. They identify with the plight of the Afghan refugees, the Kashmiris and the Palestinians. They were aware, more than most westerners, of the murderous record of the Northern Alliance in Afghanistan after they took power with the fall of the communist regime. No wonder, then, that neither the smouldering ruins of Ground Zero, still emitting acrid smoke over the Manhattan skyline weeks after the devastation, nor the deadly and mysterious anthrax attack on the USA, nor even the rational pragmatism of the Pakistan President Musharraf, seemed to them to justify the Allied war against Afghanistan. The alliance with Arab regimes created so painstakingly by the UK and the USA was treated by many British Pakistanis with cynical scepticism.

Partly the scepticism reflects the fact that Pakistani settlers in the UK share with other South Asians, as well as with West Indian immigrant-settlers, an oppositional postcolonial sensibility. This generates a suspicion *in principle* of the publicly declared good intentions of successive British governments. The postcolonial sensibility meshes with the Islamic utopianist one to create a political perspective suspicious of the good intentions of the West in general.

In itself, this does not amount to a clash of civilizations. After all, within the West too, perceptions of the conflict have differed. Hence, in the initial stages of the crisis, virtually all commentators on the terror attack in the British Press, Muslim and English alike, tended to preface their columns with reminders of the sufferings of Palestinians and Iraqi children, and of the USA's complicit role in the rise of Saddam Hussein, bin Laden and the Taliban. It is evident that neither Pakistani nor western intellectual interpretations of the current crisis are uniform. They are *meroscopic*: partial, positioned, sited and inevitably perspectival political visions.

The vulnerability of diaspora

The tragedy is, that in the decade since the Rushdie affair and Gulf war, the majority of Pakistanis in Manchester had moved on, away from religious radicalism to more positive activism for human rights. Young British Pakistanis were increasingly taking their full place in society. With the first generation of immigrants on the point of retirement, the days of strangerhood seemed to be over for many. True, there were still deprived inner city neighbourhoods in the UK where unemployed Pakistani youth clashed with police and racist groups. This happened in the northern towns of Oldham and Bradford in the summer of 2001, causing massive destruction of property and ending in fragile truces. But in the more affluent suburbs of Manchester or London, young, British born Asians, including Muslims, were entering university and embarking on managerial and professional careers.

The new global vulnerabilities that were revealed by the intensification of conflicts in the Middle East, affected not only Muslims but Asians more generally, and even diasporic Jews living in the West. Such vulnerabilities raise the question whether members of diaspora communities can ever fully cease to be strangers.

In a key article, Khachig Tololyan (2000) highlights the historical rise and fall of Armenian diaspora centres. The history of the Armenian diaspora is one marked by repeated expulsions, on the one hand, and periodic consolidations of new diasporic centres, on the other. The transition Tololyan identifies in the modern era is from exilic nationalism to diasporic transnationalism. But equally, one can view this history as one marked by alternation between alienation and consolidation, persecution, exile and peaceful sojourning. During periods of consolidation, diasporas not only prosper, but establish powerful transnational organizations and community institutions. This long and complex history means that at any one time, dominant, emergent and dying diaspora communities co-exist simultaneously in different parts of the world, some in a state of ascendency and others, in decline.

The predicament of diaspora

What must it be like to feel under siege in one's own home? The predicament for Muslims has been one of a diasporic minority having to make impossible choices. In a postnational world, the meaning of loyalty to the state has arguably been rendered ambiguous. Short of being a paid spy or terrorist, how is disloyalty to be construed? In recent years, Muslims in the UK have developed progressively focused agendas to fight for their rights as British citizens. They actively participate in electoral politics in large numbers and field a large number of local and increasingly national candidates in the different parties. The 'ethnic' vote is a significant factor in British electoral politics.

In ordinary times, the struggle for British citizenship rights and the long-term diasporic commitment to Muslim communities overseas, especially those suffering from human rights abuses (as in Bosnia, Kashmir or Palestine), are not necessarily conflicted. South Asian Muslims living in the West subscribe to the Islamic juridical position that since western democracies allow freedom of worship, Muslims owe complete allegiance to the state, defined as a 'Land of Treaty'. Only a small minority subscribes to alternative Islamic interpretations that either forbid Muslims to settle permanently in the 'Land of Unbelief' and serve in its armed forces, or define Muslims as the vanguard of Islam in the 'Land of Preaching' (see Werbner, 2000).

To the extent that the discourse of Islamic dissent is grasped as a utopian fantasy with no practical organizational backup, then young Pakistanis who join extremist

Islamist organizations, usually imported from the Middle East, are a newly emergent, deviant minority. The Taliban version of neofundamentalism (see Roy, 1994) is, in the UK, connected to the minority Deobandi Muslim stream which takes a politically quiescent stance in the UK, as it did historically in India (Metcalf, 2002). While the rhetoric deployed by this movement is a militant one of global jihad, the stress is on the inner jihad of personal purification (Metcalf, 2001). Most British Asian Muslims arrived in the UK as economic labour migrants and are committed to bourgeois economic advancement for themselves and their children, not to violent dissent.

For youngsters who have grown up in the UK, however, the sense of cosmic malaise may be grasped as a reality to be actively changed. In this, they are somewhat set apart from the underprivileged youngsters who join Asian youth gangs and who engage in violent turf fights in the inner city, sometimes with other Asian youth gangs, sometimes with white skinheads affiliated to British fascist parties. These latter youngsters may have little intention of joining a holy war in Afghanistan or Palestine. As in the rest of the Muslim world, young Islamist activists are as a rule educated and relatively privileged. In Tipton, one of the prisoners arrested in Afghanistan was a law student, the other a computer student. The young Pakistani suicide bombers in Tel Aviv in 2003 were also educated. The mistake is, then, to explain these youngsters' Islamic radicalism as the product of personal racist victimization or deprivation in the UK. If Islamic millennialism is a sense of false, fantastical empowerment in the face of perceived, almost cosmic disempowerment, it attracts those who in their own eyes are potentially powerful (that is, young, educated, successful) but have no way of affecting world politics.

The problem for Muslim diaspora leaders is how to control these young and potentially dangerous Islamic radicals *while continuing to sustain and perpetuate their own millennial rhetoric* with its demonization of America, Israel and the West and its dreams of world Islam.[4] Among British Pakistanis the social democratic camp enunciates a moderate counter-rhetoric (for example, Mahmood, 2001). But in times of international crisis, whether moderation can displace the extravagant but exciting and empowering virtual discourses of global Islam remains an open question. The fact that British Muslims feel secure enough in the UK to enunciate a discourse of political dissent in times of crisis attests to their rootedness in British society. Yet their ambivalence is tangible. It was, after all, Tony Blair, the UK Prime Minister, who invoked the image of a tolerant, peaceful Islam. But almost simultaneously, other Labour Government Ministers were perpetuating myths about Islam and its oppressive treatment of women, the unwillingness of local Muslims to integrate, even to learn English, their self-exclusion, in what emerged as a garbled set of racialized stereotypes (Werbner, 2002b).

On the surface, nothing much has changed for British Pakistanis and they increasingly go about their daily business as usual. The dozens of Pakistani-owned restaurants in Rusholme, Manchester's Asian commercial centre, glittering with their colourful neon signs, are packed with English lovers of Indian food, and British Asians are increasingly prominent in business and the arts. But events leave a trace. They become 'texts', in the sense suggested by Paul Ricoeur (1981). Taken out of time and place, they affect the reading not only of the past and present, but also of the future. The tragedy is that the global crisis precipitated on September 11 will leave its own trace, a sediment of alienation and radical estrangement which will impact in future on the way people conceive of their identity and citizenship in their country of settlement. Ultimately, living in the diaspora is a matter of continually negotiating the parameters of minority citizenship. For British Muslims, this process, which is usually peaceful, has tragically had to lurch from one confrontation to another, from the Rushdie affair to the Gulf War to the present crisis. The hope is that each time the signs are of a more mature grasp by local diaspora Muslims of what it means to be a British citizen in a global world. The danger is that diaspora Muslims in the West will increasingly withdraw from positive engagement with their English neighbours, and lose faith in the capacity of their country of settlement to recognize what they perceive to be their deepest moral commitments and aspirations.

Acknowledgements

I am grateful to participants at Irvine, SOAS, Sydney and Melbourne, to Richard Tapper and Roly Kapferer for their helpful comments. In particular, I also want to thank Ruth Levitas for her penetrating and helpful criticisms.

Notes

1   The three were sent back to the UK in 2004 after lengthy negotiations.
2   Such allegations were widely made by the British press and, as reported in the press, by non-British western security services. They were ultimately denied by Scotland Yard and M15 after a series of arrests of allegedly Muslim extremists was followed by their release in the absence of concrete evidence. In December 2002, Pakistani suspects of terror were also arrested in Scotland. Since 2001, the arrest or administrative detention of suspected 'terrorists' has increased in the UK, and has been subject to continuous debate in the Asian press.
3   This rumour spread throughout the Muslim world, appearing first in a Jordanian newspaper, and posted almost immediately on the worldwide web. Thomas Friedman, columnist for The New York Times, suggests it reflected scepticism in the Muslim world that 'Arabs could have pulled off something as complex as September 11'. 'It is a sad fact,' he comments, 'that Arab self-esteem is very low these days'. Hence bin Laden is seen as the one man 'not intimidated by America's overweening power, as the one man who dared to tell certain Arab rulers that they had no clothes, and as the one man who did something about it' (Friedman, 2002: 110, 111).
4   The extent of intergenerational authority of Pakistani parents over their British-born children is one widely debated in the British press at present, both in relation to the northern British riots and the issue of arranged, and especially 'forced' marriages.

References

Ahmed, Akbar S. (2001) 'Veiled Truth', The Guardian, G2, 22 October: 6.
Ang, Ien (2002) 'Defending the Global City', Ethnicities 2(2): 160–2.
Bassey, Armadeep (2001) 'We All Want to Die,' Sunday Mirror, 4 November: 7.

Blair, Tony (2001) 'The Tragedy is that Bin Laden is Exploiting People's Faith', extracts from the Prime Minister's speech, *The Guardian*, 12 October.

Body, Faisal (2001) 'Muslims are a Multitude, not a Lone Voice.' *Guardian Media*, 20 October: 6.

Chrisafis, Angelique (2001) 'Muslims in UK Urged to Back Peace', *The Guardian*, 10 October.

Cohen, Stanley (1972) *Folk Devils and Moral Panics: the Creation of Mods and Rockers*. London: MacGibbon & Kee.

Dodd, Vikram, A. Chrisafis and N. Hopkins (2001) 'Hoon Warns Would-be Recruits that they Face Prosecution on Return to Britain', *The Guardian*, 30 October: 3.

Eastern Eye (2001) '"Loyalty Tests" on the Cards', 9 November: 2.

Gallup Pakistan (2001) 'Gallup poll on current Pakistan crisis', [http://www.yespakistan.com/afghancrisis/gallup_survey.asp].

Gledhill, Ruth, Joanna Bale, Sam Lister and Elizabeth Judge (2001) 'Muslim Leaders Condemn Use of Force', *The Times*, 9 October: 15.

Hall, Stuart, Chas Crichter, Tony Jefferson, John Clarke and Brian Roberts (1978) *Policing the Crisis*. London: Hutchinson.

Hopkins, Nick (2001) 'British Muslims who fought with Taliban face prosecution', *The Guardian*, 20 November: 6.

Huntington, Samuel (1993) 'The Clash of Civilizations?' *Foreign Affairs* 72(3): 22–41.

Ignatieff, Michael (2001) 'What will Victory Look Like?' *The Guardian*, G2, 9 October: 3–4.

Leonard, Karen (2000) 'State, Culture, and Religion: Political Action and Representation among South Asians in North America.' *Diaspora* 9(1): 21–38.

Mahmood, Khalid MP (2001) 'The Five Myths Muslims must Deny.' *The Observer*, 11 November: 21.

Metcalf, Barbara Daly (2001) 'Piety, Persuasion and Politics: Deoband's Model of Islamic Activism' [http://www.ssrc.org/sept 11/].

Metcalf, Barbara Daly (2002) '"Traditionalist" Islamic Activism: Deoband, Tablighis and Talibs' in Craig Calhoun, Paul Price and Ashley Timmer (eds) *Understanding September 11*, pp. 53–66. New York: The New Press.

Ricoeur, Paul (1981) *Hermeneutics and the Human Sciences*, edited by J.B. Thompson. Cambridge: Cambridge University Press

Roy, Olivier (1994) *The Failure of Political Islam*. London: I.B. Taurus.

Taher, Abul (2001) 'Proud to be British', *Eastern Eye*, 23 November: 1–6.

Tololyan, Khachig (2000) 'Elites and Institutions in the Armenian Transnation', *Diaspora* 9(1): 107–36.

Travis, Alan (2001) 'British do not See Islam as Threat to Values', *The Guardian*, 12 October: 4.

Werbner, Pnina (2000) 'Divided Loyalties, Empowered Citizenship? Muslims in Britain', *Citizenship Studies* 4(3): 307–24.

Werbner, Pnina (2002a) *Imagined Diasporas among Manchester Muslims: The Public Performance of Transnational Identity Politics*. Oxford and Santa Fe: James Currey and School of American Research.

Werbner, Pnina (2002b) 'Editorial: Reproducing the Multicultural Nation', *Anthropology Today* 18(2): 3–4.

Wintour, Patrick (2001) 'Religious Schools "Must Integrate in the Community"', *The Guardian*, 14 November: 13.

Wintour, Patrick and Helen Carter (2001) 'No. 10 Moves to Stamp Out Anti-Muslim Backlash', *The Guardian*, 19 September: 9.

Wright, Oliver (2002) '"Our City is not Radicals' Haven", say Leaders', *The Times*, 19 January: 12.

Young, Hugo (2001) 'A Corrosive National Danger in our Multicultural Model', *The Guardian*, 6 November: 18.

Olivier Roy

ISLAM IN THE WEST OR WESTERN ISLAM?

The disconnect of religion and culture[1]

THE DEFINITIVE PRESENCE of a huge Muslim population in Europe will, of course, have long-term consequences. There is, nevertheless, some debate about the figures of the Muslim population, partly due to imprecise data, partly due to the difficulty of knowing who qualifies as a Muslim. Is one defined as a Muslim strictly because of one's choice to belong to that religious community, or is one a Muslim by ethnic background? Beyond the demographic aspect, the fact that Islam is taking hold in Europe seems to put into question European identity. It is clear that the rejection of Turkey's European Union candidature by European public opinion is largely linked to the fact that Turkey is a Muslim country. Furthermore, the assassination of the Dutch filmmaker Theo Van Gogh seems to have played a role in the Dutch rejection of the European Constitution in May 2005. What does the rise of Islam in Europe entail in terms of shared culture and values? Should we speak of "Islam in the West" as if Islam were the bridgehead of a different culture area, or of "Western Islam" as if a European Islam should necessarily differ from its Middle Eastern or Asian versions?

Since the late 1970s, when it became clear that the bulk of incoming immigrants would stay in Europe, two models have shaped Western European countries' immigration policies. The first model is called "multiculturalism" and is dominant in Northern Europe; the second one is "assimilationism" and has been advocated by a broad spectrum of political forces in France. This last model – an exception in a generally multiculturalist Europe – possesses new appeal for Northern European countries (Belgium, Holland, and Denmark). Both models presuppose what is perceived as a national and/or Western identity, which, for the multiculturalist approach, should coexist with other cultures. However, the assimilationist perspective assumes that the "Western" model is universal and could integrate people from various cultural backgrounds on the condition that they give up former identities.

At the end of the 1990s, however, both models were widely seen as having failed, which led to an unprecedented convergence between the different European countries.

Countries that did not consider themselves immigration societies (Italy and Spain) realized recently that, in fact, they have actually acquired a permanent Muslim population – and this is a realization that Eastern European countries will soon be having. This convergence demands a European approach to the question of what Islam in Europe means. The same issue is, it should be noted, addressed by some Islamic institutions in Europe (The European Council of Fatwa, based in London, for instance).

The model of multiculturalism failed not because of the "multi" but because of the "culturalism." The underlying idea was that a religion is embedded into a culture (or that any culture is based on a religion). Religious believers form a community with its own customs, social fabric, diet, and so on, and community leaders who maintain some sort of social control on the community. To share a faith means to share a common culture. Such self-regulation through community leaders is portrayed in an old story from Holland, in which the Jews expulsed from Spain and Portugal around 1600 were granted asylum and offered hospitality, but asked to regulate their own community themselves.

The French assimilationist model failed because it initially ignored the religious dimension of immigrants' identities, or more exactly, because it presupposed that this dimension would fade away during the process of integration. The underlying policy was to integrate the Muslims the way the Jews had been integrated in the wake of the French Revolution: to grant them "nothing as a community (nation), everything as individual citizens." But the rise of different forms of Islamic religious revival among integrated immigrants pushed the government to acknowledge the existence of a (supposedly) purely religious community (hence the creation by the state of a religious body, the French Council of Muslim Faith, in 2002, which is in itself a break from the Republican secular policy of *laïcité*).

It is clear that the way the different European countries have defined their relations with immigrants is deeply rooted in their own history and political culture. But national identities are in crisis at two levels: from above, due to European integration (which has nothing to do with Islam), and from below, due to the crisis of the "social bind" in destitute neighborhoods (in France) or big city centers (in Holland), and the inability of the school system to cope with these areas of social exclusion. Clearly, the focus on Islam is, wrongly or rightly, a focus on national and/or European identity.

In fact, both immigration models have failed because they have been unable to acknowledge and deal with what is at the root of the present forms of religious revivalism: the disconnect between religion and culture. Religious fundamentalism among Muslims in the West is not a consequence of the importation of a given original culture into the West, but of the deculturation of Islam. Pristine cultures like Islam are in crisis, as immigration changes the relation between migrants and the original culture. Second and third generations tend to prefer the language of the guest country over that of their parents' home country, and they tend to speak better French than Arabic (when they speak Arabic at all), English than Urdu, and even, but far more slowly, German than Turkish. Youth tend to adopt Western urban youth sub-culture (in terms of dress, slang, music, etc.). Fast food is more popular than traditional cuisine. Moreover, fundamentalism is itself a tool of deculturation. The Saudi Wahhabis reject anything close to a "traditional" culture; they banned music, dance, novels, and non-religious poetry. The Taliban in Afghanistan did not fight against Western influence but against the traditional Afghan culture (banning music, kite-flying, singing birds, etc.). Such a rejection of the very concept of culture appeals to a youth who feels often culturally alienated, even if socially well-integrated. Van Gogh's killer in Holland spoke better Dutch than Arabic and was not reacting to the Middle Eastern conflict or to Muslim culture. He became outraged at what he saw as blasphemy against Islam in a purely Western context.

Contemporary fundamentalism, therefore, entails a disconnect of religious markers from cultural content. For instance, "*hallal*" does not refer only to a traditional cuisine but describes any cuisine; hence, the flourishing of *hallal* fast-food restaurants among born-again Muslims in the West, but few Moroccan or Turkish traditional restaurants. This disconnect means that the issue is not a clash of cultures between West and East but the recasting of faith into what is seen as a "pure" religion based on isolated religious markers. The issue for European societies is, then, how to deal with such a surge of religious identities at a time when secularization is seen as a prerequisite for democracy and modernity.

It is an often expressed idea that the Westernization of Islam should mean the reformation of Islam. A superficial understanding of Max Weber, who has often been misread, leads to the conclusion that the modernity of a religion has to do with its theological dogma. Because it supposedly does not differentiate between religion and politics, Islam is deemed incompatible with secularization and democracy, as long as it does not undergo a deep theological reform. Such a reasoning ignores the fact that Roman Catholicism never underwent a deep theological reformation (because it would have meant the triumph of Protestantism) but, nevertheless, has been able to adapt reluctantly to modernism. Of course, there are "liberal" Muslim theologians who advocate some sort of reformation. But, for me, this is not a prerequisite for Westernization. In fact, Westernization is already at work, specifically in the more fundamentalist forms of religious expression, for two reasons. First, fundamentalism entails a clear delinking of religion and culture. And second, the new forms of religiosity are "transversal," which is common to Islam and Christianity. What is at stake is not religion (a set of dogma and rituals), but religiosity (the relationship between a believer and religion). Even if the dogmas differ, we find common forms of religiosity that explain the religious nomadism of our time (people going from religion to religion while claiming to look for the same thing).

The present forms of religiosity are based on the same patterns. There is a stress on the individual, coupled with the crisis of religious institutions. Immediate access to the "truth" is promised through faith, at the expense of studies. A contempt of history, tradition, philosophy, and literature develops, as favor for a direct, personal, emotional form of religious feeling takes precedence. And the religious community is defined not as an already existing body (church or *ummah*), but as a reconstructed community of the "chosen" by individuals. The "community" lives both in and apart from the existing society.

The space of the *ummah* is no longer a territorial one, implying a political leadership, with a nation-state and borders. In fact, most of the neo-fundamentalist movements, including the most radical one's, stopped discussing the "*dar ul islam*" (abode of Islam) in territorial terms. They consider the *ummah* to be everywhere Muslims are to be found. An interesting case is that of Hizb-ul-Tahrir, a radical (although not terrorist) movement now based in London, which advocates the revival of the Islamic Caliphate but simply skips the issue of its territorial basis: the Caliphate could be restored in a very short time if every Muslim decides that it exists and pledges loyalty to it. Thus, one can live both as a member of a specific minority group while also part of a universal community.

This dialectic of universalism/minority is interesting because it is to be found both in Islam and Christianity. Although the great majority of Americans claim to be practicing Christians, every church speaks about living as a minority in a decadent society (as illustrated by the novel *Left Behind*, in which the "saved" are a minority).[2] Even the Catholic Church acknowledges representing a minority in Europe and advocates closing ranks in difficult times. As much as religion tends to be disembedded from cultures, churches and congregations tend to be disembedded from mainstream society (a process clearly at work in Spain and Italy, where, until recently, Catholicism was seen as being at the core of the national culture).

The new dilemma for many who are born again is not how to rebuild the society on Christian or Islamic principles, but how to live integrally with that society according to one's true religious tenets. "Integralism" in this sense tends to replace "fundamentalism," and religious revivalism does not challenge the existing political or social order. The brand of fundamentalism that is thriving among many second-generation Muslim immigrants in the West is a paradoxical consequence of their own Westernization, which means first deculturation and then the recasting of Islam as a "mere" religion. Yet the same phenomena of deculturation and recasting could take different forms, such as "liberal," "mystical," or "conservative ethical" Islam.

"Liberal Islam" means delinking the religious meaning of the *Koran* and the *Sunnah* from its socio-cultural and historical context. Historically, it could be said that Islam was a progression in terms of women's conditions, compared to the previous period (*jahiliyya* or "ignorance"), but that it nevertheless had to take into account the customs of the time (for example, allowing polygamy without recommending it). If one comes back to the true spirit of the text, then, men and women should be considered equal. The same argument is used about the prohibition of alcohol: alcohol was banned because people were unable to drink moderately and thus became drunk at prayer time, but if one can drink without becoming drunk, then alcohol is permitted. Whatever the religious validity of such assertions, they clearly contribute to making Islam Western-compatible. It should be noted, however, that such a view is not dominant by definition among those who are born again and represents more the "lazy" discourse of secular or seldom-practicing Muslims when they are asked to explain their behavior.

Mystical Islam is linked with the burgeoning of Sufi orders. These brotherhoods, whether traditional or reconstructed, are wide open to converts, once again blurring the divide between West and East. Islamic Sufism fits here with the spread of New Age religious communities and cults in the West.

Conservative ethical Islam is probably the dominant trend among practicing Muslims, who could be compared to Orthodox Jews. The basic norms are taken into account, especially the diet norms: eating *hallal* and fasting during Ramadan, for instance.[3] But beside this normative dimension, norms tend to be recast into values on the model of conservative Christianity. For example, Holland. When Pym Fortuyn entered into politics, it was to protest the declarations of a Dutch-speaking Moroccan Imam who called homosexuals "sick people" and refused to grant them any rights as a minority group. Fortuyn, however, was not acting in the name of traditional Western values but in defense of the "sexual liberation" movement of the 1960s, which is largely seen by many conservative Christians as the collapse of a society based on values and principles. Interestingly enough, many Muslims in the West are recasting their religious norms in terms of Western-compatible values, but not necessarily on the liberal side. They tend, for instance, to support the anti-abortion campaign, while abortion has never been a central issue in Muslim societies (it is usually condemned, but the ban on abortion has never really been enforced).

The debate in the West is not between Islamic and Western values, but within the West: What are Western values? Where is the divide between human freedom and nature (or God)? In fact, Islam is the mirror in which Europe is looking at its own identity, but it does not offer a new culture or new values. It expresses itself inside the present debate on religious revivalism and secularism – but as part of the debate, not its cause.

Notes

1   This paper was first presented at the conference "Religion, Secularism, and the End of the West," held by the Center on Religion and Democracy and the Institute for Advanced Studies in Culture in Laxenburg/Vienna, Austria, on June 3, 2005.

2   Tim LaHaye and Jerry B. Jenkins, *Left Behind: A Novel of the Earth's Last Days* (Carol Stream: Tyndale, 1995).

3   The fast of Ramadan is, according to polls, the most respected religious norm among French Muslims, even before daily prayer.

Further reading

Akbar S. Ahmed, *Postmodernism and Islam: Predicament and Promise*, revised edition (London: Routledge, 2004)

An insightful postmodern analysis of the representations of Islam and Islamism in western contexts.

Talal Asad, *Formations of the Secular: Christianity, Islam, Modernity* (Stanford: Stanford University Press, 2003)

A sophisticated analysis of the articulation of Islam and Islamism in modern discourses about the religious and the secular.

Amel Boubekeur and Olivier Roy (eds.), *Whatever Happened to the Islamists?: Salafis, Heavy Metal Muslims, and the Lure of Consumerist Islam* (New York: Columbia University Press, 2010)

A useful overview of the metamorphosis of Islamist ideas and practices in new sociological settings.

John R. Bowen, *Can Islam Be French?: Pluralism and Pragmatism in a Secularist State* (Princeton: Princeton University Press, 2009)

An insightful study of the interaction between Islamic social and political movements and the secular institutions of the French state.

Jocelyne Césari, *When Islam and Democracy Meet: Muslims in Europe and in the United States* (New York: Palgrave, 2006)

A comprehensive overview of the political interactions between Muslim communities and the state in key European countries and the United States.

John L. Esposito and François Burgat (eds.), *Modernizing Islam: Religion in the Public Sphere in Europe and the Middle East* (New Brunswick: Rutgers University Press, 2002)

A sound compilation of texts on the contemporary processes of Islamization and modernization, East and West.

Jytte Klausen, *The Islamic Challenge: Politics and Religion in Western Europe* (Oxford: Oxford University Press, 2005)

A useful analysis of the articulation of Islam and Islamism in key European countries from the perspective of Muslim leaders.

Political Islam and political violence

Introduction

THIS NEXT SECTION introduces the reader in greater detail to the role played by political violence and addresses the issue of its apparent growing prominence in expressions of global political Islam. In the early twenty-first century in particular, the rise of so-called trans-national Islamist terror networks suddenly came to the fore in western policy and media debates. Today, some of the most controversial literature on Islamism proposes explanations of the relationship between political Islam and terrorism, and of the role of religious ideology in legitimizing this violence. Security and terrorism studies have swiftly expanded their field of expertise after 9/11 in order to provide concrete answers to pressing problems, but without necessarily paying much attention to the long-term trends and multi-layered mechanisms of Islamist militancy. In contemporary analyses of Islamism, a great deal of attention has been paid to the globalization of conflicts and power struggles from the Muslim world. From an actor's perspective this development often corresponds to a tactical change of focus from the 'near enemy' (the domestic authoritarian regimes of the Muslim world) to the 'far enemy', the international powers supporting them. Although trans-national forms of political violence have been present throughout the twentieth century, it is the globalization of a militaristic notion of 'jihad' during the Afghan conflict in the 1980s that set in motion these new dynamics of Islamist militancy. This trend gained global recognition after the attacks of 9/11 in the United States, and warranted a decade of international policies organized around the notion of 'War on Terror'.

In media and policy circles, the presentation of Islamist violence through the prism of international terrorism blurred the already complex relationship between violence and politics in the domestic context of Muslim-majority countries. As indicated earlier in the section on democratization, political violence is a common feature of politics in the Muslim world, as the 'rules of the game' imposed by these countries' authoritarian regimes rely heavily on repressive policies. Because direct forms of repression are common features of these models of governance, the Islamist forms of resistance to the state, as well as their expression of political power, commonly involve similarly violent discourses and practices. The anti-western rhetoric that commonly characterizes this domestic Islamist militancy is grounded in the assessment that international actors are supporting authoritarian regimes in the Muslim world and are encouraging them not to tolerate an Islamist opposition. Overall, however, the most common types of Islamist violence tend to have a local or national focus and they do not primarily involve international actors. Exceptions to this trend occurred during the colonial period and, more recently, during the period of the 'War on Terror' that witnessed a direct military involvement of Western states in Muslim-majority polities. In this context, two developments have been most debated in the last decade. First, there is the issue of the size of the constituency for a violent global Islamist militancy. While the size of a violent global militant community has been growing over the last couple of decades, it remains a moot point whether this constituency is viable when disconnected from concrete national-based conflicts. Second, there is the apparent growing appeal of Islamist discourses justifying violence against a wide range of targets – a trend often referred to as takfiri. The transformation of the discourse and practices of jihadism has to be seen against the background of changing global practices of warfare and securitization, and in the context of the reconfiguration of the sources of authority able to legitimize violence.

The first contribution, by Gilles Kepel, outlines how the organization of the military jihad during the Afghan mujahidin resistance against the Soviet Union in the 1980s set in motion the contemporary transnational Islamist networks spearheaded by al-Qaeda. Kepel notes in particular the failures of the jihadist movement to initiate regime change in the Muslim world, and their implications for the construction of a more global agenda for Islamist violence. Kepel outlines how the scope of jihad has been modified to put forward a longer-term perspective on change instead of a direct political victory, and how the role of individual martyrdom has become more prominent in this new jihadist discourse.

The second text, by Quintan Wiktorowicz, details the ideological and theological foundations of the contemporary Islamist discourse on violent jihad, with particular attention given to the notion of takfir (apostasy punishable by death). Wiktorowicz highlights how the recent evolution of this aspect of the Islamist discourse has enabled jihadists to expend previously narrower notions of military jihad. In this perspective, Muslim non-combatants and all those who might collude with 'enemies' of Islam can become legitimate targets. This trend also coincides with the emergence, in conflict zones, of a new brand of jihadist scholars and ideologues who have positioned themselves as the new 'authorities' on the jihad.

The next contribution, by Thomas Hegghammer, details the re-articulation of the idea and practice of military jihad in the aftermath of the invasion of Iraq. Hegghammer illustrates how the Iraqi situation has given rise to new discourses and practices regarding the legitimization of violence, the choice of the targets and the perception of the efficacy of such tactics. Iraq also provided would-be jihadists worldwide with a clear focal point for their actions, and it enabled jihadist networks to have a terrain where they could gain military experience and try out new tactics. Yet, in the course of the Iraqi insurrection, strategic divergences of views between Islamist organizations also came more visibly to the fore, thereby shedding new light on the prospects for a truly global jihadist phenomenon.

The final extract, from Faisal Devji's *Landscape of the Jihad*, outlines the future trends for the construction of violent militancy in Islamist discourses. Devji notes the transformation of a political tactic into an ethics-based discourse that empowers and hands over responsibility for violence to individual believers rather than to political and religious leaders. This process of democratization of 'legitimate' violence coincides with that of democratization of Islamic knowledge and religious authority. Violent Islamist militancy provides a narrative that enables activists to bypass complex theological and ideological disputes, thereby allowing disparate individuals and organizations to cooperate without necessarily sharing the same strategic goals.

Gilles Kepel

THE ORIGINS AND DEVELOPMENT OF THE JIHADIST MOVEMENT

From anti-communism to terrorism

THE OUTRAGE OF 11 September 2001 was the climax of actions by the radical Islamist movement from the mid-1980s, when *jihad* militants had coalesced to confront the Red Army in Afghanistan. Under the sponsorship of the United States and oil-rich monarchies of the Arabian Peninsula, the most determined activists came from Egypt, Algeria, Saudi Arabia, Pakistan and South East Asia. Indeed, even European suburbs provided personnel for the international Islamic brigades. They focused their militant activism on "the atheistic communists" of the Soviet Union, persuading people to turn a deaf ear to the Khomeinist siren voices inciting the Islamic world to rise up against "the great American Satan". As far as the US and the conservative Muslim states allied to the US were concerned, this Afghanistan *jihad* entrapped the Soviet Union, inflicting a lethal 'Vietnam' on it, and, at the same time, it prevented revolutionary Iran from acquiring the leadership of an Islamist movement that was spreading all across the world.

These two objectives were achieved. On 15 February 1989, the Red Army withdrew ignominiously from Afghanistan, the prelude to a final meltdown of the communist system for which the fall of the Berlin Wall in the autumn of that year sounded the knell. As for Iran, it did not succeed in exporting its revolution through the Muslim world with the notable exception of Shi'ite South Lebanon. In the summer of 1988 Khomeini had been obliged to sign an armistice with Saddam Hussein, then a client of the West and the oil-rich Arab states, at the end of eight years of murderous trench warfare. With this signature, Khomeini renounced his dream of setting up a sister Islamic republic in Baghdad.

Seen from Washington, the Afghanistan *jihad* seemed a double triumph, an excellent outcome. The US Army was not involved. No soldiers were killed in combat. There were no prisoners of war, no soldiers' mothers or conscientious objectors applying pressure on the executive. This was the antithesis of what had happened in Vietnam. The combatants in Afghanistan were bearded foreigners, described as 'freedom fighters' in this struggle against the 'Evil Empire'. They represented no political faction in the internal American scene. Indifferent to their fate, the US opened offices in America to recruit militants to go to Afghanistan. These collected donations, recruited among Muslim students on the campuses and organized tours for preachers from the Middle East. This final battle against the Soviet Union by means of an indirect *jihad* cost the American tax-payer next to nothing. Generally accepted estimates of costs are in the order of $US1.2 million a year, of which half were covered by the Arab Gulf states: a derisory figure when the stakes are considered.

However, the US victory carried within it a fearful ambiguity: US leaders thought they could manipulate the *jihad* and control the actors, and then wash their hands of them once the Soviet danger had disappeared. Thus, from 1989, the freedom fighters, so celebrated yesterday, switched – as we read in the US press – to being vilified as drug traffickers. Subsidies to them were stopped. You might think they had disappeared through lack of financial support from Washington; but Pandora's box had been opened. The shock of September 11 which the US experienced was partly a consequence of their own policies in the 1980s. They paid the price for no Americans killed in the *jihad* against the Red Army with the death of thousands at the World Trade Center and the Pentagon a decade later.

The chain of events that led the Islamist radicals of the *jihad* against the Soviet Union to the *jihad* against the US is complex: doctrine and geopolitics are entangled in a web of intrigue by intelligence services on all sides. In this last respect, we have at hand only fragments of information that offer more questions than answers. However, it is possible to reconstruct, with caution, the series of events that ended up in the unprecedented act of September 11.

The ambiguous legacy of the *jihad* against the Red Army in Afghanistan

The *jihad* is a central concept in Islamic doctrine, but its application has seen vicissitudes in the course of history. Literally, it means 'exertion'. For the individual believer, it is a spiritual exertion that makes him better and more pious; for the mystic it is the ecstasy that leads towards a fusion with God. This interpretation has connotations in basic religious culture – Jihad is used as a personal name – and many Muslims object when *jihad* and terrorism are used as synonyms. But the term also has a socio-political dimension with belligerent overtones that are evident in precise legal definitions. Traditionally there has been a distinction between an offensive *jihad* – giving a religious cover to the military expansion of the Islamic world, to conquest and then exploitation of the land of the unbelievers – and a defensive *jihad*, proclaimed by the *ulama* (the Islamic religious establishment) and jurists: a general mobilization for the 'homeland under threat', whenever the country is under attack from the infidels.

The first is within the realm of political authority and has no relevance for Muslims as a whole. Soldiers take part in it, and also volunteers fired by a pious zeal or attracted by the expectation of legitimate plunder.

The second does not tolerate the desertion of any believer, and overturns the hierarchy of social values and obligations. A defensive *jihad*, when proclaimed, has supreme authority. It can dispense with fasting in Ramadan, or with obedience to a prince in opposition. It is a matter of the survival of the community of believers. Each person, under threat of mortal sin, must take part in a manner appropriate to his means, by arms, if not with funds, or at the very least, by acts of charity, or by prayer. Fighting becomes the supreme virtue, and regulates the mobilization of all energies. All means justify the end, the safeguarding of the community. But this supreme arm of Islam can become a two-edged weapon. The *ulama* have always taken great care to restrict *jihad* in time and space. If it slips out of their control, it imperils the established order. It can unleash violence that can lead the community of believers to sedition and chaos, making it a sitting target for those enemies at whom this violence should be directed.

The *jihad* of defence is an obligation for each person (in Arabic, *fard ayn*) and was proclaimed immediately after the invasion of Afghanistan by the Red Army in December 1979. In Islam there is no supreme authority comparable to the Pope in Roman Catholicism. It is the prestige or charisma of this or that doctor of law, the erudition attributed to him, the network through which he operates with his sermons distributed by video and audio cassettes, that give his juridical opinion, or *fatwa*, a greater or lesser resonance. Actually the first *ulama* to be involved belonged to the *salafi* or *wahhabi* tendency, a hardline and conservative current in Islam that represents the Saudi Arabian religious establishment. They were also connected with the Muslim Brothers, a transnational organization founded in Egypt at the end of the 1920s and firmly established among the god-fearing Arab middle class. It is also represented in the *jama'at-e islami*, the Muslim Brothers' equivalent in Pakistan and the Indian subcontinent. All these movements worked for the establishment of an Islamic state based on the *shari'a*, the law inspired by sacred texts, and co-operated in a genuine anti-communism, earning them the early sympathy of Washington. In proclaiming a *jihad* against the Soviet infidels who were invading the Islamic land of Afghanistan, they were offering an alternative to the anti-Americanism propagated by the Iranian revolution. They were a safety valve for more radical movements in the Islamic world as a whole that were beginning to threaten the stability of a number of regimes.

In November 1979 the Great Mosque of Mecca was attacked and seized by militants who condemned the ruling Saudi's dependence on the USA. In October 1981, President Sadat of Egypt was assassinated by an Islamic group called Organisation of the Jihad, and in Algeria, from 1982, an Islamic underground movement inspired by Mustafa Bouyali backed an armed struggle against the Front de Liberation Nationale (FLN) state.

In Afghanistan the *jihad* had provided a foreign theatre for all these activists, to the great relief of the regimes concerned. Thus, in Egypt, most of those condemned to the most lenient punishments after Sadat's assassination – including Muhammad al-Zawahiri, bin Ladin's right-hand man – were released in 1984 and sent to Mecca in order to perform the lesser pilgrimage ('*umra*) before being put on the next flight to Peshawar. The Egyptian government saw advantages in these arrangements. Subversive elements left the Nile valley to fight for the US ally who was providing Egypt with crucial aid and military funds. If by chance they died on the battlefield, then that would be so many fewer radical Islamists.

It was much the same for the Algerian Bouyalist underground militants who had been 'exfiltrated' in the direction of Afghanistan after being arrested by the gendarmerie, or who had chosen to go into exile in order to evade repression. But the short-term political calculation of the regimes in power turned out to be mistaken. Most foreign Jihadists did not die in battle. In contact with Pakistani instructors, and under CIA supervision, they were toughened up and acquired the latest techniques of warfare, handling and discharging explosives, guerrilla warfare, tracking people, infiltration and subversive activity in general, all designed at that time to be used in the struggle against the Soviets. Later they would put them into operation in wide-ranging terrorist acts in the 1990s against those very people who had given them instruction.

Estimates of the number of foreign *Mujahidin* who passed through the training camps situated in the Pakistani tribal areas between Peshawar and the Afghan border, where the Tora Bora is situated, and in certain areas of Afghanistan beyond Soviet control, vary between several thousands to several tens of thousands of individuals. These figures are extremely imprecise and estimates are conflicting for several reasons. No reliable administration has monitored the data – the arrivals and departures. The definition and the purpose of the camps changed: most remained active between the official end of the *jihad* on 1 April 1992 (the date of the taking of Kabul by a mixed alliance of Afghan *Mujahidin*) and the US offensive against the Taliban in the autumn of 2001. It is difficult to know how far the services of the ISI (Inter Service Intelligence, the Pakistani military intelligence services), even after 1992, were carrying out activities of liaison and training. It is similarly difficult to know what was passed on to their US counterparts.

To make up for these uncertainties, the quite varied testimonies provided by the memoirs of former *Mujahidin* and statements and confessions given under interrogation or at trials, allow us to conclude that time spent in the training camps was of two kinds. Most, it seems, did not spend a long time in the camps. They were made up of a large fringe of sympathizers who were the targets of bursts of gunfire and would pose for photographs dressed in Afghan headgear and in combat fatigues, with a Kalashnikov over their shoulders. They set off full of enthusiasm, ready to provide reserves and support, hiding places and financial support as required, without having to be formed into direct operational units. Among them were sons of good Saudi families turning up with their air-conditioned jeeps and their hunting gear that they would leave as presents when they departed. There were also Islamists coming from the suburbs and inner cities of Western countries, without any material resources, who were taken care of by the organizations specialising in *da'wa* (missionary work) and humanitarian activity. Those staying for longer, by contrast, constituted a core of determined militants, much smaller in number than the 'birds of passage'. The first who tried to gather the data, in order to keep contact with those still staying on and to form them into a network, was 'Usama bin Ladin. The term, *al-Qa'ida (al-Qaeda)*, arose from US intelligence sources and was taken up by the international press. (There is no source that confirms that the militants themselves call their organization by this name.) In Arabic it means 'base': in this case, database. It designates a database of those who had known the camps and who scattered afterwards throughout the world, forming groups with whom contact was maintained by e-mail, internet and websites. The name is probably a metaphor, but it does show the unique capacity bin Ladin has had in turning the random and temporary gathering of militants in one physical place – the camps – into a network with lasting global potential. It indicates a remarkably sophisticated management system, applying communication techniques to political and subversive activity. From the early 1980s, the *Mujahidin* militants who were regrouped in Pakistan and Afghanistan anticipated the expansion of their activity world-wide in the forthcoming 10 years.

We do not have available writings or declarations from bin Ladin referring to this period. Instead, there are texts of his mentor – 'Abdullah 'Azzam, a Palestinian Islamist militant from Janin – according to whom the Afghan *jihad* was just the start of a long process. After victory, all the lands of Islam occupied by the infidels – from Mindanao in the Philippines to the Soviet Central Asian republics and including Andalusia – would be reconquered. But, beyond this millennial rhetoric, for 'Azzam, the principal objective of the *jihad* after the inevitable fall of Kabul would be the taking of Jerusalem and the restoration of Islamic rule in a Palestine liberated from Zionist occupation. This project was thwarted by 'Azzam's assassination on Friday 24 November 1989 at Peshawar on his way to the mosque. This happened during the bloody spell following the Soviet retreat from Kabul when rival sects of Afghan *Mujahidin* were arguing over the strategy of taking the capital before wasting their forces in bloody ethno-religious wars. This mysterious assassination echoed the assault in October 1988 on Zia ul-Haqq, the Pakistani dictator. Responsibility for this assassination is also still unclaimed. Zia had changed his country into a conduit for foreign aid to the *jihad*.

In each case we face one of a large number of actions from the start of the *jihad* to the autumn of 2001, none of which can be attributed precisely to any one identifiable group, either by the world of intelligence services or by university researchers. All this leaves considerable areas of doubt when one tries to make sense of it all. Nevertheless, the assassination of 'Azzam led to Palestine being deferred on the agenda of the *jihad*, not to return until after the second *Intifada*. Other countries took its place in the 1990s – the Arabian Peninsula, Bosnia, Egypt, Algeria, Tajikistan, Chechnya and Daghestan, Kashmir, the Philippines, the Albanian issues and the first far-reaching anti-American activities.

The *jihad* in Afghanistan possessed another fundamental characteristic that would have many consequences, and that has been little studied: a psychological change of heart in the Islamist movement because of the bias of the specific indoctrination undergone inside the camps. It is probably there that we must look for the origin of the brainwashing of the activists who committed the suicide missions of September 11, among others. Their written or recorded testimonies, those that have been recovered, indicate an extreme religious fanaticism of a medieval and obscurantist character, coupled moreover with a very high level of operational sophistication. In the absence of documents or of precise evidence about this aspect of life in the training camps, we have to rely on the abundance of writings that have subsequently been produced by refugees in 'Londonistan'. This is what the British capital was called when it provided a sanctuary throughout the 1990s to a number of ideologues who had passed through Afghanistan and Pakistan in the 1980s. These texts, attributed for the most part to writers like the Palestinian Abu Qatada, the Syrian Abu Mus'ab or the Egyptian Abu Hamza, appeared in the London magazine *al-Ansar*, during the Algerian *jihad* between 1993 and 1997, and provide, up to now, the best evidence of the evolution of Islamist ideology in the camps. This literature is written in a very difficult style, full of allusions and the specialized technical vocabulary of medieval *ulama*. In contrast to Islamist ideologues, such as the Egyptian Sayyid Qutb, the Pakistani Mawdudi and even Ayatollah Khomeini, who wrote to be read, discussed and easily understood by the new educated generation who were around 20 in 1970, these pamphlets have a tone of unquestionable authority, reinforced by their incomprehensible character for non-specialist readers. This authority is invested with a mystique and a religious power that are strengthened by the accumulation of countless injunctions taken from the Qur'an and above all the *hadith* – the sayings and exemplary deeds of the Prophet Muhammad.

At the present time, the Wahhabi and Salafi trend has usually provided a religious legitimacy for socially conservative regimes, like those of most of the monarchies of the Arabian Peninsula. There was hardly any opportunity to advance the *jihad* there, for the states that favoured this trend took part, as allies of the US, in a world order from which they benefited. Now this school was revived by the leaders of the Afghan Pakistan camps, who stressed the theory of *jihad*. They combined this with the more 'modern' movement of Islamists who were readers of Qutb, the Egyptian hanged in 1966 by the Nasser regime or Mawdudi, the Pakistani founder of *jama'at-e islami* (died in 1979), and who emerged from the ranks of the Muslim Brothers. For the latter, the *jihad* had priority too, but it was incorporated into a whole programme of activities – social and humanitarian work, student activism, participation in elections, etc. – that had a broader and more varied base. The convergence of the two trends produced a new ideology – Salafi-Jihadism – with the emphasis on the *jihad*. In this intellectual context and in the environment of military training in the camps, the *jihad* was understood in its most violent and fanatical sense. There was to be a ruthless armed struggle against the infidels whose scope could be endlessly extended. The *jihad* became a focus of fascination, the panacea for the world's ills and even the essence of Islam.

Such, in all probability, was the vision of the world that would provide the framework of the international combatants who passed through the camps in 1989 when the Soviet retreat gave them comfort beyond all expectations: one of the post-Yalta superpowers had suffered a lethal military defeat, thanks to a handful of *Mujahidin*, ragged partisans in the mountains confronting aerial warfare. Certainly, the ground-to-air Stinger missiles, provided by the USA, counted for more than faith in determining the military outcome. But there was no alternative but for the missiles to be carried by men. These were the Afghan *Mujahidin* – hardly ever, it seems, the foreign Jihadists – but, globally, they shared the same mystical concept of *jihad* as the famed international warriors who had emerged from the training camps. These people had been conditioned by a literalist reading of sacred texts, with minds for which the Prophet, his Companions and their immediate successors were the sole role models, and their era the just age of Islam, the paradigm for all history. They saw themselves as the ones who had shattered the Soviet empire in the same way that the first Muslims had destroyed the Sassanid Empire, opening up the lands of the East to the champions of Allah. Once this had been achieved, the first *khalifas* were able to carry the war against the other great infidel empire that dominated the known world: Byzantium. Now, the Salafi-Jihadists were ready to fight the Byzantium of today: the United States of America.

The retargeting of the *jihad* on the West

The retargeting of the *jihad* on the West reached its apogee with the attacks of September 11. It was marked by two very distinct stages. Until the mid-1990s, it was manifest mainly in guerrilla activity in Egypt, Algeria and Bosnia: these were military setbacks. The first terrorist operation on US soil was the attack against the World Trade Center in February 1993. This was also a setback which left an unpredictable future. In the second half of the decade, a series of terrorist operations had a wider, more lethal impact, which offset the lack of guerrilla success: the attacks against the marine barracks at Dhahran on Saudi territory in June 1996, against the US embassies in Tanzania and Kenya on 7 August 1998, against the destroyer *USS Cole* off Aden in October 2000 – and, finally, September 11. They bore witness to another tactic. Unable to recruit the masses in a *jihad* led by guerrillas who wished to be seen as heroes fighting infidel regimes, the more militant chose to strike at the very heart of US power. They, thereby, exposed US weaknesses. They were hoping to galvanize the Muslim masses through enormous media coverage of simultaneous actions which would inspire them to take part in the *jihad*. But from their point of view, in spite of their murderous consequences and their devastating symbolic impact, the terrorist operations failed to achieve their aim – the uprising which they anticipated. Indeed, the Taliban regime was eliminated by US military action. Even the *jihad* in Palestine, which assumed the mantle of a Holy War, finally rebounded on its activists, in spite of the numerous Israeli civilian deaths, victims of the suicide bombers.

The spread of Jihadist guerrilla warfare and its failure 1992–1997

A consequence of Saddam Hussein's invasion of Kuwait on 2 August 1990 was to open up an irreparable fault line in the heart of the Islamist movement that was to create an opposition to the moderate bourgeois tendency linked to Saudi interests. The movement opened up to more radical groups among whom were revolutionary intellectuals and militants emerging from the young urban poor. On 7 August 1990, King Fahd, Custodian of the 'Two Holy Places' (Mecca and Medina), summoned the assistance of the US Army and its allies. In the eyes of the radicals he was committing the unforgivable sin: infidel soldiers, accompanied by their Christian and Jewish clergy, would be sullying the sacred soil of the Arabian Peninsula and threatening the Holy Places. We find a clear sign of this gulf between the two tendencies of the Islamist movement in the timing of the assault that destroyed the US embassies in Kenya and Tanzania: 7 August 1998, the actual anniversary of King Fahd's appeal. For the radicals, the arrival of the infidel US Armies and their allies on Saudi soil and then their attack on Iran were of the same nature as the Soviet invasion of Afghanistan. In both cases, *dar al-Islam*, the land of Islam, was being invaded and it was legitimate to call for a *jihad* of defence against the invader. They did not succeed in finding a consensus of *ulama* as broad as at the time of Afghanistan to proclaim a *jihad* but this did not prevent the militants getting involved in action. Their minority status was offset by the utter determination and professionalism on the part of the combatants, indoctrinated and hardened in the Afghan-Pakistani training camps.

In the aftermath of the arrival of the foreign troops on Saudi land in the summer of 1990, there emerged a movement against the House of Saud in the name of Jihadi-Salafism, which called itself *Sahwa* (Awakening). The movement attracted some preachers, generally young, locally well-educated who were also in contact with Syrian and Palestinian Muslim Brother migrants in Kuwait and well-established there. The best known were Shaykh Auda and Shaykh Hawali, who were sent to jail from 1994 to 1999, and also a media-wise opponent exiled in London, Muhammad al-Masari, whose influence was, however, of short duration.

These dissidents preoccupied the Saudi regime because they challenged its legitimacy. More and more concessions were demanded for the legal and juridical powers of the *ulama* in order that the tight alliance between the monarchy and the USA could be legitimized in the name of Islam. The seizure of a large part of the educational system by the most conservative religious authorities, just as Saudi Arabia was experiencing a demographic explosion estimated (in the absence of credible statistics) as one of the most important in the world, was one of the main advantages gained by the *ulama*. They had control over a large area of study – even non-religious matters – and they planted their vision of the world into the minds of a younger generation that was beginning to feel, from the beginning of the 1990s, the effects of the drop in oil prices, exacerbated by the increase in the number of beneficiaries of oil revenues. By the end of the decade this younger generation turned out 100,000 graduates a year, of whom it was estimated that under a third found employment. It constituted, at the very heart of Saudi society, a core of disaffected young people, who were very concerned for their future, but poorly equipped. Many of them nourished resentment against the very extensive Royal Family who had privileged access to the oil revenues.

However, the religious dissidents Shaykh (Sheikh) Auda and Shaykh Hawali were unable to exploit this discontent, because a ferocious repression ensured that there was no contact between the most active preachers and the mass of young people. Moreover, the regime had to tolerate Salafi preaching, as it was always difficult to differentiate between senior *ulama* and their far-flung disciples who had been attracted by *jihad*. Shaykh bin Baz, the Mufti of the Kingdom (died 1997), and Shaykh bin 'Uthaimin, a very well-known man of religion (died 2001), ensured a balance between conservatives and radicals.

Throughout the 1990s dissidence spread, even though it was not out in the open because the most prominent militants were imprisoned after 1994. A wave of sympathy was fostered for 'Usama bin Ladin who was stripped of his Saudi nationality in 1994 and who took as a slogan a *hadith* attributed to the Prophet on his deathbed, "Chase the Jews and the Christians out of the Arabian Peninsula". In the interpretation adopted by the militants, this meant that they had to chase out the US marines stationed near the oilfields in the eastern barracks of the Kingdom and to liberate the Kingdom from US influence that had reduced it to a protectorate. This objective remained a strategic priority for the radical tendency throughout the 1990s, just as the *hadith* itself was declared in each proclamation coming from the bin Ladin network, and then from communiqués attributed to *al-Qaʿida*. It was impossible to achieve this objective in the Kingdom because of internal repression. This led to anti-US terrorism in the region, especially in the second half of the decade, and to the spread of *jihad* elsewhere.

When, in April 1992, Kabul finally fell into the hands of a coalition of Afghan *Mujahidin*, the *jihad* in Afghanistan was over. With the assassination of 'Abdullah 'Azzam the short-term hope of transferring it to Palestine disappeared. Fronts soon opened up in Egypt, Algeria, Bosnia and then in Tajikistan and Chechnya, not to speak of the switch of the Pakistani *jihad* to Kashmir, where the Islamabad authorities controlled military operations. This gave the impression that *jihad* was spreading worldwide, ensuring much enhanced publicity. According to the militants, just as Afghanistan was taken over simply by armed force, soon the infidel regimes of targeted countries had to collapse under the impact of the Jihadist-Salafist fighters and groups of sympathizers who would be formed and recruited on the spot.

In Egypt, attacks were directed at senior officials, the police, Copts and tourists. Until 1995 the forces of repression seemed to be helpless in the face of a most effective violence that reflected the quality of training in the camps. But very soon the Jihadists became cut off from their popular base. In December 1992, the Imbaba quarter of the Cairo suburbs – stronghold of the radical Islamists of the *gama'a islamiyya* – was surrounded by the army and cleansed of its militants. They no longer came to build up a base, a sanctuary, in the urban area. They had to seek refuge in the Upper Nile Valley where they carried out a guerrilla war that closed the region to foreign tourists. Their objective was to deprive the state of tourist revenue and to bring about its downfall. However, the local population, whose income depended largely on tourism and who were the first victims, turned against the rebels, preventing further Jihadist mobilization in the rural areas. At the same time, attempts to unite the Islamist movement met with no success. The devout middle class and professional liberals maintained their links with the Muslim Brothers who dreaded being drawn into violence. The followers of this organization did, however, show their solidarity with the radical militants and the *gama'a islamiyya* when their members were victims of repression and they denounced the brutalities to which they were submitted in prison. The persistence of this divide allowed the state to reclaim the initiative. From 1996, the security forces made up for their operational delays by acquiring anti-guerrilla techniques and equipment and, in Upper Egypt, inflicted severe damage on the Islamist combatants whose demoralized troops embarked on a strategy of violence. The horror created by the massacre of dozens of tourists at Luxor by *gama'a islamiyya* activists in the autumn of 1977 marked the defeat of armed dissidence. As a strategy of seizing power on the Afghan model, guerrilla *jihad* failed in the Nile valley.

In Bosnia the *jihad* strategy was of another kind: it was to take part in a civil war between Serbs, Croats and Bosnians, and to transform the war into a religious conflict. In their eyes, Bosnia was a land of Islam that had been invaded by infidels. This justified a defensive *jihad* on the pattern of Afghanistan. The combatants who came to the area were not from Bosnia – there had been no Bosnians in the Afghan-Pakistani camps. Many came from the Arabian Peninsula where, in contrast to Egypt and Algeria, it had not been possible to open up an active *jihad* front. Brought in successive batches by the Islamic humanitarian organizations that distributed relief through the mosques, they disbursed a great deal of funds. At first they were appreciated by the Bosnian population, who were encircled and suffering ethnic cleansing and massacre by the Serbian militia. But the transplant did not take root. The ferocity of the Jihadists, who had themselves been photographed brandishing recently severed heads, and their intolerance of the popular traditions of Bosnian Islam that they denounced in the name of *salafi* purity, prevented them from being absorbed into the local scene. The Dayton Accords of December 1995 signalled the end for foreign Jihadists, making their expulsion an essential condition of the Pax Americana. Further attempts to graft a *jihad* onto the troubles of Albania and then the war in Kosovo were nipped in the bud, after militants who had been sent there were captured and then sold by the Albanian authorities to the Egyptian and Saudi governments.

The *jihad* in the Balkans had been a major symbol for those in the movement who had graduated from the Afghan-Pakistani training camps. Increasingly, the camps were associated with the personality of bin Ladin. The struggle was launched on European soil and involved genuine Europeans, Islamized Slavs with blond hair. They were supported by those activist militants who were Muslim immigrants to western Europe and mainly to the United Kingdom, France and Germany. For these reasons the European states and the USA were unable to disregard the issue when confronting a challenge unfolding on the frontiers of the West. Victims of a combination of unfavourable factors, the Jihadists were unable, unlike in Afghanistan, to rely on the support or even the tolerance of the West.

Even more serious and more significant than these two setbacks was that affecting the *jihad* in Algeria. The Jihadists there were hoping to acquire power in the wake of the remarkable successes achieved under the banner of the Front Islamique du Salut (FIS) between 1989 and 1992. After its creation in 1989, the Islamist movement effectively and rapidly rallied the support of the numerous poor urban youth who were disillusioned. They were joined by the middle classes who were denied access to the political sphere and to oil revenues by the bosses of the only political party, the Front de Libération Nationale (FLN). The absence of religious dignitaries and a credible *ulama* had very quickly allowed the ideologues and the preachers of the Party to monopolize the Islamist discourse and, consequently, the FIS scored great success in the local and municipal elections in June 1990, the first free elections in Algeria since independence.

In Iran, in 1978 Khomeini had succeeded in becoming the sole representative of the Islamist discourse. He appealed simultaneously to all the social elements that made up the movement, even attracting the secular opposition to the Shah's dictatorial regime, and keeping them all united until he had taken over power. By contrast, Algeria in 1990–1991, saw the FIS split into two branches, represented respectively by Abbassi Madani and Ali Benhadj. The former, spokesman of the religious middle classes, was initially in alliance with Saudi Arabia when Saddam Hussein attacked Kuwait in August 1990. The second, the idol of the poor urban youth, was ranged on the side of Iraq and promised to put an end to all those who had "sucked the poisonous milk of France" when the FIS took power. The unity of the movement suffered as it proved incapable of holding the constituency that had swung towards them in June 1990 against the regime, without actually sharing the Islamist vision of the world. The francophone secular middle classes, now with no illusions as to the fate promised them by Ali Benhadj, gave their support to a *coup d'état*: the army intervened between the two rounds of the legislative elections on 12 January 1992 that were about to be won by the FIS. The majority of the electorate had voted for the Islamists, providing thereby a huge popular base of disaffected people who wanted to dismantle, by force if necessary, the regime that had snatched away their expected victory. Such circumstances were very favourable to the *jihad* and were quickly exploited by the Afghanistan veterans around whom the Groupe Islamique Armé (GIA) was formed. From early 1993 they were to achieve some significant military victories. Parts of the country were outside the control of the state and declared themselves "liberated Islamic zones".

These were in the mountainous areas where an underground resistance was formed (in the same places as during the War of Independence) as well as in the urban suburbs and well-populated city centres. Until the end of 1994 various ultra-radical *amirs* (*emirs*) who followed one another at the head of the GIA managed to isolate the regime and to attract Islamic leaders from the middle classes who saw in the GIA the future leadership of Algeria.

Algeria became the great cause of the Salafi-Jihadist ideologues who had taken refuge in the British capital, the 'Londonistan' of militants. They talked of the military feats of the Islamist resistance in the countryside, making them universal heroes of the cause. They edited *al-Ansar*, publishing their tales of glory and distributing their propaganda cassettes, etc. The victory in Afghanistan had ultimately left a bitter taste. By 1994 the various *Mujahidin* factions were killing each other, giving the world a wretched image of the Islamic state emerging from the triumphant *jihad* of the 1980s. Algeria would become the new Islamist promised land: rich in petroleum, close to Europe, providing a bridgehead for a global expansion of the faith – just as it had provided, in the first years of Independence, a distinctive model of a pro-Soviet Third World country. In spite of these promising beginnings, from 1995 the *jihad* in Algeria embarked on a path that would lead to failure. That year saw Jamal Zituni become the *amir* of the GIA in mysterious circumstances. The struggle also spread to France, with assassinations attributed to a network of young Islamists who had arrived from abroad or who were French converts to Islam. From this time, the movement gave itself up to a series of atrocities that ended up in alienating all popular support and bringing it into utter discredit, even among potential supporters. There were two arguments explaining the evolution of the GIA: for the Islamist moderates who had been with FIS and certain observers, the radical group had been infiltrated by *agents provocateurs* from the Algerian secret services who pushed them into making mistakes. The attacks in France, according to this logic, had been aimed at strengthening the French grip on power in Algiers which they saw as the sole barrier against barbarism, in spite of their poor democratic credentials. As for others, the radical logic of Salafi-Jihadism that had come out of the Algerian experience was all that was needed to explain the atrocities. The attacks against France were intended to put pressure on Paris to withdraw its support for Algiers in return for peace in France itself.

In the absence of unequivocal evidence, it is difficult to be absolutely clear about terrorist operations extended to the territory of a Western country. We are similarly in the dark about many other cases during that decade, when radical Islamists and secret services seemed to be in collusion. Whatever the situation, from the beginning of 1996 and the emergence of groups of 'Patriots', armed by the Algerian state, the GIA began a decline that ended up in large-scale massacres in the suburbs of Algiers in the autumn of 1997, at the same time as the massacre of tourists by the Egyptian *gama'a islamiyya* at Luxor. After this act of barbarism, which some analysts have attributed to acts of provocation, the GIA was no longer a significant factor. It gave way to tiny armed groups that had only a limited impact and did not prevent the state taking back control of more or less the whole of the territory.

The military failure of the Algerian *jihad* was a bitter blow. The reason for failure lay in the policy of spreading guerrilla warfare on the model of the struggle against the Red Army in Afghanistan. The collapse took place in 1996: in that year all hope was lost in Bosnia and in Egypt as well as in Algeria, and the balance of forces swung in favour of established authority. Only the Chechen front remained promising, but that was marginal as far as the fight against the West was concerned. It was rather in the interests of the West to weaken Russia and to prevent the export of oil from Central Asia through this region. The failure of the guerrilla strategy at this time coincided with the first of the major terrorist operations attributed to ʿUsama bin Ladin. It could be said that one strategy was substituted for another.

The terrorist phase 1996–2002

From 1996 terrorism became the main tactic of the Salafi-Jihadist movement, and the figure of ʿUsama bin Ladin became its supreme icon. However, he clashed with ʿAbdullah ʿAzzam on the action to take after the *jihad* in Afghanistan. Bin Laden also stressed the emancipation of Saudi Arabia from being an American protectorate, believing this issue should take precedence over the liberation of Palestine from the Israeli occupation. From 1989 he was regarded with suspicion by the authorities. His passport was withdrawn and he found himself under house arrest in his own country when he made a journey there from Peshawar. He managed to escape in 1991 and, until 1996, made his home in a Sudan under the influence of the Islamist ideologue Hasan al-Turabi. Opponents of Riyad and Washington mingled in a Khartoum that had adopted a sort of international Islamist radicalism. For Salafi-Jihadists evacuated from Afghanistan in the early 1990s it became a crossroads facilitating the Egyptian activists to return home after illegally crossing the frontier.

The proximity of Sudan and Somalia was probably a factor relating to the October 1993 operation *Restore Hope* that forced the US army, trapped by Jihadists, to withdraw from Somalia. Above all, it was the failed assassination of President Mubarak at Addis Ababa in June 1995 that made Sudan a pariah in the international community. It was accused by Egypt of being, if not an instigator, then a refuge of conspirators. Khartoum had just handed over the international terrorist Carlos to France and wanted to rid itself in the same way of bin Ladin, in order to regain some respectability. The refusal of the US to take him when he was offered to them leaves open a number of questions. Saudi Arabia had no wish either to accept this embarrassing gift – the execution of bin Ladin would present too many internal political problems. So, in the summer of 1996, he apparently returned to Afghanistan which the Taliban controlled as far as Kandahar, with Pakistani and American support. Just at this time they were encouraged by their patrons to seize Kabul in September.

The events of 1996, the ins and outs of which are not known in detail, were a watershed. They marked the transition from the phase of Jihadist guerrillas to the phase of sensational terrorism involving massacres. At the end of June, while the fate of bin Ladin was being discussed, a terrorist act involving a mined lorry caused many deaths among US soldiers based at Dhahran in Saudi Arabia. This operation was reminiscent of the actions against the US and French barracks in Lebanon in October 1983, attributed to Shiʾite extremists under the influence of Tehran. In spite of the accusations made immediately after Dhahran by Riyad against Iran, many today attribute the responsibility of this action to bin Ladin's network. It was particularly significant that from Afghanistan, where he was now based, he proclaimed a *jihad* against the Americans who were in the 'Land of the Two Holy Places'. Without explicitly claiming responsibility for the action, the text provided a rationale for it, and for the assaults that were to follow against the US embassies in Tanzania and Kenya in 1998, and also against the destroyer *USS Cole* on the seas off Aden in 2000. In their eyes, the US presence was tantamount to an invasion of the lands of Islam by infidels, and justified a defensive *jihad* by any means.

Beyond the fervour of religious terminology, we have to examine the objectives of these threats against the USA. Terrorism, with fanatics carrying out such misdeeds as suicide attacks, is an extremely rational tactic with specific aims. Without doubt, the destruction of the USA, the general Islamization of the whole world and other messianic visions were part of the dreams of the starry-eyed activists who emerged from the crucible of the Afghan *jihad*. But they were not achievable in the short term. Instead, one of the principal claims of bin Ladin's proclamations was regime change in Saudi Arabia, the elimination of a dynasty that controlled the country's petroleum resources. It was to be replaced by other socio-economic groups, in particular the wealthier merchants and ordinary entrepreneurs, the class to which bin Ladin belonged and from whom he had found support and whom he praised in his statement. The failure of Islamist dissidence in the Kingdom at the beginning of the 1990s showed that it was futile to expect internal change. The Saudi regime was protected by the USA, which regards it as the regulator of the oil market, guaranteeing the provision of an accessible and relatively cheap source of energy to the world. The terrorist logic was to put increasing pressure on the USA by a chain of incidents whose social and political cost would become unbearable to the US administration. This would persuade them to shift their policy towards Saudi Arabia in favour of a regime change. It is reminiscent of the strategy attributed to the GIA at the time of the murderous incidents committed in France in 1995. The social and political cost would become so high that Paris would have no other choice but to relax its policy on Algeria. In the short term this calculation proved ill-founded. The French and US authorities in both cases did not sacrifice vital interests under pressure. Such a policy would have disastrous consequences. However, in the medium term, some political circles in Paris and Washington did re-evaluate the political implications of supporting the Algerian and Saudi regimes. We will see later how this was expressed in the USA after September 11.

The four waves of anti-US attacks between 1996 and 2001 were all carried out by 'suicide bombers' (though not the attack on the World Trade Center in 1993). This is a new phenomenon in contemporary Sunni Islamist activism. Research on suicide as a political act – and we find earlier examples of this in medieval Islam, especially among the Assassins – reveals that it was originally used by Shi'ite Islamists. It was first employed on a large scale during the war launched by Saddam Hussein against the Islamic Republic of Iran in September 1980. The young Iranian *bassij* volunteers, death-defying zealots, leapt into Iraqi minefields, convinced that they would ascend into the martyrs' Paradise. The aim was to open up a route for an offensive by the regular army. This practice passed to the Arab world through the Lebanese Shi'ites of the Hezbollah and their tiny allied groups. It proved to be unstoppable. US and French contingents of the multilateral force left Lebanon following the suicide attack of 1983 and, even more, the Israeli army abandoned southern Lebanon in May 2000, reckoning that the sacrifice of the Tsahal soldiers, victims of these attacks, was too high a price to pay for the occupation. From this time, the practice of suicide bombing acquired considerable prestige beyond the Shi'ite environment in which it had been nurtured.

The Israeli retreat from southern Lebanon was interpreted in the Middle East as the first Arab military victory in memory. At Nairobi and Dar es-Salaam on 7 August 1998 and at Aden in October 2000, suicide bombings threw the US security systems into confusion. It seemed that, in the Middle East, where there was a huge imbalance of conventional and nuclear military force unquestionably favouring Israel and the USA, this tactic was re-establishing some kind of 'balance of terror'.

Thus, the tactic of terrorism worked on two fronts. In the first place, it put pressure on Tel Aviv and Washington, in the hope of forcing concessions from them – the most obvious of which were the US and French withdrawals from Beirut in 1983, the departure of US forces from Somalia in 1993 and, finally, the Israeli withdrawal from southern Lebanon after the decision of Prime Minister Barak in 2000. At the same time, the resulting prestige and aura of martyrdom of the suicide bombers, strengthened the Jihadist camp even within Muslim society. This forced the Islamists from the middle classes to follow those whom the masses saw as heroes facing up to US and Israeli enemies. It also constituted a major challenge to the Arab states whose military failure in confronting Israel seemed all the more outrageous. It threatened their legitimacy that was based on their role in defending the Arab nation, a role that was the keystone of most of these regimes. They continued forbidding any expression of pluralism, preventing any change in political élites, preserving power in the hands of the same families or the same ethnic groups.

In spite of the special character of these terrorist operations and the enormous impact of destabilization, they had not been able to force the USA to modify its policy on the Middle East, particularly on the Saudi monarchy. It was in this context that an operation was planned that would be of an entirely different order, an action that was directed at its heart.

The turning point of September 11 can only be understood in relation to two causes, two fronts under one banner: *jihad* – the American presence in Saudi Arabia, which was the pretext for the attacks of 1996, 1998 and 2000 at Dhahran, Nairobi and Dar es Salaam as well as Aden; and the Palestine issue after the launch of the second *Intifada* in autumn 2000. Bin Ladin made that explicit in the declaration issued on Al-Jazeera television on 7 October 2001. It also helps us to understand the popular support bin Ladin enjoyed as an icon of the resistance among the Arab youth and a wide section of society until the defeat of the Taliban in Afghanistan.

The launch of the second *Intifada* came at the moment when certain political actors considered that a renewal of limited confrontation with the other side would unblock the deadlock of the Oslo peace process. This was as much on the side of the Palestinian Authority as in part of the Israeli establishment. Arafat, whose administration was under attack for its authoritarianism and the corruption of his circle, remained impotent in the face of the relentless advance of Israeli settlements. The mystique of a new *Intifada* allowed him to improve his image with a younger generation that was disenchanted. It also curtailed the development of Hamas that had strengthened its influence through a range of well-organized charitable activities. These welded society together and distributed aid and subsidies, the money coming from the Arabian Peninsula. On the Israeli side, Ariel Sharon saw in the logic of confrontation with the Palestinian Authority the chance to take over the leadership of the Likud Party and then to win the elections. That was the purpose of his much publicized walk under heavy security surveillance around the mosques on Temple Mount in Jerusalem in Autumn 2000. This was the beginning of the second *al-Aqsa Intifada*, named after the mosque he went to during his walk, which deliberately provoked Palestinian anger.

The launch of the *Intifada* and the first attacks allowed Ariel Sharon to take effective power during the elections of February 2001. As for Yasir Arafat, the Israeli withdrawal from southern Lebanon had persuaded him that the Jewish state was ready for concessions. In order to avoid the spectre of violence against its civilian population, they would allow the Palestinian Authority to reassert its prestige and power with its own population. Until the summer of 2001 the situation remained unresolved. Gradually the Authority lost control of the violence, and the first suicide bombings against civilians took place, imitating the Lebanese Hezbollah and instigated by the Islamists of Hamas and the Islamic *jihad* organization. The Israeli response took the form of the destruction of the infrastructure and of targeted assassinations, carried out by missiles fired from helicopters or aeroplanes, demonstrating an immeasurable military superiority thanks to American support. All this, relayed by television, built up resentment among people throughout the Arab and Muslim world and revealed the powerlessness of the Arab populations. Their governments were unable to engage their own armies in the confrontation because of their patent technological inferiority.

Such was the context of September 11. The attacks on New York and Washington leave their mark, in terms of symbolic and spectacular images, in two ways. First there was the suicide 'bombing', on the pattern of those carried out by the radical Palestinian activists, but on a vastly greater scale. Whereas the Jenin 'martyrs' could only massacre a few dozen victims in a bus or a café in Tel Aviv, the 19 air pirates killed several thousands. The number of dead and wounded was due to the use of sophisticated tactics – the hijacking of aeroplanes. Second, this tactic would show that Israeli and US military technology that could again and again wipe out its conventional targets was not impregnable. It was vulnerable when confronted by audacious and determined adversaries who could not be traced to any one state.

For these two reasons, September 11 has gained enthusiastic support among a section of the population in the Arab and Muslim world, especially the youth, whereas the attacks of 1998 and 2000 had met with only limited approval. Bin Ladin has appeared as a hero, because he has restored the Palestine issue even though he had never before shown any interest outside the Arabian Peninsula. Nevertheless, an uneasy feeling gradually appeared that the scale of the massacre of innocents in the US transformed the attacks into a crime against humanity. As for Arab opinion, people tried to disassociate their 'hero' bin Ladin from the crime, which they attributed to the Israeli Mossad or to sinister activities of the CIA or the FBI. Some even went so far as to claim that the majority of the dead were Muslims! This was an attempt to use victimhood to the benefit of the Arab-Islamic cause. It was the first sign that it was not so easy to transform the initial response into a mass *jihad* against the West. September 11 would not be the first step in this *jihad*. This monumental provocation against the USA was bound to result in retaliation – it did lead to the invasion of the Afghanistan of the Taliban, the sanctuary of bin Ladin. By instigating the assassination of Commander Massoud on 9 September, the Salafi-Jihadists were hoping to deprive the US offensive of its principal pillar of support on the ground, and to draw the US Army into the same lethal trap as the Red Army. This would have been the third phase of the operation, when the Muslim world, galvanized by the *jihad*, would pursue their victorious attacks against a USA that had been incapacitated. This bold plan evaporated immediately following the speedy elimination of the Taliban regime by the US Army and the forces of the Northern Alliance. Although al-Qa'ida still seemed effective in spite of the tracking down of its leaders, its capacity was reduced.

With the failure of bin Ladin's partisans to transform September 11 into a mass *jihad*, some charismatic *ulama* who had supported the Afghan *jihad* against the Soviet Union condemned the attacks on American soil. The perpetrators were denied the designation of 'martyrs', their cause apparently lost. To make up for that, these same religious people followed the example of Shaykh Qardawi, who had emerged from the Egyptian Muslim Brothers and had achieved star quality with his weekly preaching on al-Jazeera television. They praised the suicide bombers in Israel as 'martyrs' within the ranks of a legitimate *jihad*. The Jewish state had, in their view, illegally occupied a portion of the land of Islam and all means to expel them were justified, including the assassination of civilians. This was based on the pretext that, in Israeli society, there were no civilians, as everyone, including women, wore military uniform.

Thus the *jihad* for the Palestinian cause was restored to centre stage. As compensation for the failure of the Jihadists in Afghanistan, it supported the second *Intifada* in its most bloody form. Furthermore, there emerged a widespread movement of solid support manifested by street demonstrations. Thus, Arab political leaders, even those tied to the USA, had to justify the suicide bombers, or at least to find excuses for them. However, in spite of blows delivered against Israel, the end result of the *jihad* into which the second *Intifada* was transformed raised a growing number of questions in Arab circles themselves. Each new outrage gave comfort to Ariel Sharon who presented himself as a representative of the West facing terrorism. The fund of sympathy for Palestinians in Europe and the USA was largely depleted, even amongst those who were most sympathetic to their national claims. The campaign to discredit Yasir Arafat found considerable support, despite the fact that the *ra'is* was received as recently as the autumn of 2000 by the American President. The Israeli bombing has more or less wiped out the administrative machinery of the Palestinian Authority. The political cost of the campaign of the suicide bombers seems to be considerable and its gains questionable. There is only the exaltation of a small minority who have locked themselves into a mentality where terrorism becomes an end in itself.

Bibliography

Bergen, Peter (2001) *Holy War: Inside the Secret World of Osama bin Laden* (London, Weidenfeld).

Cooley, John K. (1999) *Unholy Wars: Afghanistan, America and International Terrorism* (London, Pluto).

Dorronsoro, Gilles (2001) *La Révolution Afghane* (Karthala).

el Berry, Khaled (2002) *La Terre est plus belle que le Paradis* (Lattès).

Kepel, Gilles (2002) *Jihad: The Trail of Political Islam* (London, IB Tauris).

Kepel, Gilles (2003) *Bad Moon Rising: A Chronicle of the Middle East Today* (London, Saqi).

Martinez, Luis (2002) *Civil War in Algeria* (NJ, Columbia University Press).

Rashid, Ahmed (2000) *Taliban* (New Haven, Yale University Press).

Quintan Wiktorowicz

A GENEALOGY OF RADICAL ISLAM

Introduction

A l QAEDA AND THE radical fundamentalists that constitute the new "global jihadi movement" are not theological outliers. They are part of a broader community of Islamists known as "Salafis" (commonly called "Wahhabis").[1] The term "salafi" is used to denote those who follow the example of the companions (*salaf*) of the Prophet Mohammed. Salafis believe that because the companions learned about Islam directly from the Prophet, they commanded a pure understanding of the faith. Subsequent practices, in contrast, were sullied by religious innovations that infected the Muslim community over time. As a result, Muslims must purify the religion by strictly following the Qur'an, the Sunna (path or traditions of the Prophet Mohammed), and the consensus of the companions. Every behavior must be sanctioned by these religious sources.

Although there is consensus among Salafis about this understanding of Islam, there are disagreements over the use of violence. The jihadi faction believes that violence can be used to establish Islamic states and confront the United States and its allies. Nonviolent Salafis, on the other hand, emphatically reject the use of violence and instead emphasize propagation and advice (usually private) to incumbent rulers in the Muslim world.[2] These two groups demarcate the most important fissures within the Salafi community, although there are individuals and movements that do not fall neatly into either, including influential figures like Mohammed Sorour (now in London), Safar al-Hawali, and Salman al-Auda.

Understanding the genealogy of the radical jihadis necessitates identifying the key points of divergence within the Salafi community. Given a common understanding about following the strict model of the Prophet and his companions, what are the major points of disagreement? This article identifies four major points of contention among Salafis: (1) whether Muslims can call leaders apostates and wage jihad against them;

(2) the nature of a "defensive" and global jihad; (3) the permissibility of targeting civilians; and (4) the legitimacy of suicide bombings (what radicals call "martyrdom operations"). How and why did the radicals diverge from the majority of Salafis on these issues? Who supported the divergent ideological trends, and how have these trends evolved over time?

The answers to these questions lie, to a large extent, in the inherently subjective process of religious interpretation whereby immutable religious texts and principles are applied to new circumstances and issues. The Qur'an and the Sunna of the Prophet Mohammed outline numerous rules about politics, economics, society, and individual behavior, but they do not directly respond to many questions relevant to the modern period. As a result, Salafis (and other Muslims) ask themselves what the Prophet would do if he were alive today. Given the way he lived his life and the principles he followed, how would he respond to the issues facing contemporary society? It is a process of extrapolation based on independent judgment (*ijtihad*) and reasoning by analogy (*qiyas*). So, for example, what would the Prophet say about the use of weapons of mass destruction? Clearly neither the Qur'an nor the Sunna speaks directly to this issue. Some radicals, however, argue that there is evidence that the Prophet would have supported the use of weapons of mass destruction if he were alive today. Specifically, they cite the siege of Ta'if in which the Prophet authorized the use of a catapult against a walled city where enemy fighters mixed with civilians, what jihadis call the "weapon of mass destruction of his day."[3] This process of reasoning invariably leads to differences of opinion about how the Prophet would respond to current issues.

The subjective nature of this process is nicely captured by a member of the Shura Council and Military Wing of the Gamiyya Islamiyya in Egypt during a group interview in June 2002 in which leaders explained why they abandoned the violent struggle initiated by the movement during the earlier 1990s:

> Shari'ah [the straight path of Islam, Islamic law] cannot be separated from reality. You must read both the reality and the relevant text before applying the right verses to the appropriate reality. Mistakes stem from the fact that the right text is sometimes applied on irrelevant reality.[4]

The leaders cited the decision by certain members of the movement to seize property belonging to Coptic Christians as an example. One responded that, "The person who did this used to apply certain texts to the wrong reality. The Islamic ruling on seizing loot belonging to the infidels applies to wars against the infidels, such as the war against the Jews in 1973 because it was a clear war. As for applying this principle to fellow citizens who are a part of this country's fabric, it is wrong."[5]

In tracing the evolution of jihadi thought over the past few decades, it appears that many of the shifts and changes are the result of new understandings about context rather than new readings of the religious texts and concomitant principles. Jihadis continue to use the same texts, quotes, and religious evidence as other Salafis, but they have developed new understandings about context and concepts such as "belief," "defense against aggression," and "civilians." The evolution of jihadi thought is less about changing principles embedded in the religious texts than the ways in which these principles are operative in the contemporary period.

This is not to argue that theology is completely irrelevant. Certainly, individual thinkers like Taqi al-Din Ibn Taymiyya (1263–1328), Muhammad bin Abdul Wahhab (1703–1792), Mawlana Abul A'la Mawdudi (1903–1979), and Sayyid Qutb (1906–1966) offered new understandings of the religious texts that challenged dominant interpretations, but subsequent thinkers, for the most part, merely adapted these understandings to new issues, often stretching them to their logical conclusion in a way that increased the scope of permissible violence.

Charges of apostasy (*takfir*) and waging jihad at home

The vast majority of Muslims are conservative in their approach to declaring someone an apostate, a process known as *takfir*. The seriousness of the endeavor is underscored by a number of Qur'anic cautionary notes and stories about the Prophet. A few examples include:

> If a Muslim calls another *kafir* [unbeliever], then if he is a *kafir* let it be so; otherwise, he [the caller] is himself a *kafir*. (saying of the Prophet from Abu Dawud, *Book of Sunna*, edition published by Qur'an Mahal, Karachi, vol. iii, p. 484)

> No man accuses another man of being a sinner, or of being a *kafir*, but it reflects back on him if the other is not as he called him. (saying of the Prophet from Bukhari, *Book of Ethics*; Book 78, ch. 44)

> Withhold [your tongues] from those who say "There is no god but Allah" – do not call them *kafir*. Whoever calls a reciter of "There is no god but Allah" as a *kafir*, is nearer to being a *kafir* himself. (reported from Ibn Umar)[6]

Most Muslims believe that, as the Prophet said, "whoever accuses a believer of disbelief, it is as if he killed him."[7] Therefore, so long as a leader has a "mustard seed of faith" and implements the prayer, he is still considered a Muslim. (Throughout this article, the pronoun "he" is used because this is the jihadi standard. It must be recognized, however, that it encompasses both males and females.) From this perspective, a leader only becomes an apostate if he willingly implements non-Islamic law, understands that it does not represent Islam, and announces that it is superior to Islam. Otherwise, the leader could be ignorant, coerced, or driven by self-interest, failings that signify sinfulness, not apostasy. This is the line of argument represented by the Salafi mainstream.[8]

This reading of apostasy requires absolute proof of intentions, something that is nearly impossible unless the ruler publicly announces his disbelief. Nonviolent Salafis have, in fact, created a complex decision-making tree for excommunication that makes it extremely difficult to declare someone an apostate. They may charge a person with committing an *act* of apostasy, but unless that individual willingly proclaims that the act is Islamic, after clear evidence to the contrary, or announces that it is superior to Islam, he remains a Muslim. The culprit may go to Hell if he does not repent before dying, but that is for God to decide.

The nonviolent Salafis also believe it is forbidden to fight against rulers. Most cite the well-accepted prohibition against killing other Muslims, as outlined in Qur'an 4:92: "It is not for a believer to kill a believer unless (it be) by mistake."

The current jihadi argument about apostasy developed out of Egyptian and Saudi intellectual streams. The Egyptian lineage has its roots in British-controlled India. Conservative Indian Muslims were concerned that many Hindu converts to Islam were retaining earlier cultural practices and that Shi'ism and the British were undermining the purity of Sunni Islam. Hardliners reacted by drawing a sharp distinction between "true believers" and the infidels, which included Muslims who deviated from a rigid interpretation of Islam (apostates). Radical Sunni groups supporting this Manichean perspective emerged in Northern India during the 1820s and 1830s, including a movement led by Sayyid Ahmad Rai-Barelvi.[9] The conservative bent to these groups prompted the British to denote them as "Wahhabis" after the puritanical sect found on the Arabian Peninsula.

These conservatives were the intellectual predecessors to Mawlana Abul A'la Mawdudi, who in the 1930s seemed to give a "modernist cast to Sayyid Ahmad Rai-Barelvi's approach."[10] Whereas Rai-Barelvi and others rejected anything Western as antithetical to Islam, Mawdudi sought to appropriate Western technology, science, and other aspects of modernity while returning to the fundamentals of Islam. For modernists, the positive aspects of the West could be used to strengthen the Muslim community against Western imperialism. At the same time, despite this difference with earlier conservatives, Mawdudi adopted the strict distinction between belief and disbelief developed by Rai-Barelvi and his ilk.

Mawdudi's work drew extensively from Taqi al-Din Ibn Taymiyya, the best known medieval Salafi scholar, particularly his writings on the sovereignty of God.[11] One of Ibn Taymiyya's most important contributions to Salafi thought is his elaboration of the concept of *tawhid* – the unity of God. He divided the unity of God into two categories: the unity of lordship and the unity of worship. The former refers to belief in God as the sole sovereign and creator of the universe. All Muslims readily accept this. The second is affirmation of God as the only object of worship and obedience. Ibn Taymiyya reasoned that this latter component of divine unity necessitates following God's laws. The use of human-made laws is tantamount to obeying or worshipping other than God and thus apostasy. Mawdudi adopted this position and drew a sharp bifurcation between the "party of God" and the "party of Satan," which included Muslims who adhered to human-made law.

In making this argument, Mawdudi introduced his concept of "the modern jahiliyya" (circa 1939). The term "jahiliyya" refers to the "period of ignorance" (or period of paganism) preceding the advent of Islam. He argued that the deviations of self-proclaimed Muslims, the influence of imperialist powers, and the use of non-Islamic laws were akin to this earlier period of ignorance. For Mawdudi, true Muslims must struggle against this ignorance, just as the Prophet and his companions struggled against the paganism of the dominant Quraysh tribe in Mecca. In 1941, he formed the Jamaat-i-Islami as the spearhead of this struggle, a vanguard viewed as necessary to promote God's sovereignty on Earth.[12]

Mawdudi's importance for the Egyptian stream is his impact on Sayyid Qutb, often seen as the godfather of revolutionary Sunni Islam (he was executed by Nasser in 1966).[13] Qutb read Mawdudi's most influential works, including *Jihad in Islam,*

Islam and Jahiliyya, and *Principles of Islamic Government*, which were translated into Arabic beginning in the 1950s. A more direct connection existed through one of Mawdudi's most important protégés, Abdul Hasan Ali Nadvi, who was a central figure in transmitting his mentor's theories to the Arab world. In 1950, Nadvi wrote *What Did the World Lose Due to the Decline of Islam?*, a book published in Arabic that expounded on Mawdudi's theory of modern jahiliyya. When he first traveled to the Middle East in 1951, Nadvi met with Qutb, who had already read his book. Both Mawdudi and Nadvi are quoted at length in Qutb's *In the Shade of the Qu'ran*, published in 1953.[14]

In *In the Shade of the Qu'ran*, Qutb outlines his view of the modern jahiliyya, which provides the cornerstone for declaring rulers apostates and waging jihad.

> Jahiliyya (barbarity) signifies the domination (hakamiyya) of man over man, or rather the subservience to man rather than to Allah. It denotes rejection of the divinity of God and the adulation of mortals. In this sense, jahiliyya is not just a specific historical period (referring to the era preceding the advent of Islam), but a state of affairs. Such a state of human affairs existed in the past, exists today, and may exist in the future, taking the form of jahiliyya, that mirror-image and sword enemy of Islam. In any time and place human beings face that clear-cut choice: either to observe the Law of Allah in its entirety, or to apply laws laid down by man of one sort or another. In the latter case, they are in a state of jahiliyya. Man is at the crossroads and that is the choice: Islam or jahiliyya. Modern-style jahiliyya in the industrialized societies of Europe and America is essentially similar to the old-time jahiliyya in pagan and nomadic Arabia. For in both systems, man is under the dominion of man rather than Allah.[15]

Qutb brought together Mawdudi's "modern jahiliyya" and Ibn Taymiyya's argument that the unity of God requires that Muslims follow divine law, creating a synthesis that reinforced the stark distinction between the Party of God and the Party of Satan: all those who do not put faith into action through an Islamic legal system and strictly obey the commands of God are part of the modern jahiliyya and no longer Muslims. In the Middle Eastern context, this meant apostasy because most members of the "jahiliyya community" were born Muslims.

Qutb's solution to the modern jahiliyya, however, was a stark departure from Mawdudi, who sought to work within the system. Whereas Mawdudi formed a political party and social movement to promote reform, Qutb advocated jihad to establish an Islamic state. In doing so, he argued against well-established Islamic legal opinions that jihad was primarily a struggle against the soul (*jihad al-nafs*) or a defensive war to protect the Muslim community. In a kind of Islamic liberation theology, he argued that force was necessary to remove the chains of oppression so that Islamic truth could predominate. Even more importantly, because the rulers in the Muslim world used non-Islamic legal codes, they were part of the modern jahiliyya and therefore not real Muslims. As infidels, they could be fought and removed from power, because the primary objective of Muslims is to establish God's rule on earth (divine *hukm*).

Qutb's argument found its most infamous manifestation in Mohammed al-Faraj's *The Neglected Duty*.[16] Faraj was a member of Islamic Jihad and used the book as a kind of internal discussion paper to explain and defend the group's ideology.[17] The book uses several lines of argument that have become staples of jihadi discourse. First, Faraj draws on Ibn Taymiyya to argue for the centrality of jihad in faith. He uses an assortment of quotes and hadiths (stories about the Prophet) in an effort to demonstrate that "jihad is second only to belief" in Islam. This is used to elevate the importance of jihad as a "pillar of Islam," a mandatory requirement to be a Muslim. Faraj argues that jihad has become "the neglected duty" (a phrase adopted by today's jihadis), something that must be resurrected as a central pillar of the faith.

Second, he reiterates Qutb's argument that rulers who do not implement Islamic law are unbelievers and must be removed from power. This is based on a Qur'anic verse consistently cited by Al Qaeda: "Whoever does not rule by what God hath sent down – they are unbelievers" (Qur'an 5:48). In making this argument, Faraj turns to Ibn Taymiyya's fatwa against the Mongols (or Tatars). As they conquered Muslim territory, the Mongols converted to Islam, thus raising questions about whether combat against them was a legitimate jihad. Ibn Taymiyya responded by arguing that someone who professes to be a Muslim is no longer a believer if he fails to uphold Islamic law or breaks any number of major injunctions concerning society and behavior. As Johannes Jansen notes, "The list of injunctions he draws is quite long; and it is not altogether clear how many nonapplied injunctions bring the ruler (or the individual believer) to the point of no return. When does he become an apostate to be combated?"[18] For the jihadis, the rationale was clear: the Mongols continued to implement the Yasa code of Genghis Khan and were therefore no longer Muslim because they did not adhere to the unity of worship. Jihadis viewed (and continue to view) this as analogous to contemporary states where rulers have adopted Western legal codes rather than Islamic law alone.

Qutb's influence on Faraj and other Egyptian jihadis is unquestionable. He inspired an assortment of radical groups, including The Islamic Liberation Organization, Takfir wal Hijra (Excommunication and Flight), Salvation from Hell, the Gamiyya Islamiyya (Islamic Group), and Islamic Jihad. He also had an important impact on two Egyptian thinkers who have been critical for the international jihadi movement. The first is Omar Abdul Rahman, the former mufti of Islamic Jihad and the Gamiyya Islamiyya who is currently serving a life sentence for conspiracy to commit terrorism in the United States. As a graduate from al-Azhar University, Rahman had substantial cachet among the radicals inspired by Qutb. Because most of his pronouncements were oral (he is blind), there is little textual data about his views. He did, however, fervidly support Qutb's emphasis on the necessity of God's governance on earth and the use of jihad to remove apostate rulers. Rahman also argued that, "the enemy who is at the forefront of the work against Islam is America and the allies."[19] For many jihadis, Rahman replaced Abdullah Azzam, one of Al Qaeda's founders, as the theological leader of the global jihad after the latter was assassinated in 1989. His incarceration, of course, has diminished this role.

Qutb also dramatically impacted Ayman Zawhiri, Al Qaeda's second in command. In his *Knights under the Prophet's Banner*, Zawahiri calls Qutb "the most prominent theoretician of the fundamentalist movements."[20] For Zawahiri, Qutb's greatest contribution seems to have been that,

> He affirmed that the issue of unification [tawhid] in Islam is important and that the battle between Islam and its enemies is primarily an ideological

one over the issue of unification. It is also a battle over to whom authority and power should belong – to God's course and the shari'ah, to man-made laws and material principles, or to those who claim to be intermediaries between the Creator and mankind.... This affirmation greatly helped the Islamic movement to know and define its enemies.

Sayyid Qutub's [sic] call for loyalty to God's oneness and to acknowledge God's sole authority and sovereignty was the spark that ignited the Islamic revolution against the enemies of Islam at home and abroad. The bloody chapters of this revolution continue to unfold day after day.[21]

Zawahiri adopted both Qutb's Manichean view of the world and his unwavering desire to establish an Islamic state at any cost, using violence if necessary. This dichotomous struggle for God's sovereignty on earth eliminates the middle ground and sets the stage for a millennial, eschatological battle between good and evil.

Qutb's arguments inform jihadis in other countries as well. Many of his disciples fled Egypt during the massive crackdown by Nasser in the 1960s and moved to Saudi Arabia, where at least a few prominent thinkers took positions as university professors. Sayyid Qutb's brother, Mohammed, is perhaps the best example. In 1964, he published *The Jahiliyya of the Twentieth Century*, which rearticulated Sayyid's arguments (radicals often cite his *Islam: The Misunderstood Religion* as influential as well).[22] Not only did Mohammed Qutb teach Osama bin Laden at university, but he taught some future Islamist dissidents as well, including Safar al-Hawali. The Saudi government tolerated (perhaps even supported) the spread of Qutb's ideology because it coincided with their antipathy toward Nasser and foreign policy objectives vis-à-vis Egypt.

Although it is tempting to place all the blame on Sayyid Qutb for the radicalization of Islamism, the Saudis developed their own jihadi intellectual stream through Ibn Wahhab, who remains extremely influential. The Saudi jihadis recognize Qutb as a good Muslim who did good work, but they do not rely on him to the same extent as the Egyptian groups, instead using Ibn Wahhab as their direct pipeline to Ibn Taymiyya,[23] although there is some evidence that Taymiyya was less of an influence on Ibn Wahhab than is conventionally thought.[24]

Ibn Wahhab's most relevant work for the radicals is a small book titled *The Ten Voiders [or Nullifiers] of Islam* (see Table 1), which outlines ten things that automatically expel someone from the religion.[25] Three are of particular importance for the jihadis. First, a Muslim becomes a disbeliever if he associates someone or something in worshipping God. During his life, Ibn Wahhab was combating some Islamic practices he viewed as deviant polytheism, such as Sufism. Given the jihadis' emphasis on Ibn Taymiyya's argument about the unity of worship, this "voider" is also used to condemn any ruler who uses non-Islamic law.

Second, any Muslim who judges by "other than what God revealed" and believes this is superior to divine law is an apostate. For nonviolent Salafis, the two parts of this "voider" are critical: to be an apostate a ruler must not only implement non-Islamic law but also believe he is using legal means that are better than Islam. Unless the leader flagrantly admits that he has rejected Islam or believes in the supremacy of human-made law (extremely unlikely), he remains a Muslim.[26]

Table 1 The ten voiders according to Ibn Wahhab (i.e., automatic apostasy)

1)   Polytheism (associating others with God in worship)

2)   Using mediators for God (for example, praying to saints)

3)   Doubting that non-Muslims are disbelievers

4)   Judging by non-Islamic laws and believing these are superior to divine law

5)   Hating anything the Prophet Mohammed practiced

6)   Mocking Islam or the Prophet Mohammed

7)   Using or supporting magic

8)   Supporting or helping non-believers against Muslims

9)   Believing that someone has the right to stop practicing Islam

10) Turning away from Islam by not studying or practicing it

Jihadis, on the other hand, argue that actions are grounds for apostasy. For radicals, there are certain things about Islam that are "known by necessity," such as the ten voiders (some radicals use a much longer list). As a result, if a leader violates one of these, it is evidence of apostasy because he willingly flouts God's will. Like Qutb and the Egyptian radicals, the Saudi jihadis root this argument in Ibn Taymiyya's perspective on the unity of God: it requires both belief in the Creator as well as action (obeying and worshipping God).

Third, supporting or helping nonbelievers against Muslims is apostasy. This one, above all others, seems to have become the central "evidence" used by Al Qaeda to charge regimes in the Muslim world with apostasy. The movement and its supporters continually refer to the same Qur'anic verse: "O you who believe! Take not the Jews and Christians for your friends and protectors [*awliya'*]; they are but friends and protectors to each other" (Qur'an 5:51). It is important to note that there is an important grammatical ambiguity in this verse: it uses the term "wali" (pl. *awliya'*), which is an old Arabic technical term for patron, although in contemporary usage it has developed a broader connotation.[27] The jihadis use an expansive definition of *wali* to include virtually any relationship with non-Muslims.

The jihadis cite, in particular, the Saudi regime's decision to allow American troops in the kingdom to fight Iraq in 1990–1991. This was seen as taking nonbelievers as friends and helping them in a war against other Muslims (though Al Qaeda would never view Saddam Hussein as a Muslim). Bin Laden makes direct reference to this in his 1996 "Declaration of War": "The regime betrayed the Ummah [Muslim community] and joined the Kufr [unbelievers], assisting and helping them against the Muslims. It is well known that this is one of the ten 'voiders' of Islam, deeds of de-Islamisation" (his use of the term "voider" comes from Ibn Wahhab).[28]

The terms "helping" and "supporting" are inherently subjective, and Al Qaeda uses this to create an expansive understanding that includes any kind of support for the United States in its "war on terrorism." Even a word of support is considered apostasy. Take the following statement from a bin Laden tape that emerged in February 2003 as the United States was positioning to invade Iraq:

We also point out that whosoever supported the United States, including the hypocrites of Iraq or the rulers of Arab countries, those who approved their actions and followed them in this crusade war by fighting with them or providing bases and administrative support, or any form of support, even by words, to kill the Muslims in Iraq, should know that they are apostates and outside the community of Muslims. It is permissible to spill their blood and take their property. God says, "O ye who believe! Take not the Jews and the Christians for your friends and protectors: they are but friends and protectors to each other."[29]

Although it is difficult to verify, it seems that the radicalization of the Saudi Salafis comes from three sources, in addition to Ibn Wahhab himself. First, there were always some radical elements among the Saudi Salafis, what Guido Steinberg refers to as the "radical wing" of the Wahhabiyya. These elements have existed since at least the 1920s and joined the Ikhwan revolts in 1928–1929. Second, Qutb's influence was felt through his books as well as Egyptians working and teaching in Saudi Arabia after the Nasser crackdown against Islamists.[30] Third, there was a radicalization process as a result of the war against the Soviets in Afghanistan. The conflict brought together Egyptians, Saudis, and other nationalities in a conflict zone where they learned about Islam in a context of violence. This period also witnessed the influence of more radical elements coming out of the Deobandi madrasa system in Pakistan. This provided greater opportunity for exposure to the jihadi elements from Egypt and elsewhere, which likely shifted the ideology of some of the Saudi fighters. Prior to that experience, Saudi Salafis were, for the most part, pro-regime, often ferociously so because the regime supported Salafism and helped export it as part of the kingdom's foreign policy. It took Afghanistan to significantly shake that support (exacerbated in the immediate aftermath by the stationing of American troops in Saudi Arabia).

Global jihad

In Islam, there are two types of external jihad: offensive and defensive. In Islamic jurisprudence, the offensive jihad functions to promote the spread of Islam, enlightenment, and civility to the *dar al-harb* (domain of war). In most contemporary interpretations, the offensive jihad can only be waged under the leadership of the caliph (successor to the Prophet), and it is tempered by truces and various reciprocal agreements between the Islamic state and non-Muslim governments, such as guaranteed freedom of worship for Muslim minorities. Today, very few Islamists focus on this form of jihad.

The defensive jihad (*jihad al-dafaʿa*), however, is a widely accepted concept that is analogous to international norms of self-defense and Judeo-Christian just war theory.[31] According to most Islamic scholars, when an outside force invades Muslim territory it is incumbent on all Muslims to wage jihad to protect the faith and the faithful. Mutual protection is seen as a religious obligation intended to ensure the survival of the global Muslim community. At the root of defensive jihad is a theological emphasis on justness, as embodied in chapter 6, verse 151 of the Qur'an: "Do not slay the soul sanctified by God except for just cause." Defending the faith-based community against external aggression is considered a just cause *par excellence*.

Although Muslim scholars almost uniformly agree that a defensive jihad is an obligation for Muslims, the issue remained relatively dormant until the Soviet invasion of Afghanistan in 1979. At the time, the majority of scholars had accepted the argument that jihad should focus on the struggle of the soul and inner purification, what has been dubbed "the greater jihad."[32] For the jihadis, the most important objective was to challenge this perspective and inspire participation in the war against the Soviets on behalf of Muslim brothers and sisters in Afghanistan. As a result, much of the writing at this time included extensive exhortations to jihad that outlined both the duty and glory of participation.

In making this argument, jihadis relied extensively on Ibn Taymiyya, whose contribution to the ideology of jihad has more to do with the religious and moral elements of jihad rather than legalistic issues related to just war or rules of engagement in combat.[33] In his writings, he argued that, "The command to participate in jihad and the mention of its merits occur innumerable times in the Koran and Sunna. Therefore it is the best voluntary [religious] act that man can perform. All scholars agree that it is better than the hajj (greater pilgrimage) and the ʿumra (lesser pilgrimage) [performed at a time other than the Hajj], than voluntary salat [prayer] and voluntary fasting, as the Koran and Sunna indicate. The Prophet, Peace be upon him, has said: *'The head of the affair is Islam, its central pillar is the salat and its summit is the jihad.'* And he has said: *'In Paradise there are a hundred grades with intervals as wide as the distance between the sky and earth. All these God prepared for those who take part in jihad'.*"[34] [original italics]

Jihadis also drew extensively from the work of Ibn Nuhaas al-Demyati (d. 1412). In *Advice to Those Who Abstain from Fighting in the Way of Allah*, Ibn Nuhaas methodically addresses the various concerns of those who resist participating in jihad.[35] He touches on fears of death; concern for children, spouses, relatives, friends, social status, and lineage; love for material things; and desire to improve oneself before participating in battle. For each of these, Ibn Nuhaas quotes the Qurʾan and Sunna of the Prophet to argue that this life means nothing when compared with the hereafter.

Abdullah Azzam is the most important figure to resurrect active participation in defensive jihad in the contemporary period. Following in the tradition of Ibn Taymiyya and Ibn Nuhaas, parts of his writings are intended to inspire participation. In his *Join the Caravan*, he opens by arguing that, "Anybody who looks into the state of the Muslims today will find that their greatest misfortune is their abandonment of Jihad (due to love of this world and abhorrence of death)."[36] To muster support, Azzam turns to Qurʾanic verses consistently cited by Al Qaeda today, such as, "Proscribed for you is fighting, though it be hateful to you. Yet it may happen that you will hate a thing which is better for you; and it may happen that you will love a thing which is worse for you. God knows and you know not" (Qurʾan 2:216).

He also makes a more legalistic argument to demonstrate that jihad is an undeniable duty. Azzam uses Ibn Taymiyya's distinction between collective and individual duties (*fard kifayah* and *fard ʿayn*) in Islam. Collective duties are obligations that can be fulfilled by a group of Muslims on behalf of the entire Muslim community. Individual duties are those that each and every Muslim must fulfill to avoid falling into sin. In the context of jihad, Ibn Taymiyya argued that, "jihad is obligatory if it is carried out on our initiative and also if it is waged as defense. If we take the initiative, it is a collective duty [which means that] if it is fulfilled by a sufficient number [of Muslims], the obligation lapses for all others and the merit goes to those who have fulfilled it … . But if the enemy wants to attack the Muslims, then repelling him becomes a[n] [individual] duty for all those under attack and for the others in order to help him."[37]

Azzam adopted Ibn Taymiyya's reasoning and argued that if a group of Muslims trying to fulfill a duty to repel aggressors fails to do so alone, it becomes an individual obligation for those nearest the conflict zone:

> Ibn 'Abidin, the Hanafi scholar says, "(Jihad is) fard 'ayn [an individual obligation] when the enemy has attacked any of the Islamic heartland, at which point it becomes fard 'ayn on those close to the enemy…. As for those beyond them, at some distance from the enemy, it is fard kifayah [a collective duty] for them unless they are needed. The need arises when those close to the enemy fail to counter the enemy, or if they do not fail but are negligent and fail to perform jihad. In that case it becomes obligatory on those around them – fard 'ayn, just like prayer and fasting, and they may not abandon it. (The circle of people on whom jihad is fard 'ayn expands) until in this way, it becomes compulsory on the entire people of Islam, of the West and the East.[38] (original sentence structure from translation)

According to Azzam, the Afghans could not fulfill the obligation without help from other Muslims: "the jihad is in need of men and the inhabitants of Afghanistan have not met the requirement which is to expel the Disbelievers from Afghanistan. In this case, the communal obligation (fard kifayah) is overturned. It becomes individually obligatory (fard 'ayn) in Afghanistan, and remains so until enough Mujahideen [holy warriors] have gathered to expel the communists in which case it again becomes fard kifayah."[39]

Azzam also argues that this obligation is eternal. In making this claim, he is clearly influenced by Sayyid Qutb and quotes the following passage from Qutb's writing:

> If Jihad had been a transitory phenomenon in the life of the Muslim Ummah, all these sections of the Qur'anic text would not be flooded with this type of verse! Likewise, so much of the sunnah [sic] of the Messenger of Allah (may Allah bless him and grant him peace), would not be occupied with such matters…. If Jihad were a passing phenomenon of Islam, the Messenger of Allah (may Allah bless him and grant him peace) would not have said the following words to every Muslim until the Day of Judgment, "Whoever dies neither having fought (in Jihad), nor having made up his mind to do so, dies on a branch of hypocrisy."[40]

So, Azzam concludes, the jihad in Afghanistan is an eternal individual obligation. Under these circumstances, it is elevated to the status of the five pillars of Islam, necessary to be a Muslim. Azzam, like Al Qaeda later, uses a quote from Ibn Taymiyya to emphasize the importance of the defensive jihad as a religious obligation: "As for the occupying enemy who is spoiling the religion and the world, there is nothing more compulsory after faith (iman) than repelling him."[41] Building on this, Azzam argues that, "everyone not performing jihad today is forsaking a duty, just like the one who eats during the days of Ramadan without excuse, or the rich person who withholds the Zakat [religiously obligated charity] from his wealth." This means that, "The obligation of jihad today remains fard 'ayn until the liberation of the last piece of land which was in the hands of Muslims but has been occupied by the Disbelievers" (such as Spain, for example). This argument sets the stage for what Olivier Roy has termed "the nomadic jihad," an eternal struggle to "defend" Muslims from the disbelievers.[42]

The influence on Al Qaeda's current thinking is unmistakable. This is not surprising given that Azzam helped found Al Qaeda and provided the underlying rationale for the movement in an April 1988 article titled "The Solid Base" (al-Qaʾida al-Bulba), published in al-Jihad. Various Al Qaeda statements extend Azzam's argument about the obligations of the nomadic jihad to justify attacks against the United States. To apply this argument, however, the jihadis have to demonstrate that the Americans are occupying Muslim land. For bin Laden, this rationale became clear in 1990 after King Fahd ignored his offer to use Afghan war veterans to repel Saddam and instead authorized the presence of American troops in Saudi Arabia. In a 1998 fatwa, bin Laden and several other jihadis argued that, "for over seven years the United States has been occupying the lands of Islam in the holiest of places, the Arabian Peninsula, plundering its riches, dictating to its rulers, humiliating its people, terrorizing its neighbors, and turning its bases in the Peninsula into a spearhead through which to fight the neighboring Muslim peoples. If some people have formerly debated the fact of the occupation, all the people of the Peninsula have now acknowledged it."[43]

In this argument, the jihadis received support from less radical Islamists like Safar al-Hawali and Salman al-Auda, who opposed the American presence. In his 1996 "Declaration of War," for example, bin Laden explicitly references Hawali: "The imprisoned Sheikh Safar al-Hawali, may Allah hasten his release, wrote a book of seventy pages; in it he presented evidence and proof that the presence of the Americans in the Arab Peninsula is a pre-planned military occupation."[44]

Bin Laden and Al Qaeda also found comfort with the oppositional Islamists who signed the Memorandum of Advice in July 1992, which represented an unprecedented public critique of the Saudi regime's domestic and foreign policies.[45] Although many of these oppositional clerics do not support Al Qaeda's tactics and use of violence, their critique of the regime and overall opposition to the U.S. presence in the kingdom provided the fodder bin Laden needed to frame America as an occupying force supported by an un-Islamic regime, thereby justifying a defensive jihad.

The critical need for a defensive posture to legitimize jihad is apparent in Al Qaeda's penchant for framing all its actions as defensive. In a 1998 interview, bin Laden argued that, "We are carrying out the mission of the Prophet Muhammad (peace be upon him). The mission is to spread the word of God, not to indulge in massacring people. We ourselves are the target of killings, destruction, and atrocities. We are only defending ourselves. This is a defensive jihad. We want to defend our people and our land. That is why we say, if we don't get security, the Americans, too, would not get security. This is the simple formula that even an American child can understand. Live and let live."[46]

For most jihadis, this "defensive argument" was absolutely necessary to legitimate 11 September in particular. For example, immediately after the 11 September attacks, Abu Hamza al-Misri, a radical Al Qaeda supporter in London, argued that it "was done in self defense. If they did it for that reason then they are justified." He added that, "If you ask how could it be self defense in doing this in America, it is as much as it was in self defense in Hiroshima."[47]

Killing civilians[48]

The Qur'an and Sunna of the Prophet Mohammed are replete with enjoinments against killing civilians. Nonviolent Salafis and other Muslims repeatedly emphasize the following pieces of religious evidence to argue for a prohibition against targeting noncombatants:

> We decreed for the Children of Israel that whosoever kills a human being for other than manslaughter or corruption in the earth, it shall be as if he had killed all mankind, and whoso saves the life of one, it shall be as if he had saved the life of all mankind. (Qur'an 5:32)

> And fight in God's cause against those who wage war against you, but do not transgress, for God loves not the transgressors. (Qur'an 2:190)

> Set out for jihad in the name of Allah and for the sake of Allah. Do not lay hands on the old verging on death, on women, children and babes. Do not steal anything from the booty and collect together all that falls to your lot in the battlefield and do good, for Allah loves the virtuous and the pious. (Sunna of the Prophet Mohammed)

> Stop, O people, that I may give you ten rules for your guidance in the battlefield. Do not commit treachery or deviate from the right path. You must not mutilate dead bodies. Neither kill a child, nor a woman, nor an aged man. Bring no harm to the trees, nor burn them with fire, especially those which are fruitful. Slay not any of the enemy's flock, save for your food. You are likely to pass by people who have devoted their lives to monastic services; leave them alone. (Instructions given by Abu Bakr, the first caliph or successor to the Prophet Muhammed, to a Muslim army setting out to battle against the Byzantine Empire in Syria)

Although nonviolent Salafis view this kind of religious evidence as a prohibition against *purposely* targeting civilians, they do recognize the possibility of civilian casualties in the course of warfare, considered an acceptable consequence in a legitimate jihad. Islamic fighters must do everything they can to limit noncombatant casualties, but "collateral damage" (to use Western terminology) is often inevitable. This is particularly the case where the enemy uses human shields. Under these circumstances, the Islamic fighters are permitted to attack, and the responsibility for noncombatant deaths lies with the enemy.

From this perspective, only combatants can be targeted. This includes not only soldiers, political leaders responsible for waging war, and intelligence officers, but support staff outside the military and political structure as well, such as advisors who help plan the war. Although they may not be directly involved in actual fighting and combat, support personnel are considered part of the war effort, thereby making them legitimate targets.

The move toward civilian targeting seems to be a recent development with little precedent. Neither Sayyid Qutb nor Ibn Wahhab argued that civilians could be targeted during combat and war, and there was little discussion about the subject until the 1990s. As a result, Al Qaeda has reached directly back to the example of the Prophet and classical and medieval scholars such as Ibn Taymiyya, Ibn Kathir, Ibn al-Qayyim, Shawkani, Ibn al-Qasim, and Ibn Qudamah. Given the vast religious evidence from the Qur'an and Sunna emphasizing the sanctity of life and limiting attacks against noncombatants, Al Qaeda could hardly argue against noncombatant immunity. But it has broken new ground over the past decade or so to develop an expanded understanding about permissible targets in war.

The jihadi debate about civilian targeting began in the mid-1990s in response to the Algerian civil war, which erupted after the regime cancelled Parliamentary elections in January 1992 as it became clear that the Islamic Salvation Front would dominate the new government.[49] Following the coup, Islamist rebels limited attacks to government officials, military personnel, and the police. The scope and tenor of the conflict, however, escalated dramatically in 1993 with the emergence of the Armed Islamic Group (Groupes Islamiques Armé or GIA). Initially, the GIA launched broader attacks against the security services and assassinated junior ministers and members of the National Consultative Council (formed by President Mohammed Boudiaf to provide a democratic façade following the coup).

During this period, there is some evidence that bin Laden and Al Qaeda provided limited support to the GIA through Qamareddin Kharban, the leader of the "Algerian Afghans" (Algerians who had fought in Afghanistan against the Soviets). This included financial support; Al Qaeda fighters sent to Algeria; and theological cover through Al Qaeda-linked scholars like Abu Qatada, who also helped publish and distribute the GIA's *al-Ansar* bulletin (in conjunction with Abu Musab) in London.[50]

This growing relationship changed dramatically in 1996 when Antar Zouabri became the emir of the GIA. He initiated his new leadership position by issuing a fatwa charging the entire society with apostasy and authorizing attacks against any Algerian who refused to join or aid the GIA (including other armed Islamist groups). In this manner, Zouabri took Qutb's Manichean view of the world to an extreme: you are either with the GIA and thus Islamic truth or against it and thus God. The position was summed up in a GIA communiqué posted in an Algiers suburb in 1997: "There is no neutrality in this war we are waging. With the exception of those who are with us, all others are apostates and deserve to die."[51]

The fatwa shifted GIA operations away from the state and toward softer targets in society, eventually leading to widespread civilian massacres. Whereas civilians comprised only 10% of the casualties in 1992, by 1997 this figure rose to 84%.[52] Thousands were massacred. Ordinary citizens were maimed, decapitated, and burned alive. According to GIA chief Abou el-Moudhir, all of these people "have become the enemies of our fighters, from the youngest of their children to the oldest of their elderly."[53] Although there is some evidence of possible regime complicity in a few attacks, the GIA claimed responsibility for most of them.

The underlying justification for the massacres portended the later Al Qaeda justification for 11 September and purposeful civilian targeting: individuals who support the government act as surrogates and representatives of the enemy; they are thus legitimate targets. Take the GIA's rationale for attacking journalists and editors:

> The rotten apostate regime did not stop using the mercenary media to cover its crimes and rationalize its aggression. This has turned all written, seen, and heard media outlets into a tool of aggression spreading lies and rumors. It would have been an obligation for these writers to stand with their nation in these hard times and embrace the blessed jihad, but instead they have turned their pens into swords defending the low lives of apostasy and treason. Based on that, mujahidin consider every reporter and journalist working for radio and television as no different than regime apostates. GIA calls on every reporter working there to immediately stop work, otherwise the group will continue hitting hard those who do not comply. Whoever fights us with the pen will be fought with the sword.[54]

In other words, "civilian" journalists and editors were no longer noncombatants because they served the interest of the government.

The same kind of reasoning was used to attack teachers and school children: by attending government-controlled schools, they signaled support for the regime. In a statement published in the Arabic daily *al-Hayat*, the GIA warned that those who "continue their studies are helping the tyrant to ensure stability and thereby are not accomplishing the jihad." They are considered heretics and deserve death.[55]

More broadly, the GIA argued that any Algerian who did not support the GIA was tacitly supporting the regime, thereby removing their noncombatant immunity. The menu of legitimate targets was thus expanded to include almost the entire society.

The massacres sparked a debate within international jihadi circles. Supporters were frustrated by the GIA's apparent unwillingness to elaborate on the religious justification for their attacks. Some supporters initially denied GIA involvement, dismissing such claims as government propaganda (Abu Hamza al-Misri is a case in point, although he eventually withdrew his support for the movement in 1997). But when it became clear that Algerian jihadis were involved, there was widespread condemnation and opposition from the international jihadi network. Abu Qatada, considered the GIA's mufti, withdrew his support as a direct response to the massacres.[56] Allegedly dismayed by the un-Islamic nature of the massacres, bin Laden provided support for the rival GSPC (Groupe Salafiste pour la Predication et le Combat, Salafi Group for Combat and Propagation) led by former GIA emir Hassan Hattab. Zouabri became increasingly isolated and the GIA disintegrated into rival factions. He was eventually killed in February 2002.[57]

The primary concern for bin Laden and the international jihadis seems to have been that the targets were Muslims rather than infidels. According to Islamic law, Muslims cannot kill other Muslims, except under very stringent conditions (such as banditry, but even then there are restrictions). The idea of using *takfir* against such a broad portion of the population was rejected by the international jihadis. For Al Qaeda, killing apostate government officials is one thing; attacking ordinary Muslim citizens is entirely different because they have been led astray by the regime and its battalion of state clerics, who purposely obfuscate and hide Islamic truth from the people. The massacres also threatened Al Qaeda's strategy to win the hearts and minds of Muslims in its battle against the United States and its "puppets."[58]

Emerging from the debate about civilian targeting in Algeria, Al Qaeda began sharpening its position in the late 1990s with support from a consortium of

Table 2 Conditions for killing civilians according to Al Qaeda (only one condition is necessary)

---

1) The enemy has purposefully killed Muslim civilians*

2) Civilians have assisted the enemy in "deed, word, or mind"*

3) Islamic fighters cannot distinguish between combatants and non-combatants

4) There is a need to burn enemy strongholds or fields where there are civilians

5) Heavy weaponry needs to be used

6) The enemy uses civilians as human shields

7) The enemy violates a treaty with the Muslims and civilians must be killed as a lesson

---

* These are the most often cited conditions.

contemporary scholars. The movement uniformly rejected targeting Muslim civilians, unless they assisted the infidel (in which case they were no longer Muslims in any event). It also displayed great sensitivity to concerns that Muslims could be caught in the crossfire, arguing that Muslims should not mix with non-Muslims and should stay away from potential targets. Those who are killed inadvertently are considered martyrs for the cause, and blood money should be paid to the families. This argument about blood payment appears to have come from Ayman Zawhiri, who offered this solution after members of Islamic Jihad inadvertently killed a young child during an attack against Prime Minister Atif Sidqi's motorcade in Egypt in 1993.[59] This was also the solution offered for Muslims killed in the 11 September attacks.[60]

The jihadis predominantly use two lines of argument to justify targeting non-Muslim civilians (see also Table 2). First, they use a "doctrine of proportional response." Although accepting the general prohibition against killing noncombatants, the jihadis consistently draw on Ibn al-Qayyim, al-Shawkani, al-Qurtubi, Ibn Taymiyya, and others to argue that when the infidel kills Muslim civilians it becomes permissible to attack their civilians in kind. This is supported by Qur'an 2:194: "And one who attacks you, attack him in like manner as he attacked you." In his *Shadow of the Lances*, Al Qaeda spokesman Suleiman Abu Gheith argues that, "Anyone who peruses these sources reaches a single conclusion: The sages have agreed that reciprocal punishment to which the verses refer is not limited to a specific instance. It is a valid rule for punishments for infidels, for the licentious Muslims, and for oppressors."[61] In other words, if the enemy uses tactics that are prohibited according to Islam, these tactics become legal for Muslims.

To make the doctrine of proportional response operable against Americans, the jihadis have to demonstrate that the United States is purposely targeting Muslim civilians. It does so by citing a number of conflicts involving the United States in which civilians have been killed, including Afghanistan and Iraq, among others. Without actually demonstrating intent, which is critical for the use of the proportionality doctrine, the radicals conclude that the United States has strategically killed Muslims to terrorize the Islamic nation (umma). It makes this argument with particular emphasis on the Palestinian territories (and unwavering American support for Israel), in effect tapping into the widespread sense of despair felt by millions of Muslims exposed to the images of children and other civilians killed during confrontations with Israeli soldiers. In the justification for 11 September, Al Qaeda argues that,

> There currently exists an extermination effort against the Islamic peoples that has America's blessing, not just by virtue of its effective cooperation, but by America's activity. The best witness to this is what is happening with the full knowledge of the world in the Palestinian cities of Jenin, Nablus, Ramallah, and elsewhere. Every day, all can follow the atrocious slaughter going on there with American support that is aimed at children, women, and the elderly. Are Muslims not permitted to respond in the same way and kill those among the Americans who are like the Muslims they are killing? Certainly! By Allah, it is truly a right for Muslims.[62]

For Al Qaeda, the evidence points to a clear conclusion:

> It is allowed for Muslims to kill protected ones among unbelievers as an act of reciprocity. If the unbelievers have targeted Muslim women, children, and elderly, it is permissible for Muslims to respond in kind and kill those similar to those whom the unbelievers killed.[63]

For Suleiman Abu Gheith, the sheer volume of Muslims killed by the United States means that Muslims have the right to kill four million Americans in order to reach parity.[64]

Al Qaeda's use of the doctrine of proportional response hinges on its interpretation of U.S. intentions: are American troops purposely targeting civilians? If the answer is yes, even nonviolent Salafis would agree that it is permissible to target American civilians. If the answer is no, then Muslims are limited by religious edicts against killing women, children, the elderly and other noncombatants. Bombarded by images of young, stone-throwing boys shot by Israeli soldiers, most Muslims accept the argument that Israel purposely targets civilians. Increasingly, many have also come to believe that the United States is doing the same. Some argue, for example, that U.S. technology is so effective that the only way civilians can be killed is if American troops target them. Al Qaeda thus plays into widespread frustration and apprehension about American military power and the "collateral damage" of war.

The second major line of argument builds on Ibn Taymiyya, who argued that, "Since lawful warfare is essentially jihad and since its aim is that the religion is God's entirely and God's word is uppermost, therefore, according to all Muslims, those who stand in the way of this aim must be fought. As for those who cannot offer resistance or cannot fight, such as women, children, monks, old people, the blind, the handicapped and their likes, they shall not be killed, unless they actually fight with words [e.g., propaganda] and acts [e.g., spying or otherwise assisting in the warfare]."[65] This defines enemy populations in terms of their capacity to fight, in effect introducing subjectivity into the definition of "civilian."

The jihadis argue that anyone who assists the enemy in any way loses the protection of noncombatant status: "It is allowed for Muslims to kill protected ones among unbelievers on the condition that the protected ones have assisted in combat, whether in deed, word, mind, or any other form of assistance, according to the prophetic command." Perhaps the most oft-cited piece of evidence for this line of argument is a story about Duraid Ibn al-Simma, a well-known Arab poet who strongly opposed Mohammed and the message of Islam. According to tradition, he was brought to the battlefield to advise the Hawazin troops about battle procedures in a conflict against the Muslims. As a very old man, he posed no physical threat to the Muslim forces, but the intelligence he provided to the enemy made him a target and led to his death in battle.[66]

Although even nonviolent Salafis agree that individuals who directly assist combat through advice in war planning or other supportive functions are legitimate targets, Al Qaeda uses the subjectivity inherent in the "capacity to fight" threshold to dramatically broaden the menu of legitimate targets. Anyone the movement itself deems as supporting the "war against Islam" is fair game, including NGOs, journalists, academics, government consultants, and businesses.

The most important new line of thinking, without precedent in Islamic law, is the jihadi argument about personal and individual culpability in a democracy. This argument is best represented in a fatwa about 11 September issued by Hammoud al-Uqla al-Shuaybi, considered the godfather of the Saudi jihadis. In the fatwa, al-Uqla argues that:

> [W]e should know that whatever decision the non-Muslim state, America, takes — especially critical decisions which involve war — it is taken based on opinion poll and/or voting within the House of Representatives and Senate, which represent directly, the exact opinion of the people they represent — the people of America — through their representatives in the Parliament [Congress]. Based on this, any American who voted for war is like a fighter, or at least a supporter.[67]

In addition to citing Ibn Taymiyya's stance vis-à-vis the capacity of the enemy population to fight, al-Uqla also cites another ruling in which Ibn Taymiyya argued that Christians could be fought because "they assisted the enemies of the Muslims against them, and helped them with their wealth and weapons, despite the fact that they did not fight us." Al-Uqla's perspective has influenced some of his more radical jihadi students, including Ali bin Khudayr al-Khudayr, Nasir Hamad al-Fahd, and Suleiman Alwan. Alwan and al-Khudayr issued fatwas after 11 September saying that anyone who assisted the United States was an apostate. Al-Fahd issued a fatwa supporting the use of weapons of mass destruction.

This kind of argument is replicated in several Al Qaeda publications. In its justification for September 11, the movement reasons that because a democratically elected government reflects the will of the people, a war against Islam of this magnitude must have popular support. Using the term "public opinion" (*al-ra'y al-'amm*) to represent the will of the people in a democracy, Al Qaeda argues that,

> It is stupidity for a Muslim to think that the Crusader-Zionist public opinion which backs its government was waiting for some action from Muslims in order to support the Crusader war against Islam and thereby enkindle a spirit of hostility against Islam and Muslims. The Crusader-Zionist public

opinion has expended all it has in order to stand behind the nations of the cross, executing their war against Islam and Muslims from the beginning of the colonization of Islamic countries until the present day. If the successive Crusader-Zionist governments had not received support from their people, their war against Islam and Muslims would not have taken such an obvious and conspicuous form. It is something that would not attain legitimacy except by the voices of the people.[68]

Abd al Aziz bin Saleh al-Jarbu, author of *Basing the Religious Legitimacy of Destroying America*, recounts a story in which the Prophet ordered his followers to kill a woman because she sang songs to inspire the enemy warriors. "If this was the decree against anyone who sang songs of vituperation against the Messenger," he reasoned, "then it is all the more a decree against those who to this added participating in a vote approving massacres of Muslims and against those who spread shame and prostitution to Islam and the Muslims."[69]

Obviously Ibn Taymiyya did not discuss the culpability of individuals in a democracy because this was not a medieval or classical issue. The jihadis have transmogrified his line of argument and a well-established principle in Islamic jurisprudence that those who assist in combat, even if they are not soldiers, are legitimate targets. By declaring all Americans personally responsible simply because they live in a democracy, Al Qaeda has manipulated the subjective nature of defining "the capacity to fight" to justify wide-scale attacks on non-combatants.

Although GIA emir Zouabri was never considered a theological luminary and had little direct influence on theological debates about civilian targeting, his rationale for the massacres in Algeria runs throughout Al Qaeda's justification for 11 September. In both cases, the definition of "civilian" was stretched to include broad swathes of the population. So whereas Al Qaeda may have objected to killing Muslim civilians in Algeria, its logic for killing non-Muslim civilians mirrors Zouabri's reasoning.

Suicide bombings

Like civilian targeting, the issue of suicide bombings or "martyrdom operations" is relatively recent. The use of suicide bombings by Muslims began in Lebanon and was popularized by Hizballah. Tactically speaking, this influenced Palestinian groups. Theologically speaking, however, it is unlikely that Hizballah directly influenced Al Qaeda and the Sunni jihadis because its arguments derived from Shi'ite traditions of martyrdom (and it focused on military and political targets). The real debate about the religious permissibility of these kinds of operations among Salafis, in fact, did not emerge until the mid-1990s and was a response to its widespread usage by Hamas and other Palestinian factions.

What is interesting about the current jihadi arguments about suicide bombings is how little attention seems to be given to constructing a theological argument justifying such attacks. Instead, the vast majority of materials focus on extolling the virtues of martyrdom. Abdullah Azzam's *Virtues of Martyrdom in the Path of Allah* is a classic example.[70] In it, he elaborates twenty-seven points of evidence about the benefits of martyrdom. Most writings argue that the martyr has a seat in Paradise, avoids the torture of the grave, marries seventy black eyed virgins, and can advocate on behalf of seventy relatives so that they too might reach Paradise. Scholars from all ideological persuasions agree about the virtues of martyrdom.

Since the 1990s, Al Qaeda and the jihadis have been forced to address two central questions. First, are martyrdom operations suicide? This is critical because Islam explicitly prohibits suicide. Some of the more senior Salafi clerics in Saudi Arabia have argued that these attacks are prohibited. Muhammad Bin Salih Bin Uthaymin (d. 2000), for example, argues that, "as for what some people do regarding activities of suicide, tying explosives to themselves and then approaching disbelievers and detonating amongst them, then this is a case of suicide.... So whoever commits suicide then he will be considered eternally to Hell-Fire, remaining there forever."[71] In making this condemnation, the focus is on the *act* itself: consciously killing oneself.

The jihadis, however, focus on the *intent* of the perpetrator. Although he is not as radical as Al Qaeda, Yusuf al-Qaradawi outlines the basic reasoning:

> He who commits suicide kills himself for his own benefit, while he who commits martyrdom sacrifices himself for the sake of his religion and his nation. While someone who commits suicide has lost hope with himself and with the spirit of Allah, the *Mujahid* [holy warrior] is full of hope with regard to Allah's spirit and mercy. He fights his enemy and the enemy of Allah with this new weapon, which destiny has put in the hands of the weak, so that they would fight against the evil of the strong and arrogant. The *Mujahid* becomes a "human bomb" that blows up at a specific place and time, in the midst of the enemies of Allah and the homeland, leaving them helpless in the face of the brave *Shahid* [martyr] who... sold his soul to Allah, and sought the *Shahada* [Martyrdom] for the sake of Allah.[72]

Here Al Qaeda shares its view of suicide bombings as legitimate martyrdom operations with less radical, conservative Sunnis. This includes not only figures like al-Qaradawi, but also Mohammed Sayyed Tantawi, the Sheikh of al-Azhar in Egypt.[73] The jihadis thus find ample support among Muslims for the *tactic* itself.

The second question is related to targeting. Can Islamic fighters kill civilians in "martyrdom operations"? Much of the jihadi argument in answering this question is based on its justification for killing civilians in general, outlined in the previous section of this article: it challenges mainstream definitions of "innocent civilians" to include anyone who assists the enemy in "word, deed, or mind," an extremely expansive category. Its reliance on this line of reasoning stems from widespread opposition to killing civilians, even in suicide bombings. Although someone like Tantawi may support suicide bombings in principle, he and others object to killing civilians in the process. Even Muhammed al-Maqdisi, an extreme jihadi Salafi in Jordan, has cautioned against civilian targeting, although noting that in some contexts the Islamic fighters may not be able to distinguish between combatants and noncombatants.[74] From this perspective, collateral damage is permissible but should be avoided where possible.

It is because of the general consensus that Muslims cannot purposely target civilians that Al Qaeda and others must emphasize that alleged "civilians" are not really noncombatants. In the context of Israel, for example, al-Qaradawi and the jihadis frame Israel as a militarized country. Because there is mandatory military service for men and women (and reserve service after that), all men and women become legitimate targets in martyrdom operations. Some more radical elements argue that because children will one day grow up and serve in the Israeli army, they too are legitimate targets. Regardless of the nuances, Al Qaeda is careful to frame the targets of the attacks as combatants through deeds, words, and thoughts.

Conclusion and future prospects

The development of jihadi thought is characterized by the erosion of critical constraints used to limit warfare and violence in classical Islam. Whereas most Islamic scholars throughout history have defined apostates as those who clearly leave the faith by declaring themselves non-Muslims or rejecting key tenets of Islam (prayer, the prophethood of Mohammed, monotheism, etc.), jihadis claim that any leader who does not implement and follow Islamic law (as they understand it) is an apostate. Whereas most scholars reject violent uprisings to remove rulers so long as they allow the prayer and have "a mustard seed of faith," jihadis believe it is a divine duty to wage jihad against rulers who refuse to implement the radicals' interpretation of Islamic law. Whereas there is a general acceptance throughout Islamic history that civilians should not be targeted in war, Al Qaeda has defined the term "civilian" in such a way as to make everyone living in a Western democracy subject to attack (reinforced by a doctrine of proportional response that requires Muslims to kill millions of Americans). And although there is broad support for the use of suicide bombings, Al Qaeda has expanded its use to encompass attacks on ordinary civilians in Western countries rather than just military or political targets.

This trajectory indicates that the jihadis will attack increasingly wider categories of people. This is already being witnessed with regard to the Shi'ite community in Pakistan and Saudi Arabia (and to some extent Iraq because of Zarqawi's intention to seed discord between Sunnis and Shi'ites). A number of radicals declared their intention to kill Shi'ites in the early 1990s, and this has become an increasingly common position.[75] More attacks might also be expected against others in the Sunni community, in addition to state officials and government personnel.

However it plays out, the historical development of jihadi thought has been one of increasingly expansive violence, not one of limitations. In the end, this may erode popular support for Al Qaeda, as increased violence did to the GIA in Algeria, but in the meantime more groups of people will likely find themselves on the jihadi list of legitimate targets. Given the jihadi argument about proportional response and intentions to acquire weapons of mass destruction, attacks may become increasingly deadly as well.

Notes

1   Those typically called "Wahhabis" reject the term because it suggests that they follow Ibn Wahhab, a person, rather than God. This, for conservative Muslims, would be tantamount to apostasy. They instead use the term "Salafi." For more on

Salafis, see Quintan Wiktorowicz, *The Management of Islamic Activism: Salafis, the Muslim Brotherhood, and State Power in Jordan* (Albany: State University of New York Press, 2001), chapter four; Marc Sageman, *Understanding Terror Networks* (Philadelphia: University of Pennsylvania Press, 2004).

2   See Quintan Wiktorowicz "The New Global Threat: Transnational Salafis and Jihad," *Middle East Policy* 8(4) (December 2001), pp. 18–38; Michael Doran, "Somebody Else's Civil War," *Foreign Affairs* 81(1) (January/February 2002), pp. 22–42.

3   For the first fatwa on weapons of mass destruction, see the analysis of Sheikh Naser bin Hamad al-Fahd's fatwa, issued on 21 May 2003, by Reuven Paz, "YES to WMD: The First Islamist Fatwah on the Use of Weapons of Mass Destruction," *Prism Special Dispatches* 1(1) (May 2003), available at ⟨http://www.e-prism.org/images/PRISM%20Special%20dispatch%20no%201.doc⟩.

4   *Al-Musawwar*, 21 June 2002, pp. 4–22, in FBIS-NES-2002-0625.

5   Ibid.

6   From quotes provided at ⟨http://tariq.bitshop.com/misconceptions/fatwas/prohibition.htm⟩. These are the standard kinds of evidence used by nonviolent Salafis.

7   *Sahih Bukhari* 8, p. 73; 8, p. 126.

8   For the mainstream Salafi perspective on these issues and others (translated into English), see various publications at ⟨www.salafipublications.com⟩. The website is well known among Salafis as supporting the Saudi religious establishment, which is tied to the Saudi regime.

9   Email from Juan Cole, 25 March 2003.

10   Ibid.

11   For Mawdudi's perspective, see Charles J. Adams, "Mawdudi and the Islamic State," in *Voices of Resurgent Islam*, edited by John L. Esposito (Oxford: Oxford University Press, 1983), pp. 99–133; and Seyyed Vali Reza Nasr, *Mawdudi & the Making of Islamic Revivalism* (Oxford: Oxford University Press, 1995). Mawdudi's most important works are readily available online. For example, see ⟨http://www.masmn.org/Books/⟩.

12   For more on the Jamaat-i-Islami, see Seyyed Vali Nasr, *The Vanguard of the Islamic Revolution: The Jama'at-I Islami of Pakistan* (Berkeley: University of California Press, 1994).

13   For Sayyid Qutb's ideology, see Yvonne Y. Haddad, "Sayyid Qutb: Ideologue of Islamic Revival," in *Voices of Resurgent Islam*, edited by John L. Esposito (Oxford: Oxford University Press, 1983), pp. 67–98; Ahmad S. Moussalli, *Radical Islamic Fundamentalism: The Ideological and Political Discourse of Sayyid Qutb* (Syracuse: Syracuse University Press, 1994); Ibrahim M. Abu-Rabi, *Intellectual Origins of Islamic Resurgence in the Modern Arab World* (Albany: State University of New York Press, 1995); and William E. Shepard, *Sayyid Qutb and Islamic Activism: A Translation and Critical Analysis of Social Justice in Islam* (London: Brill, 1996). For his influence on radical jihadis in particular, see Emmanuel Sivan, *Radical Islam: Medieval Theology and Modern Politics* (New Haven: Yale University Press, 1985), Gilles Kepel, *Muslim Extremism in Egypt: The Prophet and Pharaoh*, trans. Jon Rothschild (Berkeley: University of California Press, 1993); Sageman, *Understanding Terror Networks*, chapter one.

14   Sivan, *Radical Islam*, p. 28.

15   As quoted in Sivan, *Radical Islam*, pp. 23–24.

16   Faraj's tract is translated in Johannes J.G. Jansen, *The Neglected Duty: The Creed of Sadat's Assassins and Islamic Resurgence in the Middle East* (New York: Macmillan Publishing Company, 1986). Also, see Kepel, *Muslim Extremism*, chapter seven.

17   Jansen, *The Neglected Duty*, p. 6.

18   Ibid., p. 97.

19   As quoted in Malika Zeghal, "Religion and Politics in Egypt: The Ulema of al-Azhar, Radical Islam, and the State (1952–1994)," *International Journal of Middle East Studies* 31(3) (August 1999), p. 395.

20   From *al-Sharq al-Awsat* published extracts of Ayman Zawahiri's *Knights under the Prophet's Banner*, FBIS-NES-2002-108, available at (www.fas.org/irp/world/para/ayman_bk.html). Qutb's influence on Zawahiri is corroborated in Montasser al-Zayyat, *The Road to Al Qaeda: The Story of Bin Laden's Right-Hand Man*, trans. Ahmed Fekry, edited by Sara Nimis (London: Pluto Press, 2004). Al-Zayyat has acted as the lawyer for a number of radical jihadis in Egypt and is well placed in the jihadi community, although many now view him as a security agent because of his central role in developing a nonviolent ideology among jihadis.

21   From *al-Sharq al-Awsat* published extracts of Ayman Zawahiri's *Knights under the Prophet's Banner*, FBIS-NES-2002-108, available at (www.fas.org/irp/world/para/ayman_bk.html).

22   *Islam: The Misunderstood Religion* is published by New Era publications and is available at (www.barnesandnoble.com).

23   Michael Doran made this observation in an e-mail. For more on Ibn Wahhab's ideology and influence, see Natana J. DeLong-Bas, *Wahhabi Islam: From Revival and Reform to Global Jihad* (Oxford: Oxford University Press, 2004).

24   DeLong-Bas, *Wahhabi Islam*.

25   See (http://www.islambasics.com/view.php?bkID=64).

26   See various publications on the topic at www.salafipublications.com

27   E-mail from Juan Cole, 12 February 2003.

28   The "Declaration" is available at (http://www.pbs.org/newshour/terrorism/international/fatwa_1996.html).

29   Originally played on *al-Jazeera*. Translated transcript available at (http://news.bbc.co.uk/2/hi/middle_east/2751019.stm).

30   E-mail from Guido Steinberg, 25 March 2003. Also, for those who read German, see Guido Steinberg, *Religion und Staat in Saudi-Arabien. Die Wahhabitischen Gelehrten 1902–1953* (Würzburg: Ergon, 2002).

31   See, for example, John Kelsay and James Turner Johnson, eds., *Just War and Jihad: Historical and Theoretical Perspectives on War and Peace in Western and Islamic Traditions* (New York: Greenwood Press, 1991); and James Turner Johnson, *The Holy War Idea in Western and Islamic Traditions* (University Park, PA: The Pennsylvania State University Press, 1997).

32   Jihadis believe that the story about the Prophet's reference to the "greater jihad" was fabricated.

33   Rudolph Peters, *Jihad in Classical and Modern Islam* (Princeton: Markus Wiener Publishers, 1996), chapter five.

34   Peters, *Jihad*, p. 47.

35   Available at (http://www.islamworld.net/advice_jihad.html).

36   Online version available at (http://www.religioscope.com/info/doc/jihad/azzam_caravan_1_foreword.htm).

37   Peters, *Jihad*, pp. 52–53.

38   Online version available at (http://www.religioscope.com/info/doc/jihad/azzam_caravan_4_part2.htm).

39   Online version available at (http://www.religioscope.com/info/doc/jihad/azzam_caravan_5_part3.htm).

40   Online version available at (http://www.religioscope.com/info/doc/jihad/azzam_caravan_3_part1.htm).

41   Ibid.

42   Olivier Roy, "The Radicalization of Sunni Conservative Fundamentalism," *ISIM Newsletter* No. 2, March 1999. Available online at (http://www.isim.nl/files/newsl_2.pdf).

43   The fatwa is available at (http://www.fas.org/irp/world/para/docs/980223-fatwa.htm).

44   Online version at (http://www.pbs.org/newshour/terrorism/international/fatwa_1996.html).

45   See Mamoun Fandy, *Saudi Arabia and the Politics of Dissent* (New York: Palgrave, 1999); and Gwenn Okruhlik, "Making Conversation Permissible: Islamism and Reform in Saudi Arabia," in *Islamic Activism: A Social Movement Theory Approach*, edited by Quintan Wiktorowicz (Bloomington: Indiana University Press, 2004).

46   As quoted in John Esposito, *Unholy War: Terror in the Name of Islam* (Oxford: Oxford University Press, 2002), p. 24.

47   *London Press Association*, 14 September 2001, FBIS-WEU_2001-0914.

48   For a more elaborate discussion of this, see Quintan Wiktorowicz and John Kaltner, "Killing in the Name of Islam: Al Qaeda's Justification for September 11," *Middle East Policy* 10(2) (Summer 2003), pp. 76–92. The article is available at (http://www.mepc.org/public_asp/journal_vol10/0306_wiktorowiczkaltner.asp).

49   For the ideological struggle in the conflict, see Mohammed Hafez, "Armed Islamist Movements and Political Violence in Algeria," *Middle East Journal* 54(4) (Autumn 2000), pp. 572–592; idem., *Why Muslims Rebel: Repression and Resistance in the Islamic World* (Boulder: Lynne Rienner, 2003), chapter five.

50   Quintan Wiktorowicz, "The GIA and GSPC in Algeria," In *In the Service of Al Qaeda: Radical Islamic Movements*, edited by Magnus Ranstorp (New York: Hurst Publishers and New York University Press, forthcoming).

51   AFP, 21 January 1997, in FBIS-NES-97-013.

52   Calculated by the author using the *Middle East Journal* "Chronology of Events."

53   AFP, 7 August 1997.

54   Armed Islamic Group communiqué issued 16 January 1995.

55   AFP, 6 August 1994, in *Joint Publications Research Service*-TOT-94-034-L.

56   Interview by author with one of Abu Qatada's associates in Jordan, 1997.

57   Wiktorowicz, "The GIA and GSPC."

58   This strategy was discussed by Zawahiri in *Knights under the Prophet's Banner*, FBIS-NES-2002-108, available at www.fas.org/irp/world/para/ayman_bk.html).

59   Ibid.

60   Translation and original Arabic available at (http://www.mepc.org/public_asp/journal_vol10/0306_wiktorowiczkaltner.asp).

61   MEMRI, "'Why We Fight America': Al-Qa'ida Spokesman Explains September 11 and Declares Intentions to Kill 4 Million Americans with Weapons of Mass Destruction," *Special Dispatch Series – No. 388*, 12 June 2002. Available at (http://www.memri.org/bin/articles.cgi? Page= subjects&Area=jihad&ID=SP38802).

62 Available at (http://www.mepc.org/public_asp/journal_vol10/0306_wiktorowiczkaltner. asp).

63 Available at (http://www.mepc.org/public_asp/journal_vol10/0306_wiktorowiczkaltner. asp).

64 MEMRI, "Why We Fight America."

65 Peters, *Jihad*, p. 49.

66 Wiktorowicz and Kaltner, "Killing in the Name of Islam," p. 88.

67 An English translation of the fatwa was posted at (www.azzam.com) after 11 September. The fatwa was dismissed by reformist Salafis in Saudi Arabia. The Council of Ulema argued that the statement was "not worth adhering to." The council also contested al-Uqla's authority to issue fatwas. See (www.fatwa-online.com/news/0011017_1.htm).

68 Translation and original Arabic available at (http://www.mepc.org/public_asp/journal_vol10/0306_wiktorowiczkaltner.asp).

69 Yigal Carmon, "Contemporary Islamist Ideology Permitting Genocidal Murder," paper presented at the Stockholm International Forum on Preventing Genocide," MEMRI *Special Report – No. 25*, 27 January 2004, available at (http://www.memri.org/bin/articles.cgi?Page=subjects& Area=jihad&ID=SR2504).

70 Available at (http://www.islamicawakening.org/viewarticle.php?articleID =1012&).

71 Available at (www.fatwa-online.com/fataawa/worship/jihaad/jih004/0010915_1. htm). See (www.fatwa-online.com) for additional fatwas along these lines.

72 As quoted in MEMRI, "Debating the Religious, Political and Moral Legitimacy of Suicide Bombings Part 1: The Debate over Religious Legitimacy," *Inquiry and Analysis Series – No. 53*, 2 May 2001. Available at (http://www.memri.org/bin/articles. cgi?Page=subjects& Area=jihad& ID=IA5301).

73 Ibid.

74 Interview with Nida'ul Islam magazine, issue 22, February–March 1998, available at (http://www.islam.org.au/articles/22/maqdisy.htm).

75 See Michael Doran, "The Saudi Paradox," *Foreign Affairs* 83(1) (January/February 2004). Available online at (http://www.foreignaffairs.org/20040101faessay83105/michael-scott-doran/the-saudi-paradox.html).

Thomas Hegghammer

GLOBAL JIHADISM AFTER THE IRAQ WAR

THERE SEEMS TO be a broad consensus among terrorism experts that the US-led invasion of Iraq in March 2003 has contributed negatively to the so-called "global war on terror." According to many analysts, the war and the subsequent occupation have increased the level of frustration in the Islamic world over American foreign policy and facilitated recruitment by militant Islamist groups.[1] Moreover, Iraq seems to have replaced Afghanistan as a training ground where a new generation of Islamist militants can acquire military expertise and build personal relationships through the experience of combat and training camps.[2]

Most analyses, however, seem to stop at the ascertainment of a vague, almost quantitative increase in the level of anti-Americanism or radicalism in Muslim communities since the Iraq War in 2003. This article will try to delve deeper into the matter and explore the qualitative changes in radical Islamist ideology since 2003. The next few pages are therefore devoted to the following research question: How has the invasion and occupation of Iraq influenced the ideological development of the so-called global jihadist movement?

This question demands a closer examination of the writings and sayings of leading radical ideologues on the issue of Iraq since the autumn of 2002, when the prospect of war caught the world's attention. Basing my analysis on key ideological texts, I will try to answer the following four subquestions: How important is Iraq to the so-called global jihadists? How united are the global jihadists in their view on the struggle for Iraq? How have the war and the occupation influenced their analysis of the overall confrontation with the US and the West? And how has their view of the enemy changed after the multinational invasion of Iraq? It must be emphasized that our focus will be on the militant and internationally-orientated Islamists, which means that moderate Islamist actors and nationalist Iraqi groups will not be considered here.

The research literature contains relatively few in-depth studies of post-September 11, 2001 ideological developments in radical Islamism.[3] This study is therefore almost entirely based on primary sources, mainly Arabic texts from radical Islamist Internet sites. These sources are often problematic and cannot provide the full answer to our research question, but they represent one of our only windows into the world of militant Islamism.

The key argument in this article is that the Iraq War gave the global jihadists a welcome focal point in their struggle against the USA, but that Iraq at the same time became so attractive as a battle front that it weakened terrorist campaigns elsewhere. Moreover, it is argued that the Iraq conflict contributed to the development of more sophisticated strategic thought in jihadist circles, and to an increase in hostility toward Europe and the Gulf countries. The main objective of this analysis is to draw a more accurate picture of the global jihadist movement and to illustrate how armed conflict can generate unexpected ideological changes within radical political movements.

Al-Qaʿida and global jihadism since 9/11

First of all, it is essential to define the notion of "global jihadism" and clarify its relation to other Islamist movements. "Islamism" – in itself a debated and polysemic term – is understood by this author as meaning "Islamic activism." It includes non-violent and violent, progressive as well as reactionary, political movements. Militant groups represent only a marginal part of the Islamist political landscape. Islamist militants relate to Islamism much in the same way that left-wing extremists and Marxist guerrilla groups relate to socialism.

Militant Islamism has its own intellectual history, in which so-called "global jihadism" represents a relatively recent phenomenon. The first modern violent Islamist groups appeared in the Middle East in the 1960s and 1970s as radical expressions of broader socio-revolutionary movements. These groups struggled for state power and their main enemies were the local political regimes. In the 1980s and 1990s, Islamism as an ideological framework was adopted by nationalist and separatist movements in many different parts of the world. This type of militant Islamist group, present in places such as Palestine and Chechnya, did not fight primarily for state power, but for a specific territory. Their principal enemies were non-Muslim states or communities that contested the same piece of land. In the mid-1990s, a third type of militant Islamism appeared, namely global jihadism. It emerged as a result of Usama bin Ladin's adoption of a doctrine in 1996 which emphasized the fight against the US over the fight against local regimes.[4] The global jihad doctrine involved a reversal of the priorities of the socio-revolutionaries and the nationalist-separatists. Global jihadist ideologues said that before an Islamic state could be established in Egypt, and before Palestine could be liberated, Muslims needed to defend the entire Islamic world against the imminent military threat posed by the US and the West.[5] Bin Ladin's brothers-in-arms, most of whom were veterans of the Afghan War in the 1980s, began launching terrorist attacks directly on Western targets in different parts of the world. These new jihadists were no longer struggling for a specific territory or for state power in a particular country. They were fighting to defend all Muslim territories at the same time. Their main opponent was no longer the local regimes ("the near enemy"), but the United States ("the far enemy") and its allies. The discourse of these global jihadists tended to highlight Muslims' suffering at the hands of the so-called

Jewish-Crusader alliance. Their texts were characterized by long enumerations of places and events which demonstrated that Muslims were victims of oppression, occupation, and war.[6]

Global jihadism found its primary operational expression in the international terrorist activity of al-Qaʿida and the so-called Afghan Arabs from the mid-1990s onwards. The term "al-Qaʿida" is very problematic and is probably most relevant to describe the organization which took shape around Usama bin Ladin in Afghanistan between 1996 and 2001.[7] Al-Qaʿida became a unique phenomenon in the history of terrorism, because it enjoyed access to a territory, which it used to apply a unique organizational concept, namely an educational institution for global terrorism and guerrilla warfare. The organization itself remained relatively small (300-500 people), but the training camps were frequented by many more (10,000-20,000 people).[8] Radicalized Muslim youth from all over the world could travel to Afghanistan and spend time in these camps. Here lies the key to understanding the extremism and the internal cohesion of the so-called "al-Qaʿida network." The training camps generated an ultra-masculine culture of violence which brutalized the volunteers and broke down their barriers to the use of violence. Recruits increased their paramilitary skills while the harsh camp life built strong personal relationships between them. Last but not least, they fell under the ideological influence of Usama bin Ladin and Ayman al-Zawahiri, who generated a feeling among the recruits of being part of a global vanguard of holy warriors, whose mission was to defend the Islamic world against attacks by the Jewish-Crusader alliance.

The US-led invasion of Afghanistan in the aftermath of 9/11 denied al-Qaʿida access to its territory, thus removing the basis for its unique organizational concept. Moreover, the top leadership was forced into hiding, presumably in the border area between Afghanistan and Pakistan, while the mid-level leadership and the lower ranks sought refuge in various countries around the world. Post-9/11 security measures restricted their mobility, reduced the number of available meeting-places, and made long-distance communication more difficult. The result was a weakening of what had been the organizational "glue" in the al-Qaʿida network, namely the strong personal relationships and the ideological unity. In 2002, the various local branches of the al-Qaʿida network were strategically disoriented, and it seemed that old ideological debates and dividing lines started reappearing. Not everyone agreed that the liberation of Afghanistan was the most important issue. What about Palestine? And what about the struggle against the local regimes in the Arab world?

One might therefore say that the invasion of Afghanistan destroyed al-Qaʿida as an organization in the analytically useful sense of the word. Instead an extremely diverse and loosely knit ideological movement emerged, which many continue to call al-Qaʿida, for lack of a better term. However, the current author prefers the term "global jihadist movement," because it better reflects the decentralized and multipolar nature of the phenomenon. This heterogeneous movement consists of actors with partially diverging political and strategic priorities. They are bound together by little more than an extreme anti-Americanism and a willingness to carry out mass-casualty attacks on Western targets. In more concrete terms, the old al-Qaʿida network seems to have split up into five regionally-defined clusters, whose centers of gravity are in Iraq, Saudi Arabia, Afghanistan/Pakistan, Southeast Asia, and Europe/North Africa.[9] These networks seem to operate relatively independently from each other, although transregional contacts are widespread. In some areas, such as Iraq and Saudi Arabia, the global jihadists have formed identifiable organizations ("al-Qaʿida in the Land of the Two Rivers" and "al-Qaʿida on the Arabian Peninsula"). In other places, such as Europe, the organizational structures are much more difficult to identify.

Two things make the global jihadists "more global" than other militant Islamists. First of all, they view the US and the West as the primary and immediate enemy, and they see their own military activity as part of a global confrontation with the Jewish-Crusader alliance. Second, their operational pattern is transnational, either in the sense that they prefer to strike at international targets in their local battle zone, or that they are willing to carry out terrorist attacks far outside of their territorial base, for example in Europe or in the US. In practice, however, the distinction between global and local jihadists is often difficult to make. For a start, all militant Islamist groups today, whether they are globally or locally oriented, use virulently anti-American rhetoric. Moreover, attacks on Western targets in places such as Iraq may also be carried out by groups with a primarily nationalist agenda. This illustrates more than anything else that the study of ideology is not an exact science and that our current concepts do not adequately capture the complex phenomenon of Islamist militancy.

These developments raise important questions. How do we identify the key ideological tendencies in a group of actors as complex and decentralized as the global jihadist movement? And how do we deal with the vast amounts of ideological material of different origin that is circulating on the Internet? A first possible step is to identify the main participants in the ideological debates. This author argues that there are five principal categories of actors that shape contemporary global jihadist ideology. The first category is represented by the leadership of the "old al-Qaʿida," i.e. Usama bin Ladin and Ayman al-Zawahiri. They have an almost mythical status in Islamist circles and still exert tremendous ideological influence. The two leaders communicate primarily through sound and video recordings diffused on Arabic television stations such as al-Jazeera and on the Internet. The statements by Bin Ladin and al-Zawahiri are often quite general in content, and their main purpose seems to be to convince and motivate believers to take up arms against the enemy. Their approximately 40 statements since the autumn of 2001 have focused on the political reasons to fight the Crusaders.[10] They rarely provide specific strategic or tactical advice, and hence their declarations are always subject to interpretation by other writers.[11]

The second category consists of the religious scholars. They are most often, though not always, older people with a formal religious education. The role of these "jihad shaykhs" is to issue fatwas clarifying what is religiously legitimate or necessary to do in the struggle against the infidels.[12] They are seldom directly connected to militant groups. Most of them have been based in Saudi Arabia, Britain, or in unknown locations. Since September 11, the vast majority of these scholars have been imprisoned, put in house arrest or otherwise silenced, but some are still active.[13] Their fatwas and books are published and distributed on the Internet by young and computer-savvy assistants drawn from the entourage of students that often surround these scholars.

The third category comprises the strategic thinkers. They tend to be in their twenties or thirties and are members of militant groups, but they are generally not involved in the front line of the military operations. They write articles and books about the best way – from a functional point of view – to fight the enemy. They are thus somewhat less concerned with theological aspects of the struggle. Their publications are also distributed on the Internet. Such strategic thinkers include Yusuf al-'Ayiri, Abu Mus'ab al-Suri, and Abu 'Umar al-Sayf.[14] Some writers are completely anonymous and are known only by their nom de plume on the Internet, such as Luis 'Atiyat Allah.[15]

The fourth category of ideological actors include the active militant organizations. Groups such as "al-Qa'ida on the Arabian Peninsula" and "al-Qa'ida in the Land of the Two Rivers" often publish their own magazines and declarations with information about their operations and texts justifying their struggle.[16] The purpose of these publications is presumably to generate a maximum of publicity about the group's activities in order to facilitate recruitment and fundraising. These texts, which are distributed on the Internet, provide important insights into how the struggle is perceived at the battlefront.

The fifth category is represented by what one might call the "grassroot radicals," i.e., the thousands of anonymous participants on radical Islamist discussion forums on the Internet, such as *al-Ansar, al-Qal'a* and *al-Islah* [the Supporters; the Citadel; Reform].[17] Every single day, hundreds of messages and commentaries are posted on these forums, which are primarily in Arabic. Subscribers can log on using fake identities and discuss politics, comment on news, and exchange rumours related to jihad fronts around the world. They can also download all the latest recordings and declarations by militant groups and leading ideologues. It is very difficult to know where these individuals come from or what they do in real life. It may seem, however, that the majority are "Internet radicals" who are not directly involved in terrorist activity.

A new focal point

The most obvious change in the global jihadist movement in recent years is that Iraq is now considered by far the most important battle arena in the fight against the Jewish-Crusader alliance. A study of the textual production of leading ideologists from 2001 until today clearly shows that the Iraq conflict became the most pressing single issue on the global jihadist agenda as early as the autumn of 2002.

The leadership of the old al-Qa'ida started referring to the looming Iraq War in early October 2002. At that time Ayman al-Zawahiri released an audio statement in which he said:

> The campaign against Iraq has aims that go beyond Iraq into the Arab Islamic world [...] Its first aim is to destroy any effective military force in the proximity of Israel. Its second aim is to consolidate the supremacy of Israel [...] America and its deputies should know that their crimes will not go unpunished.[18]

Usama bin Ladin's first reference to the Iraq War came in the audio statement entitled "Letter to the Iraqi people" in early February 2003, which opened with the following words:

> We are following up with great interest and extreme concern the Crusaders' preparations for war to occupy a former capital of Islam, loot Muslims' wealth, and install an agent government.[19]

Since then, the two leaders have issued at least 22 declarations, 17 of which make reference to Iraq, and seven of which have Iraq as its main topic. Out of the 12 statements released in 2004, only one did not mention Iraq. In comparison, Palestine is referred to in 14 of the 22 statements and was not the main topic in any of them.[20]

The religious scholars in the global jihadist movement also began dealing with the Iraq question at an early stage. As early as September 2002, the prominent radical Saudi shaykh Nasir al-Fahd released a book entitled "The Crusader Campaign in its Second Phase: The Iraq War."[21] In October 2002, al-Fahd and six other Saudi shaykhs issued a statement called "Fatwa on the Infidelity of Whoever Helps the Americans Against Muslims in Iraq."[22] Virtually all of the most prominent jihad shaykhs have since then issued statements on the necessity of fighting the crusaders in Iraq.[23] The most visible and prolific theologian on the Iraq question is undoubtedly the Kuwaiti scholar Hamid al-'Ali, who has written more than 20 fatwas on various aspects of the struggle in Iraq.[24]

The independent strategic thinkers have produced a large number of publications on how the jihadists should proceed to liberate Iraq. The first long strategic analyses that appeared in the autumn of 2002 focused on the strategic intentions behind the American campaign, and on the possible types of military operations the US might launch against Iraq.[25] Later analyses sought to provide concrete strategic advice on the way forward in Iraq. The most well-known titles include "Iraq and the Crusader Invasion – Lessons and Expectations" by Abu 'Umar al-Sayf, "Iraq – From Occupation to Liberation" by the editors of the jihadist magazine *Majallat al-Ansar*, as well as the anonymous work "Iraqi Jihad – Expectations and Dangers."[26] A good indication of the strong interest among these ideologists in the Iraq issue can be found by conducting a bibliographical search in one of the most extensive online databases for radical Islamist literature, *Minbar al-Tawhid wa'l-Jihad* [Pulpit of God's Unity and Jihad].[27] In October 2005, this database contained 59 titles that included the name "Iraq," ten with the name "Palestine," and eight with "Chechnya."

The militant organizations have written to a varying extent about Iraq in their publications, depending on their agenda and geographical location. It is interesting, however, to note that some jihadist magazines have increasingly made the jihad in Iraq the reference point for their own military activities. For example, the Saudi magazine *Sawt al-Jihad* (The Voice of Jihad) printed a number of articles in 2003 and 2004 which sought to explain how terrorist operations in Saudi Arabia supported the struggle in Iraq. They were thus legitimizing the terrorist campaign in Saudi Arabia by emphasizing its beneficial effect on the jihad in Iraq.[28]

The "grassroot radicals" also seem to have expressed gradually more and more interest in the Iraq question since 2003. Today, Iraq represents by far the most common topic of discussion on the radical Islamist Web forums. Vast quantities of videos, sound recordings, books, and declarations circulate today on these forums, and most of the material concerns the jihad in Iraq.

It is difficult to measure the evolution of the relative interest in the Iraq issue in these communities. This author made an attempt at quantifying this interest by

Table 1 Number of postings (*P*) and related readings (*R*) on different jihad fronts on the Internet forum *al-Qalʿa* on the 15th of selected months between Oct. 2003 – Jan. 2005

	Iraq		Palestine		Saudi Arabia		Afghanistan		Chechnya		Other topics	
	P	*R*	*P*	*R*	*P*	*R*	*P*	*R*	*P*	*R*	*P*	*R*
Oct 03	4	626	4	524	31	26871	0	0	0	0	28	14061
Feb 04	7	4120	1	464	7	12473	0	0	0	0	17	8265
May 04	13	11423	1	297	11	7443	0	0	1	689	26	12151
Aug 04	19	12666	2	469	3	1430	0	0	0	0	15	7532
Nov 04	6	5999	1	515	2	969	0	0	0	0	8	5652
Jan 05	18	4957	4	1258	4	2237	0	0	0	0	17	8486

examining the digital archive of the radical Islamist Web forum al-Qalʿa. By reading all the messages posted on the 15th of selected months from October 2003 to January 2005, and by classifying them by theme, I generated a data set which can be used to make some interesting observations (see Table 1). There are of course significant weaknesses and problems with these data, especially given the time intervals between each count and the uncertainties regarding the identity of the participants. Nevertheless, the data seem to support the hypothesis that the relative interest in the Iraqi jihad has increased gradually since 2003. It also seems that the focus on Iraq increased the most in the period between April – August 2004, which corresponds to the most intensive phase of the campaign of abductions of foreigners in Iraq. One may also note that the number of postings was surprisingly low in late 2003, but this may have to do with the fact that the terrorist campaign in Saudi Arabia was attracting significant attention, and that the jihadist groups inside Iraq did not yet have a fully developed media apparatus.

If it is the case that Iraq has gained the status as the most important battlefront for the global jihadist movement, it is natural to ask why this is so. How do the leading ideologues describe the struggle in Iraq, and what kind of reasons do they give regarding why Muslims should join the Iraqi jihad? This article argues that there are three major recurring arguments or themes in the global jihadist discourse on Iraq.

The first reason is that Iraq constitutes the best example today of Muslim suffering at the hands of Americans. Many ideologues emphasize that the US-led invasion of Iraq confirms Washington's evil intentions in the Middle East once and for all. The American-led coalition is described as having an appetite for Muslim territory as well as Muslim blood. In April 2004, Usama bin Ladin said:

> America has attacked Iraq and soon will also attack Iran, Saudi Arabia, Egypt, and Sudan. You should be aware the infidels cannot bear the existence of Muslims and want to capture their resources and destroy them.[29]

In October 2004, he added:

> [O]ppression and the intentional killing of innocent women and children
> is a deliberate American policy. [...] This means the oppressing and embar-
> going to death of millions as Bush Sr. did in Iraq in the greatest mass
> slaughter of children mankind has ever known, and it means the throwing
> of millions of pounds of bombs and explosives at millions of children –
> also in Iraq – as Bush Jr. did. [30]

The war and the occupation has created new and powerful symbols of Muslim suffering. Violent battles and American war crimes have introduced names such as Falluja
and Abu Ghrayb into the jihadist vocabulary. New visual symbols, such as pictures of
American soldiers torturing Iraqis, have added to the images of orange-clad prisoners
in Guantanamo Bay as powerful expressions of Muslims' suffering. These images are
very widely used in propaganda films and declarations by militant Islamist groups.

The second major topic that permeates the writings of global jihadist ideologues
is that the Iraqi jihad is a strategic crossroads in the overall struggle between Muslims
and the Crusaders. Iraq's position in the heart of the Islamic world and the Arab cultural sphere makes the country an extremely important battlefield. In the jihadist
literature, Iraq is presented as the final entrenchment in the defence against the US
entry into the region. As Bin Ladin underlined in a statement in May 2004:

> We are at a crossroads. [...] It is obvious that the great trick being pro-
> moted by the United States nowadays under the pretext of forcing the
> so-called reform on the greater Islamic world is a replica of Bremer's plan
> for Iraq, which provides for excluding religion, plundering wealth, killing
> men, terrifying people, and transgressing on that which is sacrosanct. [31]

The outcome of this final battle will have enormous consequences. If the Jews and the
Crusaders prevail, the path is open to the establishment of a Greater Israel from the
Nile to the Euphrates. In February 2003, Bin Ladin warned that:

> One of the most important objectives of the new Crusader attack is to pave
> the way and prepare the region, after its fragmentation, for the establish-
> ment of what is known as 'the Greater State of Israel,' whose borders will
> include extensive areas of Iraq and Egypt, through Syria, Lebanon, Jordan,
> all of Palestine, and large parts of the Land of the Two Holy Places. [32]

On the other hand, a victory for the jihadists would represent a major turning
point in the overall war against the Jewish – Crusader alliance. It would turn Iraq into
an important advanced base, from which the global jihadist movement can liberate
Palestine and Saudi Arabia from occupation. In the text known as "Jihadi Iraq –
Expectations and Dangers" written in late 2003, the anonymous writer explains that:

> If the Americans lose (and that is what we wish from God the Almighty),
> then the doors will open before the Islamic tide and we will have, for the

first time in our modern age, an advanced base for the Islamic renaissance and the Islamic struggle close to the Land of the Two Holy Places and the al-Aqsa Mosque.[33]

The third major theme found in jihadist writings on Iraq is that the prospects of victory are considered higher than on any other jihad front. Prominent ideologues have cited several different reasons for this, but most point out that the enormous costs and commitments undertaken by the US in Iraq represent a significant strategic advantage for the jihadists. In September 2004, Ayman al-Zawahiri described how Iraq has become a quagmire for the United States:

> As for Muslim Iraq, the mujahidin in it have turned America's plan upside down after the interim government's weakness became clear. America's defeat in Iraq [...] has become a matter of time, God willing. The Americans [...] are between two fires; if they continue, they will bleed until death, and if they withdraw, they will lose everything.[34]

Others again emphasize the fact that the US now has a large and historically unprecedented military presence in the Middle East, and that it has never been easier for the jihadists to strike directly at American targets. In December 2004, Bin Ladin summarized the strategic situation in the following passage:

> To the mujahidin: There is now a rare and golden opportunity to make America bleed in Iraq, both economically and in terms of human losses and morale. Don't miss out on this opportunity, lest you regret it.[35]

Debate and disagreement

A second and seemingly paradoxical ideological development since 2002 is that the Iraq conflict introduced new dilemmas and debates that have caused a certain amount of disagreement and division among the global jihadists. Despite the consensus on Iraq being the most important battlefront in the war between the Muslims and the Crusaders, debates emerged on two new sets of questions. The first concerned the relationship between Iraq and other jihad fronts, whereas the second regarded how the war for Iraq should be waged.

From an early stage, the jihad in Iraq was considered by global jihadists as politically legitimate and theologically uncontroversial. The Iraq battlefront was also more easily accessible for the average foreign fighter than, for example Palestine, which is enclosed by Israel, and Chechnya or Afghanistan, which are geographically and culturally peripheral to most Arabs. This new and very attractive jihad front introduced a dilemma in jihadist circles worldwide: Should we fight at home or travel to Iraq? In 2003 and 2004 one could observe debates over this question in a number of militant communities.

The debate was strongest in Saudi Arabia. There, a group known as "al-Qaʿida on the Arabian Peninsula" had launched a terrorist campaign in May 2003 with a series of large-scale attacks against Western targets in the capital, Riyadh. The campaign was controversial in the wider Islamist community because the attacks and the ensuing clashes with police involved the killing of other Muslims.[36] The group behind the campaign was also criticized for undermining the jihad in Iraq, on the basis that the events in Saudi Arabia diverted media attention away from the developments in Iraq. In December 2003, the very influential Chechnya-based Saudi shaykh Abu ʿUmar al-Sayf called upon the Saudi jihadists to end their terrorist campaign and travel to Iraq instead.[37] "Al-Qaʿida on the Arabian Peninsula" responded by publishing articles in their magazine Sawt al-Jihad arguing that the jihad in Saudi Arabia was beneficial to the struggle in Iraq because it put the US under pressure on several fronts. They also maintained that it was preferable for Saudi jihadists to stay and fight in the country they know the best.[38] The debate seems to have ended, at least temporarily, in the summer of 2004 in favour of fighting in Iraq only. By all accounts, this emerging consensus among Saudi militants has significantly undermined recruitment to "al-Qaʿida on the Arabian Peninsula."

We find indications of similar debates elsewhere, for example, in Jordan. In late 2004, Hazim al-Amin, a journalist from the Arabic newspaper al-Hayat, conducted a series of interviews with supporters of Abu Musʿab al-Zarqawi in Jordan. In one of his subsequent articles, al-Amin wrote:

> Many of the activists say they support Abu Musʿab's war in Iraq, but oppose armed operations in Jordan. One of them, Muhammad, says Abu Musʿab made a mistake by sending al-Jiyusi to carry out an operation against the Jordanian security forces. The mujahidin do not have the capacity to open up new battle-fronts, even though the leaders in the given country are infidel despots.[39]

There are also symptoms of such debates in Europe. The European jihadists have lost most of their prominent ideologues and do not produce their own publications, so it is more difficult to follow their ideological development. However, radical Internet forums can provide a glimpse into ongoing debates. For example, one could follow a discussion on the French-language forum al-Mourabitoune in the spring of 2004 over whether it was better to fight in Iraq or in Europe. Most participants favoured Iraq, while a minority preferred Europe. Asked whether he was ready to go to Iraq, one participant wrote: "No. Because the Jihad will come to us."[40] The many recent arrests of people involved in recruitment to Iraq also suggests that jihadists in Europe are investing considerable resources in the Iraqi front rather than terrorist operations on the European continent.[41]

The debate over whether Europe is a legitimate battleground in the struggle for Iraq has been most visible after the bombings in Madrid and London in 2004 and 2005. The prominent strategic thinker Abu Musʿab al-Suri expressed certain reservations about the March 11 Madrid attack and admitted that some of its victims were innocent [abria'].[42] A similar though much more intense controversy emerged after the July 7 London bombings. While many Web forum participants applauded the attacks as a long-awaited punishment to Britain for its involvement in Iraq, the influential shaykh Abu Basir al-Tartusi issued a statement strongly condemning the attack.[43] The declaration caused disbelief and confusion among grassroot jihadists, some of whom accused Abu Basir of "selling out" in order to avoid expulsion from Britain.[44]

In other words, it may seem that the strong consensus on the importance of the resistance in Iraq has contributed – at least temporarily – to an undermining of other jihad fronts. It is reasonable to assume that radical forces are being diverted away from other terrorist campaigns that are considered by many as being strategically unproductive or theologically controversial. This does not mean, however, that other fronts are being abandoned. Many global jihadists still believe that it is perfectly possible to fight on several fronts simultaneously. This is not least the case in Europe, where authorities have averted a large number of terrorist attacks by militant Islamists in the past few years.[45] Moreover, the Madrid and London attacks were carried out by people who no doubt saw their operation as an extension of the Iraqi resistance.[46]

The second major issue which has caused a certain amount of debate and disagreement is that of how to wage the jihad in Iraq. One of the main reasons for this is the overall brutalization of the methods used by militant Islamists on the Iraqi battlefield. Some groups have adopted unusual and controversial tactics, such as kidnappings and decapitations of civilians. With a few exceptions, these methods had not previously been used by radical Sunni groups before the Iraq War.[47] What is being discussed in global jihadists quarters is not so much the legitimacy, but the efficiency of such tactics. A few radical shaykhs, such as Abu Muhammad al-Maqdisi, have openly criticized these methods as counterproductive.[48] On radical Internet forums, some participants have expressed concern that the use of such methods might undermine support for the struggle. Some of the criticism seems to have been taken into account, because since the autumn of 2004, the bullet seems to have replaced the knife as the preferred means of execution among jihadist groups in Iraq.[49]

In addition to the debates over methods, there has also been some disagreement over the question of what represents legitimate targets. All global jihadists agreed very early on that Western military targets and Iraqi security forces constitute legitimate targets and that Iraqi Sunni civilians should not be targeted. Between these extremities, however, one finds several categories of targets that have been subject to debate, notably Sunni "collaborators" (e.g., drivers and interpreters), Shi'ite civilians, and Western civilians (e.g., journalists and relief workers). The question of how to deal with fellow Muslims who in some way or other help the enemy is an old and recurring issue in the jihadist literature. In the summer of 2003, the Kuwaiti shaykh Hamid al-'Ali was asked by jihadist groups in Iraq to clarify the matter. He responded in a fatwa saying: "all who serve in the enemies' ranks as collaborators [...] should be treated like the enemy," but he left it to the "fighters on the ground to" decide in each specific case.[50] The question of exactly what kind of activity constitutes collaboration has not been resolved and is a source for repeated debates. It is worth noting that Usama bin Ladin, who in the past always avoided calling explicitly for violence against other Muslims, has openly declared the new Iraqi regime and all its supporters infidels.[51]

Controversy also surrounds the targeting of Iraqi Shi'ites by Abu Mus'ab al-Zarqawi and his organization "al-Qa'ida in the Land of the Two Rivers." In the past, the global jihadist movement emphasized pan-Islamism and unity among Muslims in the face of the threat from the external enemy. Although Salafi discourse has always been virulently anti-Shi'ite, Arab Islamist militants have never in modern times targeted Shi'ites on the scale we are now witnessing in Iraq. Al-Zarqawi most likely found inspiration for this strategy during his time in Pakistan, where anti-Shi'ite violence has been common since the mid-1980s.[52] The mass-casualty attacks on Iraqi Shiʿites have drawn criticism from a number of quarters. There are indications that the leadership in the old al-Qaʿida has been sceptical to this development.[53] Some grassroot radicals have questioned the anti-Shiʿite strategy in the discussion forums.[54] However, the most notable criticism has come from the influential shaykh Abu Muhammad al-Maqdisi, who has openly criticized al-Zarqawis indiscriminate attacks on Shiʿites in Iraq.[55]

More strategic thinking

The third important ideological change since the Iraq War is that so-called "strategic studies" have been significantly developed as a distinct genre in the jihadist literature. This genre differs from other types of texts (such as fatwas or recruitment propaganda) in that its main purpose is to identify the best possible military strategy to defeat the enemy.[56] Texts in this genre have three main characteristics: they are secular in style, academic in their approach, and objective in their assessments.

"Jihadi strategic studies" have existed as a genre and way of thinking since the war in Afghanistan in the 1980s. In jihadist publications from the 1980s we find many sober strategic analyses of the struggle between the Mujahidin and the Red Army in Afghanistan. In the 1990s, strategic studies were less common as a literary genre, but survived as an intellectual tradition, not least in al-Qaʿida's training camps. It seems that this way of writing was not systematically applied in the analysis of the struggle against the USA until late 2001. In early 2002, the al-Qaʿida-affiliated Internet site "Centre for Islamic Studies and Research" and the online magazine *Majallat al-Ansar* published several interesting articles in this genre.[57] It is worth noting that Majallat al-Ansar featured a regular column called "Strategic Studies," starting from its first issue in January 2002. These articles avoided religious rhetoric and had no qualms about using Western news media and academic studies as references. They quoted classical military strategists like Karl von Clausewitz and used concepts like "fourth generation warfare."[58]

Since the autumn of 2002, the number of texts in this genre has increased considerably. In the same period we can also observe a qualitative improvement in the strategic analyses presented in these texts. Some of them are remarkably sophisticated. A particularly interesting development is the widening of the notion of strategy to include much more than purely military factors. The analyses written since 2002 seem to put increasingly more emphasis on the political, economic, and psychological dimensions of the confrontation with the US.[59] A good example of this development is the text known as "Jihadi Iraq – Expectations and Dangers."[60] Its central argument is that the only thing that will make the US leave Iraq is the economic cost of occupation. The best way of increasing the economic burden on Washington is to pressure its allies to withdraw from the coalition. The study then proceeds to a series of case studies of the domestic political situation in three European countries considered key members of the coalition. The author concludes that Spain is the most vulnerable link in the alliance, because the political leadership is weak and public opinion is massively against the Spanish presence in Iraq. The study, which was written in the autumn of 2003, recommends striking at Spanish forces at the time of the election in March 2004. The relationship between this text and the terrorist attacks on March 11, 2004 remains unclear, but "Jihadi Iraq" stands as good example of the evolution of strategic thought in the global jihadist movement.[61]

The intellectual processes behind this development were already underway when the prospects of war in Iraq caught the jihadists' attention in late 2002. However, it is argued here that the war and occupation in Iraq contributed significantly to promoting strategic studies as a genre in jihadist literature. One reason for this is that the strong legitimacy of the struggle in Iraq reduced the need for texts justifying the fight on theological grounds. As a result, the ideologues could spend less time on the question of "why jihad?" and more time on that of "how jihad?" Moreover, the elimination in 2002 and 2003 of nearly all established "jihad shaykhs" left the ideological field more open to strategic thinkers. A second reason is that the consensus on Iraq as the most important battlefront stimulated a collective intellectual effort to resolve the question of how to evict the Americans from Iraq. Radical ideologues and strategists from all over the world have been able, by means of the Internet, to participate in a "global brainstorming" about the best strategy for liberating Iraq. A third reason is that the Iraq conflict may be said to represent a more concrete and approachable strategic problem than the global jihadists have faced in a long time. After the Iraq War, the US found itself for the first time as a conventional occupying force in the heart of the Middle East. This gave the global jihadist movement a clearly defined military task: to force the Americans out of Iraq.

New enemies

A fourth ideological change in the global jihadist movement since the Iraq War is that their notion of the enemy seems to have been expanded and somewhat altered. One of the most conspicuous changes in the statements from the old al-Qaʿida leadership since the invasion of Afghanistan is that the number of specific countries highlighted as enemies has increased considerably. Bin Ladin and al-Zawahiri used to speak in general terms about the "Jewish – Crusader alliance" or refer to a small group of specific countries (particularly the US and Israel, occasionally the UK and France).[62] From the autumn of 2001 onwards, more and more different countries have been declared legitimate targets, and this tendency continued further after the invasion of Iraq in 2003. The following statement by Ayman al-Zawahiri from October 2004 is symptomatic:

> We shouldn't wait for the American, English, French, Jewish, Hungarian, Polish and South Korean forces to invade Egypt, the Arabian Peninsula, Yemen, and Algeria and then start the resistance after the occupier had already invaded us. We should start now. The interests of America, Britain, Australia, France, Norway, Poland, South Korea, and Japan are everywhere. All of them participated in the invasion of Afghanistan, Iraq, and Chechnya, they also facilitated Israel's existence.[63]

One underlying reason for this development may be that the invasions of Afghanistan and Iraq involved broad coalitions of active and passive participant countries.

Since 2003, it seems that there are particularly two categories of countries that are viewed by the global jihadists with more hostility than before. The first is America's European coalition partners and the second is Iraq's neighbours in the Gulf. After 2003, European countries seem to be described increasingly often as enemies, perhaps not only because many participated in the Iraq War, but also because they arrested and convicted large numbers of militant Islamists in recent years. Other important reasons include Europe's rejection of Bin Ladin's cease-fire proposal in April 2004, and France's ban on religious symbols in schools (known as the "hijab ban"). It should be mentioned that the global jihadists' view of Europe is not monolithic. There seems to be some disagreement, at least among the "grassroot radicals," as to whether the different countries' positions on the Iraq question should be taken into account when selecting targets for terrorist attacks. When two French journalists were kidnapped in Iraq the autumn of 2004, some participants on the radical Web forums argued that French targets should be avoided on the basis that the French opposed the war. Other participants disagreed.[64] This is yet another example of the paradoxical ideological effect of the Iraq War: the overall enmity to European countries seems to have increased, but the jihadists are divided by new debates over strategy.

There is less divergence regarding the status of Gulf countries such as Kuwait, Qatar, and Bahrain. Since 2003, there has been an increase in the number of texts and declarations condemning the Gulf countries' role as a military platform for the US-led campaign in Iraq. In their analyses of US military strategy in the region, jihadist strategic thinkers have emphasized Washington's partnership with the smaller Gulf states.[65] Some militant groups have called repeatedly for terrorist attacks in the smaller Gulf countries in order to liberate the entire Arabian Peninsula from Crusader occupation.[66] Postings mentioning Gulf states, which used to be a rarity on the jihadist discussion forums, seem to have become more frequent since the autumn of 2002. This interest has been further fuelled by the increase in the number of violent incidents in Gulf countries such as Kuwait and Qatar.

Conclusions

This article has argued that four major ideological changes have taken place in the global jihadist movement since the Iraq War. First, the invasion of Iraq gave the global jihadists a strategic and emotional focal point at a time when the movement was strategically disorientated, having lost its territorial base in Afghanistan. Second, the Iraq War and the occupation have introduced new dilemmas and questions that have caused debate and may have led to a channelling of radical forces to Iraq, possibly at the expense of other jihad fronts. Third, the occupation of Iraq contributed to the development and refinement of so-called "strategic studies" as a genre in jihadist literature. Finally, the Iraq experience has changed the jihadists' notion of the enemy and placed the Gulf countries and Europe more clearly in the spotlight.

Some of these changes were predictable before the war; others were not. Many analysts predicted that an attack on Iraq would constitute a propaganda coup for the global jihadists, who for years had been describing America as a warmonger with imperialist ambitions in the Middle East. Few people, however, had expected that Iraq would be so attractive as a battle front that it would weaken, at least in the short-run, terrorist campaigns elsewhere. And nobody could know that Spain would be the country in Europe to be hit first and hardest by Iraq-inspired terrorism.

These developments add to the many historical examples of unexpected ideological consequences of war that should inspire humility in even the most confident of analysts. Who could have known that the veterans from the first Afghan War would turn so quickly against America? Who could have predicted that the deployment of US troops in Saudi Arabia during the 1990 – 91 Gulf crisis would be interpreted by Usama bin Ladin as an occupation of Islam's holy places? Who realized that the start of the second Chechen War in 1999 would lead to such a dramatic increase in international recruitment to al-Qaʿida's training camps in Afghanistan?

We still do not know what the full consequences of the war in Iraq will be for the future of international terrorism. So far there have been surprisingly few cases of terrorism spillover from Iraq, but such attacks may very well increase in the future. What is certain, however, is that the consequences of the war will be long-lasting. Let us not forget that the current leaders of the global jihadist movement joined the first Afghan War as young recruits more than 20 years ago.

Notes

1   Richard Norton-Taylor, "Iraq War Has Swollen Ranks of al-Qaida," *Guardian*, October 16, 2003.

2   Dana Priest, "Iraq New Terror Breeding Ground," *Washington Post*, January 14, 2005.

3   Notable exceptions include Fawaz Gerges, *The Far Enemy* (Cambridge: Cambridge University Press, 2005); Guido Steinberg, *Der Nahe und Der Ferne Feind* [*The Near and the Far Enemy*] (Munich: C.H. Beck, 2005); Gilles Kepel, *The War for Muslim Minds* (Cambridge, MA: Belknap, 2004); Olivier Roy, *Globalized Islam* (New York: Columbia, 2004); Dominique Thomas, *Les Hommes d'al-Qaïda* [*The Men of al-Qaʿida*] (Paris: Michalon, 2005); Anonymous (Michael Scheuer), *Imperial Hubris* (New York: Brassey's, 2004). See also Reuven Paz' numerous PRISM papers (available at http://www.e-prism.org) for excellent shorter analyses of ongoing ideological developments.

4   Usama bin Ladin, "Declaration of War Against the Americans Occupying the Two Holy Places," signed August 23, 1996 (Reproduced in Thomas Hegghammer, *Dokumentasjon om al-Qaida* [*Documentation on al-Qaʿida*], Kjeller: FFI/Rapport 01393, 2002 [Available at http://rapporter.ffi.no/rapporter/2002/01393.pdf], pp. 123–140).

5   Ayman al-Zawahiri, "*Fursan taht Rayat al-Nabi*" ["Knights under the Prophet's Banner"], published as an article series in *al-Sharq al-Awsat*, December 2–12, 2001.

6   For an overview of texts by Usama bin Ladin and Ayman al-Zawahiri in English translation, see Thomas Hegghammer, *Dokumentasjon om al-Qaida* [*Documentation on al-Qaʿida*] Kjeller: FFI/Rapport 01393, 2002 (Available at http://rapporter.ffi.no/rapporter/2002/01393.pdf), and Thomas Hegghammer, *Al-Qaida Statements 2003–2004*, Kjeller: FFI/Rapport 01428, 2005 (Available at http://rapporter.ffi.no/rapporter/2005/01428.pdf). See also Kepel et al., *Al-Qaïda dans le texte*. Since this article was originally written, two new compilations of quality translations of Bin Ladin texts have been published: see Bruce Lawrence (ed.), *Messages to the World*

(New York: Verso, 2005); and Randall B. Hamud (ed.), *Osama bin Laden: America's Enemy in His Own Words* (San Diego: Nadeem, 2005).

7   There has been a certain amount of debate over when, and if at all, al-Qaʿida ever constituted a coherent, self-aware organization. According to one version of history, al-Qaʿida was founded as an organization in the late 1980s, as an offshoot of the Services Bureau and the brainchild of ʿAbdallah ʿAzzam (see *9/11 Commission Report*; Rohan Gunaratna, *Inside al-Qaida* (London: Hurst, 2002)). Critics (see Jason Burke, *Al-Qaeda* (London: IB Tauris, 2003)) have rightly pointed out that there are extremely few indications pre-9/11 that the name "al-Qaʿida" was ever in use by the people whom we assume to be its members. What is clear, however, is that the organizational structures around Bin Ladin became markedly more extensive, complex, and hierarchical after his move to Afghanistan in 1996. There is no doubt that by 1998–99, Bin Ladin presided over a sophisticated organization, whether the name al-Qaʿida was used internally or not.

8   *The 9/11 Commission Report*, p. 67.

9   It must be emphasized that national and regional "clusters" have always existed within the al-Qaʿida network. See Marc Sageman, *Understanding Terrorist Networks* (Philadelphia: University of Pennsylvania, 2004).

10   Hegghammer, *Dokumentasjon om al-Qaida* and Hegghammer, *Al-Qaida Statements 2003–2004*.

11   Reuven Paz, "Al-Qaʾidah's Interpreters," *PRISM Occasional Papers* 1, 1 (Available at http://www.e-prism.org.il).

12   Radical Islamist ideologues themselves use the term "scholars of jihad" [*ʿulamaʾ al-jihad*], in opposition to the "scholars of the palace" [*ʿulamaʾ al-balat*] who side with the oppressive rulers. See Ayman al-Zawahiri, *Knights under the Prophet's Banner*.

13   Examples of prominent scholars imprisoned in 2002 and 2003 include the Palestinian-Jordanian Abu Qatada al-Falastini (aka ʿUmar Mahmud Abu ʿUmar), held in the United Kingdom, and the Saudi Nasir al-Fahd and ʿAli al-Khudayr (imprisoned in Saudi Arabia). Some important figures were imprisoned in the mid-1990s, such as the Egyptian ʿUmar ʿAbd al-Rahman (imprisoned in the US) and the Palestinian-Jordanian Abu Muhammad al-Maqdisi (aka ʿIsam al-Barqawi). Al-Maqdisi regularly releases texts, presumably smuggled out from his Jordanian prison by visitors. One of the last remaining "jihad shaykhs" is the Syrian Abu Basir al-Tartusi (aka ʿAbd al-Muʾnim Halima) who is based in the UK.

14   Yusuf al-ʿAyiri was a Saudi ideologist and veteran of the first Afghan War in the 1980s. From about 2000 until his death in late May 2003, he was Usama bin Ladin's main contact in Saudi Arabia. He played an important ideological role as administrator of the website *Markaz al-Dirasat waʾl-Buhuth al-Islamiyya* [Center for Islamic Studies and Research] and as author of several innovative strategic studies. He is also believed to be the architect behind the terrorist campaign launched in Saudi Arabia in May 2003. Abu Musʿab al-Suri (aka Mustafa Sitmariam Nasir, aka ʿUmar ʿAbd al-Hakim) is a Syrian veteran from the first Afghan War who played an important role on the European jihadist scene in the 1990s, notably as Editor of the jihadist magazine *al-Ansar* [The Supporters] in London. He later disappeared from the ideological scene, only to reemerge with a much publicized "come-back statement" in December 2004. He is said by intelligence sources to have strong links to jihadists in Spain as well as to Abu Musʿab al-Zarqawi in Iraq. He lived in Spain for several years in the 1990s and acquired Spanish citizenship by marrying a Spanish convert.

See Lorenzo Vidino, "A Suri State of Affairs," *National Review Online*, May 21, 2004. Al-Suri's large ideological production is very influential and he was reportedly arrested in the Pakistani city of Quetta in early November 2005. Abu ʿUmar al-Sayf is a Saudi-born ideologist who is based in or near Chechnya. He is said to be one of the main ideological guides of Shamil Basayev's radical faction of the Chechen resistance. His books are signed "Head of the High Court of cassation in Chechnya" [*Ra'is Mahkamat al-Tamyiz al-ʾUlya fi al-Shihan*] and he is described in the Jihadist literature as "Mufti of the Mujahidin in Chechnya" [*Mufti al-Mujahidin fi al-Shihan*] or "Chief Judge and Leader of the Courts in Chechnya" [*Al-Qadi al-Awwal wa Amir al-Mahakim fi al-Shishan*]. At the end of November 2005, there were credible reports on jihadist message boards that Abu ʿUmar had been killed by Russian troops. Al-Sayf is very well respected in the global jihadist movement.

15 See for example *"Maqalatuhu Tatalaqqafuha Andiyat al-Hiwar,"* ["His Articles are Taking over the Discussion Forums"] *al-Quds al-Arabi* [London], July 23, 2002. There has been much speculation about ʿAtiyat Allah's identity; for a recent theory, see *al-Sharq al-Awsat*, October 2, 2005.

16 Al-Qaʿida on the Arabian Peninsula published three different magazines: *Sawt al-Jihad* [Voice of Jihad] (published in 29 issues), *Muʿaskar al-Battar* [Camp of the Sabre] (22 issues) and *al-Khansa* [named for a seventh century female poet who converted to Islam and urged her sons to wage jihad] (one issue). Al-Qaʿida in the Land of the Two Rivers publishes a magazine called *Dharwat al-Sanam* [Peak of the Hump], while the Salafist Group for Call and Combat (GSPC) publishes *al-Jamaʿa*. Several other magazines have been published by various groups in the past two years. Many of them are available at http://www.e-prism.org.il.

17 Other important forums at the time of writing include *Al-ikhlas, Al-hikma, Al-maʾsada Al-jihadiyya, Mufakkarat usama, Al-hisba, Al-tajdid*, and *Al-saqifa*. There may be as many as 100 jihadist discussion forums, but the majority of them attract relatively few visitors. The Internet addresses of most of these websites change so often that it would not be useful to include them here.

18 Hegghammer, *Dokumentasjon om al-Qaida*, p. 185.

19 Hegghammer, *Al-Qaida Statements 2003–2004*, p. 12.

20 See Hegghammer, *Al-Qaida Statements 2003–2004*.

21 Nasir al-Fahd, *al-Hamla al-Salibiyya fi Marhalatiha al-Thaniyya: Harb al-ʿIraq* [The Crusader Campaign in its Second Phase: The Iraq War], available at http://www.tawhed.ws. Nasir al-Fahd is a prolific and influential Saudi scholar who was the leading figure in the so-called Saudi salafi-jihadist current which emerged in Burayda and Riyadh from the late 1990s onward and which included scholars such as ʿAli al-Khudayr, Ahmad al-Khalidi, ʿAbd al-ʿAziz al-Jarbu, and several others. They were all imprisoned in late May 2003.

22 Nasir al-Fahd et al., *Fatwa fi Kufr man ʿAna al-Amrikan ʿala al-Muslimin fi'l-ʿIraq* [Fatwa on the Infidelity of Whoever Helps the Americans Against Muslims in Iraq], posted October 12, 2002 on http://www.alkhoder.com, now available on http://www.tawhed.ws; see Stéphane Lacroix, *Le Champ Politico-Religieux en Arabie Saoudite après le 11 Septembre* [The Political-Religious Field in Saudi Arabia after September 11] Master's degree thesis, Institut d'Études Politiques de Paris, 2003.

23 See for example Abu Basir al-Tartusi, *Bayan hawla Ghazuw al-Salibiyyin ʿala al-ʿIraq* [Statement Regarding the Crusaders' Invasion of Iraq], available on http://www.tawhed.ws; Abu Muhammad al-Maqdisi, *Risalat Munasara wa Munasaha li-Ikhwanina Ahl al-Sunna wa'l-Jamaʿa fi'l-ʿIraq* [Letter to Our Sunni Brothers in Iraq], available

on http://www.tawhed.ws; Ahmad al-Khalidi, *Wa-Intaqalat al-Maʿraka ila Ard al-ʿIraq* [The Battle Has Moved to Iraq], available on http://www.tawhed.ws; Sulayman al-ʿUlwan, *Risala ila Shaʿb al-ʿIraq* [Letter to the People of Iraq], available on http://www.tawhed.ws.

24   Hamid al-ʿAli is a Kuwaiti scholar and former leader of one of the two main moderate Islamist parties in Kuwait. His discourse turned noticeably more radical in 2002. Al-ʿAli has emerged as the most important *mufti* for jihadist groups operating in Iraq. He was put under house arrest in the summer of 2004, and imprisoned in May 2005. See http://www.h-alali.net.

25   The very first strategic analysis of Washington's ambitions in Iraq appeared in August 2002 in Abu ʿUbayd al-Qirshi's, *Kharif al-Ghadab al-ʿIraqi* [The Iraqi Autumn of Wrath], *Majallat al-Ansar* 16 (August 24, 2002). Later in the autumn of 2002, a larger and more influential work appeared, namely Yusuf al-ʿAyiri's *al-Harb al-Salibiyya ala al-ʿIraq* [The Crusader War on Iraq], which was published as a series of 11 articles on the website "Centre for Islamic Studies and Research."

26   Abu ʿUmar al-Sayf, *Al-ʿIraq wa Ghazuw al-Salib: Durus wa Taʾammulat* [Iraq and the Crusader Invasion: Lessons and Expectations], available on http://www.tawhed. ws; Sayf al-Din al-Ansari et al., *Al-ʿIraq: min al-Ihtilal ila al-Tahrir* [Iraq – From Occupation to Liberation], *Kitab al-Ansar* June 3, 2003, available on http://www. tawhed.ws; Anonymous, *ʿIraq al-Jihad: Amal wa Akhtar* [Iraqi Jihad – Expectations and Dangers], posted on the website Global Islamic Media on December 10, 2003, now available on http://www.mil.no/multimedia/archive/00038/_Jihadi_ Iraq__Hopes__38063a.pdf. One might also mention Yusuf al-ʿAyiri, *Mustaqbal al-ʿIraq waʾl-Jazira al-ʿArabiyya baʿd Suqut Baghdad* [The Future of Iraq and the Arabian Peninsula After the Fall of Baghdad]; and Anonymous, *Al-Khasaʾir al-Amrikiyya: mundhu Ghazwat Manhattan wa hatta al-ʿIraq* [American Losses: From the Manhattan Raid to Iraq] originally published by *al-Nida* Website, now available on http:// www.tawhed.ws. Among the many interesting articles on Iraq in the jihadist maga- zine *Majallat al-Ansar*, one might mention Abu Ayman al-Hilali, "*Al-Hujum ʿala al-ʿIraq: bayna Khalt al-Awraq wa Tartibiha*" ["The Attack on Iraq: From Mixing the Papers to Organizing Them"], *Majallat al-Ansar* 19 (October 22, 2002); Abu ʿUbayd al-Qirshi, "*Al-Marhala al-Qadima*" ["The Coming Phase"], *Majallat al-Ansar* 22 (December 5, 2002); Abu ʿUbayd al-Qirshi, "*Amrika wa Mabadiʾ al-Harb: bayna al-Nazariyya ila al-Tatbiq*" ["America and the Principles of War: from Theory to Practice"], *Majallat al-Ansar* 24 (January 2, 2003); Abu Ayman al-Hilali, "*Al-Muqawama al-ʿIraqiyya wa Fashl al-Dhariʿ al-Mukhattit al-Amriki*" ["The Iraqi Resistance and the Failure of the American Planning Arm"], *Majallat al-Ansar* 28 (April 3, 2003); and Abu ʿUbayd al-Qirshi, "*Limadha Saqatat Baghdad?*" ["Why Did Baghdad Fall?"], *Majallat al-Ansar* 29 (April 17, 2004).

27   The address of this Website is relatively stable: http://www.tawhed.ws.

28   See for example Muhammad Al-Salim, "*La Tadhhabu liʾl-ʿIraq*" ["Do Not Go to Iraq"], *Sawt al-Jihad* 7 (December 2003).

29   Hegghammer, *Al-Qaida Statements 2003–2004*, p. 30.

30   Hegghammer, *Al-Qaida Statements 2003–2004*, p. 67.

31   Hegghammer, *Al-Qaida Statements 2003–2004*, p. 60.

32   Hegghammer, *Al-Qaida Statements 2003–2004*, p. 17.

33   Anonymous, *Jihadi Iraq – Expectations and Dangers*, p. 2.

34   Hegghammer, *Al-Qaida Statements 2003–2004*, p. 63.

35   Hegghammer, *Al-Qaida Statements 2003-2004*, p. 80.

36   Lacroix and Hegghammer, *Saudi Arabia Backgrounder: Who are the Islamists?*

37   "Al-Qaʾida Leader Calls for Attacks on Americans in Iraq Rather Than on the Saudi Government in Saudi Arabia," *MEMRI Special Dispatch* 635 (available at http://www.memri.org).

38   See for example Al-Salim, "Do not go to Iraq!"; Muhammad al-Salim, *"Labayka ya ʾIraq"* ["Woe to you, Iraq"], *Sawt al-Jihad* 11 (February 2004); Anonymous, *Tasaʾulat hawla Jihad al-Salibiyyin fi Jazirat al-ʿArab* ["Questions Regarding the Jihad Against the Crusaders on the Arabian Peninsula"], *Sawt al-Jihad* 11 and 12 (February/March 2004).

39   *Al-Hayat*, December 14, 2004.

40   See http://www.ribaat.org/services/forum/showthread.php?t=17206.

41   "Terror Recruitment on the Rise in Europe," *MSNBC*, January 25, 2005. Available at http://www.msnbc.msn.com.

42   Abu Musʿab al-Suri, *Bayan Sadir ʿan Maktab al-Shaykh Abu Musʿab al-Suri* [*Statement by the Office of Abu Musʿab al-Suri*], dated December 27, 2004 and published on Islamist websites; See also Abu Musʿab al-Suri, *Daʿwat al-Muqawama al-Islamiyya al-ʿAlamiyya* [*The Call for Global Islamic Resistance*], published on Islamist websites in December 2004, p. 1,392.

43   Abu Basir al-Tartusi, *Bayan hawla al-Tafjirat allati Hasalat fi Madinat Lundun* [*Statement About the Explosions Which Took Place in London*], posted July 9, 2005 on his website http://www.abubaseer.bizland.com.

44   For a good summary of the debate, see Reuven Paz, "Islamic Legitimacy for the London Bombings," *PRISM Occasional Papers* 3, 4 (July 2005).

45   See Petter Nesser, *Jihad in Europe* (Kjeller: FFI/Rapport, 2004), available at http://www.ffi.no; and Petter Nesser, "Post-Millennium Patterns of Jihadist Terrorism in Western Europe" in *Jane's Terrorism and Insurgency Centre*, May 31, 2005, available at http://www.janes.com.

46   This is clear from the bombers' own words; see "Full text: al-Qaida Madrid claim," http://www.bbcnews.com, March 14, 2004; Vikram Dodd and Richard Norton-Taylor, "Video of 7/7 ringleader blames foreign policy," *Guardian*, September 2, 2005.

47   The Shiʿite Islamist group Hizbullah carried out many high-profile kidnappings of Western citizens in Lebanon in the 1980s. Some of the hostages were killed, though not by decapitation. The Algerian group GIA kidnapped and decapitated seven French monks in Algeria in the spring of 1996. In January 2002, the American journalist Daniel Pearl was abducted and beheaded by Sunni militants in Pakistan.

48   Abu Muhammad al-Maqdisi, *Al-Zarqawi: Munasara wa Munasaha* ["Al-Zarqawi: Support and Advice"], published July 2004 on http://www.tawhed.ws. On July 3, 2005, after being temporarily released from prison, al-Maqdisi appeared in an interview on the Qatari television network al-Jazeera and criticized al-Zarqawi for his indiscriminate use of suicide bombings and mass-casualty attacks against civilian Iraqi Shiʿites. See Bernard Haykel, "Among jihadis, a rift over suicide attacks," *New York Times*, October 12, 2005.

49   Brynjar Lia, "Internationalist Jihadist Groups in Iraq," conference paper presented in Oslo Militære Samfund, January 25, 2005.

50   Brynjar Lia, "The Rise of Salafi-Jihadi Groups in Iraq: Some Preliminary Observations," unpublished manuscript from lecture at the University of Oslo, November 20, 2003; The correspondence between al-ʿAli and the jihadists was

posted on the now-defunct website of the "Salafi Fighting Group of Iraq" [*Al-Jama'a al-Salafiyya al-Mujahida - al-'Iraq*] in the late summer of 2003.

51   Hegghammer, *Al-Qaida Statements 2003–2004*, p. 46.

52   Author's interview with Miriam Abou Zahab, Paris, October 26, 2005.

53   In January 2004, al-Zarqawi allegedly wrote a letter to Bin Ladin and al-Zawahiri proposing a new strategy that involved provoking civil war in Iraq by launching large-scale terrorist attacks on Shi'ites ("U.S. Says Files Seek Qaeda Aid in Iraq Conflict," *New York Times*, February 9, 2004). We do not know Bin Ladin's precise position on this proposal, but if al-Zarqawi did indeed write such a letter, it would indicate that he knew the content was controversial. However, the clearest indication of a disagreement on this issue was the so-called "Letter from Ayman al-Zawahiri to Abu Mus'ab al-Zarqawi," allegedly written in July 2005, in which al-Zawahiri expressed strong reservations about the anti-Shi'ite strategy in Iraq (see http://www.dni.gov/release_letter_101105.html).

54   Critics on the radical forums use two kinds of arguments: either that attacks on Shi'ites divert attention from the fight against the Crusaders (see for example http://www.islah200.org/vboard/showthread.php?t=120251); or that it is difficult to distinguish between Iraqi Sunnis and Shi'ites, hence such attacks run the risk of killing Sunni civilians (see for example http://www.qal3ati.net/vb/showthread.php?t=122778).

55   Al-Maqdisi, *Al-Zarqawi: Support and Advice*. See also the television interview with al-Maqdisi on al-Jazeera, July 3, 2005.

56   This genre is also to be distinguished from the vast literature on paramilitary tactics that circulates on the Internet. See for example the Saudi jihadist magazine *Mu'askar al-Battar*.

57   "Centre for Islamic Studies and Research" (*Markaz al-Dirasat wa'l-Buhuth al-Islamiyya*) was a radical Islamist website, which became known after 9/11 as one of the Internet sites with the closest links to the senior al-Qa'ida leadership. It ceased to exist shortly after the death of its administrator, Yusuf al-'Ayiri, in late May 2003. *Majallat al-Ansar* was a jihadist magazine issued regularly in PDF format on the Internet between early 2002 and mid-2003. The most prominent contributors to this magazine were Sayf al-Din al-Ansari, Abu 'Ubayd al-Qirshi, Abu Ayman al-Hilali, and Abu Sa'd al-Amili. The real identity and geographical base of these writers remains unknown.

58   Sample titles include Abu 'Ubayd al-Qirshi, "*al-qa'ida wa fann al-harb*" [Al-Qa'ida and the Art of War], *Majallat al-Ansar* 1 (January 15, 2002); Abu 'Ubayd al-Qirshi, "*hurub al-jil al-rabi'*" [Fourth Generation Warfare], *Majallat al-Ansar* 2 (January 28, 2002); Abu 'Ubayd al-Qirshi, "*hasad murr: al-hamla al-salibiyya ba'd sitta shuhur*" [Bitter Harvest: The Crusader Campaign After Six Months], *Majallat al-Ansar* 6 (March 29, 2002); Abu 'Ubayd al-Qirshi, "*Amrika wa'l-Hamla al-Salibiyya: ila Ayna?*" [America and the Crusader Campaign: Where Now?], *Majallat al-Ansar* 11 (June 12, 2002); Abu 'Ubayd al-Qirshi, "*Dars fi al-Harb*" ["Lesson in Warfare"], *Majallat al-Ansar* 23 (December 19, 2002).

59   See for example Abu 'Ubayd al-Qirshi, "*Harb al-Athir*" ["Information Warfare"], *Majallat al-Ansar* 21 (November 20, 2002). It should be mentioned that the tactical jihadist literature has undergone a similar development toward a greater emphasis on psychology in warfare. For example, 'Abd al-'Aziz al-Muqrin (the leader of al-Qa'ida in Saudi Arabia until his death in June 2004) wrote extensively on how to

handle and exploit the media in connection with kidnappings. See 'Abd al-'Aziz al-Muqrin, *Al-'Ulum al-'Askariyya* ["Military Science"], published on the *Sawt al-Jihad* website in September 2004, pp. 55–60.

60   Anonymous, *Iraqi Jihad – Expectations and Dangers*.

61   Brynjar Lia and Thomas Hegghammer, "Jihadi Strategic Studies," *Studies in Conflict and Terrorism,* Vol. 27, No. 5 (2004), pp. 355–75.

62   Michael Scheuer, *Through Our Enemies' Eyes* (Washington DC: Brassey's, 2002), pp. 228–36.

63   Hegghammer, *Al-Qaida Statements 2003–2004*, p. 64.

64   See for example http://www.al-qal3ah.net/vb/showthread.php?t=114188.

65   See for example Yusuf al-'Ayiri, *Al-Tawajud al-Amriki fi al-Khalij: Haqiqatuhu wa Ahdafuhu* [The American Presence in the Gulf: Truths and Aims], published in May 2003 on *al-Nida* Website, now available on http://www.tawhed.ws.

66   See for example Anonymous, *"Al-Wujud al-Amriki fi al-Khalij: Tarikh wa Dalalat"* ["The American Presence in the Gulf: History and Evidence"], *Sawt al-Jihad* 2 (October 2003); Muhammad Al-Salim, *"Ya ahl al-Kuwait"* ["O Kuwaiti People"], *Sawt al-Jihad* 13 (March 2004).

Faisal Devji

ACCOUNTING FOR AL-QAEDA

FACED WITH WHAT is new, and especially what is radically new, the scholar's conservative instinct is always to reach for some genealogy within which this novelty might be anchored and neutralized. In the case of the jihad this instinct works to place it in the genealogy of something called political Islam, where its ancestry is generally traced to Middle Eastern movements of the modern period like Salafism (an effort to follow the path of the early Muslims that includes within its ambit groups such as the Muslim Brotherhood) or Wahhabism (a militant effort to purify Islam named after the eighteenth-century thinker Muhammad ibn Abdul Wahhab, who lived in what is today Saudi Arabia, a country that claims to be founded on his principles). Indeed movements like the Salafis and Wahhabis are so central to the genealogies of political Islam that their presence is often updated or renewed by attaching their names with the prefix neo, as in neo-Wahhabi, but rarely with the prefix post.

A curious feature of such genealogies of the jihad is that they all originate in and remain focused specifically upon Sunni Islam and the Middle East, despite the fact that arguably the most successful examples of political Islam have been revolutionary Iran and the Hezbollah in Lebanon, both Shia movements, which among other things have contributed to an ostensibly Sunni jihad the language and practice of the "martyrdom operation", as its suicide attacks are known. Similarly the fact that the jihad today happens to be based for the most part outside the Middle East (in places like Chechnya, Afghanistan, Pakistan, India and the Philippines) among populations that have barely an inkling of Salafi or Wahhabi traditions, seems to have escaped the notice of scholarly genealogists. Apparently the very presence of Arab fighters or funding in such places is evidence enough that Salafi or Wahhabi Islam has been exported in sufficient measure to determine the nature of jihad there. That the reverse might be true, with Arab fighters and financiers importing the jihad from these regions to the Middle East, is not seriously considered, although it is certainly true of Al-Qaeda and the phenomenon of the so called Arab-Afghans, militants who returned after the anti-Soviet war in Afghanistan to their homes in the Middle East and founded new jihad movements there.

In general the importance of non-Arab Muslims and of non-Arab Islam to the Middle East has been underestimated, as borne out by the example of Iraq in early 2005: when Ayatullah Sistani was the country's great Shiite authority, even though he is an Iranian whose Arabic remains heavily accented by his native Farsi. Much of Sistani's authority in Iraq, moreover, derives from his control and disbursement of funds raised by Shia populations elsewhere, a very significant portion of which come from India and Pakistan. Sistani's constituency in the subcontinent, then, through his agent in Mumbai, might well hold a key to the Ayatullah's importance in Iraq. This Shiite example apart, the presence of large non-Arab working populations in the Arabian Peninsula, as well as the dominance of non-Arab Muslims in the formulation and dissemination of Islamic ideas globally, especially in languages like English, renders nonsensical any notion that the Arab Middle East is the original homeland of radical Islam.

The Taliban provides a perfect illustration of the kind of movement that has repeatedly been described as a foreign import. It was supposedly influenced by Deobandi practices from India, themselves funded and influenced by Saudi Wahhabism, and by Wahhabi practices coming directly from Saudi Arabia – both imparted in Pakistani seminaries, and both supposedly legalistic and scripturalist in the extreme. And yet the Taliban leader Mullah Omar chose in Kandahar to drape himself in a mantle belonging to the Prophet and declare himself the Commander of the Faithful, a title used for the caliphs who were meant to be Muhammad's successors – he was in fact flatteringly called a caliph by no less a person than Osama bin Laden. In what way did this coronation conform to any Deobandi or Wahhabi teaching? If anything the vision of Mullah Omar donning the Prophet's mantle suggests Sufi and especially Shia themes, since the latter believe in the apostolic succession of those members of Muhammad's family whom he famously covered with his cloak. And it is precisely such charismatic forms of authority that both the Deobandis and Wahhabis are supposed to execrate.

There is nothing more calculated to degrade the celebrated scripturalist or legalist forms of Islam associated with these groups, tied as they are to the authority of a class of scholarly commentators, than the institution of a self-proclaimed Commander of the Faithful – one who claimed, in addition, to have received divine instruction in his dreams. By acts such as these, the Taliban not only assumed an immediate superiority over their Saudi or Pakistani teachers, they also forced from the latter an acknowledgement of religious forms and practices that were barely dreamt of in the Deobandi and Wahhabi schools. Suddenly it seemed as if the direction of Islamic influence had been reversed, with teachers in the centre taking dictation from students on the periphery. And who can deny the wave of approval for all these Afghan innovations, mystical and even Shia though they might be, that swept the world of militant Sunnism? It is no accident then, that one of these militants interviewed by Jessica Stern in her book *Terror in the Name of God*, an Indonesian who had fought the jihad in Afghanistan, accused the Taliban precisely of being Sufi and of relying "on dreams and fantasies".[1]

The jihad is placed within genealogies of political Islam that are drawn up by systematic procedures of a racial, religious and regional apartheid that maintain what is essential to every genealogy: its purity. In the process any inconvenient fact – the importance of the Pakistani Mawdudi for both Shiites like Khomeini and prominent Salafi thinkers like the Egyptian Sayyid Qutb, let alone the influence of Sufism or Shiism on the jihad itself – must either be downplayed or erased outright. But the dispersed nature and global effects of the jihad are putting an increasing strain on all genealogical forms of explanation, which are very difficult to sustain when they cannot clearly be confined to some common geography, language or religious and political tradition. Accordingly, scholarly genealogies have now assumed the character almost of medieval chronicles in order to defend their purity, linking the jihad's transmission to purely individual influences and encounters. So for instance we are often reminded that Sayyid Qutb's brother Muhammad left Egypt to teach at the King Abdul Aziz University in Jeddah where he met a Jordanian-Palestinian student, Abdullah Azzam, who later went to Pakistan from where he became the chief ideologue in the Arab world of the Afghan jihad. The fact that Azzam should then have met the Saudi citizen of Yemeni ancestry Osama bin Laden in Peshawar comes as no surprise. While these individual meetings are of course important in the biographies of fighters as well as in the operations they undertake, more interesting, I think, is the possibility that they are quite irrelevant to the jihad itself as a global movement.

Can the jihad and its global effects be reduced to individual biographies and the politics of the Middle East? Is a genealogical mode of explanation at all credible in a situation where participants in the jihad come from all manner of national and religious backgrounds? Quite apart from the hijackers in New York or the bombers in Madrid who betrayed no obvious signs of Muslim piety, we know that in places like Afghanistan, too, fighters came from many different and even opposed Islamic affiliations that are generally kept far apart by scholarly genealogists. One might find in Kandahar, for example, members of the allegedly quietist or non-political group of Indian derivation, the Tablighi Jamaat, as well as those belonging to the Jamaat-e Islami, of Pakistani origin, who are committed to the establishment of an Islamic state, not to mention members of the Muslim League, a political party supposedly devoted to Pakistani nationalism. But the plethora of groups, often very exclusive, participating in the jihad does not indicate their alliance for some common cause. It may however signal the fact that a global movement like the jihad depends upon the erosion of traditional religious and political allegiances for its very existence. After all we have seen that Al-Qaeda, like other global movements, possesses an extraordinarily diverse membership, one that is not united by way of any cultic or ideological commonality, to say nothing about that of class, ethnicity or personal background. Indeed it can only function as the network it is by disrupting and disregarding old-fashioned forms of political and religious allegiance.

Confronted with bastard phenomena that would sully the legitimacy of any family history, scholars of Islam are sometimes forced to retain such purity as they can by transferring these illicit offspring to another genealogy. The favourite method of doing so is to excommunicate certain practices from lineages in the Islamic tradition and attribute them to some vaguely defined modern or Western category of kinship. A consequence of this practice, especially marked among those who are not scholars of Islam, is to deny the jihad any originality by attributing even its most spectacular effects to a Western inheritance. As Reinhard Schulze has recently remarked, such attempts to include the jihad within a political tradition of Western radicalism often means that what remains of a non-Western Islam is carefully sequestered from world history, existing within a hermetically sealed genealogy of its own.[2] This closed world, then, requires only cultural sensitivity and a respect for difference, even and especially when it is being destroyed, as the American army's much-trumpeted rules of multicultural engagement in Iraq demonstrate. Indeed some of the humiliations to which American soldiers subjected Iraqi detainees in Abu Ghraib Prison may be symptoms of the army's recognition of "cultural difference", itself apparently a familiar phrase at the prison.[3] These included male nudity, especially in the presence of women, the simulation of sexual intercourse among men, masturbation and the wearing by men of women's underwear, sometimes on their heads.[4] Surely such practices betray as much awareness of "cultural difference" as multiculturalists would like, being merely the obverse side of the latter's respect?

My description above of scholarship on the jihad is a caricature if not a travesty: it does no justice to any writer on the subject but is meant instead to be a patchwork of common yet unconvincing themes in academic writing on the jihad. Most objectionable of all is the attempt to place the jihad within a genealogy of influences emanating from something called political Islam, itself sequestered from a history of modernity more generally, to which it can at most be related as a kind of reaction. Not everyone does this, of course, and Reinhard Schulze even sets himself the formidable task of interpreting the entirety of modern Islam in terms of what he calls universal history, while Roxanne Euben's study of Sayyid Qutb, *Enemy in the Mirror*, is probably the first work to locate Islamic fundamentalism within the precincts of political philosophy.[5] If my objective above was to broach the possibility of the jihad being defined in accidental terms as a series of global effects, I, too, wish to conclude this chapter by locating it within a general history of modern times.

Fundamentalist futures

The jihad has replaced what used to be called Islamic fundamentalism at the edge of Muslim militancy. This latter had been part and parcel of Cold War politics and was concerned with the founding through revolution of an ideological state, fashioned in many respects on the communist model that was so popular in Africa and Asia following the Second World War. As Seyyed Vali Reza Nasr has shown in his two books on one of the most important fundamentalist thinkers, the Pakistani Sayyid Abul Ala Mawdudi and his Jamaat-e Islami party, communist ideas about the party as vanguard of the revolution, the state as an explicitly ideological institution meant to produce a utopian society, and the like, were central to the movement.[6] With the end of the Cold War, however, and the coming into being of a global market for transactions of all kinds, the revolutionary politics meant to institute ideological states quickly began to break down. This sort of fundamentalism, after all, had enjoyed only one success in its many decades of struggle, with the Islamic Republic of Iran. But given Iran's own economic and political stagnation as a fundamentalist state, the Muslim world was confronted with what Olivier Roy has called the failure of political Islam, in his book of the same name.[7]

Unlike fundamentalism, the jihad is not concerned with political parties, revolutions or the founding of ideological states. For someone like Ayman al-Zawahiri, who comes from a fundamentalist background in the Muslim Brotherhood, struggles in particular countries are important for two reasons: because, like the Taliban's Afghanistan, they provide a base for jihad more generally, as well as for rousing Muslims internationally. In other words the particular sites of these struggles are themselves unimportant, their territories being subordinated to a larger and even metaphysical struggle for which they have become merely instrumental. Indeed by moving between Bosnia and Afghanistan, Chechnya and Iraq, the jihad displays its fundamental indifference to these territories rather than consolidating them into a single Muslim geography. It ends by de-territorializing Islam altogether, since it is not one country or another that is important, but instead Islam itself as a global entity. So in his book *Knights Under the Banner of the Prophet*, which was smuggled out of an Afghan cave to Peshawar and thence to the Arabic newspaper *Al-Sharq al-Awsat* in London, Zawahiri describes the importance of invoking the Palestinian struggle solely in terms of a way to gain the support of Arabs and Muslims:

> The fact that must be acknowledged is that the issue of Palestine is the cause that has been firing up the feelings of the Muslim nation from Morocco to Indonesia for the past 50 years. In addition, it is a rallying point for all the Arabs, be they believers or non-believers, good or evil.[8]

This subordination of local to global struggles differs from the internationalism of revolutionary movements like communism both because it is based on the failure rather than success of local struggles, and because it implies the coming into being of a new global environment after the Cold War. The latter thus conceived is not seen by any proponent of the jihad who has voiced an opinion on the subject as an external event but as one intimately connected to the jihad itself. Osama bin Laden, Ayman al-Zawahiri and many others have repeatedly given credit for the collapse of the Soviet Union and the end of the Cold War to the holy warriors who they say defeated the Soviet army in Afghanistan. Whatever grain of truth there is in this claim, it demonstrates that the jihad is seen to have assumed a global role by participating in the Cold War. More than this, the end of the Cold War is considered to have catapulted the jihad into assuming, inadvertently, the global role of the Soviet Union as the only force willing to resist the absolute dominance of the United States. Thus Zawahiri:

> In the wake of the USSR's collapse, the United States monopolized its military superiority to dictate its wishes to numerous governments and, as a result, has succeeded in imposing security agreements on many countries. In this way the power of the governments that are affiliated with the United States grew in the sphere of pursuing the mujahideen in many countries. Doubtlessly this had an impact on the fundamentalist movement. Still this has been a new challenge that the jihadist movement confronted with methods that can reduce its impact. It did this by turning the United States into a target.[9]

It is clear from the above that the Jewish-Crusade[r] alliance, led by the United States, will not allow any Muslim force to reach power in any of the Islamic countries. It will mobilize all its power to hit it and remove it from power. Toward that end, it will open a battlefront against it that includes the entire world. It will impose sanctions on whoever helps it, if it does not declare war against them altogether. Therefore, to adjust to this new reality we must prepare ourselves for a battle that is not confined to a single region, one that includes the apostate domestic enemy and the Jewish-Crusade[r] external enemy.[10]

The impossibility of local struggles means that local causes and intentions have finally disappeared into their own effects to create an accidental or inadvertent landscape for the jihad's globalization. The local causes or intentions behind Al-Qaeda's attacks on Washington and New York, for example, have disappeared beneath the rubble of the World Trade Center. The jihad these attacks were meant to propound has become globalized in its unintended and uncontrollable effects. In the jihad itself this globalization is reflected upon by way of a new kind of history, one very different from a fundamentalist history that was linked to a Marxist dialectic culminating in revolution. In effect this is a global history that depends upon the disintegration of traditional Muslim narratives and chronologies, as much as of modern theories of ideology and revolution, so that the events of Islam's past are emancipated for very different uses in the present.

In the jihad a global history of the West is matched at every point by its effects upon the Muslim world, which is seen as being coextensive with it and forming a mirror history of the West itself. Apart from the medieval relations between Muslims, Christians and Jews, as well as the impact of European colonialism and the Cold War upon Islam, this history is composed of actions and personalities that have very little to do with Muslim tradition but are parasitical upon Western accounts of Islamic history. These include Saladin and the waging of the Crusades, the conquest and loss of Muslim Spain, Napoleon's invasion of Egypt and the decline of the Ottoman Empire. As is evident from the use of the term Crusaders for the United States and its allies, these historical subjects are by no means confined to the past but available for productive use today, very deliberately translating the history of the West into Islamic terms. For example the title of Zawahiri's *Knights Under the Banner of the Prophet* refers to the crusading Knights of the Holy Sepulchre.

This global history brings together Judaism, Christianity and Islam in a single landscape. And it is the very singularity of this landscape that renders futile any attempt to create a realm of Islamic autonomy. Yet it is also this kind of universality that fragments previous forms of Muslim solidarity and collective practice by subordinating them to a single history of the globe. Notions of Islamic universality in the past might have brought the whole world within their compass either by the narrative of conversion, or by linking all its peoples within some hierarchy of God's creation. In both cases Islam still possessed a world – and autonomy – of its own. But as all global movements, from those dedicated to the environment to those devoted to the destruction of atomic weapons so vehemently declare, there exists now only one world in which autonomy is impossible. This is also the world of the jihad. The more traditional forms of Muslim authority are broken down within the jihad, therefore, the more like other global movements such as environmentalism or the anti-globalization protests does Islam become.

Two factors make the jihad into a global movement: the failure of local struggles and the inability to control a global landscape of operations by the politics of intentionality. These factors entail a radical individuation of Islam that is as divorced from modes of collective solidarity and action based on some common history of needs, interests or ideas, as is the individuation of action in other global movements.[11] While I will attend to the nature of this individuation in another chapter, we have already seen how it manifests itself in the extraordinary diversity of the jihad's participants and their lack of cultic uniformity. Given all this, it is hardly surprising that fundamentalists, not to speak of traditional clerical and mystical groups, should vehemently oppose the jihad. So after the attacks of September the eleventh, among a whole host of Muslim objections to these actions from around the world, there was an unprecedented declaration signed by prominent clerics and fundamentalists who included leaders of the Muslim Brotherhood, Hamas and the Jamaat-e Islami:

> The undersigned, leaders of Islamic movements, are horrified by the events of Tuesday 11 September 2001 in the United States, which resulted in massive killing, destruction and attack on innocent lives. We express our deepest sympathies and sorrow. We condemn, in the strongest terms, the incidents, which are against all human and Islamic norms. This is grounded in the Noble Laws of Islam, which forbid all forms of attacks on innocents. God Almighty says in the Holy Qur'an: "No bearer of burdens can bear the burden of another." (Surah al-Isra 17: 15)[12]

Since a number of the signatories to this declaration are known neither for their fondness for the United States nor for their abstention from acts of violence against civilians, their protest recognizes the jihad's radical novelty on grounds other than the taking of innocent lives. In fact what is being objected to is not the taking of lives at all but the jihad's globalization beyond a politics of causes and intentions that is organized around shared and therefore very particular histories of needs, interests or ideas. Supporters of the jihad who criticize this position, then, invariably focus on its illogic and hypocrisy in recommending violence in some places but not others. Whatever the future of this struggle, the jihad has stolen the radical edge from fundamentalism, pushing it into an increasingly liberal stance. This has already affected the once "extremist" Muslim Brotherhood and Jamaat-e Islami, as well as the failed revolution of Algeria's Front Islamique du Salut and its military wing, the Groupe Islamique Armée. At the same time as Islamic politics in certain quarters becomes more radical, therefore, it becomes more moderate in others.

Notes

1   Jessica Stern, *Terror in the Name of God* (New York: Harper Collins, 2003), p. 75.
2   Reinhard Schulze, *A Modern History of the Islamic World*, trans. Azizeh Azodi (New York University Press, 2002).
3   See, for instance, the Pentagon's "Investigation of the Abu Ghraib detention facility and 205th Military Intelligence Brigade", in Steven Strasser (ed.), *The Abu Ghraib Investigations* (New York: Public Affairs, 2004), p. 160.

4   For details of such incidents see the two official reports included in *The Abu Ghraib Investigations*.

5   Roxanne Euben, *Enemy in the Mirror: Islamic Fundamentalism and the Limits of Modern Rationalism* (Princeton University Press, 1999).

6   Seyyed Vali Reza Nasr, *Vanguard of the Islamic Revolution: the Jamaat-i Islami of Pakistan* (Berkeley: University of California Press, 1994), and *Mawdudi and the Making of Islamic Revivalism* (New York: Oxford University Press, 1996).

7   Olivier Roy, *The Failure of Political Islam*, trans. Carol Volk (Cambridge, MA: Harvard University Press, 1994).

8   "Extracts from Al-Jihad Leader Al-Zawahiri's New Book", *al-Sharq al-Awsat*, http://www.fas.org/irp/world/para/ayman_bk.html, p. 77.

9   Ibid., pp. 44–5.

10   Ibid., p. 80.

11   Olivier Roy describes extensively this new form of Muslim individualization in the fourth chapter of his *Globalised Islam*.

12   Quoted in Quintan Wictorowicz and John Kaltner, "Killing in the Name of Islam: Al-Qaeda's Justification for September 11", *Middle East Policy Council Journal,* vol. X, no. 2, Summer 2003, p. 2.

Further reading

Jason Burke, *Al-Qaeda: The True Story of Radical Islam* (London: I. B. Tauris, 2004)

> A sound and well-informed journalistic account of the activities of the al-Qaeda network.

David Cook, *Understanding Jihad* (Berkeley: University of California Press, 2005)

> A measured scholarly depiction of traditional and new modes of understanding and practising Holy War.

Faisal Devji, *Landscape of the Jihad: Militancy, Morality, Modernity* (London: Hurst, 2005)

> A sophisticated analysis of the new militant discourse of transnational jihadist networks at the turn of the century.

Fawaz A. Gerges, *The Far Enemy: Why Jihad Went Global* (Cambridge: Cambridge University Press, 2005)

> An insightful analysis into the process of redirection of Islamist violence from domestic to international actors.

Mohammed M. Hafez, *Why Muslims Rebel: Repression and Resistance in the Islamic World* (Boulder: Lynne Rienner, 2003)

> A sound rational-choice approach to Islamist mobilization in conflict zones of the Muslim world.

Marc Sageman, *Understanding Terror Networks* (Philadelphia: University of Pennsylvania Press, 2004)

> A sound behaviouralist account of the mode of operation of the al-Qaeda organization on the international scene.

Mariam Abou Zahab and Olivier Roy, *Islamist Networks: The Afghan–Pakistan Connection* (New York: Columbia University Press, 2004)

> A well-informed account of the organization of violent Islamist militancy in the Afghan–Pakistani context.

The Globalization of Islamism

Introduction

HAVING REVIEWED SOME of the most visible aspects of political Islam in international affairs, the reader is introduced in this section to the ways in which Islamism develops globally at grassroots level. Several types of globalization have been taking place over the last few decades. Despite the increased attention paid in recent years to transnational Islamist violence, these networks are clearly not indicative of the mass phenomenon that is Islamism. To understand the globalization of political Islam it is crucial to appreciate the impact of other waves of Islamist proselytism that mobilized the Muslim communities. One of the earliest waves of this modern Islamist revival was spearheaded by the Egyptian Muslim Brotherhood from the 1930s onwards. The Muslim Brothers helped to diffuse across the Middle East a set of interpretations and approaches to the Islamic corpus which, later combining with other ideological and theological influences like Wahhabism, set the foundations for the modern discourse and practice of political Islam. These discourses and practices are important not only for the political side of Islamism, but also for the social diffusion of the movement. It could even be argued that the most expressly political aspects of the Islamist discourse – those having to do with the notion of an Islamic state – are less relevant to the globalization of political Islam than the social networks that provide the mass following for this revival. What Islamism has induced in the Muslim community worldwide is a greater realization that Islam is relevant to understanding the contemporary world, as well as a reactivation of Islamic practices that are judged by individuals and communities to be helpful in solving their everyday predicaments. This situation has been created by the simultaneous spread of a core discourse on Islamism and of transnational movements putting into practice this discourse among previously more traditional or secularized communities, both in the core regions of the Muslim world and in the global ummah.

Beside the violent aspects of transnational Islamist militancy, it is the political activism of Islamist organizations that has commonly attracted the attention of the media and policy-makers. Although important, this aspect of Islamism, especially when linked to the notion of an Islamic state or a Caliphate, only captures a part of the mass appeal and following of political Islam. Some of the transnational movements of re-Islamization are in fact so concerned with grassroots processes, with raising the individual Islamic awareness of the faithful that, like the Tablighi Jamaat, they choose to forego any direct political agenda or activities. Evidently, at the other end of the spectrum, some organizations, like al-Qaeda, are so driven by direct action against what they consider to be an impious international system oppressing the ummah that they do not get involved in grassroots social activities. In between are a range of movements that display both political and social activities, and that can choose to use violence or not. Although some of these transnational movements have clearly a global organization, strategy and objectives – such as the reconstruction of a Caliphate for the whole of the ummah according to a movement like Hizb-ut-Tahir – most of these organizations have a piecemeal approach to societal change. The global impact of political Islam therefore resembles more an incremental accumulation of interrelated but unplanned actions and interactions that challenge the dominant views and practices of western-led globalization and of the international system.

The first text, by Peter Mandaville, analyses the public sphere that underpins the construction of the contemporary ummah, as new forms of global mass communication (and particularly the internet) provide further opportunities, as well as create new challenges, for the diffusion and validation of Islamic practices. Mandaville details the mechanisms of formation of 'virtual' communities of practice and of learning that challenge the authority of both traditional religious leaders and the political leaders of Muslim-majority countries. These globalized Islamist interactions contribute to create a Muslim public sphere that is at once more open and inclusive, but that can also facilitate the diffusion of conservative and exclusionary viewpoints and practices.

The next contribution, by Barbara Metcalf, considers in detail the case of the pietist and formally apolitical movement Tablighi Jamaʿat, which is illustrative of a new form of globalized Islamist practice. Metcalf shows how a movement that started in India with a fairly traditionalist religious agenda centred on personal and communal betterment has been able to gain an audience in many western polities by proposing a worldview and lifestyle opposed to what is experienced as the excesses of individualism and consumerism. This movement has facilitated the production of communities of faith which are at the same time globalized, and yet partially insulated from their immediate westernized surroundings.

The third text, by Charles Hirschkind, details how 'Islamic' civic virtues are being cultivated at grassroots level through the social and educational work of the Islamists. Hirschkind notes the rise of an Islamic public sphere informed by the writings and debates of Islamist activists and scholars worldwide, which underpins local practices and attitudes towards ethics, the public good and the state. In Muslim-majority countries, these religious referents increasingly structure the views of the publicand shape the formal political discussions between social and political actors. Yet, this Islamist discourse is not rigidly established by ide ologues and scholars but is the product of constant negotiations and renegotiations between individuals within a globalized Islamic public sphere.

The final contribution, by Ahmet Kuru, shows how different types of Islamist movements have positioned themselves in relation to key aspects of political and cultural globalization. Considering the case of transnational movements of Turkish origin like Fetullah Gulen and Milli Gorus, Kuru indicates how these actors' different assessments of the threats and opportunities created by globalization have shaped their policies and engagement at the supranational level. Internally, both the ideological orientations of the movements and their social make-up have contributed to position them differently vis-à-vis globalization. Externally, the vagaries of Turkish domestic politics and the positioning of the Turkish state in the international system – such as its efforts to integrate the European Union – commonly constituted a trigger for specific policy choices.

Peter G. Mandaville

REIMAGINING THE *UMMAH*?

Information technology and the changing boundaries of political Islam

THIS CHAPTER DISCUSSES the role of information technology in the Islamic context and examines how the proliferation of information technology (IT) is likely to affect the ways in which the political community is imagined in Islam. Will global networks and computer-mediated communication (CMC) enable Muslims to approximate more closely to the *ummah*, the traditional model of the Islamic world community? Much of the recent literature in sociology and cultural studies suggests that the spread of IT and CMC will lead to the emergence of new forms of community (Jones 1995), but attention is rarely given to the question of how traditional notions of community are mediated and refigured through sustained contact with new technologies of communication. The complex processes commonly referred to under the rubric of globalization can serve to reify these changes, making them potentially available to much larger, and often geographically widespread, audiences. This chapter will explore some of these issues and attempt to assess the extent to which IT could provide the catalyst for a reformation of Muslim discourse. In short, we shall be inquiring as to the future of Islam in the context of globalized information technologies.

'The field [of globalization], if not controlled', warns Abu-Lughod (1991), 'can degenerate into what we might call "global-babble"'. Her preference is for an approach which tries to 'capture the ambiguities and nuances of the concrete, as they are embedded in the lives of people' (Abu-Lughod 1991: 131). The purpose of this chapter, then, is to examine the ways in which the impact of globalized communications and information technology on various forms of one particular tradition, Islam, has led both to the imagination of new political communities and to the reimagination of traditional categories of social and religious solidarity. Our exploration of the nexus between Islam and information technology will proceed as follows. After examining the original connotations attached to the notion of the *ummah*, some observations will be made as to the complex and often contradictory sociological implications of contemporary globalization. The discussion will then move on to highlight the salient issues surrounding the digitization and communication of Islamic knowledge, and the religious politics which this activity can engender. In order to developing the model of globalization as outlined in this chapter, two case studies involving encounters between Islam and IT are explored. Muslim diaspora activity on the internet is characterized as an instance of 'globalizing the local', and the controversial appearance of the internet in the Gulf is assessed as an example of 'localizing the global'. The concluding section returns to the question of information technology as a catalyst for recreating traditional models of community in Islam. Drawing on evidence presented throughout the chapter, it will be argued that the phenomenal rise of globalized IT does as much to challenge the *ummah* as to reconstitute it.

The origins of the *ummah*

How did the first Muslim community, the original *ummah*, come to be constituted at Medina (then known as Yathrib) during the seventh century, and what did this community look like? Note that this earliest period of Islamic history is particularly salient because the normative models which developed in these years eventually came to form the basis of Islamic law (*shari'a*). The authoritative deeds and dictums of the Prophet Muhammad (the *sunna*) have, along with the Quran itself, come to constitute the two primary sources of scriptural authority in Islam. The traditions of Muhammad's companions and their supporters in Medina have also been recorded, interpreted, and coded as sources of jurisprudence (*fiqh*), which carry an almost mythical warrant even today. In contemporary Muslim discourses, the themes, events, and personages of these years continue to be important points of reference and sources of inspiration. This story begins, however, with a decisive social rupture that occurred in Arabia over a thousand years ago: the *hijra*.

The migration of persecuted early Muslims from Mecca to Medina, the *hijra*, has become an enduring symbol in Islam, with a resonance that can still be heard in the names of various twentieth-century Islamist movements ranging from *al-Takfir w'al-Hijra* in Egypt to the diasporic *al-Muhajiroun* ('the emigrants') in London. In this sense the *hijra* has taken on a significance much wider than the specific historical event itself. It has come to symbolize deliverance from oppression and the condition of pre-Islamic ignorance known as *jahiliyya*. In this sense the *hijra* represents the institution of a new social paradigm in which 'the good life' accrues from submission to the will of a single divine source. As Ira Lapidus puts it:

> For Muslims the [*hijra*] has come to mean not only a change of place, but the adoption of Islam and entry into the community of Muslims. The *hijra* is the transition from the pagan to the Muslim world – from kinship to a society based on common belief.
>
> (Lapidus 1988: 27)

In theory then, the *hijra* represented an idiomatic shift with regard to the manner in which community was to be 'imagined' (Anderson 1991). Social cohesion based purely on clan and kin was seen as a source of constant strife and feuding, whereas a 'community of believers' could strive to transcend this base tribalism in the name of a greater unity. In Islam, the core doctrine of *tawhid* (unity of and in God) reflects this concern. For those who participated in the first migration, then, it was not the relatively short geographic separation between Mecca and Medina which mattered, but rather the much more dramatic (and, one would imagine, initially disorienting) split with their tribal kin-groups. These affiliations had been the crux and core of social solidarity in Arabia for centuries, and to leave them behind in the name of a new religion signified a major break with traditional practice.

The social environment which the Prophet and his followers found in Medina was significantly different from the one they had left behind in Mecca. The ruling elites of their native city had all come from a single tribe, the Quraysh, an autocratic family subdivided into several clans which wielded varying degrees of political influence. Medina, on the other hand, did not have a single hegemonic tribe, nor did it possess a clear hierarchy of clan organization. Its politics were instead dominated by disputes among various competing factions and ethnic affiliations. Medina was also home to a large Jewish community as well as a number of other Arab groupings. It was this unstable social atmosphere that actually provided Muhammad with the opportunity to settle in Medina. Facing increasingly intense persecution in Mecca because of his religious beliefs, he managed to convince the dissenting factions of Medina to enter into an alliance with him and his followers, and to accept his arbitration in settling their various disputes.

The *ummah* or world community of Muslims had, therefore, its initial incarnation in this group which accompanied Muhammad on the *hijra* in 622. It is difficult for the modern commentator to discern exactly what was implied by the term *ummah* in the context of Medinan society.[1] As it occurs in both the Quran and other primary source material from the period, we may understand the *ummah* as referring to a wide range of social groupings – anywhere from Muhammad's closest followers on one end of the scale, to all living creatures on the other.[2] The etymology of the word is also ambiguous. The instinctive tendency has been to relate it to the Arabic word *umm* which means 'mother', but it now seems more likely that the term is derived from analogues in Hebrew and Aramaic, both of which refer to notions of community or social solidarity.

The *ummah* of Medina was originally a sort of 'defence pact' which united the city's clans in a collective pledge to protect Muhammad and his followers. This alliance system was codified in a treaty of sorts, usually referred to as the Constitution of Medina. In essence this document provided a sense of overarching political logic for the anarchic settlement – exactly what the oasis city had been lacking. Because it demanded complete loyalty to Muhammad from the various factions in Medina, it also effectively prevented the formation of unstable alliances between these clans. Just who was included within the *ummah*'s original jurisdiction is however not easy to determine. This is made all the more difficult by the fact that the documents we have from this period appear to contain several disparate usages of the term, reflecting various modifications and amendments during the Medinan years. Does the *ummah* refer to relations of kinship, religion or territory? It would appear that at the time of Muhammad's arrival it included elements of all three. Certainly the *ummah* was initially confined to the major clans of Medina and several local Jewish and Christian groups, in addition to the core group of Muslim emigrants. Once the Prophet had succeeded in consolidating his authority in Medina, however, the character of the *ummah* began to evolve. It is likely that Muhammad became increasingly capable of demanding a commitment to his religion (or at the very least a renunciation of idolatry) from those seeking to enter into confederacies with his community. Impressed by the success of his raids against Meccan caravans, it soon became obvious to neighbouring nomadic tribes that the inclement political winds in eastern Arabia were blowing Muhammad's way. Many were anxious to pledge their loyalty to him in return for the shelter of his rapidly expanding *dhimmah*, a term which we might understand as referring to a 'zone of peace or security'.

The *ummah* as it existed in Medina is perhaps best characterized as a conglomerate of various communities: tribal, confessional and confederal. Certainly a good deal of traditional practice with regard to the formation of alliances and kinship ties was preserved in Muhammad's new mini-state, with the overtly religious aspects of the community confined largely to Muhammad's closest followers. As far as Allah's Messenger was concerned, however, the main imperative at this point was to bolster his numbers and to widen the basis of his popular support. If this involved the occasional pact with a pagan clan, so be it. The wholesale adoption of the new universal religion would, it was believed, arrive in due course. In this the Prophet was correct. As the propagation of Islam began in earnest during the years following Muhammad's death, so did the notion of a wider *ummah*, now understood quite specifically as a form of religious community, become increasingly prominent.

Islam and globalization

Having examined some of the original connotations of the *ummah* concept, we can now place it in the context of contemporary Islamic politics. In Muslim discourse today, the *ummah* often appears as a central normative concept appealing for unity across the global Muslim community. As discussed above, the essence of the *ummah* lies in the idea of renouncing one's factional identities (today we might speak of ethnicity or national allegiance) in the name of a greater solidarity with God: a communion of all Muslims. Since some of the central themes of globalization involve the bridging of distances and the removal of geographic barriers (e.g. the rise of a 'global village'), we might legitimately ask to what extent this phenomenon can help to bridge the distances and differences which separate the vast number of Muslim communities found in the world today. Let us begin by looking at the nature of contemporary Islam, and also at some of the ways in which it has reacted to the onset of globalization.

It is by now a commonplace to assert that Islam means different things to different people at different times. Whether we choose to talk about various 'Islams' or being 'Muslims through discourse', the underlying point is the same: within the religious tradition we call Islam there exist any number of interpretations as to what Islam is, what it means, and who possesses the authority to speak on its behalf (al-Azmeh 1997; Bowen 1993; Roff 1987). This internal diversity is the result of the various cultural, ethnic and national factors which have mediated the religion as it spread across much of the Middle East, Africa, Asia and, more recently, Western Europe and North America. The resulting syncretisms and interminglings have bequeathed to Islam a rich body of cultural material replete with difference, hybridity and, at times, contradiction. Indeed, it was the increasingly 'global' nature of Islam from the ninth century onwards that put a strain on the original *ummah*. Cracks inev- itably began to appear as the original Muslim community rapidly grew to encompass a diverse range of peoples, lands and histories.

What happens, then, when this complex world discourse comes into contact with another set of ideas which also, by its very nature, claims universal jurisdiction: the discourse of globalization? Islam, and political Islam in particular, has exhibited a wide variety of responses to globalization. Certain aspects of this phenomenon have been appropriated eagerly while others have been vociferously rejected. Indeed, aspects of globalization, such as the phenomenal rise of globalized information technologies, have been mobilized explicitly in response to other aspects, such as the perceived spread of American culture, which many Muslims find distasteful. First of all, though, what do we mean when we talk of globalization?

Even the most cursory reading of recent literature will reveal that globalization is currently one of the most ubiquitous buzzwords in social theory. The difficulty in theorizing the concept stems in part from the fact that the processes which it purports to describe often appear to contradict one other. For example, the term would seem to imply the global adoption of certain modes and norms of interaction with regard to international politics, finance and law. Increased economic interdependence, and the rise of a 'global culture' are also often included. Simultaneously, however, the same mechanisms which permit (or require) this homo- geneity of practice also produce a curious inverse side-effect: localizing the global can also at times serve to *globalize the local*. The channels which open spaces of local political community to the global outside can also be appropriated by those 'receiving' communities in order to export their own notions of the particular. As Arjun Appadurai puts it:

> The globalization of culture is not the same as its homogenization, but globalization involves the use of a variety of instruments of homogeniza- tion (armaments, advertising techniques, language hegemonies, clothing styles and the like), which are absorbed into local political and cultural economies, only to be repatriated as heterogeneous dialogues of national sovereignty, free enterprise, fundamentalism, etc.
>
> (Appadurai 1990: 307)

This model questions the common idiom of globalization which tends to portray the wholesale bulldozing of 'traditional' local cultures by the rampaging juggernaut of late Western (usually American) capitalism. A claim is not being made here that the exchange of materials is equal in both (or all) directions, only that the popular mono- flow paradigm of a globalizing Western modernity is a severe misrepresentation. The majority of academic treatments of this phenomenon have, fortunately, been far more nuanced in their analyses (Featherstone 1990; King 1991; Robertson 1992). Missing from the literature, however, is an extended study of those communities who seek to appropriate the mechanisms of globalization for their own ends, and in the process of doing so to articulate an authentic local response to 'other' value systems, of which the incoming cultural material is the embodiment. To be sure, a great deal of transnational traffic does flow from the West to the Rest, but this phenomenon is not altogether hegemonic. Significant exchange also occurs between the Rest and the West and, above all, important processes of globalization are certainly at work *within* the Rest. Indeed, the very categories 'West' and 'Rest' become analytically useless under the condition of globality because Rest is already in the West, and vice-versa.

Globalization refers to an ongoing *process* (or set of processes) in which economic, political, and cultural structures become increasingly transnational and interdependent (or integrated). Globalization also involves the geographic dispersal of systems, peoples, ideas, technologies, cultures, and information, all of which are defining characteristics of late modernity. Other key features of this phenomenon relate to the capacities engendered by the enabling technologies of globalization, of which the most salient for the present study are the rise of information technology and the growing influence of what we might term 'distanciated communities'. This latter designation alludes to those groups who make use of the infrastructural trappings of globalization (e.g. telecommunications, electronic information transfer and air travel) in order to bypass the geographical barriers to social interaction. Migrants, exiles, and diaspora groups are examples here. All are cases which involve the globalization of forces such as ethnicity and identity which, according to Appadurai, are:

> sentiments whose greatest force is in their ability to ignite intimacy into a political sentiment and turn locality into a staging ground for identity. [They] have become spread over vast and irregular spaces, as groups move, yet stay linked to one another through sophisticated media capabilities.
>
> (Appadurai 1990: 306)

In globalization, physical presence or proximity is no longer a prerequisite for the practice of community. 'Globalization concerns the intersection of presence and absence', writes Anthony Giddens, 'the interlacing of social events and social relations "at distance" with local contextualities' (Giddens 1991: 21). The concept of 'distanciation' is implicated in the ability of certain groups to engage in, sustain, or reproduce particular forms of community across great distances and in the face of competing traditions.[3]

Another key feature of this state of affairs is the way in which we are beginning to conceive of the world as an increasingly compressed space – a notion most popularly captured in Marshall McLuhan's metaphor of the 'global village', and theorized by Roland Robertson (1992) as a state of consciousness. Robertson's term 'globality' refers to a mindset, an awareness of the world as a single space. This apparent diminution of space and time is the result of several developments in global infrastructure during the twentieth century: advances in transportation give the illusion of dramatically reduced distances, and the phenomenal rise of information technology has meant that the velocity of international communication has increased exponentially. But how is the condition of globality experienced by individuals and the societies within which they go about their daily lives? What impact has globalization had upon the ways in which people conceive and imagine their senses of community and culture?

In a recent piece on large-scale social organization and the creation of community, Craig Calhoun argues that:

> [a] world knit together by *indirect relationships* poses three challenges in the realm of everyday personal existence: to make sense through abstract concepts of forms of social organization for which everyday experience gives us misleading preparation, to establish a sense of personal rootedness and continuity of existence where connections across time are mainly impersonal, and to establish a sense of place and social context when the coordination of action – and the action of our own lives – constantly transcends locality.
>
> (Calhoun 1991: 114)

The latter two (interrelated) issues have perhaps the most relevance in the context of this chapter, in that they relate to the tangible experiences of displacement, alienation and antagonism which often characterize the individual's experience of globality. In this sense, Calhoun's notion of 'indirect relationships' highlights an important aspect of the distanciated community.

The same forces which have brought about globalization have also brought about phenomenal increases in the extent to which people communicate and encounter each other across the boundaries of cultures, ethnicities, nations and other communities. Indeed, globality has been responsible for bringing about significant changes in the nature and locations of these very same boundaries. In addition, the processes of decolonization and a changing international labour environment have resulted in new dynamics of migration which have challenged (if not eradicated altogether) the very possibility of the homogeneous nation-state. Over the last fifty years or so, globalization has also given birth to transnational actors on a scale which is historically unprecedented: ethnic minorities, diaspora groups, and migrant workers are all examples of this phenomenon. When bodies travel, so do cultures. The aim is to examine the ways in which the traditions of our increasingly transnational cultures are reformulated and reimagined when forced to transcend locality.

It has emerged from this discussion that globalization is not simply about enabling community and communication. Although rapid developments in media and information technology have made communication across distances much easier, their cultural implications are actually far more complex. The rise of globalized IT should not be viewed simply as a tool for bringing different peoples together, but rather as a complex set of social processes which serves to highlight and radicalize the heterogeneity *within* any community or tradition it encounters. That is, globalization is about bridging distances, but it is also about *discovering difference*. The implications of this latter point in the context of Islam will be revealed in the sections to follow.

Islam and IT: some general issues

So how have the trappings of information technology shaped normative practice in the history of Islam, and in the lived experience of 'being Muslim'? The salience of technology in bringing about religious change has been well documented (Robinson 1993; Atiyeh 1995; Eickelman and Piscatori 1996). In early Islam, oral transmission was the preferred mode for disseminating religious knowledge, with each religious scholar (ʿalim, pl. ʿulama) granting his student a licence (ijaza) which permitted him to pass on the texts of his teacher. Literacy among wider populations, even in urban centres, was very low. This state of affairs allowed the ʿulama to maintain a virtual monopoly over the production of authoritative religious knowledge. We should note here that in a sense it is almost mistaken to speak of Islam as possessing 'holy scriptures'. The Quran is, quite literally, a recitation,[4] the literal word of God as revealed to Muhammad via the archangel Gabriel. It is a collection of words whose message resonates most strongly when read aloud – when given voice. Even to this day, the process of learning the Quran is first and foremost an exercise in memorization and oral repetition. This goes some way to explaining why the Muslim world hesitated to embrace the technologies of 'print-capitalism' even when they were readily available. It was the experience of European colonialism and the concomitant perceived decline in Muslim civilization which paved the way for the rise of print technology in the nineteenth century. The book, the pamphlet, and the newsletter were all taken up with urgency in order to counter the threat which Europe was posing to the Muslim world. The ʿulama were initially at the forefront of this revolution, using a newly expanded and more widely distributed literature base to create a much broader constituency. An inevitable side-effect of this phenomenon, however, was that the religious scholars' stranglehold over religious knowledge was broken. The core texts were now available to anyone who could read them; and to read is, of course, to interpret. As Francis Robinson puts it:

> Books … could now be consulted by any Ahmad, Mahmud or Muhammad, who could make what they will of them. Increasingly from now on any Ahmad, Mahmud or Muhammad could claim to speak for Islam. No longer was a sheaf of impeccable ijazas the buttress of authority; strong Islamic commitment would be enough.
>
> (Robinson 1993: 245)

The new media opened up new spaces of religious contestation where traditional sources of authority could be challenged by the wider public. As literacy rates began to climb almost exponentially in the twentieth century, this effect was amplified even further. The fragmentation of traditional sources of authority is hence a key theme with regard to the nexus of Islam and globalization. The rise of what we might call 'media Islam' or 'soundbite Islam' has been a major byproduct of globalized information technology. Ideas and messages now possess the capability to bridge time and space almost effortlessly, and the political implications of this new capacity are not easily overestimated.

A brief survey of various information technologies will now be undertaken in order to assess the impact of this phenomenon on Islam. Both the relevant technical aspects and religious implications of each technology will be outlined, and the discussion will then go on to provide some examples of how each is being used by Muslims today. Let me begin with what are, in a sense, the basics: those technologies which allow texts to be converted and stored in an electronic form. Of course, when these new media begin to be distributed an entirely new political dimension enters the picture. Those technologies involved in the *communication* of Islam will hence be dealt with in a separate section. The internet, in particular, provides one of the most apt examples of what was termed above 'globalizing the local'.

Digitizing Islam

The Anglo-centric nature of electronic media was for a long time a barrier to working with anything but the most well known religious texts, such as the Quran and those *hadith* collections available in English. The rise of the graphic user interface (GUI) in the mid-1980s, typified by the Apple Macintosh operating system and (from the mid-1990s) Microsoft's Windows, served to rectify this problem to some extent. The graphical nature of the interface allowed computer operators to make ready use of non-Latin scripts which had previously been difficult to render in the old command-line format. Operating systems and word processors began to become available in various non-English languages and, most notably for our purposes, in Arabic. Another important development here was the exponential increase in the storage capacity of the various magnetic media used by computers. This situation was again transformed with the advent of optical media such as the compact disc in the late 1980s. Computers graduated from storing programs and data on regular audio cassettes (very low capacity) to floppy disks (between just over 100kB to 1.4MB), to hard drives (20MB to several gigabytes), to the phenomenal array-based servers which chain together several high-capacity hard drives and provide enough capacity to store the complete contents of a large university or national library.

It is the read-only compact disc (CD-ROM), however, which has transformed the scene in recent years with its ability to easily transport chunks of data as large as 650MB between many computers. This provides enough capacity to comfortably store several multi-volume encyclopaedias, hours of high-quality sound, or even a full-length video film.

What does this mean for Islam? Given the voluminous nature of most Islamic texts, the CD-ROM has provided a medium which can contain the full contents of several works. This means that the entire Quran, several collections of Prophetical sayings (*hadith*), Quranic exegesis (*tafsir*), and other jurisprudential works (*fiqh*) can easily fit on a single disc. The availability of such collections, all hyper-linked and cross-referenced, has created a new constituency for religious texts. Where Muslims previously would have had to rely on the expertise of the 'ulama when dealing with these books, they are now all available in a single medium which can easily be searched by any computer user. According to Ziauddin Sardar:

> Instead of ploughing through bulky texts, that require a certain expertise to read, a plethora of databases on the *Quran* and *hadith* now open up these texts and make them accessible to average, non-expert, users. Increasingly, the 'ulama are being confronted by non-professional theologians who can cite chapter and verse from the fundamental sources, undermining not just their arguments but also the very basis of their authority.
>
> (Sardar 1993: 55–6)

Sardar then goes on to speculate about how all the core jurisprudential texts (the *usul al-fiqh*) might be placed on single compact disc, along with an expert-system[5] that would guide the user through the literature and, in effect, allow her to generate her own religious edicts (*fatwas*). This sort of *ijtihad* toolkit would amount to a 'virtual' *'alim*, and would pose a further challenge to the authority of the traditional religious scholars.[6] It is unlikely, however, that such a system will replace the *'ulama* any time soon. They still command enormous respect in many communities and would, in any case, surely challenge the claim that their methodologies – the product of centuries of study and exhaustive research – can be reduced to a set of coded computer instructions.

The existence of such collections on CD-ROM has nevertheless become a reality in the past few years. The Islamic Computing Centre in London has been at the fore-front of producing and distributing Arabic and Islamic materials in electronic format, and one only needs to glance at their product catalogue to confirm the enthusiasm with which Muslims have taken up this technology. In addition to several electronic Qurans (with full Arabic text, several English translations, and complete oral recita-tion on a single disc) the Centre also sells titles such as *WinHadith, WinBukhari* and *WinSeera*. Also available are several products which begin to approach the system which Sardar (1993) has envisaged. The *Islamic Law Base, Islamic Scholar* and *'Alim Multimedia 4.5* are all vast collections of religious texts such as the Quran, *hadith*, several volumes of *fiqh* covering all four Sunni schools of jurisprudence, biographies of the Prophet and his Companions, and more recent writing by figures such as Abu 'Ala Mawdudi. All of these databases can be kept open simultaneously, and material between them is cross-referenced and fully searchable. Utilities for calculating prayer times anywhere in the world and for converting between the *Hijri* and other calendar systems are also available. That is not to say that the *'ulama* have been marginalized entirely: the moon sliver must still be visible to the human eye for Ramadhan to begin, regardless of whether a computer astronomy program insists that it is there. Some religious scholars have also become quite enthusiastic about computer technology themselves. At the Center for Islamic Jurisprudence in Qom, for exam-ple, several thousand texts, both Sunni and Shi'ite, have been converted to electronic form (MacFarquhar 1996).

The rise of electronic or 'print Islam' (Eickelman 1989) has not eradicated the saliency of the oral tradition. Electronic media are as adept with sound as they are with the written word. Audio cassettes, widely available and portable, may well serve to give the oral tradition a 'new lease of life' (Robinson 1993: 250). Certainly we have heard much of the role of the audio cassette in Iran's Islamic revolution, where record-ings of Khomeini's sermons were smuggled into Iran from his Neauphle-le-Chateau headquarters near Paris and widely distributed, much to the Shah's dismay. The Friday sermon, or *khutba*, is today recorded at many mosques throughout the Muslim world, and the distribution of these recordings along with addresses by prominent ideologues such as Sayyid Qutb, Ali Shariati, and Abu-l A'la al-Mawdudi, serves to politicize Islam before a vast audience. Recordings of sermons by dissident Saudi *'ulama* such as Safar al-Hawali and Salman al-'Awda also circulate widely both inside and outside the Kingdom, and this marks the first time that material openly critical of the Saudi regime has been heard by relatively large sections of that country's population. The website of a London-based Saudi opposition group has also made Salman al-ʿAwda's sermons available over the internet using the latest audio streaming technology (*http://www.miraserve.com*).

Communicating Islam: broadcast and network technology

'It is in their use as *distributive* and *decentralized* networks', writes Sardar (1993: 55), 'that [information technology's] greatest potential lies for Muslim societies and cultures.' Sardar is undoubtedly correct insofar as political impact is obviously strongest when these media are distributed, broadcast, or otherwise made available to a wider audience. This section will examine the implications of technologies such as telecommunications, television (both terrestrial and satellite) and, finally, the internet – all of which serve to politicize Islam through their 'global reach' capabilities.

Telecommunications are undergoing something of a mini-boom in the Middle East, and sophisticated systems are already in place or planned for the urban areas of many Asian countries such as Malaysia, Indonesia and Pakistan. The latest GSM mobile technology is also available in many countries of the Gulf – Jordan, Lebanon, Pakistan –and is planned for Syria (MEED 1996). It is in the West, however, that Muslims have made the most widespread use of telecommunications technology for religious purposes. The Islamic Assembly of North America (IANA), for example, operates a Fatwa Centre which can be reached via a toll-free telephone number. The *ʿulama* of the centre will dispense edicts covering any subject to members of the Muslim community in North America (*http://www.IANAnet.org/fatwa/*). In the Middle East, activists in groups such as HAMAS have made use of Israeli cellular networks to stay in touch while moving around the West Bank and Gaza. Ironically, in one case this technology proved to be their downfall. The HAMAS bombmaker Yahya Ayash ('The Engineer') was assassinated by Israeli internal security agents using a booby-trapped cell phone packed with explosives.

An offshoot of telecommunications, the fax, has also been widely used by Muslims in the Middle East, and especially by Islamist groups seeking to question the legitimacy of various regimes. Organizations in Algeria and Egypt have made use of the fax machine in voicing protest to their respective governments, and the 'fax cascade' tactics of Saudi dissidents in London have become notorious. At the height of its activity, for example, the Committee for the Defence of Legitimate Rights (CDLR) was sending several thousand faxes per week to the Kingdom, where offices were forced to turn off fax machines at night in an effort to stem the flow. These faxes were reportedly photocopied and then distributed widely within the Kingdom (al-Massʾari 1995; 1997). The organization's efforts have certainly caught the attention of the ruling regime and its 'official' clergy. The government was even forced to take the unprecedented step of urging Saudis (via a state-owned newspaper) to ignore the CDLR's faxes (*Saudi Gazette* 1994).

Television, which in the Middle East is often state-owned and censored, is not a forum which has been extensively co-opted by Muslims for political purposes. We do find references, however, to instances where there has been a coming together of politicized Islam and television. Abu-Lughod (1997) speculates about the impact of militant Islamist groups in Egypt on the standards of dress and appearance of television presenters, and Eickelman (1989) discusses officially sanctioned religious presentation on television as a form of national discourse. Television, and satellite television in particular, certainly have, however, been the objects of protests by both official religious voices and various Islamist movements. In Algeria, for example, soldiers of the Armed Islamic Group (GIA) have in the past threatened the owners of satellite dishes (Ruthven 1995). Several Arab Gulf states and Iran have official bans in effect on the private ownership of the dishes. In practice, however, these bans are very difficult to enforce, and the countries have in some cases been forced to provide rival satellite programming in an attempt to lure viewers away from 'sinful' and 'poisoning' Western programmes (Rathmell 1997). Saudi Arabia owns a vast media empire and controls much of the premier Arabic-language satellite programming via its Middle East Broadcasting (MBC) network. In 1996, an Italian-based satellite relay company with significant Saudi investment interests was forced to terminate its contract with the BBC after its Arabic-language television service gave air time to the Saudi dissident Muhammad al-Mass'ari and showed a programme critical of Saudi Arabia's human rights record (*Reuters*, 4 September 1996).

In at least one case Islamists have also turned to satellite television as a potential political tool. The Movement for Islamic Reform (MIRA), an offshoot of the CDLR in London, has rented a broadcasting slot on a satellite and is planning to begin transmitting propaganda programmes which question the legitimacy of the Saudi regime according to religious criteria. The group is hoping to take advantage of the several hundred thousand satellite dishes currently in use in the Kingdom (al-Faqih 1997).

The internet: globalizing local discourses?

What about the internet? It is perhaps here that some of the most interesting things are happening. It should be noted, however, that while many countries in the Middle East and Asia are starting to provide internet access to their populations, the vast majority of Muslim users of the internet are in Europe and North America. If the globalization of information technology is having a discernible effect on political community in Islam, then it is to the various Muslim diaspora groups in the West, Arab, Iranian and South Asian, that we must turn to find it. Their activities can be seen as the appropriation of a global technology of Western origin which is then turned into a tool for the conduct and propagation of new hybridized practices. These are formed by inserting the normative discourse of Islam into the Western discourse of information technology. In this sense the use of the internet by Muslim diaspora groups provides one of the best examples of what was referred to above as 'globalizing the local'.

What, then, are the implications of this media revolution for those communities which inhabit global spaces? Whereas Anderson (1991) once pointed to the pioneering efforts of New World 'creoles' in the formation of imagined communities, he now speaks of the 'new creoles' of the information superhighway – political actors whose force lies in their adoption of the enabling technologies of electronic print and information transfer (Anderson 1995). However, we should not be too quick to declare that the internet is suddenly going to radically transform Muslim understandings of political community. We need to look realistically at the number of

Muslims who actually have access to this forum, and to take careful note of each socio-political setting which receives information via this network:

> Transnational theories, fixated on media and forms of alienated consciousness distinctive of late modernity, tend to overlook the social organization into which new media are brought in a rush to the new in expression. Impressed by what Simmel much earlier called 'cosmopolitanism', we overlook measures of social organization in pursuit of media effects.
>
> (Anderson 1997)

In addition, we need to make sure that we have a more nuanced understanding of those Muslim identities which use the internet. We cannot start talking about new forms of diasporic Muslim community simply because many users of the internet happen to be Muslims. To comprehend the processes by which community is created, we need also to understand the circumstances under which these Muslim identities became diasporic. That is, how do other aspects of identity influence the terms of religious discourse on the internet? Issues such as culture and religion are often discussed on the internet using methods of reasoning and debate which derive from the natural and technical sciences, rather than in the 'traditional' idiom of religious discourse which might be found back home. This reflects the nature of the professional or student life of many diaspora Muslims who are often technicians, engineers or research scientists (Anderson 1997).

Another area to be examined is the internet's impact on centre/periphery relations in the Muslim world. A country such as Malaysia, usually considered to be on the margins of Islam both in terms of geography and religious influence, has invested heavily in information and networking technologies. As a result, when searching on the internet for descriptions of educational programmes which offer formal religious training, one is far more likely to encounter the comprehensive course outlines provided by the International Islamic University of Malaysia rather than the venerable institutions of Cairo, Medina or Mashhad. Government officials in Indonesia have also recently begun to explore the potential of the internet for raising the profile of Indonesian Islam (Cohen 1996). Even the ayatollahs of Iran have jumped on the information bandwagon. Eager to propagate Shi'ite teachings, the scholars of Qom have digitized thousands of religious texts which they plan to make available over the internet. An e-mail *fatwa* service is also planned (Evans 1996).

We have to keep reminding ourselves, however, that the vast majority of the world's Muslims cannot afford to pay for internet access. When available in the Middle East and Asia, internet accounts are usually prohibitively expensive, hence subscriptions tend to be limited to elite groups who are often more sympathetic to Western bourgeois values. As noted above, it is usually amongst the diaspora Muslims of the Western world that we find the internet being appropriated for political purposes. The American media, for example, has recently been full of scare-mongering about 'radical fundamentalists' who use the United States as a fundraising base for their operations overseas. Reports often cite the internet as a primary tool for the dissemination of propaganda by Islamic militants. We are told, for example, that Islamist websites distribute the communiqués of Algerian militant groups and provide a forum for the teachings of Sheikh Omar Abdel-Rahman, the Egyptian cleric said to be behind the World Trade Center bombing (Cole 1997). In a recent piece, even Benedict Anderson seemed to sensationalize the advent of diaspora activists:

> [They] create a serious politics that is at the same time radically unaccountable. The participant rarely pays taxes in the country in which he does his politics; he is not answerable to its judicial system; he probably does not cast even an absentee ballot in its elections because he is a citizen in a different place; he need not fear prison, torture, or death, nor need his immediate family. But, well and safely positioned in the First World, he can send money and guns, circulate propaganda, and build intercontinental computer information circuits [sic], all of which can have incalculable consequences in the zones of their ultimate destinations.
>
> (Anderson 1994: 327)

A more sober examination of the situation, however, would most likely reveal that very few of the Muslim groups who have a presence on the internet are involved in this sort of activity. To be sure, there do exist several prominent sites which advertise information on 'digital jihad' and 'on-line activism', or which claim to provide resources for Islamist politicians, but it is unlikely that any of these – which are often run by students or part-time volunteers – actually have the capacity to engage in the sort of international intrigues alluded to above.[7] Recent, events, such as the terrorist attacks of 9/11 do show that the Islamic diaspora poses some threat to the US. However, the subsequent anthrax scare and the earlier bombing of the federal building in Oklahoma City, also indicate that a country such as the United States probably has more to fear from disillusioned sections of its own population or from various cult and millenarian movements than it does from the Muslim diaspora.

For the overwhelming majority of Muslims in the West, the internet is mainly a forum for the conduct of politics *within* Islam. Because very few 'official' Muslim organs, such as the Organization of the Islamic Conference, the Muslim World League or the various eminent religious schools, actually have any presence on the internet, we can characterize many of the Muslim sites which do exist as 'alternatives' (Anderson 1996). That is, in the absence of sanctioned information from recognized institutions, Muslims are increasingly taking religion into their own hands. The internet provides them with an extremely useful medium for distributing information about Islam and about the behaviour required of a 'good Muslim'. Given that most of this discourse involves diaspora Muslims, much of the conversation on these information networks tends to be about how Muslims should deal with the various cultural phenomena which they encounter in, say, Los Angeles, Manchester or The Hague. There has also been a great effort to make the classic works of religious learning as widely available as possible. Numerous websites offer various translations of the Quran and the *hadith*, and also articles by prominent contemporary Muslim thinkers. Traditional spaces such as the mosque have also not gone untouched. In 1996, for example, the Muslim Parliament of Great Britain recommended that all mosques in the UK be wired up to the network in order to provide 'porn-free access to the internet and [to] establish places where Muslims can socialise in a *halal* [permissible] environment' ('British Mosques on the Superhighway' 1996).

The internet has also served to reinforce and reify the impact of print-capitalism on traditional structures and forms of authority. Instead of having to go down to the mosque in order to elicit the advice of the local mullah, Muslims can now receive 'authoritative' religious pronouncements via the various e-mail *fatwa* services which have sprung up in recent months. The Sheikhs of al-Azhar are totally absent, but the enterprising young *'alim* who sets himself up with a colourful website in Alabama suddenly becomes a high-profile representative of Islam. Due to the largely anony-mous nature of the internet, one can also never be sure whether the 'authoritative' advice received via these services is coming from a classically trained religious scholar or a hydraulic engineer moonlighting as an amateur *'alim*. As we noted above, however, the authority of the traditional scholars is not easily undermined. Many of them, especially in the Middle East, are highly charismatic and demand a loyal following which cannot easily be poached away by an unknown computer personality. And again, the impact of these services must be measured realistically, based on the number of Muslims who actually make use of them. However, it can perhaps be said that they are having a fairly significant effect with regard to those questions which concern the details of daily life for a Muslim in the West. Diaspora Muslims are likely to find it convenient to be able to turn to one of their own – someone who has also lived Western culture – so as to receive a hearing that is sympathetic and more in tune with local contexts.

More than anything else, the internet provides a space where Muslims, who often find themselves to be a marginalized or extreme minority group in many Western communities, can go in order to find others 'like them'. It is in this sense that we can speak of the internet as allowing Muslims to create a new form of imag-ined community, or a reimagined *ummah*: 'It is imagined because the members … will never know most of their fellow-members, meet them, or even hear of them, yet in the minds of each lies the image of their communion' (Anderson 1991: 6). Hence the various Islams of the internet offer a reassuring set of symbols and terminology which attempt to reproduce familiar settings and terms of discourse in locations far remote from those in which they were originally embedded. It is inevitable when such traditions travel that various processes of cultural translation are set in motion. The resulting syncretisms then give rise to new forms of Islam, each of which is redrawn to suit the unique set of socio-cultural contingencies into which it enters. This is what we mean when we speak of globalizing the local; or to be more precise, the globalization of cultural material which is then *re-localized* in new and distant contexts.

The internet in the Persian Gulf: localizing the global?

> This internet issue has made everything else pale into insignificance. These networks are accessible to everyone; people can find political, security and pornographic materials, songs, films, and scenery there. Unfortunately, some of our officials do not pay attention to these things. I do not under-stand why they are so confused; why there is no logic to what they do; they are expanding these things. They should explain themselves.
>
> (Ayatollah Ahmad Jannati)

What happens, though, when the internet begins to spread into a region of the world populated by societies whose normative orientation takes strong issue with some of its content? The question of how globalization affects cultural dynamics in the Arab Gulf countries is extremely salient here. We need first to note that the Gulf does not by any means represent a parochial, primitive backwater. Rather it provides a fascinating case for understanding how rapid influxes of technology and industry impact upon traditional socio-cultural patterns and practices. Gulf society is itself already something of a hybrid, a merger between traditional norms and forms of social organization and the very latest in modern technology. The region's affluence is the result of its crucial role in world energy provision, and both of these factors have allowed (if not forced) the Gulf to undergo rapid processes of industrialization and modernization – processes which in other regions of the world usually occur over the space of many generations rather than in just over half a century. Given these circumstances it is inevitable that tensions emerge between the traditional and the modern. For the most part Gulf societies have demonstrated extreme flexibility and a willingness to exploit the latest trends in technology as well as the global division of labour. The presence of an enormous Asian migrant labour force is well known, and this phenomenon is prevalent at every level of social structure in the Gulf. Among Bedouin tribes in Saudi Arabia, for example, it is not uncommon to find camels being herded by a Pakistani rather than by a local Arab – likewise the trappings of modern technology. Bedouin in the UAE make extensive use of that country's GSM mobile telephone network; globalization, it would seem, has even found its way into the desert.

The arrival of the internet in the Gulf has been a complex affair. There is a distinction to be drawn here between the availability of internet access for a limited number of specialized research institutes, and the availability of accounts to the wider public. Various universities and hospitals in the Gulf had internet gateways (often via Europe) during the early 1990s, but it is only since about 1995 that private accounts have started to appear in a few locations. The reasons for this are obvious. These countries are all ruled by conservative dynastic regimes which, to varying degrees, wield overwhelming editorial control over their respective media forums. This has meant that local political issues receive virtually no coverage except via the occasional heavily veiled wording in a newspaper. All magazines, television programmes, films and videos from abroad are censored, with any references to the Gulf and its various regimes removed unless unequivocally laudatory. Bare skin and alcohol advertising are also banned, as are sexually explicit or other religiously questionable materials. Several Gulf states, such as Kuwait and Qatar, have been experimenting with a certain modicum of free press and participatory politics. Even here, however, there are tacit parameters which are not to be transgressed. For the most part, Gulf Arab society remains closed.

What happens then with the advent of the internet, a medium which, by its very nature, is heavily resistant to any attempt at control, censorship, or regulation? Governments in the Gulf find themselves in something of a quandary. On the one hand they are as anxious to take advantage of the internet as they have been to make use of every other new form of technology; its scientific and educational potential have certainly not gone unnoticed in the Gulf. On the other hand they are worried about the perceived threat to their relatively closed societies. Pornography, sex, religious and political debate – all these things would suddenly be available to Gulf citizens. In addition, countries such as Saudi Arabia and Bahrain feel themselves under threat from exiled religious opposition groups who make use of the latest information technology to question the legitimacy of the regimes. The internet services offered by groups such as the Movement for Islamic Reform in Arabia (MIRA) and the Bahrain Freedom Movement (BFM) in London have in the past been aimed primarily at fellow countrymen abroad such as students and travelling businessmen. Internet access in the Gulf would provide these groups with a much-desired constituency which had previously been reachable only via the fax (al-Faqih 1997). The challenge, then, has been to reconcile these two concerns, that is, to get hooked up to the internet as everyone else seems to be doing, while at the same time finding some sort of means to prevent citizens from accessing 'undesirable' information and images.

This latter problem has been circumvented by two main approaches. The first, as noted above, has been to severely limit internet access. Initially only specialized scientific and medical universities and research institutes were allowed onto the internet, and all material accessed was noted. This parallels the experience in Iran, where until early 1996 only higher education establishments could tap into the internet, and then only over a clogged, high-traffic route via Vienna. The second approach to internet control involves the installation of hardware and software safeguards which prevent users from accessing specific sites known to be 'bad'. The system operators keep a list of all banned locations on the central file server and any request for one of these sites by a user is refused. The websites of the various Gulf dissident organizations would, one might assume, be at the top of these lists. The enormous size of the internet tends to foil this method, however. Internet sites divide, multiply, and mirror themselves on a daily basis and it becomes impossible to keep track of where data is migrating on the internet. Hence also impossible to restrict access to all possible sites. Another method of censorship involves the computer actually searching all downloaded data, looking for references to banned keywords and scanning for graphic patterns that match those of naked bodies. This method, however, severely slows down one's connection to the internet and is likely to fail in its efforts as often as it is to succeed.

A combination of these methods has been used in those Gulf countries which do allow public access to the internet. The UAE's sole service provider Etisalat, for example, has installed a 'proxy-server system' which allows it to select the sites available to its users at any one time. The UAE is also negotiating with a British secu-rity company for the installation of an elaborate system which would allow police to monitor all requests for data sent by UAE internet accounts and would alert them whenever banned materials were requested by users (*IPS* 1997). Indeed, it is the availability of such systems which has convinced many Gulf countries to gradually phase in the availability of private internet access. Kuwait was first, followed by the UAE, Bahrain and Qatar. Oman went online in early 1997, but Saudi Arabia, the larg-est and most conservative of the Gulf states, continues to hesitate, with its advertised deadlines for the provision of private internet service constantly pushed back.

At this point it is too early to tell what the long-term impact of the internet will be on Gulf society. Its presence has, however, already provoked a number of telling incidents. Dubai's chief of police, Major General Dhahi Khalfan Tamim, has been vocal in emphasizing the need to control access to the internet, and has even found himself embroiled in a public feud with the service provider Etisalat, a rare occurrence in the Emirates. The conflict centred around the question of who possesses jurisdiction to issue licences for internet access. Dhahi claimed that the police and security forces were ultimately responsible for monitoring the flow of information in and out of the emirate, while the 60 per cent state-owned Etisalat insisted that its own expertise should have the deciding hand (*Reuters*, 18 June 1996). In other comments Dhahi has expressed fears about Israel trying to disrupt Arab countries using the internet, and has also recommended that the UAE follow the lead of Singapore in placing tight restrictions on internet access (*IPS* 1997). So it is difficult to read the politics behind an event such as the opening of the region's first internet café in Dubai. This enterprise, which brings the internet out into the open, can be understood in a number of ways. We might choose to see it as the popularization of the internet, as an indication that the internet has well and truly arrived in the Gulf. In this case its installation in a very public space, a shopping centre, represents a victory of consumer demand over state authority. Alternatively, however, we might just as easily read the situation as one of government intervention. This rendition would hold that state authorities sanctioned the establishment of an internet café precisely so that the network would be brought into the open. Instead of accessing the internet from the privacy of their own homes where government monitoring is more difficult, the café encourages potential users to go online in a very public setting. According to this logic people would be less likely to attempt to access questionable material in circumstances under which they are easily scrutinized.

The religious sector has also reacted to the arrival of the internet. Islamist deputies in Kuwait, for example, submitted a bill to that country's parliament which called on the government to be wary of 'sin-inducing' material on the internet which '[does] not suit our social values' (*Reuters*, 28 August 1996). The proposal also recommended that the government act swiftly to put control mechanisms in place. Two months later the Kuwaiti Ministry of Communications announced that it would regulate the country's main internet connection point. 'This operation', they announced, 'will give us full control of the internet in Kuwait, as well as full control of the necessary equipment. Anyone who wants to be an [internet service] provider will have to do so under certain conditions which we are currently drafting' (*Xinhua*, 4 November 1996). Although it is difficult to determine whether or not this new policy was prompted by the protests of the Islamist parliamentarians, their contemporaneous publicizing of the issue must certainly have been a factor.

In Iran users have been told that their e-mail has to comply with Islamic laws and traditions (Bogert 1995), and in the Arab Gulf countries the various regimes have worked to ensure that the internet feeds entering their societies are devoid of controversial and 'sinful' materials. By effectively reducing the content of the internet in this way and by heavily promoting their own Arabic-language sites, these countries manage to 'localize the global' to some degree. Recent plans to expand the region-specific GulfNet project is another pointer in this direction, an indication of how technologies from the 'outside' can be appropriated for purely local use. But this is only one side of the story. The arrival of networked forums such as the internet in the Gulf offers the possibility of something for which Arab Gulf society is becoming increasingly impatient: a modicum of civil society. 'We have agreed to ban sex, religion and politics on the internet to respect local laws', notes one user, 'but when someone downloads from North America and they discuss God, for example, the chatting continued and you learn something. The authorities can't do anything about this' (*Reuters*, 4 April 1996).

Spaces of public debate are few and far between in the region, with only a few of the countries only just cautiously easing back their tight controls over the media. The socio-economic situation in the Gulf, and especially in Saudi Arabia, is such that the citizens of these countries are increasingly coming to demand that they be treated *as* citizens; that is, that they be granted a certain degree of political rights. High levels of unemployment among recent graduates, for example, have spawned a generation which is largely disillusioned with the Sa'ud regime. Substantial numbers of young Saudis suddenly find themselves needing to criticize the government, but without any effective forum in which to do so. Inspired by exile groups such as the CDLR or MIRA, and by charismatic focal *'ulama*, Islamist discourse is increasingly becoming their chosen language of protest. The regime is well aware of this potential instability, and hence it is very hesitant to give the Saudi population access to computer-mediated communication. Preventing users from downloading pornography and sinful texts from 'out there' is one thing; it will be far more difficult for governments to prevent their citizens from talking to each other. The vast majority of these populations have no interest in Western pornography. For them, problems closer to home are much more pressing. Open computer networks in the Gulf would provide a means by which local political issues could be discussed and debated, responses planned, and actions coordinated. For these people the internet offers a semblance of political civility, albeit somewhat different in form from the very specific model of 'civil society' which we derive from the Western tradition of political philosophy (Seligman 1992). If we contextualize the socio-political implications of Gulf internet use in this way, then the sense in which it represents a localization of the global starts to become clear.

It has become apparent that the encounter between Islam and the globalized technologies of communication is as multifaceted as the religion itself. The advent of globalization, it has been argued, must be understood as a culturally heterogenizing force just as much as it is seen as a source of homogeneity. In this regard we spoke of how globalization can lead to increased localization and vice-versa. In the case of Islam the nature of these processes depends upon where the Muslims concerned are situated. For diaspora Muslims, globalized communication means intermingling and dialogue between disparate local interpretations of what it means to be 'Islamic'. The politics of authenticity which inevitably ensue from this also serve to further fragment traditional sources of authority, such that the locus of 'real' Islam and the identity of those who are permitted to speak on its behalf becomes ambiguous. This is, in effect, the globalization of various local Islams. In the case of the Arab Gulf countries, however, a global force such as the internet is made local in two key ways. Official censorship tries to reduce its content such that it fits within the normative constraints of Gulf Muslim society; and at the same time various religio-political communities or movements in the Gulf may attempt to appropriate it as a form of 'digital civil society', perhaps explicitly in opposition to the various ruling regimes. In a sense, the dichotomy between these two identities, the global diaspora Muslim and the local Gulf Muslim, is false. Individuals can move fluidly between these roles, picking and choosing as convenient, emphasizing and de-emphasizing different identities as the situation demands. The globalization of information technology has undoubtedly had a strong impact on Muslim politics wherever they take place: It has provided Islamists with effective new tools with which to network, disseminate information and raise their profiles abroad. Increased interaction between various 'local' conceptions of Islam (as mediated by cultural, regional, and national traditions) also serves to emphasize the religion's inherent heterogeneity.

Conclusion

In order to come to a conclusion, we need to know to what extent the globalization of information technology provides a new framework within which Muslims can reimagine the *ummah*. First and foremost, it is important to recognize that with a medium such as the internet we are dealing with forms of 'virtual community' (Rheingold 1994). These are contexts in which indirect and distanciated relationships are sustained through computer-mediated communication. To invoke Gibson's (1984) metaphor, participants in this kind of community are 'wrapped in media', such that one's corporeal existence becomes significantly de-emphasized. To what extent, though, is community created, or in this case re-created, within these contexts? On the nascent electronic frontier, it is perhaps most useful to understand community primarily as a *shared normative framework*. Community here is quite literally the product of communication; an active process. Contrast this with forms of community into which one is born or which can be 'made real' through the possession of a passport (e.g. ethnicity or nationality). Here, community is enacted through the creation of discourses based upon common modes of interpretation. This is illustrated by the fact that so many of today's virtual communities, MUDS, chat rooms, and Usenet, for example, tend to be organized according to specific themes or interests.[8] The 'order' of such worlds is often derived from the symbolic language of popular television shows, novels or films. There is no reason, therefore, why it would not be possible to develop forms of 'virtual *ummah*' whose discursive norms derive from an Islamic framework.[9]

Entry into the traditional *ummah* is, in theory, available to any individual willing to recognize the singularity of God and the prophethood of Muhammad. Historically, of course, this has not prevented the ruptures and schisms which characterize the history of any great world religion. What role could IT possibly play in unifying so polysemic a community?

Recalling our discussions above, we might envisage a virtual *ummah* playing several roles:

- Fostering social networks through which 'distanciated' Muslims can organize and communicate.
- Providing spaces for critical dialogue, debate about Islam and encounters with the Muslim 'other'. This function might be seen as comparable to that played by the diasporic mosque described by Fischer and Abedi (1992).
- Allowing Muslim political movements to locate and share resources.

- More generally, opening forums in which Muslims can find solidarity, support and like-minded people. Our discussion of Muslim diasporas on the internet above highlighted this aspect of the virtual *ummah*.

But to what extent would the original sense of the *ummah* as a new social paradigm be recreated; that is, as a form of community in which factional identities are subordinated to a greater religious whole? This aspect of the virtual *ummah* is the most problematic, but we might still want to speculate about computer-mediated communication permitting Muslims to transcend ethnic or national boundaries. If the 'common language' (or the most resonant discourse) found by a Muslim wandering through the internet is Islam rather than 'Malayness' or 'Iranianess', then to what extent might the religious aspects of her self-identity become reified?

What about politics within such a space? The internet began as a community with no centre and with no clear hegemony. As Lyon points out,

> Whatever the eventual trajectory of virtual communities, the extent to which they are able to be consequential will depend on how subjectivity and meaning are understood and mobilised within them. And if they are to be politically consequential, questions of access, participation and co-ordination would also have to be addressed.
>
> (Lyon 1997: 36)

Who would administrate the virtual *ummah*? Our earlier discussion has pointed to the fact that in the first few years of relatively widespread internet access it was the more peripheral countries of the Muslim world which hastened to create a virtual presence. As more and more 'official' organs of the Islamic world (e.g. the Organization of the Islamic Conference, the Muslim World League, etc.) come online, they may well seek to assert their hegemony in the virtual *ummah*. There has certainly been a temporary leavening effect, but for how long? Will the traditional centres and peripheries of the Muslim world simply reproduce themselves in cyberspace? The point must be made that virtual communities do not exist in a political or economic vacuum. Access to information technology requires resources in more than one sense. Prospective members of the virtual *ummah* would need both someone to pay for their internet access *and* someone to permit them the political liberty to actually make use of online resources. As we have seen in the case of the Gulf countries, this latter imperative is not always so easily secured.

Changes are undoubtedly taking place, however. Some writers, such as Dale Eickelman, speak of the onset of an Islamic Reformation. 'Increasingly in the Muslim world', he writes, 'religious beliefs are self-consciously held, explicitly expressed, and systematized. It is no longer sufficient simply to "be" Muslim and to follow Muslim practices. One must reflect upon Islam and defend one's views' (Eickelman 1998). Information technology and computer-mediated communication may serve to further radicalize this critical trend in that they allow greater numbers of people to take Islam into their own hands, opening new spaces for debate and critical dialogue. The complex nature of globalized information technology, however, ensures that there will always be extreme tensions within its effects on a given tradition. While information technology does in some senses offer the world's Muslims the capability to bridge the distances between them, it also furnishes Islam with a mirror to hold up to itself and an opportunity to gaze upon its many diverse faces.

Notes

1   Quran, Sura 2:43 – 'We have made you a community [*umma*] in the middle so that you may bear witness against mankind'. Ali and Arberry render 'in the middle' as, respectively, 'justly balanced' and 'just', a translation which I find dissatisfying since it ignores the spatial implications of the Arabic *wasat*, 'middle or centre'. Various interpretations regard this as implying that Islam is to be seen as a religion in between Christianity and Judaism (Montgomery Watt) or as the religion of Arabia which 'is in an intermediate position in the Old World' (Yusuf Ali). It may also refer to the mediatory position which Muhammad's community occupied in Medina.
2   See Quran, Sura 6:38.
3   There is an obvious link here to Benedict Anderson's concept of the 'imagined community' (Anderson 1991), and an even stronger echo can be found in some of his more recent writings (see Anderson 1994).
4   *Al-qur'an* means 'the recitation'.
5   This is a program which contains rules and guidelines which tell a computer how to process, 'think' and make decisions with particular sets of data. It is usually written in an artificial intelligence language such as PROLOG.
6   *Ijtihad* refers to independent judgements made through the interpretation and/or extrapolation of religious texts by scholars.
7   See, for example, *http://www.uoknor.edu/cybermuslims/cy_jihad.html*.
8   Multi-user Domains (MUDS) are virtual communities in which 'real' users assume the guise of a character or nickname. These communities often have elaborate infrastructures, sometimes emulating entire cities. Internet Relay Chat (IRC) allows users from all over the world to log into and 'chat' in real time on dozens of channels organized by topics of interest. Usenet is a complex electronic bulletin board on which users follow 'threads' of discussion in various newsgroups which are, again, organized according to different topics of interest.
9   In a Muslim MUD we might, for example, expect to see users adopting names which carry religious symbolism. Conversation and discussion would, presumably, take place according to Islamic discursive norms. The question of who gets to set those norms in any given context is, however, another set of issues altogether. One could easily imagine Shi'a-influenced MUDS competing with other, predominantly Sunni, domains.

References

Abu-Lughod, J. (1991) 'Going Beyond Global Babble', in Anthony D. King (ed.) *Culture, Globalization and the World-system*, London: Macmillan.
Abu-Lughod, L. (1997) 'Dramatic Reversals: Political Islam and Egyptian Television', in Joel Beinin and Joe Stark (eds) *Political Islam*, London: I. B. Tauris.
Anderson, B. (1991) *Imagined Communities*, revised edn, London: Verso.
—— (1994) 'Exodus', *Critical Inquiry*, 20.

Anderson, J. (1995) '"Cybarites", Knowledge Workers, and New Creoles on the Superhighway', *Anthropology Today*, 11.

—— (1996) 'Islam and the Globalization of Politics', paper presented to the Council on Foreign Relations Muslim Politics Study Group, NewYork City: 25 June.

—— (1997) 'Cybernauts of the Arab Diaspora: Electronic Mediation in Transnational Cultural Identities', paper presented at the Couch-Stone Symposium on 'Postmodern Culture, Global Capitalism and Democratic Action', University of Maryland, April.

Appadurai, A. (1990) 'Disjuncture and Difference in the Global Cultural Economy', in Mike Featherstone (ed.) *Global Culture: Nationalism, Globalization and Modernity*, London: Sage.

Atiyeh, G. N. (ed.) (1995) *The Book in the IslamicWorld: TheWrittenWord and Communication in the Middle East*, Albany: SUNY Press.

al-Azmeh, A. (1997) *Islams and Modernities*, 2nd edn, London: Verso.

Bogert, C. (1995) 'Chat Rooms and Chadors', *Newsweek*, 21 August.

Bowen, J. R. (1993) *Muslims Through Discourse*, Princeton: Princeton University Press.

'British Mosques on the Superhighway', at *http://www.malaysia.net/muslimedial*, 30 June 1996.

Calhoun, C. (1991) 'Indirect Relationships and Imagined Communities: Large-scale Social Integration and the Transformation of Everyday Life', in Pierre Bourdieu and James S. Coleman (eds) *Social Theory for a Changing World*, Boulder: Westview Press.

Cohen, M. (1996) 'Modern Times: Islam on the Information Highway'. *Far Eastern Economic Review*, 29 August.

Cole, R. (1997) 'IslamicTerrorists Organize, Raise Funds in U.S. while Plotting Attacks', *Associated Press*, 24 May.

Eickelman, D. F. (1989) 'National Identity and Religious Discourse in Contemporary Islam', *International Journal of Islamic and Arabic Studies*, vol. 6, 1–20.

—— (1998) 'Inside the Islamic Reformation', *Wilson Quarterly*, vol. 22, 80–9.

Eickelman, D. F. and Piscatori, J. (1996) *Muslim Politics*, Princeton: Princeton University Press.

Evans, K. (1996) 'Thoroughly Modern Mullahs', *Guardian*, 16 March.

al-Faqih, S. (1997) Personal interview. London: March.

Featherstone, M. (ed.) (1990) *Global Culture: Nationalism, Globalization and Modernity*, London: Sage.

Fischer, M. M. J. and Abedi, M. (1990) *Debating Muslims: Cultural Dialogues in Postmodernity and Tradition*, Madison: University of Wisconsin Press.

Gibson, William (1984) *Neuromancer*, NewYork: ACE.

Giddens, A. (1991) *Modernity and Self-identity*, Cambridge: Polity Press.

IPS (1997) Internet Provider Service.

Jones, S.G. (ed) (1995) *CyberSociety: Computer-Mediated Communication and Community*, London: Sage.

King, A. D. (ed.) (1991) *Culture, Globalization and theWorld-System*, London: Macmillan.

Lapidus, I. (1988) *A History of Islamic Societies*, Cambridge: Cambridge University Press.

Lyon, D. (1997) 'Cyberspace Sociality: Controversies over Computer-mediated Relationships', in Brian D. Loader (ed.) *The Governance of Cyberspace*, London: Routledge.

MacFarquhar, N. (1996) 'With Mixed Feelings, Iran Tiptoes to the Internet', *New York Times*, 8 October.

al-Mass'ari, M. (1995 and 1997) personal interviews, London, June 1995, March 1997.

MEED (1996) 'Region Joins the Global Revolution', *MEED Special Report*, 1 March.

Rathmell, A. (1997) 'Netwar in the Gulf', *Jane's Intelligence Review*, January, 29–32.

Rheingold, H. (1994) *The Virtual Community*, London: Minerva.

Robertson, R. (1992) *Globalization: Social Theory and Global Change*, London: Sage.

Robinson, F. (1993) 'Islam and the Impact of Print', *Modern Asian Studies*, vol. 27, 229–51.

Roff, W. R. (ed.) (1987) *Islam and the Political Economy of Meaning*, London: Croom Helm.

Ruthven, M. (1995) 'The West's Secret Weapon against Islam', *Sunday Times*, 1 January.

Sardar, Z. (1993) 'Paper, Printing and Compact Disks: The Making and Unmaking of Islamic Culture', *Media, Culture and Society*, vol. 15, 43–59.

Saudi Gazette (1994) 'Bin Baz Calls on Muslims to Ignore Bulletins Seeking to Split Their Ranks', 12 November.

Barbara D. Metcalf

NEW MEDINAS

The Tablighi Jama'at in America and Europe

The Tablighi Jama'at

THE TABLIGHI JAMA'AT is a quietist movement of spiritual renewal that originated some seventy years ago in British India. The movement has spread widely in areas of Indo-Pakistani migration, among Muslims of North African origin in Belgium (Dassetto 1988) and France (Kepel 1987), and thence to North Africa (Tozy and Etienne 1986), as well as to many countries of Africa and to Malaysia.[1] A succinct summary by a British Muslim reviewing "Islam in Britain" might serve as an introduction to the movement, as well as an illustration of how Tablighis are often viewed:

> The founder of the Tablighi Jamaat in India was Maulana Muhammad Ilyas (1885–1944). A student of Deoband [a reformist theological institute founded in 1867], he became disillusioned with [conventional education] and wanted to project Islam in an extroverted manner. His main thrust was to do missionary work.... The Tablighis ... travel in groups on *gasht* (tour) to bring other Muslims round to their way of thinking. They have been quite successful in this but [N.B.] like the Deobandis they are non-political.
>
> The center of the Tablighi Jamaat in Britain is Dewsbury [in West Yorkshire]. They are spread all over Britain through the mosques and are well organized. They are polite, courteous and well behaved, and can easily be spotted in the streets. They wear a cap, a beard, a long shirt which goes below the knees, and a pyjama or trousers which is shortened to be above the ankles. They might also wear a jacket and sneakers. They keep very much to themselves. (Raza 1991: 14–15)

The rationale behind the program described by Raza, as conceived by Maulana Muhammad Ilyas, was imitation of the practice of the early community of the Prophet, not only by following his *sunna* in general terms, but specifically by conducting "campaigns" to spread Islam. For Ilyas, the critical qur'anic teaching was that Muslims were "the best community" only insofar as they "enjoined the good and forbade evil" (Qur'an, sura Al Imran, 3: 110). Although military forays were impossible, active preaching was equally a "struggle in the way of God," a *jihad*. Muslims were to go out on patrols (*gasht*) and excursions or forays (*khuruj*); and they were to be led by an *amir*, a ruler or chief, who need not necessarily be a teacher or spiritual guide. Every time they left home "in the way of God," they undertook a *hijra*, recalling the move to Medina.[2] The most distinctive dimension of Muhammad Ilyas's teaching was that the duty to preach was incumbent on all Muslims, not only on the learned or spiritual elite. Outsiders labeled them the "community" (*jama'at*) of "informing" or "notifying" (*tabligh*), in reference to this earnest preaching.

Since there are no formal criteria for membership, it is impossible to measure the spread or depth of Tabligh activity with any precision. Even participation in missions is a limited measure of the movement's influence: thus a recent doctoral dissertation on a Muslim community in Bombay attributes a radical change in religious style over recent decades to Tabligh preaching despite the fact that very few participate in the weekly gatherings, let alone the missionary tours (Fazalbhoy 1990). Tabligh includes many levels of participation, from those who have virtually no other activity, to people engaged in household or paid employment who yet manage to meet the movement's standards for participation in gatherings and travel, to those who join an occasional mission, to those who may occasionally or regularly pray where Tablighis congregate and listen to their discussions. The annual gatherings, drawing participants worldwide, are one measure of the movement's growth. In the subcontinent, the numbers attending the meetings in Raiwind (Pakistan) each November and Tungi (Bangladesh) each January are widely estimated to be over one million; similar numbers participated in meetings in India, but because of fears of anti-Muslim violence, such mass meetings have in recent years been suspended there in favor of smaller gatherings.[3]

Tabligh abroad

The beginnings of Tabligh activity overseas are precisely remembered by activists today. Thus the first tour in Britain is dated to 1946; in the United States, to 1952; in France, to 1962. The change came under the leadership of Maulana Muhammad Yusuf (1917–65) as the movement's amir, a role he succeeded to upon the death of his father, Maulana Muhammad Ilyas, in 1944. From the very beginning, he encouraged a worldwide vision of the spread of the Tabligh message; that spirit continues, so that even if the traces are slight, it is important to activists that their brethren have traveled everywhere, whether to China or Alaska. It was, however, with the substantial labor, student, and professional migrations to Europe and North America, beginning in the 1960s, that a network of support and a core audience for preaching appeared and substantial Tabligh activity began.

There have, however, been other networks utilized by Tabligh missions (Gaborieau 1993: 17). A key occasion for Tabligh activity has been hajj travel, when the pious use the unavoidable companionship of travel to persuade their fellows; once in the Hijaz, they turn their attention to Arabs and others they encounter. Hence diaspora

Muslims might hear the Tabligh message while on hajj or might themselves undertake the pilgrimage as part of a Tabligh mission.

A second network has been that established by students and scholars of Islam, especially those associated with the academy known as the Nadwa-tu'l-'Ulama, located in Lucknow in north India, which has a strong tradition of Arabic scholarship and links to the Arabic-speaking world. Maulana Abu'l-Hasan 'Ali Nadwi (1914–), a distinguished scholar and international Islamic figure, who identified himself for a time with the Tabligh program, has been particularly influential among the Nadwa 'ulama.[4] Again, this influence has reached beyond the Arab world itself in a variety of ways – for example, in the interest 'Ali Miyan, as Maulana Nadwi is known, took in Muslims in Europe.[5] A third important network has been that established by trading communities, particularly Gujaratis, whose effectiveness in the diaspora may be linked to their previous experience in culturally and religiously plural societies (van der Veer 1994), an experience less true of Pakistanis and Bangladeshis. Gujaratis dominate the European center at Dewsbury (Lewis 1994: 90–94) and are prominent among active participants elsewhere. Tabligh activity has also been stimulated among North African immigrants in Belgium and France who have responded to missions from the Indian subcontinent.

Certain key figures and moments stand out in the history of early Tabligh expansion to the West. One almost legendary figure was 'Abdu'r-Rashid Arshad, a telecommunications engineer from Peshawar (in Pakistan) whose influence spread participation in Tabligh throughout the federal government's Post and Telegraph Department. Arshad not only traveled in the Indian subcontinent but also joined an early mission to England; then, thanks to overseas appointments, he was able to carry his missionary work to Japan, to the United States, and, finally, to Saudi Arabia, where he died in 1963 in an accident (Gaborieau 1992: 9).

Cherished events in the early years of Tabligh activity in Europe include the participation in a mission in London in 1946 of Dr. Zakir Husain, scholar and president of the Republic of India (1967–69), who had come to Britain for a scholarly conference. According to Maulana Muhammad Yusuf's biographer, "because of Dr. Zakir's high rank and his worldwide reputation, people paid attention to him" (Muhammad Sani Hasani n.d.: 257–58). Also significant were the visits to Britain in 1979 and 1981 of Maulana Muhammad Zakariyya Kandhalawi (1898–1982), the author of the movement's guiding books and pamphlets (Metcalf 1993a), at the invitation of his disciples engaged in founding the seminary at Dewsbury (Gaborieau 1992: 20).

Tablighis were not the first organized Muslim missionaries from the Indian subcontinent to spread to America and Europe, however. That role was played by the Ahmadis, a controversial modernizing movement that emerged in the late nineteenth century around the figure of a charismatic teacher, Mirza Ghulam Ahmad (183?–1908). The first mosque in Britain, established at Woking in 1889, was associated with Ahmadi activities for some years (Lewis 1994: 12). Ahmadis continue to be active throughout the world today, at a time when they are severely curtailed in some core Muslim areas because of the Pakistani-generated move in 1974 to label them "non-Muslims" (cf. Haider, this volume). In the United States, many African-American Muslims, who may no longer be affiliated with the Ahmadis, first heard about Islam from Ahmadi missionaries (Beverly McCloud, personal communication). Ahmadis use the same vocabulary for their work as do Tablighis, not least the non-qur'anic term *tabligh*, as did a number of ephemeral movements of the 1920s, however different the content of their teachings.[6]

Although the goal of the Tabligh movement has been to permeate mainstream Muslim life, using all mosques as bases, particular institutions have in fact come to be associated specifically with Tabligh activity. In Britain, the Dewsbury seminary, established in the early 1980s, now has some 300 students, of whom 15 percent are from overseas: the mosque of the seminary dominates the neighborhood of modest row houses, many inhabited by immigrants, in the town. The students follow a six-year course, spending one year at the original center of Tabligh work, the Banglewali Masjhi in the Nizaumddin section of New Delhi; a new five-story building adjoining the original mosque was built primarily to house members of overseas missions.[7] The central Tabligh mosque in London, the Markazi Masjid, is housed in a former synagogue, whose interior is wholly utilitarian. In Belgium, a Tabligh association and mosque were formally established in 1975 under the leadership of a Moroccan who bad gone to Bangladesh on a mission; a dozen other Tablighi mosques were built during the 1980s (Dassetto 1988: 164). In Paris, the Mosquée Omar is a bustling center of Tabligh activity (Kepel 1987: 192–201). In Canada, the Al Rashid Islamic Institute, set up in 1987, now educates fifty boys and has a Toronto mosque of its own as base (Azmi 1989). In the United States, a recent survey showed some twenty-five mosques under the control of "a group of 'evangelical' missionary Muslims called Jamaati Tableegh" (Haddad and Lummis 1987: 21).

Lack of involvement in politics does not mean that Tablighis wholly eschew utilization of facilities offered by the state. They do indeed turn to government at every level, of necessity, to negotiate permits for buildings and meetings, visas for travel, and so forth. In Belgium, Tablighis chose to organize as a voluntary association and have, apparently, wanted to make themselves visible through a council of mosques, claiming a "nonfundamentalist" voice in relation to the state (Dassetto 1988: 165–66). In Britain, Tablighis have utilized the opportunities offered to religious schools to gain local education authority support for instruction in the Dewsbury seminary (Lewis 1994: 91). The Tabligh in the West, given the exigencies and opportunities presented by state recognition, seems to have adopted a higher institutional profile than that common in India or Pakistan.

The first general annual meeting, or *ijtima'*, of the Tablighi Jama'at in North America was held in Detroit in 1980, and similar meetings have followed – for example, one in Chicago in 1988, with attendance estimated at 6,000, which would make it the largest gathering of Muslims ever held in North America (Ahmed 1991b).

A major ijtima' was held in Belgium, at Charleroi, in 1982 (Dassetto 1988: 164). The Dewsbury meeting, held each June, now attracts several thousand participants, who are lodged in the main mosque and private homes. In addition to participants from Europe and North America, mission groups come to Dewsbury from countries such as South Africa, as well as from old Muslim areas. Although the proceedings are in Urdu, translation is provided into English, French, and Arabic in various corners of the meeting rooms.[8] When I visited the Dewsbury ijtima' in 1991, I met or heard about British-born Muslims of Indo-Pakistani origin; South and East Africans, mostly of Gujarati background; Indians and Pakistanis; Canadians; British converts; and Americans. I met an African-American U.S. Army sergeant based in Germany who had converted to Islam and to Tabligh activity through the influence of another American Tablighi in Munich: he had adopted the name of one of the humble Mewati peasants won over by Maulana Ilyas in the very earliest days of Tabligh,

Muhammad Musa. He was accompanied by his wife, a former Jehovah's Witness from Philadelphia. I also met a large *jamaʿat* of South African men and women on a *chilla*, a forty-day tour that included the hajj, this ijtimaʿ in Dewsbury, and an ijtimaʿ in Los Angeles. Tabligh networks link diverse populations and far-flung geographic areas.

Most descriptions of Tabligh, like Muhammad Raza's above, implicitly define the movement as one of men – for example, by describing missionary tours, residence in mosques, and characteristic dress. In Dewsbury, I joined a gathering of women assembled in the home of a family of active participants located near the mosque where the men were gathered. Bedroom walls had been removed to turn the upper story into a single open space; mats spread on the floor allowed large numbers to gather for sitting, sleeping, and participating in discussions and talks. Women in the diaspora and elsewhere meet regularly – in Dewsbury every afternoon – for the kind of study and prayer shared by men. Women are responsible for guiding their families and other women, and, when I asked the assembled group if they had come to know Tabligh through the men in their families, they were indignant at my failure to recognize how often it was women – dating back to the Prophet's day – who had offered correct guidance to men.[9] Women travel only when accompanied by men and typically stay in homes, while men stay in mosques.

Tabligh involves fundamental reconfigurations of gender boundaries as part of its overall deemphasizing of hierarchy, evident above all in the insistence that every Muslim, poor or rich, learned or not, can participate (Metcalf 1993b). At Dewsbury in 1990, for example, one session was given over to the importance of women's participation. The preacher enjoined men to share child care in order to make this possible, citing a hadith that women were permitted to refuse even to nurse their children. If women could refuse to nurse, he argued, men were not in a position to require them to do anything. Women, therefore, could prefer to do Tabligh rather than care for children. A further mark of changes in social roles is the fact that many marriage contacts were concluded at the ijtimaʿ, presumably blessed for being undertaken on such an occasion (Syed Zainuddin, personal communication). To the extent that this meant eliminating the elaborate gifts, visits, and transactions customarily entailed in celebrating weddings, it also meant a new basis for social relations and a diminution of traditional roles defined by gender and hierarchy.

Tablighis insist on the priority of face-to-face encounters, and relationships, for communicating their message. Even in the West, they eschew the powerful new media, including cassettes and videos, that have been so effective in so many other movements. They do utilize print, however, although they emphasize a narrow range of books and use them, typically, in oral settings. A book publisher and distributor, the Idara Ishaat-E-Dini-yat (Institute for Disseminating Works on Religion), adjoining the Banglewali Masjid, has been particularly important in publishing, translating, and disseminating Tabligh-related materials. Visitors to its shop typically find the aisles crowded with crates destined for countries around the world. It translates extensively into English and, to a lesser degree, into Arabic and French (Metcalf 1993a).

In accounting for the effectiveness of Tabligh, the constitution of a new basis for social relationships, perhaps particularly felt in situations of social dislocation like immigration, is clearly significant. Ideally Tabligh groups operate on principles unlike those of the everyday world, stressing mutuality, a nonjudgmental quality, and intense, yet typically transitory, relationships, as jamaʿats group and regroup in ways that reconfigure customary patterns of hierarchy and gender. Also important to Tabligh success both in old Muslim areas and in the diaspora is the relentless apoliticism of the Tabligh: it is thus inconspicuous and regarded as at least harmless and at most, by some regimes, as beneficial and stabilizing.[10] Keeping aloof from politics has become all the more important with increased international travel and the need to secure visas to countries often suspicious of anyone who even looks like a Muslim.[11] Also powerful is the Tabligh resistance to "Western" culture in favor of presumed authentic Islamic values and imperatives, a resistance that fosters the conviction that ultimately it does not matter where one is.

Three conversations

Many of these themes are evident in the three fragments of conversations that follow, not least the spatial mobility of many engaged in Tabligh and the spatial conceptions that inform this movement. In the following three anecdotes, for example, the British Bengali funeral director was on the verge of leaving for the annual Tabligh meeting in Tungi, Bangladesh. The Pakistani scientist, while now based in Pakistan, has spent considerable time abroad and is immersed in international networks. The Canadian-born Muslim student had studied for two years in Medina and told me this story in Britain. Although brief, the fragments signal something of the coherence and autonomy of Tabligh conceptions. The first two conversations suggest how readily non-Tablighis (in this case, myself) fail to see this distinctiveness.

Conversation 1

December, 1991. We enter the modest, bustling office of an elderly energetic British Bengali, resident in Britain since he was shipwrecked as a sailor in World War II. Shortly after his arrival, having encountered Tabligh missionaries from the subcontinent seeking a place to pray, he himself became active in Tabligh. I am accompanied by a colleague, a Bangladeshi historian. Our host has dedicated his career to two essentials of Muslim life in the diaspora: halal provisions and Muslim burial arrangements. He described his many tours undertaken for Tabligh, and, being a Californian, I spoke up when he mentioned my home state to ask about the ethnic composition of the tour that went there. (The humor of his answer rests in part on the pride Bengalis typically have in their beautiful, cultured homeland.)

> *BDM*: Were you all Bengalis who went on the tour to California?
> *Interlocutor*: Why do you ask that? Allah said, "I created men and jinn that they might worship me." He did not say I created Bengalis and Californians! It's not my fault, I'm a Bengali.

Conversation 2

July 1991. A comfortable sitting room in a house in a quiet urban residential area. I have come to meet a fortyish scientist who has participated in Tabligh, and whose family, including some in the United States and in Britain, have been active in the movement. He reminds me that we met at a dinner party in Berkeley some ten years back. I am accompanied by a longtime woman friend who is a cousin of this person's wife (who is also a professional). Although all four of us arc present, the conversation is largely between myself and the scientist. It is intense and focused on my proposal to write about Tabligh. He challenges my topic on two grounds: first, the implications of writing about a movement whose members do not seek publicity and do not want to be documented, and, second (the point in the exchange below), that as an outsider in a movement that is predicated on experiential, not intellectual, understanding, I cannot be accurate in my presentation.

> *Interlocutor*: Why are you interested in Tabligh?
> *BDM*: Well, for starts, the Tablighi Jamaʿat is very unusual. It is a transnational institution but communicates something very different from the consumer culture, Westernization, whatever we usually associate with "transnational institutions." I'm interested in countering monolithic views of "Islamic fundamentalism." I'm intrigued by the organization of Tabligh, which is so intrinsic to its goals.
> *Interlocutor*: Then why not study some international social science organization? You are missing the point completely in your analysis. The only appropriate analysis of Tablighi Jamaʿat puts God at the center and sees that all else rests on His grace.

Conversation 3

The Medina Mosque, a Tablighi mosque, in Toronto. A Muslim graduate student chatting to a young Canadian Tablighi:

> *Student*: How do you feel as a Muslim about living in Canada?
> *Tablighi*: Where I am, there it is *daruʾl-islam*.

The three conversations above suggest critical parameters of what could be called a Tabligh apprehension of human society, the Divine presence, and history. The first conversation insists that national and ethnic identities do not matter. The second refuses, inter alia, to conclude as a result that we are dealing with "transnationalism." How can transnationalism be the point if nationalism is irrelevant? What is at stake are issues of a different order completely; the experiential realization of Divine grace. And in the third, what we generally take to be some vision of an Islamically organized society, "the abode of Islam," turns out to be available to any individual who – in any place, in any time – relives the prophetic example of Medina.

Beyond history and the nation-state

The issues of history and the nation are closely conjoined. If we think of modern history and its implicit assumptions, nothing has been more significant to its shaping than the nation-state. Just look at any college catalogue of courses to see the way historical study is organized in terms of nation-states, typically using that geographical framework for periods long before the nation-state existed. We smile at a book title like *Five Thousand Years of Pakistan*, but what seems implausible on the face of it is only an extreme example of the project of historical writing to shape national identities.

In the 1920s, at a time when politically oriented Muslims in British India were shaping stories about themselves, typically ones that focused on periods of past greatness, current decline, and a vision of progress and greatness once India was free, Maulana Ilyas and those associated with him chose to focus on a different kind of history, one that gave no room to national boundaries (of any kind) or to nationalism. A widespread debate of the period was over which term should be used for Indian Muslims, the chief contenders being *qaum*, with its emphasis on ethnic ties, and *millat*, a term associated with juridical arrangement established by the state. Ilyas's only term for Muslims was the ideal, apolitical *umma*, which includes all Muslims everywhere. It is striking that in letters to Maulana Muhammad Yusuf dating from the early years of work in the diaspora, the writers speak of their homeland – for example, in trying to encourage residents in America and Europe to travel there to participate in missions – as "hind-o-pak," India-Pakistan, as if the area were (still) one country (Muhammad Sani Hasani n.d.: ch. 11). Tabligh history is history without the nation-state and with no concern for worldly progress. It is what has been called "typological" history of nonlinear time created by patterns of moral significance.[12] The issue for Tablighis is not to trace linear change and causality but to identify moments when individuals have followed the pristine example of the Prophet; the goal, then, is to relive his time. All such moments are the same in essence, and contingencies of time and place are irrelevant. The importance of transcending particular space in favor of the umma is the theme of a talk given by Maulana Muhammad Yusuf shortly before his death in 1965: "Remember! The words, 'my nation, my region, and my people' all lead to disunity, and God disapproves of this more than anything else" (quoted in Wahiduddin Khan 1986: 47).

Historians of the Indian subcontinent have in recent years become deeply interested in the themes that have shaped the historical and social thought of subordinate groups who did not themselves write history (Guha and Spivak 1988; Chatterjee 1986; Chakrabarty 1992). In this quest for "subaltern histories" that do not fit the dominant narratives, whether colonial, Marxist, or nationalist, historians have sometimes seemed to search for an untouched or authentic cultural expression. In many cases, however, it is clear that the subaltern voice is in fact responding to and shaped by colonial or nationalist cultural norms.[13] In the case of Tabligh, the underlying assumptions do in fact seem to be fundamentally independent of British or nationalist concerns. At the same time, one must see the extent to which the context of British rule stimulated the movement and the fact that certain assumptions – not least the starting point of Muslim decline, decadence, failure – were shared in common.

Contemporary observers, however, write Tabligh into the dominant narratives. In Muhammad Raza's account above, intended as a value-free catalogue of movements and sects, the word *but* suggests the common criticism that Tablighis do not participate in politics as they should, whether for the sake of the state or the sake of Islam. A recent, insightful scholarly account of Tabligh makes the same judgment: that Tabligh isolates from politics significant segments of the population that might otherwise be drawn to Islamically oriented positions (Ahmed 1991b). Other critics have insisted that whatever Tablighis may think they are doing, they have contributed to ethnic separatism that can be destructive of social goals. The significance of Tabligh is thus weighed in relation to the state, a perspective of no relevance to Tablighis' own view of their activities.

Manzil-i Leila: reaching heaven

Tabligh preaching stresses over and over again how transitory this world is in contrast to the world to come. Thus, in a sermon recorded at the Mosquée Omar in Paris, the preacher sought to turn his listeners away from the ambitions and comforts of this world – perhaps all too scarce for many of them in any case – in favor of remembering judgment and the blessings they could win then:

> There are people who come and say to me, "Brother, they don't let me pray at work!" They don't let you do it, pray, at work? So? Is work God as far as you're concerned? So who provides for you? Well? When you are here, with us, you say, "God." but to your boss [using the French word *chef*] you say, "Boss! I'll drop praying so you don't get angry!" Well, just wait for the anger of the Lord of the Heavens and the Earth.

And continuing, not about the French boss, but about other Muslims who denounce those who pray, learn the Qur'an, go on missions (*al khuruj fi sabil illah*, expeditions in the path of Allah), call others to faithfulness, and spend their nights in remembering God (*dhikr*) as "dervishes," he says: "Soon, they will learn, they will see the 'dervish' who will be the first to enter Paradise!" And, he adds, the man successful in this life in worldly affairs, will be the first to enter hell (Kepel 1987: 197–98).

But what is most striking about this emphasis on Paradise is the conviction permeating Tabligh discourse that Paradise is not only in the future but now. Maulana Ilyas, the movement's founder, made that promise: "[The servant of God] will find, in this world, the pleasures of Paradise" (Troll 1985: 171). And Tablighis today insist on the same. Thus an academic, currently based in Delhi, who shifted from being a "cultural Muslim" to a faithful Tablighi while doing a Ph.D. in English literature at a British university some ten years back, used exactly that language in describing to me the intensity of the pull to missions – that to go out on them was an analogue of Paradise.

The letters printed in Maulana Yusuf's biography are permeated with the Sufi discourse that turns on the passion of the soul for the Beloved, who is ultimately God. Certain classic stories are allegories of that relationship – for example, that of the Leila referred to in the subheading above, the dark Arab beauty in pursuit of whom Majnun, his very name describing his maddened state, wanders the Arabian desert. In spatial terms, the Sufi quest is a journey, and the goal is a series of *manzil*, or stages. Muhammad Sani Hasani's chapter on the spread of Tabligh to Europe, America, and Japan is introduced with the poetic couplet "O believer, let us show you / A display of the Divine, inside the house of idols" (Muhammad Sani Hasani: 516). Places like America and Europe are houses of idols (*butkhane*), but, just as the young Canadian

Tablighi mentioned above insisted, daru'l-islam can he anywhere. Indeed, the greatest and most abiding pleasure, the divine encounter or *manzil-i leila*, may be found in the very context of infidelity, even if one is lured there by the deceptive (*majazi*) beauty of material gain.

The presence of the Divine for those engaged in Tabligh in the diaspora is not expressed abstractly but in terms of extraordinary interventions and experiences. A key teaching of Maulana Ilyas was that the work of guidance was the responsibility, not of learned scholars and Sufi shaikhs alone, but of every Muslim. This radical transformation of the role of religious leaders is at the heart of Tabligh organization (Metcalf 1993b). Moreover, ordinary people now not only fulfill the duties of guiding others but also receive the blessings, including those of "openings" (*kashf*) that, as Tablighis have explained to me, come almost immediately to those who go out on missions, in contrast to those who simply follow a Sufi path and must endure years of effort.

Hagiographies of pious 'ulama are filled with stories of the miracles (*karamat*) God works through them (see, e.g., Metcalf 1982: 176–79). Stories of Tablighis, by contrast, are filled with accounts of miracles worked through everyone. A classic pattern in such stories is that of the English literature professor noted above: people were appalled when he set out on a four-month mission, leaving his ill father behind with inadequate resources; when he returned, the father was cured. Muhammad Sani Hasani begins his account with a story he identifies as a key to the character of Tablighis:

> A small jama'at of four people set out for the United States. On ship, they went to ask permission from the captain to give the call to prayer and to pray. He demurred, saying that people would be bothered by the noise. Nonetheless, they did give the azan and pray, and people came and watched them, inviting those on the ship who were Muslims to join them. The captain was very impressed by their ethical teaching. When the ship docked, he said that it was only because of them that God had spared the ship a storm since this was the very first time he had ever sailed that route in quiet weather. (paraphrased from Muhammad Sani Hasani n.d.: 518)

In a classic Sufi account, it would have been a saint's charisma that controlled the elements.

Similarly resonant of the stories of the saints is an account of a terrible car accident that occurred during travel to an ijtima' in Detroit. On that occasion, even with others grievously wounded around him, one faithful Tablighi astonished the ambulance attendants by registering completely normal blood pressure. This was a mark, I was told, of the complete peace, *sukun*, known to participants who put their trust in God. The trope of an outsider dumbstruck at a saint's marvelous achievement is common in the stories of the saints, and here appears in the story of an ordinary Tablighi.

Tablighis cite moments of divine intervention that change the course of everyday life. At the time of the Gulf War in 1991, for example, the African-American U.S. Army sergeant mentioned above was posted in Kuwait. He was deeply troubled about engaging in a war against the Iraqis, his fellow Muslims. He turned to a Muslim elder, also in the army, who advised him to follow his military duty but to pray for help. He "prayed hard." On the verge of crossing the border into Iraq, his tank broke down and remained inoperable for the duration of the fighting. He saw no action in the war.

Travel and migration set a context for such happenings. The accounts of early Tabligh missions in Europe and America reveal an extraordinary opportunity to travel in complete dependence on God, which is always their goal. The missions arrive with no place to go, perhaps only scant knowledge of the language. A characteristic approach has been to proceed to a phone book and seek out Muslim names to set up appointments. As recounted in these letters, both the Tablighis and those they find experience the satisfactions and peace vouchsafed to the spiritually advanced: *sukun, rahat, luzzat, zauq.*

Writing of an ijtimaʿ held in Manchester in 1962, one participant recalled that in twenty years of activity, he had never encountered such faith and fear of God as in that week. He described the sight of Manchester filled with Tablighis as a veritable Bhopal (site of many large Tabligh ijtimaʿ in India) (Muhammad Sani Hasani n.d.: 525). This same participant was transfixed with admiration for converts; for example, in describing an ijtimaʿ in London where there was an American jamaʿat en route to Pakistan, including two converts, he said, "Our faith is not one-tenth of theirs" (ibid.: 524). Similarly, a Pakistani, assigned to translate for an Australian convert who had come on a mission to Pakistan, rejoiced in how much he had learned from the convert's faith, as exemplified in a comment he had made. When asked why he had come, the Australian answered, "My home is on fire," an answer the Pakistani still pondered years later. Tablighis in the diaspora and Tablighis in the homelands mutually sustain one another.

Conclusion

The worldwide spread of Tabligh has transformed the movement in significant ways. It has reinforced a change in the context of preaching to emphasize Tabligh as a counter to all that is summed up by "the West" – materialism, neglect of family, sexual promiscuity – instead of simply Tabligh as a challenge to Muslims' own forgetfulness. For those resident in Europe and North America, Tabligh insists that, whatever their original motives in coming may have been, they can choose to live out a different story than that of material advancement, assimilation, and identification with a new nation-state. In Tabligh thinking, the very fact that they have traveled is rendered positive. Tabligh assuages the ambiguities associated with materialist motivations, residence in a place associated with a secularism and consumerism they deplore, even the fact that instead of achieving worldly success, they may find themselves unemployed.

What turns out to be at stake is not *space*, the new place where they have chosen to live, but *time*, in which the past and future converge in the present (cf. Schubel, this volume). In Tabligh, participants seek to relive the highest moment of human history, the Prophet's society in Medina, and in so doing to taste the joys of the eternal happiness promised to them in Paradise ahead. Far from being on the periphery, they can make any place a center. Whatever the spiritual links to Nizamuddin may be, it is in the end ideally only the local jamaʿat, and ultimately the individual alone, that matters. Long ago Maulana Ilyas told Tablighis that each jamaʿat was to be a "traveling hospice or academy." Instead of travel or pilgrimage to a center, the center is where one is.

Tabligh can be seen as one response, that of drawing boundaries and reasserting absolute truth, in the context of the pluralism engendered by one increasingly integrated global society and ever more intrusive modern states. Tablighis reject the kind of ecumenicism that invites non-Muslims to grace their proceedings: not for them the Lord Mayor at their assemblies (cf. Werbner, this volume). Ideally, non-Muslims are not constituted as an "other" but, ultimately, rendered invisible, although, a Tablighi would insist, treated with respect. The end result, of focusing on one's own and one's community's religious life and avoiding religion in public life, converges with a secular approach to politics and religion.

If Tabligh thus seems able to deal with the problem of cultural and religious pluralism, it also offers an implicit response to the racism and disdain that pluralism often entails. The power of that racism to shape an individual's self-image is shown at its most extreme, in Salman Rushdie's Saladin Chamcha, who wants to be an Englishman, but turns into a goat: "They describe us ... and we succumb to the pictures they construct" (Rushdie 1989: 168). Tabligh ideology gives participants in the diaspora a powerful script unlike those the dominant society offers – they are reliving Medina and they are concretely blessed. In embracing that picture, the space they inhabit becomes their own.

Notes

1   See the forthcoming volume under the editorship of Muhammad Khalid Masud on Tabligh activities throughout the world, in particular, the articles by Marc Gaborieau, on the international spread of Tabligh; S. H. Azmi, on Tabligh in Canada; and Philip Lewis, on Britain. The volume is based on a workshop on the Tablighi Jamaʿat organized by the Joint Committee on the Comparative Study of Muslim Societies of the Social Science Research Council / American Council of Learned Societies and convened by James Piscatori at the Royal Commonwealth Society, London, June 1990.

2   For general background to the Tablighi Jamaʿat in the Indian subcontinent, see Haq 1972, Lokhandwala 1971, Metcalf 1982, Nadwi 1948, Troll 1985, and Wahiduddin Khan 1986.

3   For an attempt to use scientific precision in estimating participation at the Raiwind meeting, see Qurashi 1986.

4   In this regard the forthcoming work of two doctoral students is particularly important. Mariam Ghalmi is currently preparing a dissertation at the Ecole des hautes études en sciences sociales on the subject of the relationship of the Nadwa-tuʾl-ʿUlama to the Tabligh. Ahmed Mukarram, at Oxford University, is studying Maulana Abuʾl-Hasan ʿAli Nadwi himself.

5   See among Maulana Nadwi's writings Naʾi dunya men saf saf baten (Speaking Plainly to the West) (Lucknow: Majlis-i-Tahqiqat wa Nashriyyat-i-Islam, 1978) and Muslims in the West: The Message and Mission (Leicester, Eng.: Islamic Foundation, 1983).

6   For references to other "tabligh" movements, see Siddiqi 1986. On the Ahmadiyya, see Friedmann 1989. Both Khalid Masud and Marc Gaborieau have pointed out that

no one has studied the possibility of Ahmadi influence on other transnational movements.

7   I am grateful to Philip Lewis for arranging my visit to Bradford and accompanying me to Dewsbury in June 1991.

8   I am grateful to Syed Zainuddin (Aligarh University, India) and Muhammad Talib (Jamia Millia, New Delhi, India) for their firsthand descriptions of the ijtima' they attended in 1990.

9   At issue in a more extensive study of women participants would be the question of whether women's themes and interpretations differ systematically from those of men. For a study of the differing ideologies of women and men in a (far different kind of) religious movement, see Bacchetta, forthcoming.

10   In the 1960s, for example, President Mohammed Ayub Khan is reported to have directed his officials to cooperate with Tabligh activities, regarding them, unlike those of the politically oriented Islamic movements, as desirable.

11   The inability of Westerners to distinguish among Islamic groups is exemplified by the case of Lieutenant General Javed Naser, an active participant in Tabligh, who was appointed head of Inter Services Intelligence in Pakistan in March 1992, but was removed some months later as part of Pakistani efforts to ensure that the United States, apparently on the verge of declaring Pakistan a terrorist state, did not panic at the sight of his beard (*Newsline*, March–April 1992, p. 97). With thanks to Syed Vali Nasr for this and other clippings.

12   For a study of typological or mythical thinking within the Christian tradition, see Frye 1982.

13   It would, for example, seem plausible to argue that in the late-nineteenth-century chronicle Pandey discusses (1990), the zamindar was in fact very much a product of the colonial culture. We know that he was involved in conversations taking place at the local middle school, and we can speculate, at least, that he was directing his account to local officials and representing himself and his class as the people who had the town's interests at heart. Similarly, the weaver, author of a diary Pandey studies, far from being untouched, is himself the head (*sardar*) of an upwardly mobile crafts group identifying themselves no longer as *julaha* ("weaver," a category so humble that the term is also glossed "blockhead") but as *nurbaf* ("weaver of light," a positive term of Persian, hence learned, etymology).

Works cited

Ahmed, Mumtaz. 1991a. "The Politics of War: Islamic Fundamentalism in Pakistan." In *Islamic Fundamentalisms and the Gulf Crisis*, ed. James Piscatori, pp. 155–85. Chicago: University of Chicago Press.

———. 1991b. "Islamic Fundamentalism in South Asia: The Jamaat-i-Islami and the Tablighi Jamaat." In *Fundamentalisms Observed*, ed. Martin E. Marty and R. Scott Appleby, pp. 457–530. Chicago: University of Chicago Press.

Azmi, S. H. 1989. "An Analysis of Religious Divisions in the Muslim Community of Toronto." *Al Basirah* 1, 1 (January 1989): 2–9.

Bacchetta, Paola. Forthcoming. "On the Constructions of Identities in Hindu Nationalist Discourse: The Rashtriya Swayamsevak Sangh and the Rashtra Sevika Samiti." Doctoral dissertation in French. Institut d'études du développement economique et social, Université de Paris I, Panthéon-Sorbonne.

Chakrabarty, Dipesh. 1992. "Postcoloniality and the Artifice of History: Who Speaks for 'Indian' Pasts?" *Representations* 37 (Winter 1992): 1–26.

Chatterjee, Partha. 1986. *Nationalist Thought and the Colonial World: A Derivative Discourse*. London: Zed Books.

Dassetto, Felice. 1988. "The Tabligh Organization in Belgium." In *The New Islamic Presence in Western Europe*, ed. Tomas Gerholm and Y. G. Lithman, pp. 159–73. New York: Mansell, 1988.

Fazalbhoy, Nasreen. 1990. "A Sociological Investigation of Selected Problems in the Study of Islam in an Urban Setting." Doctoral dissertation, Department of Sociology, University of Delhi.

Friedmann, Yohanan. 1989. *Prophecy Continuous: Aspects of Ahmadi Religious Thought and Its Medieval Background*. Berkeley: University of California Press.

Frye, Northrop. 1982. *The Great Code: The Bible and Literature*. New York: Harcourt Brace Jovanovich.

Gaborieau, Marc. 1992. "'Abdu'r-Rahman Mewati," "'Abdu'r-Rashid Peshawari," "Iftikhar Faridi," "M. Ilyas Kandhalawi," "Muhammad Isma'il Kandhalawi," "Muhammad Yusuf Kandhalawi," and "Muhammad Zakariyya Kandhalawi." In *Dictionnaire biographique des savants et grandes figures du monde musulman périphérique du xixe siècle à nos jours*, fasc. 1, ed. Marc Gaborieau et al. Paris: Ecole des hautes études en sciences sociales, Research Group 0122.

Guha, Ranajit, and Gayatri Chakravorty Spivak, eds. 1988. *Selected Subaltern Studies*. New York: Oxford University Press.

Haddad, Yvonne Yazbeck, and Adair Lummis. 1987. *Islamic Values in the United States: A Comparative Study*. New York: Oxford University Press.

Haq, M. Anwarul. 1972. *The Faith Movement of Maulana Muhammad Ilyas*. London: George Allen & Unwin. This is largely based on Nadwi 1948 [1983].

Kepel, Gilles. 1987. *Les Banlieues de l'Islam*. Paris: Editions du seul.

Lewis, Philip. 1994. *Islamic Britain: Religion, Politics and Identity among British Muslims*. London: I. B. Tauris.

Lokhandwala, S. T., ed. 1971. *India and Contemporary Islam: Proceedings of a Seminar*. Simla: Indian Institute of Advanced Studies.

Metcalf, Barbara D. 1982. *Islamic Revival in British India: Deoband, 1860–1900*. Princeton: Princeton University Press.

——. 1993a. "Living Hadith in the Tablighi Jama'at." *Journal of Asian Studies* 52, 3 (August 1993): 584–608.

——. 1993b. "'Remaking Ourselves': Islamic Self-Fashioning in a Global Movement of Spiritual Renewal." In *Accounting for Fundamentalisms*, ed. Martin E. Marty and R. Scott Appleby, pp. 706–25. Chicago: University of Chicago Press.

Muhammad Sani Hasani. N.d. *Sawanih-i hazrat maulana muhammad yusuf kandhlawi*. Lucknow: Nadwatu'l-'ulama.

Nadwi, S. Abul Hasan Ali [Maulana Abu'l-Hasan 'Ali Nadwi]. [1948] 1983. *Life and Mission of Maulana Mohammad Ilyas*. Lucknow: Academy of Islamic Research and Publications.

——, ed. 1964. In Urdu. *Hazrat maulana muhammad ilyas aur un ki dini da'wat*. Lucknow: Tanwir Press.

Pandey, Gyanendra. 1990. "Community as History." In *The Construction of Communalism in Colonial North India*, pp. 109–57. Delhi: Oxford University Press.

Qurashi, M. M. 1986. "The Tabligh Movement: Some Observations." *Islamic Studies* 28, 3: 237–48.

Raza, Muhammad S. 1991. *Islam in Britain: Past, Present and the Future*. London: Volcano Press.

Rushdie, Salman. *The Satanic Verses*. New York: Viking, 1989.

Siddiqi, Majid. 1986. "History and Society in a Popular Rebellion: Mewat, 1920–1933." *Comparative Studies in Society and History* 28, 3 (July 1986): 442–67.

Tozy, Mohamed, and Bruno Etienne. 1986. "La Daʿwa au Maroc." In *Radicalismes islamiques*, ed. Olivier Carré and Paul Dumont. 2 vols. Paris: L'Harmattan.

Troll, Christian W. 1985. "Five Letters of Maulana Ilyas (1885–1944), the Founder of the Tablighi Jama'at, Translated, Annotated, and Introduced." In *Islam in India: Studies and Commentaries*, vol. 2: *Religion and Religious Education*, ed. Christian W. Troll, pp. 138–76. Delhi: Vikas.

Van der Veer, Peter. 1994. *Religious Nationalism: Hindus and Muslims in India*. Berkeley: University of California Press.

Wahiduddin Khan. 1986. *Tabligh Movement*. New Delhi: Maktaba Al-Risala.

Charles Hirschkind

CIVIC VIRTUE AND RELIGIOUS REASON

An Islamic counterpublic

SINCE THE RISE of modernization theory in the 1960s up through present concerns with globalization, a growing body of anthropological and sociological scholarship has explored the impact of modern media technologies on religious practice. Scholars have frequently approached this topic in terms of a polarity between what are assumed to be two contradictory processes: the deliberative and the disciplinary. Analyses focusing on the deliberative aspect have emphasized the possibilities of argument, contestation, and dialogue that have been afforded by the advent of universal modern literacy, the diffusion of printed texts, and the operation of electronic mass media.[1] Following conventional histories of the Protestant revolution, this scholarship has given particular emphasis to the role of print and other media technologies in propelling a democratization of religious authority. The new object-like quality of religion and the universal accessibility of religious texts, it is argued, transform ritual speech into individual assertion, oral mnemonics into analytical memory. Equipped with these newly found sophistications and the autonomous reasoning that they facilitate, a growing number of individuals engage with and revise the religious traditions they have inherited.

Scholars emphasizing the disciplinary functions of religious media, on the other hand, have stressed the ideological over the dialogic aspects of the phenomenon.[2] Media technologies, in this view, enable an extension of an authoritative religious discourse. The resultant public is less a sphere of discussion than one of subjection to authority, part of a project aimed at promoting and securing a uniform model of moral behavior. In short, the public arena constituted by the media practices of religious actors tends to be identified *either* as a deliberative space of argument and contestation between individuals *or* as a normative space for education in community-oriented virtue. The assumption is that the more truly deliberative a public is, the weaker its disciplinary function, and vice versa. This way of framing the inquiry reflects, in part, a tendency within liberal thought to view the individual as necessarily in conflict with the community and the forms of collective discipline that undergird it.

In this article I want to rethink this polarity between deliberative and normative models through an interrogation of the practices of public sociability tied to the production and consumption of "cassette-sermons" in Egypt. In Cairo, where I conducted fieldwork for two years, cassette-recorded sermons of popular Islamic preachers, or *khuṭabā'* (sing. *khaṭīb*), have become a ubiquitous part of the contemporary social landscape. The recorded voices of these orators can be heard to echo from within cafés, butcher shops, private homes, and most forms of public transportation throughout the city. Beyond its use as a form of pious entertainment, taped-sermon audition in Egypt has become a popular technique for the cultivation of Islamic virtues and, thus, for the creation of the modes of public sociability these virtues uphold.

In what follows, I will argue that the emphasis placed on the recuperation and cultivation of Islamic virtues by preachers and sermon audiences in Egypt needs to be seen in light of the role ascribed to those virtues in creating the ethical conditions for a domain of public deliberation and argumentation, a domain that over the course of this century has come to be seen by many Egyptian Muslims as necessary for the revival and strengthening of the Islamic community (*umma*). In contrast to a space for the formation of opinion through inter-subjective reason (Habermas 1989), this arena is geared to the deployment of the disciplining power of ethical speech, a goal that takes public deliberation as one of its modalities. As such, these emergent practices cannot be understood as simply a modernizing turn toward an increasingly individualized form of rational piety or as the deployment of religion for the task of consolidating a national culture. Rather, as I argue below, they need be analyzed in terms of a particular articulation of personal and political virtues within contemporary Islamic discourse.

The form of contemporary Islamic public enabled by the media practices I discuss, while shaped in various ways by the structures and techniques of modern publicity, exhibits a conceptual architecture that cuts across the modern distinctions between state and society, public and private, that are central to the Habermasian notion of the public sphere. In their objects, styles of reasoning, and modes of historicity, the deliberative practices that constitute this arena are grounded in evolving Islamic traditions of civic duty as these were revived and reformulated within the modern period by Egyptian reformists in the context of an engagement with the institutions, concepts, and technologies of modern political life.

Scholars of the public sphere have tended to dismiss the role of the virtues as inessential or irrelevant to processes of public debate. To predicate public deliberation and participation on the prior cultivation of a set of virtues, it is argued, only makes sense in the context of an Aristotelian notion that we, as human beings, have certain definable ends that those virtues enable us to achieve – a notion that has no place in a liberal society committed to value pluralism and individual autonomy. In the view of theorists of liberty from Hobbes to Isaiah Berlin (1969), to root political participation in civic virtue is to impose a demand on the citizen that necessarily restricts his or her individual freedom.[3] Truly rational deliberation, it is claimed, must be grounded in the autonomy of individuals and, hence, their independence from the kind of structures of discipline and authority within which virtues are learned and practiced.

Within liberal societies, this claim has what we might call descriptive purchase due to the fact that such an understanding is institutionalized in the social and political life of those societies. As a result, however, there has been a neglect within liberal scholarship of the place of discipline in preparing the liberal citizen for public life. As Burchell observes,

> What is altogether missing from this kind of controversy [over the conditions of political participation] is a sense of the citizen as a social creation, as an historical persona, whose characteristics have been developed in particular times and places through the activities of social discipline, both externally on the part of governments and internally by techniques of self-discipline and self formation. [1995:549]

Burchell demonstrates how early modern forms of civility and public life were understood to depend on Christian techniques of ethical discipline, enacted through education and institutions of social discipline (e.g., police, schools, factories), as well as through techniques of self-fashioning promoted in manuals and treatises (1995:553). By exploring the virtues and dispositions constitutive of early modern European publics, Burchell draws attention to the place of ethical discipline in creating the nondiscursive background of sentiments and habits on which public deliberation depends. This work opens up an inquiry into the relation between forms of discipline (and the virtues that at least in some social contexts are its object) and practices of civic argumentation and debate as constituted within differing traditions.

Such an inquiry is found in the works of those scholars who have challenged the Habermasian account of the secular nature of the public sphere by emphasizing the salient role played by religious associations in its development, both within Western (e.g., Zaret 1992) and non-Western (e.g., Van der Veer 1999) contexts. While I find many of the arguments of these authors convincing, my goal in this article is somewhat different. Specifically, these authors take as their starting point the public sphere as an institution of national political life and then proceed to examine how different religious actors and organizations have contributed to its constitution, its modes of association and communication, its moral bases, and its heterogeneity and plurality. My aim here, in contrast, will be to describe an emergent arena of Islamic deliberative practice that, while articulated with the discourses and practices of national political life, remains structured by goals and histories not easily accommodated within the space of the nation. As I describe below, this arena should not be understood in terms of an abandonment of politics but, rather, as an attempt to establish the conditions for the practice of a particular kind of politics. Indeed, insomuch as the moral discourse that constitutes this domain is directed at the remaking of the practices and institutions of collective life in Egypt, it is fundamentally political.

Admittedly, the concept of public elaborated within liberal theory or constituted within Western liberal democracies is also relevant to my discussion. European constitutional, legal, and political forms were gradually introduced into Egypt beginning early in the 19th century. In addition, print journalism had already become an important institution of political life by the time of the early nationalist movement in the later part of the same century. And today, despite censorship policies that sharply restrict political discussion and a total state monopoly on television broadcasts,

Egypt continues to have an active opposition press, vibrant political debate within professional unions, a multiplicity of institutes, clubs, and other associations of civic life – in short, most of the basic features of a modern public sphere. These institutions and the modes of power they deploy have in various ways been among the conditions for the emergence of the Islamic public practices I am concerned with here. My interest, however, is not to assess such practices in terms of the degree to which they correspond to or depart from our normative models of the public sphere but, rather, to describe them in their specificity, as a particular way of connecting discipline to deliberation that builds on traditions of Islamic public reasoning.

Cassette-da'wa

From their inception in the early 1970s, the production and consumption of sermon tapes has been associated with the broad movement known as *al-da'wa* (literally, a "summons" or "call"), and almost all of the preachers who make use of this medium refer to themselves, and are referred to by others, as *du'āt* (sing. *dā'iya*), that is, those who undertake da'wa. The term *da'wa* has historically encompassed a wide range of meanings. As found in the Quran, it generally refers to God's invitation, addressed to humankind and transmitted through the prophets, to live in accord with God's will.[4] Over the early centuries of Islam's development, *da'wa* came to be used increasingly to designate the content of that invitation, and in the works of some classical jurists it appears to be interchangeable with both the term *sharī'ā* (the juridical codification of God's message) and *dīn* (often translated as "religion").[5] *Da'wa* also, however, carried another sense from early in Islam's historical career, one that has been central to contemporary Islamic thought: that of a duty, incumbent on some or all members of the Islamic community, to actively encourage fellow Muslims in the pursuit of greater piety in all aspects of their lives.[6]

The notion of da'wa seems to have received little systematic elaboration from the late medieval period until early in the 20th century. Although the "rediscovery" of the notion cannot be tied to any particular figure or institution, its current salience owes primarily to its development within Islamic opposition movements earlier in the century, most notably, the Muslim Brotherhood.[7] From the late 1920s, Ḥassān al-Banna, the founder of the Brotherhood, revived the classical notion of da'wa to define the goals of the organization, namely, the restoration of the Islamic community (umma) in the face of its increasing secularization under khedival rule (Mendel 1995:295).[8] The Brotherhood was particularly critical of the marginalization of Islamic doctrines and practices within the projects of social and political reform being promoted by nationalist thinkers, as well as the failure of the established institutions of Islamic authority to oppose this process. By employing such modern political methods as print and recorded media, large-scale rallies, and training camps for the task of Islamic reform, the Brotherhood quickly went from being a local grassroots association to encourage pious conduct to becoming an international organization embodying considerable religious and political power and authority.[9]

As elaborated by al-Banna, da'wa defined the mode of action by which moral and political reform were to be brought about. Brotherhood members were advised to go to mosques, schools, cafés, clubs, and other public locations to speak with whomever would listen about Islam, the Brotherhood, and the task of building a pious Muslim society. The Brotherhood also encouraged the Islamic practice of *isti'dhān*, whereby a member of the mosque assembly asks permission to address the gathering on matters relevant to the Muslim community. This practice, which became increasingly widespread during subsequent decades, had the effect of enhancing the dialogical structure of social discourse within the mosque, thereby expanding its role as a key site of public discussion.[10] Mass media also became central to the Brotherhood's effort. Books and short tracts by contemporary religious writers, as well as magazines covering national and international events considered relevant to Muslims, were widely circulated and competed with the more secular-oriented publications of the nationalist movement. For da'wa speech and print – and, later, audio media – the sermon provided a paradigmatic rhetorical form, a practice that stood in contrast to the European models of political oratory increasingly adopted by Egyptian secular nationalists. Al-Banna's sermons in particular became massively popular in Egypt and other Arab countries and were widely distributed in book and pamphlet form.

While the Brotherhood was eventually banned by the Egyptian state and many of its members were imprisoned or driven underground, da'wa itself did not disappear. On the contrary, over the last half century da'wa has increasingly become a space for the articulation of a contestatory Islamic discourse on state and society, a discourse embodied in a diversified array of institutional forms including educational centers, preaching associations, thousands of private mosques, and an expanding network of publishing houses and other media.[11] As a result of the activity of the latter, there now exists a vast literature offering instruction in the practice of individual da'wa, understood as an ethical form of speech and action aimed at improving the moral conduct of one's fellow community members. The concept has also become a key point of reference for a wide variety of other activities in some way oriented toward promoting and fortifying the ethical practices that constitute Islamic modes of piety and community – from providing social services to the poor, to tutoring children at mosques, to selling Islamic books or tapes. As I explore below, this extensive network of commercial, welfare, and spiritual associations has provided the institutional framework for the emergence of a domain of practice and critique that, to a certain extent, remains autonomous from the interests and policies of the state.

[...]

Contestatory religion

Although the practice of da'wa does not presuppose the idea of the nation so much as that of the collective of those who practice Islamic virtues, national institutions are a necessary object of the dā'iya's discourse insomuch as they shape the conditions of social existence for Muslims in Egypt. As we know, through the processes central to modern nation building, such institutions as education, worship, social welfare, and family have been incorporated to varying degrees within the regulatory apparatuses of the modernizing state. Whether in entering into business contracts, selling wares on the street, disciplining children, adding a room to a house – in all births, marriages, and deaths – at each juncture the state is present as overseer or guarantor, defining limits, procedures, and necessary preconditions. As a consequence, in Egypt as elsewhere, modern politics and the forms of power it deploys have become a condition for the practice of many personal activities. When the state acts in ways that foreclose the possibility of living in accord with the Islamic standards promoted by the movement – such as forbidding schoolgirls from wearing head scarves, broadcasting television serials that show what is considered indecent public behavior (e.g., kissing), or cutting back on the amount of time dedicated to learning the Quran in schools – khuṭabāʿ use the mosque sermon to publicly criticize these actions,[12] a critique that is then quickly distributed on tape.

The Egyptian state is anxious about the loyalties and sensibilities of the religious subject being forged within the daʿwa movement and has sought, in response, to establish a network of secular cultural institutions as a prophylaxis. Thus, within the government-controlled press we find numerous articles calling for the development and expansion of after-school cultural activities – music, literature, debating clubs, arts, and sports. As one editorial argues in regard to the correct use of mosques,

> We should restore mosques once again to their proper function as places
> of worship, and provide young people with plenty of other accessible
> leisure activities, so that they can live like normal young people, studying
> or working in the morning, going to their place of worship to pray, and
> then in their leisure time going to the cinema, theatre or library, or taking
> part in their favorite sport. [Al-Ahram Weekly 1993]

For "normal young people," Islam – as individual spiritual practice – should stand as a brief interlude between the two primary modes of existence around which the times and spaces of daily life are arranged: work and leisure. Indeed, it is precisely this disjuncture between the kind of public subject fashioned within the daʿwa movement and one who will perform the role of national citizen inhabiting a private domain of unconditional immunity that has made culture a site of considerable struggle. For khuṭabāʿ and their audiences, the danger of Western cultural forms and popular media entertainment lies in the fact that they engender emotions and character attributes incompatible with those that in their view enable one to live as a Muslim. As a khaṭib I worked with told me, echoing a widely held opinion, "The enemies of Islam use *fann, adab, thaqāfa,* and *mūda* [art, literature, culture, and fashion] to attack Islam" – a comment explicitly acknowledging the Western and secular genealogy of these categories of discourse and practice. Much of the criticism found in cassette-sermons is directed at media entertainment, film stars, popular singers, and television serials. Thus, Shaykh Kishk's most well-known sermons are his critiques of immensely popular national icons, the singers Umm Kulthūm and Muḥammed ʿAbd al-Whāb, while khaṭib ʿUmar ʿAbd al-Kāfi is best known for having convinced a number of famous film actresses to give up their acting careers.

What is at stake here is not simply a case of political criticisms being deflected onto the safer realm of culture. For many khuṭabāʿ in Egypt, most of the programs presented on the state-controlled television engage and direct the senses toward moral dispositions – states of the soul – incompatible with the virtues on which an Islamic society rests. One response to this from proponents of daʿwa has been to develop and encourage the use of alternative, Islamic forms of popular diversion.

Thus there has been a proliferation of such things as Islamically suitable songs for weddings, Islamic summer camps for children, "Islamic theater" based around stories of early Muslim historical figures, and various forms of Islamic literature. Khuṭabāʿ frequently recommend to their audiences the use of *anāshīd* (an epic performed to music often based on the lives of Muslim heroes) or sermon tapes as media practices suitable for Islamic gatherings.

The state's attempt to control daʿwa has met two serious obstacles. One is grounded in the limited resources and capacities of the economically enfeebled Egyptian state. The second, on the other hand, owes to the very heterogeneity of the state itself. Many of the state-administered religious organizations include sizable factions sympathetic to the same religious arguments that their own institutions have been called on to officially denounce and combat. Indeed, many of the faculty members and students at the government-administered al-Azhar University that I came to know during my fieldwork also participated actively in the affairs of independent Islamic institutions associated with Islamist currents. Not surprisingly, the use of such state institutions to enact policy decisions is frequently unsuccessful: recently, for example, new legislation requiring that all khuṭabāʿ be licensed by the Ministry of Religious Affairs was strongly denounced in a series of reports put out by a group of leading Azhar scholars (ʿulamāʿ) (*al-Hayat* 1996a, 1996b). State attempts to purge these institutions of the commitments, orientations, and sensibilities that continue to link them with, and make them responsive to, Islamist currents have been only partially successful.

It is also notable that most of the well-known Egyptian khuṭabāʿ of recent years – for example, Muhammed Mitwalli al-Shaʿarāwi, Muhammed al-Ghazāli, ʿAbd al-Sabbūr Shahīn, and ʿAbd al-Hamīd Kishk – have all been affiliated at some point in their careers both with state institutions *and* with major opposition movements, primarily the Muslim Brotherhood. Shayhk Kishk, one of the most unequivocally oppositional public voices in the last 30 years, was never entirely outside of the official structures he so powerfully criticized. While Kishk worked for a brief period as an itinerant khaṭīb within the system of mosques belonging to the private daʿwa association al-Jamʿiyya al-Sharʿiyya, for most of his life he preached for the Ministry of Religious Affairs at the al-Malik mosque in the al-Hadaiq al-Qubba quarter of Cairo. Notably, he retained his position as khaṭīb at this mosque from 1964 until 1981, despite having become one of the most virulent critics of the Egyptian government and having been subject to all forms of state repression, including two periods of imprisonment. Then, after having been permanently prohibited from preaching and restricted in his personal movement and communications, he was nonetheless offered a regular weekly column in the Islamic newspaper *al-Liwāʾ al-Islāmi*, one of the papers published by the governing party.

In short, although the state has tried to harness the Islamic pedagogical, juridical, and homiletic institutions to a variety of national goals (many now tied to issues of state security), this has not led to the wholesale abandonment within these institutions of practices and discourses that articulate with the field of daʿwa.[13] As a result, many of those active in daʿwa do not categorically identify the state as an enemy or antagonist. Rather, among those involved in the movement one finds a plurality of arguments and opinions in regard to the state, ranging from outright condemnation, to distrust and ambivalence, to indifference.

While in practice da'wa may entail an oppositional stance in regard to the state in the various ways I have described, this type of public does not in its present form play a mediatory role between *state* and *society*. In other words, the practice of da'wa does not take place within, or serve to uphold, that domain of associational life referred to as civil society. Rather, the dā'iya's narrative locates itself within the temporal frame of an Islamic umma and in relation to the succession of events that characterizes its mode of historicity.[14] In this regard, when asked where the effect of the da'wa movement was most evident, rarely did those I worked with refer to "Egyptian society" or "the nation." Instead, when indicating the positive impact of da'wa most of them would refer to specific popular neighborhoods where, in their view, residents' neighborly conduct accorded with Islamic standards: assistance was provided to the sick and poor by the community, those behaving improperly (e.g., drinking, swearing, fighting, dressing inappropriately) were readily confronted by community members, and most people prayed and attended mosque regularly. While participants of this movement clearly considered themselves to be Egyptian citizens, they also cultivated sentiments, loyalties, and styles of public conduct that stood in tension with the moral and political exigencies and modes of self-identification of national citizenship.[15] In this sense, they constitute what I have called a counterpublic.

Dialogic conditions

Cassette-sermons have played a central role in the creation of the public domain I have thus far described. By allowing the sermon to move outside the more rigid framework of the mosque, the cassette medium enabled this oratorical form to become a key instrument of da'wa. Traditionally, the Friday sermon occurs within a highly structured spatial and temporal frame, as a duty upon the Muslim community as established in the exemplary practices of the Prophet.[16] As a traditional and obligatory component of Muslim weekly routine, the khaṭīb's performance anchors its authority in its location and timing, in the khaṭīb's competent enactment of a tradition-required role as established within the instituted practices of Muslim societies. During the initial years of their use, taped sermons permitted an infinite extension and replication of this performance but remained beholden to it, a mere supplement, and not a departure or transformation, of a long-standing authoritative Islamic oratorical form. Sermon speech was now displaced outside its assigned locus but only as a representation of an original founding performance to which it referred. However, with the increased popularity of such tapes, the development of tape markets, new practices of listening, association, commentary, and tape-based khuṭabā', tape sermons have become increasingly independent from the mosque performances that they reproduce: they have a signifying practice of their own, related to but not subsumable within mosque sermons.

Notably, the fact that taped sermons may be widely distributed and repeatedly listened to has meant that they are now subject to a higher degree of public scrutiny in terms of both scholarly rigor and general argument, a fact that has further accentuated the dialogicality of the practice. For example, in late 1996, the widely acclaimed Egyptian khaṭīb Muḥammed Ḥassān put out a rerecording of his most popular sermon, on the death of the Prophet, which was prefaced by a studio-recorded apology for certain errors in ḥadīth citation he had made in the original. He explicitly related the necessity of amending the original version to the cassette medium, stating, "Given the vast circulation of this tape, it was incumbent on me [by God] to study the science of ḥadīth usage. God rewards with favor people who recount ḥadīth. I corrected every ḥadīth on the tape, God willing, in accord with the books of ḥadīth so as to achieve the highest level of accuracy." In other words, the question of an error in a khaṭīb's discourse, what before would have been solely a concern of religious specialists, has become a topic to be addressed before the mass public of sermon listeners, many of whom now take an active interest in these issues. In this way, khuṭabā' are now subject to assessment by increasingly well-informed audiences.

Ḥassān's apology illustrates the way the contemporary sermon, as the privileged rhetorical form of the daʿwa movement, has come to reflect the set of demands placed on it by the new public context wherein it now circulates. Within this sphere, cassette-sermons mediate multiple forms of argument and contestation. Khuṭabā', for example, not only provide a critical commentary on trends within society, actions taken by the state, and international events seen as important to Muslims but also commonly draw attention to erroneous positions put forward by other khuṭabā' or religious scholars. Likewise, sermon listeners frequently disagree with arguments made by khuṭabā', both in content and in style. Many of my informants, for example, felt that Shaykh Kishk's style, at the time of the regime of Anwar Sadat (1970–81), of criticizing public figures directly and openly was a violation of the ethics of public criticism within Islam.[17] "In Islam," as a student named Muṣtafa put it,

> a dāʿiya should always first approach the wrongdoer [ʿāsi] directly and personally, so as to gently encourage him to correct his errors. Only if he then persists in sinning is it allowable to speak openly about his misconduct. Of course, it's fine for khuṭabā' to make general criticisms in their sermons, but naming names, like Kishk did, that just rouses people but serves no good purpose.[18]

Muṣtapha's opinion on Kishk – and other khuṭabā', for that matter – was not universally shared, and, indeed, was often contested by others. This points to another level of dialogue mediated by cassette-sermons: namely, tapes frequently serve as a catalyst for arguments between listeners about the responsibility of the khaṭīb in relation to the national state.

The virtues of civic debate

Within daʿwa literature and among the young men of my study, the performance of daʿwa is understood to be predicated on a prior cultivation of the virtues.[19] As I describe in this section, the virtues play more than an instrumental role in relation to the activity of daʿwa: as with other practices that Muslims consider duties placed on them in their status as Muslims – such as prayer, fasting, or alms giving – daʿwa has conditions of enactment that include a particular set of virtues. In this sense, it is both an activity that upholds the possibility for the virtuous performance of other Muslim practices and a virtuous act in itself.

As I mention earlier, much of the Islamic print and audio media today concerns the qualities the dāʿiya must possess in order to perform the civic duty of daʿwa. Such discourses fall within a long and continuing tradition of Islamic ethical and pedagogical writings on the virtues that uphold individual piety. Where they depart from this tradition is in addressing the virtues, not simply from an ethical point of view but also from a rhetorical one, as conditions for the persuasiveness of speech and action within the public domain of daʿwa practice. Virtuous conduct, in other words, is seen by the movement both as an end in itself and as a means internal to the dialogic process by which the reform of society is secured.

The virtues of the dāʿiya as cultivated and practiced within daily life tend to be understood behaviorally, as disciplined ways of being and acting, ways for which the body's performances and expressions constitute an integral part. They are cultivated gradually through disciplinary practices, such as prayer, Quranic recitation and memorization, hadīth study, and listening to sermons, as well as by undertaking the practice of daʿwa itself. As I mention above, one of the notable achievements of the Islamic revival movement in Egypt during the last 30 years has been a renewed interest across a wide class spectrum in learning traditional Islamic knowledges such as Quranic recitation and hadīth.

Some of the virtues specific to the practice of daʿwa are addressed within daʿwa literature under the term adab al-daʿwa (loosely, "etiquette of daʿwa") and include those qualities that ensure the orderliness and civility of public interaction. Much of daʿwa print and cassette media focuses on the task of developing these qualities. For example, a recently published book entitled *Effective Daʿwa* lists among the principles undergirding the character of the public subject the following:

> First Principle: Who takes no interest in the affairs of the Muslims is not one of them. Expressing interest in others draws them toward you. To be given concern, one must show a concern for others. This is one of the effective qualities of the Muslim individual, that he be useful to those around him. Thus, one need be skilled at placing oneself in the service of others; and extending a useful hand to others, with sincerity and free from personal interest or egoism.
>   ... Fourth Principle: Speak of good or stay silent. This means listening well and saying little. For the hurried speaker is also a hurried listener. Be a good listener and don't interrupt while your interlocutor is speaking. Rather, listen to him as you would want to be listened to. Many people fail to leave a good influence on the souls of those they meet, because they don't listen to them closely with attention and interest. [Māḍi 1995: 23, 27]

The dāʿiya, as figured by the author, must be an active and concerned citizen, one who having honed the skills of public concern and careful listening is able, through example and persuasion, to move fellow Muslims toward correct forms of comportment and social responsibility. The book provides exercises, including a list of questions at the end of each chapter, to help the reader learn and polish the requisite skills.

Similarly, a tape by the popular khaṭīb Wagdi Ghunīm entitled "The Muslim as Dāʿiya" provides the listener with a list of 13 requirements that every individual in his or her capacity as dāʿiya must adhere to. Among these he includes friendliness, gentleness of speech (*al-rifq wa al-līn*), and temperateness, as well as neatness and cleanliness.[20] Throughout the tape, Ghunīm provides numerous illustrations of how *daʿwa* should be undertaken, as in the following:

> Say we are sitting and speaking with a fellow who then gets upset. I'll say to him, "O' my brother, may God be generous with you; O' my brother, may God open your heart and mine [*yashraḥ ṣadrak wa ṣadri*]." Or say some- one is sitting nearby smoking a cigarette and then comes and offers you one. Take advantage of the opportunity. Don't try to take the pack of cigarettes away from him. No.Daʿwa always entails politeness [*adab*]. Say to him: "O' Brother, may God restore you to health. I ask God that you stop to smoke. May God protect your chest [*ṣadrak*] from your act."

The prior cultivation of such virtues as friendliness, temperateness, and gentleness of speech ensures that daʿwa, as a public act, will be conducted in a calm, respectful manner, protected from the kind of passions that would vitiate the act and the social benefit that it seeks to realize. The adab of daʿwa, in other words, entails not a simple suppression of the passions but, rather, their moderation or attunement in accord with an authoritative model of the virtues. A speech devoid of passion – what Muḥammed Ḥassān, referring to certain modern media styles, calls "cold culture [*al-thaqāfa al-bārida*] addressing only the intellect [*al-adhān*]" – lacks the rhetorical force to move the moral self toward correct behavior, the central aim of daʿwa public discourse. The men I worked with sought to achieve this attunement through disci- plinary techniques including listening to cassette-sermons, Quranic recitation, mosque lessons, and the ongoing practice of daʿwa itself.

Also necessary for the practice of daʿwa is the virtue of courage (*shajāʿa*). Indeed, courage was one of the qualities most often cited by the men I knew when they iden- tified the excellence of a particular dāʿiya. The exemplary figures here are again the khuṭabāʿ. One of the most commonly mentioned attributes of a true dāʿiya khaṭīb is his or her courage to speak the truth in the face of the quite real danger of arrest and torture by the Egyptian state. Tales of Shaykh Kishk's feats of courage while in prison, including standing undaunted before attack dogs brought into his cell, are widely known and frequently recited by daʿwa participants. In addition, many of the young men I knew in Cairo cited a lack of courage as largely responsible for the failure of people to enact daʿwa and worried that Egypt would become like the United States where (as they had heard) no one dares to speak or take action in public on the behalf of others out of fear.

The virtues of sincerity (*ikhlās*), humility (*khushūʿ*), and fear of God (*taqwa* or *khaūf*) are also frequently associated with the performance of daʿwa and are given great emphasis in sermons and manuals on the practice. As elaborated within classical Islamic moral doctrine, these dispositions endow a believer's heart with the capacities of discrimination necessary for proper moral conduct and reasoning. In the rhetorical context of public deliberation discussed here, this understanding has implications for both speaker and listener. For the speaker's discourse to result not merely in abstract understanding but in the kind of practical knowledge that impacts on how one lives, it must be imbued with those virtues that enable it to reach the heart of the listener.

This was spelled out for me by a khaṭib from whom I took lessons for over a year: "The speaker must soften the listeners for what he has to tell them. This will depend on how well they are moved by the Quranic verses, the tone of the khaṭib's voice, by the warnings of divine punishment and the promise of the Hereafter. But only if one speaks with humility, fear of God, and sincerity will their hearts open in this way, and the listeners will be moved and want to do good."

Alternatively, from the perspective of the listener, without having first imbued the heart with the requisite emotional dispositions, he or she will be incapable of actually grasping and digesting what is at stake in the discourse. The virtues, that is to say, are a condition for both the effectiveness of the dāʿiya's utterance and the listener's audition. As affective-volitional dispositions sedimented in one's character, they form the evaluative background enabling one to act and speak reasonably and effectively within the public realm.

Acknowledgments

This article is based on fieldwork carried out in Egypt between 1994 and 1996 with the support of dissertation grants from the Wenner-Gren Foundation for Anthropological Research and the Social Science Research Council. Additional funding was provided by a Charlotte Newcombe Dissertation Write-Up Fellowship and a Rockefeller Postdoctoral Fellowship at the Centre for the Study of Religion, University of Toronto. Earlier versions of the article were presented to audiences at Duke University, the University of California at Irvine, the University of Chicago, and the University of Toronto. The article has benefited from the comments of Hussein Agrama, Talal Asad, William Glover, Saba Mahmood, Donald Moore, Martina Reiker, Armando Salvatore, and Candace Vogler. I also want to thank Daniel Segal and two anonymous reviewers for their useful suggestions.

Notes

1 This progressivist account is most frequently associated with the work of Ong (1982) and Goody (1987) but also played a role in the work of such theorists of modernization as Lerner (1958). Habermas's (1989) influential discussion of the role of print and new reading practices in constituting the bourgeois public sphere has also become a key point of reference for anthropologists interested in media. For recent work on the Middle East emphasizing the deliberative aspect of Islamic publics, see Eickelman 1992, 1997, and Eickelman and Anderson 1997, as well as some of the contributions to the volume edited by Augustus Norton (1995) addressing civil society in the Middle East.

2 For scholars focusing on the ideological or disciplinary aspects of Islamic media, see Azmeh 1993, Etienne 1983, Kepel 1986, Mohammedi and Mohammedi 1994, Roy 1996, and Sivan 1990. For more complicated approaches to the entwining of dialogue and discipline in different media contexts, see Street 1993 and Warner 1990.

3 A particularly useful discussion of this issue is found in Skinner 1984.

4   For the primary Quranic reference for this interpretation, see 14:46.

5   On the history of the concept and practice of daʿwa and its classical origins, see al-Faruqi 1976, Mendel 1995, and Waardenburg 1995.

6   As a striving to adjust or reform the conduct of the community on a whole, *daʿwa* in this usage overlaps semantically with some uses of the notion of *jihād*, although in current use it usually does not express the idea of militancy sometimes indicated by the latter term.

7   The most comprehensive discussion of the history of the Muslim Brotherhood remains that in Mitchell 1993.

8   *Khedive* refers to the rulers of Egypt who governed as viceroys of the Ottoman sultan between 1867 and 1914.

9   Al-Banna understands the nation-state as a legitimate object of political loyalty and identity but one secondary to and subsumed within a broader community based on adherence to Islamic practice: "The bone of contention between us [the Muslim Brotherhood] and them [Egyptian nationalists] is that we define patriotism according to the standard of credal belief, while they define it according to territorial borders and geographical boundaries" (1978:50).

10   Throughout the history of Islam mosques have often served as the locus for a variety of practices and modes of discourse beyond those strictly devotional, including seeking and offering advice, settling disputes, and various types of instruction. Over the course of the 20th century, the Egyptian state has sought to limit the use of the mosque to activities of worship alone. Thus, the practice of *istiʿdhān*, for example, has been largely curtailed during the last 15 years by new legislation that prohibits all but state-authorized personnel from addressing the mosque attendees. The daʿwa movement that I describe here presents an ongoing challenge to these trends.

11   Zeghal's (1996) work on the institutional and intellectual evolution of al-Azhar University over the course of the 20th century provides an excellent account of the emergence of daʿwa as a sphere of religious activism outside the purview of the state. See especially Zeghal 1996: ch. 4. On the topic of Islamic publishing in Egypt, the most thorough discussion to date is found in Quijano-Gonzalez 1994.

12   A comparison can be drawn here to the Turkish government's decision to forbid the reading of the Quran in schools: the worry is that such training will orient students favorably to projects that would challenge the secular basis of the state and its goals of Europeanization.

13   The Egyptian state, it should be mentioned, has established its own institutions of daʿwa as part of its attempt to purge this field of currents not supportive of its modernizing policies. There are numerous governmental associations operating under the rubric of daʿwa, including a college at al-Azhar University (Kullīyat al-Daʿwa) set up in 1977 to train khuṭabāʿ, as well as over a dozen state-affiliated institutes of daʿwa (*maʿāhud al-daʿwa*) aimed at nonspecialists (i.e., people who are not khuṭabāʿ by profession but wish to study Islam so as to be of service to the community). These efforts, however, have failed to dislodge the popular perception that the activity of daʿwa is incompatible with the directives and policies of the state. This judgment is evident in the contrasting appellations popularly used to distinguish preachers who categorically support government positions from those willing to question state policy: while the former are referred to by the more neutral designations "khaṭīb" or "imām," the latter are generally granted the more commendatory status of "dāʿiya."

14 In this sense, the contemporary daʿwa movement is grounded on a narrative mode quite distinct from the nationalist press (or, for that matter, the novel), the genre that Anderson (1983) identified as a key enabling condition for the imaginary community of the nation. An analysis of the narrative structure of the Islamic sermons that are central to the daʿwa movement is found in Gaffney 1994 and Hirschkind 1999.

15 Compare my argument here with that of Lila Abu-Lughod (1993), who, in her work on television serials in Egypt, argues that rural audiences associate both the secular and the Islamist positions – as represented in the serial characters – with the national culture of urban elites.

16 The most thorough and interesting anthropological works on Islamic sermons are those of Antoun (1989) and Gaffney (1994). Adopting a Weberian framework of analysis, Gaffney provides a richly documented account of three contemporary preaching styles in Egypt in terms of their contrasting ideological perspectives. Antoun, working in a Jordanian context, explores aspects of sermon rhetoric, in particular how preachers use formal structures of sermon oratory to make reference to current practical issues.

17 Fischer and Abedi (1992) provide a useful overview of some of the key Islamic terms that have structured the practices of publicness within Islamic societies.

18 For an excellent analysis of the concepts and practices of Islamic public criticism as exemplified by a recent debate between a group of religious scholars (ʿulamāʾ) and the Saudi Arabian monarchy, see Asad 1993.

19 Perhaps I need to warn some readers who will think that in speaking of "virtue" I am making a moral judgment about the participants in the daʿwa movement, endorsing their actions as "admirable." Let me clarify, therefore, that no such judgment is implied. I make use of a neo-Aristotelian vocabulary simply as a means to talk about a moral psychology tied to traditions of Islamic discipline in which valued forms of behavior are inculcated.

20 All of my informants and many of the people I met in Cairo who considered daʿwa an important aspect of their lives demonstrated the latter virtue at all times, never appearing in public without freshly washed and pressed clothing, carefully groomed hair and beard, perfectly trimmed nails, and so on.

References

Abu-Lughod, Lila (1993) Find a Place for Islam: Egyptian Television Serials and the National Interest. Public Culture 5:493–513.

Al-Ahram Weekly (1993) Culture: Where the Real Battle Can Be Fought. Al-Ahram Weekly, April 15–21:7.

Anderson, Benedict (1983) Imagined Communities: Reflections on the Origin and Spread of Nationalism. London: Verso.

Antoun, Richard (1989) Muslim Preacher in the Modern World: A Jordanian Case Study in Contemporary Perspective. Princeton: Princeton University Press.

Asad, Talal (1993) The Limits of Religious Criticism in the Middle East: Notes on Islamic Public Argument. In Genealogies of Religion: Discipline and Reasons of Power in Christianity and Islam. Talal Asad, ed. Pp. 200–236. Baltimore: Johns Hopkins University Press.

Azmeh, Aziz (1993) Islams and Modernities. London: Verso

Al-Banna, Hassan (1978) Five Tracts of Hassan al-Banna (1906–1949). Charles Wendell, trans. Berkeley: University of California Press.

Berlin, Isaiah (1969) Two Concepts of Liberty. In Four Essays on Liberty. Pp. 118–172. Oxford: Oxford University Press.

Burchell, David (1995) The Attributes of Citizens: Virtue, Manners and the Activity of Citizenship. Economy and Society 24(4):540–558.

Eickelman, Dale (1992) Mass Higher Education and the Religious Imagination in Contemporary Arab Societies. American Ethnologist 19(4):643–655.

—— (1997) Reconstructing Islamic Thought in the Late Twentieth Century: Mass Education and the Mass Media. Paper presented at the Conference on Mass Media and the Transformation of Islamic Discourse, International Institute of Asian Studies, Leiden, March 18.

Eickelman, Dale, and Jon Anderson (1997) Print, Islam, and the Prospects for Civic Pluralism: New Religious Writings and Their Audiences. The Journal of Islamic Studies 8(1):43–62.

Etienne, Bruno (1983) La Moëlle de la Prédication: Essai sur le Prône Politique dans l'Islam Contemporain. Sommaire 33(4):706–720.

Al-Faruqi, Isma'il (1976) On the Nature of the Islamic Da'wah. International Review of Missions 65: 391–409.

Fischer, Michael M. J. and Mehdi, Abedi (1992) Thinking a Public Sphere in Arabic and Persian. Public Culture 6:219–230.

Gaffney, Patrick (1994) The Prophet's Pulpit: Islamic Preaching in Contemporary Egypt. Berkeley: University of California Press.

Goody, Jack (1987) The Logic of Writing and the Organization of Society. Cambridge: Cambridge University Press.

Habermas, Jürgen (1989) The Structural Transformation of the Public Sphere. Cambridge: MIT Press.

Al-Hayat (1996a) Jabhat 'Ulama al-Azhar Tutalib Tantawi bil-Tadakhul li Ta'adil Mashru' Qānun al-Du'at (The Organization of al-Azhar Scholars demands from Tantawi to intervene in the project of law of the Du'at). Al-Hayat, May 11:6.

—— (1996b) Misr: Tattajih NahūTaṣā'id al-Azma Bain Wazīr al-Auqāf wa Jabhat 'Ulama al-Azhar (Egypt: Heading toward mounting crisis between the minister of religious affairs and the Organization of al-Azhar Scholars). Al-Hayat, September 6: 1.

Hirschkind, Charles (1999) Technologies of Islamic Piety: Cassette-Sermons and the Ethics of Listening. Ph.D. dissertation, Johns Hopkins University.

Kepel, Gilles (1986) Muslim Extremism in Egypt: The Prophet and the Pharaoh. Berkeley: University of California Press.

Lerner, Daniel, (1958) The Passing of Traditional Society: Modernizing the Middle East. New York: Free Press.

Mādi, Jamāl (1995) Al-Da'wa al-Mu'athira (Effective da'wa). Mansura, Egypt: Muṭābi'al-wafā'.

Mendel, Miloš (1995) The Concept of "ad-Da'wa al-Islāmīyya": Towards a Discussion of the Islamic Reformist Religio-Political Terminology. Archiv Orientalni 63:286–304.

Mitchell, Richard (1993) [1969] The Society of the Muslim Brothers. Oxford: Oxford University Press.

Mohammedi, Annabelle, and Ali Mohammedi (1994) Small Media, Big Revolution. Minneapolis: University of Minnesota Press.

Norton, Augustus Richard, ed. (1995) Civil Society in the Middle East, vol. 1. Leiden: E. J. Brill.

Ong, Walter (1982) Orality and Literacy: The Technologization of the Word. London: Methuen Press.

Quijano-Gonzalez, Yves (1994) Les Gens du Livre: Champ Intellectuel et Édition dans l'Egypte Républicaine (1952–1993). Ph.D. dissertation, Institut d'Etudes Politiques de Paris, Mention Sciences Politiques.

Roy, Olivier (1996) The Failure of Political Islam. Cambridge, MA: Harvard University Press.

Sivan, Emmanuel (1990) The Islamic Resurgence: Civil Society Strikes Back. Journal of Contemporary History 25(3):353–364.

Skinner, Quentin (1984) The Idea of Negative Liberty: Philosophical and Historical Perspectives. In Philosophy in History: Essays on the Historiography of Philosophy. Richard Rorty, J. B. Schneewind, and Quentin Skinner, eds. Pp. 293–309. Cambridge: Cambridge University Press.

Street, Brian (1993) Cross-Cultural Approaches to Literacy. Cambridge: Cambridge University Press.

Van der Veer, Peter (1999) The Moral State: Religion, Nation, and Empire in Victorian Britain and British India. In Nation and Religion: Perspectives on Europe and Asia. Peter Van der Veer and H. Lehman, eds. Pp. 15–43. Princeton: Princeton University Press.

Waardenburg, Jacques (1995) The Da'wa of Islamic Movements. Actas, XVI Congreso Union Européenne d'Arabisants et d'Islamisants. Pp. 539–549.

Warner, Michael (1990) The Letters of the Republic: Publication and the Public Sermon in Eighteenth Century America. Cambridge, MA: Harvard University Press.

Zaret, David (1992) Religion, Science, and Printing in the Public Spheres in Seventeenth-Century England. In Habermas and the Public Sphere. Craig Calhoun, ed. Pp. 212–235. Cambridge: MIT Press.

Zeghal, Malika (1996) Gardiens de l'Islam: Les Oulemas d'Al Azhar dans l'Egypte Contemporaine. Paris: Presses de la Fondation Nationale des Sciences Politiques.

Ahmet T. Kuru

GLOBALIZATION AND DIVERSIFICATION OF ISLAMIC MOVEMENTS

Three Turkish cases

IN THE AFTERMATH of the September 11 events, debates raged about the tension between the West and the Muslim world, and between globalization and Islamic movements. Some authors were reminded of the "clash of civilization" thesis arguing an essential cultural incompatibility between the West and the Muslim world.[1] Others pointed to an antagonistic relationship between globalization, originating from and arguably controlled by the West, and Islamic movements, which resist this process. The World Trade Center was targeted because it symbolized globalization.[2] According to this perspective, what we are seeing is a tension between Jihad and McWorld.[3]

Although these arguments are exaggerations, they are not baseless speculation.[4] There are Islamic movements that oppose globalization in order to preserve their identities and ways of life. These movements see globalization as a new phase of Western colonialism. Therefore, their resistance to globalization coincides with their anti-Western mentality. They blame the West for the moral bankruptcy and other problems of the world. They also claim that democracy is anti-Islamic because it replaces God's sovereignty with that of the people.[5]

Yet, analysis of the Turkish Islamic movements indicates that Islamic movements do not have a homogenous attitude toward globalization. Some of them, for example, the Gülen movement, have supported globalization, whereas others, for example, the early Milli Görüş (National Outlook) and the Haydar Baş movements, have opposed it. The attitudes of these movements toward globalization are not only diverse but also changeable. The followers of the Milli Görüş movement, for instance, have adopted varying views on this issue, as I will explain later.

I selected the cases of the Gülen and the Milli Görüş movements because they have been the two most influential Islamic movements in Turkey. The Haydar Baş movement is marginal in comparison to these two. Yet, it is an important example of an antiglobalization Islamic movement. It is also an interesting case for examining the new anti-European Union (EU) coalition in Turkey that includes groups from Islamic, secular, nationalist, and leftist backgrounds.

Why do certain Islamic movements support globalization and others oppose it? I argue that the attitudes toward globalization and the West of the Turkish Islamic movements are contingent on two variables – opportunity structures and the normative frameworks of movements. The hypotheses that I will test are: first, the more an Islamic movement benefits from international opportunity structures shaped by globalization, the more it becomes pro-globalization; and second, the more the normative framework of an Islamic movement is tolerant and open to cross-cultural interactions, the more it becomes pro-globalization. I will test these two hypotheses on five cases: the Gülen movement, the Haydar Baş movement, the early Milli Görüş movement, the elders of the late Milli Görüş movement, and the young generation of the late Milli Görüş movement.

The fact that these movements are operating in the same country, Turkey, helps to control many domestic variables. That does not mean that this is a single-case study. My unit of analysis is a movement, not a country. Variation of social movements may be analyzed not only through cross-country analysis but also through cross-movement and cross-time comparisons.[6] This essay performs cross-sectional and longitudinal analyses by comparing social movements and their transformations since the 1990s. The cross-movement analysis of the paper explains the diversity of Islamic movements, and its cross-time examination, based on the method of process tracing,[7] explains their changes.

Are the results of this analysis generalizable or bounded by Turkey's "unique" conditions? If all Islamic movements in Turkey had a homogenous and positive attitude toward globalization, one might claim that these movements were shaped by Turkey's peculiar conditions, such as its geographical proximity to the West, historical experience as a noncolonized country, or secular and democratic regime. However, the three factors – geography, history, and regime – have existed for decades and have been experienced by all movements. Therefore, these factors can explain neither the transformations of Turkish Islamic movements since the 1990s nor the diversity among them. Instead, these movements are shaped by some generalizable factors, such as opportunity structures and the normative frameworks of movements, which affect other Islamic movements as well. Therefore, the theoretical perspective of this paper can be used to examine Islamic movements in other countries.

The movements examined here are social movements that are nonstate, nonprofit, nonviolent, and voluntary. They are also Islamic, because Islam constitutes their ideational framework and basis of solidarity.[8] Islamic movements have been analyzed by different approaches. "Essentialism" generally focuses on the alleged uniqueness, exceptionalism, or unity of the Muslim world.[9] Therefore, it examines Islamic movements through the so-called religious and cultural peculiarities. Criticism of the essentialist approach has recently become widespread.[10] The anti-essentialists, or one may call them "contextualists," have shown that Islamic phenomena are more complex than the essentialists assume. They have demonstrated the contextual change and diversity in the Muslim world as they relate to modernity,[11] liberalism,[12] and democracy.[13] The main weakness of many contextualist works, however, is their lack of causal explanation. They generally try to understand Islamic movements through an inter pretivist methodology, rather than to explain the causes of their transformation.

This paper, with very few others,[14] makes a contribution to the contextualist approach by applying the social movement literature to the analysis of Islamic movements. Additionally, it analyzes an issue neglected by contextualists – the relationship between Islamic movements and globalization.

This paper also makes two contributions to the literature on social movements. First, it fills the gap in the social movements literature mentioned by Doug McAdam: "Movements scholars have, to date, grossly undervalued the impact of *global* political and economic process in structuring the *domestic* possibilities for successful collective action."[15] To date, very few works have been published on this issue.[16] The present paper contributes to the literature by explaining the impact of globalization on both international and domestic opportunity structures and the influence of these structures on social movements.

Second, discussion of resource mobilization theory and the political process model dominated social movement literature until the late 1990s. Recently, a group of scholars has attempted to construct a "synthetic" approach, which includes different allegedly dichotomous factors.[17] This essay contributes to this synthesizing approach by analyzing both structural and agency-based factors. It analyzes the interaction between opportunity structures and the normative frameworks of movements, and the impact of this interaction on the movements' attitudes.

Scholars of political science generally avoid analyzing ideas as explanatory variables because of the risk of tautological explanations. By using normative frameworks as an explanatory variable, I do not mean that a movement constructs a pro-globalization discourse if it has a pro-globalization normative framework, which is apparently a tautology. I use the movements' normative frameworks (*Risale-i Nur* for the Gülen movement, political Islamism and conservative democracy for the groups in the Milli Görüş movement, and religio-nationalism for the Haydar Baş movement) as sets of general norms and values that do not determine, but, rather, affect the movements' attitudes on specific subjects, such as globalization.

In this regard, having a tolerant normative framework and being pro-globalization are different but closely related conditions. An Islamic movement may be defined as tolerant if it is open to inter-faith dialogue and respectful of cultural diversity. We can categorize an Islamic movement, on the other hand, as pro-globalization if it takes a position for increasing the transnational flow of people, goods, and ideas around the globe, rather than for cultural fragmentation and the ghettoization of the world. In the Turkish context, one of the best concrete signs of being pro-globalization is support for the country's integration into the EU.

In sum, having a tolerant normative framework is generally a necessary but not sufficient condition for an Islamic movement to be pro-globalization. In the case of the Gülen movement, for example, we will see that before its interaction with international opportunity structures, the movement remained indifferent toward globalization despite the fact that it has always had a tolerant normative framework. That is why I attach importance to both normative frameworks and international opportunity structures as two interconnected factors that shape Islamic movements' attitude toward globalization. In the first two sections of the paper, I will explain the interaction between globalization and opportunity structures in general, as well as in Turkey. Then, I will test the two hypotheses through the analyses of the cases.

Globalization and opportunity structures

Globalization has a plethora of definitions. In this paper, I use this term as the intensification of worldwide political, economic, and sociocultural relations.[18] Globalization, therefore, implies the increasing flow of money, goods, services, ideas, and people across national borders. Globalization has two main pillars. The first is global capitalism, which depends on the increase of *cross*-border, *open*-border, and *trans*-border economic relations.[19] The other is the development and spread of communications technologies, which shrink the world.[20]

Globalization has had an impact on both domestic and international opportunity structures that affect social movements. To understand the impact of globalization on opportunity structures, we need to disaggregate the alleged dichotomy between globalization and the nation-state. The relationship between globalization and the nation-state is not a zero-sum game. Globalization empowers the free market system at the expense of the statist regimes. Nevertheless, by no means does it eliminate the role of states in the international economic system.[21] Although globalization weakens the importance of state boundaries, states respond to this challenge by producing new forms of legality. States also remain crucial to guaranteeing a globalized legal order.[22]

Globalization challenges a specific type of state, one that aims to homogenize its citizens through sociocultural policies. It weakens state monopolies in different areas (that is, the economy, the media, and education) through a free market system and the spread of communications technologies.[23] Globalization weakens state capacity to use "social engineering" as a tool to shape society.[24] A state may try to limit the influence of globalization in order to preserve its sociocultural monopoly. That process can be "deeply anti-democratic" because it requires "an inevitable extension of the powers of the state" to suppress both the global flows and the freedom of its citizens.[25]

In this paper, I analyze two types of opportunity structures – domestic and international – which are both influenced by globalization. Domestic opportunity structures mean emerging opportunities for social movements to set up economic, media, and educational institutions as a result of the weakening of state monopolies in these three domains. By international opportunity structures, I imply three things: first, international opportunities, which emerged as a result of the decline of state monopolies in several countries, and which facilitate the institutional diffusion of transnational social movements; second, trans-border networks and resources, which support social movements ideationally and materially; and third, international institutions and norms, which support social movements repressed by their own states. There is a strong interaction between domestic opportunity structures and these three types of international opportunities.

Globalization, the state, and domestic opportunity structures in Turkey

Globalization has had an eminent impact on domestic opportunity structures in Turkey, particularly since the premiership and then presidency of Turgut Özal (1983–1993).[26] Before the Özal period, there was a substantial state monopoly on economic and even sociocultural life. The state was using import-substituting indus-trialization and controlling the market. There was a monopoly of the one-channel public television, the public radio station, and public universities. Özal led policies on economic liberalization and the development of communications technologies. The economic structure changed from an import substitution-based statist economy to an export-led liberal economy. The state control over foreign currency exchange was abolished and the Turkish *lira* became convertible. Along the same lines, the Turkish stock exchange was constituted in Istanbul. State-owned enterprises became increas-ingly privatized, and private education began to spread. Economic liberalization was strongly related to the transfer of communications technologies. In the early 1990s, the state monopoly on television and radio stations was ended. Subsequently, the number of private radio stations blossomed. The number of national television chan-nels has increased to about twenty. Recently, the use of cellular phones, fax machines, and computers has increased, as has the use of the Internet. The spread of communi-cations technologies facilitated the emergence of heterogeneous identities and cultural diversity beyond the control of the state.[27]

Economic liberalization and new communications technologies provided Islamic movements the opportunity to set up their own economic, media, and educational institutions.[28] After the decline of state monopoly in these three domains, Islamic movements became more visible in the public sphere.[29] Economic liberalization facil-itated the emergence of a new pro-Islamic bourgeoisie, the so-called Anatolian Tigers. They founded business associations (for example, MÜSİAD) as alternatives to TÜSİAD, which represents the high bourgeoisie. Moreover, the Islamic movements have developed several media networks, including television channels, radio stations, and publications. The spread of communications technologies created new public arenas for formerly marginalized people. In fact, the Muslim public is the "best organized of the new publics" in Turkey.[30] In sum, the interaction between globaliza-tion and the state has shaped domestic opportunity structures in Turkey, which has helped Islamic movements to constitute their own institutions.

In the early 1990s, Özal was leading liberal state policies aimed at engaging globalization. In the late 1990s, however, the Turkish establishment noticed a trade-off between the benefits of the engagement with globalization for the country on the one hand, and the rise of the Islamic movements at the expense of the statist regime on the other. The establishment was alerted by the rise of the Islamic movements and tended to adopt repressive state policies.[31] In the Milli Guvenlik Kurulu (National Security Council) (MGK) summit of 28 February 1997, the military directly intervened in politics in what has been described as a "soft" coup d'état.[32] This summit dictated eighteen demands that the government of pro-Islamist Prime Minister Necmettin Erbakan oppress the Islamic movements. The military gained support from other parts of the establishment,[33] such as the media, the judi-ciary, and the high bourgeoisie. The soft coup d'état claimed to be protecting *laiklik* (secularism).[34] As a part of this new process, religious education was restricted, and veiling in schools was strictly banned.[35] The military removed its allegedly Islamist officers. Pro-Islamic corporations and banks faced official discrimination and were forced to stop their financial support of Islamic movements. The change of state poli-cies from liberal to repressive with the February 28 coup changed the opportunity structures and created new domestic constraints for Islamic movements. It also created new incentives for these movements to search for alternative international opportunities.

Although all Turkish Islamic movements have experienced a relatively homogenous domestic opportunity structure, they have developed very heterogeneous attitudes toward globalization. Therefore, we need to analyze some variables other than the domestic opportunity structure, such as international opportunity structures and the normative frameworks of movements, to explain this diversification.

The Gülen movement

The Gülen movement developed a pro-globalization view in the 1990s. If my two hypotheses are correct, this movement should first, have benefited from international opportunity structures shaped by globalization, and second, have had a tolerant normative framework open to cross-cultural interactions.

The Gülen movement emerged in the late 1960s as a local group around İzmir. In the mid-1980s, it began to open educational institutions and spread to other parts of Turkey. As it spread geographically, it transformed from a local group into a nationwide social movement. Ties became more impersonal, and abstract principles prevailed instead of communitarian customs. In the 1990s, the Gülen movement experienced its second transformation. It changed from a national social movement into a transnational one by opening institutions internationally and gathering sympathizers from several nationalities.[36]

Throughout the 1990s, the Gülen movement benefited from the international opportunity structures shaped by globalization in three main ways. First, globalization has weakened the state monopoly on sociocultural and economic life in many countries. This has allowed the institutional diffusion of the Gülen movement in more than fifty countries. Second, the movement has taken advantage of the conceptual and legal framework of transnational movements and nongovernmental organizations. It has primarily benefited from the transnational Turkish diaspora, in addition to its sympathizers from different nationalities. Finally, it has employed international opportunities to balance the repression of the Turkish state. The initiator of the movement, Fethullah Gülen, has lived in the United States since 1999 because of the repressive political atmosphere of Turkey, in addition to some personal health problems.

Particularly after the collapse of the Soviet Union, the Gülen movement opened institutions in the former communist countries. Later on, it extended its education, media, and business networks to more than fifty countries. The movement has been active in a wide geographic area, from North America to East Asia. Currently, private companies and foundations affiliated with the Gülen movement operate hundreds of dormitories, preparatory schools, and high schools, in addition to six universities in Turkey and abroad.[37] They also operate a media network, including Samanyolu, a television channel with a global satellite outreach; several local and national radio stations; *Zaman*, a newspaper published in twelve different countries; *Aksiyon*, a news magazine; *The Fountain*, an international magazine in English; and about ten other magazines, which cover issues ranging from ecology, literature, and theology to popular science.

Do the opportunity structures have an independent impact on the Gülen movement's international expansion? We can answer this by analyzing the cases of failure for the movement's spread. The movement's schools and media outlets were officially closed in two countries – Uzbekistan and Afghanistan. In the early 1990s, opportunity structures helped the movement to open institutions in these countries. However, the emergence of authoritarianism in Uzbekistan and the Taliban rule in Afghanistan withered the opportunities for the movement, particularly through the state monopolies in education and the media. These two regimes resisted the impact of globalization and did not respect the legitimacy of international nongovernmental organizations. In sum, the end of the opportunity structures in these two countries meant the official closure of the Gülen movement's schools and media outlets.

Two resources have helped the Gülen movement to benefit from international opportunity structures. First, the movement has been very successful in English instruction, which has been in high demand in many countries, for example, the former Soviet republics.[38] The students of the movement's schools have won several medals in the International Scientific Olympics, in addition to achieving the top scores in nationwide university entrance examinations in Turkey. The movement has reproduced this success in many other countries. The second resource of the movement is that it has created a synergy based on cooperation between educators and businesspeople. The sympathizers of the Gülen movement have been powerful enough to establish an interest-free bank and insurance company. Without the financial donations of business, the movement's schools could not afford to operate.

The second variable that shapes the attitudes of Islamic movements toward globalization is their normative frameworks. The Gülen movement has had a tolerant normative framework that has been open to cross-cultural interactions. This has affected the movement's pro-globalization stand. Gülen's thinking has been very much influenced by the writings of Bediüzzaman Said Nursi (1876–1960).[39] Nursi's *Risale-i Nur*, a collection of approximately 120 pamphlets, is an interpretation of the Qur'an and is widely read among the Gülen movement's sympathizers. Nursi opposed violence and the politization of Islam.[40] He encouraged interfaith dialogue and appreciated globalization as early as the 1910s: "The world became a single city with the improvement of the transportation facilities. Communication facilities, such as print and the telegraph, also made the world population into a population of a single place."[41] In the late Ottoman era, Nursi defended the idea that Christians could hold administrative positions in the Empire.[42] He specifically encouraged Muslim–Christian cooperation in the struggle against materialism and atheism. During the Second World War, he was concerned about the non-Muslim war victims in Europe and held that the non-Muslim children became martyrs and the innocent adults might have gained salvation.[43] Because of Nursi's influence, the Gülen movement has always respected human dignity, and it has never regarded Christians and Jews as the "enemy." When the movement began to construct its positive discourse on globalization and the West, Nursi's influence became more visible.

Until the 1990s, the Gülen movement had focused on the spread of religious messages and had been isolated from political life. For that reason, it did not have a definitive view of globalization. In the 1990s, it became visible in the public sphere in Turkey[44] and opened institutions abroad with the help of international opportunity structures. In this period, the movement developed a positive attitude toward globalization, with an emphasis on religious tolerance, interfaith dialogue, and democracy.[45] In 1994, the movement founded the Foundation of Journalists and Writers (FJW) to organize public meetings aimed at promoting tolerance and dialogue. These two concepts became the mottos of the movement, which has interacted with different cultures and governments all around the world, and has, therefore, needed a language of engagement.[46] The FJW's meetings have regularly brought together academics, intellectuals, and religious leaders. In 1997, the FJW organized the Inter-Civilization Dialogue Congress as a reaction to the "clash of civilizations" thesis. In 1998, the FJW initiated the Eurasian Meetings that have annually brought together intellectuals from several Eurasian countries. In 2000, the FJW coordinated the meeting of the representatives of the three "Abrahamic" religions in Turkey.

The FJW has also organized the annual Abant Workshops, which have involved approximately fifty Turkish intellectuals from different ideological backgrounds. The first workshop, held in 1988, primarily discussed Islam and secularism. Its press declaration stressed that God's ontological sovereignty is compatible with the political sovereignty of the people.[47] The second workshop examined the relationships among religion, state, and society.[48] The third meeting was devoted to democracy and the rule of law. Its final declaration stressed that Islam was not a barrier to democracy.[49] The fourth workshop explored the issue of pluralism, and the fifth discussed globalization.

Since the mid-1990s, Gülen has made positive statements about globalization. He has argued that the globalization process might become an opportunity for Muslims if they would proactively contribute to this process. In his own words: "Modern means of communication and transportation have transformed the world into a large, global village.... This time is a period of interactive relations. Nations and peoples are more in need of and dependent on each other, which causes closeness in mutual relations."[50] Gülen has also claimed a relationship between globalization and democracy; as a result of globalization, "the individual comes to the fore, making it inevitable that democratic governments that respect personal rights will replace oppressive regimes."[51] According to Gülen, there is a strong connection between globalization and the necessity of tolerance:

> Although the world increasingly resembles a global village, different belief systems, races, and customs will continue to survive. Each individual is a unique being; therefore it is a utopian idea to standardize people. The harmony and peace of the global village are based on the recognition and respect of this diversity.... In other words, it depends on a global tolerance and dialogue. Otherwise, the world will result in its own end through fighting and wars.[52]

Following the 1990s, Gülen has primarily devoted his speeches, writings, and media interviews to religious tolerance and interfaith dialogue. He has met with religious leaders, including Pope John Paul II, the Panahriot Greek Patriarch Bartholomeos, and Israeli Sephardic Head Rabbi Eliyahu B. Doron.[53] Gülen's relations with Christians and Jews have been criticized by some Islamists. The Ibda-C, the fundamentalist terrorist group, reportedly plotted assassination attempts against Gülen. In fact,

Gülen is very critical of terrorism. He strongly condemned the September 11 terrorist attacks against the United States, where he has lived for six years. In his statement in the *Washington Post*, on 21 September 2001, Gülen emphasized, "Islam abhors such acts of terror. A religion that professes, 'He who unjustly kills one man kills the whole of humanity' cannot condone senseless killing of thousands."

Gülen has also frequently referred to democracy and the West in a positive manner. In 1994, he made his first public speech on democracy, in which he stressed that it was impossible to retreat from democracy in Turkey.[54] Although some Islamists strongly criticized this speech, Gülen has continued to emphasize the importance of democracy. By the same token, in an interview in 1995, he opposed anti-Western feelings: "Anti-Westernism would force us out of civilization."[55] He also acknowledged that Muslims had many things to learn from the West[56] and stated that Turkey's integration into the EU would not result in cultural assimilation for Turkish society.[57] In 2000, in a written response to questions from the *New York Times*, Gülen referred to the Western democracies as a political model for Turkey: "Standards of justice and democracy [in Turkey] must be elevated to the level of our contemporaries in the West."[58]

Gülen sees democracy as a developing and irreversible process that has not yet reached its final point. In his view, an ideal democracy should also take into consideration human concerns, even about the hereafter.[59] In his article published in *SAIS Review* in 2001, he argued that Islam and democracy are compatible. He also rejected the ideology of political Islamism: "Islam does not propose a certain unchangeable form of government or attempt to shape it. Instead, Islam establishes fundamental principles that orient a government's general character, leaving it to the people to choose the type and form of government according to time and circumstances."[60] According to Gülen, Islam does not legitimize totalitarian regimes: "Islam considers a society to be composed of conscious individuals equipped with free will."[61]

In sum, the analysis of the Gülen movement supports my two hypotheses. The movement has constructed a pro-globalization and pro-Western attitude as a result of its interaction with international opportunity structures and its tolerant normative framework. In the next section, I will test my hypotheses in a different case and search for an answer to the following question: Why does an Islamic movement become antiglobalization?

The Haydar Baş movement

The Haydar Baş movement developed an antiglobalization view in the 1990s. According to my two hypotheses, this movement should first, have not benefited from international opportunity structures shaped by globalization, and second, have had an intolerant normative framework, which has been closed to cross-cultural interactions.

The Haydar Baş movement, which takes its name from its leader, emerged as a branch of the Kadiri *tarikat*. In the 1990s, it opened institutions in different parts of Turkey, involved itself in public affairs, and became a nationwide social movement. Today, it is affiliated with two nationwide television channels (Mesaj TV and Meltem TV), a newspaper (*Yeni Mesaj*), and magazines. The movement has spread its religio-nationalist messages through its media network, and has business investments and a limited number of schools.

The Haydar Baş movement does not have a significant number of institutions in foreign countries. Therefore, it has not benefited from the international opportunities that have emerged as a result of the decline of state monopolies or that exist as trans-border networks and resources. Why did the Haydar Baş movement not open institutions in foreign countries as the Gülen movement did? The answer is twofold. The first is based on the movement's choice. The Haydar Baş movement ignores emerging international opportunities because of its religio-nationalist normative framework, which focuses on Turkey at the expense of trans-border issues. This shows the direct interaction between a movement's normative framework and its engagement with international opportunity structures. The second is based on the movement's resources. Unlike the Gülen movement, the Haydar Baş movement has had limited human, financial, and institutional resources, which has made international diffusion difficult.

Additionally, the Haydar Baş movement has not benefited from international opportunities to be saved from state repression. Whenever the movement has faced state repression, it has not referred to international norms and has not applied to international institutions. Instead, it has chosen co-optation by the state. It has frequently shown its conformity to the state in its media network.[62] As a result, it has constructed a statist discourse that opposes globalization.

In terms of the second variable, the Haydar Baş movement has had an intolerant normative framework. The movement's religio-nationalist normative framework is built on an unfriendly view of other religions. It has regarded dialogue with Christians and Jews as a threat to Islamic identity. Haydar Baş, for example, has argued that Christian missionaries constitute a severe threat by seeking to convert Turks to Christianity. Because of this perceived threat, the Haydar Baş movement, unlike the Gülen movement, has avoided interaction with non-Muslims. For that reason, the Haydar Baş movement has been very critical of the Gülen movement's activities involving interfaith dialogue. In 1998, Gülen visited the Pope in the Vatican. The Haydar Baş movement strongly criticized this visit. Similarly, in 2000, the Gülen movement organized the meeting of three Abrahamic religions in Urfa, Turkey. The Haydar Baş movement, again, condemned this meeting. In sum, for the Haydar Baş movement, spreading internationally has not been worth risking the loss of identity and solidarity. Therefore, it has perceived globalization as a challenge, avoided international integration, and aimed to preserve its identity through an antiglobalization discourse.[63]

In 2001, the Haydar Baş movement founded a political party, the Bağımsız Türkiye (Independent Turkey) Party (BTP) under the leadership of Haydar Baş. The BTP received less than 1 percent of the votes in the 2002 national elections. It has focused on the spread of the movement's religio-nationalist views. The BTP has been against globalization and has defined it as "a concept created by industrialized states after the Second World War to exploit underdeveloped and developing countries' natural resources."[64] It has also claimed that EU membership would be a type of colonialization that would violate Turkey's cultural, economic, and political independence.[65]

Haydar Baş has claimed that there are two totally contradictory civilizations, namely Western and Islamic. The former desires to oppress, to rule, and to destroy, whereas the latter wishes to help, to develop, and to construct. For him, the EU is a Christian club: "The EU put on the Euro the pictures of the doors of two cathedrals, St. Pierre and Notre Dame.... The twelve stars on the EU's flag represent the twelve apostles of Jesus."[66] Haydar Baş has also opposed globalization. In his own words:

> Globalization is a concept originating from the West which has become a façade to adamantly impose particular ideas on underdeveloped countries, such as the claim that the borders are removed and nations are cooperating by ignoring their economic, cultural, and civilizational differences. The Western countries which produced this concept, however, consolidate the Christian unity and raise walls against other countries. That is a very normal situation, because globalization is constructed to maintain the hegemony of Christian faith and civilization. In this regard, we have to be cautious against the global exploitation and destruction of local cultures. We need to take precautions to preserve our belief system, civilization, and solidarity. The primary precaution is to follow policies that prioritize nationality.[67]

The discussion on globalization among Islamic movements has strongly related to contemporary politics in Turkey: "Turkish politics ... will increasingly be organized along the lines of 'globalisers' and 'antiglobalisers' ... as opposed to cleavages based on the previous left-right or Islam-secularism axes."[68] The statist part of the Turkish establishment opposes Turkey's integration with the EU,[69] since "membership of the EU would mean breaking down the concept of the *Devlet Baba* (Father State), which holds that the state should be served by the people, not the other way round."[70] In 2001, in a symposium on the EU organized by the Turkish military academies, some generals resisted Turkey's EU membership, claiming that the EU was a "Christian club."[71] In 2002, the secretary general of the MGK, General Tuncer Kılınç, insisted that Turkey should cooperate with Russia and Iran, instead of the EU.[72] The Haydar Baş movement has agreed with this statist perspective and has cooperated with secular groups in opposing globalization and the EU.

Consequently, the Haydar Baş movement developed a negative attitude toward globalization because it has not benefited from international opportunities and has had an intolerant religio-nationalist normative framework. The Haydar Baş movement has perceived globalization to be a challenge and has resisted it to preserve its identity.

To this point, I have analyzed one clearly positive and one clearly negative view of globalization. The following section will examine a more changing and divided stand.

The Milli Görüş movement

The Milli Görüş movement had an antiglobalization and anti-Western attitude until the late 1990s. Following the February 28 coup in 1997, the movement found itself divided by the opposing views of the elders and the younger members. Ultimately, the younger generation left the movement completely. If my two hypotheses are correct, the antiglobalization attitudes of the early Milli Görüş movement and the elders of the late Milli Görüş movement should first, have not benefited from international opportunity structures, and second, have had intolerant normative frameworks. Yet the pro-globalization view of the younger generation of the late Milli Görüş movement should have had the opposite features.

The Milli Görüş movement was initiated by Erbakan. In 1970, Erbakan and his followers founded the Milli Nizam (National Order) Party (MNP). The party was disbanded following the military coup d'état in 1971. In 1972, the former cadres of the MNP founded the Milli Selamet (National Salvation) Party. That party also was disbanded, by the military coup d'état in 1980. These parties were both accused of being antisecular. When its party was disbanded, the movement founded a new one, rather than protesting radically against the state. The movement has also had links with sociocultural institutions[73] (for example, the National Youth Foundation) and media outlets (for example, *Milli Gazete*).

In 1983, the Milli Görüş movement founded the Refah (Welfare) Party (RP). The RP gained influence in the 1990s in Turkish politics and was simultaneously strengthened by the nationwide rise of Islamic movements. It became increasingly successful in national elections with the support of the new Anatolian bourgeoisie and pro-Islamic media networks. It won the mayors' seats in Turkey's two largest cities, Istanbul and Ankara, in 1994. In the national parliamentary elections, the RP increased its share of the votes from 7.2 percent in 1987 to 21.4 percent in 1995 and became the leading party.[74] Erbakan became prime minister in 1996 in the RP-True Path Party (DYP) coalition.

Until the end of the 1990s, the Milli Görüş movement did not benefit from international opportunities. It was a national movement that sought a top-down transformation of society via politics, unlike the Gülen movement, which focused on a bottom-up transformation via education. The Milli Görüş movement was restricted by Turkey[75] and did not attempt to spread out to other countries by benefiting from international opportunities, nor did it see the international institutions and norms as an opportunity to be saved from state repression. Instead, it saw international institutions and norms as extensions of the Western hegemony that collaborated with the repressive state.

In addition to the lack of international opportunities, the intolerant normative framework of the movement, political Islamism, was shaping the movement's antiglobalization view. In the 1970s, the movement sought to lead the country's development of heavy industry.[76] That discourse was consistent with the personality of Erbakan, who was a professor of mechanical engineering and worked on the Leopard tank project in Germany. In the 1980s and early 1990s, the movement used a second discourse based on welfare policies, as emphasized in the title of its party (Welfare Party). Yet, during both of these periods, the Milli Görüş movement preserved the core of its normative framework – political Islamism. Moreover, anti-Westernism was a sine qua non for the movement.[77]

The RP, therefore, had a political Islamist and anti-Western agenda. It opposed Turkey's membership in the EU. The RP was planning to found an Islamic Union and to create an Islamic currency. In late 1996 and early 1997, Erbakan visited several Muslim countries as the prime minister, and tried to organize an Islamic Union. He succeeded in creating an international cooperation organization among eight Muslim countries, referred to as the D-8 (Developing Eight). This became a topic of debate between the Gülen and the Milli Görüş movements. Gülen defined D-8 as a vain project and a "very cheap message" to Erbakan's constituency.[78] Because of these types of disagreements, the Gülen movement did not support the RP. It continued to pursue the principle of political neutrality and to establish good relations with all political parties, including the leftist ones.

The February 28 "soft" coup in 1997 ended the RP-DYP coalition and substantially impacted the Milli Görüş movement. Erbakan was forced to resign in June, 1997.[79] The RP was dissolved, and Erbakan was banned from politics in 1998 by the Turkish Supreme Court. Shortly after that, the RP's mayor of Istanbul, Tayyip Erdoğan, was imprisoned for reciting a poem, and consequently banished from political life.

Following the February 28 coup, the Milli Görüş gradually divided into two groups – the elders, led by Erbakan, and the younger generation, led by Erdoğan. Because of state repression, both of these groups tended to see international institutions and norms as opportunities for protection of their rights. Erbakan, for example, appealed to the European Court of Human Rights to overturn the dissolution of the RP and his ban from politics by the Turkish Constitutional Court.

As the Milli Görüş movement attempted to benefit from international opportunity structures, the movement's discourse toward globalization became increasingly positive. After the closure of the RP, RP's parliamentarians founded the Fazilet (Virtue) Party (FP). The FP became "one of the keenest on Turkish membership of the EU,"[80] mainly because it hoped that membership would end the limitations on freedoms and restrict the role of the military in politics.[81] The FP also began to seek a dialogue with the United States. In 1999, the official leader of the FP, Recai Kutan, visited Washington to meet with American politicians and Jewish lobby groups.[82] The FP revised its discourse and started to emphasize democracy and the rule of law. In May 1998, Kutan, in a television interview, emphasized that this revision was the main difference between the RP and the FP. He explained that the latter stressed the promotion of democracy, human rights, and political freedom. He also stressed that the leaders of the FP "had learned from their experience in the last couple of years that democracy comes first – without it, nothing else can be accomplished."[83] As Ziya Öniş points out, the political program of the FP was substantially different from that of its predecessor, the RP. The RP had possessed a strong anti-EU view, referred specifically to Islam, stressed religious and social rights, attached importance to the central government, and emphasized the strong economic role of the state. The FP, however, favored Turkey's EU membership, referred to religious rights as part of a broader agenda on democratization, emphasized individual and human rights, attached importance to decentralization and local governments, and stressed the market economy and privatization.[84]

Despite the FP's democratic discourse, Turkey's Constitutional Court dissolved the party in 2001, arguing that it had become a standard-bearer against secularism by defending the right to wear a headscarf at universities and in the Turkish Parliament. This closure deepened the disagreement between the elders led by Erbakan and the younger generation led by Erdoğan. The elders were inclined to preserve political Islamism as the normative framework, whereas the young generation was for democracy. The followers of Erbakan founded the Saadet (Felicity) Party (SP), whereas those of

Erdoğan founded the Adalet ve Kalkınma (Justice and Development) Party (AKP). The discussion about the EU became an important fault line between these two parties.

The SP returned to the anti-EU and antiglobalization discourse. Two factors were influential in this return. First, in 2001, the European Court of Human Rights rejected Erbakan's appeal of the Turkish Constitutional Court's dissolution of the RP and his ban from politics. This meant that international institutions and norms were not real opportunities for Erbakan and his new party. Second, the younger generation of the Milli Görüş, who were resisting the old political Islamist normative framework, were gone. The elder generation, led by Erbakan again, monopolized the Milli Görüş movement. They easily reemphasized political Islamism. In sum, the end of international opportunities and the return to an intolerant normative framework marked the movement's return to antiglobalizationism, thus supporting my two hypotheses. With its political Islamist discourse, the SP received only 2.5 percent of the national votes in the elections of 3 November 2002.

The younger generation of the Milli Görüş movement, however, abandoned their political Islamist views. In 2000, the two leaders of the younger generation, Erdoğan and Bülent Arınç, emphasized their pro-democratic ideas in interviews with *Zaman*, which was affiliated with the Gülen movement. Erdoğan stressed that he had "internalized democracy,"[85] and Arınç declared that they had no intention of founding an Islamic state.[86] A third leading figure, Abdullah Gül, contributed to that discussion by saying that a religious party was detrimental to religion itself.[87] Additionally, the members of the younger generation have participated in the above-mentioned Abant Workshops organized by the Gülen movement to discuss issues such as democracy and secularism.[88]

The AKP has become a leading supporter of Turkey's membership in the EU. In 2002, Erdoğan pointed to the EU as the only alternative political project for Turkey: "We support Turkey's EU membership for not remaining in a suburb of civilization as a backward country in a changing and globalizing world."[89] In the November 2002 elections, the AKP won 34.3 percent of the national votes and 363 of 550 seats in the Parliament. Erdoğan visited several European capitals to ask for support for Turkey's membership. During his long trip, Erdoğan argued that Turkey's membership would be the best response to the thesis of the "clash of civilizations."[90]

Why has the AKP developed a pro-globalization perspective? Let me explain this using my two hypotheses. First, it has benefited from international opportunities. Even after the November 2003 elections, the AKP was still in a legitimacy crisis. The Turkish establishment was accusing the AKP of hiding its Islamist agenda. Erdoğan was still banned from politics. Under these circumstances, the party received tremendous support from the EU countries and the United States. Erdoğan visited almost every member country of the EU, as only the chairman of a party, but was received as the elected leader of Turkey. Similarly, he met with President George W. Bush in the White House. In these visits, Erdoğan gained international leverage to solve the domestic legitimacy crisis. Finally, the Turkish Parliament amended the Constitution to allow Erdoğan to participate in politics, and Erdoğan became prime minister. Second, the AKP rejected political Islamism,[91] and identified its normative framework as "conservative democracy."[92] Erdoğan stresses that the AKP is not a part of the Milli Görüş movement, which is still affiliated with political Islamism.[93] In sum, as a result of international opportunities and the new tolerant normative framework – conservative democracy – the AKP has developed a pro-globalization view.

The role of the February 28 coup in the transformation of the Milli Görüş movement has been ardently debated in Turkey. My analysis argues that the February 28 coup played a role in this transformation by leading Islamic movements to search for alternative international opportunities and to criticize political Islamism. The theoretical implication of this argument is that changes in the opportunity structures have an impact on the normative frameworks of movements. Yet, the February 28 coup played only an unintentional and intervening role in the transformation of Islamic movements because different movements interpreted this coup differently.

Conclusion

The diverse attitudes of Turkish Islamic movements toward globalization depend on two variables: opportunity structures and the normative frameworks of movements. The Gülen movement and the younger generation of the late Milli Görüş movement developed positive attitudes toward globalization because they benefited from international opportunities and they had tolerant normative frameworks (*Risale-i Nur* and conservative democracy). The Haydar Baş movement, the early Milli Görüş movement, and the elders of the late Milli Görüş movement developed antiglobalization views because they did not benefit from international opportunities and had intolerant normative frameworks (religio-nationalism in the first case and political Islamism in the second and third cases).

The present paper indicated that Islamic movements needed to be analyzed through the social movement literature, rather than so-called religious essentials. It showed the contextual diversity of Islamic movements in Turkey. Although these movements have shared the same religious heritage (Sunni Islam), they have formed different attitudes. These movements have modified their discourses according to changing circumstances. In this regard, their attitudes toward globalization and the West are contingent. The contingency of the relationship between Islamic movements and the West provides us with an optimistic vision for resolving current misunderstandings, prejudices, and conflicts.[94] The policy advice of the paper would be that international institutions should continue to provide opportunities to Islamic movements, which are repressed by their states, in order to integrate these movements into the process of globalization.

My contributions to the social movement literature are twofold. First, I explained the impact of globalization on domestic and international opportunity structures. Second, I provided a theoretical framework that combines structural and agency-based factors, on the one hand, and the impacts of interests and ideas, on the other. I stressed that opportunity structures are not the only determining factors in social movements. Although Islamic movements exist under similar conditions, they evaluate and perceive opportunity structures through the lenses of their normative frameworks. On the other hand, the changes in domestic and international opportunity structures impact the normative frameworks of movements. In sum, both normative frameworks and international opportunity structures shape a movement's attitude toward globalization, but neither is sufficient on its own. Therefore, analyses of social movements must have a process-oriented perspective that emphasizes the interaction between opportunity structures and the normative frameworks of movements.

This paper did not claim to provide an exhaustive analysis of Islamic movements and globalization. Some relevant issues, such as the relationship between Islamic movements' understandings of social justice and global capitalism, need further analysis.[95] Additionally, the paper did not touch upon the cultural aspect of globalization. Scholars have discussed whether globalization has implied a Western cultural hegemony.[96] The positions of Islamic movements on this discussion are another subject for future studies.

Notes

1　Samuel P. Huntington, *The Clash of Civilizations and the Remaking of World Order* (New York: Simon & Schuster, 1996).

2　For the relationship between September 11 and globalization, see Walter LaFeber, "The Post September 11 Debate over Empire, Globalization, and Fragmentation." *Political Science Quarterly* 117 (Spring 2002): 1–17.

3　Benjamin R. Barber, *Jihad vs. McWorld: How Globalism and Tribalism Are Reshaping the World* (New York: Ballantine Books, 1996).

4　Fred Halliday, *Islam & the Myth of Confrontation: Religion and Politics in the Middle East* (New York: I.B. Tauris, 1996), 110–111.

5　Anti-Western Islamic movements generally refer to Sayyid Qutb (d. 1966) "who offers a critique of modernity as *jahiliyya*, a kind of global pathology." Roxanne L. Euben, "Mapping Modernities, 'Islamic' and 'Western'" in Fred R. Dallmayr, ed., *Border Crossings: Toward a Comparative Political Theory* (Lanham, MD: Lexington Books, 1999), 19.

6　Dieter Rucht, "The Impact of National Contexts on Social Movement Structures: A Cross-Movement and Cross-National Comparison" in Doug McAdam, John D. McCarthy, and Mayer N. Zald, eds., *Comparative Perspectives on Social Movements: Political Opportunities, Mobilizing Structures, and Cultural Framings* (New York: Cambridge University Press, 1996), 193–199.

7　See James Mahoney, "Strategies of Causal Inference in Small-N Analysis," *Sociological Method & Research* 28 (May 2000): 412–415; Andrew Bennett and Alexander L. George, "Process Tracing in Case Study Research," paper presented at the MacArthur Foundation Workshop on Case Study Methods, Harvard University, 17–19 October 1997.

8　For discussions on religious and socioeconomic dimensions of Islamic movements, see Edmund Burke, "Islam and Social Movements: Methodological Reflections" in Edmund Burke, III and Ira Lapidus, eds., *Islam, Politics, and Social Movements* (Berkeley: University of California Press, 1988), 17–37.

9　Huntington, *The Clash of Civilizations*, 174–179, 209–218, 254–258; Bernard Lewis, *What Went Wrong? The Clash Between Islam and Modernity in the Middle East* (New York: Perennial, 2003); Bernard Lewis, "The Roots of Muslim Rage," *The Atlantic Monthly* 266 (September 1990): 47–60.

10　Edward D. Said, *Orientalism* (New York: Pantheon Books, 1979); Dale F. Eickelman and James P. Piscatori, *Muslim Politics* (Princeton, NJ: Princeton University Press, 1996); Talal Asad, *Genealogies of Religion: Discipline and Reasons of Power in Christianity and Islam* (Baltimore, MD: Johns Hopkins University Press, 1993); Aziz al-Azmeh, *Islams and Modernities* (New York: Verso, 1996).

11   Nilüfer Göle, *The Forbidden Modern: Civilization and Veiling* (Ann Arbor: University of Michigan Press, 1996).

12   Charles Kurzman, ed., *Liberal Islam: A Sourcebook* (New York: Oxford University Press, 1998).

13   Robert W. Heffner, *Civil Islam: Muslims and Democratization in Indonesia* (Princeton, NJ: Princeton University Press, 2000).

14   Quintan Wiktorowicz, ed., *Islamic Activism: A Social Movement Theory Approach* (Bloomington: Indiana University Press, 2003); Christopher Alexander, "Opportunities, Organizations, and Ideas: Islamists and Workers in Tunisia and Algeria," *International Journal of Middle East Studies* 32 (November 2000): 465–490; Ziad Munson, "Islamic Mobilization: Social Movements Theory and the Egyptian Muslim Brotherhood," *The Sociological Quarterly* 42 (Fall 2001): 487–510.

15   Doug McAdam, "Conceptual Origins, Current Problems, Future Directions" in McAdam, McCarthy, and Zald, eds., *Comparative Perspectives on Social Movements*, 34: emphases original.

16   See, for two of the rare examples, John A. Guidry, Michael D. Kennedy, and Mayer N. Zald, eds., *Globalizations and Social Movements: Culture, Power, and the Transnational Public Sphere* (Ann Arbor: University of Michigan Press, 2000); Donatella della Porta, Hanspeter Kriesi, and Dieter Rucht, eds., *Social Movements in a Globalizing World* (New York: St. Martin's Press, 1999).

17   Doug McAdam, Sidney Tarrow, and Charles Tilly, "Toward an Integrated Perspective on Social Movements and Revolution" in Mark Irving Lichbach and Alan S. Zuckerman, eds., *Comparative Politics: Rationality, Culture, and Structure* (New York: Cambridge University Press, 1997), 142–173; McAdam, McCarthy, and Zald, eds., *Comparative Perspectives on Social Movements*; Sidney G. Tarrow, *Power in Movement: Social Movements and Contentious Politics* (New York: Cambridge University Press, 1998); Doug McAdam, Sidney Tarrow, and Charles Tilly, *Dynamics of Contention* (New York: Cambridge University Press, 2001); Charles Kurzman, "Structural Opportunity and Perceived Opportunity in Social-Movement Theory: The Iranian Revolution of 1979," *American Sociological Review* 61 (February 1996): 153–170.

18   Anthony Giddens, *The Consequences of Modernity* (Stanford, CA: Stanford University Press, 1990), 64. See also John Baylis and Steve Smith, eds., *The Globalization of World Politics* (New York: Oxford University Press, 1998); James H. Mittleman, *The Globalization Syndrome: Transformation and Resistance* (Princeton, NJ: Princeton University Press, 2000).

19   Jan Art Scholte, "Global Capitalism and the State," *International Affairs* 73 (July 1997): 430–432.

20   See Jeffrey James, *Globalization, Information Technology and Development* (New York: St. Martin's Press, 1999).

21   Peter Evans, "The Eclipse of the State? Reflections on Stateness in an Era of Globalization," *World Politics* 50 (October 1997): 62–87.

22   Saskia Sassen, *Losing Control? Sovereignty in an Age of Globalization* (New York: Columbia University Press, 1996), 24–26; Saskia Sassen, "Whose City Is It? Globalization and the Formation of New Claims," *Public Culture* 8 (Winter 1996): 213.

23   Annabelle Sreberny-Mohammadi, "Introduction" in Sandra Braman and Annabelle Sreberny-Mohammadi, eds., *Globalization, Communication and Transnational Civil Society* (Cresskill, NJ: Hampton Press, 1996), 1–19.

24   Paul Hirst and Grahame Thompson, *Globalization in Question: The International Economy and the Possibilities of Governance* (Malden, MA: Polity Press, 1999), 263.

25   Peter Martin, "Une obligation morale [The Moral Case for Globalization]," *Le Monde Diplomatique* (June 1997): 14.

26   For Özal's presidency, see Metin Heper and Menderes Çınar, "Parliamentary Government with a Strong President: The Post-1989 Turkish Experience," *Political Science Quarterly* 111 (Fall 1996): 493–497.

27   Haluk Şahin and Asu Aksoy, "Global Media and Cultural Identity in Turkey," *Journal of Communication* 43 (Spring 1993): 36.

28   Ali Bulaç argues that Muslims should appreciate globalization, which weakens the nation-state and empowers individuals. Ali Bulaç, "Küreselleşme Kimi Tehdit Ediyor? [Whom does Globalization Challenge?]," *Zaman*, 24 July 2001; "Küreselleşme İslamı Tehdit Ediyor mu? (Does Globalization Challenge Islam?]," *Zaman*, 25 July 2001.

29   See Nilüfer Göle, "Snapshots of Islamic Modernities," *Daedalus* 129 (Winter 2000): 91–117.

30   Jenny B. White, "Amplifying Trust: Community and Communication in Turkey" in Dale F. Eickelman and John W. Anderson, eds., *New Media in the Muslim World: The Emerging Public Sphere* (Bloomington: Indiana University Press, 1999), 177.

31   M. Hakan Yavuz, "Cleansing Islam from the Public Sphere," *Journal of International Affairs* 54 (2000): 21–42.

32   Ben Lombardi, "Turkey – The Return of the Reluctant Generals?" *Political Science Quarterly* 112 (Summer 1997): 214–215.

33   I prefer to use the term "establishment" rather than the "state," for avoiding the false state–society dichotomy. See, for the blurry boundaries between state and society, Joel S. Migdal, *State in Society: Studying How the States and Societies Transform and Constitute One Another* (New York: Cambridge University Press, 2001).

34   For the difference between *laïcité* (secularism) as a regime and *laïcisme* (secularism) as an ideology in Turkey, see Semih Vaner, "Introduction," *Cahiers d'Études sur la Méditerranée Orientale et le Monde Turco-Iranien* 27 (January–June 1999): 11–12.

35   See Nuh Gönültaş, "Vatan Dayak Yemediğin Yerdir! (Motherland Is Where You Are not Beaten!]," *Zaman*, 29 September 2000.

36   The author's personal interviews and observations in Turkey, Turkmenistan, and the United States in the Gülen movement's institutions.

37   See M. Hakan Yavuz, "Towards an Islamic Liberalism? The Nurcu Movement and Fethullah Gülen," *The Middle East Journal* 53 (Autumn 1999): 599; See also Elisabeth Özdalga, "Worldly Asceticism in Islamic Casting: Fethullah Gülen's Inspired Piety and Activism." *Critique: Critical Middle Eastern Studies* 17 (Fall 2000): 83–104.

38   See Ahmet T. Kuru, "Between the State and Cultural Zones: Nation-Building in Turkmenistan," *Central Asian Survey* 21 (March 2002): 83–84.

39   See the special issue of *The Muslim World* 89 (July–October 1999), edited by M. Hakan Yavuz. See also Ibrahim M. Abu-Rabi, ed., *Islam at the Crossroads: On the Life and Thought of Bediüzzaman Said Nursi* (Albany. NY: SUNY Press, 2003).

40   Bediüzzaman Said Nursi, "Mektubat [The Letters]" in *Risale-i Nur Külliyatı* [The Epistles of Light] (İstanbul: Nesil Yayncılık, 1996), 366–368.

41   Bediüzzaman Said Nursi, "Muhakemat [The Reasoning]" (İstanbul, 1912] in *Risale-i Nur Külliyatı*, 1997.

42   Bediüzzaman Said Nursi, "Münazarat [The Debates]" in *Risale-i Nur Külliyatı* ,1945. See also Zeki Saritoprak, "Said Nursi's Teachings on the People of the Book: A Case Study of Islamic Social Policy in the Early Twentieth Century," *Islam and Christian–Muslim Relations* 11 (October 2000): 321–332.

43   Bediüzzaman Said Nursi, "Kastamonu Lahikası [The Kastamonu Letters]" in *Risale-i Nur Küliyatı* 1651.

44   Uğur Kömeçoğlu, "Kutsal ile Kamusal: Fethullah Gülen Cemaat Hareketi [The Sacred and the Public: The Fethullah Gülen Communal Movement]" in Nilüfer Göle, ed., *İslamın Yeni Kamusal Yüzleri* [Islam's New Public Faces] (İstanbul: Metis, 2000), 148–194.

45   Hüseyin Gülerce, "Yeni Dinamikler [New Dynamics]," *Zaman*, 19 June 2001.

46   See Bekim Agai, "The Gülen Movement's Islamic Ethic of Education" in M. Hakan Yavuz and John L. Esposito, eds., *Turkish Islam and the Secular State: The Gülen Movement* (Syracuse, NY: Syracuse University Press, 2003), 48–68.

47   *İslam ve Laiklik* [Islam and Secularism] (İstanbul: Gazeteciler ve Yazarlar Vakfı, 1998).

48   *Din, Devlet, Toplum* [Religion, State, and Society] (İstanbul: Gazeteciler ve Yazarlar Vakfı, 1999).

49   *Demokratik Hukuk Devleti* [Democratic State and the Rule of Law] (İstanbul: Gazeteciler ve Yazarlar Vakfı, 2000).

50   Fethullah Gülen, "At the Threshold of the New Millennium," *The Fountain* 3 (January–March 2000): 7.

51   Ibid., 8.

52   Quoted in Nevval Sevindi, *Fethullah Gülen ile Global Hoşgörü ve New York Sohbeti* [Global Tolerance and the New York Interview with Fethullah Gülen] (İstanbul: Timaş, 2002), 42.

53   See Ali Ünal and Alphonse Williams, eds., *Advocate of Dialogue: Fethullah Gülen* (Fairfax: The Fountain. 2001).

54   Eyüp Can, *Fethullah Gülen Hocaefendi ile Ufuk Turu* [The Tour d'Horizon with Fethullah Gülen Hocaefendi] (İstanbul: Milliyet Yayıları, 1996), 129.

55   Ibid., 43.

56   For Gülen's views on Western modernity, see Ahmet T. Kuru, "Fethullah Gülen's Search for a Middle Way between Modernity and Muslim Tradition" in Yavuz and Esposito, eds., *Turkish Islam and the Secular State*, 115–130.

57   Can, *Fethullah Gülen Hocaefendi*, 43. For Gülen's ideas on the EU, see Hasan Kösebalaban, "The Making of Enemy and Friend: Fethullah Gülen's National-Security Identity" in Yavuz and Esposito, eds., *Turkish Islam and the Secular State*, 170–183.

58   Douglas Frantz, "Turkey Assails a Revered Islamic Moderate," *New York Times*, 25 August 2000.

59   Nevval Sevindi, *Fethullah Gülen ile New York Sohbeti* (İstanbul: Sabah Kitapları, 1997), 78.

60   Fethullah Gülen, "A Comparative Approach to Islam and Democracy," translated by Elvan Ceylan, *SAIS Review* 21 (Summer–Fall 2001): 134.

61   Ibid., 135.

62   Taha Kıvanç, "Tarikatlerle Temas [Contact with *Tariqats*]," *Yeni Şafak*, 3 July 2001.

63   See, for the similarities between nationalist and anti-globalist discourses, Fred Halliday, "The Middle East and the Politics of Differential Integration" in Toy Dodge

and Richard Higgot, eds., *Globalization and the Middle East: Islam, Economy, Society, and Politics* (London: Royal Institute of International Affairs, 2002), 41.

64   Bağımsız Türkiye Partisi, "Küreselleşme Nedir [What is Globalization]?" 20 May 2003, accessed on the website of the BTP at http://www.btp.org.tr/index. php?temelgorusler=1, 15 June 2003.

65   Bağımsız Türkiye Partisi, "AB'ye Basvuru [Application to the EU]," accessed on the website of the BTP at http://www.btp.org.tr/basvuru.htm, 30 May 2002.

66   Haydar Baş, "Haftanın Sohbeti [The Interview of the Week]," *Yeni Mesaj*, 26 April 2002. See also Haydar Baş, "Türk Milleti İkinci Sevr'e Müsaade Etmeyecektir [The Turkish Nation Will Not Allow the Second Sevres Treaty]," *Yeni Mesaj*, 16 August 2002.

67   Haydar Baş, "Küreselleşme ile Örtülen Gerçekler [The Facts Hidden by Globalization]," *Yeni Mesaj*, 19 May 2001. See also Haydar Baş, "Küreselleşme ve ABD Hegemonyası [Globalization and the American Hegemony]," *Yeni Mesaj*, 28 July 2001.

68   Ziya Öniş, "Globalization, Democratization and the Far Right: Turkey's Nationalist Action Party in Critical Perspective," *Democratization* 10 (Spring 2003): 33–34.

69   See, for these changing perspectives about the EU in Turkey, Hasan Kösebalaban, "Turkey's EU Membership: A Clash of Security Cultures," *Middle East Policy* 9 (June 2002): 130–146.

70   "Is It Adieu to Ataturk?," *The Economist*, 18 December 1999, 43.

71   "AB Hristiyan Kulübü [EU, A Christian Club]," *Radikal*, 14 January 2001.

72   "AB'den Destek Yok, Doğu'ya Bak [No Support from the EU, Turn to the East]," *Hürriyet*, 7 March 2002.

73   See Ali Bayramoğlu, *Türkiye'de İslami Hareket: Sosyolojik Bir Bakış* [The Islamic Movement in Turkey: A Sociological Perspective] (İstanbul: Patika, 2001), 64.

74   M. Hakan Yavuz, *Islamic Political Identity in Turkey* (New York: Oxford University Press, 2003), 240.

75   The Milli Görüş movement has also a branch in Germany. That branch, however, does not have a major impact on the movement's attitude toward globalization.

76   Haldun Gülalp, "Modernization Policies and Islamist Politics in Turkey" in Sibel Bozdoğan and Reşat Kasaba, eds., *Rethinking Modernity and National Identity in Turkey* (Seattle: University of Washington Press, 1997), 59.

77   İhsan D. Dağı, *Kimlik, Söylem ve Siyaset: Doğu-Batı Ayrımında Refah Partisi Geleneği* [Identity, Discourse, and Politics: The Tradition of Welfare Party in the Crossroads of the East and the West] (Ankara: İmge Kitabevi, 1998).

78   Sevindi, *Fethullah Gülen ile New York Sohbeti*, 33.

79   Michael M. Gunter, "The Silent Coup: The Secularist-Islamist Struggle in Turkey," *Journal of Asian and Middle Eastern Studies* 21 (Spring 1998): 11.

80   "Ataturk's Long Shadow (Founder of Modern Turkish Nation-state)," *The Economist*, 10 June 2000, 3.

81   Reşat Kasaba and Sibel Bozdoğan, "Turkey at a Crossroad," *Journal of International Affairs* 54 (Fall 2000): 18.

82   "Turkey's Islamists: The Reformers Make Their Bids," *The Economist*, 13 November 1999, 57.

83   Quoted in Haldun Gülalp, "The Poverty of Democracy in Turkey: The Refah Party Episode," *New Perspectives on Turkey* 21 (Fall 1999): 54.

84 Ziya Öniş, "Political Islam at the Crossroads: From Hegemony to Co-existence," *Contemporary Politics* 7 (December 2001): 281–298. See also Ziya Öniş, "Neoliberal Globalization and the Democracy Paradox: The Turkish General Election of 1999," *Journal of International Affairs* 54 (Fall 2000): 304.

85 Erdoğan's interview with Eyüp Can, *Zaman*, 6 February 2000.

86 Arınç's interview with Mehmet Gündem, *Zaman*, 6 February 2000.

87 "Siyasal Islam Yol Ayrımında [Political Islam at the Crossroads]," *Hürriyet*, 8 February 2000.

88 In addition to these politicians, one of the main thinkers of Islamism, Ali Bulaç, declared that political Islamism was dead. He called for a new "civil" Islamism. Interview of Ali Bulaç, *Aksiyon*, 7–13 November 1998.

89 "Tayyip Erdoğan: Avrupa Birliğinden Yanayız [Tayyip Erdoğan: We Are for the EU]," *Zaman*, 10 March 2002.

90 "Erdoğan AB ve Kıbrıs İçin Radikal 'Çözüm Paketi' Önerdi [Erdoğan Proposed a Radical "Solution Packet"]," *Zaman*, 21 November 2002.

91 The author's personal interview with an AKP Congressperson, September 2003, Ankara, Turkey. For the AKP's view on political Islamism and secularism, see Ahmet T. Kuru, "Reinterpretation of Secularism in Turkey: The Case of the Justice and Development Party" in M. Hakan Yavuz, ed., *Transition of Turkish Politics: The Justice and Development Party* (Salt Lake City: University of Utah Press, 2005, forthcoming).

92 Yalçın Akdoğan, *Muhafazakar Demokrasi* (Ankara: AK Parti, 2003).

93 "Erdoğan: Milli Görüş' ün Değil Demokrat Parti'nin Devamıyız [Erdoğan: We Are the Successor of the Democrat Party, not the Milli Görüş]," *Zaman*, 17 May 2003.

94 See Fred Halliday, "West Encountering Islam: Islamophobia Reconsidered" in Ali Mohammadi, ed., *Islam Encountering Globalization* (New York: Routledge Courzon, 2002), 21.

95 See, for some Muslim concerns about global economic inequality, Ahmet Taşgetiren, "Öteki Küresellşme [The Other Globalization]," *Yeni Şafak*, 23 July 2001; Ali Bulaç, "Küresel Yoksullaşma [Global Poverty]," *Zaman*, 10 July 2002.

96 Ali A. Mazrui, "Pretender to Universalism: Western Culture in a Globalizing Age," *Journal of Muslim Minority Affairs* 21 (April 2001): 11–24; Robert J. Holton, *Globalization and the Nation-State* (New York: Macmillan Press, 1998), 161–205; Jonathan Xavier Inda and Renato Rosaldo, "Introduction: A World in Motion" in Jonathan Xavier Inda and Renato Rosaldo, eds., *The Anthropology of Globalization: A Reader* (Malden, MA.: Blackwell, 2002), 9–26; Ibrahim M. Abu-Rabi, "Globalization: A Contemporary Islamic Response?" *The American Journal of Islamic Social Sciences* 15 (Fall 1998): 26–33; Murad Wilfried Hofman, "Globalization and the Muslim Future," *Middle East Affairs Journal* 6 (Fall–Winter 2000): 5–18.

Further reading

Mohammed Ayoob, *The Many Faces of Political Islam: Religion and Politics in the Muslim World* (Ann Arbor: The University of Michigan Press, 2007)
> A well-informed overview of the contemporary expressions of political Islam on the international scene.

Faisal Devji, *The Terrorist in Search of Humanity: Militant Islam and Global Politics* (New York: Columbia University Press, 2008)
> A probing analysis into the new patterns of articulation of global jihadism in the post-9/11 period.

Kai Hafez (ed.), *The Islamic World and the West: An Introduction to Political Cultures and International Relations*, trans. M. A. Kenny (Leiden: Brill, 2000)
> A useful collection of theoretical considerations and empirical studies of the contemporary expressions of Islamism worldwide.

Mahmood Mamdani, *Good Muslim, Bad Muslim: America, the Cold War, and the Roots of Terror* (New York: Three Leaves Press, 2004)
> A critical analysis of the interactions between militant Islam and US foreign policy actors in conflict situations.

Peter Mandaville, *Transnational Muslim Politics: Reimagining the Umma* (London: Routledge 2003)
> An insightful perspective into the articulation of new transnational Islamist discourses and practices.

Ali Mohammadi (ed.), *Islam Encountering Globalization* (London: Routledge, 2002)
> A collection of well-informed essays on the insertion of Islam and Islamism into the multifaceted processes of contemporary globalization.

Olivier Roy, Globalized Islam: *The Search for a New Ummah* (New York: Columbia University Press, 2004)
> A sophisticated and comprehensive analysis of the main trends organizing Islamism at the global level today.

SECTION EIGHT

The future of political Islam

Introduction

THE CONTINUITIES AND ruptures of the Islamist movement are analysed in this final section of the Reader, with a view to outlining the prospects for the phenomenon in the coming years and decades. The safest way to explore the future of political Islam is to begin by considering what Islamism is not likely to become. In the first instance, it is useful to note that this phenomenon is not going to be modelled on the al-Qaeda type of activism that captured the headlines for most of the first decade of the twenty-first century. The novelty of this brand of political Islam was that it sought to articulate at the international level the views and demands of a global Muslim constituency, and that it used violence to make other international players pay attention to this constituency. What has become ever clearer over time is that this type of militant Islamist network is not the most effective form of organization to articulate the views, needs, aspirations and practices of a (would-be) global Muslim community. Despite a lack of active mass support, the al-Qaeda phenomenon and its spin-offs are not going to disappear suddenly, especially as its militant discourse becomes more individualized. In the short-term, this type of violent global militancy is going to continue to benefit from the aggressive foreign policy choices and military actions of the international actors involved in the 'War on Terror', even if specific groups will be weakened or destroyed in the process. However, as Muslim constituencies previously marginalized in the Islamist movement – like the western-based communities – gain recognition and are included in the ordinary forms of militancy of mass Islamist movements, the overall prominence of the violent Islamist transnationalism can only diminish proportionally. Overall, this type of activism cannot withstand the competition from more mainstream Islamist political and social networks in the long run, as it is not concerned with the local social and political implications of its militancy.

For these reasons, socially-oriented Islamist movements concerned with the re-Islamization of the masses have a better opportunity to grow in strength, both in the core regions of the Muslim world and in new diasporic regions where Muslim minorities now live permanently. From a grassroots perspective, the success of specific organizations, discourses and practices will depend primarily on devising appropriate articulations between the social and the political. In particular, it will hinge on the ability of individual and communal initiatives to link up with the legal, institutional and political structures that organize the polities in which these movements now operate. Some of these networks (like the Gülen movement) have clearly thought about these linkages in more depth than others (like the Tablighi), and this may prove a useful long-term strategy. Finally, the emergence and entrenchment of Islamist political parties is increasingly likely to become a feature of political Islam in Muslim-majority countries in the longer term. The politics of the Muslim world are directly influenced by the way in which these formal Islamist organizations are included in – or excluded from – the system of government and the ruling elite in the region and, in their turn, how they interact with other types of (secular) opposition movements. This routinization of Islamist politics does not necessarily involve a takeover of the state but it means that they have a voice in the formal political decision-making process that reflects the popular appeal of the Islamist movement. In its turn, this situation will facilitate the establishment of a stable internal party structure, hierarchy and decision-making process within Islamist organizations that have up to now been forced to operate underground.

The first extract, from Graham Fuller's *The Future of Political Islam*, highlights some of the key considerations regarding the future of political Islam from the perspective of 'the West', and particularly western governments. Fuller indicates how the views held by dominant international actors and institutions towards the Islamization of politics in the Muslim world shape the opportunities and constraints for engaging with Islamism. Although there are opportunities for coexistence and collaboration, conflict and distrust are repeatedly generated by self-fulfilling prophecies about impending clashes.

From a policy perspective, the text by Daniel Brumberg highlights that in international affairs the endorsement of an Islamist agenda does not in itself tie up Islamist movements to a very specific domestic or foreign policy. These policies can equally well favour the international status quo than challenge it, they can be pro- or anti-western, they can be populist or elitist, and so on. What remains crucial, however, is the way in which this Islamist agenda is articulated in its domestic political environment, which can be 'dissonant' when there are opportunities for contestation, or 'harmonic' when a hegemonic system controls the polity and when only a dramatic regime change can shift the balance of power.

The third contribution, by Saba Mahmood, details the micro-processes of the formation of Islamist identity in a modern Muslim majority society. Mahmood indicates how common misconceptions regarding the mechanisms of production of Islamist identity have hindered the understanding of how social processes frame the dynamics of the Islamist phenomenon. The processes of social production of Islamist views and practices at the grassroots level constitute the springboard for the elaboration of more explicitly political discourses and behaviours. They have to be seen as reflecting informed and legitimate socio-political choices that aim at creating a different type of societal order, and not merely as the outcome of misguided views about politics induced by socio-economic hardship and intellectual poverty.

The final text, from Jenny White, considers the socio-political evolution of an Islamist movement that has come to play the part of a 'normal' political party in the emerging democratic system of a Muslim-majority country, Turkey. White analyses the continuities and the ruptures that characterize this particular articulation of Islamism, and reflects on the implications of the Turkish case for other states and Islamist organizations in the region. Ultimately, the routinization of the politics of Islamism will depend on the institutionalization of Islamist actors as organizations that can effectively and legitimately govern Muslim polities.

Graham E. Fuller

THE FUTURE OF POLITICAL ISLAM
Its dilemmas and options

FOR ALL THEIR NEARLY unrivaled influence in the Muslim world today, Islamists face one supreme question: will they be able to rise to the challenges that confront today's ineffective leaderships and any potential leaders of the future? Islamists are good at identifying and articulating the grievances, but to succeed they must move beyond their present roles if they wish to remain relevant to societies' needs.

Islamism as ideology?

The analysis throughout this book argues that *political Islam cannot properly be viewed as an alternative to other ideologies such as democracy, fascism, socialism, liberalism, and communism.* It cannot be put anywhere clearly on an ideological spectrum. It is far more useful to see it as a cultural variant, an alternative vocabulary in which to dress any one of these ideological trends. It is hard to argue that Islamism is a distinct program in itself, even though we can identify certain predispositions such as a conservative social agenda, a call for political change, a defensive cultural/nationalist bent, and a rhetorical call for adoption of Islamic law that means many different things in practice. This is a political movement that makes Islam the centerpiece of its own political culture and then proceeds to improvise on what this means in the local political context. *Islamism is therefore not an ideology, but a religious-cultural-political framework for engagement on issues that most concern politically engaged Muslims.*

The Islam that says no

Islamists must develop a clear, positive, specific, and constructive agenda for society and state. If the quest for "authenticity" in Islam – defined in opposition to the quasi-Westernized authoritarian status quo – becomes the dominant goal of Islamist parties, the chances are good they will remain trapped in a quixotic quest – one that condemns them to a permanent negative role as guardians of self-defined cultural gates lacking forward vision. The parties will come to represent only "the Islam that says no," a negative and joyless approach obsessively focused on what is forbidden and wrong. There is very little agenda, especially among the fundamentalist, for what is inspiring, joyful, constructive, or forward-looking. Yet one key function of all religion is to instill inspiration, joy, and meaning into one's vision of life. The "Islam that says no" fails entirely in this enterprise. This narrow and reactive approach is intensified by a concentration upon the threats to Islam from the outside world – a defensive posture based on rejection of the external world rather than focusing on the positive goal of improving governance and society in the Muslim world. In the end it is only through genuine strengthening and improvement of Muslim governance that Muslim societies can resist Western domination and adopt viable alternative approaches.

The fundamentalist Islamists have demonstrated a particular tendency to reduce Islam to the symbolism of Shari'a law and then sometimes even reduce Shari'a to family law and the code of penalties (hudud) as somehow representing Islam in its most "authentic" or quintessential form. Such a posture will reduce Islamists to little more than nuisance value in their societies. They thus abdicate responsibility for grappling with the really hard issues of making Islamic values relevant and applicable to today's complex social and economic issues. Olivier Roy suggests that the very inability of politically active Islamists to withstand the repressive power of the state has propelled numbers of them toward this more apolitical and fundamentalist view of increasing irrelevance.[1]

Defense of tradition, or change?

Islamists often seem caught between two poles: guardians of tradition, or vanguard of change. Most of them recognize that change is essential across Muslim society. But pursuit of a reformist role requires them to cooperate, or even compete with liberal secularists. In philosophical terms, reaching a compromise is manageable, but in the rougher world of practical politics, each party is competing for a slice of the electorate. Islamists cannot neglect courting the conservative constituency of society, but that may automatically condemn them to adopt highly conservative positions and even to support the social status quo. In Kuwait the Muslim Brotherhood has already split over whether to support women's voting rights. The debate has led to formation of at least two different movements among Islamists, one fundamentalist (salafi/Wahhabi), the other Brotherhood-based and more moderate.

How should the Islamists deal with the liberals? If they expend their ammunition on attacking the liberals, as they often do in Egypt and Kuwait on social and cultural issues, they are in reality supporting the state agenda – which is to weaken liberal reformers and block change. The Islamists are in effect weakening the forces of change that would benefit the Islamists themselves through increased political openness. Their risk in concentrating upon politics is that it inevitably leads to pursuit of tactical advantage at the expense of longer-range ideological or strategic influence. In times of hardship, any community or ideology tends to revert back to basics, to the purity of their ideals. Thus Islamists may be retreating back to hardcore interpretations of Islam, particularly on social issues: limiting the participation of women in society, calling for tighter dress codes, intensified calls to censoring literature and ban art, insisting on separate male and female education, and opposing liberalization of Family Law.

A conservative–liberal split among Islamists?

As Islamist movements continue to proliferate, liberal Islamists will eventually be led to break sharply with conservative and fundamentalist Islamists. Which group will fare better? It depends on the time, country, and local circumstances. In Pakistan, for example, we witness the disturbing spectacle of a strong policy-oriented mainstream Islamist organization, the Jama'at-i Islami, under severe pressure from the narrower and much more radical Islamist groups that assume more uncompromising lines on Kashmir, sectarianism, and social issues. The badly deteriorating situation in Pakistan contributes to the rise of more extreme Islamist groups there. But in Turkey, where there is (relative) prosperity and no sense of an imploding state and society, the mainstream Islamist party (Refah/Fazilet/AK) is strong, Islamist radicals are few, and the movement is rivaled on the social level only by the even more modernist and apolitical Nur Islamic movement of Fethullah Gülen.

But these fault lines may not readily lead to splits. Islamists have historically been reluctant to engage in public criticism of other Islamist movements, especially when they all feel themselves under the gun from local regimes as well as from hostile Western governments. But after 11 September, we are beginning to see sharper divisions emerging among fundamentalists and moderate Islamists. Such thoughtful public debates and critiques are in fact essential if the intellectual and ideological environment of the movement is to evolve and mature.

Islamism moves to the left?

A key contention of this book is the astonishing absence at this point of a "left" on the political spectrum in most of the Muslim world – leading to the question of whether Islamists will take advantage of this vacuum. Communists and socialists, who flourished during much of the Cold War period, have now lost importance and figure very little in Muslim politics. Yet "the left" cannot disappear; it is an integral part of the political spectrum anywhere that focuses upon burning social and economic causes and issues. How radical will Islamist movements ever seek to be – not in terms of violence or bloodshed, but in advancing a dynamic social and economic agenda directed particularly toward amelioration of mass grievances? The heavy Islamist emphasis on justice ('adl) would seem to lead naturally to a more radical position on social and economic issues. Yet to date, Islamist movements have demonstrated remarkable social and economic conservatism, especially in view of the pressing need for deeply rooted social and economic reform across the Muslim world. Their timidity so far raises a serious question again about just how "opportunist" Islamist parties really are.

In Pakistan and Egypt the Islamists have opposed serious land reform that is desperately needed. In Pakistan they have also opposed extension of the income tax where it is the rich who benefit most from its absence. In Kuwait most Islamists have opposed suffrage for women. While Islam is certainly not a radical religion, one of its principle goals – a more just political and social order – should in principle spur Islamists to adopt more radical policies of reform and economic and social justice. Perhaps the most ubiquitous feature of Islamism, the struggle against corruption, constitutes the most radical Islamist challenge to the status quo anywhere – a significant start. But the great questions of gross maldistribution of economic benefits, huge disparities in income, and feudal systems of landholding and human control remain largely outside the Islamist critique. Iran, in fact, is the only place where Islamists have taken up a more radical social and economic agenda. Will Islamists yield to the temptation to adopt more radical socioeconomic policies down the road, especially as social grievances reach higher levels, offering a rich mine for political gain? A columnist for *al-Hayat*, Joseph Samaha asks whether Islamists have by now gained enough legitimacy in the political order of so many Muslim countries that they are now content to abandon the quest for "the great change" and are everywhere willing simply to settle for a piece of the political game based on the status quo.[2]

The dangers of Islamist reaction-based policies

Will useful Western political values be rejected simply because their provenance is perceived as tainted, and the Western political agenda suspicious? Islamists will need to determine what it is they are really rejecting, the ideas themselves or their source. The problem is not made easier when Western projection of its own political values into foreign policy has been frequently selective, uneven, self-serving, and characterized by double standards and convenience. The message is corrupted by the messenger.

Yet Islamists regularly fall into this trap of conflating the two. One example is attitudes toward Iraq. Most Muslims are well aware that Saddam Hussein has violated nearly all Islamic precepts of just rule and has harshly oppressed and killed Islamists and slaughtered hundreds of thousands of Muslims in neighboring Iran and Kuwait. Yet when Saddam is confronted by Western armies, large numbers of Islamists – indeed, most Muslims – perceive Western military intervention as an even greater threat. Saddam is a hero simply because he stands up to America. Similarly, the NATO war against Serbian ethnic cleansing in Kosovo in 1999 came in for heavy criticism by many Islamists and other Muslims who showed greater concern over NATO muscle-flexing in a new region than the fact that NATO was actually protecting Kosovar Muslims in Europe against the oppression of Serbian Christians.

When American Vice President Al Gore publicly criticized Malaysian Prime Minister Mahathir Mohammad for his 1999 slanders and show trial against Anwar Ibrahim, a popular and distinguished Islamist leader, large numbers of Malaysians took offense, not because they disagreed but because it appeared to represent unwarranted Western interference in offering criticism of the Malaysia. And in 2001, while acknowledging that the 11 September attack on the World Trade Center was a crime, nearly all Muslims strongly opposed the American military attack on Afghanistan and the overthrow of the Taleban government in the U.S. War Against Terrorism. Yet the Muslim world in previous years had nearly unanimously opposed the Taleban regime as representing a primitive and embarrassing form of Islam. In the end another American attack against a Muslim country was perceived as worse than either the regime or its fall. Such knee-jerk reactions indicate something is badly amiss on both sides.

In short, Islamists show greater obsession with attacking the perceived "enemies of Islam" than they are with developing their own independent values. Only when Islamists can liberate themselves from this type of knee-jerk reaction will they be free to proclaim their own values, which may or may not coincide with Western values or interests.[3]

Islamism and Shari'a (Islamic law)

Is the Shari'a really the central theme or focus of Islamists, or do they have broader goals? Fundamentalist Islamists in particular single out the Shari'a as the essential element, the *sine qua non* for the creation of a genuine Islamic state and society. All of this overlooks the debate over the very issue of what "Shari'a" really is. Is it to be narrowly understood as no more than the Islamic legal code (*fiqh*) as constructed by *ulama* over time? Islamist modernists reject this narrow and traditional view. Or is Shari'a a far broader concept of alternative "ways" to God in its original meaning?

Even full application of Shari'a law, in the eyes of many Islamists, is not enough in itself to constitute everything an Islamic state is meant to be. Shari'a law can be applied more or less fully and yet the state still prove incapable of wise and just governance on the grander political, economic, and societal issues. Something more is clearly needed, something that can be inspired by Islam or derived from Islam, but it will require human wisdom and legal sensibility. As most of Islam is concerned with moral principles, understandings of the world, and Man's relationship to God and society.

It is difficult, however, for the non-Muslim observer to question the centrality of the Shari'a, not only for the Islamic state but even as the chief agenda of Islamist parties. *Yet even to the outside observer there is no visible correlation between application of Shari'a law and the attainment of a better society and governance in today's Muslim world.* Few would deny the importance of the values of the Shari'a in theological and philosophical terms, but one can still *question its centrality in meeting the major dilemmas of Muslims today.* Are the leading states approximating full application of Shari'a today – Saudi Arabia, Pakistan, Iran, Afghanistan under the Taleban, or Sudan – demonstrating any greater success in governance? *The basic reality is that no Muslim state has made any significant progress toward creation of a more ideal society as it has come ever closer to full application of Shari'a law.* These regimes have not advanced toward a more ideal society in traditional "worldly" measures, shared by Islamists, such as economic improvement, educational policy, justice in society, social tranquility, equity of the economic order, better governance, cultural attainments, national power, or social support for the regime.

Of course the Shari'a is central to the Islamic concept of strengthening the moral understanding of individuals and society. But the Shari'a is largely operating in the moral sphere of human life and is not equipped – indeed, is not *intended* to deal with the practical political, social, and economic problems that plague all modern societies and states. These problems, while possessing a moral component for which the Shari'a can provide some very general guidelines, are usually of a more technical, administrative, institutional, or legal nature involving the evolution of political society within a contemporary political structure. Indeed, many modernist Islamists emphasize that the Shari'a is not some magic pill or a module that one simply plugs in with instant results. Islamists in the Indonesian Muhammadiya point out that they are concerned with "far more important issues than application of Shari'a": they seek to strengthen a Muslim nation's education, health, economy, and society – a task that represents the "greater Shari'a" or path of God.

The failings of contemporary state and society run deep, requiring reform and change in the direction of good governance. Islam's stress on the concept of just governance and a just society can serve as an inspiration for bold change even if it is not a blueprint. But because of the symbolic power and politicized nature of invoking Shari'a today, even modernist Islamists tread carefully to avoid seeming de-evaluation of the role of Shari'a in contemporary life.

Every one of the societies mentioned above that have made major strides toward full application of Shari'a to one degree or another still suffers significantly from social injustice, economic inequity, major corruption, lack of answerability from the ruler, administrative incompetence, poor governance, and unwillingness to permit popular participation in the political process. Every one of them, starting with Iran, is still mired in the classic questions: whose Islam, or which kind of Islamism, are we talking about? Is the government answerable to the people? Do the people have a say in what they want? Who has the right to interpret Islam – or any other ideology? Has life significantly improved on either the material or moral level? Any examination of these societies reveals that the problem of corruption, brutality, exclusion, arbitrariness, bad policies, struggles for power, abused institutions – all still exist, despite serious efforts to create Islamic government and a serious role for the Shari'a. While no one can expect perfect governance, *in principle we should be able to expect some serious progress toward improvement in these areas as serious steps are made toward greater application of the Shari'a. In fact we see in most of these states policies and conditions that are at least as bad as states that give little or no weight to Shari'a.*

Now, let's be clear. This is not a failing of Islam itself. Few Islamists would claim that political Islam is the same thing as Islam. The problem is that Islam has not yet been interpreted freshly, boldly, and widely enough as it might apply to contemporary political and social conditions. Islamists have not made clear distinctions between what issues are related to Islam and what are "secular" political issues. The deeper values of Islam have not been made relevant or applied to what are nearly universal political problems in the political and social life of human beings. Islamic concepts as demonstrated in its *fiqh* (the body of Islamic jurisprudence) and political philosophy are largely linked to historic time, place, and circumstance, making them difficult to apply today without serious rethinking or *ijtihad*.

God did not, of course, hand down the Shari'a; he transmitted the Qur'an, which the Prophet sought to implement according to his best understanding – as seen in the Traditions of the Prophet – and human scholars created the Shari'a based on these two sources. Shari'a law is thus a man-made compilation over many centuries of various jurisprudents' understanding of how the Qur'an and the Traditions could be more concretely applied to what was premodern society. Interpretations and emphasis can and do differ over time in accordance with contemporary reality.

In fact, I find it far easier to accept the vague slogan that "Islam is the solution" than the more concrete thought that "the Shari'a is the solution." The first idea suggests that Islam offers a rich body of philosophical and moral thought that can offer general guidance, insight, and wisdom to troubled contemporary societies. The second idea suggests that *there already exists a concrete body of law that will automatically answer all needs if only fully applied*. The *hudud* (Islamic punishments) certainly offer no automatic remedy: whether a thief is jailed, or his hand amputated, will not greatly change the moral problem of theft. The real social issue of crime is whether harsher or less harsh punishment is more effective – a debate conducted in all societies.

Shari'a is actually deeply aware of differing social conditions that might produce theft and gives judges wide legal latitude in its interpretation and application. Adultery, too, can be made punishable by law, however harshly, if society desires, but the exact type of punishment is not central to the argument of morality. Is stoning (going back to the Old Testament) closer to God's will than lethal injection if society decides to apply the death penalty for adultery? *Fiqh* is bound in time to an Islamic past, many of whose features are long gone and rarely interpreted in a contemporary light today. Slavery, for example, has been a nearly universal human institution of all societies since the beginning of mankind; it is mentioned in the Old Testament, the New Testament, and the Qur'an as well, and legislation regarding the proper treatment of slaves was made in the Shari'a, but today hardly any Muslim suggests a return to those days.

Conservative social values have been maintained by every society in history in a manner relative to its time. But how realistic are those specific traditional conservative policies, designed for a premodern era, in the face of the social, economic, and technological realities of today? Today women are universally a part of the labor force, a birth-control pill exists, and widely diverse social mores are practiced; these are all appropriate subjects for debate from both a conservative or liberal position. Conservative social values are fine, but they have weight, impact, and acceptance only to the extent that they are relevant to contemporary realities and needs. *Islamic moral principles can be made permanently relevant through regular reinterpretation in accordance with existing realities and community consensus.*

Integrating western and Islamic political culture

The irony for political Islam in the twenty-first century is that *only the integration of broad aspects of Western political thought and political experience will enable Islamism to survive as a meaningful political force* – particularly in the area of democratic institutions. But conversely, *the evolution of broader political thought in the Muslim world cannot decisively advance or flourish unless it specifically comes to incorporate and digest Islamic political thought and traditions as well*. Western political models for governance in the Muslim world will shrivel like transplanted trees unless they include the nourishment of Islamic culture from which political Islam emerges. This process is both inevitable and essential for the advancement of genuine and "authentic" political thought in the Muslim world.

After all, there is no "authentic" thought today; all of world thinking draws on earlier traditions from different civilizations at different times. Even ancient Greek thought, long thought to be the original root of Western culture, now is understood itself to have drawn heavily upon earlier Near Eastern civilizations. If Islamist thought draws upon "Western" thought today, it is drawing upon modern institutions that have their roots in the Near East.

It is only when Islamic political and social thought itself – long restricted or frozen – begins to evolve through interaction with external forces that real intellectual growth and institutional development will emerge. At the same time, efforts in the Muslim world to advance political and social thought *totally independent of the framework of Islamic culture* is doomed to be fractured, unintegrated, rootless, and alienated.

Thus the superficial "Westernization" we see at the elite level in the Muslim world provides a misleading measure of genuine political and intellectual progress within these societies, even if it commands superficial Western admiration. Westernization-by-fiat represents the imposition of a Western overlay on top of Islamic culture and practice, primarily benefiting the elites but failing to reach down into the roots of Muslim society and culture. It is not surprising that we see backlash on the part of the majorities of these populations who feel their traditional values ignored and themselves left behind in the modernization process of the elites. Indeed, "Westernization" and "secularism" have gotten a bad name when they are perceived locally as the reigning ideology of despotic and often corrupt rule that enjoys strong Western support.

Interestingly, the efforts by various Muslim regimes to assume protective Islamic coloration in hope of satisfying the masses and gaining greater Islamic legitimacy have been much less serious than the efforts by political Islam to grapple with Western concepts. Traditional Islamic culture has been compelled to integrate Western ideas selectively because it perceives their value in a future Islamic order. Islamism has no option but to come to terms selectively with Western political values as the reigning body of political thought at a global level. The result has been more positive than negative in engendering genuine political evolution in a context that does not lobotomize Islamic tradition.

Islamist movements, then, represent the first serious intellectual interaction between the two forces of Islamic and Western political thought in ways designed to bring about some kind of true integration rather than modernization through a walling off of tradition. Some Islamists (and most Westernizers) are happy with walls between the two cultures, but most people are not. They realize that the interplay of cultures and civilizations will not advance as long as one key element in the process is absent. Thus political Islam in the end becomes a primary vehicle for the confrontation, debate, inculcation, integration, and reconciliation of these grand cultural forces of Islamic and Western culture at the most essential level, bringing about gradual accommodation and rapprochement on both the intellectual and grassroots level. Naturally there is no one "political Islam," and different groups will move toward acceptance and integration – or rejection – of selected Western political ideas and institutions at different rates. But the process is inevitable.

Turkey will be the first country to succeed in reaching a genuine reconciliation and integration of Islamist and Western liberal democratic tradition. I am referring not to Turkey's Kemalist secularist elite that essentially rejects the Islamic experience, but to the new synthesis emerging in Turkey through gradual admission of modernist

Islamists into social and political institutions. This is happening because Turkey has advanced farther in establishing modern institutions of democratic governance than any other Muslim state, an evolution shared by its Islamists. So Turkey's task now is to open up fully its democratizing system and to reach back to integrate those social and ideological elements that were left behind or excluded during the forced Westernization project. Most of Turkey's elite is already on the way to recognizing this inevitability: they appreciate necessity of this integration in the interests of social harmony, and they recognize that the pressures from these excluded social elements can no longer be easily ignored in a democratic state that aspires to membership in the European Union.

Islam and leadership

Islamist movements are *potentially* capable of providing leadership in most of their chosen policy arenas, and many are already doing so. But even if Islamists find guidance in Islamic values for a broad range of contemporary questions, they must still demonstrate that the *specific inspiration* that they avow is relevant to the problems at hand. If it is not relevant, it is not the fault of Islam but of their own faulty understanding, interpretation, and lack of political imagination and talent. Different Islamists in different countries will come up with different ways to understand and apply Islamic guidance. No one can predict how successful they will be, but they represent at least one popular force bidding to open the political order inside presently largely unsuccessful authoritarian states. Islamist movements will remain on the political scene for a long time until eclipsed by those with better answers and better organization.

Is there anything new about Islamism's current broad range of political and social activity? Yes, Islamic movements in the past could mobilize the public on an *ad hoc* basis on specific issues – such as the Indian Mutiny against the British, or the anti-British movement over tobacco taxes in Iran early in the twentieth century, or the anti-colonial struggle in Algeria. But while individual Islamic leaders periodically employed Islamic rhetoric to mobilize the public on specific issues, the modern Islamist movement is no longer an ad hoc coalition. It consists of a standing organization with formal organizational rules, major funding, a staff, and involved in an ever-evolving political and social agenda. This does not mean that Islamism is a monolith. Islamists learned a lot by watching the mobilization techniques of the communists and Arab nationalists in the middle of the last century, the first such movements to aim for mass mobilization.

Notes

1 Roy in a personal exchange with the author.
2 Joseph Samaha, "Are the Islamists going mainstream?" *Mideast Mirror*, 9 June 1999.
3 Fahmi Howeidi, "Why Moslems should support NATO in its punishment of the Serb butchers," in *Mideast Mirror*, 6 April 1999, citing *al-Ahram*; and al-Effendi, Abdelwahhab, "Why Arab commentators should be cheering NATO," *Mideast Mirror*, 20 April 1999, citing *al-Quds al-ʾArabi*.

Daniel Brumberg

ISLAMISTS AND THE POLITICS OF CONSENSUS

ONE OF THE GREATEST barriers to illuminating political Islam is the belief that Islam demands a specific form of politics. Although some might think this idea long dead, it has lately reappeared in the guise of cultural relativism. Thus two scholars of Islam argue, "In Islamic history, there are a number of very important concepts and images.... These are the foundations for the Islamic perception of democracy ... [based on] core concepts ... central to the political position of virtually all Muslims."[1] While defining these concepts in different ways, most Muslims are said to aspire to a culturally authentic "Islamic democracy" whose core trait is a consensual rather than a win-or-lose, majoritarian vision of politics.[2]

This is a dubious thesis. To say that someone is Muslim tells us little regarding that person's views on politics. The supposition that there is one Muslim identity that trumps all others is erroneous. Muslims may be secular, traditional, or orthodox; they may also think of themselves as belonging to ethnic groups – Kurds in Iraq, Turkey, Iran, and Syria; or Berbers in Morocco and Algeria – whose customs and values can take precedence over Islamic identity. Nor is political identity shaped strictly by religion. While Islamists invariably speak in the language of "authenticity," their Islam is a *political construct* that borrows from both Western and Islamic political thought. Because the resulting amalgam of ideas and symbols points in many and even contradictory directions, in no sense can it be said that the Islamic faith itself requires consensual politics.

This does not mean that some form of consensual politics would be inappropriate. Indeed, democracy in the Islamic world might well fare best where political institutions, rules, and procedures allow all (or most) voices to be represented. But this has little to do with Islam. Indeed, if Islam guaranteed a high level of consensus, it would in fact provide an ideal basis for majoritarian democracy, that is, one in which those who lose elections sit in opposition while those who win exercise legitimate political power. It is precisely the *absence* of unity that requires political institutions emphasizing agreement and cooperation. Power-sharing is necessary not only because

Muslims differ as to the most beneficial relationship of mosque and state but also because such divisions often provoke concerns that election victors will impose their particular vision of Islam on others. By promising inclusion, power-sharing could allay such fears in ways that promote accommodation. Hence the key questions: Will Islamists share power with groups that espouse alternative notions of political community? What conditions will help or hinder consensus-based politics?

Autocracy with democrats

Writing in 1972, when Arab nationalism still overshadowed Islamism, Ilya Harik remarked that the central problem in the Arab world is "the imposition of uniformity on a pluralistic social reality, with nationalism as the mold and reality as the mosaic."[3] In their efforts to press the cause of unity, Islamists have a clear advantage over Arab nationalists: Islamists speak for a monotheistic faith that inspires the loyalty of most Muslims. Inasmuch as Islam evokes the ideal of one *umma* or community, it offers an array of symbols that Islamists can use to legitimate unitary – or what I call *harmonic* – ideologies and programs.

   Some hold that this quest for unity is so intrinsic to Islamism that it virtually precludes the forging of pluralistic power-sharing pacts. Thus John Waterbury writes that Algeria's Islamic Salvation Front (FIS) "in no way resembles [Poland's] Solidarity." The latter struck an agreement with General Jaruzelski because Solidarity's aims focused on the pragmatics of economic and political power rather than existential issues such as religious identity. But unlike Solidarity, Islamists "do not oppose, or wish to replace, incumbent power blocs because they are undemocratic but because they have no sense of mission."[4] This crusade to ensure that the state's primary mission is to guarantee one overarching ideology has invariably alarmed women's organizations, ethnic minorities such as Berbers and Kurds, secular intellectuals and professionals, and of course military officers, who have gladly invoked such fears to justify autocracy. The resulting alliance between potential democrats and police states offers an inverted image of political reform in Eastern Europe and the wider Third World. In the latter cases, none-too-democratic elites nonetheless found democratic institutions and procedures useful for dealing with regime-versus-opposition conflicts, thereby paving the way for "democracy without democrats." In the Middle East, by contrast, fear of Islamist victories has produced "autocracy *with* democrats," as key groups that might choose democracy absent an Islamist threat now actively support or at least tolerate autocrats. As one secular Algerian said of his country's 1992 coup, "when faced by a choice between FIS's Ali Belhadj and General Khaled Nezzar, I chose the general."[5]

   Even a brief look at Arab states suggests how pervasive this logic is. In Iraq, Syria, and Bahrain, ethnoreligious minorities have enforced autocracies in part because they fear the consequences of democratization. This anxiety has grown in direct proportion to the length of their incumbency. The longer they have used repression to survive, the more autocrats rightly fear that reform will lead to their being toppled or even killed. The military-based regimes in Egypt and until recently Algeria (though that could change again) are stuck in the same trap. While their rulers are, for the most part, Sunni Muslims and thus do not represent ethnoreligious minorities, their efforts to narrow the scope of democratic participation have sometimes received tacit support from key groups that fear the consequences of full-fledged democratization. Yet by quarantining both Islamist and secular voices, these regimes have fettered potential democrats while alienating Islamists who might favor accommodation. Even rulers who might accept reform are stymied amid the increasing political isolation that results from this strategy, and are finding it harder and harder to climb out of the very hole into which they have helped to dig themselves.

Although the picture seems bleak, it is not without some brighter spots. In Kuwait, both Islamist and secular members of parliament have maintained an uneasy détente with the royal family since 1992. In Turkey, two Islamist parties compete in elections; one of them (the Saadet or Contentment Party) holds 48 seats in the 550-member Grand National Assembly. In Algeria, a multiparty coalition dominated by the two government-oriented parties includes two Islamist parties that together won 27 percent of the seats in the 1997 National People's Assembly elections. Further afield, in Indonesia, several Islamist parties have shared power in a succession of fractious cabinets since the June 1999 elections. And in Morocco and Bahrain, it is likely that Islamists will make gains in parliamentary elections set for autumn 2002. There may be a trend toward inclusion, even if most of the regimes that have made room for Islamists are unlikely to allow a leap from hobbled pluralism to competitive democracy.[6]

Which states are more likely to dig themselves out of autocracy rather than get buried by it? Those scholars who argue that Islam is intrinsically illiberal, or who define away the problem by offering relativist concepts of "Islamic democracy," offer little in the way of explanation, and of prediction still less. Yet instrumentalist accounts that reduce Islamism to little more than a source of rationalizing ideologies are equally limiting. Islamist ideologies may be "constructed," but they are shaped by and encapsulated within a *multitude* of ideal social, political, and cultural identities and interests that can contradict as well as complement one another. Thus the challenge is not to figure out whether Islamism is "essentially" democratic versus autocratic, or liberal versus illiberal. Instead, it is to see whether this or that Islamist group is acting within a hegemonic political arena where the game is to shut out alternative approaches, or else within a competitive – let's call it *dissonant* – arena where Islamists, like other players, find themselves pushed to accommodate the logic of power-sharing.

What do I mean by "dissonant"? Consider Lebanon: There the ideological, cultural, and political divisions between and within the Islamic and Christian communities have been institutionalized in a consociational system that not only offers all key groups representation but, just as important, creates constraints that make it unlikely that any one Islamist group will have either the means or the inclination to impose a single ideological vision on the state. Thus while Lebanon's Hezbollah is not, philosophically speaking, a champion of pluralism, in practice its leaders do not and *cannot* favor the imposition of an Islamic state. While one might argue that the decisive constraint on Hezbollah is the presence of Syrian troops, even absent this check it is difficult to imagine Hezbollah pursuing a hegemonic project, since doing so would surely spark another civil war (a war that Hezbollah's leaders know they cannot win, and which could draw Syrian or Israeli involvement). In short, a dissonant political field has this paradoxical quality: It invites competition and conflict, but can also create incentives for sharing power.

Lebanon is not the only example of dissonance in the Islamic world. The tendency to treat it as an exceptional case is a consequence of many factors, not least of

which is the facile account of Islamism critiqued above. But the failure to grasp fully
the political significance of dissonance also reflects a poverty of sociological imagination. For as Arend Lijphart argues, identity cleavages come in many forms: religious,
ethnic, linguistic, social, and even ideological.[7] Viewed through this expansive prism,
we can see dissonance even in countries whose leaders have denied its existence.
Consider Algeria, where despite decades of rule by a single party that spoke in the
name of *le peuple*, society is a mosaic of crosscutting and overlapping cleavages based
on clans, ideology (Islamism versus secularism, state socialism versus the market),
and ethnicity (Berbers versus Arabs). The effort to repress these differences led
to autocracy (1962–88), to a failed experiment in pluralistic politics (1989–91), to
the bloody civil war that exploded after the army pulled the plug on elections in
1992, and finally to a regime which, since 1997, has tried to institutionalize dissonance by selectively incorporating Islamist, Berber, secular-democratic, and military-
bureaucratic groups through a controlled system of party representation.

Algeria's urgent attempt to create a more competitive playing field reminds us
that the mere existence of social, cultural, or ideological differences is insufficient to
create ideological and political dissonance. Instead, a dissonant political arena is a
product of a lengthy state-building dynamic that institutionalizes competing visions of
community in different organizations, associations, or political parties. However
autocratic, such *dissonant states* create a multipolar arena that abets competition and
negotiation. By contrast, *harmonic states* – meaning those which attempt to create
unity or its appearance through repression, cooptation, or distraction – create a uni-
polar field that can easily become a place for deadly games of "winner takes all"
between rulers and their opponents.[8]

We can readily trace the implications of these contrasting dynamics for politics
in predominantly Muslim countries. By distancing themselves from the cultural,
religious, or ideological project of any one group, dissonant states not only serve
as arbiters of competing identities; more decisively, they leave institutional and
ideological legacies that make it difficult for any one Islamist party to impose its views
on the state itself. This competitive field opens up the space for negotiating power-
sharing arrangements. By contrast, harmonic states not only coopt or repress rival
Islamist voices and institutions; through schools, media, and government-controlled
mosques, such states spread an image of themselves as the supreme representative of
a united cultural community that by its very nature lives in peace. The more successfully they spread this utopian vision, the more likely it is that harmonic states will
spawn the very Islamist radicals who then bitterly damn such states for shirking their
duty to champion "the Arab nation" or "the Islamic *umma*." And once radicals fill the
ideological and institutional vacuum, the space for accommodation can get fatally
narrow. Algeria learned this lesson the hard way. Saudi Arabia – the harmonic Islamic
autocracy *par excellence* – must constantly suffer allegations from its clergy that it has
failed to carry out its holy mission.

Contrasting Indonesia and Algeria

While dissonant states create incentives for power-sharing and harmonic states produce the opposite, statecraft can play a vital role in determining whether leaders will

reap the benefits of dissonance or minimize the liabilities of hegemony. To appreciate the interplay of state-building legacies and statecraft, we can briefly consider the cases of Indonesia and Algeria.

Indonesia is the Islamic world's best example of dissonant state building. While 90 percent of its 228 million people are Muslims, since roughly 1900 its society has been marked by two overlapping ideological and institutional divides: between nationalists and Muslims, and between Muslims and other Muslims. The latter cleavage emerged in the 1920s as a reaction to the creation of Muhammadiyah, a movement inspired by Arab reformists that sought – much to the chagrin of rural Javanese Muslims – to rid Islam in Indonesia of pre-Islamic or Sufi-mystical practices. Rural Muslims responded to this illiberal project by creating the Awakening of Traditional Religious Leaders (Nahdlatul Ulema or NU). NU's leaders held that the only way to defend their 40 million members from the "modernizing" impulse of Muhammadiyah was to embrace the principle that the state could never serve as a vehicle of Islamization. Although some Islamists sought to transform Indonesia into a hegemonic state, by the 1970s a dissonant political field was the firm reality.

So long as President Suharto (1967–98) enforced this ban, NU backed him. But when he began flirting with Islamist autocrats in the early 1990s, NU began pushing for democracy. Abdurrahman Wahid was one of several Islamic leaders who moved NU toward pluralism, winning support from younger people in both NU and Muhammadiyah. By the late 1990s, the political arena featured Islamist autocrats and Islamist pluralists, secular nationalists, and the military, a secular if illiberal force in Indonesian politics. When Suharto fell in 1998 and reform got underway, the new party system reflected the three-way split of nationalists, Islamist pluralists, and Islamist autocrats. Wahid and his party steered between the first and the second of these three groups, thus emerging as a key power broker. But after Wahid was elected president in October 1999, he failed to capitalize on the legacy of dissonance he had inherited. Although a democrat, he responded to the efforts of other Islamist and secular leaders to influence (or manipulate) his policies by dismissing potential rivals from the cabinet. His erratic statecraft led to his resignation in July 2001.

On becoming president, Vice-President Megawati Sukarnoputri formed a cabinet with leaders from all the major parties. Yet this effort to sustain power-sharing faces obstacles, not least of which is a severe economic crisis that is eroding support for moderate Islamic parties. Moreover, Wahid's resignation has undercut his party's capacity to serve as a balancer between Megawati's secular-nationalist base and the more autocratic Islamist parties. Hamzah Haz, a former leader of one of the latter groups, is now vice-president. He is currently supporting the call of several small Islamist parties to insert language in the 1945 Constitution that effectively favors the application of Islamic law (shari῾a). This effort will probably fail because most Indonesians, including many pious Muslims, oppose it. Yet many doubt that Megawati has the leadership skills to ensure that Indonesia's experiment in pluralistic power-sharing will survive.

Algeria offers a telling contrast to Indonesia. I have already alluded to the recent Algerian civil war as the paradoxical and tragic fruit of a longstanding harmonic state. Some argue that had the FIS taken power in 1992, the Islamists' political and economic incompetence would have cured Algeria of its lingering taste for utopia. After all, a significant part of the FIS support was a protest vote, not an endorsement of Islamism. Yet the same could be said about Iran in 1979. In both cases, Islamist elites and their well-organized backers sought a hegemonic state. Had the FIS prevailed, it might have followed in the footsteps of the Islamic Republic of Iran by building control mechanisms strong enough to survive the inevitable discrediting of its utopian ideology. As Iran's more recent experience demonstrates, even the most profound legitimacy crisis may fail to undermine a state's autocratic institutions.

Algeria's current leaders have concluded that they cannot rule without a modicum of legitimacy, or in total defiance of their country's multivocal social and ideological fabric. Since the 1997 parliamentary elections, they have tried to invent a dissonant political order by promoting a multiparty government that includes two Islamist parties, the Renaissance Movement and the Movement for a Peaceful Society. While both benefit from government patronage, the latter has garnered a measure of credibility as an advocate for an Islamic alternative that repudiates violence and the notion of an Islamic state. Yet embedding dissonance at this late date is not easy: Recent polls show that 48 percent of voters attribute little credibility to the party system.[9] State-controlled inclusion of Islamists is certainly preferable to total exclusion, but unless rulers have the ingenuity and guts to give opposition parties real power, this tactic may invite frustration rather than enhance legitimacy. Forward-looking statecraft is thus essential, a point that Algeria's leaders will want to keep in mind as they struggle to transcend a legacy of conflict whose final chapter is not yet written.

Notes

1   John L. Esposito and John O. Voll, *Islam and Democracy* (Oxford: Oxford University Press, 1996), 23. Esposito repeats this argument, albeit more equivocally, in *Unholy War: Terror in the Name of Islam* (Oxford: Oxford University Press, 2002), 145.

2   John L. Esposito and John O. Voll, *Islam and Democracy*, 18 and 19.

3   Iliya F. Harik, "The Ethnic Revolution and Political Integration in the Middle East," *International Journal of Middle East Studies* 3 (July 1972): 310.

4   John Waterbury, "Democracy Without Democrats? The Potential for Political Liberalization in the Middle East," in Ghassan Salamé, ed., *Democracy Without Democrats? The Renewal of Politics in the Muslim World* (London: I.B. Tauris, 1994), 39.

5   Interview, Algiers, 18 February 2002.

6   Thomas Carothers, "The End of the Transition Paradigm," *Journal of Democracy* 13 (January 2002): 5–21.

7   Arend Lijphart, *Democracy in Plural Societies: A Comparative Exploration* (New Haven: Yale University Press, 1977).

8   For an elaboration of this argument, see Daniel Brumberg, "Dissonant Politics in Iran and Indonesia," *Political Science Quarterly* 116 (Fall 2001): 381–411.

9   "Près de la moitié des Algériens désespèrent des parties politiques," *www.algeria-interface.com/new/article.php?rub=2*. Access date: 29 April 2002.

Saba Mahmood

ETHICAL FORMATION AND POLITICS OF INDIVIDUAL AUTONOMY IN CONTEMPORARY EGYPT*

WITHIN THE VAST LITERATURE produced on contemporary Islam, Islamist movements have often been analyzed through the lens of identity politics. The increasing emphasis on Islamic forms of behavior among Muslims in the Middle East has been commonly read as a recoding of nationalist sentiments in religious idioms, a recoding that does not so much replace Arab nationalism as recast its political sentiment in Islamic symbols. The growing interest in Islamic rituals such as donning the veil, performing collective prayers, and listening to sermons are understood to enfold existent forms of Arab nationalism into particularistic expressions of religious belonging, a development that has, if anything, narrowed the scope of nationalist politics by making the figure of the Muslim paradigmatic of the citizen-subject. This continuity between Islamism and nationalism would appear to be all the more pronounced with regard to the question of gender since both ideologies appear to cast women as the repositories of tradition and culture, their bodies made the potent symbols of collective identity.

Indeed, it is not difficult to find examples of the laminated character of Islamist-nationalist discourse in Egypt today, a country that remains one of the premiere cultural centers of the Islamist movement in the Middle East. A number of Egyptian Islamists, for instance, speak about the veil as an expression of Arab-Muslim identity, while many of their secular-oriented critics view Islam as constitutive of the cultural terrain upon which the Egyptian nation has acquired its unique historical character. In contrast to these views, however, a strong current within the Islamist movement – which I will gloss here as the "piety movement" – is highly critical of this nationalist-identitarian view of Islam and directs its organizational efforts at combating the practical effects of this interpretation. The critique put forward by this movement is

*Social Research, 70(3), 2003, pp. 837–68, www.socres.org

not simply that the nationalist-identitarian view vitiates the religious character of Islam in rendering it a political ideology. Rather, their criticism is that such a view reduces Islamic ritual practices to the status of cultural customs, thereby radically transforming the role such practices have played historically in the realization of a pious life. However abstruse this might sound to secular ears, debates about how to interpret and enact the variety of embodied Islamic injunctions pervade Egyptian public life, and even political discussions often devolve upon questions about the proper role ascribed to the performance of these practices.

In what follows I want to argue that, in order to understand the importance of these debates to public life in Egypt, we need to bring questions of ethics to bear upon politics and vice-versa, and thus complicate the separation of these realms so commonly assumed in liberal political theory. Specifically, I will show that different conceptions of ritual and bodily behavior among Egyptian Muslims presuppose radically different imaginaries of collective and individual freedom; as such, debates about ritual performance represent a key site from which one can understand contrastive visions of self, community, and authority that constitute different strands of the Islamist movement in Egypt today. Toward the end of this essay, I will show how an analytical vocabulary drawn from liberal and communitarian discussions of self and community remains inadequate to the task of understanding the kind of social imaginary presupposed by certain narratives of personhood prevalent within the Islamist movement.

The issues I raise in this article about the place of social authority in the constitution of the self extend recent discussions about the disciplinary character of the public sphere. Contrary to earlier Habermasian theories that stressed the communicative and deliberative aspects of the public sphere, one in which preformed rational subjects engaged in a free exchange of ideas and critique, a number of recent scholars have drawn attention to how the public sphere is also a space for the creation of particular kinds of subjects and for the cultivation of those capacities and orientations that enable participation within this sphere (Burchell, 1995; Calhoun, 1992; Hirschkind, 2001; Salvatore, 1998; Warner, 1990). While much of this literature focuses on the technologies of discipline through which public subjects come to be produced, relatively little attention has been paid to the contrasting conceptions of social authority that undergird such disciplinary practices in specific cultural and historical locations. This is an attempt at addressing this lacuna through an analysis of the radically different understandings of authority presupposed by two models of ethical self-fashioning at the heart of Egyptian public life today, and how this difference affects the possibility of politics as it is currently practiced.

I draw upon two years of ethnographic fieldwork that I conducted among a women's piety movement based in the mosques of Cairo, Egypt. The women's mosque movement is part of a larger current within the Islamic Revival (*al-Sahwa al-Islamiyya*), which is concerned with securing the conditions enabling the practice of Islamic modes of piety through practical activities such as preaching, establishing Islamic institutions (mosques, Islamic schools, printing presses, and so on), and engaging in a range of welfare activities.[1] The primary focus of the women's mosque movement is teaching and studying Islamic scriptures, social practices, and forms of bodily comportment considered germane to the cultivation of the ideal virtuous self.

The ubiquitous popularity of the movement has grown so that even relatively small neighborhood mosques hold religious lessons for women organized by local residents. The attendance at these lessons varies from 25 to 500 women who come from a diverse array of socioeconomic backgrounds.

According to the participants, the women's mosque movement emerged about 25 years ago in response to the perception that religious knowledge, as a means to organizing daily conduct, had become increasingly marginalized under modern structures of secular governance. This trend is seen to have reduced Islamic knowledge (both as a mode of conduct as well as a set of principles) to an abstract system of beliefs that has no direct bearing on the practicalities of daily living. The women's mosque movement, therefore, seeks to preserve those virtues, ethical capacities, and forms of reasoning that the participants perceive to have become unavailable or inaccessible to ordinary Muslims. The practical efforts of the mosque movement are directed at instructing Muslims not only in the proper performance of religious duties and acts of worship but, more important, familiarizing them with the practical implications of the exegetical tradition of the Qur'an and the *hadith* (the authoritative record of the prophet's exemplary speech and action). Instruction in this tradition, however, is geared less toward inculcating a scholarly knowledge of the texts than providing a practical understanding of how these texts should guide one's conduct in daily affairs.[2]

Insofar as the mosque movement aims to make Egyptian society more religiously devout within the existing structures and policies of the state, it is distinct from the state-oriented Islamist political groups that have been the focus of most academic studies of the Islamist movement. Yet the women's mosque movement should not be understood as a withdrawal from sociopolitical engagement insomuch as the form of piety it seeks to realize entails the transformation of many aspects of social life in Egypt. It is not surprising, therefore, that in the last five years the Egyptian government has increased its surveillance of mosque groups and now requires male and female preachers, regardless of their prior religious training, to enroll in a two-year state-run program in order to be able to preach in the mosques.[3]

Notably, unlike similar women's groups in Iran and Indonesia, the Egyptian women's mosque movement exhibits no interest in reinterpreting the male exegetical tradition from a feminist stance, but is exclusively grounded in the established interpretive tradition of Sunni Islam associated with the four schools of Islamic law (Hanbali, Shafaʾi, Maliki, and Hanafi). While I have explored the paradox such a movement poses to the study of gender and feminist politics elsewhere (see Mahmood, 2001), in this article I want to explore how a consideration of debates about bodily performative behavior forces us to revise our understanding of the relation between ethics and politics within the contemporary Islamic Revival.

Folklorizing Islam

An important aspect of the mosque movement's critique of the secularization of Egyptian society focuses upon the ways in which the understanding and performance of acts of religious obligations, called ʿ*ibadat* in Islamic jurisprudence, have been transformed in the modern period. The participants argue that Islamic forms of embodied behavior – such as fasting, praying, veiling – have increasingly acquired the status of customs or conventions in the popular imagination, a kind of "Muslim folklore," undertaken as a form of entertainment or as a means to display a religio-cultural identity. According to them, this has led to a decline in another understanding of worship, one in which rituals are performed as a means to the training and realization of piety in the entirety of one's life. Part of the aim of the mosque movement is to restore this understanding of rituals and forms of bodily comportment by teaching women the requisite skills involved in its practice.

Consider the views of Hajja Nur, a mosque teacher who, until the government transferred her to another mosque, drew a weekly crowd of 500 women at the peak of her career. She told me that:

> It is the project of the government and the secularists to transform religion (al-din) into conventions or customs ('ada). People may not even know that they are doing this, but in fact what they do in actual behavior is to turn religion into no more than a folkloric custom! An example of this is the use of the veil (hijab). When you [Saba] as a foreigner look at Egyptian society right now and see all these women wearing the veil, you must remember that a lot of them wear it as a custom, rather than a religious duty that also entails other responsibilities. These people are in fact no different than those who argue against the veil and who say that the veil is [an expression of] culture [and therefore a matter of personal choice], rather than a religious command. So what we have to do is to educate Muslim women that it is not enough to wear the veil, but that the veil must also lead us to behave truly modestly in our daily life, a challenge that far exceeds the simple act of donning the veil.

I would like to highlight the distinction Hajja Nur makes between a bodily practice that is part of the larger project of becoming a pious Muslim in the entirety of one's life, and a practice that is Islamic in form and style but does not necessarily serve as a means to the training and realization of this pious self. Hajja Nur's remarks imply a critique of those forms of Islamic practice whose raison d'être is to signal an identity or tradition and are, therefore, in her view, shorn of their ability to contribute to the formation of an ethical disposition. As will become clear later, women like Hajja Nur understand forms of bodily practice (such as veiling) to not simply *express* the self but also *shape* the self that they are supposed to signify.

Hajja Nur's position may be contrasted not only with the views of many Egyptian secularists for whom the veil is indeed an outdated regional custom that has mistakenly been assigned the status of a divine injunction,[4] but, far more interestingly, with an interpretation of the veil popular among fellow Islamists. Consider for example the views expressed by a prominent Islamist leader, Adil Hussein, who served as the general secretary of the leading Islamist political party in Egypt, Hizb al-Amal (Labor Party), until his death two years ago. The Islamist newspaper published by Adil Hussein's party often criticizes the larger piety movement for its preoccupation with the minutiae of ritual bodily practices at the expense of ignoring, as one author put it, "real questions of truth, justice, and freedom." The following is an excerpt from an interview with Adil Hussein in a documentary on the Islamic Revival where he spells out why he thinks the veil is important:

> In this period of [Islamic] Revival and renewed pride in ourselves and our past, why should we not take pride in the symbols that distinguish us from others [like the veil]? So we say that the first condition is that clothing should be modest. But why can't we add a second condition that we would like this dress to be a continuation of what we have created in this region, like the Indian sari? ... Why can't we have our own dress which expresses decency, a requirement of Islam, as well as the special beauty that would be the mark of our society which has excelled in the arts and civilization? (York, 1992)

Hussein clearly regards the veil to be one symbol among others of an Islamic identity, culture, and civilization; a symbol, moreover, that is no different than the sari in this regard, which marks the regional particularity of South Asia. In Hussein's view, the increased popularity of the veil is a sign of the vitality of the Islamic Revival, which in turn is interpreted as the Arab-Muslim world's awakening to its true cultural heritage. Note how distinct this understanding is from that of Hajja Nur: the meaning of the veil for her is not exhausted by its significance as a sign (of a civilization, culture, or identity), but encompasses an entire way of being and acting, one that can only be learned through the act of veiling. To summarize the differences between the two views, one might say that for nationalists like Hussein, bodily practices stand in a relationship of significance to one's identity in a way that they do not for pietists like Hajja Nur; for the latter, these practices are exercises of ethical self-making that may or may not signify the self they help construct. These differences are of considerable import because, as I will argue later, they presume contrastive understandings of what constitutes personhood and what its appropriate relationship to social authority should be – differences that are crucial to an analysis of the embattled character of the Egyptian polity today.

Form and content

To date, debates about the proper interpretation of religious obligations (such as veiling, fasting, or praying) remain inconsequential to most analyses of the sociopolitical landscape created by the Islamic Revival in the last 40 years. Scholars have tended to treat questions of bodily form as superficial particularities through which more profound cultural meanings find expression. Even in those instances where bodily practices (such as veiling and praying) are considered within political analyses, they are understood as symbols deployed by social movements toward political ends, serving at best as vehicles for the expression of group interests. The specific conception of bodily practices and the forms they take, in other words, are not themselves seen to have political implications. This tendency is in part a product of the normative liberal conception of politics, one separate from the domain of ethics and moral conduct, and is in part a reflection of how the field of ethics and moral conduct has been shaped in the modern period.

Historian and cultural critic Jeffery Minson has argued persuasively that within post-Enlightenment thought, the relative lack of attention paid to the morphology of moral actions, to their precise shape and form, is largely a legacy of humanist ethics, particularly in its Kantian formulation (Minson, 1993). For Kant, morality proper was primarily a rational matter that entailed the exercise of the faculty of reason, shorn of the specific context (of social virtues, habit, character formation, and so on) in which the act unfolded. The Kantian legacy, I would add, becomes particularly important in light of the tradition of Aristotelian ethics it displaces, one in which morality was both realized through, and manifest in, outward behavioral forms. Against this tradition, Kant argued that a moral act could only be moral to the extent that it was not a result of habituated virtue but a product of the critical faculty of reason, which in turn was understood to be universally valid.[5] This meant that one acted morally in spite of one's inclinations, habits, and disposition rather than because of them. Kant's emphasis on the intention with which a moral act was undertaken, as a necessary if insufficient condition of morality proper, stands in contrast with the value ascribed to the particular form a moral act took in the Aristotelian worldview.[6] The question of motivation, deliberation, and choice in the Aristotelian tradition was important too, of course, but only from the standpoint of actual practices.

One consequence of this Kantian conception of ethics is the relative lack of attention paid to the manifest form ethical practices take, and a general demotion of conduct, social demeanor, and etiquette in our analyses of moral systems. As Minson points out, even scholars like Pierre Bourdieu, whose work focuses on practices of dress, physical bearing, and styles of comportment – things that Bourdieu calls "the practical mnemonics" of a culture – consider these practices interesting only insofar as a rational evaluation reveals them to be the signs and symbols of a much deeper and more fundamental reality of social structures and cultural logics (Minson, 1993: 31).[7] I would extend Minson's insight and go a step further to say that what is lacking in Bourdieu is a consideration of how different concepts of subject formation require different kinds of bodily capacities and demeanors within specific discursive (rather than cultural or class) contexts.

I would like to suggest a somewhat different analytical approach here, glossed as "positive ethics" (Colebrook, 1998), in which the particularity of form that ethics takes is not a contingent but a necessary aspect of understanding its substantive content. Originally grounded in the tradition of Ancient Greek philosophy, and more recently expanded by Michel Foucault, ethics in this formulation is founded upon particular forms of discursive practice, instantiated through sets of procedures, techniques, and exercises through which highly specific ethical-moral subjects come to be formed (Colebrook, 1998; Davidson, 1994; Foucault, 1997; Hadot, 2002; Martin, Gutman, and Hutton, 1988). An inquiry into ethics from this perspective requires that one examine not simply the values enshrined in moral codes, but the different ways in which people live these codes. Thus, what is relevant here is not so much whether people follow moral regulations or break them, but the relationships they establish between the various constituent elements of the self (body, reason, emotion, volition, and so on) and a particular moral code or norm. In this view, the specific styles and formal expressions that characterize one's relationship to a moral code are not contingent but necessary means for understanding the kind of relationship established between the self and structures of social authority, between what one is, what one wants, and what kind of work one performs on oneself in order to realize a particular modality of being or personhood.

Despite some important overlaps between the approach I propose here and a longstanding tradition of anthropological scholarship on the cultural construction of personhood (as in the work of Marcel Mauss, Erving Goffman, and Margaret Mead), it is important to clarify a few key differences. First, the approach to ethical self-formation I have outlined does not assume a homogenous notion of a self that is coextensive with a given culture, structure, or temporality. Rather, as will become clear, different configurations of personhood cohabit the same cultural and historical space, and each configuration is a product of a specific discursive formation rather than of the culture at large.[8] Second, my analytical framing focuses not on the meanings that particular practices of the self signify or their symbolic and hermeneutical value, but on the work embodied practices perform in crafting a particular assemblage of the self. Let me elaborate what I mean through a couple of ethnographic examples.

Prayer rituals

Among the women I worked with, the condition of piety was described as the quality of "being close to God": a manner of being and acting that suffused all of one's acts, both religious and worldly in character. According to the mosque participants, among the minimal requirements critical to the formation of a virtuous Muslim is the act of praying five times a day. The performance of ritual prayer called *salat* is considered to be so centrally important in Islam that whether someone who does not pray regularly can qualify as a Muslim has been a subject of intense debate among theologians. Despite the doctrinal importance of salat, it was surprising to me that mosque participants considered the desire to pray five times a day (with its minimal conditions of performance) an object of pedagogy. Many of the mosque participants did not pray diligently and seemed to lack the requisite will to accomplish what was required of them. Since such states of will were not assumed to be natural by the teachers, or their followers, women took extra care to teach each other the means by which the desire to pray could be cultivated and strengthened in the course of conducting the sort of routine, mundane actions that occupied most women during the day.

The complicated relationship between the performance of salat and one's daily activities was revealed to me in a conversation with three women, all of whom regularly attended lessons in different mosques of their choice in Cairo. They were known in the mosque circles not only for their articulate command of a variety of complex issues, but also for their dedication to pursuing increasingly higher levels of religious exactitude. The setting for this conversation was a mosque in downtown Cairo. Since all three women worked as clerks in the local state bureaucracy in the same building, it was convenient for them to meet in the neighboring mosque in the late afternoons after work on a weekly basis. Their discussions sometimes attracted other women, who had come to the mosque to pray. In this instance, a young woman in her early twenties had been sitting and listening intently when she suddenly interrupted the discussion to ask a question about one of the five basic prayers required of Muslims, a prayer known as *al-fajr*. This prayer is performed right after dawn breaks and before sunrise. Many Muslims I know consider it the most demanding and difficult of prayers because it is hard to leave the comfort of sleep to wash and pray and also because the period within which it must be performed is very short. This young woman expressed the difficulty she encountered in performing the task of getting up for the morning prayer and asked the group what she should do about it. Mona, a member of the group who is in her mid-thirties, turned to the young woman with a concerned expression on her face and asked, "Do you mean to say that you are unable to get up for the morning prayer habitually and consistently?" The girl nodded in agreement. Bearing the same concerned expression on her face, Mona said, "You mean to say that you forbid yourself the reward of the morning prayer? This surely is an indication of *ghafla* on your part?" The young woman looked somewhat perturbed and guilty but persisted and asked, "What does ghafla mean?" Mona replied that it refers to what you do in the day: if your mind is mostly occupied with things that are not related to God, then you are in a state of ghafla (which literally means carelessness or negligence).

Looking puzzled, the young woman asked, "What do you mean what I do in the day? What does my saying of the prayer [salat] have to do with what I do in the day?" Mona answered: "It means what your day-to-day deeds are. For example, what do you look at in the day? Do you look at things that are prohibited to us by God, such as immodest images of women and men? What do you say to people in the day? Do you insult people when you get angry and use abusive language? How do you feel when you see someone doing an act of disobedience? Do you get sad? Does it hurt you when you see someone committing a sin or does it not affect you? These are the things that have an effect on your heart, and they hinder or impede your ability to get up and say the morning prayer. [The constant] guarding against disobedience and sins wakes you up for the morning prayer. You see, salat is not just what you say with your mouth and what you do with your limbs. It is a state of your heart. So when you do things in a day for God and avoid other things because of Him, it means you're thinking about Him, and therefore it becomes easy for you to strive for Him against yourself and your desires. If you correct these issues, you will be able to rise up for the morning prayer as well."

Responding to the young woman's look of consternation, Mona asked her, "What is it that annoys you the most in your life?" The young woman answered that her sister fought with her a lot, and this bothered her and made her angry most days. Mona replied: "You, for example, can think of God when your sister fights with you and not fight back with her because He commands us to control our anger and be patient. For if you do get angry, you know that you will just gather more sins, but if you are quiet then you are beginning to organize your affairs on account of God and not in accord with your temperament. And then you will realize that your sister will lose the ability to make you angry, and you will become more desirous of God. You will begin to notice that if you say the morning prayer, it will also make your daily affairs easier, and if you don't pray it will make them hard." At this point, we moved back to our previous discussion, and the young woman stayed with us until the end.

The answer that Mona provided to this young woman is not a customary answer, such as invoking the fear of God's retribution for habitually failing to perform one's daily prayers. Mona's response encompasses a remarkable exposition of key principles that are at the center of this economy of moral cultivation, principles that as we will see later are quite distinct from other understandings of the practice of prayer in Egypt today. To begin with, note the ways in which ordinary tasks in daily life are made to attach to the performance of consummate worship in Mona's account. When Mona links the ability to pray to the vigilance with which one conducts the practical chores of daily life, all mundane activities – like getting angry with one's sister, the things one hears and looks at, the way one speaks – become a place for securing and honing particular moral capacities. Significantly, when Mona advises the young woman to refrain from getting angry with her sister, it is important that she do so with the intention of pleasing god (rather than for other reasons, such as controlling her blood pressure, or avoiding sibling conflict). The reigning assumption here is that religious and worldly acts performed repeatedly, with the right kind of intention, eventually root the behavior within ones senses so much so that one's ability to obey God is not a matter of exercising one's will, but issues forth almost spontaneously and effort-lessly from a pious disposition. In this understanding, intention, something that we associate with interiority, is conjoined with outward bodily acts in a manner that the two cannot be conceptually separated.[9]

The complicated relationship between learning, memory, experience, and the self undergirding the model of pedagogy suggested in Mona's answer has at times been discussed by scholars through the Latin term *habitus*, meaning an acquired faculty in which the body, mind, and emotions are simultaneously trained to achieve competence at something (such as meditation, dancing, or playing a musical instru-ment). The term *habitus* has become best known in the social sciences through the work of Pierre Bourdieu, who uses it as a theoretical concept to understand how the structural and class positions of individual subjects come to be embodied as dis-positions – largely through unconscious processes (1977). My own work draws upon a longer and richer history of this term, however, one that addresses the centrality of gestural capacities in certain traditions of moral cultivation. Aristotelian in origin and adopted within Christianity and Islam, habitus in this formulation is concerned with ethical formation and presupposes a specific pedagogical process by which moral character is acquired. Specifically, in this pedagogical model moral virtues (such as modesty, honesty, fortitude) are acquired through a coordination of outward behavior (for example, bodily acts, social demeanor) with inward dispositions (for example, emotional states, thoughts, intentions) through the repeated performance of acts that entail those particular virtues or vices.

In the *Nichomachean Ethics*, Aristotle addresses this pedagogical principle in the following manner: "Moral virtue comes about as a result of habit, whence also its name *ethike* is one that is formed by a slight variation from the word *ethos* (habit). From this it is also plain that none of the moral virtues arise in you by nature; for nothing that exists by nature can form a habit contrary to nature.... . For the things we have to learn before we can do them, we learn by doing them ... we become just by doing just acts, temperate by doing temperate acts, brave by doing brave acts" (1941: 592–93). The appeal of this notion to Muslim and Christian theologians is not hard to understand given its emphasis on human activity and deliberation, rather than nature or divine grace, as determinants of moral conduct. While a virtuous habitus is acquired through virtuous habits, the two are not to be confused: unlike habits, habi-tus once acquired through assiduous practice takes root in character and is considered to be largely unchangeable.

A similar understanding of habituated learning and moral formation is found in the writings of a number of Islamic thinkers, such as Abu Hamid al-Ghazali, but also al-Miskawayh, Ibn Khaldun, and Ibn Rushd. Ibn Khaludun for example, uses the term *malaka*, translated as habitus, which he describes as an inner quality developed through outer practice until that quality comes to regulate and govern one's behavior without conscious deliberation (Lapidus, 1984). In *The Muqadimmah*, Ibn Khaldun writes, "A habitus is a firmly rooted quality acquired by doing a certain action and repeating it time after time, until the form of that action is firmly fixed [in one's disposition]. A habitus corresponds to the original action after which it was formed" (1958: 346). Malaka, therefore, is an acquired excellence at a moral or a practical craft, and as with other skills, achieving malaka in faith rises from practice, is perfected by practice, and then governs all actions and practices. This is only one of the legacies of Aristotelian tradition that is alive and well in contemporary Islam; the other, as I suggested earlier, is a conception of morality in which the precise behavioral form of a moral action is as important as the motivation with which it is performed.

Prayer and citizenship

As I mentioned earlier, this understanding of ritual and performative behavior is not one shared by all Egyptian Muslims. Consider, for example, Mona Hilmi's interpretation of the performance of prayer (salat). Hilmi is a columnist who writes for *Ruz al-Yusuf*, a popular weekly magazine that represents a liberal-nationalist perspective in the Egyptian press. What prompted the appearance of her article was the arrest of several teenagers from upper-middle-class and upper-class families for allegedly participating in "devil worship" (*'abdat al-shaitan*). This incident was widely reported in the Egyptian press and, in part, prompted a discussion about the appropriate role of religion – in particular ritual worship – in Egyptian society. Hilmi writes:

> The issue is not whether people perform rituals, and acts of worship either to get recompense or reward, or out of fear of God, or the desire to show off in front of other people. The issue instead is how rituals and worship prepare for the creation of a type of person who thinks freely, is capable of enlightened criticism on important daily issues, of distinguishing between form and essence, between means and ends, between secondary and basic issues. The biggest challenge is how to transform love for God inside every citizen [*mawatin wa mawatina*] into continuous self-criticism of our daily behaviors and manners, and into an awakening of innovative/creative revolutionary thought that is against the subjugation of the human being and the destruction of his dignity (Hilmi, 1997: 81).

Clearly, Hilmi's argument engages the importance of religious practice in Egyptian society, but it is an interpretation of ritual practice that is quite distinct from the one that Mona and her friends espoused. First, Hilmi and the women with whom I worked voice clear differences about the kind of person to be created in the process of performing ritual obligations. Hilmi imbues her view of what a human being should become with the language and goals of liberal-nationalist thought. For example, the highest goal of worship for her is to create a human being capable of "enlightened criticism on important daily issues" and "revolutionary thought that is against the subjugation of human beings" (1997: 81). As a result, Hilmi addresses "the citizen" (*mawatin wa mawatina*) in her call to duty rather than "the faithful" (*mu'min wa mu'mina*) or "slaves of God" (*'ibad Allah*), the terms more commonly used by the women with whom I worked. In contrast, for many of the mosque participants, the ultimate goal of worship was the natural and effortless performance of the virtue of submission to God. Even though women like Mona subjected their daily activities to self-criticism (as the author recommends), it was done to secure God's approval and pleasure rather than to hone those capacities referred to by Hilmi and central to the definition of the modern autonomous citizen. I do not mean to suggest that the discourses of nationalism have been inconsequential in the development of the mosque movement or that the modern state and its forms of power (social, political, and economic) have not shaped in important ways the lives of the women with whom I worked. My point is simply that the inculcation of ideals of enlightened citizenship was not the aim of worship for the women of the mosque movement as it seems to be for Hilmi.

A far more important distinction between Mona's and Hilmi's views, one that is central to my overall argument, turns upon the means and end relationship that the ritual of salat articulates for each. For Hilmi, it seems that the goal of creating modern autonomous citizens remains independent of the means she proposes (that is, Islamic rituals); indeed, various modern societies, it appears, have accomplished the same goal through other means. In Hilmi's schema, therefore, the means (ritual salat) and the end (the model liberal citizen) can be characterized without reference to each other; and a number of quite different means may be employed to achieve one and the same end. In other words, whereas rituals such as salat may, in Hilmi's view, be usefully enlisted for the project of creating a self-critical citizenry, they are not necessary but contingent acts in the process. Hence Hilmi emphasizes the citizen's ability to distinguish between essence and form – that is, between an inner meaning conceptually independent from the outward performances that express it – and the dangers of conflating the two.

In contrast, for members of the piety movement, ritual acts of worship are the sole and ineluctable means of forming pious dispositions. For women like Mona, the performance of prayer is not simply the expression of a pious self but is the means by which the pious self is created. Moreover, in this worldview, neither consummate prayer nor a pious disposition is possible without the performance of salat in the prescribed and codified manner and attitude. As such, outward bodily gestures and acts (such as salat or wearing the veil) are an indispensable aspect of the pious self in two senses: first in the sense that the self can acquire its particular form only through the performance of the precise bodily enactments; *and* second in the sense that the prescribed bodily forms are the necessary attributes of the self. The point I want to stress is that the conceptual articulation of bodily behavior in relation to oneself and others differs in these two imaginaries and, by extension, the implications for power and authority vary as well.

Politics and ethical form

In order to interrogate the political implications of these distinct economies of moral action, let me dwell for a moment on the relationship between the interiority and exteriority of the subject that informed the pedagogical model of the pietists with whom I worked. As I have described, the mosque participants did not regard authorized models of behavior as an external social imposition that constrained the individual. Rather, they viewed socially prescribed forms of conduct as the potentialities, the "scaffolding" if you will, through which the self is realized. It is precisely this self-willed obedience to religiously prescribed social conventions – what is often perceived as blind and uncritical emulation of norms – that elicits the critique that such movements only serve to reproduce the existing patriarchal order and prevent women from distinguishing their "own desires and aspirations" from those that are "socially dictated." For some scholars of gender, women of the kind I worked with are often seen as depriving themselves of the ability to enact an ethics of freedom, one founded on their capacity to distinguish their own (true) desires from (external) religious and cultural demands.

Such criticism turns upon an imaginary of freedom, one deeply indebted to liberal political theory, in which an individual is considered to be free on the condition that she act autonomously, and that her actions be the result of her own choice and free will, rather than of custom, tradition, transcendental will, or social coercion. Autonomy in this conception of freedom is a procedural principle, and not an ontological or substantive feature of the subject, in that it delimits the necessary condition for the enactment of the ethic of freedom (see Schneewind, 1998). On this view, even illiberal actions can arguably be tolerated if it is determined that they are undertaken by a freely consenting individual who "acted on her own accord." Political theorist John Christman gives the example of a person who chooses out of her own free will to be someone else's slave (1991). In keeping with the procedural account of autonomy in liberalism, Christman argues, the only way in which we can consider such a person free is if we can make a determination that the process by which she acquired her desire for slavery was indeed the result of her "own thinking and reflection," unencumbered by social and cultural influences. In other words, it is not the substance of desire but its "origin that matters in liberal judgments about autonomy" (Christman, 1991: 359).

It is in keeping with this logic that I am often told that the women of the mosque movement exemplify the liberal autonomous subject precisely because they are enacting their own desires for piety, despite the social obstacles they face, and not following the conventional roles assigned to women. Hence a true liberal, I am told, should be tolerant of this movement even if she disagrees with the movement's larger goals. In such a view, well captured in Christman's formulation of the "voluntary slave," what is assumed is not only that conventional forms of behavior can be distinguished from one's true desires, but also that such a distinction is universal. The point I would like to emphasize here is that this model of human action presupposes that there is a natural disjuncture between a person's "true" desires and those that are socially prescribed. The politics that ensues from this disjuncture aims to identify moments and places where conventional norms impede the realization of an individual's real desires, or at least obfuscate the distinction between what is truly one's own and what is socially required.

The model of self presupposed by this position dramatically contrasts with the one that conceptually and practically shaped the activities of the women I worked with. The account I have presented of the mosque movement shows that the distinction between the subject's real desires and obligatory social conventions – a distinction at the center of liberal, and at times progressive, thought – cannot be assumed, precisely because socially prescribed forms of behavior constitute the conditions for the emergence of the self as such and are integral to its realization. One of the issues such a conception of self raises is: How does one rethink the question of individual freedom in a context where the distinction between the subject's own desires and socially prescribed performances cannot be so easily presumed, and where submission to certain forms of (external) authority is a condition for the self to achieve its potentiality? What kind of politics would be deemed desirable and viable in a discursive tradition that regards conventions (socially prescribed performances) as necessary to the self's realization?

The argument I am making here should not be confused with the one made by communitarian philosophers (Sandel, 1998; Taylor, 1985a, 1985c) and their feminist interlocutors (Benhabib, 1992; Friedman, 1997; Meyers, 1989; Nedelsky, 1989; Young, 1990) who have argued that liberalism has an anemic and anomic model of the individual, one that does not take full account of the ways in which the individual is socially produced and personifies the social within herself. According to many of these thinkers, recognition of the socially embedded character of the individual would rectify the autonomizing tendency within liberalism. But what remains unproblematized by these critics is the distinction between the individual and the social: even among the communitarians and their feminist interlocutors, the interiority of the subject remains a valorized space to which one turns in order to realize one's interests and to distinguish those fears and aspirations that are one's own from those that are socially imposed.

For example, Charles Taylor, in criticizing the concept of atomism underlying various strands of liberal theory,[10] argues that the capacity for freedom requires not only "a certain understanding of self, one in which the aspirations to autonomy and self-direction become conceivable," but also requires that this self-understanding be sustained and defined "in conversation with others or through the common understanding which underlies the practices of our society" (Taylor, 1985a: 209). What is notable here is that Taylor does not discard the notion that autonomy is central to the exercise of freedom, but rather emphasizes the social conditions that are necessary for its production and flourishing. Furthermore, autonomy, for Taylor, means not simply acting as one wants (the Hobbesian requirement of negative freedom), but consists in achieving "a certain condition of self-clairvoyance and self-understanding" in order to be able to prioritize and assess conflicting desires, fears, and aspirations within oneself on one level, and, on another level, to be able to sort out what is in one's best interest from what is socially required (1985c: 229). In other words, the exercise of freedom for Taylor turns upon not only the ability to distance oneself from the social, but also, more importantly, to turn one's gaze critically to reflect upon oneself to determine the horizon of possibilities and strategies through which one acts upon the world.

Seyla Benhabib, as a critical interlocutor of communitarian critics, proposes a feminist communicative ethics that builds upon both the work of communitarian philosophers like Sandel and Taylor, and "deontological" liberal theorists such as John Rawls and Jurgen Habermas, who have argued for the priority of the right over the good (Benhabib, 1992).[11] What Benhabib finds useful in the communitarian critique is the recognition of the socially embedded quality of the individual and the need for a particular structure of the social that makes the ideal of autonomy possible and sustainable in the first place. Benhabib is right to point out, however, that this tendency is not limited to the communitarians alone but shares something critical with a conception of communicative ethics that is Habermasian and Rawlsian in origin but often assumed to be the opposite of communitarian views of the social and the individual (Benhabib, 1992: 71-76). What these contentious ethical conceptions share, Benhabib argues, is an understanding of the self that upholds moral autonomy as a necessary "right of the self to challenge religion, tradition and social dogma, but also the right of the self to distance from social roles and their content or to assume 'reflexive social distance'" (Benhabib, 1992: 73). Benhabib finds this bridge between the communitarians and the deontologists to be of critical importance in order to build a feminist conception of ethics that is predicated upon a critique of an ahistorical and atomistic notion of the self. What Benhabib's argument makes evident is that even feminist renditions of the communitarian point of view aim to establish a balance between social belonging and critical reflection wherein critical reflection is understood fundamentally as an autonomous exercise.[12]

It should be clear by now that the liberal communitarian framework is not appropriate for the analysis of conceptions of the self and its relationship to authority that were prevalent among the women of the mosque movement. Ultimately, a person for whom self-realization is a matter of excavating herself (developing, what Taylor calls, "self-clairvoyance"), or sorting out her own interests from those that are social and collective (what Benhabib calls "the right of the self to distance from social roles and their content"), looks to a different set of strategies and horizons than a subject for whom the principle ideals and tools of self-reference reside outside of herself. This is one reason I have tried to use the analytical language of ethical formation to describe the process of moral cultivation (note, the relevant term here is "cultivation" and not "inculcation"). My argument therefore has not focused on contextualizing the individual within a particular structure of the social. Rather, my aim has been to bring questions of subject formation into dialogue with an old anthropological interest in culturally specific conceptions of social authority.

What, the reader might ask, does this have to do with politics or the public sphere? By way of an answer, I would recall the powerful challenge political theorist William Connolly (1999) has recently thrown to a rationalist account of the public sphere, one that tends to assume that public culture and political engagement is primarily an exercise in the critical faculty of reason and an abstract mode of deliberation. In criticizing this assumption, Connolly argues that political judgments do not simply entail the evaluation of abstract moral principles, but issue forth from "visceral modes of appraisal" that draw their force from an intersubjective level of being and acting. The analysis I have presented here extends Connolly's insight by exploring how specific conceptions of social authority make possible the embodied capacities – what Connolly calls the "visceral register" – that underlie public life. Indeed, once we recognize that political formations presuppose not only distinct modes of reasoning, but also depend upon affective modes of assessment, then an analysis of ethical practices of self-formation takes on a new, distinctly political, relevance. My arguments in this article, in other words, suggest that we think through the problematic of politics in a way that is adequate to the variable understandings of the self and its embodied powers.

Finally, I would like to point out that this analytical approach to ethics and politics is particularly suited for the study of the kind of Islamist movement with which

I worked. This is because the form of activism practiced by the mosque participants does not mobilize an entire set of arguments that rely on what we normatively associate with the realm of politics, such as participating in the electoral process, challenging the state, making identitarian claims, or using the judicial system to create room for an expanded public religiosity. As a result, it is very easy to miss the political implications of the piety movement and to regard them, as many scholars of Islamism have done, as movements of moral reform that seek to bring about change in social mores but have little to reveal about the political landscape of contemporary Muslim societies. I hope that my arguments in this essay have addressed both the misguided set of assumptions that theoretically secure such a reading and the descriptive evidence that should lead us to revise it.

Notes

1   For an analysis of the changes instituted within the public sphere by the piety movement in Egypt, see Hirschkind (2001), Salvatore (1998).

2   This aspect of the movement is characteristic of a key development in modern Islam wherein the proliferation of Islamic knowledge and sources in the last century has been geared toward the concerns of ordinary men and women rather than religious scholars. See Eickelman and Anderson (1997); Messick (1996); Schulze (1987); Starrett (1995).

3   For a fuller discussion of this tension between the state and women's mosque groups, see Mahmood (2004).

4   See, for example, the views of Said Ashmawi, a well-known Egyptian intellectual who is known for his "secular" interpretations of a range of Islamic issues. Ashmawi (1994a, 1994b).

5   Kant is explicit in his objection to morality that is a result of habituated virtues, acquired through the long process of character formation: "When the firm resolve to comply with one's duty has become a habit, it is called *virtue* also in a legal sense, in its *empirical character* (*virtues phaenomenon*). Virtue here has the abiding maxim of *lawful* actions.... Virtue, in this sense, is accordingly acquired little by little, and to some it means a long habituation (in the observance of law), in virtue of which a human being, through gradual reformation of conduct and consolidation of his maxims, passes from a propensity to vice to its opposite. But not the slightest *change of heart* is necessary for this; only a change of *mores.* . . . *However*, that a human being should become not merely *legally* good, but *morally* good (pleasing to God) i.e., virtuous according to the intelligible character [of virtue] (*virtus noumenon*) and thus in need of no other incentive to recognize a duty except the representation of duty itself – that, so long as the foundation of the maxims of the human being remains impure, cannot be effected through gradual *reform* but must rather be effected through a *revolution* in the disposition of human being. . . . And so a new man can come about only through a kind of rebirth, as it were a new creation ... and a change of heart" (Kant, 1998: 68).

6   This does not mean that for Kant morality was purely an individual matter guided by personal preference; rather an act was moral only insofar as it was made in accord with a universally valid form of rationality. As Charles Taylor points out, Kant's moral imperative combines two features: everyone is obligated to act in

accord with reason, and "it is an essential feature of reason that it be valid for everyone, for all rational creatures alike. That is the basis of the first form of Kant's categorical imperative: that I should act only according to a maxim which I could at the same time will as a universal law. For if I am right to will something, then everyone is right to will it, and it must thus be something that could be willed for everybody" (Taylor, 1985b: 323).

7   When Bourdieu considers the variety of practices that characterize a particular social group (such as the style of eating, socializing, and entertainment), he is primarily concerned with how these practices embody and symbolize the *doxa* and ethos of the social class or cultural group to which these practices belong. See, for example, Bourdieu (1977, 1984). One may argue, however, that the significance of an embodied practice is not exhausted by its ability to function as an index of social status or class. The specificity of a bodily practice is also interesting for the kind of relationship it presupposes to the act it constitutes, wherein the conceptual understanding of the act itself would change were we to analyze the bodily form it takes. For an extended discussion of what is at stake in this difference of analytical focus, see chapter 4 of my forthcoming book (2004).

8   In this respect my argument differs from that of James Faubion, who has also argued for the productive application of Foucault's work on ethics to anthropology. Faubion suggests that Foucault's elaboration of ethics can be usefully mapped onto culturally specific notions of the self – such as the Haagen and Greek conceptions of personhood (2001: 90). In contrast, I am suggesting that there is no single conception of the self that corresponds to the discursive practices of a given culture, but that many different conceptions may exist simultaneously and perhaps in tension with one another, depending upon the particular regime of truth to which they accede.

9   For an excellent discussion of this understanding of ritual behavior, one that has informed my own analysis of practices of the piety movement, see Asad (1993).

10   Taylor describes atomism as "a vision of society as in some sense constituted by individuals for the fulfillment of ends which [are] primarily individual" – a notion that underlies social contract theory in particular, but also informs other strands of liberalism (1985a: 187).

11   This is in contrast to communitarian theorists like Taylor and Sandel, who have linked their critique of the impoverished notion of the unencumbered self in liberalism to the primacy placed on the conception of individual rights over a shared vision of the collective good of a given society.

12   That communitarian views embody this tension between the social and the individual is not entirely surprising given their Romantic legacy. As Charles Larmore points out, a range of Romantics – from Burke to Herder to Rousseau – seem to have embraced, to varying degrees, the notion of a private interiorized subjectivity, which, even though they recognized it was a product of the larger community, nonetheless, had to be distinct from the community in order to be "true to itself" (Larmore, 1996: 66–85).

References

Aristotle. *The Basic Works of Aristotle*. Ed. Richard McKeon. New York: Random House, 1941.

Asad, Talal. *Genealogies of Religion: Discipline and Reasons of Power in Christianity and Islam.* Baltimore: Johns Hopkins Press, 1993.

Ashmawi, Said Muhammed. "Al-hijab laisa farida" ("The Veil Is Not Obligatory").
    Ruz al-Yusuf, 13 June 1994a: 22–25.

———— . "Fatwa al-hijab ghair shara'iyya" ("The Fatwa on the Veil is Illegitimate").
    Ruz al-Yusuf, 8 August 1994b: 28–31.

Benhabib, Seyla. *Situating the Self: Gender, Community and Postmodernism in Contemporary
    Ethics*. New York: Routledge, 1992.

Bourdieu, Pierre. *Outline of a Theory of Practice*. Cambridge: Cambridge University Press,
    1977.

———— . *Distinction: A Social Critique of the Judgment of Taste*. Cambridge: Harvard University
    Press, 1984.

Burchell, David. "The Attributes of Citizens: Virtue, Manners and the Activity of
    Citizenship." *Economy and Society* 24:4 (1995): 540–558.

Calhoun, Craig. *Habermas and the Public Sphere*. Cambridge: MIT Press, 1992.

Christman, John. "Liberalism and Individual Positive Freedom." *Ethics* 101 (1991): 343–359.

Colebrook, Claire. "Ethics, Positivity, and Gender: Foucault, Aristotle, and the Care of
    the Self." *Philosophy Today* 42:1/4 (1998): 40–52.

Connolly, William. *Why I am not a Secularist*. Minneapolis: University of Minnesota Press,
    1999.

Davidson, Arnold. "Ethics as Ascetics: Foucault, the History of Ethics, and Ancient
    Thought." In *Foucault and the Writing of History*. Ed. J. Goldstein. Cambridge:
    Blackwell, 1994.

Eickelman, Dale, and Jon Anderson. "Print, Islam, and the Prospects for Civic Pluralism:
    New Religious Writings and Their Audiences." *Journal of Islamic Studies* 8:1 (1997):
    43–62.

Faubion, James. "Toward an Anthropology of Ethics: Foucault and the Pedagogies of
    Autopoiesis." *Representations* 74 (2001): 83–105.

Foucault, Michel. *Michel Foucault: Ethics, Subjectivity, and Truth*. Ed. Paul Rabinow. New
    York: The New Press, 1997.

Friedman, Marilyn. "Autonomy and Social Relationships: Rethinking the Feminist
    Critique." *Feminists Rethink the Self*. Ed. D. T. Meyers. Boulder: Westview Press,
    1997.

Hadot, Pierre. *What is Ancient Philosophy?* Cambridge: Harvard University Press, 2002.

Hilmi, Mona. "Abdat al-shaitan wa 'abdat al-siramik" ("Worship of the Devil and Worship
    of Ceramic"). *Ruz al-Yusuf* 3583:2 (1997): 80–81.

Hirschkind, Charles. "Civic Virtue and Religious Reason: An Islamic Counter-Public."
    Cultural Anthropology 16:1 (2001): 3–34.

Ibn Khaldun. *The Muqaddimah*. Trans. F. Rosenthal. New York: Pantheon Books, 1958.

Kant, Immanuel. *Religion within the Boundaries of Mere Reason and Other Writings*. Eds.
    A. Wood and G. di Giovanni. Cambridge: Cambridge University Press, 1998.

Lapidus, Ira. "Knowledge, Virtue and Action: The Classical Muslim Conception of Adab
    and the Nature of Religious Fulfillment in Islam." *Moral Conduct and Authority*. Ed.
    B. D. Metcalf. Berkeley: University of California Press, 1984.

Larmore, Charles. *The Romantic Legacy*. New York: Columbia University Press, 1996.

Mahmood, Saba. "Feminist Theory, Embodiment, and the Docile Agent: Some Reflections
    on the Egyptian Islamic Revival." *Cultural Anthropology* 6:2 (2001): 202–236.

———— . *Pious Formations: The Islamic Revival and the Subject of Feminism*. Princeton University
    Press, 2004.

Martin, Luther, Huck Gutman, and Patrick Hutton, eds. *Technologies of the Self: A Seminar
    of Michel Foucault*. Amherst: University of Massachusetts Press, 1988.

Messick, Brinkley. "Media Muftis: Radio Fatwas in Yemen." *Islamic Legal Interpretation: Muftis and their Fatwas*. Eds. M. K. Masud, B. Messick, and D. Powers. Cambridge: Harvard University Press, 1996.

Meyers, Diana. *Self, Society, and Personal Choice*. New York: Columbia University Press, 1989.

Minson, Jeffrey. *Questions of Conduct*. New York: St. Martin's Press, 1993.

Nedelsky, Jennifer. "Reconceiving Autonomy: Sources, Thoughts and Possibilities." *Yale Journal of Law and Feminism* 1:1 (1989): 7–36.

Salvatore, Armando. "Staging Virtue: The Disembodiment of Self-Correctness and the Making of Islam as Public Norm." *Islam, Motor or Challenge of Modernity*. Vol. 1. *Bielfield Yearbook of the Sociology of Islam*. Ed. G. Stauth. Hamburg: Lit Verlag, 1998.

Sandel, Michael. *Liberalism and the Limits of Justice*. Cambridge: Cambridge University Press, 1998.

Schneewind, John. *The Invention of Autonomy: A History of Modern Moral Philosophy*. Cambridge: Cambridge University Press, 1998.

Schulze, Reinhard. "Mass Culture and Islamic Cultural Production in 19th Century Middle East." *Mass Culture, Popular Culture, and Social Life in the Middle East*. Eds. G. Stauth and S. Zubaida. Boulder: Westview Press, 1987.

Starrett, Gregory. "The Political Economy of Religious Commodities in Cairo." *American Anthropologist* 97:1 (1995): 51–68.

Taylor, Charles. "Atomism." *Philosophy and the Human Sciences: Philosophical Papers (2)*. Cambridge: Cambridge University Press, 1985a.

——— . "Kant's Theory of Freedom." *Philosophy and the Human Sciences: Philosophical Papers (2)*. Cambridge: Cambridge University Press, 1985b.

——— . "What's Wrong with Negative Liberty." *Philosophy and the Human Sciences: Philosophical Papers (2)*. Cambridge: Cambridge University Press, 1985c.

Warner, Michael. *The Letters of the Republic: Publication and the Public Sermon in Eighteenth-Century America*. Cambridge: Harvard University Press, 1990.

Young, Iris. *Justice and the Politics of Difference*. Princeton: Princeton University Press, 1990.

York, Steve. *Remaking the World*. Alexandria, Va.: PBS Video, 1992.

Jenny B. White

THE END OF ISLAMISM? TURKEY'S MUSLIMHOOD MODEL

THE RADICAL PERIOD is over, predicted Akıf Beki, Ankara correspondent for the Islamist television station Kanal 7.[1] Islamism has become "religion," relegated to the civil realm, found only in religious communities, no longer in the state. "There has been a civil-ization. Islamism has become Muslimhood." This diagnosis was echoed by Mehmet Aydın, noted Islamic scholar and minister in the new Justice and Development Party (AKP) government. The formerly Islamist AKP won national elections on November 3, 2002, with enough votes to form a government.[2] The party, Aydın insisted, no longer accepts the label "moderate Islamist." Rather, party members consider themselves to be "moderate Muslims" whose religious ethics inspire their public service as individuals but cannot be construed as part of their identities as political actors in the public sphere. "AKP is a political movement and the movement's actors have a very warm, close relationship, primarily as individuals, to … religious experience…. At the moment, I believe that all the ministers are fasting…. We are religious people, but our actions in the public sphere … do not have a religious side or theological meaning. Where is there a religious side? There's a link in our values. Just because I've become a politician, I'm not about to leave the values I believe in by the wayside." As parallels, he noted President George W. Bush's personal religiosity and championing of "faith-based programs," as well as the close relationship between church and state in some European countries. He pointed out that the noted Islamist scholar Ali Bulaç had distanced himself entirely from Islamism, saying that it was a period that was now over, as people lived their beliefs within a pluralist framework.

Has Islam become individual, personal practice distinct from the public and political realms, as these voices claim, despite the presence of Islam-inspired devout Muslims in those realms? If so, how does this compare to the vision of the followers of Mustafa Kemal Atatürk, founder of the Turkish Republic, of a pristinely secular, modern public and political realm, with religion relegated to the private sphere?

In Turkey, a series of secularist governments, backed by a fiercely Kemalist military, have implemented this model by setting legal curbs on religious expression in public. Religious insignia of all kinds, whether turban or Roman collar, are forbidden on the streets; women's head coverings, while tolerated on the street, are banned in government offices, the civil service, and many university classrooms, and more subtly discouraged in other workplaces and arenas. The state has replaced the *ulema* with a Ministry of Religious Affairs that trains and oversees all religious specialists, vets sermons, supervises mosques and religious schools, and issues advice about how to be a good Muslim that the state feels is compatible with a rational, scientific, secular society. The new AKP government challenges this by agreeing that religion is personal but arguing that, as such, it can be incorporated into the public and political spheres without compromising the secular state system. Kemalists, however, would likely conclude that the secular nature of the state is not safe in the hands of individuals in whose lives religion plays such an important role that they feel the need to fast and pray while doing their public duty (for instance, in the prime ministry).

Thus, the issue that has emerged as a major area of dispute under the new government is the boundaries of the private and the public, the personal, the civil, and the political. The Kemalist model seems to imply that a modern, secular democratic system requires not just certain practices in the public arena, but also a certain kind of person. When a secular person enters the political realm, she becomes secularist; when an Islamic believer enters the political realm, she becomes, by definition, Islamist. The Muslimhood model challenges this by asserting that believing Muslims can be secular politicians, that their qualities of personhood not only do not disqualify them from running the secular governmental machinery, but may even benefit the political realm by inserting personal ethics and a moral stance. On November 3, 2002, Turkey's voters seemed to agree when they elected the Islam-inspired AKP to head the government and threw out the corrupt and ineffectual centrist parties.

What is the evidence for the death of Islamism in Turkey and the rise of a personalized Muslimhood? Can this work as a political formula? If so, can this serve as a more general model for Islamic (or "Muslim") governance, or does it reflect characteristics and circumstances unique to Turkey? Are there alternative trends and actors that might contradict or undercut the personalization and privatization of Islam and the Muslimization of politics and the public sphere?

The personalization of Islam

Günter Seufert has suggested that Islam in Turkey has become increasingly detached from personal identity and become a means of expression.[3] He linked this to the development since the 1980s of a consumer society in which identity can be demonstrated through purchased goods, and items are advertised by playing on identities. This implies a change in political focus as well. He argued that, whereas in the past, Turks might have asked, "What does an Islamic identity say about national identity?" now they are asking, "What does the nation mean for a Muslim?" "How does democracy fit with Islam?" has become "What does Islam mean for democracy?"

While the Kemalist state has long laid claim to the right to define Islam through its Ministry of Religious Affairs, the new AKP government is challenging this definition, and the market and media are wresting control over defining a "Muslim" away from the state and, perhaps, even away from Islamic groups and movements. Navaro-Yashin (2002) describes the fashion industry that has grown up around a form of veiling, *tesettür*, that has been associated with political Islam. At a *tesettür* fashion show, a woman watching the veiled models striding down the runway told Navaro-Yashin that she welcomed the elaboration of an explicitly middle class form of veiling. She had recently begun to veil, she revealed, and the sales staff in her usual shops no longer recognized her, treating her as if she couldn't afford to shop there. If she wore couture *tesettür*, she reasoned, that wouldn't happen (Navaro-Yashin 2002). The 1990s saw the spread of Islamist gated communities and department stores. During Ramazan in November 2002, the special holiday pages in major newspapers gave advice on such topics as whether or not sushi and lobster were permitted foods and how to take care of the skin while fasting. Subjects generally were approached from a pluralist angle, pointing out different Islamic interpretations and variations by region and country. Scientific explanations were amended to religious ones; for instance, explaining that research by veterinarians had revealed substances harmful to human beings in the flesh of animals like pigs, dogs, and lions. This was true as well for newspapers, like *Zaman*, associated with the Islamic movement. At the mammoth annual Fatih Book Fair, held in the courtyard of the Sultan Ahmet Mosque, people crowded the stands. The book fair is self-consciously Islamic and the patrons dress the part. The book displays, however, sometimes present surprising contrasts, with translations of Dostoyevski, Gogol, Turgenev, and Jack London next to *The Big Islamic Catechism*, and Steinbeck and George Orwell sharing a shelf with *Islam's Smiling Face* and *Army and Commander in Islam*. One stand advertised a sale on Malcolm X, another a computer program for learning prayers in Arabic, a problem for most Turks, who do not understand Arabic. Shoppers, however, often reached over more esoteric offerings and picked up books like *Test Your Child's IQ* and slim, colorful volumes for children about Islam and prayer, including talking books that made the sounds of the Arabic alphabet.

Recently, the Mevlevi, or whirling dervishes, have begun appearing in popular music and video clips and on entertainment shows on television. This is a radical departure from their previous public performances in which the public was told not to clap, since this was a religious ceremony, not a form of entertainment. On a late-night program on Show TV in November 2002, the female host exchanged light banter with a sexy, blonde Turkish singer, both in low-cut evening gowns, then introduced a small group of young men dressed as (and presented as) dervishes, along with a musician who played Sufi music to accompany them while they whirled for the cameras. One of the dervishes was a young boy of seven, the son of the musician. (Classic Mevlana performances also often included at least one young apprentice dervish.) When the whirling ended, the hostess asked the boy to announce, "Stay tuned. After the commercials, we'll be right back." This was still unusual enough to merit a lightly shocked article on the entertainment page of *Sabah* newspaper, where the journalist Yüksel Aytuğ criticized the show's host for asking the young dervish, "How long have you been turning?" Spinning-tops "turn," he admonished, but dervishes "whirl" and they do so in a ceremony with deep religious and philosophical meaning. They are not dancers or entertainers (November 24, 2002, 30).

Despite unease with the desacralization of religious practices, it appears to be becoming more common. An article in the newspaper *Milliyet* featured a musician that taught children Sufi whirling as a game and planned to put together a show around Sufi whirling and music by a South African singer (November 14, 2002). A more Islamically oriented newspaper advised women to finger prayer beads to reduce stress (*Zaman*, October 28, 2002). Another newspaper showed an actress wearing a *muska*, or amulet, as a fashion accessory over a tight bathing suit. Cultural and musical syncretism is not new in Turkey, but the incorporation of religious practices into such risqué formats would have been thought highly inappropriate until recently and unleashed a negative reaction. As Seufert pointed out, however, over the last four or five years, objects and practices associated with an Islamic identity have come to be dislodged from their religious moorings and become available, primarily via the marketplace and media, to those whose primary identity is not Islamic, but who are interested in demonstrating that they are Muslim. Muslimhood, in other words, has become fashionable.

The death of Islamism

What has become of the much-discussed Islamism of the 1980s and 1990s? According to Akıf Beki, it is a failed project, a trend that has played itself out. Until the 1970s, he explained, Islam was understood as orthodox religious tradition, not as an ideology, or something that belonged in the political or civic realms. During that decade, influences from India and Egypt made themselves felt with the translation of Mawdudi, Hasan al-Banna and Sayyid Qutb. This brought with it a sense of alienation from and reaction against the West. Their ideas gained a following and began a radical trend that advocated a political project, control over the state so as to set up an Islamic government. By the 1990s, however, this state-centric approach had shown itself to be a dead end in Turkey. It proved impossible to gain control of the state except by political struggle, and radicals were not prepared to wage an armed fight. The final failure was on February 28, 1997, when the National Security Council, the liaison institution between the military and the government, pushed the Islamist prime minister, Necmettin Erbakan (Welfare Party) out of power in what has come to be known as a "soft coup." Erbakan himself, Beki went on, had irritated many in the Muslim community with his confrontational politics, and they were glad to see him go. Islamist ideas, along with the anti-Western "complex," began to be reevaluated and rejected. Another factor was the increasing cultural interaction between Islamist and non-Islamist intellectual circles that led Islamists to be influenced by multicultural approaches. In the 1990s, Beki argued, Islam as ideology was replaced by Islam as religion, centered on the Qur'an.

One of the main arenas for the interaction of Islamists and non-Islamists have been the annual Abant meetings, sponsored by the followers of Fethullah Gülen, an Islamic movement centered on education. These meetings brought together Islamist and secularist intellectuals and politicians from across the ideological spectrum, as well as representatives of Turkey's other major Islamic sect, the Alevi. Since 1998, they have gathered for several days each year in the picturesque mountain town of Abant, halfway between Ankara and Istanbul, to hash out positions on topics like the relation of Islam to laicism (1998), religion and society (1999), state and law (2000), pluralism and social reconciliation (2001), and globalization in light of the "spirit of

Abant" (2002). A book of proceedings is published after every meeting and a joint position statement is issued. The platform expresses support for democracy, human rights, and individual freedoms, arguing that these are entirely in accord with Islamic principles. There is no contradiction between religion and rationality: divine inspiration can better be understood in the light shed by the rational accumulation of knowledge. "Religious identity is individual" (*Abant Platformu* 2000, 316–17). It is communal insofar as religion is a component of a person's culture and a source of common values. Mehmet Aydın, one of the organizers, defined the "Abant spirit" as respect for different bodies of knowledge and ideas in Turkey and an attempt to see them represented; respect for the "honor" of knowledge and ideas, even if different, and a willingness to let the discussion go wherever it leads; an open mind and heart, being democratic and courageous; giving importance to the logic of the dialogue; and attempting, at the end of the discussions, to capture a shared common denominator that may not represent everyone's views in their entirety, but enough to recognize their contribution. The Abant meetings are designed to make of this "spirit" of reconciliation a "usable" model (2002, 101–2).

Muslim actors: groups

Participants in the Abant meetings comprise organized religious sects or groups as well as individual thinkers who may or may not be associated with particular strains of thought about Islam and its place in the public sphere. Some prominent secularist thinkers also participate. First I will discuss two Muslim groups, the Fethullahcılar and the Alevi, quite different, but well represented in Turkish society and the public sphere and both arguably representative of moderate streams in Turkish Islam. The sponsors of the Abant meetings, the Fethullahcılar, are followers of the retired preacher Fethullah Gülen. Gülen's movement consists of a network of nominally independent organizations in Turkey's major cities united around Gülen's teachings and supporting a publishing and media empire and educational initiative. Gülen's movement is an offshoot of the Nurcu movement, based on the writings of Said Nursi (1877–1960) that argue that there is no contradiction between religion and science. The Nurcu spread in Turkey in the 1950s and held a particular appeal for those educated in the secular school system. Gülen's followers include many teachers, students, businessmen, and educated professionals.

Gülen seeks to "Islamize Turkish nationalism; recreate a legitimate link between state and religion; emphasize democracy and tolerance; and encourage links with Turkish republics" (Aras 1998, 29). He believes that Turks share with Central Asian Turks a knowledge-based, nonpolitical form of Islamic interpretation, influenced by Sufi tradition. He differentiates this "Turkish-Muslim identity" from Arab Islam, arguing that Turkish Muslims are more tolerant and open to dialogue with all parts of society, including other religions and sects. He promotes the seeking of knowledge as a religious value and integration with the Western world, even if that means incorporating Western technology, clothing, and, to some extent, lifestyle. In his writings, he emphasizes that religion is a private matter and its requirements should not be imposed on anyone. Instead, the Fethullahcılar spread their message by sponsoring schools, dormitories, summer camps, and reading circles. Gülen-financed schools can be found in Turkey and abroad, primarily in Central Asia and the Balkans. The Fethullahcılar put on conferences to which they often invite internationally known scholars to discuss themes like Islam, democracy and civil society. They own a popular television station (STV) and a newspaper (*Zaman*) and publish large numbers of books and periodicals.

In the 1980s, the Turkish military and government encouraged a model of nationalist religion, which came to be known as the Turkish-Islamic synthesis, in a bid to counter the appeal of leftist ideologies. Gülen's brand of Turkish Islam, with its emphasis on Islamic education and belief in the compatibility of religious ethics and modern state institutions, seemed ideal and initially was supported. Major politicians accepted invitations to dine and speak with Gülen. However, as Islamist politics grew in popularity through the 1990s, especially at the ballot box, Gülen and his followers were accused of dissembling and, in reality, wishing to turn Turkey into an Islamic state. For the past several years, the frail leader has lived in the United States, where he initially came for medical treatment, unable to return to Turkey under threat of arrest. His movement, however, retains its momentum. It is too early to say whether the AKP government will allow him to return, since the military, the courts, and, to some extent, the police, have acted relatively independently of the government in the past. However, the prime minister in 2002, Abdullah Gül, and other members of his government have attended Abant meetings in the past, and Minister Mehmet Aydın was one of the organizers.

The Alevi are a non-Sunni syncretistic Muslim minority estimated to make up between 20 and 25 percent of the Turkish population. For centuries, they have been marginalized and sometimes persecuted by the Sunni majority for their beliefs, which some consider heretical. They do not subscribe to the Sunni requirements regarding prayer and fasting, and their ceremonies, at which music plays a prominent role, are not gender segregated. Although traditionally socially liberal and politically to the left of center, the Alevi are often overlooked in discussions of moderate Islam in Turkey. This may be due to their association with leftist activities in the turbulent 1960s and 1970s. In the 1980s, however, the Alevis, much like the Fethullahcılar, were perceived to be allies of the state in countering the perceived new threat of Islamism. They were granted permission to reopen their lodges, closed along with other Islamic institutions after the founding of the Republic, and to practice and hold their *cem* ceremonies openly. This has led to what some have called an Alevi revival or repoliticization, including the founding of numerous Alevi associations and foundations and local and national radio stations. In 1989, they issued an "Alevi Manifesto" in which they demanded unconditional acceptance of their religious community and their specific culture by the public and the state, and an end to all discrimination.

That discrimination at times has been severe. The Ministry of Religious Affairs is Sunni-dominated and disproportionately supports Sunni education and activities. As recently as 1995, several people in a café in an Alevi neighborhood were killed in a drive-by shooting, probably by right-wing nationalists. When community residents marched on the police station to protest their inactivity, the police, many of whom are sympathetic to the nationalists, retaliated, killing several residents. The ensuing riots left at least a dozen people dead and over a hundred wounded. That same year, outsiders broke into several university campuses and beat up students eating lunch during Ramazan, the month of fasting. When students protested police inactivity, they were beaten. When a guest on a television entertainment show made a joke that the Alevi have no morals and have group sex during their ceremonies, Alevis tried to set the television station on fire. A former high official at the Ministry of Religious Affairs, himself an Alevi, went on television to calm the situation and reassure the Alevi that they were integrated into Turkish society.

Since the end of the 1980s, however, the Alevis, under the leadership of an educated and politically active Alevi elite, organized in powerful associations, have become a force in Turkish politics and society. The explosion of interest in Alevis by the Turkish media, scholars, and politicians in Turkey and abroad raised Alevi visibility in the public sphere. Participation in Alevi activities increased, particularly in the cities. People were more willing to present themselves as Alevi (Erdemir 2002, 2). These events led to ongoing discussions about what exactly Alevi religion and culture are, particularly among younger, urban, educated Alevis who have lost touch with the inward-looking tribal traditions of traditional religious leaders, the *dedes* (Vorhoff 1997, 56).

Like the Sunni Islamist movement, Alevi presence in the public sphere has taken the form of mass demonstrations, civic organizations, and media publications – books, periodicals, and newspapers. Some of these publications have changed their content to cater to the move in reader interest from socialist politics to cultural commentary about Alevi rituals, music, and personalities (Vorhoff 1997, 57). This has fed a crisis in authority within the Alevi community. The analytical dissection and publicization of Alevi identity and the creation of Alevi civic institutions over the last decade has created a public body of knowledge about Alevi identity that is often at odds with the more esoteric knowledge of the *dedes* and threatens their authority, based on their membership in holy lineages (Massicard 2001). The new public represents what one might call a different market, representing many different interests, including a desire for religious consumption. Unlike the more intimate ceremonies of the past, the new urban *cems*, held in great, modern halls, may involve hundreds of people, many strangers to one another. Although they provide a welcome opportunity to establish networks that cross village, lineage, and regional ties, some participants are disturbed by their "folkloric" aspect, viewing urban *cem* ceremonies as nothing more than public performances that have lost the authenticity of traditional ceremonies (Erdemir 2002, 9).

Thus, the new Alevi presence in the public sphere is characterized by internal generational, rural/urban, and ethnic divisions, but also by the desacralization of religious ceremonies as Alevi Muslimhood becomes a fashionable identity. What this identity entails will likely be the result of competition in the marketplace of religious consumption, rather than of tradition or politics. Erman and Göker remain skeptical about whether "the recognition of Alevi difference(s) will aid the creation of a more pluralistic political system" (2000, 115). Like Sunni Islamists, Alevis are now riven by social class divisions that may make it impossible to develop an identity politics founded on cultural and religious aspects that address all the needs and interests of a diverse following.

The Justice and Development Party (AKP) seems, at first glance, the most successful manifestation of Islam in the public and political realm. The party is the latest in a series of overtly Islam-inspired parties since the 1960s, each, in turn, closed down by the state (in the 1980s and 1990s, these were the Welfare and Virtue Parties).

With each new party, the platform changed and constituency broadened until, by the 2002 election, the AK Party was supported by a spectrum that included peasants and urbanites, poor and wealthy, as well as intellectuals. Its success at the polls was due, in part, to an intensive, personalized method of mobilizing and to an ability to translate its platform of social justice into a local cultural language of neighborliness and mutual obligation (White 2002). Islam as an ideology played a relatively restrained supporting role in Virtue Party mobilization, quite different from the strident Islamism of its predecessor, Erbakan's Welfare Party.

This evolution toward moderate, nonconfrontational Islamic participation was the harbinger of a further receding of Islam into a cultural, ethical stance under the AKP. What caused this moderation and movement from a strident Islam oriented toward changing the state to a model of Muslims doing politics within the state? The chastening effect of continual closings played a role, as did the ability of banned parties to reconstitute themselves to compete again. The decline of other political parties opened the field to competition by a younger generation of politicians. The AK Party is led by the charismatic Recep Tayyip Erdoğan, a former soccer player, businessman, and mayor of Istanbul, who replaced the patronage-based politics of Necmettin Erbakan, leader of the previous Islamist parties, with a more participatory, populist grassroots political style. Market and media created crosscurrents of ideas and practices, uprooting previous meanings.

In the remainder of this essay, I will focus on the special circumstances of Turkish Islamic thinkers that led to a rejection of Arab reformist Islam in favor of what they consider to be a Turkish brand of Islamic philosophy that influences the present government. The movement toward a Turkish Islamic philosophy in some ways parallels the personalization and privatization of Islam and desacralization of Islamic practices discussed above, allowing a fractured new public to position themselves in a variety of ways within an Islamic idiom. In other words, the Muslimhood model does not create a unitary body of thought, goals, or practices, but projects a pluralist vision of an Islamic public sphere that reflects more closely the diverse nature of Islam in Turkey, but also contains within it contradictions that may sow the seed of dissent.

Muslim thinkers: the reformists

The annual meetings of intellectuals at Abant and a number of AKP, Alevi, and Gülen sponsored publications, meetings, and educational events have reinforced the Abant model that promotes compatibility with and, indeed, the necessity of pluralism, democracy, and individual rights in a Muslim society. A group of prominent reformist intellectuals, based at Ankara University's School of Theology, has developed a stream of Islamic thought that seeks to develop a new form of interiority of Islamic belief in Turkey – religion as human nature or an internal state, not society's religion or tradition.

This puts them in an ambiguous relationship with some orthodox and overtly political forms of Islamism, but very much in line with the Abant model and the trends of personalization of Islam and Muslimization of the public and political spheres discussed above. In other words, reformist intellectual currents and the effects of market and media seem similarly aligned in encouraging a movement toward personalization of Islam, or Muslimhood, and away from a politicized Islamism.

Some of the main figures among the Reformists (Yenilikçiler), as they call themselves, are Mehmet Aydın, Mehmed Said Hatiboğlu, M. Hayrı Kırbaşoğlu, Ömer Özsoy, Salih Akdemir, Yaşar Nuri Öztürk, and Hidayet Şefkatlı Tuksal, one of the few women prominent in the movement. Mehmet Aydın was born in Elazig in 1943. He graduated from Ankara University's School of Theology in 1966 and the following year, with support from the Turkish Ministry of Education, went to Edinburgh University in England for a doctorate in philosophy. When he returned in 1972, he began teaching in the School of Islamic Sciences at Ankara University and also taught philosophy at Middle East Technical University. In 1984, he moved to Dokuz Eylül University, where he was dean from 1993 to 1999. In fall of 2002, he became a minister in the new AKP government. He is considered to be a modernist and has published ten books on Islam and philosophy, including *Turkish Contribution to Philosophy* (in English, 1985), and *Why?* (in Turkish, 2002), which consists of reflections on September 11. In this collection of his newspaper columns, he suggests that rather than a clash of civilizations, the attacks of September 11 and Muslim responses to it are symptoms of the Muslim world's inability to get its own house in order, understand the West, and explain Islam to the West. This is exacerbated by the Muslim world's lack of understanding of Western languages and, thus, of the West's sociology, social psychology, politics, ideology, and strategic vision. The same, he continues, can be said of the West with regard to the Muslim world.

Many of the Reformists are professors at Ankara University's School of Theology, known as a hotbed of modernism, and most have published extensively. Ömer Özsoy is considered by some to be an Islamic feminist. M. Hayri Kirbaşoğlu, born in Manisa in 1954, specializes in the study and exegesis of *hadith*, the sayings of the Prophet Muhammed as handed down by chains of more or less reliable sources. His "scientific" evaluations of several popular collections of *hadith* have led him to doubt their veracity.

Salih Akdemir represents the less orthodox stream of the Reformists. He does not believe that Islam requires women to cover their heads; he supports gender-mixed student housing and the controversial Muslim practice of temporary marriage. Unlike some of his colleagues, he reportedly does not live an orthodox Islamic lifestyle. He practices an individualistic approach to Islam and argues that Islam is "human nature," not tradition. He is inspired by Jung's notion of collective conscience and he believes that, in this regard, all religions are the same. "Allah is inside all of us....You use a computer, don't you? ... Allah put inside the angels a diskette; they say whatever is on the diskette; but inside Adam he put a copy of his own hard drive. This potential, this humanity created by Allah, can develop into something like Nietzsche's superior man. The last human being will carry all the godly characteristics.... But with ... our two-faced leaders in Turkey, in America, in Europe, this humanity isn't going anywhere. It's really all slavery. They lift the chains a bit and give them a bit of bread and their eyes widen." The requirements of the Qur'an, he argues, cannot simply be brought into the present. One has to make changes, adapt it to new situations, bring new solutions to bear. He reinterprets Islamic texts by means of semantic analyses. One of his new projects is called the "Transcendental Unity of Semitic Religions."[4] Although *shari'ah* law has been a basic Islamist goal, the Reformers focus on the Qur'an, rather than on the more questionable "Arab" interpretations. Their own analyses draw on eclectic methods and sources. Among Islamist activists, there is no consensus over the meaning of *shari'ah,* with some using it simply as a metaphor for a just society with no change in laws required, while others focus on the legality of marrying four wives.

Another heterodox scholar is Yaşar Nuri Öztürk, born in Bayburt in 1945. He has degrees in law, theology, and Islamic philosophy and, after practicing law for a time, joined the faculty of Marmara University. In 1993, he was appointed dean of the School of Theology at Istanbul University. He is the author of nineteen books and, through his newspaper columns and television appearances, has a broader presence in the public arena than most other Reformists. In the 2002 elections, he was a candidate not for the AK Party, but for the left-of-center and traditionally secularist Republican Peoples' Party (RPP); he is now a member of parliament. His ideas are especially popular with elite secularists. That and his reputation as a gadfly has somewhat tarnished his repute as an Islamic scholar.

Two other names deserve mention here, those of Ismet Özel and Ali Bulaç, representing what some have called Left Islam. (See Meeker 1991 for analyses of their writings and a list of publications.) Their publications and public appearances have been influential among believers and secularists alike. Ismet Özel is a well-known poet and columnist in several radical Islamist newspapers. He teaches French and comparative literature at Bilgi University, an institution known for the left or liberal orientation of its faculty. He was born in 1944 in Kayseri, in central Anatolia, the sixth child of a police official. He studied political science at Ankara University and French literature and language at Hacettepe University. In the 1960s he was well known as a leftist, but by the 1980s had begun to look to Islam instead for solutions. In his first book, *Three Problems: Technique, Civilization, Alienation* (in Turkish), he argues that the central problem for contemporary Muslims is not whether and how "Western science and technology can be integrated with Islamic belief and practice," but rather "the reconstitution of an Islamic way of life, an objective that begins with the individual reconstituting his personal thought and practice" (Meeker 1991, 211). His writings rely heavily on Western philosophers and thinkers. One young theology student admitted to me that he finds Özel's writings "impenetrable."

Ali Bulaç was born in 1951 in Mardin. He spent seven years in a *madrasa* receiving an Islamic education and later studied sociology at Istanbul University. He knows Arabic and is familiar with classical Islamic writers. His first book, *Concepts and Orders of Our Times* (in Turkish), in the late 1970s became what Meeker calls a "kind of manifesto for Muslim intellectuals" (1991, 197–98) and has sold over forty thousand copies. In the book, Bulaç analyzes capitalism, scientific socialism, and fascism as attempts to come to grips with class conflict. At the end of the book, he suggests that Islam provides a means to cope with contemporary conditions by forming the basis of an alternative "moral social order in which property rights are recognized but the rich become the willing guardians of the poor" (Meeker 1991, 200). Bulaç argues that it is not necessary to use Western principles and institutions to confront the Western challenge. The task of the Muslim intellectual "is not to rework Islam so that it takes the form of yet one more modernist construction, but to show how its beliefs and practices remain a sufficient foundation for community in contemporary life" (Meeker 1991, 201). Although Bulaç is heavily involved in Gülen-sponsored publications and the Abant meetings, his and Özel's work represents a distinct stream of Islamic Reformist thought that rejects Western solutions, despite reference to Western authors in making this argument.

As befits a modernist institution, Reformist debates are carried out over the Internet, and some of these intellectuals have personal Web pages. The Reformists also publish a well-respected journal, *Islamiyat*, described as modernist liberal. The journal is the brainchild of Mehmet Aydın and his graduate students. The journal first appeared in 1998. Each issue is centered on a theme; some of the most influential issues have taken up Islam and democracy (1999), increasing worldliness (2001), religion and violence (2002, no. 1), and the Islamic Left (2002, no. 2). The issue on religion and violence included articles about violence in Judaism and Christianity, as well as Islam, with separate evaluations of *jihad* and wife-beating in light of the Qur'an. Writings by Fazlur Rahman appear in several issues, translated from English. *Islamiyat* is linked to a publishing house that issues Turkish-language books by reformists, including translations of contemporary Arab authors like Muhammed Âbid el-Câbirî (*Restructuring Contemporary Arab-Islamic Thought*), Emîn el-Hûlî (*Reformist Approaches to Arab-Islamic Culture*), and Ahmed en-Naîm (*Reform in Islamic Law*). The publication list also includes a book on semantics as a new science of meaning (by F. R. Palmer) and a book on Islamic views on reincarnation. There is little reference to classic Arab Islamic writers. Both Aydın and Özsoy confirmed that the translation of works by Fazlur Rahman in the 1970s "started the ball rolling" and that his remains the decisive imprint on the Reformist movement. Through Rahman, Özsoy explained, "the Turks gained access to Muhammad 'Abduh and other Arab Islamist thinkers."

However, Aydın explained that recent transnational Islamic rethinking had little impact in Turkey "because Turkish Islamic scholars and writers haven't traveled much and many don't speak English or Arabic.... Few outsiders understand Turkish.... Professor Kirbaşoğlu is known in the Arab world to some extent because he taught in Saudi Arabia. However, for the most part, none of our publications have been translated into other languages.... I believe there are significant numbers of people who think along the same lines, but we are not aware of them." As a result of their training at Turkish and European universities, Reformists tend to be fluent in French, English, and other European languages. Aydın, Özsoy and Akdemir told me that they read Arabic. However, their conversations were peppered with examples from the Western canon, ranging from Freud to Heidegger, not Arab sources.

The Reformists' emphasis on Muslim inferiority requires them to differentiate between religion and culture. It is here that perceived differences from Arab Islam become most apparent. Özsoy: "Since Islam has been an imperial religion from the beginning, it has the capacity to take on different cultural forms. This allows nations to preserve their characteristics after becoming Muslim. This is, in fact, the result of Islam being a humanistic and realistic religion. Of course, we should not make the mistake of equating ethnic and national character with Islam. In the final analysis, Islam is nothing but the average of what contemporary Muslims are. However, I have always weighed the significance of this. I mean, while reading the Qur'an, to what extent am I facing an Arab reality and to what extent the demands of Allah? We have to distinguish between these."[5]

Arab Islam acts as a foil, highlighting the greater democratic potential of Turkish Islam. Salih Akdemir explained that in the Middle East religion was understood as a relationship of slavery between God and man, so no democracy was possible. Turkish Muslimhood, on the other hand, "is moderate, comfortable," according to Mehmet Aydın. "[We have] a rooted history.... If you ask me, religious tolerance was greater in Ottoman times than in the present.... It didn't emerge with the Republic; there is an 800 to 900 year history." He gave as an example the acceptance of Jews after the founding of the Republic. "Secondly, Turkish Islam was, of course, culturally influenced to some extent by its Central Asian roots. [For this reason,] in my youth relations between men and women in the villages were extremely comfortable." He suggested that, although one says "Islam" very easily in English, in fact, for Turkey a better word might be "Muslimhood."

Islamiyat is read by other intellectuals and has little currency beyond the circle of theologians and Islamic scholars, yet is one of the most vibrant arenas for new Islamic thinking in Turkey. This begs the question of why we should care about a group with such a limited audience. This is perhaps best answered by pointing to Aydın's new position as minister in the prime minister's inner circle. While disclaiming Islamism, these intellectuals have brought their Muslim approach and Muslimhood model into the government, albeit as individuals. As we shall see below, this does not solve the problem presented by Muslim ideas and practices spilling into public and political space in an entrenched secular (or laicist) system. However, it suggests new possibilities for negotiating these contradictions that would have been impossible with an overtly political Islamism, which would only have been able to resolve the problem by replacing the secular system with an Islamic one.

Reformist influences have been felt in the most unlikely places in the political sphere. During the election campaign, Deniz Baykal, the leader of the RPP, Turkey's most secular, socialist-oriented party, founded by Ataturk himself, created a media stir when he said, "From Muhammad Iqbal to Sayyid Qutb, Islamic thinkers have been social democrats" (*Sabah*, October 28, 2002). Forced to respond to media outrage that he would put the Egyptian "founder of political Islam" on the same level as Mevlana and Haci Bektaş, Baykal explained that he was not interested in Qutb's political views, but in his ideas about social justice and anticapitalist views and belief that "social democracy is Islamic." In his response, he referred to the Reformist Yaşar Nuri Öztürk, who had translated Qutb and who was standing as an RPP candidate for parliament. Far from helping the RPP gain votes in the more orthodox countryside, Öztürk may have lost some of those votes by suggesting that the call to prayer be changed from Arabic to Turkish. Nevertheless, the party stood by him as a bearer of enlightened and modern religious knowledge (*Milliyet*, November 12, 2002). Another party member insisted defensively that "[i]n our youth, we didn't just read [Qutb]; we read Marx too!" (*Sabah*, October 28, 2002). After the election, the presence of an Islamic scholar representing the RPP in parliament presented a slightly humorous benefit when a new independent candidate from the rural east balked at wearing the traditional gold jacket pin given him when he entered parliament. Öztürk was able to reassure him that gold was not *haram*, religiously forbidden (*Milliyet*, November 14, 2002).

The relation of Reformists to Islamic political movements varies. Özsoy takes a critical stance with respect to the conservative Islamist parties under Erbakan, but is more favorably inclined toward the AKP, not because it is Islamist, but because it is not. "In Turkey, only a fraction of the so-called Islamists regards [Erbakan's political Islamist] tradition with sympathy. A significant portion has joined other religious communities and the larger body is loyal to the state and regards [the Ministry of] Religious Affairs highly.... Just as a party that defends solely the rights of Kurds or a party that promotes the Alevis is not healthy, an Islamist party is [not healthy either]....AK Party [on the other hand] has votes coming from people from different walks of life [and] a diverse body of deputies in the National Assembly. For instance, we have scholars from our faculty [in parliament]. People who are very enlightened; following a reformist interpretation of Islam, and not as a fantasy but as people who have internalized this and know what they are doing.... Professor Mehmet Aydın is the most prominent of them. [This is not just] about the AK Party. The people walking down the street have a conception of Islam as well, which is partially influenced by reformist Islam. Islam never stops." Not surprisingly, Reformist ideas have faced criticism from more orthodox Muslims and Islamists, but their influence with AKP inserts their ideas into the mainstream. Their ideas also seem to find support in the general population. A national poll showed that while most Turks considered themselves to be devout Muslims and prayed regularly, most also believed that Islam had no place in politics (Çarkoğu & Toprak 2000).

Public and private spheres

Politics is contestation over what is private and what is public or political. That is, it is an interpretive struggle, not just an issue of control over space. How is that space defined? What are its boundaries? How are the ideas and practices that take place there evaluated? One might consider this a subset of a larger contestation over the place of "tradition" and "modernity," or Islam and secularism. In Turkey, these issues are front and center, as reformist Muslims try to bring their personal Muslimhood onto the public stage in schools, in government, in the streets, and within a laic system. While a secular system requires the separation of matters of church and state, a laic system commands secularism and forbids religion in the public and political spheres and is set up to enforce it. Özsoy describes this form of laicism, as it is practiced by the Turkish state, as a form of atheism, where religion is expected not to exist at all in certain arenas. Islamists and "public Muslims" have come up short against this seemingly immovable barrier. Erdoğan's two daughters study in the United States because they would not be allowed to cover their heads in Turkish schools. Özsoy complained that "this is a faculty of theology [but] our students ... have to uncover their heads. A large number of our students can't attend classes; others attend wearing wigs. No separation between public and private sphere is left. [The classroom] is defined as public sphere." When it was founded in 2001, the AKP had been warned by the Constitutional Court that it faced closure because six of the party founders wore head scarves; it is illegal for women wearing head scarves to found a political party. Just two weeks after coming to power, the AKP government faced the first major challenge to its Muslimhood model. Protocol required Bülent Arınç, the new speaker of parliament, to see secularist President Ahmet Sezer off at the airport. Since Mrs. Sezer would be there, protocol required that Arınç bring his wife as well. The following day, the photo on the front page of all the major newspapers showed President Sezer shaking hands with a veiled Mrs. Arınç. It did not take long for Sezer to remind the AKP government that this had been an illegal act, not to be repeated. Veiling is not permitted in the political arena, whether in parliament or on the airport runway. Several days later, the heads of the branches of the military paid the new government a routine welcome visit. After spending twenty minutes with the prime minister, they spent exactly two minutes, as timed by waiting journalists, in the office of Mr. Arınç. The message was clear. AKP was not to step over the line again.

This presented an interesting dilemma and occasioned a great deal of public debate in the media and in people's homes about whether and under what circumstances religious symbols like the veil could appear in the public sphere and what exactly constituted the public sphere. Some suggested that a differentiation should be made between those who provide service on behalf of the state (like teachers and members of parliament) and those who receive services (like students and ordinary citizens), with only direct representatives of state service being required to adhere to the restrictions on religious symbolism. This debate has opened a hitherto closed door to redefining the meaning of the public arena by differentiating between society and the state. For many Turks, however, the public is irrevocably political. At present, Kemalist opposition to contracting the parameters of the public sphere retains the upper hand. The Kemalists are concerned to ensure that society remains secular, at least in its public face. The Muslimhood model provides both a challenge and an opportunity to rethink these policies. In so doing, it is useful to point out that the meanings of the concepts of public and private and veiling itself already are contested and have begun to change.

Within the Islamist movement itself, the differentiation between a public and private sphere also has become negotiable and ill-defined. Aggressive marketing has created a middle-class and elite Islamist style that sets itself off against the "unconscious" veiling of the masses. The "new Islamic woman" takes part in previously male-dominated activities in the public sphere, whether political activism or shopping. Veiled political activists from working-class backgrounds also aspire to the well-publicized role of "new Islamic woman," dressing the part as prescribed by advertisements and Islamist magazines aimed at women. Eventually, however, many are forced by economic circumstances to retreat into seclusion within the patriarchal family and the home, an arena set off in Islamist ideology as private in opposition to public. This "private" arena itself has been valorized by the market, resulting in a new bourgeois Islamic home environment marked by certain purchased commodities. This stands in contrast to an Islamic home marked primarily by religiously supported female virtues (like virginity, motherhood, housekeeping, and seclusion). A woman may move between being a "new Islamic woman" and being a secluded housewife, depending on her class and education. Both are legitimated with reference to Islamic doctrine. Veiling itself is a powerful symbol both of Islamist women's right to act in public as well as their duty to remain secluded in the home. Male Islamist activists are more likely than their female colleagues to emphasize the latter over the former. While the veil acts as a visible, unifying political symbol under certain circumstances, the heterogeneity of economic circumstances and motivations of its wearers indicates potential fractures within the movement, particularly along lines of social class and gender, about Islamic definitions of the proper constitution of public and private and women's place within them.

Özsoy believes that "the differentiation of a public and private sphere may be a legal and sociological necessity, but with regard to religion, it is an anachronism ..... There is a famous story told about the Prophet Muhammed's companion, Omar .... It is said that Omar, the Caliph, had two groups of candles. During working hours when he was caliph, he would use the state's candle, but from the moment he thought he had moved to his private life, he used his private candle. Although this doesn't give us a technical way to separate private from public sphere ... it gives us some clues that can be pursued. [We can find such clues] in the life of the Prophet (PBUH) as well." His point is that Muslims can reconcile themselves to laicism[6] if they understand it as simply a "technology" (which candle do I use where?), rather than as an ideology (am I a laicist or Islamist?). "When laicism is presented as a paradigm against religion it is not possible to say that religious people are at peace with it. However, when it is perceived as a detail, a technique of state formation, in that sense, we don't see that they have a problem together." The question of who will be allowed to use both candles, however, is not addressed.

This functional view of secularism and laicism is echoed by both Tayyip Erdoğan and Mehmet Aydın. "Islam is a religion, and a party is just a political institution," Erdoğan explained. "Secularism is just a style of management. When a person chooses Islam, he becomes Muslim, but he can choose secularism as a style of administration.... Secularism is an important part of democracy. [It] establishes the administrative structure of this country" (*Washington Post*, November 10, 2002, B1–2). Aydın agrees that secularism is compatible with democracy in a Muslim society, but insists on defining secular in a nonideological sense as working in conformity with the rule of law in a fully functioning democracy. "I do not want it in other terms. If you say, I will secularize the culture, for instance, [and impose] an educational model in which religious terminology has no place; this doesn't work."

Many people believe that defining public and private by differentiating between service giver and service provider might be a "technical" solution to the seemingly intractable question of whether veiled women may attend schools. Özsoy, however, does not agree. "I do not think this is right in principle because I believe dress is a fundamental right. There are definitely some criteria that will define and limit it .... For instance, I must not have the freedom to come here totally naked .... This can be called custom, tradition, or moral appropriateness. But it must be regulated by law. [Otherwise,] I believe such restrictions are wrong in principle, whether it be for a service provider or service taker in the public sphere."

Aydın accepts some form of laicism as necessary in a Muslim country to guard the state against a chaos of Islamic interpretation. He believes that laicism is natural to the Turkish interpretation of Islam, because a laic state, for instance, ensures that men and women are equal (as he believes they were in early Central Asian Turkic communities). He argued that the state must be laic because [otherwise] there would be too many people who would claim the right to interpret the law. The result would be a situation like that of "the Vatican and Protestants, or the Reformation and counter-Reformation." For a Muslim country like Turkey, he said, he would advocate laicism "as it is meant in Holland." By this he means a more benign and liberal definition of what is allowed in public space, rather than a redefinition of the space. I suggested the term "secularism," but he didn't like it and suggested "secularity" as something more "natural."

Public culture

The present debates about what form of clothing and behavior belongs where might well be less a clash of distinct secularist (or laicist) versus Islamist ideologies than the most recent manifestation of a long process of differentiation of personal experience from provincial propriety versus urban mores. As Meeker points out, as a result of continual two-directional urbanization, Turkish citizens, whether in village or city, have been required more and more to differentiate between family space and social space, social and public space, school and work, weekend and weekday, community of origin and community of migration (which could include places as far away as Germany and Saudi Arabia), and to adjust their behaviors and attitudes appropriately (1994, 40). Official Kemalism did not provide many answers to the dilemmas faced by people trying to come up with a moral roadmap for unfamiliar contexts, and left- and right-wing political ideologies of the 1960s and 1970s were suppressed. In the 1980s and 1990s, many Turks focused their hopes on developing civil society; for others, the answers lay in provincial modes of propriety that were common even in cities, unacknowledged by secular nationalist ideology. These norms and patterns of speech and behavior involved, among other things, rituals of cleanliness, distinct ideas of personal status and rights, and a focus on "intimacy, loyalty, interpersonal transparency and affection" and mutual support (Meeker 1994, 37), and were anchored in a local and oral Islamic ethic.

This widespread language and ethic, unacknowledged and even demonized by the Kemalists, served as a powerful foundation for Islamist politics. It is important to note that early Islamic parties, like the National Salvation Party (NSP) in the 1970s, did not do well in elections. Toprak (1981, 101) suggests that this is because religion by itself was not a sufficient factor for mobilization. It was not until the 1990s that an Islamic party began to organize and mobilize people on the basis of what Meeker calls a provincial "Islamic language of being" (1994, 31), rather than on the basis of local interests. (The NSP catered to provincial small businessmen fearful of big business.) That change allowed Islamic politics to expand beyond specific interests to attract people across a wide spectrum who perceived in the party a familiar and time-honored strategy for dealing with life's difficulties and change.

These developments have been exacerbated by economic decline and privatization of state industries in the 1980s and 1990s. There is a perceptible nostalgia for traditional strategies and institutions that, in retrospect, seemed to provide solutions. There is a diffuse but discernible nostalgia for a sheltering authority. This can be seen in the recent popularity of films and film series about rural *aghas* who are gruff and demanding, but care about their people, protect them, and meet their needs. The Ottoman Empire, moth-balled since 1923 by the Republic, has been dusted off to provide models for everything from tolerant multiculturalism to veiling styles and architectural models for summer resorts. The Welfare and Virtue Parties that preceded AKP put forward Ottoman-inspired ideas ranging from Bulaç's scheme for *millet*-style religious federalism to charity programs in which wealthy families, in effect, "adopt" poor families. AKP was successful primarily because it organized and mobilized people on the basis of neighborhood networks built around the very characteristics described in Meeker's provincial propriety. The links between neighborhood networks, civic organizations, and political party – a powerful nexus I call vernacular politics (White 2002) – created a broad national movement, flexible enough to incorporate a great variety of people. The masses, in effect, were mobilized on the basis of familiar personal ties and obligations, and their energies and interests channeled into a national political program. Vernacular politics made the line between personal and political, and between local and national, obsolete.

The rehabilitation of provincial modes of propriety as the bases for new urban, modern Muslim identities and national political mobilization became possible with the development of an aggressive media. Television and radio were effectively deregulated in the 1980s as cable and satellite television made it impossible to control. There also was a publication explosion. The Turkish–Islamic synthesis of the 1980s meant that the government allowed a great variety of Islamic ideas and material to be published and broadcast. The newly opened economy of the 1980s brought wealth to conservative and provincial entrepreneurs. The Özal government brought them into the bureaucracy. All of these things led to the development of a new Islamist public culture. Almost immediately, it came into conflict with official public culture. Veiling developed a popular, chic style and began to appear in areas of the city, particularly middle-class areas, formerly the exclusive realm of secularists, and Islamic ideas were debated in the media.

Muslimization of the public

There are, in other words, multiple challenges to the laicist definition of the boundaries and content of the public sphere, from media and market forces, from Muslim intellectuals and politicians, and from ordinary citizens looking for strategies for self-expression. Yet, at the same time, there is widespread concern about the social manifestations of other kinds of difference that seem to be on the rise: an acceptance of lifestyle differences only if they are segregated; a politically unmoored and intolerant Muslimhood that divides people within the same social class, the same neighborhood. A secularist friend worried that AKP's plan to move authority for such things as education and health care from the central state into the hands of local authorities would lead to dangerous differences between, say, school districts, with one allowing head scarves and the other not. He worried it would lead to segregation, "like U.S. blacks," but based on lifestyle. Ayşe Böhürler, the Islamist writer and television personality, complained about Negrofication (*zencileştirme*).[7] Two relatively new terms, "white Turks" and "black Turks," have come into wide use to refer to urban, secular, left-of-center Turks, on the one hand, and rural (or "reactionary," uncivilized) Islamist conservatives on the other. A middle-aged desk clerk in a touristic hotel who has lived his entire life in Fatih, arguably Istanbul's most religiously conservative neighborhood, described a creeping division between residents who are more devout and those less observant. Whereas in the past, they lived mixed together, he explained, now there is less tolerance. More religiously observant residents are disturbed by the more open clothing and lifestyles of their neighbors. They have, over time, become geographically segregated, so that those living behind the mosque tend to be more observant than those living in front of the mosque.

Is Islamist politics dead? Some questions

Many politicians and intellectuals argue that Islam has ceased to play a direct role in politics, other than inspiring direction. They claim that Islam in both the public and private spheres has become pluralist, multicultural, and modern. The meanings of Islamic symbols and practices seem to be diffusing as they are marketed and popularized. Yet society seems ever more rent by differences that people associate with differing positions with regard to Islamic lifestyle. Also, real forces (the military, the secularist/laicist establishment, beginning with the president and the courts) dispute the presence of what they consider political symbols, like the veil, in public and civic space. That is, they point to a continuation of Islam in politics. Is this simply a matter of definition – Where is the public sphere? Is the veil really a public symbol or just a personal fashion choice? Is Islamic ideology truly dead? – Or is the redefinition of public and private a sleight of hand that makes Muslim values and practices appear to be personal choices even when government ministers are seen to fast and pray together?

The Muslimhood model and Abant model of reconciliation are promising, but without a viable political framework, the problem is not solved. A young urban planner at Middle East Technical University in Ankara compared this to the conundrum of the famed Gordian Knot. Alexander the Great cut the Gordian Knot, which could not be undone, with his sword. "It's a solution," said the urban planner, "but a trivial one. The knot is not undone. In other words, it's not really a solution." This is true whether the army intervenes to keep the government free of Islamic politicians, or whether Muslim politicians bring their ideas and practices into the secular government. To undo the Gordian Knot, he said, one needs democracy. For Özsoy, this does not pose a problem. "Once a fellow citizen asked me if Islam and democracy are compatible. I answered him as follows.... If Muslims want it, it is. [This is] because there is no such abstract Islam outside of the way in which Muslims have shaped and brought it to the historical scene." This interpretation reflects both the individualism of the Reformist position and the differentiation of religion from its traditional and cultural historical baggage, separating a Turkish from an Arab Islam. The November 2003 car bombings in Istanbul, apparently planned by Al-Qaeda with the assistance of a local, hitherto unimportant radical Islamist group, can be expected to reinforce this suspicion of Arab Islam and lead AKP to further distance itself from any radical Islamic elements that might still remain within the party.

Can the Muslimhood model travel?

The Abant model is seen by many as something that can travel, if only other Muslim countries could overcome their internal barriers (attributed to culture, bad governments, etc.). The Muslimhood model, on the other hand, even though it is based on a universalist conception of human character, is perceived to be more strongly expressed in Turkey because of the characteristics of Turkish Islam (Central Asian Sufism) and Ottoman history. Aydın, however, has a more optimistic view: "If we stay in power another five years ... there are some things we need to fix in Turkey.... Turkish society is religious. If we can put into place the best model of a democratic law state in a religious Muslim society, then it's impossible for Syria and Iraq not to be affected by this.... Much radicalism derives from politics, from economic problems. If you have a very narrow definition of nationalism, ethnicity goes up in flames. If you interpret Islam as allowing only this, and all the rest is forbidden, you will have serious problems. In the Islamic world, radicalism derives from fifty years of politicians who have not solved people's economic problems and now try to use religion to clear the way before them. Also, the appearance of radicalism in the Islamic world is linked to Israel's politics, which desperately needs to be solved."

Certain elements present themselves, however, that may be less transferable. Radical Islamism in Turkey as inspired by transnational trends died because of a general realization that a *shari'ah*-based state was not a practicable goal due to state and military resistance, a popular lack of support for Islam in politics, and the recognition that Arab Islam differs from Turkish Islam, which is more individualistic and moderate. There was an all-around moderating effect as representatives of different groups and positions communicated at Abant meetings and in the media. These trends were reflected intellectually by theologian Renewers and politically by AKP. AKP's model of Muslimhood limits Islam in politics to ethical and moral inspiration of individual behavior and individual choice. The party supports democracy because it guarantees freedom of individual belief and expression and, thus, religious expression and its own survival.

Repression of Islamist participation in public life has not led to movement away from a civil sphere to violent radicalism because (1) the repressing mechanisms of state and military enjoy widespread legitimacy and support; the military (in polls ranked the most trusted institution) and the state are both entwined with the heroic nationalist legacy of Ataturk; (2) repressed political figures and parties generally are able to reconfigure and struggle for a new place within a competitive political system. This leads to two questions: (1) whether, in the absence of repression, the other factors mentioned above would have been sufficient to moderate the Islamist impetus; (2) whether the Muslimhood model could survive a system without such repressive mechanisms (an AKP aim). It is conceivable that Muslim ideals might become absorbed and diffused in the secular "technology" of state, or that Muslims might be outflanked by less liberal elements of society.

AKP came to power in part because its message matched religiocultural provincial ethical and behavioral norms that, despite the universalist and individualist claims of the Muslimhood theorists, are not necessarily liberal or based on individualism. Rather, rights in this social paradigm are derived from community membership and obedience to communal norms. While the provincial code protects guests and travelers, it is not particularly conducive to tolerance of behavioral aberration among fellow residents. Due to urbanization and the growth of both Islamic and non-Islamic commercial media, what had been a provincial code has become elaborated into nationally valorized identities, linked in a diffuse way to Islam, with differences among people encoded in symbols like the veil and terminology like black and white Turk. The divisiveness is expressed most obviously in a continuing battle over what constitutes public space (parliament? university classrooms? the street? state occasions?) and who controls what can and cannot appear there. This comes out in such disputes as the permissibility of veiling or, in neighborhoods like Fatih, secular dress in public places, whether women's proper place is in parliament or in the home, and whether or not alcohol sale and consumption should be prohibited in sidewalk restaurants (where nondrinking Muslim passers-by might be offended at the sight).

These dilemmas illustrate an interesting difference between social and political trends. While politics and intellectual discourse on Islam seem to be moving into the realm of democracy, tolerance, and individualism, society is becoming more polarized along the lines of perceived lifestyle differences. Speaker Arınç's protocol dilemma was the first sign of the legally entrenched nature of secularist practices and definition of the public sphere, heedless of the new government's attempts to explain Islamicized practices as individual, rather than public, choices.

Notes

1 Interview with author, Ankara, November 30, 2002. (Unless otherwise specified, further quotations will refer to the interview first referenced.)
2 Interview with author, Ankara, November 25, 2002.
3 Interview with author, Istanbul, November 23, 2002.
4 Interview with author, Ankara, November 29, 2002.
5 Interview with author, Ankara, November 29, 2002.
6 The Turkish term *laiklik* has been translated as both "laicism" or "secularism."
7 Discussion with author, Istanbul, November 28, 2002.

References

Abant Platformu. 2000. Istanbul: Gazeteciler ve Yazarlar Vakfı Yayınları.

Aras, Bülent. 1998. "Turkish Islam's Moderate Face." *Middle East Quarterly* 5, no. 3: 23–29.

Aydın, Mehmet. 2002. *Niçin?* Istanbul: Zaman Kitap.

—— . 1985. *Turkish Contribution to Philosophical Culture*. Istanbul: AKM Yayınevi.

Çarkoğu, Ali, and B. Toprak. 2000. *Türkiye'de Din, Toplum ve Siyaset*. Istanbul: Türkiye Ekonomik ve Sosyal Etüdler Vakfı.

Erman, Tahire, and E. Göker. 2000. "Alevi Politics in Contemporary Turkey." *Middle Eastern Studies* 36, no. 4 (October): 99–118.

Erdemir, Aykan, 2002. "Alternative Modernities? 'Modern' Alevis and Alevi Alternatives." Paper presented at Symposium "Local Modernities: Islamic Cultural Practices as Sites of Agency, Mediation and Change," MIT, Boston, October 5.

Massicard, Elise. 2001. "Local Productions of Alevi Knowledge." *Istanbuler Almanach* no. 5: 70–74.

Meeker, Michael. 1991. "The New Muslim Intellectuals in the Republic of Turkey." In *Islam in Modern Turkey: Religion, Politics and Literature in a Secular State*, edited by Richard Tapper, pp. 189–219. London: I. B. Tauris.

—— . 1994. "Oral Culture, Media Culture, and the Islamic Resurgence in Turkey." In *Exploring the Written in Anthropology*, edited by Eduardo P. Archetti, pp. 31–64. Oslo: Scandinavian University Press.

Navaro-Yashin, Yael. 2002. "The Market for Identities: Secularism, Islamism, Commodities." In *The Everyday of Modern Turkey*, edited by Deniz Kandiyoti, pp. 153–221. London: I. B. Tauris.

Toprak, Binnaz. 1981. *Islam and Political Development in Turkey*. Leiden: E. J. Brill.

Vorhoff, Karin. 1997. "Vom Schweigen Zum Schreiben: Alewitische Presse in der Türkei Heute." *Istanbuler Almanach* no. 1: 55–60.

White, Jenny B. 2002. *Islamist Mobilization in Turkey: A Study in Vernacular Politics*. Seattle: University of Washington Press.

Further reading

Abdullahi Ahmed An-Naim, *Islam and the Secular State: Negotiating the Future of Shariʾa* (Cambridge: Harvard University Press, 2008)
  A sophisticated investigation of the mechanisms and possibilities of interaction between Islamic law and secular state institutions.

Asef Bayat, *Making Islam Democratic: Social Movements and the Post-Islamist Turn* (Stanford: Stanford University Press, 2007)
  An insightful study of the internal transformation of political Islam and of the changing role of Islamism in Muslim politics.

Michaelle Browers and Charles Kurzman (eds.), *An Islamic Reformation?* (Lanham: Lexington Books, 2004)
  A useful collection of texts connecting modern Islamist discourses to an overarching set of theological debates.

François Burgat, *Islamism in the Shadow of al-Qaeda*, trans. P. Hutchinson (Austin: University of Texas Press, 2008)
  A useful overview of the recent transformations of Islamism in a security context shaped by the confrontation between al-Qaeda and state security apparatuses.

Graham E. Fuller, *The Future of Political Islam* (London: Palgrave Macmillan, 2004)
  A sound and well-informed overview of the key issues and challenges facing political Islam in the contemporary international context.

Robert W. Hefner (ed.), *Remaking Muslim Politics: Pluralism, Contestation, Democratization* (Princeton: Princeton University Press, 2004)
  A very informative collection of essays reviewing the processes of political liberalization involving Islamist movements in the Muslim world.

Armando Salvatore and Dale F. Eickelman (eds.), *Public Islam and the Common Good* (Leiden: Brill, 2004)
  A useful compilation of essays on the multifaceted reconstruction of a modern Islamic public sphere and political discourse.

Index

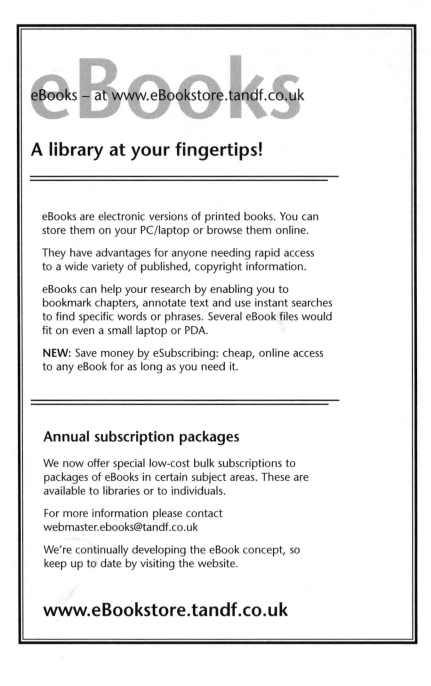